Lecture Notes in Computer Science 1601
Edited by G. Goos, J. Hartmanis and J.

T0259905

Springer

Berlin
Heidelberg
New York
Barcelona
Hong Kong
London
Milan
Paris
Singapore
Tokyo

Joost-Pieter Katoen (Ed.)

Formal Methods for Real-Time and Probabilistic Systems

5th International AMAST Workshop, ARTS'99
Bamberg, Germany, May 26-28, 1999
Proceedings

 Springer

Series Editors

Gerhard Goos, Karlsruhe University, Germany
Juris Hartmanis, Cornell University, NY, USA
Jan van Leeuwen, Utrecht University, The Netherlands

Volume Editor

Joost-Pieter Katoen
University of Erlangen-Nürnberg, Lehrstuhl für Informatik
Martensstr. 3, D-91058 Erlangen, Germany
E-mail: katoen@informatik.uni-erlangen.de

Currently at:
University of Twente, Formal Methods and Tools Group
P.O. Box 217, 7500 AE Enschede, The Netherlands
E-mail: katoen@cs.utwente.nl

Cataloging-in-Publication data applied for

Die Deutsche Bibliothek - CIP-Einheitsaufnahme

Formal methods for real time and probabilistic systems :
proceedings / 5th International AMAST Workshop, ARTS '99,
Bamberg, Germany, May 26 - 28, 1999. Joost-Pieter Katoen (ed.). -
Berlin ; Heidelberg ; New York ; Barcelona ; Hong Kong ; London ;
Milan ; Paris ; Singapore ; Tokyo : Springer, 1999
  (Lecture notes in computer science ; Vol. 1601)
  ISBN 3-540-66010-0

CR Subject Classification (1998): C.3, C.2.4, D.2, D.3, F.3

ISSN 0302-9743
ISBN 3-540-66010-0 Springer-Verlag Berlin Heidelberg New York

© Springer-Verlag Berlin Heidelberg 1999
Printed in Germany

Typesetting: Camera-ready by author
SPIN 10704800   06/3142 – 5 4 3 2 1 0   Printed on acid-free paper

Foreword

The aim of the ARTS'99 workshop is to bring together researchers and practitioners interested in the design of real-time and probabilistic systems. It is intended to cover the whole spectrum of development and application of specification, verification, analysis and construction techniques for real-time and probabilistic systems. Being a workshop under the umbrella of the AMAST movement (Algebraic Methodology And Software Technology), ARTS is intended to provide a forum for the presentation of approaches that are based on a clear mathematical basis. Aspects of real-time and probabilistic systems for the workshop include (but are not limited to): compositional construction and verification techniques, automatic and machine-supported verification, case studies, formal methods for performance analysis, semantics, algorithms and tools, and hybrid systems.

ARTS'99 was organised by the Lehrstuhl für Informatik 7 at the University of Erlangen-Nürnberg and took place at the Städtliche Volkshochschule in Bamberg (Oberfranken), Germany from May 26–28, 1999. Previous editions of ARTS workshops were organized by the University of Iowa, USA (1993), University of Bordeaux, France (1995), Brigham Young University, USA (1996), and General Systems Development, Mallorca, Spain (1997). Previous proceedings appeared as LNCS 1231 or as books in the AMAST Series of Computing.

The Program Committee selected 17 papers from a total of 33 submissions. Each submitted paper was sent to three Program Committee members, who were often assisted by sub-referees. During a one-week discussion via e-mail, the Program Committee has made the selection of the papers on the basis of the reviews. This volume contains the 17 selected papers plus 3 invited papers (in either full or abstract form).

I would like to thank the Program Committee members and the sub-referees for their efforts. I also like to thank the invited speakers for giving a talk at the workshop and for their contribution to the proceedings. Special thanks to Ulrich Herzog, Chris Moog, Teodor Rus, Diego Latella and Ruth Abraham (Springer-Verlag) for their support. Without their help, this event would not have been possible.

March 1999

Joost-Pieter Katoen
Program Chair
ARTS'99

Invited Speakers

Bengt Jonsson   (Uppsala University, Sweden)
Frits W. Vaandrager (University of Nijmegen, The Netherlands)
Moshe Y. Vardi   (Rice University, USA)

Steering Committee

Manfred Broy   (Technical University of Munich, Germany)
Edmund Clarke (Carnegie Mellon University, USA)
Ulrich Herzog   (University of Erlangen-Nürnberg, Germany)
Zohar Manna   (Stanford University, USA)
Maurice Nivat   (University of Paris 6, France)
Amir Pnueli   (Weizmann Institute of Science, Israel)
Teodor Rus   (Chair, University of Iowa, USA)

Program Committee

Rajeev Alur   (University of Pennsylvania, USA)
Jos Baeten   (Eindhoven University of Technology, The Netherlands)
Christel Baier   (University of Mannheim, Germany)
Miquel Bertran   (University of Ramon Llull, Spain)
Antonio Cerone   (University of South Australia, Australia)
Rance Cleaveland   (SUNY at Stony Brook, USA)
Jim Davies   (Oxford University, UK)
Colin Fidge   (University of Queensland, Australia)
David de Frutos   (University of Madrid, Spain)
Hubert Garavel   (INRIA Rhone-Alpes, France)
Constance Heitmeyer (Naval Research Laboratory, USA)
Tom Henzinger   (University of Berkeley, USA)
Jane Hillston   (University of Edinburgh, UK)
Joost-Pieter Katoen (University of Erlangen-Nürnberg, Germany, Chair)
Rom Langerak   (University of Twente, The Netherlands)
Kim G. Larsen   (Aalborg University, Denmark)
Diego Latella   (CNR-CNUCE, Italy)
Jonathan Ostroff   (University of York, Canada)
Steve Schneider   (Royal Holloway, UK)
Roberto Segala   (University of Bologna, Italy)
Walter Vogler   (University of Augsburg, Germany)

Organising Committee

Joost-Pieter Katoen
Chris Moog

Referees

Luca Aceto	Luis Fernando Llana Díaz
Suzanna Andova	Gerald Lüttgen
Myla Archer	Mieke Massink
Marco Bernardo	Radu Mateescu
Elmar Bihler	Joachim Meyer-Kayser
Andrea Bondavalli	Annabelle McIver
Howard Bowman	Faron Moller
Mario Bravetti	Gethin Norman
Franck van Breugel	Manuel Núñez
Graham Clarke	Richard Paige
Alex Cowie	Prakash Panangaden
Luca de Alfaro	Adriano Peron
Pedro D'Argenio	Rob Pooley
Henrik Ejersbo Jensen	Jean-Francois Raskin
Stephen Gilmore	Michel Reniers
Holger Hermanns	Arend Rensink
Anna Ingólfsdóttir	Theo C. Ruys
Lars Jenner	Markus Siegle
Lennard Kerber	Graeme Smith
Ulrich Klehmet	Scott Smolka
Kåre Kristoffersen	Nigel Thomas
Marta Kwiatkowska	Axel Wabenhorst
Yassim Lakhnech	John Žic
Karl Lermer	Gerard Zwaan

Sponsoring Institutions

C.N.R. Istituto CNUCE, Pisa, Italy
German Research Council (Deutsche Forschungsgemeinschaft)

Table of Contents

Fully Abstract Characterization of Probabilistic May Testing

Bengt Jonsson and Wang Yi

Department of Computer Systems, Uppsala University
Box 325, S-751 05 Uppsala, SWEDEN
{bengt,yi}@docs.uu.se

Abstract. In this paper, to develop a refinement relation for probabilistic and nondeterministic systems, we study a notion of probabilistic testing, that extends the testing framework of de Nicola and Hennessy for nondeterministic processes to the probabilistic setting. We present a model of *probabilistic computation trees*, which corresponds to the classic trace model for non-probabilistic systems. Our main contribution is a fully abstract characterization of the may-testing preorder which is essential for the probabilistic setting. The characterization is given based on convex closures of probabilistic computation trees.

1 Introduction

To study probabilistic phenomena such as randomization and failure rates in distributed computing, many researchers have focused on extending models and methods that have proven successful for nonprobabilistic systems to the probabilistic setting. In the non-probabilistic setting, transition systems are well-established as a basic semantic model for concurrent and distributed systems (e.g. [16, 17, 19]).

In the literature, the model of transition systems has been extended to the probabilistic case by adding a mechanism for representing probabilistic choice (e.g. [26, 6, 7, 14, 18, 20, 21, 22]). In the non-probabilistic case there are two principal methods for reasoning about systems: to specify and prove properties in some logic and to establish a preorder or equivalence relation between two transition systems. Both are very useful e.g. in a stepwise development process. An abstract transition system model can be analyzed by proving properties in some logic. The abstract model can then be refined in a sequence of steps, where correctness is preserved in each step by establishing a preorder relation between the refined transition system and the refining one. To keep it manageable, it is often necessary to decompose the transition system model, implying that compositionality is an important property of a preorder.

In this paper, we use probabilistic transition systems to describe processes, which may contain probabilistic and nondeterministic choices independently.

J.-P. Katoen (Ed.): ARTS'99, LNCS 1601, pp. 1–18, 1999.

This model is essentially that by Wang and Larsen [31], the so-called alternating model by Hansson and Jonsson[7], the concurrent Markov chain model [28], has also been studied by Segala and Lynch [25, 23]; it can also be seen as a nondeterministic extension of the purely probabilistic automata of Rabin [22] or the reactive model by Larsen and Skou [14] that do not include any nondeterministic choice construct. To develop a notion of refinement for probabilistic and nondeterministic systems, we study the testing framework of [31], that extend the work by de Nicola and Hennessy [5] to the probabilistic setting. The idea is to define the preorders in terms of the ability of systems to pass tests. Tests are simply processes with the additional ability to report success or failure, and so this set-up has the advantage of basing the preorder on a notion of "observation" (in this case through synchronization), which yields automatically compositional preorders.

Over the past years, a number of models for describing probabilistic aspects of transition systems in the form of e.g. Markov chains, Process Algebras, Timed Petri Nets, etc. have been proposed [6, 8, 9, 14, 15, 18, 20, 21, 27]. Logics and associated methods for probabilistic systems can be found in e.g. [4, 8, 9, 13, 14]. Several (bi)simulation-based preorders between probabilistic systems have been investigated, e.g. [6]. Segala and Lynch [24] and Wang [30] present simulation-based preorders for probabilistic processes. These are not based on some independent notion of "testing". Testing-based preorders of probabilistic processes have also been studied by Christoff [2] and by Cleaveland, Smolka, and Zwarico [3] and by Yuen et al. [32, 29]. These works consider a pure probabilistic model [26], and therefore their preorders do not capture the notion of refinement in the sense of being "less nondeterministic". The work which is closest to the current one is by Segala [23], who define essentially the same testing preorders as in this work. Segala does not develop a characterization of the testing preorder in terms of objects like "traces" or "trees", but proves that when defining the compositional testing preorder, then it suffices to consider a unique "canonical" context: the compositional precongruence is obtained by comparing systems composed with this canonical context.

This paper is a continuation of our earlier work [11, 12]. The purpose is to provide a more detailed and also simplified presentation of the technical contents of [12]. The characterization theorem presented in this paper is based on a slightly different model, that of probabilistic computation trees which is a natural probabilistic extension of the classic trace model for CSP [10]. Our main contribution is simplified fully abstract characterization of the may-testing preorder for probabilistic processes. The characterization is given based on convex closures of probabilistic computation trees. In [12] we have outlined how a fully abstract characterization of must-testing can be constructed in a similar manner.

The rest of the paper is organized as follows: in Section 2, we present the necessary definitions for probabilistic transition systems and testing semantics for such systems. Section 3 develops the notion of probabilistic computation trees extending the classic trace model to probabilistic setting. Section 4 establishes a characterization theorem for the may-testing preorder. Section 5 gives some concluding remarks.

2   Preliminaries

We consider a model of probabilistic transition systems, containing probabilistic and nondeterministic choices as independent concepts. We study a notion of testing for these systems where tests may be probabilistic, implying that testers are capable of copying internal states.

A *probability distribution* on a finite set S is a function $\pi : S \to [0, 1]$ such that $\sum_{s \in S} \pi(s) = 1$. Let $Dist(S)$ denote the set of probability distributions on S. If π is a probability distribution on S and ρ is a probability distribution on T, then $\pi \times \rho$ is a probability distribution on $S \times T$, defined by $(\pi \times \rho)(\langle s, t \rangle) = \pi(s) * \rho(t)$. A *partial distribution* on S is a function $\pi : S \to [0, 1]$ such that $\sum_{s \in S} \pi(s) \leq 1$.

We assume a set Act of atomic actions, ranged over by a and b.

Definition 1. *A (probabilistic) process is a tuple $\langle S, \longrightarrow, \pi_0 \rangle$, where*

- *S is a non-empty finite set of states,*
- *$\longrightarrow \subseteq S \times Act \times Dist(S)$ is a finite transition relation, and*
- *$\pi_0 \in Dist(S)$ is an initial distribution on S.*

We shall use $s \xrightarrow{a} \pi$ to denote that $\langle s, a, \pi \rangle \in \longrightarrow$.   □

We may view the distributions as probabilistic states and the others as nondeterministic states. By definition, a probabilistic process is always alternating between probabilistic states and nondeterministic ones. In many cases when it is understood from the context, we will identify a distributions that assigns only probability 1 to a single state s with the state s.

To study compositionality, we define a synchronous parallel composition operator for probabilistic transition systems, in which two processes $\mathcal{P}$ and $\mathcal{Q}$ execute in parallel while synchronizing on all actions in Act.

Definition 2. *Let $\mathcal{P} = \langle S, \longrightarrow, \pi_0 \rangle$ and $\mathcal{Q} = \langle T, \longrightarrow, \rho_0 \rangle$ be two processes. The composition of $\mathcal{P}$ and $\mathcal{Q}$, denoted $\mathcal{P} \| \mathcal{Q}$ is a process $\langle U, \longrightarrow, \varrho_0 \rangle$, where*

- *$U = S \times T$. A pair $\langle s, t \rangle \in U$ is denoted $s \| t$.*
- *$\longrightarrow \subseteq U \times Act \times Dist(U)$ is defined by*
  $s \| t \xrightarrow{a} \pi \times \rho$ iff $s \xrightarrow{a} \pi$ and $t \xrightarrow{a} \rho$,
- *$\varrho_0 = \pi_0 \times \rho_0$ is the initial distribution.*   □

Note that the parallel composition operator enjoys all the desired properties such as commutativity and associativity that a parallel composition operator in a process algebra should possess. Note also that the class of probabilisitic transition systems is closed under the operator.

An *initial state* of a process $\mathcal{P} = \langle S, \longrightarrow, \pi_0 \rangle$ is a state $s \in S$ such that $\pi_0(s) > 0$. A state s is *reachable* in $\mathcal{P}$ if there is a sequence $s_0 s_1 \ldots s_n$ where s_0 is initial, $s = s_n$, and for each $0 \le i < n$ there is a distribution π_{i+1} such that $s_i \xrightarrow{a_i} \pi_{i+1}$ and $\pi_{i+1}(s_{i+1}) > 0$. A distribution $\pi \in Dist(S)$ is *reachable* in $\mathcal{P}$ if it is either the initial distribution or if $s \xrightarrow{a} \pi$ for some a and state s which is reachable in $\mathcal{P}$.

A *finite tree* is a process $\langle S, \longrightarrow, \pi_0 \rangle$ with all states being reachable, in which for each state s, there is exactly one reachable distribution π with $\pi(s) > 0$, and for each noninitial distribution π there is exactly one s and a such that $s \xrightarrow{a} \pi$, and further there is no s and a such that $s \xrightarrow{a} \pi_0$. We shall be concerned with an important class of finite trees known as *resolutions*.

Definition 3. *A finite tree is a resolution if for each state s there is at most one action a and distribution π, such that $s \xrightarrow{a} \pi$.* □

In the following, we will use long arrow $\longrightarrow$ for transitions of processes, and short arrow $\rightarrow$ for transitions of resolutions.

Following Wang and Larsen [31], we define tests as processes that are finite trees where the leaves are labeled by "success".

Definition 4. *A (probabilistic) test is a tuple $\langle T, \longrightarrow, \rho_0, \mathcal{F} \rangle$, where*

- $\langle T, \longrightarrow, \rho_0 \rangle$ *is a (probabilistic) process*
- $\mathcal{F} \subseteq T$ *is a set of* success-states, *each of which is terminal.* □

In the following, we will assume that tests are finite trees. However note that a process is not necessarily a finite tree.

A test $\mathcal{T}$ is applied to a process $\mathcal{P}$ by putting the process $\mathcal{P}$ in parallel with the test $\mathcal{T}$ and observing whether the test reaches a success state.

We define a testing system as the parallel composition of a process and a test.

Definition 5. *Let $\mathcal{P} = \langle S, \longrightarrow, \pi_0 \rangle$ be a process and $\mathcal{T} = \langle T, \longrightarrow, \rho_0, \mathcal{F} \rangle$ be a test. The composition of $\mathcal{P}$ and $\mathcal{T}$, denoted $\mathcal{P} \| \mathcal{T}$ is a test $\langle \mathcal{U}, \longrightarrow, \varrho_0, \mathcal{G} \rangle$, also called a testing system, where*

- $\langle \mathcal{U}, \longrightarrow, \varrho_0 \rangle = \langle S, \longrightarrow, \pi_0 \rangle \| \langle T, \longrightarrow, \rho_0 \rangle$,
- $\mathcal{G} = S \times \mathcal{F}$ *is the set of success states.* □

Note that as tests are finite trees, testing systems will be finite trees.

Note also that the probabilistic choice of tests correspond to the copying ability of testers, which required to characterize observational equivalence for nondeterministic processes as a testing equivalence [1].

Since each state may have several outgoing transitions in $\mathcal{P}\|\mathcal{T}$, we cannot compute a unique "probability of success" (i.e., reaching a success-state). The probability of success depends on the sequence of "choices" between outgoing transitions made both by $\mathcal{P}$ and by $\mathcal{T}$ during the course of executing $\mathcal{P}\|\mathcal{T}$. This problem disappears if the testing system happens to be a resolution, which however is not true in general. We therefore factor $\mathcal{P}\|\mathcal{T}$ into resolutions, each of which represents a sequence of such choices, and which can therefore be assigned a unique probability of success. Alternatively, we could imagine that there is a *scheduler* that decides the outcome of the next nondeterministic choice; each scheduler would then give rise to a resolution of $\mathcal{P}\|\mathcal{T}$.

Definition 6. *Let $\mathcal{P} = \langle S, \longrightarrow, \pi_0 \rangle$ be a finite tree, and let $\mathcal{C} = \langle C, \rightarrow, \theta_0 \rangle$ be a resolution. Then $\mathcal{C}$ is a resolution of $\mathcal{P}$ if*

- *$C \subseteq S$,*
- *$c \xrightarrow{a} \theta$ in C implies $c \xrightarrow{a} \theta$ in $\mathcal{P}$, and*
- *$\theta_0 = \pi_0$.* □

Intuitively, a resolution of $\mathcal{P}$ is a "subtree" of $\mathcal{P}$ which only contains probabilistic choices.

If c is a state of the resolution $\mathcal{C}$, let $\sigma_C(c)$ denote the probability of reaching c within $\mathcal{C}$. More precisely, if $c_0 c_1 \cdots c_n$ is a sequence where c_0 is initial, $c = c_n$, and for each $0 \leq i < n$ we have $c_i \xrightarrow{a_{i+1}} \theta_{i+1}$ for some a_{i+1} and θ_{i+1}, then we define

$$\sigma_C(c) = \theta_0(c_0) * \theta_1(c_1) * \cdots * \theta_n(c_n)$$

A resolution of a testing system can be assigned some probability of success. The set of resolutions defines a set of probabilities of success of $\mathcal{P}\|\mathcal{T}$, as follows.

Definition 7. *Let $\mathcal{P}\|\mathcal{T} = \langle \mathcal{U}, \longrightarrow, \varrho_0, \mathcal{G} \rangle$ be a testing system, and let $\mathcal{C} = \langle C, \rightarrow, \theta_0 \rangle$ be a resolution of $\mathcal{P}\|\mathcal{T}$. The expected outcome $\omega(\mathcal{C})$ of $\mathcal{C}$ is defined by*

$$\omega(\mathcal{C}) = \sum_{s\|t \in (\mathcal{G} \cap C)} \sigma_C(s\|t)$$

We use $\Omega(\mathcal{P}\|\mathcal{T})$ to denote the set of expected outcomes $\omega(\mathcal{C})$ of resolutions $\mathcal{C}$ of $\mathcal{P}\|\mathcal{T}$. □

We now define a may-preorder of testing, which abstract from the set of possible expected outcomes when testing a process $\mathcal{P}$ by a test $\mathcal{T}$: *may* testing considers the highest possible expected outcome of $\mathcal{P}\|\mathcal{T}$.

Definition 8. *Given two processes* $\mathcal{P}$ *and* $\mathcal{Q}$,

- $\mathcal{P} \sqsubseteq_{may} \mathcal{Q}$ *if* $\forall \mathcal{T} : \sup \Omega(\mathcal{P} \| \mathcal{T}) \geq \sup \Omega(\mathcal{Q} \| \mathcal{T})$ ⃞

Intuitively, the preorder $\sqsubseteq_{may}$ refines processes with respect to "safety properties". We can regard the success-states of a tester as states that define when the tester has observed some "bad" or "unacceptable" behavior. A process then refines another one if it has a smaller potential for "bad behavior" with respect to any test. In the definition of $\mathcal{P} \sqsubseteq_{may} \mathcal{Q}$, this means that the maximal probability of observing bad behavior of $\mathcal{Q}$ should not exceed the maximal probability of observing bad behavior of $\mathcal{P}$.

A useful property of $\sqsubseteq_{may}$ is that it is compositional in the sense that they are precongruences with respect to our parallel composition operator [12] i.e. for all processes P, Q, R, $P \sqsubseteq_{may} Q$ implies $P \| R \sqsubseteq_{may} Q \| R$.

3 Probabilistic Computation Trees

In this section, we study alternative characterizations of the testing preorder defined in Definition 8. Our intention is to derive a characterization that is similar in spirit to the trace model developed for CSP and CCS. In this model, a process is characterized by a set of traces. Each trace represents a behavior of a process in a particular context, and therefore the preorder corresponds to inclusion between traces, since a process denoted by a larger set of traces has more possibilities to interact with its environment. In our probabilistic setting, we will try to find the analogies of traces, and characterize processes as sets of such objects.

To define the $\sqsubseteq_{may}$ preorder, we will define objects that correspond to traces in standard CSP [10]. A trace in CSP is just a sequence of actions that can be performed by a process from its initial state. It represents a possible contribution of the process to a particular execution, e.g., when interacting with a test process.

To arrive at "traces" in our context, let us consider what is really the contribution by a process to an execution. First, the initial distribution of the process is "copied" to a number of instances, corresponding to different outcomes of the initial probabilistic choice of the tester. From each combination of initial states of the process and tester, the testing system synchronizes an outgoing transition from the process with an outgoing transition of the tester. the result of such a transition will be a distribution, in which the distribution of the process is copied into a number of instances, corresponding to different outcomes of the probabilistic choice in the tester after the synchronizing transition.

In summary, the contribution by the process is described by a tree-like structure in which the process chooses one outgoing transition for each outcome of a probabilistic choice, and in which each probability distribution in a transition is copied a number of times. We are thus lead to the following inductive definition of a *probabilistic computation tree.*

Definition 9. *A* Probabilistic Computation Tree *(PCT) is a triple $\phi = \langle U, \delta, u_0 \rangle$, where*

- *U is a finite set of nodes,*
- *δ is a mapping which assigns to each node in U a finite set of partial distributions over $Act \times U$. The mapping δ is required to induce a tree structure on U, where u is an immediate ancestor of v iff v is contained in a distribution in $\delta(u)$,*
- *u_0 is the root of the tree.* □

We shall use probabilistic computation trees to characterize the behaviour of a process. In general, a process may contain a set of such trees.

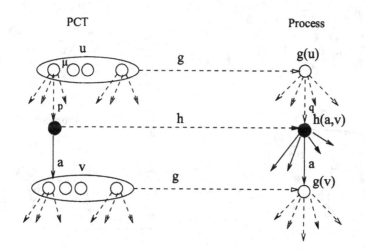

Fig. 1. Mapping a Probabilistic Computation Tree to a Process where $g(u) = \pi$, $p = \mu(a, v)$, $q = \pi(h(a, v))$, and $p \leq q$.

Definition 10. *Let $\mathcal{P} = \langle S, \longrightarrow, \pi_0 \rangle$ be a process and $\phi = \langle U, \delta, u_0 \rangle$ be a probabilistic computation tree. Then ϕ is a probabilistic computation tree of $\mathcal{P}$ if there is a mapping $g : U \mapsto Dist(S)$ such that*

- *$g(u_0) = \pi_0$ and*
- *if $g(u) = \pi$, then for each distribution $\mu \in \delta(u)$ there is an injective mapping $h : (Act \times U) \mapsto S$ such that for all (a, v) with $\mu(a, v) > 0$, we have $h(a, v) \xrightarrow{a} g(v)$ and $\mu(a, v) \leq \pi(h(a, v))$* □

The above definition has the form of a commuting diagram, which is described in Figure 1. Intuitively, the definition states that a probabilistic computation tree ϕ is a behaviour of a process iff the structure of ϕ can be simulated by that of $\mathcal{P}$. Alternatively, we may view a probabilistic computation tree as describing a set of different choices that can be made by a process. Each outcome of such a choice is modeled by a distribution over the initial states of the process together with the initial actions that are chosen. Since each state s in a distribution π of a process in general has several outgoing transitions, there can be a distribution μ for each combination of chosen next transitions from the states in π. Different combinations of transitions from states in π_0 are represented by the initial distributions of ϕ.

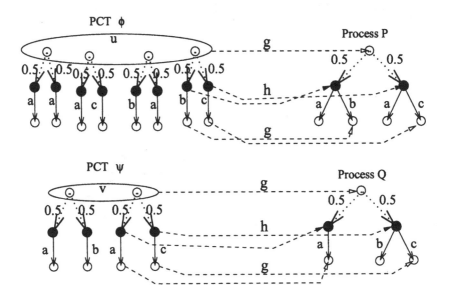

Fig. 2. Two example processes with a probabilistic computation tree.

As an example, in Figure 2 we show a probabilistic computation tree ϕ of a process $\mathcal{P}$ and a probabilistic computation tree ψ of a process $\mathcal{Q}$. In this case, the probabilistic computation trees contain a distribution for each combination of "initial transitions" in the corresponding processes. Note that the probabilistic computation tree ψ is also a probabilistic computation tree of $\mathcal{P}$ (which will imply that $\mathcal{P} \sqsubseteq_{may} \mathcal{Q}$). However, there is no obvious mapping from states of $\mathcal{Q}$ to "simulating" states of $\mathcal{P}$; for example the right state of $\mathcal{Q}$ cannot be simulated by any state of $\mathcal{P}$, which is the reason for defining $\sqsubseteq_{may}$ in terms of the probabilistic computation trees derived from a process.

We shall consider each process as a set of probabilistic computation trees, and our final goal is to characterize the may-testing preorder in terms of such trees.

We first study the inter relationship between probabilistic computation trees and tests.

The following notion of *completion* describes how a probabilistic computation tree contributes to a resolution for a given test.

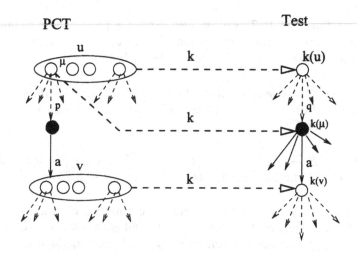

Fig. 3. *Completion* from a Probabilistic Computation Tree to a Test where $p = \rho(k(\mu)) > 0$ and $q = \mu(\langle a, u \rangle) > 0$.

Definition 11. *Let $\phi = \langle U, \delta, u_0 \rangle$ be a probabilistic computation tree, and $\mathcal{T} = \langle T, \longrightarrow, \rho_0, \mathcal{F} \rangle$ be a test. A completion from ϕ to $\mathcal{T}$ is a mapping k from U to $Dist(T)$ and from reachable distributions of ϕ to T such that*

- *$k(u_0) = \rho_0$ and*
- *if $k(u) = \rho$, then for each $\mu \in \delta(u)$, we have*
  - *$\rho(k(\mu)) > 0$ and*
  - *whenever $\mu(\langle a, u \rangle) > 0$, then $k(\mu) \xrightarrow{a} k(u)$.*   □

This definition has the form of a commuting diagram, which is described in Figure 3. Note that given a test and a probabilistic computation tree, each *completion* gives exact one resolution. The following definition states how to construct the resolution.

Definition 12. *Given a completion k from ϕ to $\mathcal{T}$, define the resolution $k(\phi)(\mathcal{T})$ as $\mathcal{C} = \langle C, \rightarrow, \theta_0 \rangle$, where*

- *C contains all pairs in the form*
  - *$\langle a, u \rangle \| k(\mu)$ such that $\mu(\langle a, u \rangle) > 0$ or*
  - *$\cdot \| k(\mu)$ where $\cdot$ is a particular element, denoting a terminated computation tree.*

$- \rightarrow$ *contains all transitions of form* $\langle a, u \rangle \| k(\mu) \xrightarrow{a} \theta(u)$ *where the distribution*
θ *is defined by*
  - $\theta(\langle a, u \rangle \| k(\mu)) = \mu(\langle a, u \rangle) * k(u)(k(\mu))$ *and*
  - $\theta(\cdot \| k(\mu)) = 1 - |\mu|.$
$- \; \theta_0 = \theta(u_0).$ □

Given a resolution $\mathcal{C}$ of $\mathcal{P} \| \mathcal{T}$, we can also extract a probabilistic computation tree ϕ which represents the contribution of $\mathcal{P}$ in $\mathcal{C}$. We can also extract the correspondence between ϕ and $\mathcal{T}$ as a completion from ϕ to $\mathcal{T}$.

Lemma 1. *Let $\mathcal{P}$ be a process and $\mathcal{T}$ be a test. For each resolution $\mathcal{C}$ of $\mathcal{P} \| \mathcal{T}$ there is a probabilistic computation tree ϕ of $\mathcal{P}$ and a completion k from ϕ to $\mathcal{T}$ such that $\mathcal{C} = k(\phi)(\mathcal{T})$.*   □

Proof. Let $\mathcal{P} = \langle S, \longrightarrow, \pi_0 \rangle$, let $\mathcal{T} = \langle T, \longrightarrow, \rho_0, \mathcal{F} \rangle$, and let $\mathcal{C} = \langle C, \rightarrow, \theta_0 \rangle$. We define the probabilistic computation tree $\phi = \langle U, \delta, u_0 \rangle$ as follows:

  - U contains a state $u_{\pi,\rho}$ for each reachable distribution of form $\pi \| \rho$ in $\mathcal{C}$,
  - δ is defined as follows: for each $u_{\pi,\rho} \in U$ and each state t with $\rho(t) > 0$, the set $\delta(u_{\pi,\rho})$ contains a distribution $\mu_{\pi,t}$ such that $\mu_{\pi,t}\langle a, u_{\pi',\rho'} \rangle) = \pi(s)$ where s is the unique state in S such that $s \| t \xrightarrow{a} \pi' \times \rho'$ is a transition of $\mathcal{C}$.
  - $u_0 = u_{\pi_0, \rho_0}.$

We now define the completion k from ϕ to $\mathcal{T}$ by $k(u_{\pi,\rho}) = \rho$ and $k(\mu_{\pi,t}) = t$.

We first check that ϕ is a probabilistic computation tree of $\mathcal{P}$ according to Definition 10. Define the mapping g by $g(\mu_{\pi,\rho}) = \pi$. For a distribution $\mu_{\pi,t}$ in $\delta(u_{\pi,\rho})$, define the mapping g from pairs of form $\langle a, u_{\pi',\rho'} \rangle)$ with $\mu_{\pi,t}(\langle a, u_{\pi',\rho'} \rangle)) > 0$ to S by $g(\langle a, u_{\pi',\rho'} \rangle)) = s$, where s is such that $\mathcal{C}$ has a transition of form $s \| t \xrightarrow{a} \pi' \times \rho'$. This implies that $g(\langle a, u_{\pi',\rho'} \rangle) \xrightarrow{a} g(u_{\pi',\rho'})$. By the definition of g, we also have $\mu_{\pi,t}(\langle a, u_{\pi',\rho'} \rangle)) = g(\mu_{\pi,\rho})(g(\langle a, u_{\pi',\rho'} \rangle))$.

We next check that k is a completion from ϕ to $\mathcal{T}$. Let $\mu_{\pi,t}$ be a distribution in $\delta(u_{\pi,\rho})$. We immediately get $\rho(t) > 0$, implying that $k(u_{\pi,\rho})(k(\mu_{\pi,t})) > 0$. If $\mu_{\pi,t}(\langle a, u_{\pi',\rho'} \rangle) > 0$ then $\mathcal{C}$ has a transition $s \| t \xrightarrow{a} \pi_i \times \rho'$, meaning that $t \xrightarrow{a} \rho'$, i.e., $k(\mu_{\pi,t}) \xrightarrow{a} k(u_{\pi',\rho'})$.

Finally, we check that $\mathcal{C}$ is isomorphic to $k(\phi)(\mathcal{T})$. Consider the definition of $k(\phi)(\mathcal{T})$.

  - The states of $k(\phi)(\mathcal{T})$ are defined to be all pairs of form
    - $\langle a, u \rangle \| k(\mu)$ such that $\mu(\langle a, u \rangle) > 0$. We identify $\langle a, u \rangle \| k(\mu)$ with the state $g(\langle a, u \rangle) \| k(\mu)$ of $\mathcal{C}$ or
    - $\cdot \| k(\mu)$. We identify $\cdot \| k(\mu)$ with all states of form $s \| k(\mu)$ which are in $\mathcal{C}$ but are not of the form $g(\langle a, u \rangle) \| k(\mu)$ for any a, u, and μ. Intuitively, these are states that have no outgoing transition in $\mathcal{C}$.

- For each $u = u_{\pi,\rho}$, we find that the distribution $\theta(u)$ is equal to $\pi \times \rho$ on those states of $\mathcal{C}$ that have an outgoing transition in $\mathcal{C}$.
- The transitions of $k(\phi)(\mathcal{T})$ are all transitions of form $\langle a, u \rangle \| k(\mu) \xrightarrow{a} \theta(u)$. Now, if $\langle a, u \rangle \| k(\mu)$ is a state, then $\mu(\langle a, u \rangle) > 0$, implying that that for some π, t, π' and ρ' we have $\mu = \mu_{\pi,t}$, $u = u_{\pi',\rho'}$, which by the definition of ϕ implies that $s \| t \xrightarrow{a} \pi' \times \rho'$. Noting that $\theta(u_{\pi',\rho'}) = \pi' \times \rho'$ concludes the proof.
- Noting that $\theta(u_{\pi_0,\rho_0}) = \pi_0 \times \rho_0$ shows that the initial distribution of $k(\phi)(\mathcal{T})$ is that of $\mathcal{C}$. $\qquad\square$

In summary, each resolution in the testing system for a given process and a given test corresponds to a probabilistic computation tree of the process and vice versa. If a *completion* is given then the correspondence is one-to-one. Our next lemma claims that the expected outcome of such a resolution can be calculated directly using the completion.

First, we need some notation. Let $\sigma_\phi(u)$ denote the probability of reaching u in ϕ. We can define this inductively as follows:

- Let $\sigma_\phi(u) = 1$ if u is the root of ϕ.
- If $\delta(u)$ contains a distribution μ with $\mu(u') > 0$, then $\sigma_\phi(u') = \mu(u') * \sigma_\phi(u)$.

Similarly, let $\sigma_\mathcal{T}(t)$ denote the probability of reaching t in the test $\mathcal{T}$. For a distribution ρ on states of $\mathcal{T}$, let $\omega(\rho)$ denote the probability $\sum_{t \in \mathcal{F}} \rho(t)$ of a successful state in ρ.

Lemma 2. *Given a probabilistic computation tree $\phi = \langle U, \delta, u_0 \rangle$ and a completion k from ϕ to a test $\mathcal{T}$, then the expected outcome $\omega(k(\phi)(\mathcal{T}))$ of $k(\phi)(\mathcal{T})$ can be calculated as*

$$\sum_{u \in U} \sigma_\phi(u) * \sigma_\mathcal{T}(k(u)) * \omega(k(u))$$

$\qquad\square$

Proof. It follows from definition 7 and 12. $\qquad\square$

That is, the expected outcome of $k(\phi)(\mathcal{T})$ can be calculated by summing for each node u in ϕ the probability of reaching the combination of u and its corresponding distribution $k(u)$ in the test, and multiplying that probability by the probability $\omega(k(u))$ that the test has at that point reached an accepting state.

4   Characterization Theorem

In Definition 12 and Lemma 1 we have established a relationship between probabilistic computation trees of $\mathcal{P}$ and resolutions of $\mathcal{P} \| \mathcal{T}$. This relationship immediately allows us to conclude that if the probabilistic computation trees of

Q are included in those of $\mathcal{P}$ then $\mathcal{P} \sqsubseteq_{may} Q$. The converse, however, does not hold. Intuitively, this is due to the following facts.

1. If ϕ_1 and ϕ_2 are probabilistic computation trees of a process, which have the same structure, only with different values assigned to the probability distributions, then the expected outcome of a resolution which corresponds to "a convex combination" (we will later make this notion precise) of ϕ_1 and ϕ_2 must always lie between the expected outcomes of resolutions that correspond to ϕ_1 and ϕ_2.
2. Deferring a probabilistic choice restricts the possibilities for a test, and hence does not increase the set of possible outcomes.
3. Making a nondeterministic choice earlier also restricts the possibilities for a test, and hence does not increase the set of possible outcomes.

We define a criterion of "covering a probabilistic computation tree by a convex combination of other probabilistic computation trees" which captures these three transformations.

Definition 13. *Let $\phi = \langle U, \delta, u_0 \rangle$ and $\psi = \langle V, \delta, v_0 \rangle$ be probabilistic computation trees. A covering from ϕ to ψ is a function h from nodes of ϕ to nodes of ψ and from reachable distributions of ϕ to reachable distributions of ψ such that*

- *whenever $\mu \in \delta(u)$ then $h(\mu) \in \delta(h(u))$,*
- *whenever $\mu(\langle a, u \rangle) > 0$ then $h(\mu)(\langle a, h(u) \rangle) > 0$, and*
- *$h(u_0) = v_0$.* □

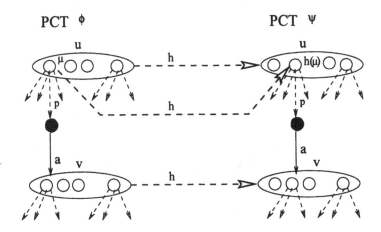

Fig. 4. *Covering* between Probabilistic Computation Trees where $p = \mu(a, v) > 0$ and $q = \pi(h(a, v)) > 0$.

We illustrate the definition in Figure 4. Intuitively, a covering from ϕ to ψ shows how ϕ can emulate ψ when composed with an arbitrary test T in the sense that if l is a completion of ψ by T, then $l \circ h$ is a completion of ϕ by T. This is stated in the following lemma.

Lemma 3. *Assume that $T = \langle T, \longrightarrow, \rho_0, \mathcal{F} \rangle$ is a test, and ϕ and ψ are probabilistic computation trees. Let l be a completion from ψ to T, and h be a covering from ϕ to ψ. Then $l \circ h$ is a completion from ϕ to T.* $\square$

Proof. Let $k = l \circ h$. We check the conditions in Definition 11.

- if $\mu \in \delta(u)$ then if $h(\mu) \in \delta(h(u))$ implying that $h(l)(u)(h(l)(\mu)) > 0$ implying that $k(u)(k(\mu)) > 0$,
- whenever $\mu(\langle a, u \rangle) > 0$ we have $h(\mu)(\langle a, h(u) \rangle) > 0$ implying $h(l)(\mu) \xrightarrow{a} h(l)(u)$, implying $k(\mu) \xrightarrow{a} k(u)$,
- $k(u_0) = h(l(u_0)) = \rho_0$. $\square$

We generalize the notion of *covering* to set of probabilistic computation trees.

Definition 14. *Assume a probabilistic computation tree $\psi = \langle V, \delta, v_0 \rangle$ and a set of such trees $\{\phi_1, \phi_2 \ldots \phi_n\}$. We say that ψ is covered by by a convex combination of (or simply covered by) $\phi_1, \ldots, \phi_n$ if*

- *there are nonnegative real numbers $\lambda_1, \lambda_2 \ldots \lambda_n$ with $\sum_{i=1}^{n} \lambda_i = 1$ and*
- *for each ϕ_i, there is a covering h_i from ϕ_i to ψ*

such that for all nodes $v \in V$ we have

$$\sigma_\psi(v) \leq \sum_{i=1}^{n} \left(\lambda_i * \sum_{v = h_i(u)} \sigma_{\phi_i}(u) \right)$$

$\square$

To establish our main result, we need the following fact from linear algebra.

Lemma 4. *Assume that x and $y_1, \ldots, y_n$ are vectors in R^m with nonnegative coordinates. If for each vector z in R^m with nonnegative coordinates there is a vector y_i such that $\langle x, z \rangle \leq \langle y_i, z \rangle$ where $\langle u, v \rangle$ is the standard inner product, then there are nonnegative real numbers $\lambda_1, \ldots, \lambda_n$ with $\sum_i \lambda_i = 1$ such that $x \leq \sum_i \lambda_i * y_i$ where the inequality $\leq$ holds in each coordinate.* $\square$

We can now state the characterization theorem for $\sqsubseteq_{may}$.

Theorem 1. $\mathcal{P} \sqsubseteq_{may} \mathcal{Q}$ *if and only if each probabilistic computation tree of* $\mathcal{Q}$ *is covered by a convex combination of probabilistic computation trees of* $\mathcal{P}$. $\quad\square$

Proof. We first treat the if-direction. Let $\mathcal{T} = \langle T, \longrightarrow, \rho_0, \mathcal{F} \rangle$ be a test, and consider a maximal resolution $\mathcal{D} = \langle D, \rightarrow, \vartheta_0 \rangle$ of $\mathcal{Q} \| \mathcal{T}$. By Lemma 1, there is a probabilistic computation tree ψ of $\mathcal{Q}$ such that $\mathcal{D} \in l(\psi)(\mathcal{T})$. By assumption, there are chains $\phi_1, \ldots, \phi_n$ of $\mathcal{P}$ and nonnegative numbers $\lambda_1, \ldots, \lambda_n$ with $\sum_i \lambda_i = 1$ such that for each $i = 1, \ldots, n$ there is a covering h_i from ϕ_i to ψ such that for all states v of ψ we have

$$\sigma_\psi(v) \leq \sum_{i=1}^n \left(\lambda_i * \sum_{v = h_i(u)} \sigma_{\phi_i}(u) \right)$$

Consider a fixed ϕ_i of $\mathcal{P}$. By Lemma 3, if $h_i(u_i) \| t$ is a state of $l(\psi)(\mathcal{T})$, then $u_i \| t$ is a state of $k(\phi_i)(\mathcal{T})$. Thus, by the definition of covering we can conclude

$$\omega(\mathcal{D}) \leq \sum_{i=1}^n \lambda_i * \omega(\mathcal{C}_i)$$

Since $\sum_i \lambda_i = 1$ there must be an i such that $\omega(\mathcal{D}) \leq \omega(\mathcal{C}_i)$. The proof now follows by observing that the resolution $\mathcal{C}_i$ can be extended to a maximal resolution $\mathcal{C}_i'$ such that $\omega(\mathcal{C}_i') \geq \omega(\mathcal{C}_i)$.

We then treat the only if-direction. Assume that $\mathcal{P} \sqsubseteq_{may} \mathcal{Q}$. Let $\psi = \langle V, \delta, v_0 \rangle$ be a probabilistic computation tree of $\mathcal{Q}$. We must prove that ψ is covered by a convex combination of probabilistic computation trees of $\mathcal{P}$. The idea of the proof is the following. Assume an arbitrary mapping $\mathbf{z} : V \mapsto [0, 1]$ from nodes of ψ to real numbers between 0 and 1. From ψ and $\mathbf{z}$ we will construct a test $\mathcal{T}_{\psi, \mathbf{z}}$ and a completion l from ψ to $\mathcal{T}_{\psi, \mathbf{z}}$ such that for each $v \in V$, the probability that $\mathcal{T}_{\psi, \mathbf{z}}$ reaches a success state which in $l(\psi)(\mathcal{T}_{\psi, \mathbf{z}})$ occurs in parallel with v is proportional to $\sigma_\psi(v) * \mathbf{z}(v)$. This probability can be expressed as the product of the probability $\sigma_{\mathcal{T}_{\psi, \mathbf{z}}}(l(v))$ that $\mathcal{T}_{\psi, \mathbf{z}}$ reaches the distribution that corresponds to v, and the proportion $\omega(l(v))$ of success states in the distribution $l(v)$. In other words, there is a $K > 0$ such that for each $v \in V$, we have

$$\sigma_{\mathcal{T}_{\psi, \mathbf{z}}}(l(v)) * \omega(l(v)) = K * \mathbf{z}(v)$$

This implies that the probability that $l(\psi)(\mathcal{T}_{\psi, \mathbf{z}})$ reaches a success state of form $v \| t$ for some t is equal to

$$\sigma_\psi(v) * \sigma_{\mathcal{T}_{\psi, \mathbf{z}}}(l(v)) * \omega(l(v)) = K * \sigma_\psi(v) * \mathbf{z}(v)$$

Thus, the probability that $l(\psi)(\mathcal{T}_{\psi, \mathbf{z}})$ reaches a success state is

$$\begin{aligned}
&\omega(l(\psi)(\mathcal{T}_{\psi, \mathbf{z}})) \\
&= \sum_{v \in V} \sigma_\psi(v) * \sigma_{\mathcal{T}_{\psi, \mathbf{z}}}(l(v)) * \omega(l(v)) \\
&= K * \sum_{v \in V} (\sigma_\psi(v) * \mathbf{z}(v))
\end{aligned}$$

Consider now an arbitrary resolution $\mathcal{C}$ of $\mathcal{P} \| \mathcal{T}_{\psi,\mathbf{z}}$. By Lemma 1 there is a probabilistic computation tree ϕ of $\mathcal{P}$ and a completion k from ϕ to $\mathcal{T}_{\psi,\mathbf{z}}$ such that $\mathcal{C} = k(\phi)(\mathcal{T}_{\psi,\mathbf{z}})$. Define the function h by letting $v = h(u)$ iff $k(u) = l(v)$, and by letting $\nu = h(\mu)$ iff $k(\mu) = l(\nu)$. It will turn out that h is a covering from ϕ to ψ. By Lemma 2 it follows that $k = l \circ h$ and that the probability that $l(\phi)(\mathcal{T}_{\psi,\mathbf{z}})$ reaches a success state satisfies

$$\begin{aligned}
&\omega(k(\phi)(\mathcal{T}_{\psi,\mathbf{z}})) \\
&= \sum_{v \in V} \sum_{v = h(u)} \left[\sigma_\phi(u) * \sigma_{\mathcal{T}_{\psi,\mathbf{z}}}(l(v)) * \omega(l(v)) \right] \\
&= K * \sum_{v \in V} \left[\left(\sum_{v = h(u)} \sigma_\phi(u) \right) * \mathbf{z}(v) \right]
\end{aligned}$$

Thus, by the assumption that $\mathcal{P} \sqsubseteq_{may} \mathcal{Q}$, we get that for any probabilistic computation tree ψ of $\mathcal{Q}$ and any $\mathbf{z} : V \mapsto [0,1]$ there must be a probabilistic computation tree ϕ of $\mathcal{P}$ such that

$$\sum_{v \in V} (\sigma_\psi(v) * \mathbf{z}(v)) \leq \sum_{v \in V} \left[\left(\sum_{v = h(u)} \sigma_\phi(u) \right) * \mathbf{z}(v) \right]$$

Since $\mathbf{z}$ is arbitrary, there must by Lemma 4 be nonnegative real numbers $\lambda_1, \ldots, \lambda_n$ with $\sum_i \lambda_i = 1$ and chains $\phi_1, \ldots, \phi_n$ of $\mathcal{P}$ such that for each nonterminal node v of ψ, we have

$$\sigma_\psi(v) \leq \sum_{i=1}^{n} \left(\lambda_i * \sum_{v = h_i(u)} \sigma_{\phi_i}(u) \right)$$

Since we earlier proved that each such h_i is a covering from ϕ_i to ψ, the theorem is proven.

It remains to construct the test $\mathcal{T}_{\psi,\mathbf{z}}$. This is done as the tuple $\langle T, \longrightarrow, \rho_0, \mathcal{F} \rangle$ where

- T consists of
  - one state t_ν for each reachable distribution $\nu \in Dist(\mathcal{A}ct \times V)$ of ψ, and
  - one state t_v for each reachable state v of ψ,
- Define $l(\nu) = t_\nu$.
- The test $\mathcal{T}_{\psi,\mathbf{z}}$ has one reachable distribution, defined as $l(v)$, for each $v \in V$, which satisfies, either
  - $l(v)(t') > 0$ iff $t' = t_{\nu'}$ for ν' with $\nu' \in \delta(v)$, and
  - $l(v)(t') \geq 0$ iff $t' = t_v$.
- $\longrightarrow$ contains a transition $t_\nu \xrightarrow{b} l(v)$ for each reachable distribution ν in ψ, and for each pair $\langle b, v \rangle$ with $\nu(\langle b, v \rangle) > 0$.
- $\rho_0 = l(v_0)$.
- $\mathcal{F}$ is the set of states of form t_v for $v \in V$.

The probabilities in $T_{\psi,\mathbf{z}}$ are assigned so that for some normalization constant $K > 0$ we have that for each $v \in V$:

$$K * \mathbf{z}(v) = \sigma_{T_{\psi,\mathbf{z}}}(t_v) = \sigma_{T_{\psi,\mathbf{z}}}(l(v)) * \omega(l(v))$$

where $\sigma_{T_{\psi,\mathbf{z}}}(l(v))$ is the probability of reaching the distribution $l(v)$ within $T_{\psi,\mathbf{z}}$, and $\omega(l(v))$ is simply $l(v)(t_v)$, i.e., the probability of reaching the success state t_v within the distribution $l(v)$.

We should check that the mapping l as defined above is really a completion from ψ to $T_{\psi,\mathbf{z}}$. We check the conditions in Definition 11.

- Let $v \in V$, and if $\nu \in \delta(v)$. By the definition of $k(v)$ we have $k(v)(k(\nu)) > 0$.
- Let $\nu(\langle a, v \rangle) > 0$. By the definition of $\longrightarrow$ we have $k(\nu) \overset{a}{\longrightarrow} k(v)$.
- By definition, $k(v_0) = \rho_0$.

We next check that the function h is indeed a covering from ϕ to ψ. Recall that a state of ϕ is of form $u_{\pi,\rho}$, where π is a reachable distribution in $\mathcal{P}$ and ρ is a reachable distribution in $T_{\psi,\mathbf{z}}$. By the construction of $T_{\psi,\mathbf{z}}$, the distribution ρ is $l(v)$ for some $v \in V$. Since $k(u_{\pi,l(v)})$ is defined to be $l(v)$, we have $h(u_{\pi,l(v)}) = v$. This is well defined, since l is injective and ranges over all reachable distributions of $T_{\psi,\mathbf{z}}$. We check the conditions in Definition 13.

- Let $\mu \in \delta(u)$. By the proof of Lemma 1 this means that $\mu = \mu_{\pi,t}$ and $u = u_{\pi,\rho}$ with $\rho(t) > 0$. By the construction of $T_{\psi,\mathbf{z}}$, This means that $\rho = l(v)$ and that $t = l(\nu)$ where $\nu \in \delta(v)$.
- Let $\mu(\langle a, u \rangle) > 0$. By the proof of Lemma 1 this means that $\mu = \mu_{\pi,t}$ and $u = u_{\pi',\rho'}$, with $t \overset{a}{\longrightarrow} \rho'$. By the construction of $T_{\psi,\mathbf{z}}$, This means that $t = l(\nu)$ and that $\rho' = l(v)$ where $\nu(\langle a, v \rangle) > 0$.
- $h(u_0) = v_0$ is trivial. □

5   Conclusion

Transition systems are well-established as a basic semantic model for concurrent and distributed systems (e.g. [16, 17, 19]). To study probabilistic behaviours, various extensions to the model of transition systems have been proposed. One of these extensions is probabilistic transition systems (see e.g. [31, 12, 25, 23]) in which the concept of probabilistic choice is independent from that of nondeterministic choice. Thus, one can reason about nondeterministic e.g. underspecification and stochastic behaviours in one framework. To developed a semantical basis of refinement for probabilistic transition systems, we have studied the notion of probabilistic testing and the associated compositional testing preorders, developed by Wang and Larsen [31], which extends the testing framework of de Nicola and Hennessy [5] for nonprobabilistic processes.

We have developed a model of *probabilistic computation trees*. We believe that the model of probabilistic computation trees is a natural probabilistic extension of the classic trace model for CSP [10]. Our main contribution is a fully abstract characterization of the may-testing preorder. The characterization is given based on convex closures of probabilistic computation trees.

References

[1] Samson Abramsky. Observation equivalence as a testing equivalence. *Theoretical Computer Science*, 53(2,3):225–241, 1987.

[2] I. Christoff. Testing equivalences and fully abstract models for probabilistic processes. In Baeten, editor, *Proc. CONCUR, Amsterdam*, volume 458 of *Lecture Notes in Computer Science*, pages 126–140. Springer Verlag, 1990.

[3] R. Cleaveland, S. Smolka, and A. Zwarico. Testing preorders for probabilistic processes. In *Proc. ICALP '92*, 1992.

[4] C. Courcoubetis and M. Yannakakis. The complexity of probabilistic verification. In *Proc. 29th Annual Symp. Foundations of Computer Science*, pages 338–345, 1988.

[5] R. de Nicola and M. Hennessy. Testing equivalences for processes. *Theoretical Computer Science*, 34:83–133, 1984.

[6] A. Giacalone, C. Jou, and S.A. Smolka. Algebraic reasoning for probabilistic concurrent systems. In *Proc. IFIP TC2 Working Conference on Programming Concepts and Methods*, Sea of Galilee, April 1990.

[7] H. Hansson and B. Jonsson. A calculus for communicating systems with time and probabilities. In *Proc. 11th IEEE Real-Time Systems Symposium*, Orlando, Florida, 1990.

[8] H. Hansson and B. Jonsson. A logic for reasoning about time and reliability. *Formal Aspects of Computing*, 6:512–535, 1994.

[9] S. Hart and M. Sharir. Probabilistic temporal logics for finite and bounded models. In *Proc. 16th ACM Symp. on Theory of Computing*, pages 1–13, 1984.

[10] C. A. R. Hoare. *Communicating Sequential Processes*. Prentice-Hall, 1985.

[11] B. Jonsson, C. Ho-Stuart, and Wang Yi. Testing and refinement for nondeterministic and probabilistic processes. In Langmaack, de Roever, and Vytopil, editors, *Formal Techniques in Real-Time and Fault-Tolerant Systems*, volume 863 of *Lecture Notes in Computer Science*, pages 418–430. Springer Verlag, 1994.

[12] B. Jonsson and Wang Yi. Compositional testing preorders for probabilistic processes. In *Proc. 10th IEEE Int. Symp. on Logic in Computer Science*, pages 431–441, 1995.

[13] D. Kozen. A probabilistic pdl. In *Proc. 15th ACM Symp. on Theory of Computing*, pages 291–297, 1983.

[14] K.G. Larsen and A. Skou. Bisimulation through probabilistic testing. *Information and Control*, 94(1):1–28, 1991.

[15] Gavin Lowe. *Probabilities and Priorities in Timed CSP*. D. Phil thesis, Oxford, 1993.

[16] Z. Manna and A. Pnueli. The anchored version of the temporal framework. In de Bakker, de Roever, and Rozenberg, editors, *Linear Time, Branching Time and Partial Order in Logics and Models for Concurrency*, volume 354 of *Lecture Notes in Computer Science*, pages 201–284. Springer Verlag, 1989.

[17] R. Milner. *Communication and Concurrency*. Prentice-Hall, 1989.

[18] M.K. Molloy. Performance analysis using stochastic Petri nets. *IEEE Trans. on Computers*, C-31(9):913–917, Sept. 1982.

[19] G. Plotkin. A structural approach to operational semantics. Technical Report DAIMI FN-19, Computer Science Department, Aarhus University, Denmark, 1981.

[20] A. Pnueli and L. Zuck. Verification of multiprocess probabilistic protocols. *Distributed Computing*, 1(1):53–72, 1986.

[21] S. Purushothaman and P.A. Subrahmanyam. Reasoning about probabilistic behavior in concurrent systems. *IEEE Trans. on Software Engineering*, SE-13(6):740–745, June 1989.

[22] M.O. Rabin. Probabilistic automata. *Information and Control*, 6:230–245, 1963.

[23] R. Segala. A compositional trace-based semantics for probabilistic automata. In *Proc. CONCUR '95, 6th Int. Conf. on Concurrency Theory*, volume 962 of *Lecture Notes in Computer Science*, pages 234–248. Springer Verlag, 1995.

[24] R. Segala and N. Lynch. Probabilistic simulations for probabilistic processes. In Jonsson and Parrow, editors, *Proc. CONCUR '94, 5th Int. Conf. on Concurrency Theory*, number 836 in Lecture Notes in Computer Science, pages 481–496. Springer Verlag, 1994.

[25] R. Segala and N.A. Lynch. Probabilistic simulations for probabilistic processes. *Nordic Journal of Computing*, 2(2):250–273, 1995.

[26] R. van Glabbeek, S.A. Smolka, B. Steffen, and C. Tofts. Reactive, generative, and stratified models of probabilistic processes. In *Proc. 5th IEEE Int. Symp. on Logic in Computer Science*, pages 130–141, 1990.

[27] M. Y. Vardi and P. Wolper. An automata-theoretic approach to automatic program verification. In *Proc. 1st IEEE Int. Symp. on Logic in Computer Science*, pages 332–344, June 1986.

[28] M.Y. Vardi. Automatic verification of probabilistic concurrent finite-state programs. In *Proc. 26th Annual Symp. Foundations of Computer Science*, pages 327–338, 1985.

[29] S.-H. Wu, S.A. Smolka, and E.W. Stark. Composition and behaviors of probabilistic I/O-Automata. In Jonsson and Parrow, editors, *Proc. CONCUR '94, 5th Int. Conf. on Concurrency Theory*, number 836 in Lecture Notes in Computer Science, pages 513–528. Springer Verlag, 1994.

[30] Wang Yi. Algebraic reasoning for real-time probabilistic processes with uncertain information. In Langmaack, de Roever, and Vytopil, editors, *Formal Techniques in Real-Time and Fault-Tolerant Systems*, volume 863 of *Lecture Notes in Computer Science*, pages 680–693. Springer Verlag, 1994.

[31] Wang Yi and K. Larsen. Testing probabilistic and nondeterministic processes. In *Protocol Specification, Testing, and Verification XII*, 1992.

[32] S. Yuen, R. Cleaveland, Z. Dayar, and S.A. Smolka. Fully abstract characterizations of testing preorders for probabilistic processes. In Jonsson and Parrow, editors, *Proc. CONCUR '94, 5th Int. Conf. on Concurrency Theory*, number 836 in Lecture Notes in Computer Science, pages 497–512. Springer Verlag, 1994.

Quantitative Program Logic and Performance in Probabilistic Distributed Algorithms

Annabelle K. McIver

Programming Research Group, Oxford University, UK.
anabel@comlab.ox.ac.uk,
http://www.comlab.ox.ac.uk/oucl/groups/probs.
The work is supported by the EPSRC.

Abstract. In this paper we show how quantitative program logic [14] provides a formal framework in which to promote standard techniques of program analysis to a context where probability and nondeterminism interact, a situation common to probabilistic distributed algorithms. We show that overall performance can be formulated directly in the logic and that it can be derived from local properties of components. We illustrate the methods with an analysis of performance of the probabilistic dining philosophers [10].

1 Introduction

Distributed systems consist of a number of independent components whose interleaved behaviour typically generates much nondeterminism; the addition of probability incurs an extra layer of complexity. Our principal aims here are to illustrate how, using 'quantitative program logic' [14], familiar techniques from standard programming paradigms easily extend to the probabilistic context, and that they can be used even to evaluate performance.

Examples of all our program techniques — compositional reasoning, μ-calculus treatments of temporal logic and fairness — can be found in the general literature [2, 9]; the novel aspects of the present work lie in their smooth extension via the quantitative logic, and our exploitation of the extended type (of reals rather than Booleans) in our formulation of performance operators as explicit μ-calculus expressions in the logic. The advantages are not merely cosmetic: by making performance and correctness objects of the same kind we discover that performance can be calculated directly from local properties of components. Locality has particular significance here since in practice it reduces system-wide analysis to the analysis of a single component in isolation from the others, vastly simplifying arguments. And finally, it is worth mentioning that though our primary theme is proof, our estimated performance of the random dining philosophers [10] is still lower than some other published analyses [11].

Our presentation is in three sections. In Sec. 2 and Sec. 3 we set out the programming model, the quantitative program logic and the μ-calculus formulations for probabilistic temporal logic and performance. Some properties of the

J.-P. Katoen (Ed.): ARTS'99, LNCS 1601, pp. 19–33, 1999.

operators are also explained in those sections. In Sec. 4 we analyse the dining philosophers.

We uniformly use S for the state space and $\mathcal{D}S$ for discrete probability distributions over S. We also use ':=' for 'is defined to be' and '.' for function application. We lift ordinary arithmetic operators pointwise to operators between functions: addition $(+)$; multiplication $(\times)$; maximum $(\sqcup)$ and minimum $(\sqcap)$. Other notation is introduced as needed.

2   Program Logic and Estimating Probabilities

Operationally we model probabilistic sequential programs [14, 7] (compare also [3, 11]) as functions from (initial) state to *sets* of distributions over (final) states. Intuitively that describes a computation proceeding in two (indivisible) stages: a nondeterministic choice, immediately followed by a probabilistic choice, where the probability refers to the possible final states reachable from a given initial state. In this view the role of nondeterminism is to allow an arbitrary selection over some range of probability distributions; however the agent making that selection can only influence the weights of the probabilistic transitions, not their *actual* resolution once those weights have been picked. That behaviour is precisely the kind exhibited by an 'adversary scheduler' assumed of many distributed algorithms [11]. We shall discuss schedulers in more detail in Sec. 4.

Unlike other authors we shall not use the operational model directly for program analysis. We introduce it only as an aid to intuition and in practice we use the quantitative program logic introduced elsewhere [14, 15]: it is equivalent to the operational view and is analytically more attractive. The idea, first suggested by Kozen [8] for deterministic programs, is to extract information about probabilistic choices by considering 'expected values'. Ordinary program logic [4] identifies preconditions that guarantee post conditions, in contrast, for probabilistic programs, the *probability*, rather than the certainty of achieving a post condition is of interest, and Kozen's insight was to formulate that as the result of averaging certain real-valued functions of the state over the final distributions determined by the program. Thus, the quantitative logic we use is an extension of Kozen's (since our programs are both nondeterministic and probabilistic) and is based on *expectations* (real-valued functions of the state rather than Boolean-valued predicates). We denote the space of expectations by $\mathcal{E}S(:=S \to \mathbb{R})$, and we define the semantics of a probabilistic program r as $wp.r$, an *expectation transformer* [14].

Definition 2.1 Let $r \colon S \to \mathbb{P}(\mathcal{D}S)$ be a program taking initial states in S to sets of final distributions over S. Then the *least possible*[1] pre-expectation at state s of program r, with respect to post-expectation A in $\mathcal{E}S$, is defined

---

[1] This interpretation is the same as the *greatest guaranteed* pre-expectation used elsewhere [14].

$$wp.r.A.s \quad := \quad (\sqcap F{:}r.s \cdot \int_F A) \, ,$$

where $\int_F A$ denotes the integral of A with respect to distribution F.[2]   □

In the special case that A is a $\{0, 1\}$-valued — a *characteristic* expectation — we may identify a predicate which is *true* exactly at those states where A evaluates to 1, and then the above interpretation makes $wp.r.A.s$ the least possible probability that r terminates in a state satisfying that predicate. To economise on notation we often pun a characteristic expectation with its associated predicate, saying that 's satisfies A' when strictly speaking we mean $A.s = 1$. The context should dispel confusion, however. Other distinguished functions are the constants $\underline{1}$ and $\underline{0}$ evaluating everywhere to 1 and 0 respectively and thus corresponding to *true* and *false*. We also write $\overline{A}$ for the negation of A (equivalent to $\underline{1} - A$).

By taking the minimum over a set of distributions in Def. 2.1, we are adopting the demonic interpretation for nondeterministic choice, and for many applications it is the most useful, since it generalises the 'for all' modality of transition semantics [1]. Thus if $wp.r.A.s = p$ say for some real p then *all* (probabilistic) transitions in $r.s$ ensure a probability of at least p of achieving A. For our application to performance, however, upper bounds have more significance: thus we define also the dual of $wp.r$, generalising the 'exists' modality [1]. (Compare also upper and lower probability estimates [3].)

Definition 2.2 Let $r{:}S \to \mathbb{P}(\mathcal{D}S)$ be a program, taking initial states in S to sets of final distributions over S. Then the *greatest possible* pre-expectation at state s of program r, with respect to post-expectation A in $\mathcal{E}S$, is defined[3]

$$\widetilde{wp}.r.A.s \quad := \quad \underline{1} - wp.r.(\underline{1} - A).s \, .$$

□

The semantics for a (restricted) programming language, sufficient for the applications of later sections, is set out in Fig. 1. It is essentially the same as for ordinary predicate transformers [4] except for probabilistic choice which is defined as the weighted average of the pre-expectations of its operands.

To illustrate the logic we consider the program set out in Fig. 2, for which we calculate the least possible probability that the variable b is set to *true* after a single execution. From Def. 2.1 that is given by $wp.\text{Chooser}.\{b = true\}$, where $\{e = v\}$ denotes the predicate (i.e. characteristic expectation) 'e is equal to v'. From Fig. 1 we see that in order to evaluate the conditional choice in Chooser, we need to consider each of the options separately.

We calculate the '$b = false$' case first. Denoting equivalence of expectations by $\equiv$, we reason:

---

[2] In fact $\int_F A$ is just $\sum_{s:S} A.s \times F.s$ because S is finite and and F is discrete [5]. We use the $\int$-notation because it is less cluttered, and to be consistent with the more general case.

[3] This is equivalent to interpreting nondeterministic choice as maximum, and so $\widetilde{wp}.r.A.s = (\sqcup F{:}r.s \cdot \int_F A)$. It is similar to an angelic interpretation for nondeterminism.

assignment	$wp.(x := E).A := A[E/x]$
probabilistic choice	$wp.(r \ {}_p\oplus r').A := p(wp.r.A) + (1-p)(wp.r'.A)$
nondeterministic choice	$wp.(r\|r').A := wp.r.A \sqcap wp.r'.A$
sequential composition	$wp.(r;r').A := wp.r.(wp.r'.A)$
conditional choice	$wp.(r \text{ if } B \text{ else } r').A := B \times wp.r.A + \overline{B} \times wp.r'.A$

A is in $\mathcal{ES}$ and E is an expression in the program variables. The expression $A[E/x]$ denotes replacement of variable x by E in A. The real p satisfies $0 \le p \le 1$, and pA means 'expectation A scaled by p'. Finally B is Boolean-valued when it appears in a program statement but is interpreted as a $\{0,1\}$-valued expectation in the semantics.

Fig. 1. Probabilistic wp semantics. Nondeterminism is interpreted demonically.

$$\text{Chooser} := (b := true) \text{ if } \{b = true\} \text{ else } (b := true)\|(b := true \ {}_{1/2}\oplus b := false)$$

If b is *false* initially then it can be either set to *true* unconditionally, or only with probability $1/2$: the choice between those two options is resolved nondeterministically.

Fig. 2. Randomised Chooser with a Boolean-valued variable b.

$$wp.((b := true)\|(b := true \ {}_{1/2}\oplus b := false)).\{b = true\}$$

$$ \text{nondeterministic choice}$$

$\equiv \quad wp.(b := true).\{b = true\} \sqcap wp.(b := true \ {}_{1/2}\oplus b := false).\{b = true\}$

$$ \text{assignment}$$

$\equiv \quad \{true = true\} \sqcap wp.(b := true \ {}_{1/2}\oplus b := false).\{b = true\}$

$$ \text{see below}$$

$\equiv \quad \underline{1} \sqcap (wp.(b := true \ {}_{1/2}\oplus b := false).\{b = true\})$

$$ \text{probabilistic choice}$$

$\equiv \quad \underline{1} \sqcap (1/2(wp.(b := true).\{b = true\}) + 1/2(wp.(b := false).\{b = true\}))$

$$ \text{assignment}$$

$\equiv \quad \underline{1} \sqcap (\{true = true\}/2 + \{false = true\}/2)$

$$ \text{see below}$$

$\equiv \quad \underline{1} \sqcap (1/2 \times \underline{1} + 1/2 \times \underline{0})$

$\equiv \quad \underline{1/2} \ . \text{arithmetic}$

For the deferred justifications, we use the equivalences $\{true = true\} \equiv \underline{1}$ and $\{false = true\} \equiv \underline{0}$.

A similar (though easier) calculation follows for the '$b = true$' case, resulting in $wp.(b := true).\{b = true\} \equiv \underline{1}$, and putting the two together with the rule for conditional choice we find

$$wp.\text{Chooser}.\{b = true\} \equiv \{b = true\} + \{b = false\}/2 , \qquad (1)$$

implying that there is a probability of at *least* $1/2$ of achieving $\{b = true\}$ if execution of Chooser begins at $\{b = false\}$ and of (at least) 1 if execution begins at $\{b = true\}$.

In contrast, we can calculate the *greatest possible* probability of reaching $\{b = false\}$ using Def. 2.2:

$$
\left.
\begin{array}{lll}
& \widetilde{wp}.\text{Chooser}.\{b = false\} & \\
\equiv & 1 - wp.\text{Chooser}.(\underline{1} - \{b = false\}) & \text{Def. 2.2} \\
\equiv & 1 - wp.\text{Chooser}.\{b = true\} & b \text{ is Boolean-valued} \\
\equiv & 1 - (\{b = true\} + \{b = false\}/2) & (1) \\
\equiv & \{b = false\}/2 \ , &
\end{array}
\right\} \quad (2)
$$

yielding a probability of at *most* $1/2$ if execution begins at $\{b = false\}$ and 0 if it begins at $\{b = true\}$ — there is no execution from $\{b = true\}$ to $\{b = false\}$.

In this section we have considered maximum and minimum probabilities using wp and $\widetilde{wp}$ for a single execution of a program. In the next section we extend the ideas to temporal-style semantics.

3   Computation Trees and Fixed Points

In this section we consider arbitrarily many executions of a fixed program denoted $\bigcirc$. Later we shall interpret it as wp.prog for some program prog, but for the moment we adopt an abstract view. (We shall also use $\widetilde{\bigcirc}$ to be interpreted as $\widetilde{wp}$.prog.) Ordinary program semantics of such systems are computation trees [1], with each arc of the tree representing a transition determined by $\bigcirc$. A *path* in the tree represents the effect of some number of executions of $\bigcirc$, and is defined by a sequence whose entries are (labelled by) the states connecting contiguous arcs. When $\bigcirc$ contains probabilistic choices, the probabilistic transitions in $\bigcirc$ generate (sets of) probability distributions over paths of the computation tree: probabilities over finite paths may be calculated directly, and they determine a well defined probability distribution over all paths.[4] Our aim for this section is, as for the state-to-state transition model, to extract probabilistic information about the paths by interpreting 'path operators' (defined with expectation transformers) over the computation trees, again avoiding direct reference to the underlying path-distributions.

Standard treatments of tree-based semantics often use μ-calculus expressions in the program logic [9], and it turns out [16] that such formulations for the temporal properties 'eventually' and 'always' have straightforward generalisations in the quantitative logic by replacing $\vee$ and $\wedge$ in those expressions by $\sqcup$ and $\sqcap$ respectively. The resulting operators, $\Diamond$ and $\square$ (set out in Fig. 3), when applied to a characteristic expectation A return the probability (rather than the certainty) that eventually or always A holds of the paths in the computation tree.

---

[4] It is usually called the Borel measure over cones [5].

But in the more general setting we can do more: for the reals support a wider range of operators (than do Booleans), promising greater expressivity; indeed as well as correctness we can also express *performance* directly within the logic. Our first performance measure denoted ΔA, (also set out in Fig. 3) expresses the expected length of the path in the computation tree until predicate A holds. In the context of program analysis it corresponds to the expected *number* of (repeated) executions of $\bigcirc$ required until A holds.

least possible eventually	$\diamond A := (\mu X \cdot A \sqcup \bigcirc X)$
greatest possible eventually	$\widetilde{\diamond} A := (\mu X \cdot A \sqcup \widetilde{\bigcirc} X)$
least possible always	$\square A := (\nu X \cdot A \sqcap \bigcirc X)$
greatest possible always	$\widetilde{\square} A := (\nu X \cdot A \sqcap \widetilde{\bigcirc} X)$
least possible time to A	$\Delta A := (\mu X \cdot \underline{0} \text{ if } A \text{ else } (\underline{1} + \bigcirc X))$
greatest possible time to A	$\widetilde{\Delta} A := (\mu X \cdot \underline{0} \text{ if } A \text{ else } (\underline{1} + \widetilde{\bigcirc} X))$

A is $\{0, 1\}$-valued.

Fig. 3. Expectation operators with respect to a distribution over the computation tree generated by $\bigcirc$.

To make the link between the fixed-point expression for ΔA in Fig. 3 and expected length of the computation path to reach A we unfold the fixed point once: if A holds it returns 0 — no more steps are required to achieve A along the path; otherwise we obtain a '1+' — at least one more step is required to reach A[5]. A formal justification is given elsewhere [13].

In general the μ-calculus expressions correspond to the 'for all' or 'exists' fragments of temporal logic [1] according to whether they are defined with $\bigcirc$ or $\widetilde{\bigcirc}$. For example $\widetilde{\diamond} A$ defined with $\widetilde{\bigcirc}$ returns the maximum possible probability that a path satisfies eventually A. Also $\widetilde{\Delta} A$ gives an upper bound on the number of steps required to reach A.

The introduction of fixed points requires a notion of partial order on $\mathcal{E}S$, and here we use one induced by *probabilistic implication* $\Rrightarrow$ (defined next with its variants) extending ordinary Boolean implication:

$$\Rrightarrow \text{ 'everywhere no more than'}$$
$$\equiv \text{ 'everywhere equal to'}$$
$$\Lleftarrow \text{ 'everywhere no less than' .}$$

---

[5] An equivalent formulation for $\widetilde{\Delta} A$ is $(\mu X \cdot \overline{A} \times (1 + \widetilde{\bigcirc} X))$. We shall use this more succinct form in our calculations rather than that set out in Fig. 3, which is helpful only in that it is close to the informal explanation.

In fact we define fixed points within certain subsets of $\mathcal{E}S$ because the existence of the fixed points are assured in spaces that have a least or greatest element and the whole of $\mathcal{E}S$ has neither.[6] We are careful however to choose subsets that suit our interpretation. Thus for least fixed points (μ) we take the non-negative expectations: the least element is $\underline{0}$, and our applications — average times and probabilities of events — are all the result of averaging over non-negative expectations. For greatest fixed points (ν) we restrict to expectations bounded above by $\underline{1}$: the greatest element is $\underline{1}$ and we use greatest fixed points only to express probabilities which involve averaging over characteristic expectations, themselves bounded above by $\underline{1}$. We set out the full technical details elsewhere [16].

feasibility	$\widetilde{\diamond} A \Rrightarrow \underline{1}$
duality	If $A \Rrightarrow \underline{1}$ then $\widetilde{\diamond} A \equiv \underline{1} - \Box(\underline{1} - A)$
invariants	If $I \Rrightarrow \bigcirc I$ and $I \Rrightarrow A$ then $I \Rrightarrow \Box A$

A is $\{0, 1\}$-valued and I are in $\mathcal{E}S$.

Fig. 4. Some properties of the path operators

The first property of Fig. 4 are general to expectation operators whereas the latter two apply only to fixed points. In particular the invariant law extends the notion of ordinary program invariants: an expectation I in $\mathcal{E}S$ is said to be an *invariant* of $\bigcirc$ provided $\bigcirc I \Lleftarrow I$. When I takes arbitrary values, the invariant law says that the probability that A always holds along the paths with initial state s is at least $I.s$. This property is fundamental to our treatment of 'rounds' in the next section.

We end this section with a small example illustrating $\widetilde{\triangle}$. We use the program Chooser set out in Fig. 2 above, (hence $\bigcirc$ is interpreted as $\widetilde{wp}$.Chooser), and we wish to calculate $\triangle\{b = true\}$ an upper bound on the expected number of times Chooser must be executed until b is set to *true*. In a simple case where there is a probability of success on each execution (specifically here if Chooser sets b to *true*) elementary probability theory implies that the expected time to success is the result of summing over a geometric distribution; in contrast the calculation below shows how to find that time using our program logic. (In fact since Chooser is nondeterministic, probability theory is not applicable, and the analysis requires a more general framework such as this one.) We note first that $\widetilde{\triangle}\{b = true\}$ evaluated at '$b = true$' is 0 (for b is already set to *true*). Thus we

---

[6] We also assume continuity of the operators concerned [14].

know that $\widetilde{\triangle}\{b = true\} \equiv q\{b = false\}$, for some non-negative real, q which we must determine (where recall that we use qA to mean 'A scaled by q'). With that in mind, we reason

$$\widetilde{\triangle}\{b = true\}$$

$\qquad\qquad\qquad\qquad\qquad\qquad\qquad$ definition $\widetilde{\triangle}$; Fig. 3 and footnote 5

$$\equiv \quad \overline{\{b = true\}} \times (\underline{1} + \widetilde{wp}.\text{Chooser}.(\widetilde{\triangle}\{b = true\}))$$

$\qquad\qquad\qquad\qquad\qquad\qquad\qquad \widetilde{\triangle}\{b = true\} \equiv q\{b = false\}$

$$\equiv \quad \{b = false\} \times (\underline{1} + \widetilde{wp}.\text{Chooser}.(q\{b = false\}))$$

$\qquad\qquad\qquad\qquad\qquad\qquad\qquad\qquad\qquad\qquad \text{see below}$

$$\equiv \quad \{b = false\} \times (\underline{1} + q(\widetilde{wp}.\text{Chooser}.\{b = false\}))$$

$\qquad\qquad\qquad\qquad\qquad\qquad\qquad\qquad\qquad\qquad \text{from (2)}$

$$\equiv \quad \{b = false\} \times (\underline{1} + q\{b = false\}/2) \;.$$

For the deferred justification we are using the scaling property of $\widetilde{wp}.$Chooser which allows us to distribute the scalar q. [7]

Now evaluating at '$b = false$' we deduce from the above equality that

$$q = 1 + q/2 \;,$$

giving $q = 2$, and (unsurprisingly) an *upper bound* of 2 on the number of executions of Chooser required to achieve success.

4   Fair Adversary Schedulers and Counting Rounds

We now illustrate our operators above by considering Rabin and Lehmann's randomised solution [10] to the well-known problem of the dining philosophers. The problem is usually presented as a number of philosophers $P_1, .., P_N$ seated around a table, who variously think (T) or eat (E). In order to eat they must pick up two forks, each shared between neighbouring philosophers, where the i'th philosopher has left, right neighbours respectively P_{i-1} and P_{i+1} (with subscripts numbered modulo N). The problem is to find a distributed protocol guaranteeing that some philosopher will eventually eat (in the case that some philosopher is continuously hungry). Randomisation is used here to obtain a symmetrical solution in the sense that philosophers execute identical code — any non-random solution cannot both guarantee eating and be symmetrical [10].

The aim for this section is to calculate upper bounds on the expected time until some philosopher eats, and since we are only interested in the time to eat we have excluded the details following that event. The algorithm set out in Fig. 5 represents the behaviour of the i'th philosopher, where each atomic step is numbered. A philosopher is only able to execute a step provided he is scheduled and when he is, he executes exactly one of the steps, without interference from

---

[7] Scaling is a standard property of expectation operators from probability theory [20] which also holds here. Others are monotonicity and continuity. In fact only distribution of addition fails: nondeterminism forces a weakening of that axiom; compare suplinearity of Fig. 7.

the other philosophers. Fig. 5 then describes a philosopher as follows: initially he decides randomly which fork to pick up first; next he persists with his decision until he finally picks it up, only putting it down later if he finds that his other fork is already taken by his neighbour. We have omitted the details relating to the shared fork variables, and for ease of presentation we use labels T, E, l, r etc. to denote a philospher's state, rather than the explicit variable assignments they imply. Thus, for example, if P_i is in state L_i or P_{i-1} is in state R_{i-1}, it means the variable representing the shared fork (between P_i and P_{i-1}) has been set to a value that means 'taken'. The distributed system can now be defined as repeated executions of the program $\|_{1 \leq i \leq N} P_i$, together with a fairness condition, discussed next.

$$
\begin{aligned}
1. \ & \textbf{if } T_i && \to l_{i \ 1/2} \oplus r_i \\[4pt]
2. \ & \| \ (l_i \vee r_i) && \to \textbf{if } (l_i \wedge \neg R_{i-1}) \to L_i \\
& && \| \ (l_i \wedge R_{i-1}) \ \to l_i \\
& && \| \ (r_i \wedge \neg L_{i+1}) \to R_i \\
& && \| \ (r_i \wedge L_{i+1}) \ \to r_i \\
& && \textbf{fi} \\[4pt]
3. \ & \| \ (L_i \vee R_i) && \to \textbf{if } (L_i \wedge \neg R_{i-1}) \to E_i \\
& && \| \ (L_i \wedge R_{i-1}) \ \to \mathbb{L}_i \\
& && \| \ (R_i \wedge \neg L_{i+1}) \to E_i \\
& && \| \ (R_i \wedge L_{i+1}) \ \to \mathbb{R}_i \\
& && \textbf{fi} \\[4pt]
4. \ & \| \ (\mathbb{L}_i \vee \mathbb{R}_i) && \to T_i \\
& \textbf{fi}
\end{aligned}
$$

The state T_i represents thinking, l_i (r_i) that a philosopher will attempt to pick up the left (right) fork next time he is scheduled, L_i (R_i) that he is holding only the left (right) fork, $\mathbb{L}_i$ ($\mathbb{R}_i$) that he will put down the left (right) fork next time he is scheduled and E_i that he eats. The use of state as a Boolean means 'is in that state'; as a statement it means 'is set to that state'.

Fig. 5. The i'th philosopher's algorithm [10].

A fundamental assumption of distributed systems is that of a scheduler. Roughly speaking it is the mechanism that manages the nondeterminism in $\|_{1 \leq i \leq N} P_i$, and its only constraint here is fairness: if a philosopher is continuously hungry (or 'enabled') then he must eventually be scheduled (and for simplicity we assume that philosophers are either enabled or eating). That assumption, of course, means that counting atomic steps is pointless — any particular philosopher may be ignored for an arbitrary long interval whilst other philosophers are scheduled. Instead we count *rounds*, an interval in which each philosopher has been scheduled at least once — and fairness guarantees that rounds exist.

However there is a problem: recall that the tree semantics for a distributed system is composed of paths (denoted by t) in which arcs represent the effect of atomic steps, therefore interpreting the performance measure $\widetilde{\Delta}$ directly over that tree would not estimate rounds. We must do something else: we construct a new tree, one in which $\widetilde{\bigcirc}$ is associated with the effect of a round rather than an atomic step, and we interpret $\widetilde{\Delta}$ over that. We map each path t (a sequence of states with successors determined by atomic steps) to t' (a sequence of states with successors determined by rounds) as follows: first t is divided into contiguous subsequences, each one containing a round (we have omitted the precise details of how this can be done); t' is the projection of t onto the states at the delimiters.[8] Now interpreting $\widetilde{\Delta}$ over the resulting tree will correctly provide an estimate of numbers of rounds rather than atomic steps; however we require more, namely a bound that dominates all possible such interpretations.

We assume some program Round which represents the overall effect of a round — it is the sequential composition, in some order, of some number of atomic steps (where each step is determined by some P_i in this case). To abstract from that order and how rounds are delimited, we assume no more about Round's behaviour except the following: we require Round to terminate and that each P_i appears somewhere in the sequential composition. The trick now is to specify those requirements (i.e. to define 'round') in a way that allows promotion of atomic-step properties to round properties: we use the technique of invariants.

$$
\left.
\begin{array}{ll}
\textit{local invariants} & \text{If } I \text{ is in } \mathcal{ES} \text{ and } wp.(\|_{1 \leq i \leq N} P_i).I \Lleftarrow I \text{ then} \\
& \quad wp.\text{Round}.I \Lleftarrow I \ . \\
\textit{fair progress} & \text{If } I, I' \text{ in } \mathcal{ES} \text{ are both local invariants and} \\
& \quad \text{there is some } i \text{ such that } wp.P_i.I \Lleftarrow I' \text{ then} \\
& \quad wp.\text{Round}.I \Lleftarrow I' \ ,
\end{array}
\right\} \quad (3)
$$

where an invariant I is said to be *local* if $wp.P_i.I \Lleftarrow I$ for all i, equivalently if $wp.(\|_{1 \leq i \leq N} P_i).I \Lleftarrow I$. This technique is very powerful, for although local invariants may be difficult to find, they are easy to check.

The fair progress property is specific to computations in the context of fair execution. It states that if an invariant I' holds initially, and if from within that invariant some (helpful) P_i establishes a second invariant I, then I must hold at the end of the round — fairness must guarantee that P_i executes at some stage in the round, and no matter how the round begins if I' holds initially, invariance ensures that it holds at that stage; after which the now established invariant I continues to hold, no matter how the round is completed. The local invariant property is a special case of that, and in fact implies termination of Round. Termination is specified by the property $wp.\text{Round}.\underline{1} \Lleftarrow \underline{1}$ which follows from the local invariant rule with I taken to be $\underline{1}$.

---

[8] This is effectively sequentially composing the atomic steps.

The problem of counting rounds now becomes one of interpreting $\bigcirc$ as $\widetilde{wp}$.Round in the definition of $\widetilde{\triangle}$, but then only using properties (3) to deduce properties of wp.Round (hence of $\widetilde{wp}$.Round, Def. 2.2). With those conventions we can specify the expected time to the first eating event as $\widetilde{\triangle}(\exists i \cdot E_i)$, and our next task is to consider how in general to estimate upper bounds on $\widetilde{\triangle}A$, for some A, using only local invariants.

We introduce a second performance operator set out in Fig. 6 which counts steps in a different way. Informally $\#A$ counts the expected number of times that A holds ever along paths in the computation tree. If A holds in the current state on a path, it is deemed to be one more visit to A; similarly unfolding the fixed point once reveals a corresponding '1+' in that case [9]. The new performance operator is related to $\widetilde{\triangle}A$ by observing that for characteristic A the number of times A holds on the path is at least as great as the length of the path until $\overline{A}$ holds. Other properties of $\#$ are set out in Fig. 7. (Note that with this notation we have returned briefly to the abstract notions of Sec. 3.)

The connection between performance and local invariants is to be found in the visit-eventually rule. It generalises a result from Markov processes [5] which says that the expected number of visits to A is the probability that A is ever reached ($\widetilde{\Diamond}A$) conditioned on the event that it is never revisited (probability $1-p$). Its relevance here is that an upper bound on $\widetilde{\Diamond}A/(1-p)$ (and hence on $\widetilde{\#}A$) may be calculated from upper bounds on both $\widetilde{\Diamond}A$ and $\overline{\bigcirc}\widetilde{\Diamond}A$, both of which are implied by *lower bounds* on local invariants, and the next theorem sets out how to do that.

least possible visits to A	$\#A := (\mu X \cdot (\bigcirc X) \ \textbf{if} \ \overline{A} \ \textbf{else} \ A + \bigcirc X)$
greatest possible visits to A	$\widetilde{\#}A := (\mu X \cdot (\widetilde{\bigcirc}X) \ \textbf{if} \ \overline{A} \ \textbf{else} \ A + \widetilde{\bigcirc}X)$

A is $\{0, 1\}$-valued.

Fig. 6. The expected number of visits.

Theorem 4.1 Consider a distributed system defined by processes $P_1, ..., P_N$ arbitrated by a fair scheduler. Given an expectation A and local invariants I, I' such that $A \Rrightarrow 1-I$ and $I' \Rrightarrow wp.P_i.I$ for some i, then $\widetilde{\#}A$, the maximal possible number of times that A holds (after executions of Round) is given by

$$\widetilde{\#}A \Rrightarrow 1/(1-q) \ ,$$

---

[9] A more succinct form for $\widetilde{\#}A$ is given by $(\mu X \cdot A + \widetilde{\bigcirc}X)$.

suplinearity $\widetilde{\#}(A + B) \Rrightarrow \widetilde{\#}A + \widetilde{\#}B$

visit-reach $\widetilde{\triangle A} \Rrightarrow \widetilde{\#}A$
with equality if $\overline{A} \Rrightarrow \bigcirc\overline{A}$

visit-eventually $\widetilde{\#}A \Rrightarrow \widetilde{\Diamond}A/(1-p)$,
where $p := (\sqcup s : A \cdot \widetilde{\bigcirc}(\widetilde{\Diamond}A).s)$.

A is $\{0, 1\}$-valued. We write $(\sqcup s : A \cdot f.s)$ for the maximum value of $f.s$ when s ranges over the (predicate) A. In the visit-eventually rule, p is the greatest possible probability that A is ever revisited; if $p = 1$ that upper bound is formally infinite.

Fig. 7. Some properties of expected visits

---

where $q := 1 - (\sqcap s : A \cdot I'.s)$ and $\widetilde{\bigcirc}$ is defined to be $\widetilde{wp}.\text{Round}$ in the definition of $\widetilde{\#}$.

Proof: Using the notation of the visit-eventually property of Fig. 7 we see that an upper bound on $\widetilde{\#}A$ is given by upper bounds on both $\widetilde{\Diamond}A$ and p. By appealing to feasibility (Fig. 4) and arithmetic we deduce immediately that $\widetilde{\#}A \Rrightarrow 1/(1-q)$ for any $q \geq p$. All that remains is to calculate the condition on q. We begin by estimating an upper bound for $\widetilde{wp}.\text{Round}.(\widetilde{\Diamond}A)$.

$$
\begin{array}{lll}
& \widetilde{wp}.\text{Round}.(\widetilde{\Diamond}A) & \text{Fig. 7} \\
& & \text{monotonicity, footnote 7; } A \Rrightarrow \underline{1} - I \\
\Rrightarrow & \widetilde{wp}.\text{Round}.(\widetilde{\Diamond}(\underline{1} - I)) & \\
\equiv & \widetilde{wp}.\text{Round}.(\underline{1} - \square(\underline{1} - (\underline{1} - I))) & \text{duality, Fig. 4} \\
\equiv & \widetilde{wp}.\text{Round}.(\underline{1} - \square I) & \text{arithmetic} \\
\Rrightarrow & \widetilde{wp}.\text{Round}.(\underline{1} - I) & I \Rrightarrow \square I; \text{ invariants, Fig. 4} \\
\equiv & \underline{1} - wp.\text{Round}.I & \text{Def. 2.2} \\
\Rrightarrow & \underline{1} - I' , & \text{fair progress, (3)}
\end{array}
\quad (4)
$$

where in the last step we are using our assumption that there is some philosopher such that $wp.P_i.I \not\Lleftarrow I'$ for local invariant I'. Next we bound q:

$$
\begin{array}{lll}
& q \geq p & \\
\text{if} & q \geq (\sqcup s : A \cdot \widetilde{wp}.\text{Round}(\widetilde{\Diamond}A).s) & \text{definition } p, \text{ Fig. 7} \\
\text{if} & q \geq (\sqcup s : A \cdot (\underline{1} - I').s) & (4) \\
\text{if} & q \geq 1 - (\sqcap s : A \cdot I'.s) , & \text{arithmetic}
\end{array}
$$

as required. $\square$

Finally we are in a position to tackle the dining philosophers: our principal tools will be Thm. 4.1 and suplinearity of Fig. 7 — the latter property allows the problem to be decomposed, making application of Thm. 4.1 easier (since it is then applied to fragments of the state space rather than to the whole state space). Deciding how to choose an appropriate decomposition often depends on the *probabilistic invariant* properties, and we discuss them next.

Ordinary program invariants are predicates that are maintained; probabilistic invariants, on the other hand, describe predicates that are maintained *only with some probability*, and we end this section by illustrating one such for the dining philosophers.

Consider first the case first when two philosophers (P_i and P_{i+1}) are in the configuration $(l_i \vee L_i) \wedge (r_{i+1} \vee R_{i+1})$. Informally we reason that the configuration is maintained unless one of P_i or P_{i+1} eats: other philosophers cannot disturb it, and inspection of P_i shows that l_i can only evolve to L_i, and that L_i can only evolve to E_i (since P_{i+1} is in state $r_{i+1} \vee R_{i+1}$). More generally we reason that $A := (\exists i \cdot (l_i \vee L_i) \wedge (r_{i+1} \vee R_{i+1}) \vee E_i)$ is always maintained, if it is ever established.

Next, to factor in probability, we look for a property that is only maintained with some probability. Again we consider the neighbours P_i and P_{i+1} but this time for the the the configuration $(l_i \vee L_i) \wedge T_{i+1}$. As before the configuration can only evolve to eating, unless P_{i+1} is scheduled, and when it is the state r_{i+1} (and thus A) is established with probability 1/2; hence defining A' to be

$$(\exists i \cdot (l_i \vee L_i) \wedge T_{i+1}) \wedge \overline{A} ,$$

we argue that if $A \vee A'$ ever holds, then it must *continue to hold* with probability at least 1/2. Expressed in the logic, we say that that $A + A'/2$ is a local invariant. Checking formally that $wp.P_i.(A + A'/2) \Lleftarrow A + A'/2$ confirms that fact. (Notice that the invariants are expressions over the whole state space, however we only need check invariance with respect to a *single* philosopher.)

Finally if we define $I := A$ and $I' := A + A'/2$ the remarks above imply that Thm. 4.1 provides an upper bound of $\underline{2}$ on $\widetilde{\#}A'$. Intuition tells us that the bound must be finite since from probability theory [5] A' cannot be visited infinitely often if there is always a probability of 1/2 of reaching an ordinary invariant A, disjoint from A'.

Calculations such as the above are required to find individual upper bounds on the return visits to a collection of predicates whose union implies the whole space. The particular invariant properties of the algorithm provide the best guide for choosing a decomposition. For example, if I is a (standard) local invariant and J is a predicate disjoint from I, and if $\bigcirc.I.s = p$ for all s in J, where $0 < p < 1$ then $I + pJ$ is also a (probabilistic) invariant. Thus I and J might form part of a suitable decomposition. (We would put $I' := I + pJ$ to deduce a maximum of $1/(1-p)$ visits to J.) But whatever the decomposition, the most important feature of this method is that once invariants are discovered, verifying that they satisfy the properties of Thm. 4.1 is straightforward in the logic.

The precise decomposition used for the analysis of the dining philosophers follows that of the correctness proof (appearing elsewhere [17]), and it gives a total expected time to first eating of no more than 33 (compare 63 of [11]). The details of those calculations are set out elsewhere [12].

5   Conclusion

In this paper we have shown how ordinary correctness techniques of distributed algorithms can be applied to probabilistic programs by using quantitative program logic, and that the methods apply even in the evaluation of performance. This treatment differs from other approaches to performance analysis of probabilistic algorithms [11, 3, 6] in that we do not refer explicitly to the distribution over computation paths; neither do we factor out the nondeterminism as a first step nor do we analyse the behaviour of the composed system: instead we use compositionality of local properties thus simplifying our formal reasoning. Other approaches using expectations [19, 8] do not treat nondeterminism and thus are not applicable to distributed algorithms like this at all.

Acknowledgements

This paper reports work carried out at Oxford within a project supported by the *EPSRC* — Carroll Morgan and Jeff Sanders are also members of that project.

References

[1] M. Ben-Ari, A. Pnueli, and Z. Manna. The temporal logic of branching time. *Acta Informatica*, 20:207–226, 1983.

[2] K. M. Chandy and J. Misra. *Parallel Program Design: A Foundation*. Addison-Wesley, Reading, Mass., 1988.

[3] L. de Alfaro. Temporal logics for the specification of performance and reliability. *Proceedings of STACS '97*, LNCS volume 1200, 1997.

[4] E.W. Dijkstra. *A Discipline of Programming*. Prentice Hall International, Englewood Cliffs, N.J., 1976.

[5] W. Feller. *An Introduction to Probability Theory and its Applications*, volume 1. Wiley, second edition, 1971.

[6] H. Hansson and B. Jonsson. A logic for reasoning about time and probability. *Formal Aspects of Computing*, 6(5):512–535, 1994.

[7] Jifeng He, K.Seidel, and A. K. McIver. Probabilistic models for the guarded command language. *Science of Computer Programming*, 28(2,3):171–192, January 1997.

[8] D. Kozen. A probabilistic PDL. In *Proceedings of the 15th ACM Symposium on Theory of Computing*, New York, 1983. ACM.

[9] D. Kozen. Results on the propositional μ-calculus. *Theoretical Computer Science*, 27:333–354, 1983.

[10] D. Lehmann and M. O. Rabin. On the advantages of free choice: a symmetric and fully-distributed solution to the Dining Philosophers Problem. In *Proceedings of the 8th Annual ACM Symposium on Principles of Programming Languages*, pages 133–138, New York, 1981. ACM.

[11] N. Lynch, I. Saias, and R. Segala. Proving time bounds for randomized distributed algorithms. *Proceedings of 13th Annual Symposium on Principles of Distributed Algorithms*, pages 314–323, 1994.

[12] A.K. McIver. Quantitative program logic and efficiency in probabilistic distributed algorithms. Technical report. See QLE98 at *http* [18].

[13] A.K. McIver. Reasoning about efficiency within a probabilistic mu-calculus. 1998. Submitted to pre-LICS98 workshop on Probabilistic Methods in Verification.

[14] C. C. Morgan, A. K. McIver, and K. Seidel. Probabilistic predicate transformers. *ACM Transactions on Programming Languages and Systems*, 18(3):325–353, May 1996.

[15] Carroll Morgan. The generalised substitution language extended to probabilistic programs. In *Proceedings of B'98: the Second International B Conference. See B98 at* http *[18]*, number 1397 in LNCS. Springer Verlag, April 1998.

[16] Carroll Morgan and Annabelle McIver. A probabilistic temporal calculus based on expectations. In Lindsay Groves and Steve Reeves, editors, *Proc. Formal Methods Pacific '97*. Springer Verlag Singapore, July 1997. Available at [18].

[17] C.C. Morgan and A.K. McIver. Correctness proof for the randomised dining philosophers. See RDP96 at *http* [18].

[18] PSG. Probabilistic Systems Group: Collected reports.
http://www.comlab.ox.ac.uk/oucl/groups/probs/bibliography.html.

[19] M. Sharir, A. Pnueli, and S. Hart. Verification of probabilistic programs. *SIAM Journal on Computing*, 13(2):292–314, May 1984.

[20] P. Whittle. *Probability via expectations*. Wiley, second edition, 1980.

Establishing Qualitative Properties for Probabilistic Lossy Channel Systems: An Algorithmic Approach

Christel Baier and Bettina Engelen *

Universität Mannheim,
Fakultät für Mathematik & Informatik,
D7, 27, 68131 Mannheim, Germany
{baier,bengelen}@pi2.informatik.uni-mannheim.de
FAX: ++49/621/292-5364

Abstract. Lossy channel systems (LCSs) are models for communicating systems where the subprocesses are linked via unbounded FIFO channels which might lose messages. Link protocols, such as the Alternating Bit Protocol and HDLC can be modelled with these systems. The decidability of several verification problems of LCSs has been investigated by Abdulla & Jonsson [AJ93, AJ94], e.g. they have shown that the reachability problem for LCSs is decidable while LTL model checking is not. In this paper, we consider *probabilistic* LCSs (which are LCSs where the transitions are augmented with appropriate probabilities) as introduced by [IN97] and show that the question of whether or not a linear time property holds with probability 1 is decidable. More precisely, we show how $LTL_{\setminus X}$ model checking for (certain types of) probabilistic LCSs can be reduced to a reachability problem in a (non-probabilistic) LCS where the latter can be solved with the methods of [AJ93].[1]

1 Introduction

Traditional algorithmic verification methods for parallel systems are limited to finite state systems and fail for systems with an infinite state space, such as real-time programs with continuous clocks or programs that operate with unbounded data structures or protocols for processes that communicate via unbounded channels. Typically, such systems are modelled by a finite state machine that specifies the control part. The transitions between the control states are equipped with conditions (e.g. about the values of a counter or a clock or about the messages in a channel). The behaviour of such a system is then given by a (possibly infinite) transition system whose global states consist of a control state and an auxiliary component whose values range over an infinite domain (e.g. the interpretations for a counter or a clock or the contents of certain channels). Even a wide range

---

* The second author is sponsored by the DFG-Project MA 794/3-1.
[1] Here, $LTL_{\setminus X}$ denotes standard linear time logic without next step.

of verification problems for such infinite systems is undecidable, various authors developed verification algorithms for special types of infinite systems.

This paper is concerned with model checking algorithms for communication protocols where the (sub-)processes are linked via unbounded FIFO channels. Dealing with *perfect* channels, in which case one gets the same expressiveness as Turing Machines, most verification problems are undecidable [BZ83]. Several link protocols, like the Alternating Bit Protocol [BSW69] or HDLC [ISO79], are designed to work correctly even for unreliable channels. For such faulty systems, various verification problems can be solved automatically. Finkel [Fin94] considered *completely specified protocols* modelled by channel systems where the channels might lose their first message and showed that the termination problem is solvable. Abdulla & Jonsson [AJ93] present algorithms for a reachability analysis (see also [AKP97]) and the verification against (certain types of) safety and eventually properties for *lossy channel systems* (LCSs), i.e. channel systems that may lose arbitrary messages. Abdulla & Kindahl [AK95] have shown that also the task of establishing a branching time relation (simulation or bisimulation) between a LCS and a finite transition system can be automated. Decidability results for other types of unreliable FIFO systems have been developed e.g. by Cécé, Finkel & Iyer [CFI96] (where channel systems with insertion or duplication errors are considered) and Bouajjani & Mayr [BM98] (where lossy vector addition systems are investigated). Even if validating faulty channel systems is easier than reasoning about perfect channel systems, some verification problems are still undecidable for unreliable channel systems. Abdulla & Jonsson [AJ94] show the undecidability of model checking for LCSs against LTL or CTL specifications or establishing "eventually" properties under fairness assumptions about the channels.[2]

We follow here the approach of Iyer & Narasimha [IN97] and consider *probabilistic LCSs* (PLCSs for short). In PLCSs, one assumes that the failure rate of the channels is known and deals with a constant $\wp$ that stands for the probability that one of the channels loses a message. The other transitions are equipped with "weights" that yield the probabilities for the possible steps of the global states and turn the transition system for the underlying LCS into a (possibly infinite) Markov chain.

For probabilistic systems modelled by Markov chains, various (deductive and algorithmic) verification methods have been proposed in the literature, but only a minority of them is applicable for PLCSs. Most of the algorithmic methods are formulated for *finite* Markov chains and hence are not applicable for PLCSs, see e.g. [VW86, CY88, CC91, CC92, HT92, HJ94, CY95, IN96, BH97]. Even some of the axiomatic methods, see e.g. [HS86, JS90, LS92], fail for PLCSs since they are designed for *bounded* (or even finite) Markov chains.[3]

---

[2] To overcome the limitations of algorithmic verification methods for LCSs due to undecidability results, [ABJ98] propose (possibly non-terminating) symbolic verification techniques based on a "on the fly" reachability analysis.

[3] Boundedness of a Markov chain means that there is an upper bound $\epsilon > 0$ for the non-zero transition probabilities. In the Markov chain for a PLCS, the probability

In this paper, we shrink our attention to temporal logical specifications; more precisely, to specifications given by formulas of propositional linear time temporal logic LTL. When interpreting a LTL formula f over the states of a Markov chain, the probability for f to hold in a state s, i.e. the probability measure of all paths starting in s and satisfying f, can be viewed as the "truth value" for f in state s. Thus, LTL can serve as specification formalism for both *qualitative* and *quantitative* temporal properties. In the former case, a LTL specification just consists of a LTL formula f; satisfaction of f in a state s means that f holds for *almost all* paths starting in s (i.e. with probability 1). Lehmann & Shelah [LS82] present sound and complete axiomatizations for (a logic that subsumes) LTL interpreted over Markov chains of arbitrary size; thus, the framework of [LS82] can serve as a proof-theoretic method for verifying qualitative properties for PLCSs. Quantitative properties can be expressed by a LTL formula f and a lower bound probability p; satisfaction in a state s means that the probability for f is beyond the given lower bound p.[4] In [IN97], an *approximative quantitative analysis* for PLCSs (i.e. an algorithm for approximating the probabilities for a $LTL_{\backslash X}$ formula f to hold in the initial state of a PLCS) is proposed. Here, $LTL_{\backslash X}$ means LTL without the next step operator X. This method yields a model checking procedure for verifying quantitative $LTL_{\backslash X}$ specifications with respect to a tolerence ϵ but it fails for qualitative properties (because of the tolerance).[5]

The main contribution of this paper is a verification algorithm for establishing qualitative properties specified by $LTL_{\backslash X}$ formulas for PLCSs. We use the ω-automaton approach à la Wolper, Vardi & Sistla [WVS83] and construct an ω-automaton $\mathcal{A}_f$ for the given formula f. Then, we define the product $\mathcal{PL} \times \mathcal{A}_f$ of the given PLCS $\mathcal{PL}$ and the ω-automaton $\mathcal{A}_f$ (yielding a new PLCS) and a formula f' of the form $f' = \bigvee \Diamond \Box (a_j \wedge \Diamond b_j)$ with atomic propositions a_j, b_j such that the probability for f to hold for $\mathcal{PL}$ equals the probability for f' to hold for $\mathcal{PL} \times \mathcal{A}_f$.

For finite Markov chains, it is well-known that whether or not a qualitative property can be established does not depend on the precise probability but just on the topology of the underlying directed graph [HSP83]. More precisely, qualitative properties of the type $f' = \bigvee \Diamond \Box (a_j \wedge \Diamond b_j)$ can be established by analyzing the bottom strongly connected components. This does not longer hold when we deal with infinite (bounded or unbounded) Markov chains. For an example, consider the system of Figure 1. The qualitative property stating that s_0

---

for the loss of a concrete message tends to 0 if the channel length tends to ∞; thus, they fail to be bounded.

[4] In the branching time framework (where one distinguishes between state and path formulas), the state formulas typically also assert that the probability for a certain event lies in a given interval; thus, the state formulas can be viewed as (special types of) quantitative LTL specifications. See e.g. [HJ94, ASBS95, BdA95].

[5] The tolerance ϵ specifies how precise the approximated value should be. I.e. the difference between the computed value q' and the precise probability q for the formula to hold in the initial state of the given PLCS is at most ϵ.

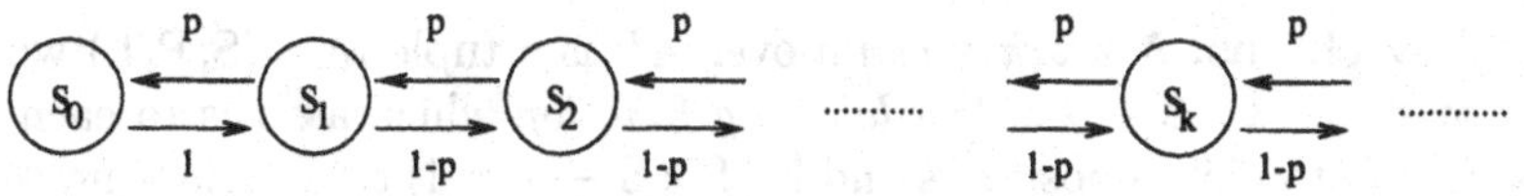

Fig. 1. An infinite (bounded) Markov chain

is visited infinitely many times cannot be established unless $p \geq \frac{1}{2}$.[6] To avoid a scenario as for the Markov chain in Figure 1 with $p < 1/2$ where a reachability analysis cannot help for establishing qualitative properties, we make an additional assumption about the underlying PLCS and require *probabilistic input enabledness*. This assumption allows us to reduce the question of whether a qualitative property specified by a formula f' as above is satisfied to a reachability problem in the underlying (non-probabilistic) LCS where the latter is solvable with conventional methods [AJ93, AKP97].

The reason why we do not deal with the next step operator will be explained in Section 4. Roughly speaking, the lack of next step ensures the invariance of the formulas with respect to losing a message. This is essential for characterizing the probability for f to hold for a PLCS $\mathcal{PL}$ by the probability for the above mentioned formula f' in the product system $\mathcal{PL} \times \mathcal{A}_f$. (See Lemma 2.)

Organization of the paper: In Section 2 we briefly explain our notations concerning Markov chains and linear time logic $LTL_{\backslash X}$ with its interpretation over Markov chains. The definitions of LCSs and PLCSs and related notations are given in Section 3. Our model checking algorithm is presented in Section 4. Section 5 concludes the paper.

This paper contents only the proof sketches. In the full paper [BER99] the complete proofs can be found.

Throughout the paper, we work with a finite non-empty set AP of atomic propositions which we use in the context of labelled Markov chains, $LTL_{\backslash X}$ formulas and LCSs. The reader should be familiar with basic notions of probability theory, see e.g. [Fel68, Bre68], further on with the main concepts of the temporal logic and model checking approach, see e.g. [CES86, Eme90, MP92], and also with the connection between temporal logic and ω-automaton, see e.g. [Tho90, Var96].

2   Preliminaries: Markov Chains and $LTL_{\backslash X}$

In the literature, a wide range of models for probabilistic processes is proposed. In this paper, we deal with (discrete time, labelled) Markov chains which is one of the basic models for specifying probabilistic systems. We briefly explain our notations concerning Markov chains and linear time logic $LTL_{\backslash X}$ with its interpretation over Markov chains.

---

[6] This observation follows with standard arguments of Markov chain theory ("random walks"). For $p < \frac{1}{2}$, the probability to reach s_0 from s_k is $p^k/(1-p)^k < 1$.

Markov chains: A *Markov chain* over AP is a tuple $M = (S, P, L)$ where S is a set of *states*, $L : S \longrightarrow 2^{AP}$ a *labelling function* which assigns to each state $s \in S$ a set of atomic propositions and $P : S \times S \longrightarrow [0, 1]$ a *transition probability function* such that for all $s \in S$: $P(s, t) > 0$ for at most countably many states $t \in S$ and $\sum_{t \in S} P(s, t) = 1$.

Execution sequences arise by resolving the probabilistic choices. Formally, an *execution sequence* in M is a nonempty (finite or infinite) sequence $\pi = s_0, s_1, s_2, \ldots$ where s_i are states and $P(s_{i-1}, s_i) > 0$, $i = 1, 2, \ldots$. An infinite execution sequence π is also called a *path*. We denote by $word(\pi)$ the to π associated sequence of atomic propositions, i.e. $word(\pi) = L(s_0), L(s_1), L(s_2), \ldots$. The first state of π is denoted by $first(\pi)$. $\pi(k)$ denotes the $(k+1)$-th state of π, i.e. if $\pi = s_0, s_1, s_2, \ldots$ then $\pi(k) = s_k$. $Reach_M(s)$ denotes the set of states that are reachable from s, i.e. $Reach_M(s)$ is the set of states $\pi(k)$ where π is a path with $first(\pi) = s$. $Path_M(s)$ denotes the set of paths π with $first(\pi) = s$ and $Path_{fin,M}(s)$ denotes the set of finite paths starting in s. For $s \in S$, let $\Sigma_M(s)$ be the smallest σ-algebra on $Path_M(s)$ which contains the basic cylinders $\{\pi \in Path_M(s) : \rho$ is a prefix of $\pi\}$ where ρ ranges over all finite execution sequences starting in s. The probability measure $Prob_M$ on $\Sigma_M(s)$ is the unique measure with

$$Prob_M \{ \pi \in Path_M(s) : \rho \text{ is a prefix of } \pi \} = P(\rho)$$

where $P(s_0, s_1, \ldots, s_k) = P(s_0, s_1) \cdot P(s_1, s_2) \cdot \ldots \cdot P(s_{k-1}, s_k)$. If it is clear from the context, we omit the subscript M and briefly write $Path(s)$, $Reach(s)$, etc..

Linear Time Logic $LTL_{\backslash X}$:

$$f ::= tt \mid a \mid f_1 \wedge f_2 \mid \neg f \mid f_1 \mathcal{U} f_2$$

$LTL_{\backslash X}$ formulas are build from the above grammar where a is an atomic proposition $(a \in AP)$ and $\mathcal{U}$ the temporal operator "until". As usual, operators for modelling "eventually" or "always" can be derived by $\Diamond f = tt \, \mathcal{U} \, f$ and $\Box f = \neg \Diamond \neg f$. The interpretation of $LTL_{\backslash X}$ formulas over the paths and states of a Markov chain is as follows. Let $M = (S, P, L)$ be a Markov chain over AP. The satisfaction relation (denoted $\models_M$ or briefly $\models$) for path formulas is as in the non-probabilistic case, i.e. it is given by: $\pi \models a$ iff $\pi(0) \models a$, $\pi \models f_1 \wedge f_2$ iff $\pi \models f_i$, $i = 1, 2$, $\pi \models \neg f$ iff $\pi \not\models f$ and $\pi \models f_1 \mathcal{U} f_2$ iff there exists $k \geq 0$ with $\pi \uparrow i \models f_1$, $i = 0, 1, \ldots, k-1$ and $\pi \uparrow k \models f_2$.[7]

For $s \in S$, we define the "truth value" $p_s^M(f)$ (or briefly $p_s(f)$) as the measure of all paths that start in s and satisfy f, i.e. $p_s(f) = Prob \{\pi \in Path(s) : \pi \models f\}$. The satisfaction relation for the states (also denoted $\models_M$ or $\models$) is given by $s \models f$ iff $p_s(f) = 1$.

3 Probabilistic Lossy Channel Systems

We recall the definitions of (non-probabilistic and probabilistic) LCSs as introduced by [AJ93] and [IN97]. A LCS models the behaviour of a number of

---

[7] Here, $\pi \uparrow k$ denotes the k-th suffix of π, i.e. the path $\pi(k), \pi(k+1), \pi(k+2), \ldots$.

processes which communicate over certain unreliable channels. The control part of a LCS is specified by a finite state machine with (conditional) action-labelled transitions. The transitions can either be labelled by τ (which stands for an autonomous (internal) move for one of the processes) or by a communication action $c?m$ (where a process receives message m from channel c) or $c!m$ (where a process sends message m via channel c). The global behaviour depends on the current control state s and the contents of the channels. While the enabledness of the internal actions τ and the output actions $c!m$ just depends on the control state, enabledness of an input action $c?m$ requires that m is the first message of c and that the current control state s has an outgoing transition labelled by $c?m$.

The effect of an input action $c?m$ is that the first message m is removed from c while the output action $c!m$ inserts m at the end of c. The internal action τ does not change the channel contents. Moreover, in each global state, any messages in a channel can be lost in which case the control state does not change.

Definition 1. (cf. [AJ93]) *A Lossy Channel System (LCS) is a tuple* $\mathcal{L} = (S_{control}, s_0, L, Ch, Mess, \hookrightarrow)$ *where*

- $S_{control}$ *is a finite set of* control states,
- $s_0 \in S_{control}$ *is an initial* control state,
- L *is a labelling function, i.e.* $L : S_{control} \longrightarrow 2^{AP}$,
- Ch *is a finite set of* channels,
- $Mess$ *is a finite set of* messages,
- $\hookrightarrow \subseteq S_{control} \times Act \times S_{control}$

where $SendAct = \{c!m : c \in Ch, m \in Mess\}$, $RecAct = \{c?m : c \in Ch, m \in Mess\}$ *and* $Act = SendAct \cup RecAct \cup \{\tau\}$.[8]

The (global) behaviour of a LCS can be formalized by an action-labelled transition system (which might have infinitely many states). We use the action set $Act_\ell = Act \cup \{\ell_{c,i} : c \in Ch, i = 0, 1, 2, \ldots\}$ where the auxiliary labels $\ell_{c,i}$ denote that the i-th message of channel c is lost. The global states are pairs $\mathsf{s} = \langle s, w \rangle$ consisting of a control state s and an additional component w that gives rise about the channel contents. Formally, w is a function $Ch \longrightarrow Mess^*$ which assigns to each channel c a finite string $w.c$ of messages. We use the symbol $\emptyset$ to denote both the empty string and the function that assigns to any channel c the empty string. For $c \in Mess^*$, $c \neq \emptyset$, $first(c)$ is the first message in c. $|c|$ denotes the length of c; i.e. $|\emptyset| = 0$ and $|m_1 \ldots m_k| = k$. $w[c := x]$ denotes the unique function $w' : Ch \longrightarrow Mess^*$ with $w'.c = x$ and $w'.d = w.d$ for $d \neq c$. The total channel length $|w|$ is defined as the sum over the lengths of the contents of the vector w; i.e. $|w| = \sum_{c \in Ch} |w.c|$. Further on, $|\mathsf{s}| = |w|$ and $\mathsf{s}.c = w.c$ for the global state $\mathsf{s} = \langle s, w \rangle$. The transition system associated with $\mathcal{L}$ is

$$\mathsf{TS}(\mathcal{L}) \;=\; (S_{global}, \longrightarrow, \mathsf{L}, \mathsf{s}_0)$$

---

[8] The finite representation of a LCS in the sense of Definition 1 just specifies the control part. Since the loss of messages does not affect the control state, transitions obtained by losing a message are not specified by the transition relation $\hookrightarrow$.

where $S_{global} = S_{control} \times (Ch \longrightarrow Mess^*)$, $s_0 = \langle s_0, \emptyset \rangle$ is the *initial global state* and $L(\langle s, w \rangle) = L(s)$ for all $\langle s, w \rangle \in S_{global}$. Furthermore the transition relation $\longrightarrow \subseteq S_{global} \times Act_\ell \times S_{global}$ is the smallest set such that, for $w = m_1 m_2 \ldots m_k$:

- If $s \xrightarrow{c!m} t$ then $\langle s, w \rangle \xrightarrow{c!m} \langle t, w[c := m_1 \ldots m_k m]\rangle$.
- If $s \xrightarrow{c?m} t$ and $k \geq 1$ then $\langle s, w[c := mm_1 \ldots m_k]\rangle \xrightarrow{c?m} \langle t, w \rangle$.
- If $k \geq 1$ and $i \in \{1, \ldots, k\}$ then $\langle s, w \rangle \xrightarrow{\ell_{c,i}} \langle s, w[c := m_1 \ldots m_{i-1} m_{i+1} \ldots m_k]\rangle$.
- If $s \xrightarrow{\tau} t$ then $\langle s, w \rangle \xrightarrow{\tau} \langle t, w \rangle$.

We write $\mathsf{s} \xrightarrow{\ell} \mathsf{t}$ iff $\mathsf{s} \xrightarrow{\ell_{c,i}} \mathsf{t}$ for some c and i and $\mathsf{s} \xrightarrow{\alpha} \mathsf{t}$ iff $\mathsf{s} \xrightarrow{\alpha} \mathsf{t}$ for some global state t. We define $act(\mathsf{s})$ to be the set of actions $\alpha \in Act$ that are *enabled* in the global state s. Formally, $act(\mathsf{s}) = \{\alpha \in Act : \mathsf{s} \xrightarrow{\alpha}\}$. In what follows, we require that in all global states at least one action is enabled. This is guaranteed by the requirement that, for any control state s, there is some action $\alpha \in SendAct \cup \{\tau\}$ and control state t with $s \xrightarrow{\alpha} t$.[9]

Definition 2. (cf. [IN97]) *A PLCS is a tuple* $\mathcal{PL} = (\mathcal{L}, P_{control}, \wp)$ *where* $\mathcal{L}$ *is a LCS,* $\wp \in]0, 1[$ *the* failure probability *and*

$$P_{control} : S_{control} \times Act \times S_{control} \longrightarrow [0, 1]$$

a function with $P_{control}(s, \alpha, t) > 0$ *iff* $s \xrightarrow{\alpha} t$.

The Markov chain associated with a PLCS $\mathcal{PL} = (\mathcal{L}, P_{control}, \wp)$ arises by augmenting the transitions of the transition system $TS(\mathcal{L})$ with probabilities.[10] In any global state s where $|\mathsf{s}| \neq 0$, the probability for losing one of the messages is $\wp$ where all transitions $\mathsf{s} \xrightarrow{\ell_{c,i}} \mathsf{t}$ have equal probability. The other transition probabilities (for the transitions labelled by actions $\alpha \in Act$) are derived from $P_{control}$ (that assigns "weights" to the transitions) with the help of the *normalization function* $\nu : S_{global} \longrightarrow \mathbb{R}_{>0}$ which is defined by:

$$\nu(\langle s, w \rangle) = \sum_{\alpha \in act(\langle s, w \rangle)} P_{control}(s, \alpha)$$

where $P_{control}(s, \alpha) = \sum_t P_{control}(s, \alpha, t)$.[11] The conditional probability (under the assumption that no message will be lost in the next step) for an α-labelled transition $\langle s, w \rangle \xrightarrow{\alpha} \langle s', w' \rangle$ is given by the "weight" $P_{control}(s, \alpha, s')$ divided by $\nu(\langle s, w \rangle)$. We define the action-labelled transition probability function

---

[9] Note that for any control state s where the system has terminated we may assume that there is a τ-loop, i.e. $s \xrightarrow{\tau} s$.

[10] First, we define the probabilities for the action-labelled transitions. Then, we abstract from the action-labels and deal with the probabilities $P_{global}(\mathsf{s}, \mathsf{t})$ to move from s to t via any action.

[11] Since we assume that any control state s has at least one transition $s \xrightarrow{\alpha} t$ for some $\alpha \in SendAct \cup \{\tau\}$, the normalization factor $\nu(\langle s, w \rangle)$ is always > 0.

$P_{global} : S_{global} \times Act_\ell \times S_{global} \longrightarrow [0,1]$ as follows. If $\alpha \in Act$, $\langle s, w \rangle \xrightarrow{\alpha} \langle s', w' \rangle$, $|w| \neq 0$ then

$$P_{global}(\langle s, w \rangle, \alpha, \langle s', w' \rangle) = \frac{1 - \wp}{\nu(\langle s, w \rangle)} \cdot P_{control}(s, \alpha, s').$$

For the loss of a message, corresponding to the transition $s \xrightarrow{\ell_{c,i}} t$[12], we define

$$P_{global}(s, \ell_{c,i}, t) = \frac{\wp}{|s|}.$$

For the global states with empty channels we put $P_{global}(\langle s, \emptyset \rangle, \alpha, \langle s', w' \rangle) = P_{control}(s, \alpha, s')/\nu(\langle s, \emptyset \rangle)$. In all remaining cases, we define $P_{global}(s, \alpha, t) = 0$. We define

$$P_{global}(s, \alpha) = \sum_{t \in S_{global}} P_{global}(s, \alpha, t), \quad P_{global}(s, t) = \sum_{\alpha \in Act_\ell} P_{global}(s, \alpha, t).$$

The Markov chain[13] associated with $\mathcal{PL}$ is $MC(\mathcal{PL}) = (S_{global}, P_{global}, L, s_0)$ where P_{global} is viewed as a function $S_{global} \times S_{global} \longrightarrow [0,1]$. Dealing with $LTL_{\setminus X}$ as formalism for specifying qualitative properties for PLCSs, we deal with the satisfaction relation $\mathcal{PL} \models f$ iff $s_0 \models_{MC(\mathcal{PL})} f$ where $s_0 = \langle s_0, \emptyset \rangle$ is the initial global state of $MC(\mathcal{PL})$.

4 Model Checking

In this section, we describe a $LTL_{\setminus X}$ model checking procedure for PLCSs. More precisely, the input of our algorithm is a PLCS $\mathcal{PL}$ and a $LTL_{\setminus X}$ formula f; the output is "yes" or "no" depending on whether or not $\mathcal{PL} \models f$. The basic idea of our method is the reduction of the $LTL_{\setminus X}$ model checking problem to a reachability problem in a (non-probabilistic) LCS where the latter can be solved with the methods proposed in [AJ93] or [AKP97].

Before we explain how our algorithm works we briefly sketch the algorithmic methods that have been developed for verifying finite probabilistic systems against LTL formulas.

Courcoubetis & Yannakakis [CY88] deal with finite Markov chains and present an algorithm that is based on a recursive procedure that successively removes the temporal modalities from the formula (i.e. replaces each subformula g whose outermost operator is a temporal operator, e.g. $\mathcal{U}$, by a new atomic proposition a_g) where at the same time each state s of the underlying Markov chain M is splitted into the two states $\langle s, a_g \rangle$ and $\langle s, \neg a_g \rangle$. The transition probabilities in the new Markov chain M_g are computed with the help of the probabilities $p_s(g)$

---

[12] Note that $|s| \neq 0$ because we cannot lose a message from the empty channel.

[13] To be precisely, we deal with a *pointed* Markov chain by which we mean a Markov chain that is endowed with an initial state. For simplicity, we briefly refer to "pointed Markov chains" as "Markov chains".

for the path formula g. This method is very tricky and elegant for finite Markov chains but it seems to be not adequate for infinite systems (like PLCSs) since it would require the computation of infinitely many transition probabilities.

An alternative method is based on the ω-automaton approach proposed by Vardi & Wolper [Var85, VW86]. This approach has been used later by several other authors, see e.g. [CY95, IN96, dA97, BK98]. The basic idea behind the ω-automata theoretic approach can be sketched as follows. The starting point is a probabilistic system S, e.g. described by a Markov chain or Markov decision process, and a linear time formula f. Using well-known methods, one constructs an ω-automaton $\mathcal{A}_f$ for the formula f and defines a new probabilistic system $S \times \mathcal{A}_f$ by taking the "product" $S \times \mathcal{A}_f$ of S and $\mathcal{A}_f$. From the acceptance condition of $\mathcal{A}_f$, a set V' of states in $S \times \mathcal{A}_f$ can be derived such that the probability that f holds in a state $\mathbf{s}$ agrees with the probability for a certain state $\mathbf{s}'$ in $S \times \mathcal{A}_f$ to reach a state in V'.

Similar ideas are used in the tableau-based method of Pnueli & Zuck [PZ93] where the "product" of the probabilistic system and the "tableau" for f (obtained from the Fischer-Ladner closure of f) is analyzed.

In this paper, we follow the approachs of [dA97, BK98] and use a deterministic Rabin automaton to get an alternative characterization of the probability that a $LTL_{\backslash X}$ formula f holds in a global state.[14]

We recall the basic definitions and explain our notations. A *deterministic Rabin automaton* $\mathcal{A}$ is a tuple $(Q, q_0, Alph, \delta, AccCond)$ where

- Q is a non-empty finite set of states,
- $q_0 \in Q$ is the initial state,
- $Alph$ is a finite alphabet,
- $\delta : Q \times Alph \longrightarrow Q$ is the transition function,
- $AccCond$ is the acceptance condition, i.e. $AccCond \subseteq 2^Q \times 2^Q$.

An infinite sequence $\mathbf{p} = p_0, p_1, p_2, \ldots \in Q^\omega$ is said to satisfy the acceptance condition of the automaton $\mathcal{A}$ (denoted $\mathbf{p} \models AccCond$) iff there exists $(A, B) \in AccCond$ such that $inf(\mathbf{p}) \subseteq A$ and $inf(\mathbf{p}) \cap B \neq \emptyset$. Here, $inf(\mathbf{p})$ denotes the set of automaton states that occur infinitely often in $\mathbf{p}$.

A *run* $\mathbf{r}$ of $\mathcal{A}$ over an infinite word $a_0, a_1, a_2, \ldots \in Alph^\omega$ is a sequence $\mathbf{r} = q_0, q_1, q_2, \ldots \in Q^\omega$ (starting in the initial state q_0 of $\mathcal{A}$) with $q_{i+1} = \delta(q_i, a_i)$ for all $i \geq 0$. A run $\mathbf{r}$ of $\mathcal{A}$ is called *accepting* iff $\mathbf{r} \models AccCond$. A word $\mathbf{a} = a_0, a_1, a_2 \ldots \in Alph^\omega$ is called *accepted* iff there is an accepting run $\mathbf{r}$ over $\mathbf{a}$. Let $AccWords(\mathcal{A})$ denote the set of accepting words.

It is well-known [WVS83, Saf88, VW94] that, for any LTL formula f (in particular, for any $LTL_{\backslash X}$ formula) with atomic propositions in AP, a deterministic Rabin automaton $\mathcal{A}_f$ with the alphabet $Alph = 2^{AP}$ can be constructed such that $AccWords(\mathcal{A}_f)$ is exactly the set of infinite words $\mathbf{a} = a_0, a_1, \ldots$ over 2^{AP}

---

[14] [dA97, BK98] deal with finite probabilistic systems with non-determinism, i.e. Markov Decision Processes rather than Markov chains. It is still open whether or not a *non-deterministic* ω-automaton would still be sufficient for our purposes as it is the case for finite Markov chains [CY95, IN96].

where f is true.[15] The product $M \times \mathcal{A}_f$ of a Markov chain $M = (S, P, L)$ and the automaton $\mathcal{A}_f$ is defined as follows.

$$M \times \mathcal{A}_f = (S \times Q, P', L')$$

where $L'(\langle s, q \rangle) = L(s)$ and

$$P'(\langle s, q \rangle, \langle t, p \rangle) = \begin{cases} P(s, t) & \text{if } p = \delta(q, L(t)) \\ 0 & \text{otherwise.} \end{cases}$$

Let $AccCond = \{(A_j, B_j) : j = 1, \dots, k\}$ be the acceptance condition of $\mathcal{A}_f$. Hence we define $A'_j = S \times A_j$, $B'_j = S \times B_j$. Let V'_j be the smallest set such that $V'_j \subseteq A'_j$ and $Reach_{M \times \mathcal{A}_f}(v') \subseteq V'_j$, $Reach_{M \times \mathcal{A}_f}(v') \cap B'_j \neq \emptyset$ for all $v' \in V'_j$.[16] Let $V' = V'_1 \cup \dots \cup V'_k$. As in [dA97, BK98] it can be shown that

(*) $Prob_M \{\pi \in Path_M(s) : \pi \models f\} = Prob_{M \times \mathcal{A}_f} \{\pi \in Path_{M \times \mathcal{A}_f}(s') : \pi \models \Diamond V'\}.$

for all states $s \in S$. Here, s' denotes the state $\langle s, \delta(q_0, L(s)) \rangle$ and $\pi \models \Diamond V'$ is an abbreviation of "π will eventually reach a state of V'". Thus, the test whether $p_s(f) = 1$ can be done by first computing $\mathcal{A}_f$ and then performing a probabilistic reachability analysis in the product $M \times \mathcal{A}_f$ to check whether

(**) $Prob_{M \times \mathcal{A}_f} \{\pi \in Path_{M \times \mathcal{A}_f}(s') : \pi \models \Diamond V'\} = 1.$

For finite Markov chains, the latter (the test of (**)) can be done with non-probabilistic (graph theoretical) methods.[17] In our case, where we deal with infinite Markov chains obtained by a PLCS (i.e. Markov chains of the form $M = MC(\mathcal{PL})$), condition (*) still holds but it is not clear (at least not for the authors) how to test condition (**). The problem is that the reachability algorithm of [AJ93] (or [AKP97]) cannot be applied since the underlying transition system of the so obtained Markov chain $MC(\mathcal{PL}) \times \mathcal{A}_f$ might not be the transition system of a LCS (see Remark 1). For this reason, we do not deal with the product $MC(\mathcal{PL}) \times \mathcal{A}_f$ but switch to the product of the PLCS $\mathcal{PL}$ and the automaton $\mathcal{A}_f$ (which yields a new PLCS $\mathcal{PL} \times \mathcal{A}_f$) and then show how to apply conventional methods for a reachability analysis in the LCS $\mathcal{L} \times \mathcal{A}_f$ to reason about the probabilities in $MC(\mathcal{PL} \times \mathcal{A}_f)$.

4.1   The Product of a PLCS and an ω-Automaton

In the sequel, let $\mathcal{PL}$ be a PLCS and $\mathcal{A}$ a deterministic Rabin automaton with the alphabet 2^{AP} where the components of $\mathcal{PL}$ and $\mathcal{A}$ are as before; i.e. $\mathcal{PL} = (\mathcal{L}, P_{control}, \wp)$ and $\mathcal{A} = (Q, q_0, 2^{AP}, \delta, AccCond)$ where $\mathcal{L}$ is as in Definition 1 and $AccCond = \{(A_j, B_j) : j = 1, \dots, k\}$.

---

[15] Here, satisfaction of LTL formulas interpreted over infinite words over 2^{AP} is defined in the obvious way.

[16] The existence of such a set V'_j can be shown with the help of Tarski's fixed point theorem for monotonic set-valued operators.

[17] One just has to check whether all states reachable from the state s' via an execution sequence that does not pass V' can reach a V'-state.

Definition 3. $\mathcal{PL} \times \mathcal{A}$ *denotes the PLCS* $(\mathcal{L} \times \mathcal{A}, P_{\mathcal{A}}, \wp)$ *where*

$$\mathcal{L} \times \mathcal{A} = (S_{control} \times Q, \langle s_0, p_0 \rangle, L_{\mathcal{A}}, Ch, Mess, \hookrightarrow_{\mathcal{A}})$$

with $p_0 = \delta(q_0, L(s_0))$, $L_{\mathcal{A}}(\langle s, q \rangle) = L(s)$ *and*

$$\langle s, q \rangle \stackrel{\alpha}{\hookrightarrow}_{\mathcal{A}} \langle t, p \rangle \quad \text{iff} \quad s \stackrel{\alpha}{\hookrightarrow} t \text{ and } p = \delta(q, L(t))$$

and, if $\langle s, q \rangle \stackrel{\alpha}{\hookrightarrow}_{\mathcal{A}} \langle t, p \rangle$ *then* $P_{\mathcal{A}}(\langle s, q \rangle, \alpha, \langle t, p \rangle) = P_{control}(s, \alpha, t)$.

We use the notation $\langle s, w, q \rangle \in S_{control} \times (Ch \longrightarrow Mess^*) \times Q$ rather than $\langle \langle s, q \rangle, w \rangle$ for the global states in MC($\mathcal{PL} \times \mathcal{A}$).

Remark 1. The Markov chain MC($\mathcal{PL} \times \mathcal{A}$) induced by $\mathcal{PL} \times \mathcal{A}$ differs from the product MC($\mathcal{PL}$) $\times \mathcal{A}$. We assume that $q \neq q'$. We regard the loss of messages in both constructions. Let $q' = \delta(q, L(s))$ and $w : Ch \longrightarrow Mess^*$ such that $w.c = m_1 \ldots m_{i-1} m_i m_{i+1} \ldots m_k$ and $w' = w[c := m_1 \ldots m_{i-1} m_{i+1} \ldots m_k]$. In MC($\mathcal{PL}$) $\times \mathcal{A}$, the state $\langle s, w, q \rangle$ can move to $\langle s, w', q' \rangle$ (via the action $\ell_{c,i}$), but possibly not to the state $\langle s, w', q \rangle$. In MC($\mathcal{PL} \times \mathcal{A}$), we have

$$\langle s, w, q \rangle \xrightarrow{\ell_{c,i}}_{\mathcal{A}} \langle s, w', q \rangle .$$

Thus, $P'(\langle s, w, q \rangle, \langle s, w', q \rangle) = 0 < P_{global}(\langle s, w, q \rangle, \langle s, w', q \rangle)$ is possible.[18] This signifies that it is possible that the underlying graph of the Markov chain MC($\mathcal{PL}$) $\times \mathcal{A}$ cannot be obtained by the transition system of a LCS. ∎

We now assume that $\mathcal{A} = \mathcal{A}_f$ is a deterministic automaton for a $LTL_{\backslash X}$ formula f. Recall that $p_s^M(f)$ denotes $Prob_M \{\pi \in Path_M(s) : \pi \models_M f\}$.

Lemma 1. *Let* s *be a global state in* $\mathcal{PL}$ *and* $s' = \langle s, \delta(q_0, L(s)) \rangle$. *Then,*

$$p_s^{MC(\mathcal{PL})}(f) = p_{s'}^{MC(\mathcal{PL} \times \mathcal{A}_f)}(f).$$

Proof. Easy verification. ∎

For the construction $M \times \mathcal{A}_f$, the projection of a path π in $M \times \mathcal{A}_f$ to the automaton states yields a run in $\mathcal{A}_f$ which is accepting iff $\pi \models f$. Unfortunately, the projection of the paths in MC($\mathcal{PL} \times \mathcal{A}_f$) to the automaton states does not yield a run in $\mathcal{A}_f$ since the loss of a message (more precisely, a step of the form $\langle s, w, q \rangle \xrightarrow{\ell} \langle s, w', q \rangle$ where $\delta(q, L(s)) \neq q$) does not correspond to a transition in $\mathcal{A}_f$. However, the loss of a message does not affect the control and automaton state and hence can be viewed as a *stutter step*. Since we do not deal with the next step operator and since the atomic propositions only depend on the control components (but not on the channel contents), the formula f is insensitive with respect to such stutter steps [BCG88]. Thus, $\pi \models f$ iff r is accepting where r is the run induced by the sequence of automaton states that results from π by removing all stutter steps.

Let $A'_j = S_{control} \times A_j$, $B'_j = S_{control} \times B_j$. In the sequel, we treat A'_j, B'_j as atomic propositions with the obvious meaning; e.g. $A'_j \in L_{\mathcal{A}}(\langle s, q \rangle)$ if $\langle s, q \rangle \in A'_j$.

---

[18] Note that the control state (which consists in $\mathcal{L} \times \mathcal{A}$ of a control state in $\mathcal{L}$ and an automaton state) does not change if a message is lost.

Lemma 2. *For any path π in* $\mathsf{MC}(\mathcal{PL} \times \mathcal{A}_f)$:

$$\pi \models f \quad \textit{iff} \quad \pi \models \bigvee_{1 \le j \le k} \Diamond\Box(A'_j \wedge \Diamond B'_j).$$

Proof. (Sketch) We denote by $\equiv_{st}$ the stuttering equivalence relation for infinite sequences $x_0, x_1, x_2, \ldots$ over an arbitrary set X.[19] Let $\mathbf{a} = a_0, a_1, \ldots$ and $\mathbf{a}' = a'_0, a'_1, \ldots$ be infinite sequences over 2^{AP}. Since f is invariant under stutter steps we get:

(1) If $\mathbf{a} \equiv_{st} \mathbf{a}'$ then $\mathbf{a} \models f$ iff $\mathbf{a}' \models f$.

If $\mathbf{p} = p_0, p_1, \ldots$ and $\mathbf{p}' = p'_0, p'_1, \ldots$ are infinite sequences over Q then:

(2) If $\mathbf{p} \equiv_{st} \mathbf{p}'$ then $\mathbf{p} \models AccCond$ iff $\mathbf{p}' \models AccCond$.

Let π be a path in $\mathsf{MC}(\mathcal{PL} \times \mathcal{A}_f)$ and $\pi(i) = \langle s_i, w_i, p_i \rangle$. For any i, we choose some $\alpha_i \in Act \cup \{\ell\}$ such that $\pi(i) \xrightarrow{\alpha_i} \pi(i+1)$. Clearly, there are infinitely many indices i with $\alpha_i \ne \ell$. Let $\langle s'_0, w'_0, p'_0 \rangle, \langle s'_1, w'_1, p'_1 \rangle, \ldots$ be the sequence that results from π by removing the i-th tuple $\pi(i) = \langle s_i, w_i, p_i \rangle$ if $\alpha_i = \ell$. Let

$$\mathbf{a} = L(s_0), L(s_1), \ldots, \quad \mathbf{a}' = L(s'_0), L(s'_1), \ldots, \quad \mathbf{p} = p_0, p_1, \ldots, \quad \mathbf{p}' = p'_0, p'_1, \ldots.$$

We have $\langle s_i, p_i \rangle = \langle s_{i+1}, p_{i+1} \rangle$ for all indices i with $\alpha_i = \ell$. Thus, $\mathbf{a} \equiv_{st} \mathbf{a}'$ and $\mathbf{p} \equiv_{st} \mathbf{p}'$. By definition of $\mathcal{PL} \times \mathcal{A}_f$, we have $p'_{i+1} = \delta(p'_i, L(s'_{i+1}))$, $i = 0, 1, 2, \ldots$. Thus, $\mathbf{p}'$ is a run over $\mathbf{a}'$. Hence,

$$\mathbf{a}' \models f \quad \text{iff} \quad \mathbf{a}' \in AccWords(\mathcal{A}_f) \quad \text{iff} \quad \mathbf{p}' \models AccCond.$$

By (1) and (2) $\pi \models f$ iff $\mathbf{a} \models f$ iff $\mathbf{a}' \models f$ iff $\mathbf{p}' \models AccCond$ iff $\mathbf{p} \models AccCond$. Clearly, $\mathbf{p} \models AccCond$ is an equivalent formulation for $\pi \models \bigvee_j \Diamond\Box(A'_j \wedge \Diamond B'_j)$. ∎

4.2   Probabilistic Input Enabledness

Because of Lemma 1 and Lemma 2 we can shrink our attention to formulas of the form $\bigvee \Diamond\Box(a_j \wedge \Diamond b_j)$ where a_j, b_j are atomic propositions. We aim at a condition that allows to establish qualitative properties specified by formulas of this type by analyzing the graph of the underlying LCS. For this, we need a condition that allows us to abstract from the concrete transition probabilities. In contrast to the finite-state case, for infinite Markov chains, the precise transition probabilities might be essential for establishing qualitative properties.

Example 1. The Markov chain of Figure 1 can be viewed as the Markov chain associated with a PLCS consisting of a single control state s, one channel c, one message m, the transition $s \xrightarrow{c!m} s$ and the failure probability $\wp = p$. Then, the state s_k of Figure 1 represents the global state $\langle s, m^k \rangle$ in which the total channel length is k. The qualitative property stating that the initial global state s_0 is visited infinitely often holds for $p \ge 1/2$ but not for $p < 1/2$. ∎

The problem in the above example is that, for $p < 1/2$, with non-zero probability, the channels grow in an "uncontrolled" way. To prevent such situations,

---

[19] I.e. $\equiv_{st}$ is the smallest equivalence relation on X^ω which identifies all sequences $x_0, x_1, \ldots, x_{i-1}, x_i, x_{i+1}, \ldots$ and $x_0, x_1, \ldots, x_{i-1}, x_{i+1}, \ldots$ where $x_i = x_{i+1}$.

we shrink our attention to *probabilistic input enabled* PLCSs. Probabilistic input enabledness is a condition which ensures that with probability at least $1/2$ any global state s moves within one step to a global state t where $|t| = |s| - 1$ and which guarantees that almost all executions visit infinitely many global states where all channels are empty (see Lemma 3). In particular, it ensures that with probability 1 any message m received in a certain channel c will either be lost or will be consumed by a process (via the action $c?m$).

The formal definition of probabilistic input enabledness can be viewed as a probabilistic "variant" of the standard notion of input enabledness for I/O-automata, see [LT87, Lyn95]. In fact we work with a slightly different meaning of input enabledness. For I/O-automata, communication works synchronously and input enabledness guarantees that the output of messages cannot be blocked. This effect is already obtained for systems where the communication works asynchronously (as for LCSs). Our notion of input enabledness can be viewed as a condition that asserts some kind of "channel fairness" as it rules out the pathological case where a certain message m (produced and send by a process via the action $c!m$) is totally ignored (i.e. never lost nor consumed via the action $c?m$). We adapt the notion of input enabledness for I/O-automata (which asserts that in any (global) state all input actions are enabled) for PLCSs in such a way that, for any global state s where $|s| \geq 1$, the probability for any input action $c?m$ is "sufficiently" large.

Definition 4. *A PLCS* $\mathcal{PL}$ *is called* probabilistic input enabled *iff for all* $s \in S_{control}$ *and all* $c \in Ch$, $m \in Mess$:

$$P_{control}(s, c?m) \geq (1 - 2\wp) \cdot \left(\sum_{\alpha \in SendAct \cup \{\tau\}} P_{control}(s, \alpha) \right).$$

It should be noticed that any PLCS with failure probability $\wp \geq 1/2$ is probabilistic input enabled. Clearly, with $\mathcal{PL}$, also the product $\mathcal{PL} \times \mathcal{A}$ is probabilistic input enabled. In the sequel, we assume that $\mathcal{PL} = (\mathcal{L}, P_{control}, \wp)$ is a probabilistic input enabled PLCS where $\mathcal{L}$ is as in Definition 1.

Let $S_\emptyset = \{s \in S_{global} : |s| = 0\}$ be the set of all global states where all channels are empty. We write $\pi \models \Box \Diamond S_\emptyset$ to denote that π passes infinitely many global states in $S_\emptyset$, i.e. $|\pi(i)| = 0$ for infinitely many indices i.

Lemma 3. *For all global states* s:

$$\sum_{\substack{t \\ |t| = |s| - 1}} P_{global}(s, t) \geq \tfrac{1}{2}.$$

and $Prob\{\pi \in Path(s) : \pi \models \Box \Diamond S_\emptyset \} = 1$.

Proof. (Sketch) The first part is an easy verification. For the second part it suffices to show that $p(s) = 1$ for all global states s where $p(s) = Prob\{\pi \in$

$Path(s) : \pi \models \Diamond S_\emptyset\}$. We put $p(k) = \min\{ p(s) : s \in S_{global}, |s| \leq k\}$. Then, $1 = p(0) \geq p(1) \geq \dots$. Let $s \in S_{global}$, $|s| = k$ where $k \geq 1$. Then,

$$
\begin{aligned}
p(s) =& \sum_{\substack{t \\ |t| \in \{k, k+1\}}} \mathsf{P}_{global}(s,t) \cdot p(t) + \sum_{\substack{t \\ |t| = k-1}} \mathsf{P}_{global}(s,t) \cdot p(t) \\
\geq& \sum_{\substack{t \\ |t| \in \{k, k+1\}}} \mathsf{P}_{global}(s,t) \cdot p(k+1) + \sum_{\substack{t \\ |t| = k-1}} \mathsf{P}_{global}(s,t) \cdot p(k-1) \\
\geq& (1 - Q(k, k-1)) \cdot p(k+1) + Q(k, k-1) \cdot p(k-1),
\end{aligned}
$$

where $Q(k, k-1) = \min\{\mathsf{P}_{global}(s,t) : s,t \in S_{global}, |s| = |t| + 1 \leq k\}$. By Lemma 3, we get $Q(k, k-1) \geq \frac{1}{2}$. Let $p = \inf_{k \geq 1} Q(k, k-1)$. Then, $p(k) \geq (1 - p) \cdot p(k+1) + p \cdot p(k-1)$. This yields a similar situation as in Figure 1, where $p(k)$ can be viewed as the probability to reach s_0 from s_k, and (since $p \geq \frac{1}{2}$) we get $p(k) = 1$ for all $k \geq 1$. ■

We now show how, for probabilistic input enabled PLCSs, qualitative properties specified by a formula $f' = \bigvee \Diamond \Box (a_j \wedge \Diamond b_j)$ can be established by proving a qualitative eventually property $\Diamond U$ where U is a finite set of control states. For showing that $p_s(\Diamond U) = 1$, we use a reachability analysis in the underlying (non-probabilistic) LCS.[20] More precisely, the set U is defined by means of the *bottom strongly connected components* (BSCCs for short) of the directed graph $G_\emptyset(\mathcal{L})$ whose nodes represent the global states $\langle s, \emptyset \rangle$ and whose edges represent the reachability relation between them. The condition $p_s(\Diamond U) = 1$ can shown to be equivalent to $p_s(\Diamond \overline{U}) = 0$ where $\overline{U}$ characterizes all global states $\langle s, \emptyset \rangle$ that belong to a BSCC of $G_\emptyset(\mathcal{L})$ and that are not contained in U. To check whether $p_s(\Diamond \overline{U}) = 0$, it suffices to show that the global state s cannot reach a global state $\langle \overline{u}, \emptyset \rangle$ where $\overline{u} \in \overline{U}$.

Definition 5. *Let $\mathcal{L}$ be a LCS as in Definition 1. We define*

$$ G_\emptyset(\mathcal{L}) = (S_{control}, \leadsto_\mathcal{L}) $$

where the relation $\leadsto_\mathcal{L} \subseteq S_{control} \times S_{control}$ is given by $s \leadsto_\mathcal{L} t$ iff the global state $\langle t, \emptyset \rangle$ is reachable from the global state $\langle s, \emptyset \rangle$ in $\mathsf{TS}(\mathcal{L})$.

If $U \subseteq S_{control}$ then we write $s \leadsto_\mathcal{L} U$ iff $s \leadsto_\mathcal{L} u$ for some $u \in U$. $s \not\leadsto_\mathcal{L} U$ denotes that there is no $u \in U$ with $s \leadsto_\mathcal{L} u$.

Let $a_j, b_j \in AP$ and $A_j = \{s \in S_{control} : a_j \in L(s)\}$, $B_j = \{s \in S_{control} : b_j \in L(s)\}$. Let U_j be the union of all BSCCs C of $G_\emptyset(\mathcal{L})$ such that $C \subseteq A_j$ and $C \cap B_j \neq \emptyset$, $j = 1, \dots, k$, and $U = U_1 \cup \dots \cup U_k$; consequently $\overline{U}$ is the union of all BSCCs C of $G_\emptyset(\mathcal{L})$ such that, for all $j \in \{1, \dots, k\}$, either $C \not\subseteq A_j$ or $C \cap B_j = \emptyset$.

---

[20] We write $p_s(\Diamond U)$ to denote the probability for the global state s to reach a global state of the form $\langle u, w \rangle$ for some $u \in U$.

Lemma 4. *For all control states s:*

$$Prob\left\{\pi \in Path(\langle s, \emptyset \rangle) : \pi \models \bigvee_{1 \leq j \leq k} \Diamond\Box(a_j \wedge \Diamond b_j)\right\} = 1 \quad \text{iff} \quad s \not\leadsto_{\mathcal{L}} \overline{U}.$$

Proof. (Sketch) Let U_j be the union of all BSCCs C of $G_\emptyset(\mathcal{L})$ such that $C \subseteq A_j$ and $C \cap B_j \neq \emptyset$, $j = 1, \ldots, k$, and $U = U_1 \cup \ldots \cup U_k$. For any global state s, we define $\Pi_{BSCC}(s)$ to be the set of paths $\pi \in Path(s)$ such that, for some BSCC C, all global states $\langle t, \emptyset \rangle$, $t \in C$, are visited infinitely often. Using Lemma 3, one can show that

(1) $Prob(\Pi_{BSCC}(s)) = 1$ \qquad (2) $p_s(\Diamond U) + p_s(\Diamond\overline{U}) = 1$

for all global states s. It is easy to see that $\pi \models \Diamond\Box(a_j \wedge \Diamond b_j)$ iff $\pi \models \Diamond U_j$ for any path $\pi \in \Pi_{BSCC}(s)$. By (1) and (2), we get:

$$p_s\left(\bigvee_{1 \leq j \leq k} \Diamond\Box(a_j \wedge \Diamond b_j)\right) = p_s(\Diamond U) = 1 - p_s(\Diamond\overline{U}).$$

Hence, $p_s\left(\bigvee_{1 \leq j \leq k} \Diamond\Box(a_j \wedge \Diamond b_j)\right) = 1$ iff $p_s(\Diamond\overline{U}) = 0$. Since any global state $\langle \overline{u}, w \rangle$ can reach the state $\langle \overline{u}, \emptyset \rangle$ (via losing all messages), we have $p_s(\Diamond\overline{U}) = 0$ iff s cannot reach a global state of the form $\langle \overline{u}, \emptyset \rangle$ where $\overline{u} \in \overline{U}$. ∎

4.3   The Model Checking Algorithm

Combining Lemma 1, 2 and 4 we get the following theorem which builds the basis of our model checking algorithm.

Theorem 1. *Let $\mathcal{PL} = (\mathcal{L}, P_{control}, \wp)$ be a probabilistic input enabled PLCS where $\mathcal{L}$ is as in Definition 1, f a $LTL_{\backslash X}$ formula and A_f a deterministic Rabin automaton for f. Let $\overline{U}'$ be the union of all BSCCs C' of the directed graph $G_\emptyset(\mathcal{L} \times A_f)$ such that, for all $j \in \{1, \ldots, k\}$, either $C' \not\subseteq A_j'$ or $C' \cap B_j' = \emptyset$. Then,*

$$\mathcal{PL} \models f \quad \text{iff} \quad s_0' \not\leadsto_{\mathcal{L} \times A_f} \overline{U}'.$$

Here, $s_0' = \langle s_0, \delta(q_0, L(s_0)) \rangle$ denotes the initial control state of $\mathcal{L} \times A_f$ and A_j', B_j' are as in Lemma 2.

With all the above preliminaries, we are now able to formulate our model checking algorithm. (see Figure 2). The input is a probabilistic input enabled PLCS $\mathcal{PL}$ and a $LTL_{\backslash X}$ formula f. First, we construct a deterministic Rabin automaton A_f for f and the LCS $\mathcal{L} \times A_f$. Then, we compute the reachability relation $\leadsto_{\mathcal{L} \times A_f}$ for the LCS $\mathcal{L} \times A_f$ which yields the graph $G_\emptyset(\mathcal{L} \times A_f)$. For this, we may apply the methods of [AJ93] (or [AKP97]).

Using standard methods of graph theory, we calculate the BSCCs of the graph $G_\emptyset(\mathcal{L} \times A_f)$ and obtain the set $\overline{U}'$ (defined as in Theorem 1). Finally, we check whether the initial control state s_0' of $\mathcal{L} \times A_f$ can reach a node of $\overline{U}'$ with respect to the edge relation $\leadsto_{\mathcal{L} \times A_f}$.

Input: a probabilistic input enabled PLCS $\mathcal{PL} = (\mathcal{L}, P_{control}, \wp)$ and a $LTL_{\backslash X}$
   formula f

Output: if $\mathcal{PL} \models f$ then **yes** else **no**

Method:

1. Compute the deterministic Rabin automaton $\mathcal{A}_f$ for the formula f.
2. Compute the LCS $\mathcal{L} \times \mathcal{A}_f$.
3. Compute the reachability relation $\leadsto_{\mathcal{L} \times \mathcal{A}_f}$ (which yields the graph $G_\emptyset(\mathcal{L} \times \mathcal{A}_f)$).
4. Compute the set $\overline{U}'$ (defined as in Theorem 1) by means of the BSCCs in $G_\emptyset(\mathcal{L} \times \mathcal{A}_f)$.
5. If $s_0' \not\leadsto_{\mathcal{L} \times \mathcal{A}_f} \overline{U}'$ then return **yes** else return **no**.

Fig. 2. The $LTL_{\backslash X}$ model checking algorithm

5   Conclusion and Future Work

We have shown that, for probabilistic input enabled PLCSs, model checking against qualitative $LTL_{\backslash X}$ specifications is decidable. This should be contrasted with the undecidability of LTL model checking for (non-probabilistic) LCSs [AJ94].[21] Thus, adding appropriate transition probabilities to a LCS, can be viewed as a technique to overcome the limitations of algorithmic verification that are due to undecidability results.

Whether or not the probabilistic input enabledness is a necessary condition is still open. The correctness of our method is based on the observation that, with probability 1, a BSCC C of the graph $G_\emptyset(\mathcal{L})$ is reached and that all states of C are visited infinitely often. This property holds for probabilistic input enabled systems (see Lemma 4) but is wrong for general PLCSs (see Example 1).

In this paper, we used the interpretation of a PLCS by a (sequential) Markov chain as proposed in [IN97]. This model is adequate e.g. if the underlying parallel composition for the processes that communicate via the channels is a probabilistic shuffle operator in the style of [BBS92]. This kind of parallel composition assumes a scheduler that decides randomly (according to the "weights" specified by the function $P_{control}$) which of the processes performs the next step. Alternatively, the global behaviour of a PLCS could be described by a model for probabilistic systems with non-determinism (such as concurrent Markov chains [Var85] or the more general models of [BdA95, Seg95, BK98]), where the non-determinism can be used to describe the interleaving behaviour of the communicating processes.

---

[21] Note that in the probabilistic setting, a linear time formula f is viewed to hold in a state s iff f holds on *almost all* paths starting in s (but f might be wrong on some paths) while, in the non-probabilistic case, f is viewed to be correct for a state s iff f holds on *all* paths starting in s.

Unfortunately, we cannot report on experimental results. The implementation of our algorithm (combined with the methods of [AJ93] or [AKP97]), case studies and a complexity analysis will be future topics. Moreover, we intend to investigate how our algorithm can be modified for probabilistic systems with non-determinism and an interpretation of $LTL_{\setminus X}$ formulas over PLCSs that involve (process) fairness, i.e. an interpretation in the style $\mathcal{PL} \models f$ iff f holds with probability 1 for any fair scheduler. Another future direction is to study a CTL^*-like temporal logic that combines $LTL_{\setminus X}$ and the branching time logic of [HS86] where state formulas of the form $\forall f$ (asserting that f holds with probability 1) are considered.

References

[ABJ98]   P. Abdulla, A. Bouajjani, and B. Jonsson. On-the-fly analysis of systems with unbounded, lossy FIFO channels. *LNCS*, 1427:305–318, 1998.

[AJ93]   P. Abdulla and B. Jonsson. Verifying programs with unreliable channels. *Proc. LICS'93*, pages 160–170, 1993. The full version with the same title has been published in *Information and Computation*, 127:91–101, 1996.

[AJ94]   P. Abdulla and B. Jonsson. Undecidable verification problems for programs with unreliable channels. *LNCS*, 820:316–327, 1994. The full version with the same title has been published in *Information and Computation*, 130:71–90, 1996.

[AK95]   P. Abdulla and M. Kindahl. Decidability of simulation and bisimulation between lossy channel systems and finite state systems. *LNCS*, 962:333–347, 1995.

[AKP97]   P. Abdulla, M. Kindahl, and D. Peled. An improved search strategy for lossy channel systems. In *PSTV/FORTE*. Chapman-Hall, 1997.

[ASBS95] A. Aziz, V. Singhal, R. Brayton, and A. Sangiovanni-Vincentelli. It usually works: The temporal logic of stochastic systems. *Proc. CAV'95*, 939:155–165, 1995.

[BBS92]   J. Baeten, J. Bergstra, and S. Smolka. Axiomatizing probabilistic processes: ACP with generative probabilities (extended abstract). *CONCUR'92*, 630:472–485, 1992. The full version with the same title has been published in *Information and Computation*, 122:234–255, 1995.

[BCG88]   M. Browne, E. Clarke, and O. Grumberg. Characterizing finite Kripke structures in propositional temporal logic. *Theoretical Computer Science*, 59:115–131, 1988.

[BdA95]   A. Bianco and L. de Alfaro. Model checking of probabilistic and nondeterministic systems. *LNCS*, 1026:499–513, 1995.

[BER99]   C. Baier, B. Engelen, and M. Roggenbach. Establishing Qualitative Properties for Probabilistic Lossy Channel Systems. Technical Report 3/99, Universität Mannheim, Fakultät für Mathematik und Informatik, 1999.

[BH97]   C. Baier and H. Hermanns. Weak bisimulation for fully probabilistic processes. *LNCS*, 1254:119–130, 1997.

[BK98]   C. Baier and M. Kwiatkowska. Model checking for a probabilistic branching time logic with fairness. *Distributed Computing*, 11:125–155, 1998.

[BM98]   A. Bouajjani and R. Mayr. Model checking lossy vector addition systems. 1998. To appear in *Proc. STACS'99, LNCS*.

[Bre68]   L. Breiman. *Probability*. Addison-Wesley Publishing Company, 1968.

[BSW69]   K. Bartlett, R. Scantlebury, and P. Wilkinson. A note on reliable full-duplex transmission over half-duplex links. *Communications of the ACM*, 12(5):260–261, 1969.

[BZ83]   D. Brand and P. Zafiropulo. On communicating finite-state machines. *Journal of the ACM*, 30(2):323–342, 1983.

[CC91]   L. Christoff and I. Christoff. Efficient algorithms for verification of equivalences for probabilistic processes. *Proc. CAV'91, LNCS*, 575:310–321, 1991.

[CC92]   L. Christoff and I. Christoff. Reasoning about safety and liveness properties for probabilistic processes. *Proc. 12th Conference on Foundations of Software Technology and Theoretical Computer Science, LNCS*, 652:342–355, 1992.

[CES86]   E. Clarke, E. Emerson, and A. Sistla. Automatic verification of finite-state concurrent systems using temporal logic specifications. *ACM Transactions on Programming Languages and Systems*, 8(2):244–263, 1986.

[CFI96]   G. Cécé, A. Finkel, and S. Iyer. Unreliable channels are easier to verify than perfect channels. *Information and Computation*, 124(1):20–31, 1996.

[CY88]   C. Courcoubetis and M. Yannakakis. Verifying temporal properties of finite-state probabilistic programs. *Proc. FOCS'88*, pages 338–345, 1988.

[CY95]   C. Courcoubetis and M. Yannakakis. The complexity of probabilistic verification. *Journal of the ACM*, 42(4):857–907, 1995.

[dA97]   L. de Alfaro. Temporal logics for the specification of performance and reliability. *Proc. STACS'97, LNCS*, 1200:165–176, 1997.

[Eme90]   E. Emerson. Temporal and modal logic. *Handbook of Theoretical Computer Science*, B:995–1072, 1990.

[Fel68]   W. Feller. *An Introduction to Probability Theory and its Application*. John Wiley and Sons, New York, 1968.

[Fin94]   A. Finkel. Decidability of the termination problem for completely specified protocols. *Distributed Computing*, 7(3):129–135, 1994.

[HJ94]   H. Hansson and B. Jonsson. A logic for reasoning about time and reliability. *Formal Aspects of Computing*, 6(5):512–535, 1994.

[HS86]   S. Hart and M. Sharir. Probabilistic propositional temporal logics. *Information and Control*, 70(2/3):97–155, 1986. This is the extended version of "Probabilistic Temporal Logics for Finite and Bounded Models". In *Proc. STOCS'84*, 1–13, 1984.

[HSP83]   S. Hart, M. Sharir, and A. Pnueli. Termination of probabilistic concurrent program. *ACM Transactions on Programming Languages and Systems*, 5(3):356–380, 1983.

[HT92]   T. Huynh and L. Tian. On some equivalence relations for probabilistic processes. *Fundamenta Informaticae*, 17:211–234, 1992.

[IN96]   P. Iyer and M. Narasimha. "Almost always" and "sometime definitely" are not enough: Probabilistic quantifiers and probabilistic model-checking. Technical Report TR-96-16, Department of Computer Science, North Carolina State University, 1996.

[IN97]   P. Iyer and M. Narasimha. Probabilistic lossy channel systems. *Proc. TAPSOFT'97, LNCS*, 1214:667–681, 1997.

[ISO79]   ISO. Data communications - HDLC procedures - elements of procedures. Technical Report TR-ISO-4335, International Standards Organization, Geneva, 1979.

[JS90]   C. Jou and S. Smolka. Equivalences, congruences, and complete axiomatizations for probabilistic processes. In *Proc. CONCUR'90, LNCS*, 458:367–383, 1990.

[LS82]   D. Lehmann and S. Shelah. Reasoning about time and chance. *Information and Control*, 53(3):165–198, 1982.

[LS92]   K. Larsen and A. Skou. Compositional verification of probabilistic processes. In *CONCUR'92, LNCS*, 630:456–471, 1992.

[LT87]   N. Lynch and M. Tuttle. Hierarchical Correctness Proofs For Distributed Algorithms. *PODC'87*, pages 137–151, 1987.

[Lyn95]   N. Lynch. *Distributed Algorithms*. Morgan Kaufmann Series in Data Management Systems. Morgan Kaufmann Publishers, 1995.

[MP92]   Z. Manna and A. Pnueli. *The Temporal Logic of Reactive and Concurrent Systems-Specification*. Springer-Verlag, 1992.

[PZ93]   A. Pnueli and L. Zuck. Probabilistic Verification. *Information and Computation*, 103(1):1–29, 1993. This is the extended version of "Probabilistic Verification by Tableaux". In *Proc. LICS'86*, 322–331, 1986.

[Saf88]   S. Safra. On the complexity of ω-automata. *FOCS'88*, pages 319–327, 1988.

[Seg95]   R. Segala. *Modeling and Verification of Randomized Distributed Real-Time Systems*. PhD thesis, Massachusetts Institute of Technology, 1995.

[Tho90]   W. Thomas. Automata on infinite objects. *Handbook of Theoretical Computer Science*, B:133–191, 1990.

[Var85]   M. Vardi. Automatic verification of probabilistic concurrent finite-state programs. *FOCS'85*, pages 327–338, 1985.

[Var96]   M. Vardi. An automata-theoretic approach to linear temporal logic. *LNCS*, 1043:238–266, 1996.

[VW86]   M. Vardi and P. Wolper. An automata-theoretic approach to automatic program verification. *LICS '86*, pages 332–345, 1986.

[VW94]   M. Vardi and P. Wolper. Reasoning about infinite computations. *Information and Computation*, 115(1):1–37, 1994.

[WVS83]   P. Wolper, M. Vardi, and A. Sistla. Reasoning about infinite computation paths (extended abstract). *FOCS'83*, pages 185–194, 1983.

Root Contention in IEEE 1394

Mariëlle Stoelinga and Frits Vaandrager

Computing Science Institute, University of Nijmegen
P.O. Box 9010, 6500 GL Nijmegen, The Netherlands
{marielle,fvaan}@cs.kun.nl

Abstract. The model of probabilistic I/O automata of Segala and Lynch is used for the formal specification and analysis of the root contention protocol from the physical layer of the IEEE 1394 ("FireWire") standard. In our model of the protocol both randomization and real-time play an essential role. In order to make our verification easier to understand we introduce several intermediate automata in between the implementation and the specification automaton. This allows us to use very simple notions of refinement rather than the more general but also very complex simulation relations which have been proposed by Segala and Lynch.

1   Introduction

Recently, the analysis of probabilistic, distributed algorithms and protocols has gained new attention. Various methods and formalisms have been extended with probabilities, and several case studies have been carried out using these formalisms, c.f. [14, 17].

This report verifies a small sub-protocol of IEEE 1394, called root contention. The IEEE 1394 high performance serial bus has been developed for interconnecting computer and consumer equipment such as multimedia PCs, digital cameras, VCRs, and CD players. The bus is "hot-pluggable", i.e. equipment can be added and removed at any time, and allows quick, reliable and inexpensive high-bandwidth transfer of digitized video and audio. Although originally developed by Apple (FireWire), the version documented in [9] has been accepted as a standard by IEEE in 1996. More than seventy companies — including Sun, Microsoft, Lucent Technologies, Philips, IBM, and Adaptec — have joined in the development of the IEEE 1394 bus, and related consumer electronics and software. Hence there is a good chance that IEEE 1394 will become the future standard for connecting digital multimedia equipment. Various parts of IEEE have been specified and/or verified formally, see for instance [5, 11, 12]. However, as far as we know, root contention has not.

Root contention in IEEE 1394 is a simple but realistic protocol that involves both real-time and randomization. The verification in this report is carried out in the probabilistic automaton model of Segala and Lynch [18, 20]. Following the tradition, the correctness of the protocol is proven by establishing a probabilistic simulation between the implementation and the specification, both probabilistic automata.

J.-P. Katoen (Ed.): ARTS'99, LNCS 1601, pp. 53–74, 1999.

The probabilistic simulation relations from [18, 20] are rather complex. In order to simplify the simulation proofs, this report introduces the notions of probabilistic step refinement and of probabilistic hyperstep refinement. These are special case of the simulations in [18, 20].

The strategy followed in the simulation proof is the following. Given the protocol automaton Impl and the abstract specification Spec, we define three intermediate automata I1, I2, and I3. First, I1 abstracts from the message passing in Impl but keeps the same probabilistic choices and most of the timing information. Next, I2 abstracts from all the timing information in Impl, and I3 abstracts from the probabilistic choice in I3. The introduction of the intermediate automata allows us to separate our concerns. The simulation between Impl and I1 is easy from probabilistic point of view and its proof mainly involves traditional, non-probabilistic techniques like proving invariants. The remaining simulations between automata I2, I3 and Spec deal with probabilistic choice, but since these automata are small this is not so difficult anymore.

This paper is organized as follows. After some mathematical preliminaries in Section 2, Section 3 introduces the probabilistic automaton model. Section 4 describes the root contention protocol, both informally and formally. Then Section 5 defines the intermediate automata and established the simulation relations. Finally, Section 6 presents the conclusions and some topics for future research.

2   Probability Distributions

This section recalls a few basic notions from probability theory and introduces some notation.

Definition 1. *Let $\mathcal{I}$ be an index set and let $x_i \in [0, \infty]$ for all $i \in \mathcal{I}$. Define $\sum_{i \in \mathcal{I}} x_i$ by*

1. $\sum_{i \in \emptyset} x_i \triangleq 0$
2. $\sum_{i \in \mathcal{I}} x_i \triangleq x_{i_1} + x_{i_2} + x_{i_3} + \cdots + x_{i_n}$, *if $\mathcal{I} = \{i_1, i_2, i_3, \ldots, i_n\}$ is a finite set with $n > 0$ elements*
3. $\sum_{i \in \mathcal{I}} x_i \triangleq \sup\{\sum_{i \in \mathcal{J}} x_i \mid \mathcal{J} \subseteq \mathcal{I}$ *is finite*$\}$, *if $\mathcal{I}$ is infinite.*

Here $\sup X$ denotes the supremum of X. Notice that $\sum_{i \in \mathbb{N}} x_i = \sum_{i=0}^{\infty} x_i$ because the summation order is irrelevant, due to the fact that $x_i \geq 0$.

Definition 2. *A probability distribution over set X is a function $\mu : X \to [0, 1]$ such that $\sum_{x \in X} \mu(x) = 1$. We write $support(\mu) \triangleq \{x \in X \mid \mu(x) > 0\}$. It follows from the definitions that this is a countable set. We denote the set of all probability distributions over X by $\Pi(X)$.*

We denote a probability distribution μ on a countable domain by enumerating it as a set of pairs. So, if $\text{Dom}(\mu) = \{x_1, x_2 \ldots\}$ then denote μ by $\{x_1 \mapsto f(x_1), x_2 \mapsto f(x_2) \ldots\}$. If the domain of μ is known, then we often leave out elements of probability zero. For instance, the probability distribution assigning probability one to an element $x \in X$ is denoted by $\{x \mapsto 1\}$, irrespective of X. Such distribution is called the *Dirac distribution* over x. The *uniform distribution* over a finite set with $n > 0$ elements, say $\{x_1, \ldots, x_n\}$, is given by $\{x_1 \mapsto \frac{1}{n}, \ldots, x_n \mapsto \frac{1}{n}\}$.

Definition 3. *Let X and Y be sets, $\mu \in \Pi(X)$ and $\nu \in \Pi(Y)$. The* product *of μ and ν, notation $\mu \times \nu$, is the probability distribution $\kappa : X \times Y \to [0,1]$ satisfying $\kappa(x,y) = \mu(x) \cdot \nu(y)$.*

Definition 4. *Let X and Y be sets, $\mu \in \Pi(X)$ and $f : X \to Y$. The* image of *μ under f, notation $f_*(\mu)$, is the probability distribution $\nu \in \Pi(Y)$ satisfying $\nu(y) = \sum_{x \in f^{-1}(y)} \mu(x)$.*

3 Probabilistic Automata

This section presents the model of probabilistic automata and two extensions, probabilistic I/O automata and timed probabilistic I/O automata. We assume that the reader is familiar with non-probabilistic (timed) automata and their simulation relations, see e.g. [13, 15] for an introduction and for the notations used in this paper.

3.1 The Basic Model

This section recalls the basic probabilistic automaton model from [18, 20], and introduces the notions of probabilistic step refinement and probabilistic hyper-step refinement.

Definition 5. *A* probabilistic automaton *A consists of four components:*

1. *A set $states_A$ of states.*
2. *A nonempty set $start_A \subseteq states_A$ of start states.*
3. *An action signature $sig_A = (ext_A, int_A)$, consisting of external and internal actions respectively; we define the set of actions as $act_A \triangleq ext_A \cup int_A$.*
4. *A transition relation $trans_A \subseteq states_A \times act_A \times \Pi(states_A)$.*

We write $s \xrightarrow{a}_A \mu$ for $(s, a, \mu) \in trans_A$, and $s \xrightarrow{a}_A s'$ for $s \xrightarrow{a}_A \{s' \mapsto 1\}$.

Sometimes, a more general definition of probabilistic automata is given where $trans_A \subseteq states_A \times \Pi(act_A \times states_A)$. In this context the probabilistic automata from the definition are called *simple* probabilistic automata.

Definition 6. *Let A be a probabilistic automaton. The automaton A^-, the* non-probabilistic variant *of A, which behaves like A but discards all probabilistic information, is defined by:*

1. *$states_{A^-} = states_A$.*
2. *$start_{A^-} = start_A$.*

3. $sig_{A^-} = sig_A$.
4. $trans_{A^-} = \{(s, a, s') \mid \exists \mu : s \xrightarrow{a}_A \mu \wedge \mu(s') > 0\}$.

Define $reach_A$, the set of reachable states of A, to be the set of reachable states of A^-.

An execution (execution fragment, trace) of a probabilistic automaton A is an execution (execution fragment, trace) of A^-. The set of executions (execution fragments, traces) and finite executions (execution fragments, traces) of A are respectively denoted by $execs(A)(frags(A), traces(A))$ and by $execs^*(A)$ $(frags^*(A), traces^*(A))$.

Definition 7. *If A is a probabilistic automaton and $X \subseteq ext_A$, then $hide(A, X)$ is the probabilistic automaton $(states_A, start_A, (ext_A \setminus X, int_A \cup X), trans_A)$.*

Definition 8. *We say that two probabilistic automata A_1 and A_2 are compatible if $int_{A_1} \cap act_{A_2} = act_{A_1} \cap int_{A_2} = \emptyset$. If A_1 and A_2 are compatible then their parallel composition, notation $A_1 \parallel A_2$, is the probabilistic automaton A defined by:*

- $states_A = states_{A_1} \times states_{A_2}$.
- $start_A = start_{A_1} \times start_{A_2}$.
- $sig_A = (ext_{A_1} \cup ext_{A_2}, int_{A_1} \cup int_{A_2})$.
- $trans_A$ is the set of triples $((s_1, s_2), a, \mu_1 \times \mu_2)$ such that for $i = 1, 2$, if $a \in act_{A_i}$ then $(s_i, a, \mu_i) \in trans_{A_i}$, otherwise $\mu_i = \{s_i \mapsto 1\}$.

Informally, within a composition two probabilistic automata synchronize on their common actions and evolve independently on others. Whenever synchronization occurs, the state reached is obtained by choosing a state independently for both automata.

Probabilistic Step Refinements The simplest form of simulations between probabilistic automata that we consider are the probabilistic step refinements. These are mappings from the states of one automaton to the states of another automaton that preserve initial states and probabilistic transitions.

Definition 9. *Let A and B be two probabilistic automata with $ext_A = ext_B$. A probabilistic step refinement from A to B is a function $r : states_A \rightarrow states_B$ such that:*

1. *for all $s \in start_A, r(s) \in start_B$;*
2. *for all steps $s \xrightarrow{a}_A \mu$ with $s \in reach_A$, one of the following conditions holds:*
   (a) $r(s) \xrightarrow{d}_B r_*(\mu)$, or
   (b) $a \in int_A \wedge r(s) \xrightarrow{b}_B r_*(\mu)$, for some $b \in int_B$, or
   (c) $a \in int_A \wedge r_*(\mu) = \{r(s) \mapsto 1\}$.

We write $A \sqsubseteq_{\text{PSR}} B$ if there is a probabilistic step refinement from A to B. Note that condition 2(c) is equivalent to $a \in int_A \wedge \forall s'[\mu(s') > 0 \Rightarrow r(s') = r(s)]$.

Probabilistic Hyperstep Refinements Probabilistic hyperstep refinements generalize the probabilistic step refinements introduced above. They are a special case of the probabilistic forward simulations of Segala and Lynch [18, 20].

Definition 10. *Let X, Y be sets and $R \subseteq X \times \Pi(Y)$. The lifting of R is the relation $R_{**} \subseteq \Pi(X) \times \Pi(Y)$ given by: $(\mu, \nu) \in R_{**}$ if and only if there is a choice function $r : support(\mu) \to \Pi(Y)$ for R, i.e., a function such that $(x, r(x)) \in R$ for all $x \in support(\mu)$, satisfying*

$$\nu(y) = \sum_{x \in \text{supp}(\mu)} \mu(x) \cdot r(x)(y).$$

The idea is that we obtain ν by choosing the probability distribution $r(x)$ with probability $\mu(x)$.

Example 1. Given a probabilistic automaton A and an action $a \in act_A$, we can lift the relation $\xrightarrow{a}$ over $states_A \times \Pi(states_A)$ to the relation $\xrightarrow{a}_{**}$ over $\Pi(states_A) \times \Pi(states_A)$. For instance, if $s_1 \xrightarrow{a} \mu_1$, $s_2 \xrightarrow{a} \mu_2$ and $s_1 \neq s_2$, then

$$\{s_1 \mapsto \tfrac{1}{3}, s_2 \mapsto \tfrac{2}{3}\} \xrightarrow{a}_{**} \tfrac{1}{3} \cdot \mu_1 + \tfrac{2}{3} \cdot \mu_2.$$

Intuitively, if $s_1 \xrightarrow{a} \mu_1$, $s_2 \xrightarrow{a} \mu_2$ and the probability to be in s_1 is $\tfrac{1}{3}$ and to be in s_2 is $\tfrac{2}{3}$, then we choose the next state according to μ_1 with probability $\tfrac{1}{3}$ and according to μ_2 with probability $\tfrac{2}{3}$. If there is another a–transition, say $s_2 \xrightarrow{a} \nu$, then we can also choose the next state according to μ_1 with probability $\tfrac{1}{3}$ and according to ν with probability $\tfrac{2}{3}$. Hence

$$\{s_1 \mapsto \tfrac{1}{3}, s_2 \mapsto \tfrac{2}{3}\} \xrightarrow{a}_{**} \tfrac{1}{3} \cdot \mu_1 + \tfrac{2}{3} \cdot \nu.$$

We do *not* have

$$\{s_1 \mapsto \tfrac{1}{3}, s_2 \mapsto \tfrac{2}{3}\} \xrightarrow{a}_{**} \tfrac{1}{3} \cdot \mu_1 + \tfrac{1}{3} \cdot \mu_2 + \tfrac{1}{3} \cdot \nu.$$

Definition 11. *Let A and B be probabilistic automaton with $ext_A = ext_B$. A probabilistic hyperstep refinement from A to B is a function $h : states_A \to \Pi(states_B)$ such that:*

1. *for all $s \in start_A$, $h(s) = \{s' \mapsto 1\}$ for some $s' \in start_B$;*
2. *for all steps $s \xrightarrow{a}_A \mu$ with $s \in reach_A$, one of the following conditions holds:*
   (a) *$h(s) \xrightarrow{a}_{B**} h_{**}(\mu)$, or*
   (b) *$a \in int_A \wedge h(s) \xrightarrow{b}_{B**} h_{**}(\mu)$, for some $b \in int_B$, or*
   (c) *$a \in int_A \wedge h(s) = h_{**}(\mu)$.*

Write $A \sqsubseteq_{\text{PHSR}}$ if there is a probabilistic hyperstep refinement from A to B.

Segala [18] describes the behavior of probabilistic automata in terms of *trace distributions*, and proposes inclusion of trace distributions, notation $\sqsubseteq_{\mathrm{TD}}$, as an implementation relation between probabilistic automata that preserves safety properties. The following theorem states that probabilistic (hyper-)step refinements are a sound proof method for establishing trace distribution inclusion.

Theorem 1. *Let A and B be probabilistic automata with $ext_A = ext_B$.*

1. *If $A \sqsubseteq_{\mathrm{PSR}} B$ then $A \sqsubseteq_{\mathrm{PHSR}}$.*
2. *If $A \sqsubseteq_{\mathrm{PHSR}}$ then $A \sqsubseteq_{\mathrm{TD}} B$.*

Proof. For (1), suppose that $A \sqsubseteq_{\mathrm{PSR}} B$. Then there exists a probabilistic step refinement r from A to B. Let $R : states_A \rightarrow \Pi(states_B)$ be given by $R(s) = \{r(s) \mapsto 1\}$. It is routine to check that R is a probabilistic hyperstep refinement from A to B. Use that

$$R_{**}(\mu) = r_*(\mu),$$
$$s \xrightarrow{a}_B \nu \Leftrightarrow \{s \mapsto 1\} \xrightarrow{a}_{B**} \nu.$$

Hence $A \sqsubseteq_{\mathrm{PHSR}}$.

For (2), suppose that $A \sqsubseteq_{\mathrm{PHSR}}$. Then there exists a probabilistic hyperstep refinement R from A to B. We claim that R is a probabilistic forward simulation in the sense of [18, 20]. Now $A \sqsubseteq_{\mathrm{TD}} B$ follows from the soundness result for probabilistic forward simulations, see Proposition 8.7.1 in [18]. For a simple, direct proof of (2) we refer to [22].

3.2   Probabilistic I/O Automata

This section defines the probabilistic I/O automaton model, an extension of probabilistic automata with a distinction between input and output actions, and with a notion of fair behavior.

Definition 12. *A probabilistic I/O automaton A is a probabilistic automaton enriched with*

1. *a partition of ext_A into input actions in_A and output actions out_A, and*
2. *a task partition $tasks_A$, which is an equivalence relation over $out_A \cup int_A$ with countably many equivalence classes.*

We require that A is input enabled, which means that for all $s \in states_A$ and all $a \in in_A$, there is a μ such that $s \xrightarrow{a}_A \mu$.

As probabilistic I/O automata are enriched probabilistic automata, we can use the notions of nonprobabilistic variant, reachable state, execution (fragment) and trace also for probabilistic I/O automata.

Definition 13. *Let A be a probabilistic I/O automaton. An execution of A is fair if the following conditions hold for each class C of $tasks_A$:*

1. If α is finite then C is not enabled in the final states of α.
2. If α is infinite, then α contains either infinitely many actions from C or infinitely many occurrences of states in which no action in C is enabled.

Similarly, a trace of A is fair in A if it is the trace of a fair execution of A. The sets of fair executions and fair traces of A are denoted by $fexecs(A)$ and $ftraces(A)$ respectively.

Definition 14. Let A and B be probabilistic automata with $ext_A = ext_B$. Let r be a mapping from $states_A$ to $states_B$. Then r induces a relation $\tilde{r} \subseteq frags(A) \times frags(B)$ as follows: if $\alpha = s_0a_1s_1 \cdots \in frags(A)$, $\mathcal{I}$ is the index set of α, $\beta = t_0b_1t_1 \cdots \in frags(B)$ and $\mathcal{J}$ is the index set of β, then $\alpha\tilde{r}\beta$ if and only if there is a surjective, nondecreasing index mapping $m : \mathcal{I} \to \mathcal{J}$, such that for all $i \in \mathcal{I}$, $j \in \mathcal{J}$,

1. $m(0) = 0$
2. $r(s_i) = t_{m(i)}$
3. if $i > 0$ then either of the following conditions holds
    (a) $a_i = b_{m(i)} \wedge m(i) = m(i-1) + 1$ or
    (b) $a_i \in int_A \wedge b_{m(i)} \in int_B \wedge m(i) = m(i-1) + 1$ or
    (c) $a_i \in int_A \wedge m(i) = m(i-1)$.

In [17], fair trace distribution inclusion, notation $\sqsubseteq_{\text{FTD}}$, is proposed as an implementation relation between probabilistic I/O automata that preserves both safety and liveness properties.

Claim ([22]). Let A and B be probabilistic I/O automata. Let r be a probabilistic step refinement from A to B that relates each fair execution of A only to fair executions of B. Then $A \sqsubseteq_{\text{FTD}} B$.

3.3   Timed Probabilistic I/O Automata

Definition 15. A timed probabilistic I/O automaton A is a probabilistic automaton enriched with a partition of ext_A into input actions in_A, output actions out_A, and the set $\mathbb{R}^{>0}$ of positive real numbers or time-passage actions. We require[1] that, for all $s, s', s'' \in states_A$ and $d, d' \in \mathbb{R}^{>0}$ with $d' < d$,

1. A is input enabled,
2. each step labelled with a time-passage action leads to a Dirac distribution,
3. (Time determinism) if $s \xrightarrow{d}_A s'$ and $s \xrightarrow{d}_A s''$ then $s' = s''$.
4. (Wang's axiom) $s \xrightarrow{d}_A s'$ iff $\exists s'' : s \xrightarrow{d'}_A s''$ and $s'' \xrightarrow{d-d'}_A s'$.

As timed probabilistic I/O automata are enriched probabilistic automata, we can use the notions of nonprobabilistic variant, reachable state, and execution (fragment), also for timed probabilistic I/O automata.

We say that an execution α of A is diverging if the sum of the time-passage actions in α diverges to ∞.

---

[1] For simplicity the conditions here are slightly more restrictive than those in [15].

Definition 16. *Let A, B be probabilistic or timed probabilistic I/O automata. A function r is a probabilistic (hyper)step refinement from A to B if r is a probabilistic (hyper)step refinement from the underlying probabilistic automaton of A to the underlying probabilistic automaton of B.*

In [22], it is argued that, under certain assumptions (met by the automata studied in this paper), $\sqsubseteq_{TD}$ can be used as a safety and liveness preserving implementation relation between timed I/O automata. In addition, the relation $\sqsubseteq_{DFTD}$ is proposed as a safety and liveness preserving implementation relation between timed probabilistic I/O automata and probabilistic I/O automata.

Claim ([22]). Let A be a timed probabilistic I/O automaton and let B be a probabilistic I/O automaton. Let r be a probabilistic step refinement from $hide(A, \mathbb{R}^{>0})$ to B that relates each divergent execution of A only to fair executions of B. Then $A \sqsubseteq_{DFTD} B$.

4   Description of the Protocol

The IEEE 1394 serial bus protocol has been designed for communication between multimedia equipement. In the IEEE 1394 standard, components connected to the bus are referred to as nodes. Each node has a number of ports which are used for bidirectional connections to (other) nodes. Each port has at most one connection.

The protocol has several layers, of which the physical layer is the lowest. Within this layer a number of phases are identified. The protocol enters the so-called tree identify phase whenever a bus reset occurs, for instance when a connection is added or removed. The task of this phase is to check whether the network topology is a tree and, if so, to elect a leader among the nodes in this tree.

This is done by constructing a spanning tree in the network and electing the root of the tree as leader. Informally, the basic idea of the protocol is as follows: leaf nodes send a "parent request" message to their neighbor. When a node has received a parent request from all but one of its neighbors it sends a parent request to its remaining neighbor. In this way the tree grows from the leafs to a root. If a node has received parent requests from all its neighbors, it knows that it is has been elected as the root of the tree. It is possible that at the end of the tree identify phase two nodes send parent request messages to each other; this situation is called root contention. In this paper we will be concerned with the formal verification and analysis of the root contention protocol which is run in this case. After completion of the root contention protocol, one of the two nodes has become root of the network.

Lynch [13, p501] describes an abstract version of the tree identify protocol and suggests to elect the node with the larger unique identifier (UID) as the root in case of root contention. Since during the tree identify phase no UID's are available (these will be assigned during a later phase of the physical layer protocol), a probabilistic algorithm has been chosen that is fully symmetric and does not require the presence of UID's.

Let us, for simplicity, refer to the two contending nodes as node 1 and node 2. The timed probabilistic I/O automata describing the behavior of these nodes are given in Figure 1, using the IOA syntax of [6] extended with a simple form of probabilistic choice. Roughly, the protocol works as follows. When a node i has detected root contention it first flips a coin (i.e., performs the action Flip(i)). If head comes up then it waits a short time, somewhere in the interval $[\delta_{fast}, \Delta_{fast}]$. If tail comes up then it waits a long time, somewhere in the interval $[\delta_{slow}, \Delta_{slow}]$. So $0 \leq \delta_{fast} \leq \Delta_{fast} < \delta_{slow} \leq \Delta_{slow}$. After the waiting period has elapsed, either no message from the contender has been received, or a parent request message has arrived. In the first case the node sends a request message to its contender (i.e., performs the action Send(i, req)), in the second case it sends an acknowledgement message (i.e., performs the action Send(i, ack)). As soon as a node has sent an acknowledgement it declares itself to be the root (via the action Root(i)), and whenever a node has received an acknowledgement it assumes that its contender will become root and it declares itself child (via the action Child(i)). If a node that has sent a request subsequently receives a request, then it concludes that there is root contention again, and the protocol starts all over again. The basic idea behind the protocol is that if the outcomes of the coin flips are different, the node with outcome tail (i.e., the slow one) will become root. And since with probability one the outcomes of the two coin flips will eventually be different, the root contention protocol will terminate (with probability one).

The timed probabilistic I/O automaton for node i (i = 1, 2), displayed in Figure 1, has five state variables: variable **status** tells whether the node has become $root$, $child$, or whether its status is still $unknown$; variable **coin** records the outcome of the coin flip; variable **snt** records the last value (if any) that has been sent to the contender and may take values req, ack or $\perp$; similarly **rec** records the last value that has been received (if any); variable **x**, finally, models the arbitration timer that records the time that has elapsed since root contention has been detected. We use two auxiliary functions mindelay and maxdelay from Toss to Reals given by, for c $\in$ Toss,

$$\text{mindelay(c)} \triangleq \textbf{if } c = head \textbf{ then } \delta_{fast} \textbf{ else } \delta_{slow}$$

$$\text{maxdelay(c)} \triangleq \textbf{if } c = head \textbf{ then } \Delta_{fast} \textbf{ else } \Delta_{slow}$$

Now it should not be difficult to understand the precondition/effect style definitions in Figure 1, except maybe for the definition of the Time(d) transitions. This part states that time will not progress if the status of the node is unknown and (1) an acknowledgement has been sent, or (2) an acknowledgement has been received, or (3) a parent request has both been sent and received. In the first case the automaton will instantaneously perform a Root(i) action, in the second case it will perform a Child(i) action, and in the third case there is contention and

```
type P = enumeration of 1, 2
type M = enumeration of  ⊥, req, ack
type Status = enumeration of  unknown, root, child
type Toss = enumeration of  head, tail
automaton Node(i: P)
    states
        status : Status := unknown,
        coin : Toss,
        snt : M := req,
        rec : M := req,
        x : Reals := 0
    signature
        input Receive(const i, m: M) where m ≠⊥
        output Send(const i, m: M) where m ≠⊥,
                Root(const i)
        internal Flip(const i),
                Child(const i)
        delay Time(d: Reals) where d > 0
    transitions
        internal Flip(i)
            pre status = unknown ∧ snt = req ∧ rec = req
            eff coin := { head ½
                          tail  ½ ;
                x := 0;
                snt :=⊥;
                rec :=⊥
        output Send(i, m)
            pre status = unknown ∧ snt =⊥
                ∧ x ≥ mindelay(coin)
                ∧ m = if rec =⊥ then req else ack
            eff snt := m
        input Receive(i, m)
            eff rec := m
        output Root(i)
            pre status = unknown ∧ snt = ack
            eff status := root
        internal Child(i)
            pre status = unknown ∧ rec = ack
            eff status := child
        delay Time(d)
            pre status = unknown ⇒
                (snt ≠ ack ∧ rec ≠ ack ∧ ¬(snt = req ∧ rec = req)
                ∧ snt =⊥⇒ x + d ≤ maxdelay(coin))
            eff x := x + d
```

Fig. 1. Node automaton.

the automaton will flip a coin.[2] The last clause in the precondition of Time(d) enforces that a Send(i, m) action is performed within either Δ_{fast} or Δ_{slow} time after the coin flip (depending on the outcome). Once the status of the automaton has become *root* or *child* there are no more restrictions on time passage.

The two automata for node 1 and node 2 communicate via wires, which are modeled as the timed probabilistic automata Wire(1, 2) and Wire(2, 1) specified in Figure 2. We assume an upper bound $\Gamma \geq 0$ on the communication delay.

```
automaton Wire(i: P, j: P)
    states
        msg : M :=⊥,
        x : Reals := 0
    signature
        input Send(const i, m: M)  where m ≠⊥
        output Receive(const j, m: M) where m ≠⊥
        delay Time(d: Reals)  where d > 0
    transitions
        input Send(i, m)
            eff msg := m;
                x := 0
        output Receive(j, m)
            pre m = msg
            eff msg :=⊥
        delay Time(d)
            pre msg ≠⊥ ⇒ x + d ≤ Γ
            eff x := x + d
```

Fig. 2. Wire automaton.

The full system can now be described as the parallel composition of the two node automata and the two wire automata, with all synchronization actions hidden (see Figure 3).

```
Impl ≜ hide Send(i, m), Receive(i, m) for i : P, m : M in
            compose Node(1); Wire(1, 2); Node(2); Wire(2, 1)
```

Fig. 3. The full system.

---

[2] Note that in each of these three cases we abstract in our model from the computation time required to perform these actions.

Remark 1. As Segala [18] points out in his thesis, it would be useful to study the theory of *receptiveness* [19] in the context of randomization. As far as we know, nobody has taken up this challenge yet. Intuitively, an automaton is receptive if it does not constrain its environment, for instance by not accepting certain inputs or by preventing time to pass beyond a certain point. Behavior inclusion is used as an implementation relation in the I/O automata framework and we exclude trivial implementations by requiring that an implementation is receptive.

If we replace all probabilistic choices by nondeterministic choices in the automata of this section, then the resulting timed I/O automata are receptive in the sense of [19]. Even with a more restrictive definition of receptivity, in which we allow the environment to resolve all probabilistic choices, the automata of this section remain receptive.

5   Verification and Analysis

Of course the key correctness property of the root contention protocol which we would like to prove is that eventually exactly one node is designated as root. This correctness property is described by the two state probabilistic I/O automaton Spec of Figure 4.

```
automaton Spec
    states
        done : Bool := false
    signature
        output Root(i: P)
    transitions
        output Root(i)
            pre done = false
            eff done = true
    tasks
        One block
```

Fig. 4. Specification.

We will establish that Impl implements Spec, provided the following two constraints on the parameters are met:

$$\Gamma < \delta_{\text{fast}} \tag{1}$$

$$\Delta_{\text{fast}} + 2\Gamma < \delta_{\text{slow}} \tag{2}$$

Within our proof, we introduce three intermediate automata I1, I2 and I3, and prove that

$$\text{Impl} \sqsubseteq_{\text{TD}} \text{I1} \sqsubseteq_{\text{TD}} \text{I2} \sqsubseteq_{\text{TD}} \text{I3} \sqsubseteq_{\text{TD}} \text{Spec}.$$

These results (or more precisely the refinements that are established in their proofs) are then used to obtain that

$$\texttt{Impl} \sqsubseteq_{TD} \texttt{I1} \sqsubseteq_{DFTD} \texttt{I2} \sqsubseteq_{FTD} \texttt{I3} \sqsubseteq_{FTD} \texttt{Spec.}$$

I1 is a timed probabilistic I/O automaton, which abstracts from all the message passing in Impl, while preserving the probabilistic choices as well as most information about the timing of the Root(i) events. I2 is a probabilistic I/O automaton which is identical to I1, except that all real-time information has been omitted. In I3 the two coin flips from each node of the protocol are combined into a single probabilistic transition.

5.1 Invariants

We will show that there exists a probabilistic step refinement from Impl to an intermediate automaton I1. In order to establish a refinement, we first need to introduce a number of invariants for automaton Impl.

We use subscripts 1 and 2 to refer to the state variables of Node(1) and Node(2), respectively, and subscripts 12 and 21 to refer to the state variables of Wire(1, 2) and Wire(2, 1), respectively. So, x_1 denotes the clock variable of Node(1), x_{12} the clock variable of Wire(1, 2), etc. Within formulas we further use the following abbreviations, for $i \in P$,

$$\text{Cont}(i) \overset{\Delta}{=} \texttt{snt}_i = req \land (\texttt{rec}_i = req \lor \texttt{msg}_{ji} = req)$$
$$\text{Wait}(i) \overset{\Delta}{=} \texttt{snt}_i = \texttt{rec}_i = \perp$$
$$\delta_i \overset{\Delta}{=} \text{mindelay}(\texttt{coin}_i)$$
$$\Delta_i \overset{\Delta}{=} \text{maxdelay}(\texttt{coin}_i)$$

Predicate Cont(i) states that node i has either detected contention (a request has both been sent and received) or will do so in the near future (the node has sent a request and will receive one soon). Predicate Wait(i) states that node has flipped the coin and is waiting for the delay time to expire; no message has been received yet. State function δ_i gives the minimum delay time for node i, and state function Δ_i the maximum delay time (both state functions depend on the outcome of the coin flip).

We claim that assertions (3)-(19) below are invariants of automaton Impl.

$$x_i \geq 0 \tag{3}$$
$$\texttt{status}_i = unknown \land \texttt{snt}_i \neq req \Rightarrow x_i \leq \Delta_i \tag{4}$$
$$\texttt{snt}_i = ack \Rightarrow x_i \geq \delta_i \tag{5}$$
$$\texttt{status}_i = root \Rightarrow \texttt{snt}_i = ack \tag{6}$$
$$\texttt{status}_i = child \Rightarrow \texttt{rec}_i = ack \tag{7}$$

$$x_{ij} \geq 0 \tag{8}$$

$$msg_{ij} \neq \bot \Rightarrow x_{ij} \leq \Gamma \tag{9}$$

$$Cont(i) \Leftrightarrow Cont(j) \Rightarrow | x_i - x_j | \leq \Gamma \tag{10}$$

$$Cont(i) \wedge \neg Cont(j) \Rightarrow Wait(j) \wedge msg_{ij} = \bot \wedge x_j \leq \Gamma \tag{11}$$

$$msg_{ij} \neq \bot \Rightarrow rec_j = \bot \tag{12}$$

$$msg_{ij} = \bot \Rightarrow snt_i = \bot \vee rec_j \neq \bot \vee Cont(i) \tag{13}$$

$$msg_{ij} = req \wedge \neg Wait(i) \Rightarrow snt_i = req \wedge snt_j \neq ack \wedge$$
$$\delta_i \leq x_i - x_{ij} \leq \Delta_i \tag{14}$$

$$msg_{ij} = req \wedge Wait(i) \Rightarrow snt_j = req \wedge x_i \leq x_{ij} \tag{15}$$

$$snt_i = \bot \wedge rec_i = req \Rightarrow snt_j = req \wedge rec_j = \bot \wedge x_j \geq \delta_j \tag{16}$$

$$rec_i = ack \Rightarrow snt_j = ack \tag{17}$$

$$msg_{ij} = ack \Rightarrow snt_i = ack \tag{18}$$

$$snt_i = ack \Rightarrow rec_i = snt_j = req \wedge rec_j \neq req \wedge x_j \geq \delta_j \tag{19}$$

Assertions (3)-(9) are local invariants, which can be proven straightforwardly for automata Node(i) and Wire(i, j) in isolation. Most of the time nodes 1 and 2 are either both in contention or both not in contention. Assertion (10) states that in these cases the values of the clocks of the two nodes differ by at most Γ. Assertion (11) expresses that the only case where node i is in contention but the other node j is not occurs when j has just flipped a coin but the request message that j sent to i has not yet arrived or been processed. If a channel contains a message then nothing has been received at the end of this channel (12). If the channel from i to j is empty then either no message has been sent into the channel at i, or a message has been received at j, or we have a situation where i is in contention and j has just flipped a coin and moved to a new phase (13). If the channel from i to j contains a request message then there are two possible cases. Either i has sent the message and is waiting for a reply (14), or there is contention and i has just flipped a coin (15). If i has received a request message without having sent anything, then j has sent this message but has not received anything (16). The last three invariants deal with situations where there is an acknowledgement somewhere in the system (17)-(19). In these cases the global state is almost completely determined: if an acknowledgement is in a channel or has been received then it has been sent, and if a node has sent an acknowledgement then it has received a request, which in turn has been sent by the other node.

The proofs of the following two lemmas are tedious but completely standard since they only refer to the non-probabilistic automaton $Impl^-$. Detailed proofs can be obtained via URL http://www.cs.kun.nl/~fvaan/PAPERS/SVproofs.

Lemma 1. *Suppose state s satisfies assertions (3)-(19) and $s \overset{Send(i,\, m)}{\rightarrow} s'$. Then $s \models msg_{ij} = rec_j = \bot$ and $s' \models Cont(i) \Leftrightarrow Cont(j)$.*

Lemma 2. *Assertions (3)-(19) hold for all reachable states of Impl.*

Remark 2. The first constraint on the timing parameters ($\Gamma < \delta_{fast}$) is used in the proof of Lemma 1 and ensures that there can never be two messages travelling in a wire at the same time. This property allows for a very simple model of the wires, in which a new message overwrites an old message. The constraint is not needed to prove the correctness of the algorithm. Nevertheless, since the constraint is implied by the standard, we decided to include it as an assumption in our analysis.

5.2   The First Intermediate Automaton

Intermediate automaton I1 is displayed in Figure 5. This probabilistic timed I/O automaton records the status for each of the two nodes to be either *init*, *head*, *tail*, or *done*. In addition I1 maintains a clock x to impose timing constraints

```
automaton I1
    type Phase = enumeration of init, head, tail, done
    states
        phase : Array[P, Phase] := constant(init),
        x : Reals := 0
    signature
        output Root(i: P)
        internal Flip(i: P),
                 Retry(c: Toss)
        delay Time(d: Reals)  where d > 0
    transitions
        internal Flip(i)
            pre phase[i] = init
            eff phase[i] := { head  ½
                              tail   ½   ;
                if phase[next(i)] ≠ init then x := 0
        output Root(i)
            pre {phase[1], phase[2]} ⊆ {head, tail}
                ∧ ¬(phase[i] = head ∧ phase[next(i)] = tail)
                ∧ x ≥ mindelay(phase[i]) − Γ
            eff phase := constant(done)
        internal Retry(c)
            pre phase = constant(c)
                ∧ x ≥ mindelay(c)
            eff phase := constant(init);
                x := 0
        delay Time(d)
            pre  init ∈ {phase[1], phase[2]}  ⇒  x + d ≤ Γ
                ∧ {phase[1], phase[2]} ⊆ {head, tail}  ⇒
                    x + d ≤ max(maxdelay(phase[1]), maxdelay(phase[2]))
            eff x := x + d
```

Fig. 5. Intermediate automaton I1.

between events. Apart from the delay action there are three actions: Flip(i), which corresponds to node i flipping a coin, Root(i), which corresponds to node i declaring itself to be the root, and Retry(c), which models the restart of the protocol in the case where the outcome of both coin flips is c. Node i performs a (probabilistic) Flip(i) action in its initial state. A Root(i) transition may occur if both nodes have flipped a coin and it is *not* the case that the outcome for i is *head* and for j *tail*. A Retry(c) transition may occur if both nodes have flipped c. Clock x is used to express that both nodes flip their coin within time Γ after the (re-)start of the protocol. In addition it ensures that subsequently (depending on the outcome of the coin flips) at least $\delta_{fast} - \Gamma$ or $\delta_{slow} - \Gamma$ time and at most Δ_{fast} or Δ_{slow} time will elapse before either a Root(i) or a Retry(c) action occurs.

Proposition 1. Impl $\sqsubseteq_{TD}$ I1. *More specifically the conjunction, for* i $\in$ P, *of*

$$phase[i] = \text{if } status_1 = root \lor status_2 = root \text{ then } done \text{ else}$$
$$\text{if Cont(i) then } init \text{ else } coin_i \text{ fi fi}$$
$$x = \text{if Cont(1)} \lor \text{Cont(2) then } min(x_{12}, x_{21}) \text{ else } min(x_1, x_2)$$

determines a probabilistic step refinement from Impl *to* I1.

Proof. Routine. See http://www.cs.kun.nl/~fvaan/PAPERS/SVproofs.

Remark 3. The second constraint on the timing parameters ($\Delta_{fast} + 2\Gamma < \delta_{slow}$) is used in the proof of Proposition 1 and ensures that contention may only occur if the outcomes of both coin flips are the same. This property is needed to prove termination of the algorithm (with probability 1).

Remark 4. Figure 6 gives the values for some of the relevant parameters of the protocol as listed in the standard IEEE 1394 [9] and in the more recent draft standard IEEE 1394a [10]. Interestingly, the values in two documents are different. Given our timing constraints (1) and (2), this leads to a maximum value for

Timing constant	Min (1394)	Max (1394)	Min (1394a)	Max (1394a)
ROOT_CONTENT_FAST	0.24μs	0.26μs	0.76μs	0.80μs
ROOT_CONTENT_SLOW	0.57μs	0.60μs	1.60μs	1.64μs

Fig. 6. Timing parameters.

Γ of $\frac{0.57-0.26}{2}\mu s = 0.155\mu s$ for IEEE 1394, and $\frac{1.60-0.8}{2}\mu s = 0.4\mu s$ for the draft IEEE 1394a. With the maximal signal velocity of $5.05ns/meter$ that is specified in both documents, this gives a maximum cable length of appr. 31 meter for IEEE 1394 and 79 meter for IEEE 1394a. However, these values should be viewed as upper bounds since within our model we have not taken into account the processing times of signals. IEEE 1394 specifies a maximum cable length of 4.5 meter.

Remark 5. In [16] it is claimed that if both nodes happen to select slow timing or if both nodes select fast timing, contention results again. This is incorrect. In automaton I1 each of the two nodes may become root if both nodes happen to select the same timing delay. This may also occur within a real-world implementation of the protocol: if in the implementation the timing parameters of one node are close to their minimum values, in the other node close to their maximum values, and if the communication delay is small, then it may occur that a message of node i arrives at node j before the timing delay of node j has expired. In fact, by instantiating the timing parameters differently in different devices (for instance via some random mechanism!) one may reduce the expected time to resolve contention. Unfortunately, a more detailed analysis of this phenomenon falls outside the scope of this paper.

Remark 6. Another way in which the performance of the protocol could be improved is by repeatedly polling the input during the timing delay, rather than checking it only at the end. We suggest that, if the process receives a request when the timing delay has not yet expired, then it immediately sends an acknowledgement (and declares itself root). If the process has not received a request during the timing delay, then it sends a request and proceeds as the current implementation. In a situation where node i flips head and selects a timing delay of δ_{fast} and the other node j flips tail and selects a timing delay of Δ_{slow}, our version elects a leader within at most $\delta_{\text{fast}} + 3\Gamma$, whereas in the current version this upperbound is $\Delta_{\text{slow}} + 3\Gamma$.

5.3 The Second Intermediate Automaton

In Figure 7 the second intermediate automaton I2 is described. I2 is a probabilistic I/O automaton that is identical to I1 except that all real-time information has been abstracted away; instead a (trivial) task partition is included. The proof of the following Proposition 2 is easy: the projection function π from I1 to I2 trivially is a probabilistic step refinement (after hiding of the time delays).

Proposition 2. I1 $\sqsubseteq_{\text{TD}}$ I2.

Proposition 3. *If $\alpha \in execs(I1)$ is diverging π relates α and β, then β is fair.*

The result formulated in the Proposition 3 above follows by the fact that a diverging execution of I1 either contains infinitely many Retry actions, or contains an infinite suffix with a Root(i) transition followed by an infinite number of delay transitions. Now the claim at the end of Section 3.3 implies I1 $\sqsubseteq_{\text{DFTF}}$ I2.

5.4 The Third Intermediate Automaton

Figure 8 gives the IOA code for the probabilistic I/O automaton I3. This automaton abstracts from I2 since it only has a single probabilistic transition.

```
automaton I2
    states
        phase : Array[P, Phase] := constant(init)
    signature
        output Root(i: P)
        internal Flip(i: P),
                 Retry(c: Toss)
    transitions
        internal Flip(i)
            pre phase[i] = init
            eff phase[i] := { head  ½
                            { tail  ½
        output Root(i)
            pre {phase[1], phase[2]} ⊆ {head, tail}
                ∧ ¬(phase[i] = head ∧ phase[next(i)] = tail)
            eff phase := constant(done)
        internal Retry(c)
            pre phase = constant(c)
            eff phase := constant(init)
    tasks
        One block
```

Fig. 7. Intermediate automaton I2.

```
automaton I3
    type Loc = enumeration of init, win₁, win₂, same, done
    states
        loc : Loc := init
    signature
        output Root(i: P)
        internal Flips,
                 Retry
    transitions
        internal Flips
            pre loc = init
                        { win₁  ¼
            eff loc := { win₂  ¼
                        { same  ½
        output Root(i)
            pre loc ∈ {winᵢ, same}
            eff loc := done
        internal Retry
            pre loc = same
            eff loc := init
    tasks
        One block
```

Fig. 8. Intermediate automaton I3.

Within automaton I3, *init* is the initial state and *done* is the final state in which a root has been elected. The remaining states win_1, win_2, *same* correspond to situations in which both processes have flipped but no leader has been elected yet. The value win_i indicates that the results are different and the outcome of i equals tail. In state *same* both coin flips have yielded the same result.

Proposition 4. I2 $\sqsubseteq_{TD}$ I3. *More specifically, the following function r from (reachable) states of I2 to discrete probability spaces over states of I3 is a probabilistic hyper step refinement from I2 to I3 (we represent a state with a list containing the values of its variables):*

$$r(init, init) = \{init \mapsto 1\}$$
$$r(head, init) = \{win_2 \mapsto \tfrac{1}{2}, same \mapsto \tfrac{1}{2}\}$$
$$r(init, head) = \{win_1 \mapsto \tfrac{1}{2}, same \mapsto \tfrac{1}{2}\}$$
$$r(tail, init) = \{win_1 \mapsto \tfrac{1}{2}, same \mapsto \tfrac{1}{2}\}$$
$$r(init, tail) = \{win_2 \mapsto \tfrac{1}{2}, same \mapsto \tfrac{1}{2}\}$$
$$r(head, head) = \{same \mapsto 1\}$$
$$r(tail, tail) = \{same \mapsto 1\}$$
$$r(head, tail) = \{win_2 \mapsto 1\}$$
$$r(tail, head) = \{win_1 \mapsto 1\}$$
$$r(done, done) = \{done \mapsto 1\}$$

The proofs of the following Propositions 5 and 6 can be found in [21]. These proofs are the only places in our verification where nontrivial probabilistic reasoning takes place: establishing $\sqsubseteq_{FTD}$ basically amounts to proving that the probabilistic mechanism in the protocol ensures termination with probability 1. Note that the automata involved are all very simple: I2 has 10 states, I3 has 5 states, and **Spec** has 2 states.

Proposition 5. I2 $\sqsubseteq_{FTD}$ I3.

Proposition 6.

1. I3 $\sqsubseteq_{TD}$ **Spec**. *More specifically, the function determined by the predicate done $\Leftrightarrow$ loc $= 4$ is a probabilistic step refinement from I3 to* **Spec**.
2. I3 $\sqsubseteq_{FTD}$ **Spec**.

6   Concluding Remarks

In order to make our verification easier to understand, we introduced three auxiliary automata in between the implementation and the specification automaton. We also used the simpler notion of probabilistic (hyper)step refinement rather than the more general but also complex simulation relations (especially in the timed case!) which have been proposed by Segala and Lynch [18, 20]. The complexity of the definitions in [18, 20] is mainly due to the fact that a single step in one machine can in general be simulated by a sequence of steps in the other machine with the same external behavior. In the probabilistic case this means that a probabilistic transition in one machine can be simulated by a tree like structure in the other machine. In the simulations that we use in this paper, a single transition in one machine is simulated by at most one transition in the other machine. In our case study we were able to carry out the correctness proof by using only probabilistic (hyper)step refinements. However, it is easy to come up with counterexamples which show that this is not possible in general. Griffioen and Vaandrager [7] introduce various notions of *normed simulations* and prove that these notions together constitute a complete proof method for establishing trace inclusion between (nonprobabilistic, untimed automata). In normed simulations a single step in one machine is always simulated by at most one step in the other machine. We think that it is possible to come up with a complete method for proving trace distribution inclusion between probabilistic automata by defining probabilistic versions of the normed simulations of [7].

For timed automata, trace inclusion is in general not an appropriate implementation relation. In [15] the coarser notion of *timed* trace inclusion is advocated instead. Similarly, [18] suggests the notion of timed trace distribution inclusion as an implementation relation between probabilistic timed automata. Since trace distribution inclusion implies timed trace distribution inclusion, and the two preorders coincide for most practical cases, we prefer to use the much simpler proof techniques for trace distribution inclusion.

The idea to introduce auxiliary automata in a simulation proof has been studied in many papers, see for instance [1]. The verification reported in this paper indicates that the introduction of auxiliary automata can be very useful in the probabilistic case: it allowed us to first deal with the nonprobabilistic and real-time behavior of the protocol, basically without being bothered by the complications of randomization; nontrivial probabilistic analysis was only required for automata with 10 states or less.

As a final remark we would like to point out that the root contention protocol which we discussed in this paper is essentially finite state. It is therefore an interesting challenge for tool builders to analyze this protocol fully automatically. Most of the verification effort in our case study was not concerned with randomization at all, but just consisted of standard invariant proofs. In fact, one could use existing tools for the analysis of timed automata such as UPPAAL [3], KRONOS [4] and HyTech [8] to check these invariants. It would be especially interesting to derive the constraints on the timing parameters fully automatically (at the moment only HyTech [8] can do parametric analysis). Tool support will be essential for the analysis of more detailed models of the protocol in which also computation delays have been taken into account.

Acknowledgement

We thank Judi Romijn for her explanation of some subtle points in IEEE 1394, and for her constructive criticism on early versions of our I/O automata model.

References

[1] M. Abadi and L. Lamport. The existence of refinement mappings. *Theoretical Computer Science*, 82(2):253–284, 1991.

[2] R. Alur, T.A. Henzinger, and E.D. Sontag, editors. *Hybrid Systems III*, volume 1066 of *Lecture Notes in Computer Science*. Springer-Verlag, 1996.

[3] J. Bengtsson, K.G. Larsen, F. Larsson, P. Pettersson, and Wang Yi. UPPAAL: a tool suite for the automatic verification of real-time systems. In Alur et al. [2], pages 232–243.

[4] C. Daws, A. Olivero, S. Tripakis, and S. Yovine. The tool KRONOS. In Alur et al. [2], pages 208–219.

[5] M.C.A. Devillers, W.O.D. Griffioen, J.M.T Romijn, and F.W. Vaandrager. Verification of a leader election protocol — formal methods applied to IEEE 1394. Technical Report CSI-R9728, Computing Science Institute, University of Nijmegen, December 1997. Submitted.

[6] S.J. Garland, N.A. Lynch, and M. Vaziri. IOA: A language for specifiying, programming, and validating distributed systems, September 1997. Available through URL http://larch.lcs.mit.edu:8001/~garland/ioaLanguage.html.

[7] W.O.D. Griffioen and F.W. Vaandrager. Normed simulations. In A.J. Hu and M.Y. Vardi, editors, *Proceedings of the 8th International Conference on Computer Aided Verification*, Vancouver, BC, Canada, volume 1427 of *Lecture Notes in Computer Science*, pages 332–344. Springer-Verlag, June/July 1998.

[8] T.A. Henzinger and P.-H. Ho. HyTech: The Cornell HYbrid TECHnology Tool. In U.H. Engberg, K.G. Larsen, and A. Skou, editors, *Proceedings of the Workshop on Tools and Algorithms for the Construction and Analysis of Systems*, Aarhus, Denmark, volume NS-95-2 of *BRICS Notes Series*, pages 29–43. Department of Computer Science, University of Aarhus, May 1995.

[9] IEEE Computer Society. IEEE Standard for a High Performance Serial Bus. Std 1394-1995, August 1996.

[10] IEEE Computer Society. P1394a Draft Standard for a High Performance Serial Bus (Supplement). Draft 2.0, March 1998.

[11] L. Kühne, J. Hooman, and W.P. de Roever. Towards mechanical verification of parts of the IEEE P1394 serial bus. In I. Lovrek, editor, *Proceedings of the 2nd International Workshop on Applied Formal Methods in System Design*, Zagreb, pages 73–85, 1997.

[12] S.P. Luttik. Description and formal specification of the Link layer of P1394. In I. Lovrek, editor, *Proceedings of the 2nd International Workshop on Applied Formal Methods in System Design*, Zagreb, pages 43–56, 1997. Also available as Report SEN-R9706, CWI, Amsterdam. See URL http://www.cwi.nl/~luttik/.

[13] N.A. Lynch. *Distributed Algorithms*. Morgan Kaufmann Publishers, Inc., San Fransisco, California, 1996.

[14] N.A. Lynch, I. Saias, and R. Segala. Proving time bounds for randomized distributed algorithms. In *Proceedings of the 13th Annual ACM Symposium on the Principles of Distributed Computing*, pages 314–323, Los Angeles, CA, August 1994.

[15] N.A. Lynch and F.W. Vaandrager. Forward and backward simulations, II: Timing-based systems. *Information and Computation*, 128(1):1–25, July 1996.
[16] MindShare, Inc, and D. Anderson. *FireWire System Architecture: IEEE 1394*. Addison Wesley, 1998.
[17] A. Pogosyants, R. Segala, and N.A. Lynch. Verification of the randomized consensus algorithm of Aspnes and Herlihy: a case study. In M. Mavronicolas and Ph. Tsigas, editors, *Proceedings of 11th International Workshop on Distributed Algorithms (WDAG'97)*, Saarbrucken, Germany, September 1997, volume 1320 of *Lecture Notes in Computer Science*, pages 111–125. Springer-Verlag, 1997. Also, Technical Memo MIT/LCS/TM-555, Laboratory for Computer Science, Massachusetts Institute of Technology.
[18] R. Segala. *Modeling and Verification of Randomized Distributed Real-Time Systems*. PhD thesis, Department of Electrical Engineering and Computer Science, Massachusetts Institute of Technology, June 1995. Available as Technical Report MIT/LCS/TR-676.
[19] R. Segala, R. Gawlick, J.F. Søgaard-Andersen, and N.A. Lynch. Liveness in timed and untimed systems. *Information and Computation*, 141(2):119–171, March 1998.
[20] R. Segala and N.A. Lynch. Probabilistic simulations for probabilistic processes. *Nordic Journal of Computing*, 2(2):250–273, 1995.
[21] M.I.A. Stoelinga. Gambling for leadership: Root contention in IEEE 1394. Technical Report CSI-R9904, Computing Science Institute, University of Nijmegen, 1999.
[22] M.I.A. Stoelinga and F.W. Vaandrager. Gambling together in Monte Carlo: Step refinements for probabilistic automata. Technical Report CSI-R99xx, Computing Science Institute, University of Nijmegen, 1999. To appear.

Automatic Verification of Real-Time Systems with Discrete Probability Distributions

Marta Kwiatkowska[1][*], Gethin Norman[1][*], Roberto Segala[2][**], and Jeremy Sproston[1]

[1] University of Birmingham, Birmingham B15 2TT, United Kingdom
{M.Z.Kwiatkowska,G.Norman,J.Sproston}@cs.bham.ac.uk
[2] Università di Bologna, Mura Anteo Zamboni 7, 40127 Bologna, Italy
segala@cs.unibo.it

Abstract. We consider the timed automata model of [3], which allows the analysis of real-time systems expressed in terms of quantitative timing constraints. Traditional approaches to real-time system description express the model purely in terms of nondeterminism; however, we may wish to express the likelihood of the system making certain transitions. In this paper, we present a model for real-time systems augmented with discrete probability distributions. Furthermore, using the algorithm of [5] with fairness, we develop a model checking method for such models against temporal logic properties which can refer both to timing properties and probabilities, such as, "with probability 0.6 or greater, the clock x remains below 5 until clock y exceeds 2".

1 Introduction

The proliferation of digital technology embedded into real-life environments has led to increased interest in computer systems expressed in terms of quantitative timing constraints. Examples of such *real-time systems* include communication protocols, digital circuits with uncertain delay lengths, and media synchronization protocols. A number of frameworks exist within which the formal reasoning and analysis of such systems can be carried out. A formalism that has received much attention, both in terms of theoretical and practical developments, is that of *timed automata*; in particular, the theory of automatically verifying timed automata against properties of a real-time temporal logic is advanced, and is supported by a number of tools [6, 8].

Traditional approaches to the formal description of real-time systems express the system model purely in terms of nondeterminism. However, it may be desirable to express the relative likelihood of the system exhibiting certain behaviour. For example, we may wish to model a system for which the likelihood of a certain event occurring changes with respect to the amount of time elapsed. This notion is particularly important when considering fault-tolerant systems. Furthermore,

---

[*] supported in part by EPSRC grant GR/M04617
[**] supported in part by EPSRC grant GR/M13046

J.-P. Katoen (Ed.): ARTS'99, LNCS 1601, pp. 75–95, 1999.
© Springer-Verlag Berlin Heidelberg 1999

we may also wish to refer to the likelihood of certain temporal logic properties being satisfied by the real-time system, and to have a model checking algorithm for verifying the truth of these assertions. The remit of this paper is to address these problems.

Therefore, we present a model for real-time systems that are described partially in terms of discrete probability distributions, and an automatic verification method for this model against a new, probabilistic real-time logic. The system model is called a *probabilistic timed graph*, and differs from the timed automata based model of [2] in the following respects. Firstly, the edge relation of probabilistic timed graphs is both nondeterministic and probabilistic in nature. More precisely, instead of making a purely nondeterministic choice over the set of currently enabled edges, we choose amongst the set of enabled discrete probability distributions, each of which is defined over a finite set of edges. We then make a probabilistic choice as to which edge to take according to the selected distribution. As with usual timed automata techniques, the underlying model of time is assumed to be *dense*; that is, the time domain is modelled by the reals ($\mathbb{R}$) or rationals ($\mathbb{Q}$). However, in contrast to [2], probabilistic timed graphs are defined over *weakly monotonic time*, which allows us to express the notion of more than one system event occurring at a given point in time.

Furthermore, we adapt the specification language commonly used for stating real-time system requirements, TCTL (Timed Computation Tree Logic) [14], to cater for probability. A common approach taken in probabilistic temporal logics is to augment certain formulae with a parameter referring to a bound on probability which must be satisfied for the formula to be true. For example, $[\phi_1 \exists \mathcal{U} \phi_2]_{\geq p}$ is true if the probability of $[\phi_1 \exists \mathcal{U} \phi_2]$ is at least p. Therefore, we develop our specification language, PTCTL (Probabilistic Timed Computation Tree Logic), by adding such probabilistic operators to TCTL. The resulting logic allows us to express such quality of service properties as, "with probability 0.7, there will be a response between 5 and 7 time units after a query".

The denseness of the time domain means that the state space of timed automata is infinite. Therefore, automatic verification of timed automata is performed by constructing a finite-state quotient of the system model. This quotient takes the form of a state-labelled transition system which represents all of the timed automaton's behaviours, and which can be analyzed using analogues of traditional model checking techniques. We adopt this method in order to construct a finite quotient of probabilistic timed graphs; naturally, the transitions of the resulting model are both nondeterministic and probabilistic in nature, and therefore the model checking methods employed must accommodate this characteristic. The verification algorithms of [5] are used for this purpose. However, they are defined with respect to PBTL (Probabilistic Branching Time Logic), which does not allow the expression of dense timing constraints. Hence, we present a method for translating a given PTCTL formula into a corresponding PBTL formula. The model checking algorithm of [5] is then used to verify the PBTL properties over our probabilistic-nondeterministic quotient structure, the results of which allow us to conclude whether the original probabilistic timed graph satisfied its PTCTL specification. Furthermore, the verification methods of [5] allow us to model check *fair* paths of the quotient construction. In the context of real-time systems, fair paths correspond to behaviours which allow the progress of time, a notion which also corresponds to realisable behaviours.

An example of a real-time system which could be subject to these techniques is the bounded retransmission protocol, which is modelled as a network of purely nondeterministic timed automata in [9]. Each communication channel is represented as a timed automaton which features a nondeterministic choice over two edges, one of which corresponds to the correct transmission of the message, the other to the message's loss. Using our framework, the relative likelihood of such a loss occurring could be represented by replacing this nondeterministic choice by a probabilistic choice between the two edges; for example, a probabilistic timed graph could be used to model that a message is lost with probability 0.05 each time a communication channel is used. Similarly, the system requirements of the bounded retransmission protocol could be expanded to admit reasoning about the probability of certain system behaviours. For instance, we may require that, with probability at least 0.99, any data chunk transmitted by the sender is successfully processed by the receiver within 10 time units.

The model presented in this paper has similarities with other frameworks for probabilistic real-time systems. In particular, the approach of [10] is also to augment timed automata with discrete probability distributions; however, these distributions are obtained by normalization of edge-labelling weights. Furthermore, the model checking algorithm of [10] is with respect to an action-based logic, rather than a state-based logic such as PTCTL. A dense time, automata-based model with discrete and *continuous* probability distributions is presented in [1], along with a quotient construction and TCTL model checking method similar to that of [2]. However, the model of Alur et al. does not permit any nondeterministic choice, and its use of continuous probability distributions, while a highly expressive modelling mechanism, does not permit the model to be automatically verified against logics which include bounds on probability. Furthermore, note that the temporal logic of [11] has syntactic similarities with the logic PTCTL, although this former logic is interpreted with respect to discrete, not dense time.

The paper proceeds as follows. Section 2 introduces some preliminary concepts and notation relating to execution sequences. Section 3 presents the underlying model of our probabilistic timed graphs, which are used to interpret formulae of the logic, PTCTL, introduced in section 4. Probabilistic timed graphs are defined in section 5 as our model for probabilistic-nondeterministic real-time systems, and a method for translating them into their underlying probabilistic timed structure is presented. Section 6 explores the model checking problem for probabilistic timed graphs, and presents a finite-state quotient construction for this model, a method for translating a PTCTL formula into a series of equivalent PBTL formulae, and finally a verification method. To conclude, section 7 analyzes the complexity of the model checking technique, and suggests further directions of research.

2   Preliminaries

Labelled paths (or execution sequences) are non-empty finite or infinite sequences of the form:

$$\omega = \sigma_0 \xrightarrow{l_0} \sigma_1 \xrightarrow{l_1} \sigma_2 \xrightarrow{l_2} \cdots$$

where σ_i are states and l_i are labels for transitions. We use the following notation for such paths. Take any path ω. Then the first state of ω is denoted by $first(\omega)$. If ω is finite then the last state of ω is denoted by $last(\omega)$. The length of a path, $|\omega|$, is defined in the usual way: if ω is the finite path $\omega = \sigma_0 \xrightarrow{l_0} \sigma_1 \xrightarrow{l_1} \cdots \xrightarrow{l_{n-1}} \sigma_n$, then $|\omega| = n$; if ω is an infinite path, then we let $|\omega| = \infty$. If $k \le |\omega|$ then $\omega(k)$ denotes the k-th state of ω and $step(\omega, k)$ is the label of the k-th step (that is, $\omega(k) = \sigma_k$ and $step(\omega, k) = l_k$). $\omega^{(k)}$ is the k-th prefix of ω; that is, if $k < |\omega|$ then $\omega^{(k)} = \sigma_0 \xrightarrow{l_0} \sigma_1 \xrightarrow{l_1} \cdots \xrightarrow{l_{k-1}} \sigma_k$, and if $k \ge |\omega|$ then $\omega^{(k)} = \omega$. If $\omega = \sigma_0 \xrightarrow{l_0} \sigma_1 \xrightarrow{l_1} \cdots \xrightarrow{l_{n-1}} \sigma_n$ is a finite path and $\omega' = \sigma_0' \xrightarrow{l_0'} \sigma_1' \xrightarrow{l_1'} \cdots$ is a finite or infinite path with $last(\omega) = first(\omega')$, then we let the *concatenation* of ω and ω' be:

$$\omega\omega' = \sigma_0 \xrightarrow{l_0} \sigma_1 \xrightarrow{l_1} \sigma_2 \cdots \xrightarrow{l_{n-1}} \sigma_n \xrightarrow{l_0'} \sigma_1' \xrightarrow{l_1'} \cdots$$

3   Probabilistic Timed Structures

In this section, we introduce an underlying model for probabilistic timed graphs, called *probabilistic timed structures*, which are obtained by augmenting the timed structures of [13] with a probabilistic choice over transitions. More precisely, instead of a nondeterministic choice over transitions that consist of a real-valued duration and a next state, as is the case in traditional timed structures, the transition function of probabilistic timed structures results in a choice over pairs consisting of a duration and a *discrete probability distribution* over next states.

Let AP be a set of atomic propositions. A *clock* x is a real-valued variable which increases at the same rate as real-time. Let $\mathcal{X}$ be a set of clocks, and let $\nu : \mathcal{X} \to \mathbb{R}$ be a function assigning a real value to each of the clocks in this set. Such a function is called a *clock valuation*. For some $C \subseteq \mathcal{X}$ we write $\nu[C \mapsto 0]$ for the clock valuation that assigns 0 to all clocks in C, and agrees with ν for all clocks in $\mathcal{X} \setminus C$ (informally, we write $\nu[x \mapsto 0]$ if C contains the single clock x). In addition, for some $t \in \mathbb{R}$, $\nu + t$ denotes the clock valuation for which all clocks x in $\mathcal{X}$ take the value $\nu(x) + t$.

Definition 1 (State). *A state σ is an interpretation of all propositions and a valuation over the set of clocks: σ assigns to each proposition a in AP a boolean value (therefore, $\sigma(a) \in \{\text{true}, \text{false}\}$) and to each clock in $\mathcal{X}$ a non-negative real (therefore, $\sigma(x) \in \mathbb{R}$).*

We denote the set of discrete probability distributions over a set S by $\mu(S)$. Therefore, each $p \in \mu(S)$ is a function $p : S \to [0, 1]$ such that $\sum_{s \in S} p(s) = 1$.

Definition 2 (Probabilistic Timed Structure). *A probabilistic timed structure $\mathcal{M}$, is a tuple (Σ, Tr, End) where Σ is a set of states, Tr is a function which assigns to each state $\sigma \in \Sigma$ a set $Tr(\sigma)$ of pairs of the form (t, p) where $t \in \mathbb{R}$ and $p \in \mu(\Sigma)$, and End is a set of states from which time is allowed to increase without bound.*

$Tr(\sigma)$ is the set of transitions that can be nondeterministically chosen in state σ. Each transition takes the form (t, p), where t represents the duration of the transition and p is the probability distribution used over the set of successor states. Therefore, given the nondeterministic choice of $(t, p) \in Tr(\sigma)$ in state σ, then, after t time units have elapsed, a probabilistic transition is made to state σ' with probability $p(\sigma')$.

Paths in a probabilistic timed structure arise by resolving both the nondeterministic and probabilistic choices. A *path* of the probabilistic timed structure $\mathcal{M} = (\Sigma, Tr, End)$ is a non-empty finite or infinite sequence:

$$\omega = \sigma_0 \xrightarrow{t_0, p_0} \sigma_1 \xrightarrow{t_1, p_1} \sigma_2 \xrightarrow{t_2, p_2} \cdots$$

where $\sigma_i \in \Sigma$, $(t_i, p_i) \in Tr(\sigma_i)$ and $p_i(\sigma_{i+1}) > 0$ for all $0 \le i \le |\omega|$.

Sets of labelled paths are denoted in the following way. $Path_{fin}$ is the set of finite paths, and $Path_{fin}(\sigma)$ is the set of paths in $Path_{fin}$ such that $\omega(0) = \sigma$. $Path_{ful}$ is the set of paths such that $\omega \in Path_{ful}$ if either ω is infinite, or ω is finite and $last(\omega) \in End$. $Path_{ful}(\sigma)$ is the set of paths in $Path_{ful}$ such that $\omega(0) = \sigma$.

Consider an infinite path ω of $\mathcal{M}$. A *position* of ω is a pair (i, t'), where $i \in \mathbb{N}$ and $t' \in \mathbb{R}$ such that $0 \le t' \le t_i$. The *state at position* (i, t'), denoted by $\sigma_i + t'$, assigns $\sigma_i(a)$ to each proposition a in AP, and $\sigma_i(x) + t'$ to each clock x in $\mathcal{X}$. Given a path ω, $i, j \in \mathbb{N}$ and $t, t' \in \mathbb{R}$ such that $i \le |\omega|$, $t \le t_i$ and $t' \le t_j$, then we say that the position (j, t') *precedes* the position (i, t), written $(j, t') \prec (i, t)$, iff $j < i$, or $j = i$ and $t' < t$.

Definition 3 (Duration of a Path). *For any path ω of a probabilistic timed structure $\mathcal{M}$ and $0 \le i \le |\omega|$ we define $\mathcal{D}_\omega(i)$, the elapsed time until the ith transition, as follows: $\mathcal{D}_\omega(0) = 0$ and for any $1 \le i \le |\omega|$:*

$$\mathcal{D}_\omega(i) = \sum_{j=0}^{i-1} t_j.$$

We now introduce *adversaries* of probabilistic timed structures as functions which resolve all the nondeterministic choices of the model.

Definition 4 (Adversary of a Probabilistic Timed Structure). *An adversary (or scheduler) of a probabilistic timed structure $\mathcal{M} = (\Sigma, Tr, End)$ is a function A mapping every finite path ω of $\mathcal{M}$ to a pair (t, p) such that $A(\omega) \in Tr(last(\omega))$. Let $\mathcal{A}$ be the set of all adversaries of $\mathcal{M}$.*

For an adversary A of a probabilistic timed structure $\mathcal{M} = (\Sigma, Tr, End)$ we define $Path_{fin}^A$ to be the set of finite paths such that $step(\omega, i) = A(\omega^{(i)})$ for all $1 \leq i \leq |\omega|$, and $Path_{ful}^A$ to be the set of paths in $Path_{ful}$ such that $step(\omega, i) = A(\omega^{(i)})$ for all $i \in \mathbb{N}$.

With each adversary we associate a sequential Markov chain, which can be viewed as a set of paths in $\mathcal{M}$. Formally, if A is an adversary of the probabilistic timed structure $\mathcal{M}$, then $MC^A = (Path_{fin}^A, \mathbf{P}^A)$ is a Markov chain where:

$$\mathbf{P}^A(\omega, \omega') = \begin{cases} p(\sigma) & \text{if } A(\omega) = (t, p) \text{ and } \omega' = \omega \xrightarrow{t,p} \sigma \\ 0 & \text{otherwise} \end{cases}$$

Definition 5 (Divergent Adversary). *An adversary A of a probabilistic timed structure (Σ, Tr, End) is divergent if and only if for any infinite path $\omega \in Path_{ful}^A$ and $t \in \mathbb{R}$, there exists $j \in \mathbb{N}$ such that $\mathcal{D}_\omega(j) > t$. Let $\mathcal{A}_{div}$ be the set of all divergent adversaries.*

Note that this definition of divergent adversaries corresponds to a common restriction imposed in the study of real-time systems, namely that of *time-divergence*. The traditional interpretation of this requirement is that runs of the real-time system that are not time-divergent can be disregarded during analysis, because they do not represent realisable behaviour; in our case, consideration of the class of divergent adversaries means that nondeterministic choice is resolved in such a way as to result only in time-divergent paths.

For any probabilistic timed structure, let $\mathcal{F}_{Path}$ be the smallest σ-algebra on $Path_{ful}$ which contains the sets:

$$\{\omega \mid \omega \in Path_{ful} \text{ and } \omega' \text{ is a prefix of } \omega\}$$

for all $\omega' \in Path_{fin}$.

We now define a measure *Prob* on the σ-algebra $\mathcal{F}_{Path}$, by first defining the following function on the set of finite paths $Path_{fin}$.

Definition 6. *Let $Prob_{fin} : Path_{fin} \rightarrow [0, 1]$ be the mapping inductively defined on the length of paths in $Path_{fin}$ as follows. If $|\omega| = 0$, then $Prob_{fin}(\omega) = 1$. Now consider any path ω such that $|\omega| = n + 1$. If $\omega^{(n)} = \omega'$ let:*

$$Prob_{fin}(\omega) = Prob_{fin}(\omega') \cdot \mathbf{P}^A(\omega', \omega)$$

where A is any adversary such that $A(\omega') = (t, p)$ and $\omega = \omega' \xrightarrow{t,p} \sigma$.

Definition 7. *The measure Prob on $\mathcal{F}_{Path}$ is the unique measure such that:*

$$Prob(\{\omega \mid \omega \in Path_{ful} \text{ and } \omega' \text{ is a prefix of } \omega\}) = Prob_{fin}(\omega').$$

4   Probabilistic Timed Computation Tree Logic

We now describe the probabilistic real-time logic PTCTL (Probabilistic Timed Computation Tree Logic) which can be used to specify properties of probabilistic timed systems. PTCTL synthesizes elements from two extensions of the branching temporal logic CTL, namely the real-time temporal logic TCTL [14] and the essentially equivalent, probabilistic temporal logics pCTL and PBTL [7, 5]. In particular, the temporal operator $\mathcal{U}$ ("until") and the path quantifiers $\forall$ and $\exists$ ("for all" and "there exists", respectively) are taken from CTL, the freeze quantifier $z.\phi$ and the facility to refer directly to clock values are taken from TCTL, and the probabilistic operators $[\phi_1 \exists \mathcal{U} \phi_2]_{\sqsupseteq \lambda}$ and $[\phi_1 \forall \mathcal{U} \phi_2]_{\sqsupseteq \lambda}$ are taken from PBTL. Note that the freeze quantifier $z.\phi$ is used to reset the clock z, so that ϕ is evaluated from a state at which $z = 0$. Using our new logic, we can express properties such as, "with probability 0.6 or greater, the value of the system clock x does not exceed 3 before 5 time units have elapsed", which is represented as the PTCTL formula $z.[(x \leq 3) \forall \mathcal{U} (z = 5)]_{\geq 0.6}$.

As with TCTL, PTCTL employs a set of clock variables in order to express timing properties; for this purpose, we introduce a set of *formula clocks*, $\mathcal{Z}$, which is disjoint from $\mathcal{X}$. Such clocks are assigned values by a *formula clock valuation* $\mathcal{E} : \mathcal{Z} \rightarrow \mathbb{R}$, which uses the notation for clock valuations in the standard way.

Definition 8 (Atomic Formulae). *Let* $\mathcal{C}$ *be a set of clocks. A set of atomic formulae* $\mathrm{AF}_\mathcal{C}$ *is defined inductively by the syntax:*

$$\varphi ::= c \leq k \mid k \leq c \mid \neg \varphi \mid \varphi \vee \varphi$$

where $c \in \mathcal{C}$ *and* $k \in \mathbb{N}$*. Atomic formulae of the form* $c \leq k$ *or* $k \leq c$ *are called minimal atomic formulae.*

Definition 9 (Syntax of PTCTL). *The syntax of PTCTL is defined as follows:*

$$\phi ::= \textbf{true} \mid a \mid \varphi \mid \phi \wedge \phi \mid \neg \phi \mid z.\phi \mid [\phi \, \exists \mathcal{U} \, \phi]_{\sqsupseteq \lambda} \mid [\phi \, \forall \mathcal{U} \, \phi]_{\sqsupseteq \lambda}$$

where $a \in \mathrm{AP}$ *is an atomic proposition,* $\varphi \in \mathrm{AF}_{\mathcal{X} \cup \mathcal{Z}}$ *is an atomic formula,* $z \in \mathcal{Z}$, $\lambda \in [0,1]$*, and* $\sqsupseteq$ *is either* $\geq$ *or* $>$*.*

Note that the values of system clocks in $\mathcal{X}$ and formula clocks in $\mathcal{Z}$ can be obtained from a state and a formula clock valuation, respectively. Then, if $\varphi \in \mathrm{AF}_{\mathcal{X} \cup \mathcal{Z}}$, and given a state σ and a formula clock valuation $\mathcal{E}$, we denote by $\varphi[\sigma, \mathcal{E}]$ the boolean value obtained by replacing each occurrence of a system clock $x \in \mathcal{X}$ in φ by $\sigma(x)$, and each occurrence of a formula clock $z \in \mathcal{Z}$ in φ by $\mathcal{E}(z)$.

Definition 10 (Satisfaction Relation for PTCTL). *Given a probabilistic timed structure* $\mathcal{M}$ *and a set* $\mathcal{A}$ *of adversaries of* $\mathcal{M}$*, then for any state* σ *of* $\mathcal{M}$*, formula clock valuation* $\mathcal{E}$*, and PTCTL formula* ϕ*, the satisfaction relation* $\sigma, \mathcal{E} \models_\mathcal{A} \phi$ *is defined inductively as follows:*

$$\sigma, \mathcal{E} \models_A \text{true} \qquad \text{for all } \sigma \text{ and } \mathcal{E}$$

$$\sigma, \mathcal{E} \models_A a \qquad \Leftrightarrow \sigma(a) = \text{true}$$

$$\sigma, \mathcal{E} \models_A \varphi \qquad \Leftrightarrow \varphi[\sigma, \mathcal{E}] = \text{true}$$

$$\sigma, \mathcal{E} \models_A \phi_1 \wedge \phi_2 \qquad \Leftrightarrow \sigma, \mathcal{E} \models_A \phi_1 \text{ and } \sigma, \mathcal{E} \models_A \phi_2$$

$$\sigma, \mathcal{E} \models_A \neg\phi \qquad \Leftrightarrow \sigma, \mathcal{E} \not\models_A \phi$$

$$\sigma, \mathcal{E} \models_A z.\phi \qquad \Leftrightarrow \sigma, \mathcal{E}[z \mapsto 0] \models_A \phi$$

$$\sigma, \mathcal{E} \models_A [\phi_1 \exists \mathcal{U} \phi_2]_{\sqsupseteq \lambda} \Leftrightarrow Prob(\{\omega \mid \omega \in Path_{ful}^A(\sigma) \ \& \ \omega, \mathcal{E} \models_A \phi_1 \mathcal{U} \phi_2\}) \sqsupseteq \lambda$$
$$\text{for some } A \in \mathcal{A}$$

$$\sigma, \mathcal{E} \models_A [\phi_1 \forall \mathcal{U} \phi_2]_{\sqsupseteq \lambda} \Leftrightarrow Prob(\{\omega \mid \omega \in Path_{ful}^A(\sigma) \ \& \ \omega, \mathcal{E} \models_A \phi_1 \mathcal{U} \phi_2\}) \sqsupseteq \lambda$$
$$\text{for all } A \in \mathcal{A}$$

$$\omega, \mathcal{E} \models_A \phi_1 \mathcal{U} \phi_2 \qquad \Leftrightarrow \text{there exists } i \in \mathbb{N}, \text{ and } 0 \leq t \leq t_i \text{ such that}$$
$$\omega(i) + t, \mathcal{E} + \mathcal{D}_\omega(i) + t \models_A \phi_2, \text{ and for all } j \in \mathbb{N}$$
$$\text{and } t' \in \mathbb{R} \text{ such that } t' \leq t_j \text{ and } (j, t') \prec (i, t),$$
$$\omega(j) + t', \mathcal{E} + \mathcal{D}_\omega(j) + t' \models_A \phi_1 \vee \phi_2$$

5 Probabilistic Timed Graphs

This section introduces *probabilistic timed graphs* as a modelling framework for real-time systems with probability. This formalism is derived from timed graphs [2], a variant of timed automata for which model checking of TCTL properties can be performed. Here, we extend timed graphs with discrete probability distributions over edges, so that the choice of the next location of the graph is now probabilistic, in addition to nondeterministic, in nature. Furthermore, we incorporate *invariant conditions* [14] into the probabilistic timed graph in order to enforce upper bounds on the time at which certain probabilistic choices are made.

Definition 11 (Probabilistic Timed Graph). *A probabilistic timed graph is a tuple* $G = (\mathcal{S}, L, s_{init}, \mathcal{X}, inv, prob, \langle \tau_s \rangle_{s \in \mathcal{S}})$ *where*

- *a finite set $\mathcal{S}$ of nodes,*
- *a function $L : \mathcal{S} \longrightarrow 2^{AP}$ assigning to each node of the graph the set of atomic propositions that are true in that node,*
- *a start node $s_{init} \in \mathcal{S}$,*
- *a finite set $\mathcal{X}$ of clocks,*
- *a function $inv : \mathcal{S} \longrightarrow AF_{\mathcal{X}}$ assigning to each node an invariant condition,*
- *a function $prob : \mathcal{S} \longrightarrow \mathcal{P}_n(\mu(\mathcal{S} \times 2^{\mathcal{X}}))$ assigning to each node a (finite non-empty) set of discrete probability distributions on $\mathcal{S} \times 2^{\mathcal{X}}$,*
- *a family of functions $\langle \tau_s \rangle_{s \in \mathcal{S}}$ where for any $s \in \mathcal{S}$: $\tau_s : prob(s) \longrightarrow AF_{\mathcal{X}}$ assigns to each $p_s \in prob(s)$ an enabling condition.*

For simplicity, the invariant and enabling conditions are subject to the following assumption: if, in some state in the execution of G, allowing any amount of time to elapse would violate the invariant condition of the current node, then the enabling condition of at least one probability distribution is satisfied. [1]

---

[1] Another solution is to identify an additional discrete probability distribution $p_s^{inv} \in \mu(\mathcal{S} \times 2^{\mathcal{X}})$ with each $s \in \mathcal{S}$, which becomes enabled in s at the points for which progression of any amount of time would violate the node's invariant $inv(s)$.

The system starts in node s_{init} with all of its clocks initialized to 0. The values of all the clocks increase uniformly with time. At any point in time, if the system is in node s and the invariant condition will not be violated by letting time advance, then the system can either (a) remain in its current node and let time advance, or (b) make a *state transition* if there exists a distribution $p_s \in prob(s)$ whose corresponding enabling condition $\tau_s(p_s)$ is satisfied by the current values of the clocks. Alternatively, if the invariant condition will be violated by letting time advance then the system must make a state transition. State transitions are instantaneous and consist of the following two steps performed in succession: firstly, the system makes a *nondeterministic choice* between the set of distributions $p_s \in prob(s)$ whose corresponding enabling condition $\tau_s(p_s)$ is satisfied by the current values of the clocks. [2] Secondly, supposing that the probability distribution p_s is chosen, the system then makes a *probabilistic transition* according to p_s; that is, for any $s' \in S$ and $C \subseteq \mathcal{X}$, the probability the system will make a state transition to node s', and reset all the clocks in C to 0, is given by $p_s(s', C)$.

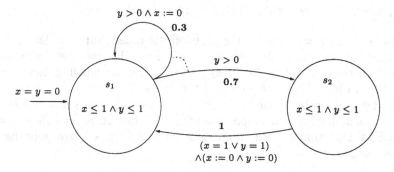

Figure 1. The probabilistic timed graph G_1.

Example. An example of a probabilistic timed graph is given in Figure 1. Control of G_1 initially resides in node s_1, with the system clocks, x and y, each set to 0. Node s_1 has two outgoing edges, both of which have the same enabling condition, $(y > 0)$, and are defined with respect to the probability distribution p_{s_1}, as denoted by the dashed arc connecting the edges at their source. The bold numerals labelling the edges refer to the probabilities of the edges being taken, while assignment labels such as $x := 0$ refer to clock resets. Therefore, the diagram states that when the value of y exceeds 0 and a nondeterministic choice has been made to take an edge according to p_{s_1}, with probability 0.3 control returns to s_1 with the value of x reset to 0, and with probability 0.7 control switches to node s_2. More formally, $p_{s_1}(s_1, \{x\}) = 0.3$ and $p_{s_1}(s_2, \emptyset) = 0.7$. Also note that the invariant condition of s_1, which is shown within the body of the node, states that the probabilistic timed graph cannot allow time to pass if doing

---

[2] In the case in which we have the special probability distribution, p_s^{inv}, then this distribution *must* be taken at this point.

so would take the value of either x or y above 1; in such a case, a probabilistic choice over the outgoing edges would be forced. The behaviour of the system when control resides in s_2 takes a similar form.

Obtaining a Probabilistic Timed Structure from a Probabilistic Timed Graph. This section will now show that the behaviour of a probabilistic timed graph can be formally stated in terms of a probabilistic timed structure. First, the following notation must be introduced. A *system clock valuation* for the set of clocks $\mathcal{X}$ is a function $\nu : \mathcal{X} \longrightarrow \mathbb{R}$. Let $\Gamma(\mathcal{X})$ denote the set of all system clock valuations for all the clocks of $\mathcal{X}$. The standard notation for clock valuations, as introduced in section 3, is used for system clock valuations ν.

Let $\varphi \in \mathrm{AF}_{\mathcal{X}}$ and $\nu \in \Gamma(\mathcal{X})$. Then $\varphi[\nu]$ is the boolean value obtained by replacing each occurrence of a clock $x \in \mathcal{X}$ in φ by $\nu(x)$. If $\varphi[\nu] = \mathbf{true}$ then we say that ν *satisfies* φ.

Definition 12 (State of a Probabilistic Timed Graph). *A* state *of G is a tuple $\langle s, \nu \rangle$, where $s \in S$ and $\nu \in \Gamma(\mathcal{X})$ such that ν satisfies $inv(s)$.*

To uniquely identify each node of the probabilistic timed graph, we let a_s be an atomic proposition that is true only in node s. Formally, we extend the set of atomic propositions to $\mathrm{AP}' = \mathrm{AP} \cup \{a_s \mid s \in S\}$, and the labelling function to $L' : S \to 2^{\mathrm{AP}'}$, where $L'(s) = L(s) \cup \{a_s\}$ for all $s \in S$.

We now define a probabilistic timed structure to formally define the behaviour of a probabilistic timed graph. Note that this definition also allows us to interpret PTCTL formulae with atomic propositions from AP' over a probabilistic timed graph.

Definition 13. *For any probabilistic timed graph G, let $\mathcal{M}^G = (\Sigma^G, Tr^G, End^G)$ be the probabilistic timed structure defined as follows:*

- *Σ^G is the set of states of G. For a given state of G, $\langle s, \nu \rangle$, then the corresponding state of $\mathcal{M}^G$ obtained by letting $\langle s, \nu \rangle(a) = \mathbf{true}$, if $a \in L'(s)$, for all $a \in \mathrm{AP}'$, and $\mathbf{false}$ otherwise, and letting $\langle s, \nu \rangle(x) = \nu(x)$ for all $x \in \mathcal{X}$.*
- *Take any $\langle s, \nu \rangle \in \Sigma^G$. Then $(t, p) \in Tr^G(\langle s, \nu \rangle)$, where $t \in \mathbb{R}$ and $p \in \mu(S \times \Gamma(\mathcal{X}))$, if and only if there exists $p_s \in prob(s)$ such that*
  1. *the clock valuation $\nu + t$ satisfies $\tau_s(p_s)$,*
  2. *$(\nu + t')$ satisfies the invariant condition $inv(s)$ for all $0 \leq t' \leq t$,*
  3. *for any $\langle s', \nu' \rangle$:*

$$p(\langle s', \nu' \rangle) = \sum_{\substack{C \subseteq \mathcal{X} \ \& \\ (\nu + t)[C \mapsto 0] = \nu'}} p_s(s', C) .$$

- *End^G comprises of states $\langle s, \nu \rangle$, for which, for any $t \in \mathbb{R}$, $\nu + t$ satisfies $inv(s)$.*

It is now possible to define the set $\mathcal{A}^G$ of adversaries of $\mathcal{M}^G$ using Definition 4.

6   Model Checking Probabilistic Timed Graphs

Note that, because all clocks are real-valued, the state space of a probabilistic timed graph is infinite. However, it was noted in [3] that the space of clock valuations of a timed graph can be partitioned into a finite set of *clock regions*, each containing a finite or infinite number of valuations which, as noted by [2], satisfy the same TCTL formulae. Combination of this partitioning with the transition systems of a timed graph induces a structure called a *region graph*, which can be used for model checking. This section will show that a similar construction can be used for model checking probabilistic timed graphs against PTCTL formulae.

Equivalence of Clock Valuations.

Definition 14. *For any $x \in \mathcal{X}$ let k_x be the largest constant the system clock x is compared to in any of the invariant or enabling conditions.*

Furthermore, for any $\nu \in \Gamma(\mathcal{X})$ and $x \in \mathcal{X}$, x is relevant *for ν if $\nu(x) \le k_x$.*

Definition 15. *For any $t \in \mathbb{R}$, $\lfloor t \rfloor$ denotes its integral part. Then, for any $t, t' \in \mathbb{R}$, t and t' agree on their integral parts if and only if:*

1. $\lfloor t \rfloor = \lfloor t' \rfloor$,
2. *both t and t' are integers or neither is an integer.*

Definition 16 (Clock equivalence). *For clock valuations ν and ν' in $\Gamma(\mathcal{X})$, $\nu \cong \nu'$ if and only if the following conditions are satisfied:*

1. $\forall x \in \mathcal{X}$ *either $\nu(x)$ and $\nu'(x)$ agree on their integral parts, or x is not relevant for both ν and ν',*
2. $\forall x, x' \in \mathcal{X}$ *that are relevant for ν, then $\nu(x) - \nu(x')$ and $\nu'(x) - \nu'(x')$ agree on their integral parts.*

Lemma 1. *Let $\nu, \nu' \in \Gamma(\mathcal{X})$ such that $\nu \cong \nu'$. Then the following conditions hold:*

(a) $\nu[C \mapsto 0] \cong \nu'[C \mapsto 0]$ *for all $C \subseteq \mathcal{X}$,*
(b) *for any $x \in \mathcal{X}$, x is relevant for ν if and only if x is relevant for ν',*
(c) *for any atomic formula $\varphi \in \mathrm{AF}_{\mathcal{X}}$, ν satisfies φ if and only if ν' satisfies φ.*

Proof. The proof follows from the definition of $\cong$. $\qquad\qquad\square$

Let $[\nu]$ denote the equivalence class to which ν belongs, and we refer to elements such as $\langle s, [\nu] \rangle$ as *regions*.

We now extend the concept of clock equivalence to formula clocks. Let $(\nu, \mathcal{E})$: $\mathcal{X} \cup \mathcal{Z} \to \mathbb{R}$ be the clock valuation that assigns a real value to each of the system and formula clocks, and let $\Gamma^*(\mathcal{X} \cup \mathcal{Z})$ be the set of all such valuations for G.

For a $(\nu, \mathcal{E}) \in \Gamma^*(\mathcal{X} \cup \mathcal{Z})$, and $C \subseteq \mathcal{X} \cup \mathcal{Z}$, we use the notation $(\nu, \mathcal{E})[C \mapsto 0]$ in the usual way. For some $t \in \mathbb{R}$, $(\nu + t, \mathcal{E} + t)$ denotes the clock valuation for which all clocks c in $\mathcal{X} \cup \mathcal{Z}$ take the value $(\nu, \mathcal{E})(c) + t$.

The equivalence relation for such a valuation is defined with respect to a particular PTCTL formula ϕ. For each formula clock $z \in \mathcal{Z}$, we let k_z be the largest constant that z is compared to in the atomic formulae of ϕ, and extend the notion of relevance of Definition 15 to formula clocks in the natural way. Let $\mathcal{E}'$ be the restriction of $\mathcal{E}$ over the clocks of $\mathcal{Z}$ that are referred to in ϕ. We can then extend the equivalence relation from $\cong$ to $\cong^*$ simply by taking $(\nu, \mathcal{E}')$ instead of ν and $\mathcal{X} \cup \mathcal{Z}$ instead of $\mathcal{X}$; the definition of equivalence classes of the form $[\nu, \mathcal{E}']$ then follows in an obvious manner. Furthermore, Lemma 1 holds for $\cong^*$. Because our construction of the equivalence classes will always be with respect to a particular ϕ, we henceforth write $\mathcal{E}$ for $\mathcal{E}'$. An element of the form $\langle s, [\nu, \mathcal{E}] \rangle$ is called an *augmented region*.

Let α be an equivalence class of the form $[\nu, \mathcal{E}]$. Then $\alpha[C \mapsto 0]$ denotes the equivalence class obtained from α by setting all of the clocks in C to 0, and let clock $c \in \mathcal{X} \cup \mathcal{Z}$ be *relevant* for α if $(\nu, \mathcal{E})(c) \leq k_c$, where $(\nu, \mathcal{E})$ is some clock valuation such that $(\nu, \mathcal{E}) \in \alpha$.

The Region Graph. We now define an edge relation over the augmented regions to obtain the *region graph*. The non-probabilistic region construction of [2] results in a state-labelled transition system, which can be model checked using well-established methods. However, in our case the region graph takes the form of a concurrent probabilistic system [5] (and is also equivalent to the probabilistic-nondeterministic systems of [7]), for which there exist model checking techniques for temporal logics with probability bounds.

First, we require some preliminary definitions.

Definition 17 (Satisfaction of formulae). *Let α be an equivalence class of $\Gamma^*(\mathcal{X} \cup \mathcal{Z})$ and $\varphi \in \mathrm{AF}_{\mathcal{X} \cup \mathcal{Z}}$ be an atomic formula. Then α satisfies φ if and only if, for any $(\nu, \mathcal{E}) \in \alpha$, the value of φ after substituting each occurrence of $x \in \mathcal{X}$ with $\nu(x)$, and each occurrence of $z \in \mathcal{Z}$ with $\mathcal{E}(z)$, is true. (Note that the value of φ will be the same for all $(\nu, \mathcal{E}) \in \alpha$, by Lemma 1(c).)*

Definition 18 (Successor Region). *Let α and β be distinct equivalence classes of $\Gamma^*(\mathcal{X} \cup \mathcal{Z})$. The equivalence class β is said to be the successor of α if and only if, for each $(\nu, \mathcal{E}) \in \alpha$, there exists a positive $t \in \mathbb{R}$ such that $(\nu + t, \mathcal{E} + t) \in \beta$, and $(\nu + t', \mathcal{E} + t') \in \alpha \cup \beta$ for all $t' \leq t$. We then denote the equivalence class β by $succ(\alpha)$.*

The successor relation can be extended to augmented regions in the following way: $\langle s', \beta \rangle$ is the successor region of $\langle s, \alpha \rangle$ if $s' = s$ and $\beta = succ(\alpha)$.

Definition 19 (End Class). *Let α be an equivalence class of $\Gamma^*(\mathcal{X} \cup \mathcal{Z})$. The class α is an end class if and only if for all $c \in \mathcal{X} \cup \mathcal{Z}$, c is not relevant for α. Furthermore, for any $s \in \mathcal{S}$, $\langle s, \alpha \rangle$ is an end region.*

We now define a region graph which captures both the probabilistic transitions in G and the movement to new regions due to the passage of time.

Definition 20 (Region Graph). *The region graph $R(G, \phi)$ is defined to be the graph $(V^*, Steps^*, End^*)$. The vertex set V^* is the set of augmented regions, and the set $End^* \subseteq V^*$ comprises of the set of end regions. The edge function $Steps^* : V^* \longrightarrow \mathcal{P}_{fn}(\mu(V^*))$ includes two types of transitions:* [3]

passage of time: *if α is not an end class and the invariant condition $inv(s)$ is satisfied by $succ(\alpha)$, then $p_{succ}^{s;\alpha} \in Steps^*(\langle s, \alpha \rangle)$ where for any $\langle s', \beta \rangle \in V^*$:*

$$p_{succ}^{s,\alpha}(\langle s', \beta \rangle) = \begin{cases} 1 \text{ if } \langle s', \beta \rangle = \langle s, succ(\alpha) \rangle \\ 0 \text{ otherwise.} \end{cases}$$

state transitions of G: *$p_{p_s}^{s,\alpha} \in Steps^*(\langle s, \alpha \rangle)$ if there exists $p_s \in prob(s)$ and α satisfies the enabling condition $\tau_s(p_s)$ such that for any $s' \in S$ and equivalence class β:*

$$p_{p_s}^{s,\alpha}(\langle s', \beta \rangle) = \sum_{\substack{C \subseteq \mathcal{X} \text{ \&} \\ [C \mapsto 0]\alpha = \beta}} p_s(s', C).$$

Definition 21 (Path on the Region Graph). *Given an augmented region $\langle s, \alpha \rangle$, a $\langle s, \alpha \rangle$-path is a finite or infinite path of the form:*

$$\omega^* = \langle s_0, \alpha_0 \rangle \xrightarrow{p^{s_0,\alpha_0}} \langle s_1, \alpha_1 \rangle \xrightarrow{p^{s_1,\alpha_1}} \langle s_2, \alpha_2 \rangle \xrightarrow{p^{s_2,\alpha_2}} \cdots$$

where $\langle s_0, \alpha_0 \rangle = \langle s, \alpha \rangle$, $s_i \in S$, α_i is an equivalence class of $\Gamma^*(\mathcal{X} \cup \mathcal{Z})$ and $p^{s_i,\alpha_i} \in Steps^*(\langle s_i, \alpha_i \rangle)$ such that $p^{s_i,\alpha_i}(\langle s_{i+1}, \alpha_{i+1} \rangle) > 0$.

We define adversaries on the region graph $R(G, \phi)$ as follows:

Definition 22 (Adversaries on the Region Graph). *An adversary A^* on the region graph is a function A^* mapping every finite path ω^* of $R(G, \Phi)$ to a distribution p such that $p \in Steps^*(last(\omega^*))$.*

We can then define the sets of paths $Path^*_{fin}$ and $Path^*_{ful}$, and those associated with an adversary, $Path^{A^*}_{fin}$ and $Path^{A^*}_{ful}$, as before. Note that end regions take the role of end states in the definition of the finite paths of $Path^*_{ful}$ and $Path^{A^*}_{ful}$.

With each adversary A^* we can associate a Markov chain. If A^* is an adversary of the region graph $R(G, \phi)$, then $MC^{A^*} = (Path^{A^*}_{fin}, \mathbf{P}^{A^*})$ is a Markov chain where, for the augmented regions $\langle s, \alpha \rangle$, $\langle s', \alpha' \rangle$, and $last(\omega^*) = \langle s, \alpha \rangle$:

$$\mathbf{P}^{A^*}(\omega^*, \omega'^*) = \begin{cases} p^{s,\alpha}(\langle s', \alpha' \rangle) \text{ if } A^*(\omega^*) = p^{s,\alpha} \text{ and } \omega'^* = \omega^* \xrightarrow{p^{s,\alpha}} \langle s', \alpha' \rangle \\ 0 \qquad\qquad \text{otherwise} \end{cases}$$

---

[3] If the model includes the distributions p_s^{inv} then we need to add an extra condition in the definition.

Definition 23 (Divergent Adversaries on the Region Graph). *An adversary A^* is* divergent *if and only if for all infinite paths $\omega^* \in Path_{ful}^{A^*}$, there exist infinitely many $n \in \mathbb{N}$ such that one of the following holds:*

1. *$\omega^*(n)$ is an end region,*
2. *$\omega^*(n+1)$ is the successor region of $\omega^*(n)$.*

Let $\mathcal{A}_{div}^*$ be the set of divergent adversaries on the region graph.

Such divergent adversaries on the region graph $R(G, \phi)$ correspond to an infinite number of adversaries on the underlying probabilistic timed structure $\mathcal{M}^G$, some of which will be divergent in the sense of Definition 5. Conversely, for any divergent adversary of $\mathcal{M}^G$, there exists a corresponding divergent adversary on $R(G, \phi)$. We observe that the notion of divergent paths of $R(G, \phi)$ induced by adversaries in $\mathcal{A}_{div}^*$ differs from that of *fair paths* of the region graph as presented in [2] because of our assumption of weakly monotonic time.

As in, for example, [5, 7], we define the function $Prob^*$ as the unique measure on the σ-algebra $\mathcal{F}_{Path}^*$.

Model Checking. A method for model checking probabilistic timed graphs against PTCTL formulae will now be presented. This approach takes the form of three steps: construction of the region graph as a finite state representation of the probabilistic timed graph in question, obtaining a formula of an extension of the probabilistic logic PBTL, and then resolving this new formula on the region graph.

First, we turn our attention to the structure over which the PBTL formula will be resolved. Formulae of PBTL are interpreted over 'PBTL-structures', which are concurrent probabilistic systems extended with a vertex labelling function. As our region graph $R(G, \phi)$ is a concurrent probabilistic system, adding an appropriately defined labelling function will convert it into a PBTL-structure which we will call a *labelled region graph*. We define AF_ϕ as the set of minimal atomic formulae appearing in the given PTCTL formula ϕ. For every atomic formula in $\varphi \in \mathrm{AF}_\phi$, we extend the set AP with the atomic proposition a_φ. We denote the resulting set of atomic propositions by AP^*.

Definition 24 (Labelled Region Graph). *For a given region graph $R(G, \phi)$, we define its associated* labelled region graph *by $(R(G, \phi), L^*)$, where the vertex labelling function, $L^* : V^* \to 2^{\mathrm{AP}^*}$, is defined by the following. For a given $\langle s, [\nu, \mathcal{E}] \rangle$, we let:*

$$L^*(\langle s, [\nu, \mathcal{E}] \rangle) = \{a \in L(s)\} \cup \{a_\varphi \mid [\nu, \mathcal{E}] \text{ satisfies } \varphi, \ \varphi \in \mathrm{AF}_\phi\}$$

Next, we present an adjusted syntax of PBTL. Note that we omit PBTL's 'bounded until' operator, because an equivalent, dense time concept can be defined by nesting a PTCTL until operator within a freeze quantifier, and its 'next step' operator, which has no analogue in the case of dense real-time. However, we extend PBTL with a freeze quantifier expression.

Definition 25 (Syntax of PBTL). *The syntax of* PBTL *is defined as follows:*

$$\Phi ::= \text{true} \mid a \mid \Phi \wedge \Phi \mid \neg\Phi \mid z.\Phi \mid [\Phi \exists\mathcal{U}\ \Phi]_{\sqsupseteq\lambda} \mid [\Phi \forall\mathcal{U}\ \Phi]_{\sqsupseteq\lambda}$$

where $a \in \text{AP}^*$ *is an atomic proposition,* $z \in \mathcal{Z}$, $\lambda \in [0,1]$, *and* $\sqsupseteq$ *is either* $\geq$ *or* $>$.

Definition 26 (Satisfaction Relation for PBTL). *Given a labelled region graph* $(R(G,\phi), L^*)$ *and a set* $\mathcal{A}^*$ *of adversaries on* $R(G,\phi)$, *then for any augmented region* $\langle s, [\nu, \mathcal{E}]\rangle$ *of* $R(G,\phi)$, *and PBTL formula* Φ, *the satisfaction relation* $\langle s, [\nu, \mathcal{E}]\rangle \models_{\mathcal{A}^*} \Phi$ *is defined inductively as follows:*

$$
\begin{aligned}
\langle s, [\nu, \mathcal{E}]\rangle \models_{\mathcal{A}^*} \text{true} \quad & \text{for all } \langle s, [\nu, \mathcal{E}]\rangle \\
\langle s, [\nu, \mathcal{E}]\rangle \models_{\mathcal{A}^*} a \quad & \Leftrightarrow a \in L^*(\langle s, [\nu, \mathcal{E}]\rangle) \\
\langle s, [\nu, \mathcal{E}]\rangle \models_{\mathcal{A}^*} \Phi_1 \wedge \Phi_2 \quad & \Leftrightarrow \langle s, [\nu, \mathcal{E}]\rangle \models_{\mathcal{A}^*} \Phi_1 \text{ and } \langle s, [\nu, \mathcal{E}]\rangle \models_{\mathcal{A}^*} \Phi_2 \\
\langle s, [\nu, \mathcal{E}]\rangle \models_{\mathcal{A}^*} \neg\Phi \quad & \Leftrightarrow \langle s, [\nu, \mathcal{E}]\rangle \not\models_{\mathcal{A}^*} \Phi \\
\langle s, [\nu, \mathcal{E}]\rangle \models_{\mathcal{A}^*} z.\Phi \quad & \Leftrightarrow \langle s, [\nu, \mathcal{E}[z \mapsto 0]]\rangle \models_{\mathcal{A}^*} \Phi \\
\langle s, [\nu, \mathcal{E}]\rangle \models_{\mathcal{A}^*} [\Phi_1 \exists\mathcal{U}\ \Phi_2]_{\sqsupseteq\lambda} \quad & \Leftrightarrow Prob^*(\{\omega \mid \omega \in Path_{ful}^{A^*}(\langle s, [\nu, \mathcal{E}]\rangle)) \ \& \\
& \quad\quad \omega \models_{\mathcal{A}^*} \Phi_1\ \mathcal{U}\ \Phi_2\}) \sqsupseteq \lambda \text{ for some } A^* \in \mathcal{A}^* \\
\langle s, [\nu, \mathcal{E}]\rangle \models_{\mathcal{A}^*} [\Phi_1 \forall\mathcal{U}\ \Phi_2]_{\sqsupseteq\lambda} \quad & \Leftrightarrow Prob^*(\{\omega \mid \omega \in Path_{ful}^{A^*}(\langle s, [\nu, \mathcal{E}]\rangle)) \ \& \\
& \quad\quad \omega \models_{\mathcal{A}^*} \Phi_1\ \mathcal{U}\ \Phi_2\}) \sqsupseteq \lambda \text{ for all } A^* \in \mathcal{A}^* \\
\omega \models_{\mathcal{A}^*} \Phi_1\ \mathcal{U}\ \Phi_2 \quad & \Leftrightarrow \text{there exists } i \in \mathbb{N}, \text{ such that } \omega(i) \models_{\mathcal{A}^*} \Phi_2, \\
& \quad\quad \text{and for all } j \in \mathbb{N} \text{ such that } 0 \leq j < i \text{ and} \\
& \quad\quad \omega(j) \models_{\mathcal{A}^*} \Phi_1
\end{aligned}
$$

Furthermore, a PBTL formula, Φ, can be *derived from* a PTCTL formula, ϕ, by applying the following rules inductively:

Subformula of ϕ_i	Subformula of Φ_i
true	true
a	a
φ	a_φ
$\phi_1 \wedge \phi_2$	$\Phi_1 \wedge \Phi_2$
$\neg\phi$	$\neg\Phi$
$z.\phi$	$z.\Phi$
$[\phi_1 \exists\mathcal{U}\ \phi_2]_{\sqsupseteq\lambda}$	$[\Phi_1 \exists\mathcal{U}\ \Phi_2]_{\sqsupseteq\lambda}$
$[\phi_1 \forall\mathcal{U}\ \phi_2]_{\sqsupseteq\lambda}$	$[\Phi_1 \forall\mathcal{U}\ \Phi_2]_{\sqsupseteq\lambda}$

Figure 2 presents the region construction of the probabilistic timed graph of Figure 1. As before, the probabilistic transitions are linked with an arc at their source vertex. In order for the reader to easily comprehend the behaviour of the region graph, each vertex has been labelled with a constraint that is satisfied by all of the clock valuations within that augmented region. Consider the following PTCTL formula:

$$\phi_1 = [(y = 0)\exists\mathcal{U}[(x > 0)\exists\mathcal{U}(y = 0)]_{\geq 0.7}]_{\geq 1}.$$

ϕ_1 can be interpreted over this graph by first converting it into the equivalent PBTL formula:

$$\Phi_1 = [a_{(y=0)}\exists\mathcal{U}[a_{(x>0)}\exists\mathcal{U}a_{(y=0)}]_{\geq 0.7}]_{\geq 1}.$$

Φ_1 is satisfied by this region graph, and therefore we conclude that the probabilistic timed graph G_1 satisfies ϕ_1. Note that the following PTCTL formula, ϕ_2, is *not* satisfied by the region graph:

$$\phi_2 = [(y = 0)\exists\mathcal{U}[(x > 0)\exists\mathcal{U}(y = 0)]_{>0.7}]_{\geq 1}$$

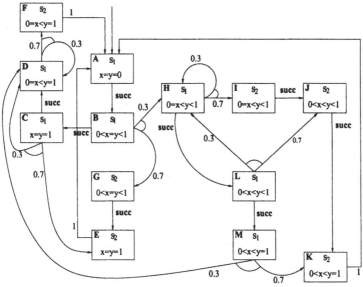

Figure 2. The region graph of the probabilistic timed graph G_1.

Proposition 1. (Correctness of the model checking procedure) *Given the probabilistic timed graph G, state $\langle s, \nu \rangle$ of $\mathcal{M}^G$ and formula clock valuation $\mathcal{E}$ satisfies the PTCTL formula ϕ if and only if vertex $\langle s, [\nu, \mathcal{E}] \rangle$ of $(R(G, \phi), L^*)$ satisfies the PBTL formula Φ, where Φ is derived from ϕ.*

Proof. Before considering any temporal or probabilistic operators, we must be convinced that subformulae comprising only of atomic propositions, atomic formulae, boolean connectives and freeze quantifiers are resolved satisfactorily. We proceed to show this by induction on the structure of ϕ.

If $\phi = $ true, then ϕ will be true for all states of $\mathcal{M}^G$ and all formula clock valuations. Here ϕ derives $\Phi = $ true, which is true for all vertices in $(R(G, \phi), L^*)$.

If $\phi = a$, where $a \in AP$, then it is true for state $\langle s, \nu \rangle$ of $\mathcal{M}^G$ and all formula clock valuations if and only if $\langle s, \nu \rangle(a) = $ true. We also know that $\langle s, \nu \rangle(a) = $ true if and only if $a \in L(s)$. By Definition 24, $a \in L^*(\langle s, [\nu, \mathcal{E}] \rangle)$ if $a \in L(s)$, so $\Phi = a$ is true for the vertex $\langle s, [\nu, \mathcal{E}] \rangle$.

If $\phi = \varphi$, where φ is a minimal atomic formula, then the state $\langle s, \nu \rangle$ of $\mathcal{M}^G$ and formula clock valuation $\mathcal{E}$ satisfies φ if $\varphi[\sigma, \mathcal{E}] = $ true. Then, from Definition 24, $a_\varphi \in L^*(\langle s, [\nu, \mathcal{E}] \rangle)$. Because $\Phi = a_\varphi$, and Φ is derived from ϕ, both ϕ and Φ resolve to true in $\langle s, \nu \rangle, \mathcal{E}$ and $\langle s, [\nu, \mathcal{E}] \rangle$ respectively.

The cases of the boolean connectives, $\neg$ and $\wedge$, are self-evident.

If $\phi = z.\phi_1$, then, for a given state $\langle s, \nu \rangle$ and formula clock valuation $\mathcal{E}$ that satisfies ϕ, we know that the augmented region $\langle s, [\nu, \mathcal{E}] \rangle$ will also satisfy $z.\Phi_1$, by observing the following argument. By Definition 10

$$\langle s, \nu \rangle, \mathcal{E} \models_{\mathcal{A}^G_{div}} z.\phi \Leftrightarrow \langle s, \nu \rangle, \mathcal{E}[z \mapsto 0] \models_{\mathcal{A}^G_{div}} \phi$$
$$\Leftrightarrow \langle s, [\nu, \mathcal{E}[z \mapsto 0]] \rangle \models_{\mathcal{A}^*_{div}} \Phi \quad \text{by induction}$$
$$\Leftrightarrow \langle s, [\nu, \mathcal{E}] \rangle \models_{\mathcal{A}^*_{div}} z.\Phi \quad \text{by Definition 26}$$

Now we show that $\langle s, \nu \rangle, \mathcal{E} \models_{\mathcal{A}^G_{div}} [\phi_1 \exists \mathcal{U} \phi_2]_{\sqsupseteq \lambda}$, if and only if $\langle s, [\nu, \mathcal{E}] \rangle \models_{\mathcal{A}^*_{div}} [\Phi_1 \exists \mathcal{U} \Phi_2]_{\sqsupseteq \lambda}$. Our presentation is split into three sections:

1. showing that, for a path ω of $\mathcal{M}^G$, a corresponding path of $(R(G, \phi), L^*)$, $[\omega]$, can be constructed. Furthermore, both of these paths have the same corresponding notion of divergence; that is, ω is divergent if and only if $[\omega]$ is divergent. It also follows that, given path ω^* of the region graph, we can construct ω such that $[\omega] = \omega^*$.

2. showing that the two paths ω and $[\omega]$ are associated with the same probability value.

3. showing $\omega, \mathcal{E} \models_{\mathcal{A}^G_{div}} \phi_1 \mathcal{U} \phi_2$ if and only if $[\omega] \models_{\mathcal{A}^*_{div}} \Phi_1 \mathcal{U} \Phi_2$, where the initial augmented state of $[\omega]$ comprises of $\mathcal{E}$.

1. Consider the following property, which shall henceforth be referred to as the *sequence property*. Take a particular node of G, $s \in \mathcal{S}$, and a clock valuation $(\nu, \mathcal{E})$, and consider the sequence of equivalence classes, $[\nu + d_1, \mathcal{E} + d_1], ..., [\nu + d_k, \mathcal{E} + d_k]$, where each equivalence class satisfies $inv(s)$, for all $1 \leq i \leq k$, $d_i \in \mathbb{R}$, and for all $1 \leq l < k$, $succ([\nu + d_l, \mathcal{E} + d_l]) = [\nu + d_{l+1}, \mathcal{E} + d_{l+1}]$. Then, for the time value $d \in \mathbb{R}$, where $d_1 \leq d \leq d_k$, we know that $(\nu + d, \mathcal{E} + d) \cong^* (\nu + d_j, \mathcal{E} + d_j)$, for some $1 \leq j \leq k$. We can then write $(\nu + d, \mathcal{E} + d) \in [\nu + d_j, \mathcal{E} + d_j]$.

The sequence property allows us to state the following. Consider the path ω of $\mathcal{M}^G$, such that:

$$\omega = \langle s_0, \nu_0 \rangle \xrightarrow{t_0, p_0} \langle s_1, \nu_1 \rangle \xrightarrow{t_1, p_1} \cdots$$

Take a particular $i \geq 0$. From $\langle s_i, \nu_i \rangle$, and letting t_i time units elapse, we may cross into a number of equivalence classes before making the next edge transition. We let m_i be this number. Let $v_{i0} = \langle s_i, [\nu_i, \mathcal{E} + \mathcal{D}_\omega(i)] \rangle$, and $v_{ij} = \langle s_i, [\nu_i + d_j, \mathcal{E} + \mathcal{D}_\omega(i) + d_j] \rangle$ for some $1 \leq j \leq m_i$, and $d_j \in \mathbb{R}$. Then we can construct the finite path $[\omega_i]$ of the region graph, such that:

$$[\omega_i] = v_{i0} \xrightarrow{p_{succ}^{v_{i0}}} v_{i1} \xrightarrow{p_{succ}^{v_{i1}}} \cdots v_{im_i} \xrightarrow{p_{p_{s_i}}^{v_{im_i}}} v_{(i+1)0} .$$

Let $[\omega] = [\omega_0][\omega_1] \cdots$ be the concatenation of all such segments.

This construction also works in the opposite direction. Let $\langle s, \alpha_1 \rangle \to \cdots \to \langle s, \alpha_n \rangle$ be a path through the region graph such that all of its edges correspond to p_{succ}^{s, α_i} transitions. Now suppose that $\langle s, \alpha_n \rangle \xrightarrow{p_{p_s}^{s, \alpha}} \langle s', \alpha' \rangle$. Then, assuming that we have a partially constructed, finite path ω of $\mathcal{M}^G$ such that $|\omega| = i$, and $(\nu_i, \mathcal{E} + \mathcal{D}_\omega(i)) \in \alpha_i$, then it follows that ω can be extended by the transition $\langle s_i, \nu_i \rangle \xrightarrow{(t_i, p_i)} \langle s_{i+1}, \nu_{i+1} \rangle$, where $t_i \in \mathbb{R}$ and p_i is derived from p_s in the usual way. Therefore, we have a method for constructing infinite or finite paths of $\mathcal{M}^G$

from paths of $(R(G, \phi), L^*)$. We note that such paths may be finite if the region graph reaches an end class from which no transitions are enabled, and that paths induced by divergent adversaries of the region graph will guarantee the existence of corresponding time-divergent paths of $\mathcal{M}^G$. Then it follows that, given ω^* of $(R(G, \phi), L^*)$, we can construct ω of $\mathcal{M}^G$ such that $[\omega] = \omega^*$.

2. Now we must show that the probability value associated with the paths ω and $[\omega]$ are the same. Consider the segment of ω, $\omega_i = \langle s_i, \nu_i \rangle \xrightarrow{t_i, p_i} \langle s_{i+1}, \nu_{i+1} \rangle$, and the segment of $[\omega]$:

$$[\omega_i] = v_{i0} \xrightarrow[p_{succ}^{v_{i0}}]{} v_{i1} \xrightarrow[p_{succ}^{v_{i1}}]{} \cdots v_{im_i} \xrightarrow[p_{p_{s_i}}^{v_{im_i}}]{} v_{(i+1)0} \ .$$

We wish to show that $Prob_{fin}(\omega_i) = Prob^*_{fin}([\omega_i])$. Consider the transition $v_{ij} \xrightarrow[p_{succ}]{v_{ij}} v_{i(j+1)}$, for $1 \le j < m_i$. Then, from the sequence property and the above construction of $[\omega]$, we know that $v_{i(j+1)}$ is a time successor of v_{ij}, and therefore $p_{succ}^{v_{ij}} = 1$. Therefore, our problem reduces to showing that:

$$Prob_{fin}(\langle s_i, \nu_i \rangle \xrightarrow{t_i, p_i} \langle s_{i+1}, \nu_{i+1} \rangle) = Prob^*_{fin}(v_{im_i} \xrightarrow[p_{p_{s_i}}]{v_{im_i}} v_{(i+1)0}) \ .$$

By the definitions of $Prob$ and $Prob^*$, this reduces to showing that:

$$p_i(\langle s_{i+1}, \nu_{i+1} \rangle) = p_{p_{s_i}}^{v_{im_i}}(\langle s_i, [\nu_{i+1}, \mathcal{E} + \mathcal{D}_\omega(i+1)] \rangle) \ .$$

Firstly, we note that $\nu_i + t_i \in [\nu_i + d_{m_i}]$. Because all of the system clock valuations in $[\nu_i + d_{m_i}]$ will enable the same probability distributions, we know that the same distributions are enabled in $\langle s_i, \nu_i + t_i \rangle$ and $v_{im_i} = \langle s_i, [\nu_i + d_{m_i}, \mathcal{E} + \mathcal{D}_\omega(i) + d_{m_i}] \rangle$. Furthermore, the move from $\langle s_i, \nu_i + t_i \rangle$ to $\langle s_{i+1}, \nu_{i+1} \rangle$ in $\mathcal{M}^G$, and from v_{im_i} to $v_{(i+1)0}$ in $R(G, \phi)$, will correspond to the choice of the *same* probability distribution of G. We denote this distribution by p_{s_i}. Recall from Definition 13 that:

$$p_i(\langle s_{i+1}, \nu_{i+1} \rangle) = \sum_{\substack{C \subseteq \mathcal{X} \ \& \\ (\nu_i + t_i)[\overline{C} \mapsto 0] = \nu_{i+1}}} p_{s_i}(s_{i+1}, C) \ ,$$

and from the definition of the region graph:

$$p_{p_{s_i}}^{s_i, \alpha}(\langle s_{i+1}, \beta \rangle) = \sum_{\substack{C \subseteq \mathcal{X} \ \& \\ \alpha[\overline{C} \mapsto 0] = \beta}} p_{s_i}(s_{i+1}, C) \ ,$$

where $\alpha = [\nu_i + d_{m_i}, \mathcal{E} + \mathcal{D}_\omega(i) + d_{m_i}]$ and $\beta = [\nu_{i+1}, \mathcal{E} + \mathcal{D}_\omega(i+1) + d_{i+1}]$. We know that, for any $C \subseteq \mathcal{X}$, $(\nu_i + t_i)[C \mapsto 0] \in [\nu_i + d_{m_i}][C \mapsto 0]$, and, trivially, that $\nu_{i+1} \in [\nu_{i+1}]$, and so the combinations of $C \subseteq \mathcal{X}$ used in both summations above will be the same. Therefore, the same probability values will be summed in the case of $\mathcal{M}^G$ and that of $R(G, \phi)$, and we can conclude that $p_i(\langle s_{i+1}, \nu_{i+1} \rangle) = p_{p_{s_i}}^{s_i, \alpha}(\langle s_{i+1}, \beta \rangle)$. We can repeat such a process for all $i \in \mathbb{N}$ and, by the definitions of $Prob$ and $Prob^*$, show that the probability value associated with the paths ω and $[\omega]$ are the same.

3. Next we prove $\omega, \mathcal{E} \models_{\mathcal{A}_{div}^G} \phi_1 \mathcal{U} \phi_2$ if and only if $[\omega] \models_{\mathcal{A}_{div}^*} \Phi_1 \mathcal{U} \Phi_2$. If $\omega(i) = \langle s_i, \nu_i \rangle$ for all $i \in \mathbb{N}$, then $\omega, \mathcal{E} \models_{\mathcal{A}_{div}^G} \phi_1 \mathcal{U} \phi_2$

$\Leftrightarrow \exists i \in \mathbb{N}$ and $0 \leq t \leq t_i$ such that $\omega(i) + t, \mathcal{E} + \mathcal{D}_\omega(i) + t \models_{\mathcal{A}_{div}^G} \phi_2$
and $\forall j \in \mathbb{N}$ and $t' \in \mathbb{R}$ such that $t' \leq t_j$ & $(j, t') \prec (i, t)$,
$\omega(j) + t', \mathcal{E} + \mathcal{D}_\omega(j) + t' \models_{\mathcal{A}_{div}^G} \phi_1 \vee \phi_2$

by Definition 10

$\Leftrightarrow \exists i \in \mathbb{N}$ and $0 \leq t \leq t_i$ such that $\langle s_i, [\nu_i + t, \mathcal{E} + \mathcal{D}_\omega(i) + t] \rangle \models_{\mathcal{A}_{div}^*} \Phi_2$
and $\forall j \in \mathbb{N}$ and $t' \in \mathbb{R}$ such that $t' \leq t_j$ & $(j, t') \prec (i, t)$,
$\langle s_j, [\nu_j + t', \mathcal{E} + \mathcal{D}_\omega(j) + t'] \rangle \models_{\mathcal{A}_{div}^*} \Phi_1 \vee \Phi_2$

by induction

$\Leftrightarrow \exists i' \in \mathbb{N}$ such that $[\omega](i') \models_{\mathcal{A}_{div}^*} \Phi_2$ and $[\omega](j') \models_{\mathcal{A}_{div}^*} \Phi_1 \vee \Phi_2 \; \forall j' \leq i'$

by construction of $[\omega]$

$\Leftrightarrow [\omega] \models_{\mathcal{A}_{div}^*} \Phi_1 \mathcal{U} \Phi_2$

by Definition 26

It follows by the definition of adversaries, both on probabilistic timed structures and the region graph, and the construction of **1**, that for all $A \in \mathcal{A}_{div}^G$, there exists an adversary $[A] \in \mathcal{A}_{div}^*$ such that, for some $\mathcal{E}$,

$$Path_{ful}^{[A]}(\langle s, [\nu, \mathcal{E}] \rangle) = \{[\omega] \mid \omega \in Path_{ful}^A(\langle s, \nu \rangle)\}.$$

Conversely, given a path in the region graph, we can construct a path of $\mathcal{M}^G$ (see [2]). Using this construction, we can show that, for all adversaries $A^* \in \mathcal{A}_{div}^*$ of the region graph, there exists an adversary $A \in \mathcal{A}_{div}^G$ such that $[A] = A^*$.

From **2**, we know that the probability values associated with ω and $[\omega]$ are the same. Then we can conclude that:

$$Prob^*\{\omega^* \mid \omega^* \in Path_{ful}^{A^*}\} = Prob\{\omega \mid \omega \in Path_{ful}^A\}$$

for some $A \in \mathcal{A}_{div}^G$. □

Using the transformation presented above, we can obtain a PBTL formula, Φ, from the PTCTL formula, ϕ. Now we can use the model checking algorithm of [5] in order to verify whether the PBTL formula Φ holds in an initial state of the region graph, $\langle s_{init}, [\nu^0, \mathcal{E}] \rangle$, where, for all $x \in \mathcal{X}$, $(\nu^0, \mathcal{E})(x) = 0$ and $\mathcal{E}$ is an arbitrary formula clock valuation.

7   Conclusions

We conclude with a brief analysis of the complexity of our method. The time complexity of PBTL model checking is polynomial in the size of the system (measured by the number of states and transitions) and linear in the size of the formula [5] (see also the recent improvement [4]). Since the translation from PTCTL to the extended PBTL has no effect on the size of the formula, it follows that the model checking for PTCTL against probabilistic timed systems will be polynomial in the size of the region graph and linear in the size of the PTCTL formula. Note that the addition of probability distributions to timed automata does not significantly increase the size of the region graph over the size of the non-probabilistic region graph, and that the freeze quantifier formulae we have added to PBTL can be handled in a straightforward manner.

Future work could address the potential inefficiencies of this method. Model checking of real-time systems is expensive, with its complexity being exponential in the number of clocks and the magnitude of their upper bounds (denoted by k_c in our presentation). However, a number of techniques for combating this inefficiency have been developed (see [16]), and could be applied in this context.

Another potential avenue of research is the application of the methods of this paper to *hybrid automata*, a model for discrete-continuous systems which allows more general continuous dynamics than timed automata. In particular, it is known that certain classes of hybrid automata are reducible to timed automata [12], and other classes have finite bisimilarity quotients [15], both of which may be particularly adaptable to probabilistic extensions.

References

[1] R. Alur, C. Courcoubetis, and D. Dill. Model-checking for probabilistic real-time systems. In *Automata, Languages and Programming: Proceedings of the 18th ICALP*, Lecture Notes in Computer Science 510, pages 115–126, 1991.

[2] R. Alur, C. Courcoubetis, and D. Dill. Model-checking in dense real-time. *Information and Computation*, 104(1):2–34, 1993. Preliminary version appears in the Proc. of 5th LICS, 1990.

[3] R. Alur and D. Dill. A theory of timed automata. *Theoretical Computer Science*, 126:183–235, 1994. Preliminary version appears in Proc. 17th ICALP, 1990, LNCS 443.

[4] C. Baier. Personal communication, 1998.

[5] C. Baier and M. Kwiatkowska. Model checking for a probabilistic branching time logic with fairness. *Distributed Computing*, 11:125–155, 1998.

[6] J. Bengtsson, K. Larsen, F. Larsson, P. Pettersson, W. Yi, and C. Weise. New generation of UPPAAL. In *Proceedings of the International Workshop on Software Tools for Technology Transfer*, Aalborg, Denmark, July 1998.

[7] A. Bianco and L. de Alfaro. Model checking of probabilistic and nondeterministic systems. In *Foundations of Software Technology and Theoretical Computer Science*, volume 1026 of *Lecture Notes in Computer Science*, pages 499–513, 1995.

[8] M. Bozga, C. Daws, O. Maler, A. Olivero, S. Tripakis, and S. Yovine. Kronos: a model-checking tool for real-time systems. In *Proc. of the 10th Conference on Computer-Aided Verification*, Vancouver, Canada, 28 June - 2 July 1998. Springer Verlag.

[9] P. D'Argenio, J.-P. Katoen, T. Ruys, and J. Tretmans. Modeling and verifying a bounded retransmission protocol. In Z. Brezocnik and T. Kapus, editors, *Proc. of COST 247 International Workshop on Applied Formal Methods in System Design*, Maribor, Slovenia, Technical Report. University of Maribor, 1996.

[10] H. Gregersen and H. E. Jensen. Formal design of reliable real time systems. Master's thesis, Department of Mathematics and Computer Science, Aalborg University, 1995.

[11] H. Hansson and B. Jonsson. A logic for reasoning about time and reliability. *Formal Aspects of Computing*, 6(5):512–535, 1994.

[12] T. Henzinger, P. Kopke, A. Puri, and P. Varaiya. What's decidable about hybrid automata? *Journal of Computer and System Sciences*, 57(1):94–124, Aug. 1998.

[13] T. Henzinger and O. Kupferman. From quantity to quality. In O. Maler, editor, *HART 97: Hybrid and Real-time Systems*, Lecture Notes in Computer Science 1201, pages 48–62. Springer-Verlag, 1997.

[14] T. Henzinger, X. Nicollin, J. Sifakis, and S. Yovine. Symbolic model checking for real-time systems. *Information and Computation*, 111(2):193–244, 1994. Special issue for LICS 92.

[15] G. Lafferriere, G. Pappas, and S. Yovine. Decidable hybrid systems. Technical Report UCB/ERL M98/39, University of California at Berkeley, June 1998.

[16] S. Yovine. Model checking timed automata. In G. Rozenberg and F. Vaandrager, editors, *Embedded Systems*, volume 1494 of *Lecture Notes in Computer Science*. Springer, 1998.

ProbVerus: Probabilistic Symbolic Model Checking

Vicky Hartonas-Garmhausen[1], Sergio Campos[2], Ed Clarke[3]

[1]Carnegie Mellon University, Department of Engineering and Public Policy,
5000 Forbes Avenue, Pittsburgh, PA 15213, USA
hartonas@cs.cmu.edu
[2]Federal University of Minas, Gerais, Brasil
scampos@dcc.ufmg.br
[3]Carnegie Mellon University, Department of Computer Science,
5000 Forbes Avenue, Pittsburgh, PA 15213, USA
emc@cs.cmu.edu

Abstract. Model checking can tell us whether a system is correct; probabilistic model checking can also tell us whether a system is timely and reliable. Moreover, probabilistic model checking allows one to verify properties that may not be true with probability one, but may still hold with an acceptable probability. The challenge in developing a probabilistic model checker able to handle realistic systems is the construction of the state space and the necessity to solve huge systems of linear equations. To address this problem, we have developed ProbVerus, a tool for the formal verification of probabilistic real-time systems. ProbVerus is an implementation of probabilistic computation tree logic (PCTL) model checking using symbolic techniques. We present ProbVerus, demonstrate its use with a simple manufacturing example, and report the current status of the tool. With ProbVerus, we have been able to analyze, within minutes, the safety logic of a railway interlocking controller with 10^{27} states.

1 Introduction

The large size and high complexity of real-world mission-critical systems makes the verification of these systems an extremely difficult problem. To study the complete system, one must also include the system's interface with the environment. Physical systems are stochastic in nature and randomization makes the verification of probabilistic systems even more difficult due to its nonintuitive effects. At the same time, industries such as the transportation, pharmaceutical, chemical, and nuclear, are required to meet this challenge being constantly under the scrutiny of process and product specification. There is a great need for industrial-strength formal methods as well as real-world case studies that can demonstrate their feasibility.

Probabilistic model checking is a method for the formal verification of stochastic systems. The state of the art in probabilistic verification research includes numerous theoretical studies that have lead to efficient algorithms; for example, there is an LTL model checking algorithm which is exponential in the size of the formula and polynomial in the size of the Markov chain [9]. The bottleneck in developing a probabilistic model checker able to handle realistic systems is the construction of the state space and

J.-P. Katoen (Ed.): ARTS'99, LNCS 1601, pp. 96-110, 1999.

the necessity to solve huge systems of linear equations. This paper proposes a novel approach; it presents an implementation of probabilistic model checking using multi terminal binary decision diagrams (MTBDDs) to perform the probability calculations. MTBDDs, introduced in [8], differ from binary decision diagrams (BDDs) in that the leaves may have values other than 0 and 1; in this case the leaves contain transition probabilities. Hachtel et al. have used algebraic decision diagrams ADDs (same as MTBDDs) in the Markovian steady state analysis of large finite state machines (with up to 10^{27} states) [10]. MTBDDs can be integrated with a symbolic model checker and have the potential to outperform other matrix representations because they are very compact, by eliminating redundancy and allowing computations on sets of states rather than on individual states. While it is difficult to provide precise time complexity estimates for probabilistic model checking using MTBDDs, the success of BDDs in practice made the MTBDD representation worthwhile to explore.

We have developed ProbVerus, a probabilistic symbolic model checker, which combines Probabilistic Computation Tree Logic (PCTL) model checking [11] and symbolic techniques. PCTL, which allows the expression of time and probability, has been selected for its expressive power and the simplicity of the verification algorithms it involves. Sections 2 and 3 introduce the building blocks of ProbVerus, PCTL and MTBDDs. Section 4 describes ProbVerus with a short run down of the syntax and the semantics of ProbVerus programs.

In section 5 we demonstrate the use of ProbVerus in the verification of engineering systems by modeling and analyzing the reliability of a simple manufacturing system. By extending model checking to the analysis of probabilistic systems, we have been able to model the stochastic behavior of manufacturing systems: arrival time of successive raw workpieces, processing time on a machine, machine setup time, material handling time, message transmission time, lifetime of a tool, time to failure of a machine or a robot, repair time, and so on. Probabilistic model checking allows us to verify properties of these systems, such as "the probability of the system reaching a deadlock within the first 12 hours of operation is 2%". Such information is extremely useful in the design of such capital-intensive systems since deadlocks and unscheduled downtime of equipment due to failures are major factors on system performance. Section 6 reports the current status of ProbVerus and concludes with a discussion of the feasibility of the approach in realistic applications.

2 Probabilistic Computation Tree Logic

We use Probabilistic real time Computation Tree Logic (PCTL) introduced in [11]. PCTL augments Clarke, Emerson, and Sistla's CTL [7] with time and probability. The temporal operators (**F**, **G**, **U**) are extended with time bounds and probabilities ($\mathbf{F}^{\leq t}_{\geq p}$, $\mathbf{G}^{\leq t}_{\geq p}$, $\mathbf{U}^{\leq t}_{\geq p}$). The expressive power of the resulting logic is illustrated by the following examples:

- $req\,\mathbf{U}^{\leq t}_{\geq p}\,ack$: there is at least a probability p that there is an acknowledgment to the request within t units and req will be true until ack becomes true.

- $\mathbf{G}_{\geq p}^{\leq t}$ *Sysfail*: there is no system failure *Sysfail* for t time units with a probability of at least p.

- $\mathbf{F}_{\geq p}^{\leq t}$ *alarm*: there is a probability of at least p that an alarm will be generated within t time units.

PCTL formulas are interpreted over finite state discrete-time Markov chains. This model has been used in the analysis of complex probabilistic systems, such as dependability analysis of fault-tolerant real-time control systems and performance analysis of commercial computer systems and networks. The Markov model has been the standard model used for probabilistic model checking (Hart and Sharir [13], Lehman and Shelah [16], Vardi [17], Hansson and Jonsson [11], Alur, Courcoubetis, and Dill [1], Courcoubetis and Yannakakis [9], Aziz el al [2]).

Markov models are constructed from states and state transitions; a state describes the system at one time instant; a state transition describes the change in state at one tick. In discrete-time models, all state transitions occur at fixed intervals and are assigned probabilities. The basic underlying assumption is that the probability of a next state transition depends only on the current state. For reliability analyses, the Markov model fits with the standard assumption of constant failure rates, exponentially distributed interarrival times for failures, and Poisson arrivals of failures. Reliability models usually assume that repair of a failed system restores it so that the failure rate of the repaired system is the same as if no failure had occurred. This assumption is valid during the useful life cycle of a component, but not accurate for components that improve with time (burn-in period) or components subject to wear and aging (wear-out period). This assumption is made nevertheless to allow for analytic solutions.

Model of Computation. PCTL formulas are interpreted over labelled discrete time Markov chains. Formally, a *labelled Markov chain* is a tuple (S, s^i, T, L), where

- S is a finite set of *states*,

- s^i is an *initial state*,

- T is the *transition relation* $T = S \times S \rightarrow [0, 1]$ such that for all s in S we have
$$\sum_{s' \in S} T(s, s') = 1,$$

- L is a *labeling function* assigning atomic propositions to states, $L: S \rightarrow 2^{AP}$

A path π from a state s_0 is an infinite sequence $\pi = s_0\ s_1\ s_2 \dots s_n \dots$ of states with s_0 as the first state and nonzero transition probabilities $P(s_{i-1}, s_i) > 0$, $i=1, 2, \dots$. The first state is denoted by $first(\pi)$, the $k{+}1$th state of path π is denoted by $\pi(k)$. A prefix of π of length k is defined by $s_0 \rightarrow s_1 \rightarrow \dots \rightarrow s_k$. We define the probability measure *Prob* on the probability space $\langle Path_\omega(s), \Sigma(s) \rangle$, where $Path_\omega(s)$ is the set of infinite paths π with $first(\pi){=}s$, and $\Sigma(s)$ is the smallest σ-algebra on $Path_\omega(s)$ that contains the paths $\{\pi \in Path_\omega(s) : \tau \text{ is a prefix of } \pi\}$ where τ ranges over all finite execution sequences starting in s. The probability measure *Prob* on $Path_\omega(s)$ is the unique measure with

$$Prob\{\pi \in Path_\omega(s) : \tau \text{ is a prefix of } \pi\} =$$

$$P(\tau) = P(s_0 s_1 \dots s_k) = T(s_0, s_1) T(s_1, s_2) \dots T(s_{k-1}, s_k)$$

Syntax and Semantics of PCTL. PCTL formulas are state formulas, i.e they represent properties of states. Given a probabilistic process P described by a labelled Markov chain $M = (S, s^i, T, L)$, PCTL formulas are defined inductively as follows:

- Each atomic proposition is a state formula.

- If f_1 and f_2 are state formulas, then so are $\neg f_1$ and $(f_1 \wedge f_2)$.

- If f_1 and f_2 are state formulas and t is a nonnegative integer, then $f_1 \mathbf{U}^{\leq t} f_2$ (strong until) and $f_1 \mathbf{U}^{\leq t} f_2$ (weak until) are path formulas.

- If f is a path formula and p is a real number with $0 \leq p \leq 1$, then $[f]_{\geq p}$ and $[f]_{> p}$ are state formulas.

For a given state s, formulas $[f]_{\geq p}$ and $[f]_{> p}$ express that the probability of paths starting in s fulfilling the path formula f is at least p and greater than p, respectively. We discuss only the bounded operators.

The operator $\mathbf{U}$ is the *strong until* operator and $\mathbf{U}$ is the *weak until* operator. Intuitively, $[f_1 \mathbf{U}^{\leq t} f_2]_{\geq p}$ means that with a probability of at least p both f_2 will become true within t units and f_1 will hold until f_2 becomes true. $[f_1 \mathbf{U}^{\leq t} f_2]_{\geq p}$ means that there is at least a probability p that either f_1 will remain true for t time units, or that both f_2 will become true within t time units and that f_1 will hold until f_2 becomes true.

The truth of PCTL formulas for a labelled Markov chain $M = (S, s^i, T, L)$ is defined by the satisfaction relation $s \models_M f$ which intuitively means that the state formula is true at state s in M. To define the satisfaction relation for states we also use the relation $\sigma \models_M f$ which intuitively means that the path σ satisfies a path formula f in M. The relations are defined inductively as follows:

$s \models_M a$ if and only if the atomic proposition $a \in L(s)$

$s \models_M \neg f$ if and only if not $s \models_M f$

$s \models_M f_1 \wedge f_2$ if and only if $s \models_M f_1$ and $s \models_M f_2$

$s \models_M f_1 \vee f_2$ if and only if $s \models_M f_1$ or $s \models_M f_2$

$s \models_M f_1 \rightarrow f_2$ if and only if $s \models_M \neg f_1$ or $s \models_M f_2$

$\sigma \models_M f_1 \mathbf{U}^{\leq t} f_2$ if and only if there exists $i \leq t$ such that $\sigma(i) \models_M f_2$ and $\forall j : 0 \leq j < i : \sigma(j) \models_M f_1$

$\sigma \models_M f_1 \mathbf{U}^{\leq t} f_2$ if and only if $\sigma \models_M f_1 \mathbf{U}^{\leq t} f_2$ or $\forall j : 0 \leq j \leq t : \sigma(j) \models_M f_1$

$s \models_M [f_1 U^{\leq t} f_2]_{\geq p}$ if and only if the probability measure of the set of paths σ from s for which $\sigma \models_M [f_1 U^{\leq t} f_2]$ is at least p.

$s \models_M [f_1 U^{\leq t} f_2]_{\geq p}$ if and only if the probability measure of the set of paths σ from s for which $\sigma \models_M [f_1 U^{\leq t} f_2]$ is at least p.

$s \models_M [f_1 U^{\leq t} f_2]_{>p}$ if and only if the probability measure of the set of paths σ from s for which $\sigma \models_M [f_1 U^{\leq t} f_2]$ is greater than p.

$s \models_M [f_1 U^{\leq t} f_2]_{>p}$ if and only if the probability measure of the set of paths σ from s for which $\sigma \models_M [f_1 U^{\leq t} f_2]$ is greater than p.

By definition,

$$M \models \Phi \text{ if and only if } s^i \models \Phi$$

i.e., process P satisfies a PCTL formula Φ if and only if its initial state s^i satisfies Φ. We use the shorthand notation:

$$f_1 U^{\leq t}_{\geq p} f_2 \text{ for } [f_1 U^{\leq t} f_2]_{\geq p}$$

$$f_1 U^{\leq t}_{\geq p} f_2 \text{ for } [f_1 U^{\leq t} f_2]_{\geq p}$$

Formulas $f_1 U^{\leq t}_{>p} f_2$ and $f_1 U^{\leq t}_{>p} f_2$ have analogous meanings.

Model Checking in PCTL . Next we describe the model checking algorithm, which labels the states of a labelled Markov chain $M = (S, s^i, T, L)$ with the PCTL formula $f_1 U^{\leq t}_{\geq p} f_2$. We introduce the function $p(s, t)$ for $s \in S$ and t a non-negative integer, defined as the measure of the set of paths π starting in s which satisfy $f_1 U^{\leq t} f_2$:

$$p(s, t) = Prob\{\pi \in Path_\omega(s) : \sigma \text{ is a prefix of } \pi \text{ and } \sigma \models_M f_1 U^{\leq t} f_2\}$$

The probability function $p(s, t)$ satisfies the following recurrence equation. For $t \geq 1$:

$$p(s, t) = \text{if } s \models_M f_2 \text{ then } 1$$

$$\text{else if } s \not\models_M f_1 \text{ then } 0$$

$$\text{else } \sum_{s' \in S} T(s, s') \times p(s', t-1)$$

For $t = 0$, $p(s, t) = \text{if } s \models_M f_2$ then 1 else 0.

The proof of the above recurrence equation can be found in [11].

This recurrence equation leads to the following algorithm, which computes $\bar{p}(s,t)$ and labels states with $f_1 \mathbf{U}^{\leq t}_{\geq p} f_2$ if $\bar{p}(s, t)$ is greater or equal to the given probability p.

1. Build the transition probability matrix P

$$P[s_k, s_l] = \begin{cases} T[s_k, s_l] \text{ if } s_k \models f_1 \text{ and } s_k \not\models f_2 \\ 1 \text{ if } k = l \text{ and } s_k \models f_2 \text{ or } (s_k \not\models f_1 \text{ and } s_k \not\models f_2) \\ 0 \text{ otherwise} \end{cases}$$

2. Create a vector $\bar{v}$ indexed by the states such that the i-th element of $\bar{v}$ is set to 1 if $s_i \models f_2$ and 0 otherwise.

3. Compute P^t, the t-th power of the transition probability matrix.

4. Multiply matrix P^t by the vector $\bar{v}$: $\bar{p}(s, t) = P^t \bar{v}$

5. $s \models f_1 \mathbf{U}^{\leq t}_{\geq p} f_2$ if $\bar{p}(s, t) \geq p$.

6. $M \models f_1 \mathbf{U}^{\leq t}_{\geq p} f_2$ if and only if the initial state $s^i \models f_1 \mathbf{U}^{\leq t}_{\geq p} f_2$.

3 Multi-terminal Binary Decision Diagrams

BDDs are a canonical representation of boolean functions $f: \{0, 1\}^n \rightarrow \{0, 1\}$ proposed by Bryant [3]. They are often more compact than traditional normal forms, such as conjunctive normal form and disjunctive normal form, and can be manipulated efficiently. For these reasons, BDDs have found wide use in CAD applications, including symbolic simulation, verification of combinational logic, and verification of sequential circuits. In 1993 Clarke et. al [8] showed that BDDs can be generalized to represent functions $f: \{0, 1\}^n \rightarrow D$ where D is any set of values. Such diagrams are called multi terminal binary decision diagrams (MTBDDs). MTBDDs can be used to represent D-valued matrices efficiently.

MTBDD Representation of Labelled Markov Chains. Let $M = (S, s^i, T, L)$ be a labelled Markov chain. We fix an ordering of atomic propositions and identify each state with the boolean n-tuple $e(s)$ of atomic propositions that are true in that state. The transition probabilities are arguments of the function $F: \{0,1\}^{2n} \rightarrow [0,1]$, $F(x_1, y_1,..., x_n, y_n) = P((x_1,..., x_n)(y_1,..., y_n))$ which allows us to represent the transition probability matrix by an MTBDD over $(x_1, y_1,..., x_n, y_n)$.

The following example illustrates the MTBDD representation of the transition probability matrix: consider a single machine which may be in one of the following states: *setup, processing, down*. Figure 1 shows the state transition diagram, which captures the transitions between the possible states. After the setup operation, the machine starts processing, it makes a transition to the processing state with probability 1. In the processing state, there are two possibilities, the machine finishes processing

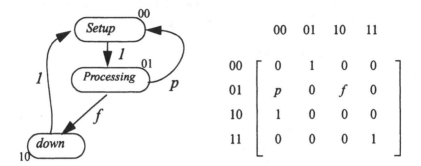

Figure 1. State Transition Graph and corresponding Transition Probability Matrix

and goes to the setup state, or the machine fails. We label the transition *setup → processing* with p and the transition *processing → down* with f, such that $p+f=1$. After the machine is repaired, it returns to the *setup* state with probability 1.

For simplicity, we use two atomic propositions, a_1 and a_2, to label the states: $L(setup) = \varnothing$, $L(processing) = \{a_1\}$, $L(down) = \{a_2\}$. We fix the order of a_1 and a_2 and encode the states as follows, $e(setup) = 00$, $e(processing) = 01$, $e(down) = 10$. Figures 2 and 3 show the function F, and the corresponding MTBDD respectively.

$$F(x_1, y_1, x_2, y_2) = \begin{cases} 1 \text{ if } x_1y_1x_2y_2 \in \{0001, 1000, 1111\} \\[1em] p \text{ if } x_1y_1x_2y_2 = 0010 \\[1em] f \text{ if } x_1y_1x_2y_2 = 0110 \\[1em] 0 \text{ otherwise} \end{cases}$$

Figure 2. Function $F(x_1, y_1, x_2, y_2)$

4 ProbVerus

ProbVerus is an implementation of PCTL model checking using symbolic techniques. It is an extension of Verus [6], a verification tool which combines powerful symbolic model checking techniques and efficient quantitative algorithms for computing minimum and maximum time delays between two events. Verus has been already used to verify several real-time systems: an aircraft controller, the PCI local bus, and a robotics controller [4, 5]. By extending Verus with PCTL model checking and MTBDDs we have created a single verification environment in which we have access to correctness checking, performance analysis, and reliability analysis of a single model of the system.

ProbVerus features a language which is designed especially to simplify writing probabilistic real-time programs. It is based on the core Verus language, an imperative

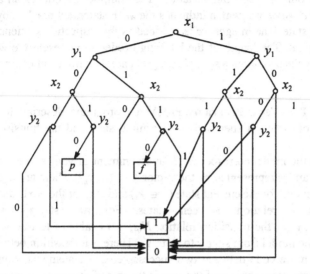

Figure 3. MTBDD representation of the Transition Probability Matrix

language with a syntax similar to C, that is enriched by special constructs that allow the straightforward expression of timing and stochastic behavior. Designers can use ProbVerus to verify models that are very close to the actual implementation expressing time and probabilities in a natural and accurate way.

Syntax of the ProbVerus Language. The ProbVerus language includes primary expressions, boolean expressions, assignments, sequential execution, conditionals, probabilistic choice, and loops:

stmt   ::= wait(1) | $v = expr$ | stmt$_1$; stmt$_2$ |

　　　　　while $cond$ stmt | if $cond$ stmt$_1$ else stmt$_2$

　　　　　pselect(p_1 : stmt$_1$; ... p_m : stmt$_m$)

　　　　　where $p_1 ... p_m \in [0, 1]$ with $p_1 + ... + p_m = 1$.

where
- *Var* is a set of boolean variables
- $v \in Var$
- *expr* are Verus expressions
- *expr*::= true | false | v | $expr_1$ ∥ $expr_2$ | $expr_1$ && $expr_2$ | !$expr$
- *cond* is a boolean expression

ProbVerus only has boolean variables. The compiler introduces an auxiliary variable, the *wait counter wc*, which indicates the `wait` statement reached by the program in the current state. The integer *wc* is encoded as the respective sequence of booleans to suit the format. The length of the bitstring needed to represent the *wait counter* is fixed and the values of *wc* in a specific program are determined at compile time of that program.

Semantics of ProbVerus Programs. ProbVerus programs describe Markov chains, the behavior of which is specified by the initial state and the transition probability matrix.

A *state* in the model corresponds to an assignment of values to the state variables $v_1, v_2, ..., v_n$ and is represented by the vector $\langle v_1, ..., v_n \rangle$. There are two copies of the state variables: one for the current state ($v \in V$) and one for the next state ($v' \in V'$). A *transition* is a relation between states. For two states $s = \langle v_1, ..., v_n \rangle$ $s' = \langle v'_1, ..., v'_n \rangle$, the transition relation $N(s, s')$ evaluates to true when there is a transition in the model from state s to state s'. There is a transition between two states s and s' when the code between two successive `wait` statements changes state s to state s'. An important feature of the tool is the use of the `wait` statement to synchronize concurrent processes, control time (time elapses by one unit at each `wait`), and update the values of the global program states. By executing a block of code between two consecutive `wait` statements atomically, thus collapsing contiguous statements to one transition, leads to models with fewer states, which allows the verification of much larger systems. The *transition relation* of the program is obtained by taking the disjunction of all relations between `wait` statements. A *path* in the transition graph is defined as a sequence of states $s_0, s_1, s_2, ...$ such that $N(s_i, s_{i+1})$ is true for every $i \geq 0$. All computations are performed on states reachable from the initial state set.

Our stochastic model does not consider nondeterminism; we define one initial state by assigning fixed values to all the state variables before the first `wait` statement. Verus restricts the set of accepted programs to those for which a `wait` statement is traversed at each loop iteration. The last statement of every accepted program ends with the statement

```
while (true) wait(1);
```

which guarantees that the final state is observed.

The semantics of ProbVerus programs is computed statement by statement using the following function R:

$$R: \text{stmt} \times M \times M \times N \rightarrow M \times M \times N \times B$$

where M is the set of matrices $m: ST \times ST \rightarrow [0,1]$, ST is the state space, N is the set of naturals, B is the set of booleans.

R has the following arguments:

- statement stmt,

- matrix $r: ST \times ST \rightarrow [0,1]$ containing the probabilities of the transitions in the program since the last wait statement, and

- transition probability matrix $m: ST \times ST \rightarrow [0, 1]$ accumulated between the previously executed wait statements

- $w \in N$ represents the number of syntactic occurrences of the wait statement encountered so far

Given the matrix r, the matrix m, and the counter w, which describe the program until the execution of statement stmt, function $R[\![\text{stmt}]\!] \langle r, m, w \rangle$ produces the matrix r', the matrix m', the counter w', which describe the program after executing stmt, and determines the value of $b \in B$, which is *true* if a wait statement is traversed in each control path through stmt.

[15] defines $R[\![\text{stmt}]\!] \langle r, m, w \rangle$ for the individual statements and includes a proof that the global transition probability matrix of a ProbVerus program is a stochastic matrix, i.e. the entries of the matrix are real numbers in the [0, 1.0] range and the sum of the elements of each row is equal to 1.

Implementation of PCTL Model Checking. We have implemented the *strong until* operator (algorithm on page 101), and the $F^{\leq t}_{\geq p}$, and $G^{\leq t}_{\geq p}$ operators and from the dual formulas [11]:

$$F^{\leq t}_{\geq p} f \equiv true \; U^{\leq t}_{\geq p} f$$

$$G^{\leq t}_{\geq p} f \equiv \neg F^{\leq t}_{>(1-p)} (\neg f)$$

All probability calculations are performed with MTBDDs and make use of the following operators:

APPLY Operator: The *APPLY* operator allows elementwise application of the binary operator *op* to two MTBDDs. If Q_1 and Q_2 are two MTBDDs, and *op* is an operation on the real numbers, then $APPLY(Q_1, Q_2, op)$ yields an MTBDD which represents the function $f(Q_1) \; op \; f(Q_2)$, where $f(Q_1)$ is the formula associated with Q_1, and $f(Q_2)$ the formula associated with Q_2.

Matrix and Vector Operators: The standard operations on matrices and vectors have corresponding operations on the MTBDDs that represent them, such as multiplication of a matrix by a vector or multiplication of two matrices. These operations benefit from the recursive structure of the MTBDD-representation of the respective matrices.

5 A Manufacturing Example

In this section we illustrate the use of ProbVerus with a simple example. We model the stochastic behavior and check stochastic properties of a small automated manufacturing system comprised of two numerically controlled machines *M1* and *M2* that are identical in all respects. Each machine is modeled as a Discrete Time Markov Chain (DTMC) that has three states: (0) the machine is being setup, (1) the machine is processing, and (2) the machine is undergoing repair following a breakdown. Figure 4 shows the state transition diagram, which captures the transitions among these three states. Each arc is labeled with the corresponding one-step transition probability; each transition corresponds to advancing the discrete time one time unit.

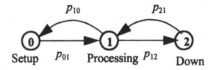

Figure 4. DTMC model of fail-prone machine under resume policy

After the setup operation the machine starts processing, hence after state 0 the next state is with certainty state 1 ($p_{01}=1$). If the current state is state 1, the next state is state 0 or state 2 with probabilities

$$p_{10} = \text{Prob\{processing finishes before failure\}}$$

$$p_{12} = \text{Prob\{failure occurs before finishing of processing\}}$$

After undergoing repair the machine resumes the processing operation, hence if the current state is state 2, then the next state is always state 1 ($p_{21}=1$).

We can describe the behavior of the above machine in ProbVerus as follows.

Figure 6 displays the DTMC model of the AMS comprised of the two machines M1 and M2. In state **s0** the two machines are being setup. In state **s1** one of the two machines is processing and in state **s2** both machines are processing. While a machine is processing, there are two possibilities: either the machine finishes and returns to the setup state or the machine fails. In **s3** one of the machines fails which then moves for repair in state **s4**. The system is down when both machines are under repair (state **s5**).

Using ProbVerus, we have modeled the AMS of Figure 6 and checked the PCTL formula $F^{\leq t}_{\geq p}$ AMS_is_down, which states that AMS will fail, i.e. that it will reach a state labeled with AMS_is_down (machine M1 is down and machine M2 is down), within t

```
Machine = Setup;
wait(1.0);

while (Machine != Down) {
        if ( Machine == Setup) {
                Machine = Processing;
                wait(1.0);
        }
        else if ( Machine == Processing) {
                pselect {p10: Machine = Setup; p12: Machine = Down;};
                wait(1.0);
        }
}
Machine = Processing;

while (true) {wait(1.0);}
```

Figure 5. ProbVerus model of a fail-prone machine

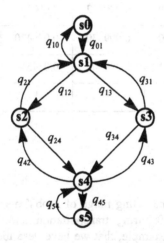

Figure 6. State Transition Graph of a Two-Machine Manufacturing System

units after the setup of the system with non-zero probability p. We have used the following one-step transition probabilities:

$q_{01}=1$,

$q_{10}=0.1663$, $q_{12}=0.8316$, $q_{13}=0.0021$,

$q_{21}=0.987654$, $q_{24}=0.0123456$,

$q_{31}=0.04762$, $q_{34}=0.95238$,

$q_{42}=0.19802$, $q_{43}=0.79208$, $q_{45}=0.0099$,

$q_{54}=1$,

to compute the probabilities of reaching the state where both machines are down for the first 5 time units of operation of the AMS, as seen in Table 1. For example, after 4 time units all states are labeled with the $F^{\leq 4}_{\geq 0,00012}$ AMS_is_down since $P(s_i, 4) \geq 0,000121$ for all the states s_i. Such properties are expressible in PCTL since PCTL formulas are interpreted over DTMCs, where each transition of the Markov chain corresponds to one time unit.

Table 1. Successive values of p of $F^{\leq t}_{\geq p}$ AMS_is_down

state/ time	0	1	2	3	4	5
s_0	0	0.000000	0.000000	0.000000	0.000121	0.000121
s_1	0	0.000000	0.000000	0.000000	0.000121	0.000333
s_2	0	0.000000	0.000122	0.000122	0.000334	0.000335
s_3	0	0.000000	0.009430	0.009430	0.016570	0.016570
s_4	0	0.009901	0.009900	0.017394	0.017394	0.023100
s_5	1	1	1	1	1	1

6 Current Status

We have been testing the modeling range of ProbVerus with success in a series of application domains: manufacturing, transportation, and fault-tolerant industrial process control systems. The example, that we have described, demonstrates that Prob-Verus provides the language to describe the stochastic behavior of manufacturing systems in a straightforward manner. PCTL allows the expression of the stochastic properties, which is critical information when designing automated manufacturing systems and analyzing their performance, availability, and reliability. Moreover, probabilistic model checking allows us to combine the performance (quantitative timing analysis) and reliability (quantitative probability analysis) early in the design phase of manufacturing systems. This is significant because real-world automated manufacturing systems must meet competitive levels of productivity and pay-back ratio where high costs are involved.

An important question is how our techniques scale up to large systems. Our largest case study is based on ACC ("Apparato Centrale a Calcolatore") [14], a complex industrial safety-critical system developed by Ansaldo Transporti for the control of medium and large-size railway stations. A set of qualitative (e.g. safety, liveness) and quantitative (e.g. response times and probabilities) properties have been automatically analyzed. Despite the complexity of the system (the model has about 10^{27} states) specifications were checked in 329 seconds using a Sparc 10 with dual processors and 256Mb of memory. During the verification of the ACC design, we discovered a subtle and anomalous behavior leading to a deadlock of the system. The anomalous behavior was pinpointed by an automatically generated counterexample trace, showing precisely the behavior leading to the violating state. The same behavior blocked the entire operation during a field test of an earlier version of the system. When we modeled possible failures in the communication between the controller and the physical devices, i.e. when the control variables of the *safety logic* are not in agreement with the values of the corresponding physical level crossing variables, then safety specifications were violated. Therefore, a failure in the sensing operation may lead to a CLEAR_SIGNAL although the gate may be still moving, or the actual level crossing is not closed. We have computed the probability of reaching unsafe states within seconds. Our numerical analysis has been performed assuming a serial link between the controller and the physical devices for which reliability information is published. Vital railway controllers, such as the ACC system, implement appropriate error recovery mechanisms for the occurrence of vital/non-vital communication failures, which have not been modeled. Our probabilistic analysis has intended to illustrate the valuable information probabilistic model checking can provide to the engineers who design and validate safety-critical systems.

7 Conclusions and Future Work

This paper presents a new tool for the formal verification of stochastic systems. We have implemented PCTL model checking using multi terminal binary decision diagrams (MTBDDs) within the Verus verification tool. The PCTL logic allows the expression of time and probabilities which are needed for the verification of stochastic systems, such as fault-tolerant real-time control systems, networks, and manufacturing systems. BDDs and MTBDDs provide a compact representation of the model by representing sets of states rather than individual states. Moreover, symbolic techniques are amenable to efficient verification algorithms. By extending Verus, we have created an environment which allows the verification and quantitative analysis of a single model using CTL, RTCTL, and PCTL model checking. While model checking can tell us whether a system is correct, probabilistic model checking can also tell us whether the system is timely and reliable. Moreover, an advantage of probabilistic model checkers over non-probabilistic model checkers is that it allows one to verify properties that may not be true with probability equal to one, but may still hold with some acceptable probability. ProbVerus allows the safety analysis and verification to take place concurrently with the system design so that design errors are detected and corrected prior to the traditional test phase. The use of symbolic techniques (BDDs and MTBDDs) in contrast to an explicit-state implementation of PCTL model checking makes it possible to analyze larger systems making probabilistic symbolic model checking a feasible approach worth further development.

References

1. R. Alur, C. Courcoubetis, D. Dill. Model Checking for Probabilistic Real-time Systems. Automata, Languages, and Programming 18th International Colloquium Proceedings; Madrid, Spain; 8-12 July 1991.
2. A. Aziz, V. Singhal, F. Balarin, R. K. Brayton, A.L. Sangiovanni-Vincentelli. It usually works: the temporal logic of stochastic systems. In Proceedings of CAV'95.
3. R. E. Bryant. Graph-based algorithms for boolean function manipulation. IEEE Transactions on Computers, C-35(8), 1986.
4. S. Campos, E. Clarke, W. Marrero, M. Minea and H. Hiraishi, Computing quantitative characteristics of finite-state real-time systems. In IEEE Real-Time Systems Symposium, 1994.
5. S. Campos and E. Clarke, Real-time symbolic model checking for discrete time models. In AMAST Series in Computing: Theories and Experiences for Real-Time System Development. T. Rus, C. Rattray, editors. World Scientific Publishing Company, 1995.
6. S. V. Campos. A Quantitative Approach to the Formal Verification of Real-Time Systems. Ph.D. Thesis, School of Computer Science, Carnegie Mellon University, 1996.
7. E. M. Clarke, E. A. Emerson. Synthesis of Synchronization Skeletons for Branching Time Temporal Logic. Logic of Programs: Workshop, Yorktown Heights, NY, May 1981, volume 131 of Lecture Notes in Computer Science. Springer Verlag, 1981.
8. E. M. Clarke, M. Fujita, P.C. McGeer, K. McMillan, J. C.-Y. Yang, X. Zhao. Multi-Terminal Binary Decision Diagrams: An Efficient Data Structure for Matrix Representation. IWLS '93: International Workshop on Logic Synthesis. Tahoe City, May 1993.
9. C. Courcoubetis, M. Yannakakis. The Complexity of Probabilistic Verification. Journal of the Association for Computing Machinery, Vol. 42, No. 4, July 1995.
10. G. Hachtel, E. Macii, A. Pardo, F.Somenzi. Markovian Analysis of Large Finite State Machines. IEEE Transactions on Computer-Aided Design of Integrated Circuits and Systems, Vol. 15. No. 12, December 1996.
11. H. Hansson and B. Jonsson. A Framework for Reasoning about Time and Reliability. In Proceedings of 10th IEEE Real Time System Symposium, pp. 102-111, 1989.
12. H. Hansson. Time and Probability in Formal Design of Distributed Systems. Elsevier, 1994.
13. S. Hart and M. Sharir. Probabilistic Temporal Logics for Finite and Bounded Models. In Proceedings of the ACM Symposium on the Theory of Computing, pp. 1-13, 1984.
14. V. Hartonas-Garmhausen, S. Campos, A. Cimatti, E. Clarke, F. Giunchiglia. Verification of a Safety-Critical Railway Interlocking System with Real-Time Constraints. In Proceedings of FTCS-28 The Twenty-Eighth Annual International Symposium on Fault-Tolerant Computing, pages 458-463, June, 1998.
15. V. Hartonas-Garmhausen. Probabilistic Symbolic Model Checking with Engineering Models and Applications. Ph.D. Thesis. Carnegie Institute of Technology, Carnegie Mellon University, 1998.
16. D. Lehmann and S. Shelah. Reasoning with time and chance. Information and Control 53, pp. 165-198, 1982.
17. M. Vardi. Automatic verification of probabilistic concurrent finite-state programs. In Proceedings of the 26th IEEE Symposium on Foundations of Computer Science. IEEE, New York, pp. 327-338, 1985.

Process Algebra with Probabilistic Choice*

Suzana Andova

Department of Computing Science
Eindhoven University of Technology
P.O.Box 513, 5600 Eindhoven, The Netherlands
suzana@win.tue.nl

Abstract. Published results show that various models may be obtained by combining parallel composition with probability and with or without non-determinism. In this paper we treat this problem in the setting of process algebra in the form of *ACP*. First, probabilities are introduced by an operator for the internal probabilistic choice. In this way we obtain the Basic Process Algebra with probabilistic choice *prBPA*. Afterwards, *prBPA* is extended with parallel composition to ACP_π^+. We give the axiom system for ACP_π^+ and a complete operational semantics that preserves the interleaving model for the dynamic concurrent processes. Considering the PAR protocol, a communication protocol that can be used in the case of unreliable channels, we investigate the applicability of ACP_π^+. Using in addition only the priority operator and the pre-abstraction operator we obtain a recursive specification of the behaviour of the protocol that can be viewed as a Markov chain.

1 Introduction

Due to the increasing complexity and the number of components of real-life parallel systems, the probability that a system or some of its components will be subject to failure during the work is increased, as well. This means that very often it is desirable or even necessary to "predict" chances of failure occurring in the system. Therefore, it is insufficient to assume that the system is reliable and to specify it under this assumption, but there is a need to describe the probabilistic behaviour of the components and the system as a whole. For the last ten years various traditional specification formalisms have been extended with a notion of probabilistic behaviour for different models of probabilistic processes.

Besides this new, probabilistic approach in modelling concurrent systems, non-determinism still has an essential role specially due to interleaving of activities of independent components of a system. In treating non-determinism mainly two different approaches have been followed, one approach which allows both non-deterministic and probabilistic choices (e.g. concurrent Markov chains [16], the alternating model [12]), and one where only probabilistic choice is allowed ([14,10,11,13,6,9]).

* Research is supported by PROMACS project, SION 612-10-000 of the Netherlands Organisation for Scientific Research (NWO)

J.-P. Katoen (Ed.): ARTS'99, LNCS 1601, pp. 111–129, 1999.
© Springer-Verlag Berlin Heidelberg 1999

The objective of this paper is to introduce a probabilistic version of ACP ([3,7]) where non-determinism and probability are combined.

Following the idea of ACP-like process algebra for interleaving parallel composition, we first investigated a probabilistic version of ACP, $prACP$, where the axiom $x \parallel y = x \Lleft y + y \Lleft x + x \mid y$ holds for arbitrary processes x and y. This axiom leads to a situation where processes that depend on each other in their probabilistic behaviour are involved in merging atomic actions of x with those of y. In Section 3 we give an example of merge of parallel processes and point out an unwanted outcome that occurs. So we rejected this approach, as it is not suitable for specification of some concurrent systems such as for example PAR protocol.

Thus, we propose in this paper a new variant of the extension of $prBPA$ by parallel composition. We still keep the idea of the interleaving model but this time only for dynamic processes (processes that do only trivial probabilistic transition with probability 1). This novel process algebra has a more complex axiom system than $prACP$ in [1]. But an advantage here is a simple and intuitively clear operational semantics. We use an extra quaternary operator $\llbracket$, called merge with memory, which helps in axiomatising the merge of dynamic processes. This operator is not necessary in the sense that an equivalent algebra, called ACP_π, can be obtained by adding new axioms without any extra operators. These two process algebras, ACP_π and the presented ACP_π^+ are equivalent but only for processes that do not contain the $\Lleft$, $\mid$ and $\llbracket$ operators. This version of combining probabilities and parallel composition in the framework of interleaving approach is proposed in [9] where the authors use bundle probabilistic transition systems.

The operational semantics of ACP_π^+ is based on the alternating model of [12] and it is defined by a term deduction system of which the signature contains an extended set of constants (each atomic action has a dynamic counterpart) and of which the deduction rules include two transition types: probabilistic and action transition. The probability associated to a probabilistic transition is determined by the value of a probability distribution function. In the construction of the term models we use probabilistic bisimulation as proposed by Larsen and Skou ([14]) and we show soundness and completeness of the term model with respect to proposed axiom systems.

Dealing with the PAR protocol ([15]) a communication protocol used in cases of unreliable channels, we investigate the applicability of ACP_π^+. We give a specification in ACP_π^+ of the constituent processes of the protocol and of the whole system. In order to do performance analysis, non-determinism has to be resolved. Using in addition only the priority operator and the pre-abstraction operator [2] we obtain a recursive specification of the behaviour of the protocol that can be viewed as a Markov chain.

2   Basic Process Algebra

We give a brief introduction of Basic Process Algebra with probabilistic choice and a complete operational semantics.

The signature of Basic Process Algebra with probabilistic choice, *prBPA*, consists of a (finite) set of constants $A = \{a, b, c, \ldots\}$, a special constant $\delta \notin A$ (we usually denote $A_\delta = A \cup \{\delta\}$) and the binary operators: $+$ (non-deterministic choice), $\cdot$ (sequential composition) and $\boxplus_\pi$ (probabilistic choice) for each $\pi \in \langle 0, 1 \rangle$. The probabilistic choice operator is modeled after the partial choice operator of [5]. Intuitively, process $x \boxplus_\pi y$ behaves like x with probability π and behaves like y with probability $1 - \pi$. The choice is already made, and cannot be influenced by the environment. We can observe the outcome, and the probability distribution of the possible outcomes. The axioms for $+$ and $\cdot$ are standard axioms for BPA_δ ([3]) (Table 1, $a \in A$), except that axiom $A3$ $(x + x = x)$ is restricted to atomic actions. $A3$ is restricted, because it does not hold anymore for processes that contain the new choice operator. In our intuition about combining non-determinism and probabilistic choice, the "top" operator is the probabilistic choice, that is we consider that the probabilistic choice is made first and later non-deterministic choice. In such a way in the process $(a \boxplus_\pi b) + (a \boxplus_\pi b)$ non-deterministic choice between actions a and b is possible with a certain probability which is not a case in the process $a \boxplus_\pi b$. The axioms for the new operators are shown in Table 2 ($\pi \in \langle 0, 1 \rangle$).

$$
\begin{array}{lll}
x + y & = y + x & A1 \\
(x + y) + z & = x + (y + z) & A2 \\
a + a & = a & AA3 \\
(x + y) \cdot z & = x \cdot z + y \cdot z & A4 \\
(x \cdot y) \cdot z & = x \cdot (y \cdot z) & A5 \\
x + \delta & = x & A6 \\
\delta \cdot x & = \delta & A7
\end{array}
$$

Table 1. BPA_δ with restricted $A3$.

$$
\begin{array}{lll}
x \boxplus_\pi y & = y \boxplus_{1-\pi} x & Pr\,AC1 \\
x \boxplus_\pi (y \boxplus_\rho z) & = (x \boxplus_{\frac{\pi}{\pi + \rho - \pi\rho}} y) \boxplus_{\pi + \rho - \pi\rho} z & Pr\,AC2 \\
x \boxplus_\pi x & = x & Pr\,AC3 \\
(x \boxplus_\pi y) \cdot z & = x \cdot z \boxplus_\pi y \cdot z & Pr\,AC4 \\
(x \boxplus_\pi y) + z & = (x + z) \boxplus_\pi (y + z) & Pr\,AC5
\end{array}
$$

Table 2. Additional axioms for *prBPA*.

We introduce abbreviations in order to deal with probabilistic sums of several arguments:

$$
x \boxplus_\pi y \boxplus_\rho z \equiv x \boxplus_\pi (y \boxplus_{\frac{\rho}{1-\pi}} z) \qquad (\pi + \rho < 1)
$$
$$
x \boxplus_\pi y \boxplus_\rho z \boxplus_\sigma w \equiv x \boxplus_\pi (y \boxplus_{\frac{\rho}{1-\pi}} z \boxplus_{\frac{\sigma}{1-\pi}} w) \qquad (\pi + \rho + \sigma < 1), \text{ etc.}
$$

Example 1. By this example we show the interpretation of non-determinism when it is combined with probabilistic choice. In Figure 1 the transition systems for the processes are shown.

$$(a \boxplus_{\frac{1}{2}} b) + (c \boxplus_{\frac{1}{3}} d) = (a + c) \boxplus_{\frac{1}{6}} (a + d) \boxplus_{\frac{1}{3}} (b + c) \boxplus_{\frac{1}{6}} (b + d).$$

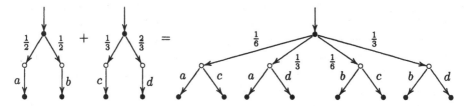

Fig. 1. An example of non-deterministic choice between probabilistic processes

In [5], the authors propose a method for verification which is based on a partial ordering of processes. They introduce the realization axiom $x \leq x \boxplus y$, which says that x has less static non-determinism than $x \boxplus y$. By the following proposition we show that this approach cannot be followed in the framework of *prBPA* because such a partial ordering of processes cannot be defined when probabilities are involved.

Proposition 1. *If prBPA $\vdash p = q \boxplus_\pi p$ for some probability $\pi \in \langle 0, 1 \rangle$, then prBPA $\vdash p \approx q$, where $p \approx q$ denotes the probability of p be equal to q has a limit of 1.* □

We define basic terms as representatives of classes of closed terms. Theorem 2, the Elimination theorem, shows that each closed term can be reduced to a basic term. We distinguish two types of basic terms: terms that are constants or that have a non-deterministic choice or a sequential composition as the outermost operator (we denote a set of these terms by $\mathcal{B}_+$) and the basic terms of the second type are such that have a probabilistic choice as the outermost operator. The precise definition of basic *prBPA* terms is given in [1].

Remark. If we consider terms that only differ in the order of the summands to be identical (i.e. we work modulo axioms $A1$, $A2$, $PrAC1$ and $PrAC2$) we have that the basic terms are exactly the terms of the form

$$x \equiv x_1 \quad \text{or} \tag{1}$$

$$x \equiv x_1 \boxplus_{\pi_1} x_2 \boxplus_{\pi_2} x_3 \ldots x_{n-1} \boxplus_{\pi_{n-1}} x_n \text{ and } n > 1 \tag{2}$$

where for each $i, 1 \leq i \leq n$, $x_i \equiv \sum_{j<l_i} a_{ij} t_{ij} + \sum_{k<m_i} b_{ik}$ for certain atomic actions a_{ij} and b_{ik}, basic terms t_{ij} and $n, m_i, l_i \in \mathbb{N}$. We have the convention that: $\sum_{j<0} s_j \equiv \delta$.

Theorem 2 *(Elimination theorem) Let p be a closed prBPA term. Then there is a basic prBPA term q such that prBPA ⊢ p = q.*   □

Further, by $\mathcal{SP}$ (the set of static processes) we will denote the set of all closed terms over the signature of *prBPA*, Σ_{prBPA}. By **D** we denote a set of closed *prBPA* terms of which an associated basic term, which exists by the Elimination theorem, is a term from $\mathcal{B}_+$.

2.1   Structured Operational Semantics of *prBPA*

The operational semantics consists of two types of transition rules, probabilistic transitions and action transitions and it is based on the alternating model as it is proposed in [12]. Each process in our model may make either probabilistic transitions or atomic transitions, but not both. Action transitions are labelled with atomic actions: $\overset{a}{\rightarrow}$. Although in the presentation of processes as probabilistic transition systems we will use labelled probabilistic transitions as $\overset{\pi}{\rightarrow}$, in the formal description of the operational semantics probabilistic transitions are unlabelled: $\rightsquigarrow$. If process p may do a probabilistic transition to process x, there is a non-zero probability with which process p may behave as process x. The probability that this transition may happen is determined by a probability distribution function $\mu(p, x)$.

In order to distinguish processes that may do a probabilistic transition and processes that may do an action transition we consider a term deduction system with a signature different from the signature of *prBPA* by the addition of new constants. If A is the set of atomic actions of *prBPA* then we define the set of dynamic atomic actions $\breve{A}_\delta = \{\breve{a} \mid a \in A_\delta\}$. By a symbol $\breve{a}$, $(a \neq \delta)$ we denote a process that can successfully terminate by executing a. Further we will write $\breve{\Sigma}_{prBPA}$ for $(A_\delta \cup \breve{A}_\delta, +, \cdot, \boxplus_\pi)$.

Definition 3 *We define the set of dynamic processes $\mathcal{DP}$ (processes that may do an action transition) in the following way:*

1. $\breve{A}_\delta \subseteq \mathcal{DP}$;
2. $s \in \mathcal{DP}, t \in \mathcal{SP} \Rightarrow s \cdot t \in \mathcal{DP}$;
3. $t, s \in \mathcal{DP} \Rightarrow t + s \in \mathcal{DP}$.

By $\mathcal{PR}$ we denote the set of all static and dynamic processes, that is $\mathcal{PR} = \mathcal{SP} \cup \mathcal{DP}$. Moreover, there is a bijection from **D** to $\mathcal{DP}$.

The operational semantics of *prBPA* is given by the term deduction system $\breve{T} = (\breve{\Sigma}_{prBPA}, D)$ induced by the deduction rules shown in Table 3 where a is a variable that ranges over the set A, and the probability distribution function as it is defined in Definition 4.

$$a \rightsquigarrow \breve{a} \qquad \delta \rightsquigarrow \breve{\delta} \qquad \frac{p \rightsquigarrow x}{p \cdot q \rightsquigarrow x \cdot q}$$

$$\frac{p \rightsquigarrow x, q \rightsquigarrow y}{p + q \rightsquigarrow x + y} \qquad \frac{p \rightsquigarrow x}{p \boxplus_\pi q \rightsquigarrow x, q \boxplus_\pi p \rightsquigarrow x}$$

$$\breve{a} \xrightarrow{a} \sqrt{} \qquad \frac{x \xrightarrow{a} x'}{x \cdot y \xrightarrow{a} x' \cdot y} \qquad \frac{x \xrightarrow{a} \sqrt{}}{x \cdot y \xrightarrow{a} y}$$

$$\frac{x \xrightarrow{a} x'}{x + y \xrightarrow{a} x', y + x \xrightarrow{a} x'} \qquad \frac{x \xrightarrow{a} \sqrt{}}{x + y \xrightarrow{a} \sqrt{}, y + x \xrightarrow{a} \sqrt{}}$$

Table 3. Deduction rules of *prBPA*.

Definition 4 *(Probability distribution function) We define a probability distribution function* $\mu : \mathcal{PR} \times \mathcal{PR} \to [0,1]$ *as follows: for each* $x \in \mathcal{PR}$

$$
\begin{aligned}
\mu(a, \breve{a}) &= 1, \\
\mu(\delta, \breve{\delta}) &= 1, \\
\mu(p \cdot q, x' \cdot q) &= \mu(p, x'), \\
\mu(p + q, x' + x'') &= \mu(p, x')\mu(q, x''), \\
\mu(p \boxplus_\pi q, x) &= \pi\mu(p, x) + (1 - \pi)\mu(q, x), \\
\mu(p, x) &= 0 \ \text{otherwise}.
\end{aligned}
$$

Because in the construction of the term model we use the Larsen-Skou probabilistic bisimulation relation (Definition 7) we need to extend the probability distribution function to the power set of $\mathcal{PR}$.

Definition 5 *We define the map* $\mu^* : PR \times 2^{\mathcal{PR}} \to [0,1]$ *as: for each* $M \subseteq \mathcal{PR}$

$$\mu^*(p, M) = \sum_{x \in M} \mu(p, x).$$

Proposition 6. *The map* μ^* *is well defined.* □

From now on we will denote $\mu^*(p, M)$ simply by $\mu(p, M)$.

Definition 7 *Let* R *be an equivalence relation on the set of processes* $\mathcal{PR}$. R *is a probabilistic bisimulation if the following four clauses are satisfied:*

1. *If* pRq *and* $p \rightsquigarrow s$, *then there is a term* t *such that* $q \rightsquigarrow t$ *and* sRt;
2. *If* sRt *and* $s \xrightarrow{a} p$ *for some* $a \in A$, *then there is a term* q *such that* $t \xrightarrow{a} q$ *and* pRq;

3. If sRt and $s \xrightarrow{a} \sqrt{}$, then $t \xrightarrow{a} \sqrt{}$;

4. If pRq, then $\mu(p, M) = \mu(q, M)$ for each $M \in \mathcal{PR}/R$.

We say that p is *probabilistically bisimilar* to q, denote $p \leftrightarrow q$, if there is a probabilistic bisimulation R such that pRq.

Below we give some obtained technical results. The detailed proofs of these propositions are given in [1].

Proposition 8. *If p is a $\mathcal{SP}$ term and $p \rightsquigarrow x$, then $x \in \mathcal{DP}$.*   □

Proposition 9. *If x is a $\mathcal{DP}$ term and $x \xrightarrow{a} y$ for some $a \in A$, then $y \in \mathcal{SP}$.*   □

Remark. From Proposition 8 and 9 it follows easily that we may consider:

1. $\rightsquigarrow \subseteq \mathcal{SP} \times \mathcal{DP}$,
2. $\xrightarrow{a} \subseteq \mathcal{DP} \times \mathcal{SP}$,
3. $\xrightarrow{a} \sqrt{} \subseteq \mathcal{DP}$,
4. for every probabilistic bisimulation R we have $R \subseteq \mathcal{SP} \times \mathcal{SP} \cup \mathcal{DP} \times \mathcal{DP}$.

Theorem 10 $\leftrightarrow$ *is a congruence relation on prBPA.*   □

Theorem 11 *(Soundness) Let p and q be closed prBPA terms. If $prBPA \vdash p = q$ then $p \leftrightarrow q$.*   □

Proposition 12. *Let p be a closed prBPA term and $a \in A$ and let $op(p)$ be the number of operators of p. Then:*

i. *if $p \rightsquigarrow \breve{x}$ then $prBPA \vdash p = x$ and $\mu(p, \breve{x}) = 1$ and $op(x) \leq op(p)$ or $prBPA \vdash p = x \boxplus_{\mu(p,\breve{x})} q$ for some $q \in \mathcal{SP}$ and $\mu(p, \breve{x}) < 1$;*

ii. *if $\breve{p} \xrightarrow{a} \sqrt{}$ then $prBPA \vdash p = a + p$;*

iii. *if $\breve{p} \xrightarrow{a} q$ then $prBPA \vdash p = a \cdot q + p$.*   □

Lemma 13 *If p, q and r are closed prBPA terms and $\pi \in \langle 0, 1 \rangle$ such that $p \boxplus_\pi q \leftrightarrow p \boxplus_\pi r$, then $q \leftrightarrow r$.*   □

Theorem 14 *(Completeness) Let p and q be closed prBPA terms. If $p \leftrightarrow q$ then $prBPA \vdash p = q$.*   □

3   Extension with Merge and Communication

Published results concerning design of probabilistic concurrent systems show various possibilities for combining parallel composition with probability with or without non-determinism. Different approaches lead to various formalisms and theories that treat this problem as well as various semantics. Following the idea of ACP-like process algebra for interleaving parallel composition, we studied a probabilistic version of ACP, $prACP$ in [1], where the choice of the process which executes the next action is considered to be non-deterministic choice, and where according to this, the axiom $x \parallel y = x \lfloor\!\lfloor y + y \lfloor\!\lfloor x + x \mid y$ holds for arbitrary processes x and y. In this way we obtain a theory with very simple set of axioms (if we do not consider the axioms for the new operator, these axioms are in essence the same as those of ACP), but unfortunately it is not the case with the associated complete operational semantics which defines the term model of this process algebra where the crucial deduction rule (for parallel composition) is

$$\frac{p \rightsquigarrow x, q \rightsquigarrow y, p \rightsquigarrow x', q \rightsquigarrow y'}{p \parallel q \rightsquigarrow x \lfloor\!\lfloor q + y \lfloor\!\lfloor p + x' \mid y'}.$$ In [1] we give an example of an application of this

process algebra for specification and performance analysis of concurrent systems, considering the Alternating Bit Protocol. But we realised that this approach to parallel composition does not give the anticipate results for some concurrent probabilistic processes, as the following example shows.

Let us consider the processes $P \equiv send_1$ and $Q \equiv read_1 \boxplus_\pi fail$. The process P executes the action $send_1$ which may be treated as "send a datum at the port 1" and the process Q executes the action $read_1$ with probability π, that is with probability π it reads the datum at the port 1, or executes the action $fail$ with probability $1 - \pi$, that is it fails with probability $1 - \pi$ and no further communication with the process P is possible. We remark that this situation is a realistic one when an unreliable transmission channel is designed (Section 4). We define a communication action $comm_1 = send_1 \mid read_1$. By intuition we expect that the behaviour of the whole system $\partial_H(P \parallel Q)$, for $H = \{send_1, read_1\}$, is described by the process $comm_1 \boxplus_\pi fail \cdot \delta$. But we obtain the following equation:

$$prACP \vdash \partial_H(P \parallel Q) = comm_1 \boxplus_{\pi^2} fail \cdot \delta \boxplus_{(1-\pi)^2} (fail \cdot \delta + comm_1) \boxplus_{(1-\pi)\pi} \delta.$$
As a consequence of the axiom mentioned above and the interpretation given of the non-deterministic choice between probabilistic processes, a possibility to combine probabilistically dependent processes $fail$ and $comm_1$ in a non-deterministic choice arises. Moreover, there is a non-zero probability with which deadlock may occur. It is obvious that this process does not satisfy our intuition about the behaviour of the parallel composition given above.

In order to overcome this difficulty, we propose in this paper a new variant of the extension of $prBPA$ by parallel composition. Again, we want to keep the idea of the interleaving model but only for dynamic processes. For instance, let us consider the processes $X = a \boxplus_{\frac{1}{2}} b$ and $Y = c \boxplus_{\frac{1}{3}} d$. Since X may execute a with probability $\frac{1}{2}$ and Y may execute c with probability $\frac{1}{3}$, the probability of merging a and c in the parallel composition $X \parallel Y$ is exactly the product of the separate probabilities, so it is $\frac{1}{6}$. After the first action occurrence, for instance if a has been performed, an outcome among the actions c and d has not been known yet, so each of these two actions may be performed in accordance with the given probabilities. In Figure 2 the transition system of $X \parallel Y$ is shown, where $a \mid c = e$, $a \mid d = f$, $b \mid c = g$ and $b \mid d = h$. This version of combining probabilities and parallel composition with the interleaving reasoning is proposed in [9] where authors use bundle probabilistic transition systems.

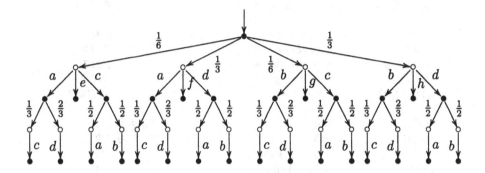

Fig. 2. An example of parallel composition of probabilistic processes.

3.1   Process Algebra

Below we give a definition (the signature and the axiom system) of the probabilistic version of ACP, called Algebra of communicating processes with probabilistic choice ACP_π^+, where + stands for the extra merge operator added to this algebra. We remark that this probabilistic version of ACP has a more complex axiom system than the algebra proposed in [1]. But an advantage here is a simple and intuitively clear operational semantics.

The signature of ACP_π^+ consists of the operators of $prBPA$, three binary operators: $\parallel$ (merge), $\rlap{\parallel}\,\_$ (left merge) and $\mid$ (communication merge), a unary operator ∂_H (encapsulation) where $H \subseteq A$ and a quaternary operator $\rlap{]}[$ (merge with memory). The axioms of the new operators are given in Table 4 together with the conditional axioms given in Table 5 and 6.

The idea behind the merge with memory operator is to delay a merge of two concurrent processes (the first and the third arguments) as long as at least one of them has a possibility for nontrivial probabilistic choice (the axioms $PrMM2$ and $PrMM3$). If none of them has a possibility for a nontrivial probabilistic choice (the condition $x = x + x$ & $y = y + y$), then the processes may be merged. The other two auxiliary arguments (the second and fourth) help in the realisation of the interleaving model as it was mentioned in the previous example. Actually, they contain the two processes which have started parallel composition, because in further derivation these processes may get lost.

$x \parallel y$	$= (x,x) \,]\!\![\, (y,y)$	$PrMM1$
$(x \boxplus_\pi x', z) \,]\!\![\, (y,w)$	$= (x,z) \,]\!\![\, (y,w) \boxplus_\pi (x',z) \,]\!\![\, (y,w)$	$PrMM2$
$(x,z) \,]\!\![\, (y \boxplus_\pi y', w)$	$= (x,z) \,]\!\![\, (y,w) \boxplus_\pi (x,z) \,]\!\![\, (y',w)$	$PrMM3$
$a \mathbin{\lfloor\!\lfloor} x$	$= a \cdot x$	$CM2$
$a \cdot x \mathbin{\lfloor\!\lfloor} y$	$= a \cdot (x \parallel y)$	$CM3$
$(x+y) \mathbin{\lfloor\!\lfloor} z$	$= x \mathbin{\lfloor\!\lfloor} z + y \mathbin{\lfloor\!\lfloor} z$	$CM4$
$(x \boxplus_\pi y) \mathbin{\lfloor\!\lfloor} z$	$= x \mathbin{\lfloor\!\lfloor} z \boxplus_\pi y \mathbin{\lfloor\!\lfloor} z$	$PrCM1$
$a \mid b \cdot x$	$= (a \mid b) \cdot x$	$CM5$
$a \cdot x \mid b$	$= (a \mid b) \cdot x$	$CM6$
$a \cdot x \mid b \cdot y$	$= (a \mid b) \cdot (x \parallel y)$	$CM7$
$(x \boxplus_\pi y) \mid z$	$= x \mid z \boxplus_\pi y \mid z$	$PrCM6$
$x \mid (y \boxplus_\pi z)$	$= x \mid y \boxplus_\pi x \mid z$	$PrCM7$
$\partial_H(a)$	$= a$	if $a \notin H$ $D1$
$\partial_H(a)$	$= \delta$	if $a \in H$ $D2$
$\partial_H(x+y)$	$= \partial_H(x) + \partial_H(y)$	$D3$
$\partial_H(x \cdot y)$	$= \partial_H(x) \cdot \partial_H(y)$	$D4$
$\partial_H(x \boxplus_\pi y)$	$= \partial_H(x) \boxplus_\pi \partial_H(y)$	$PrD4$

Table 4. Additional axioms for ACP_π^+.

$$x = x + x, y = y + y \Rightarrow (x,z) \,]\!\![\, (y,w) = x \mathbin{\lfloor\!\lfloor} w + y \mathbin{\lfloor\!\lfloor} z + x \mid y$$

Table 5. Merge for Dynamic processes (DyM).

The axiom system contains three conditional axioms. All they have a condition of form: $p = p+p$. In the terms of equalities (in the theory) $ACP_\pi^+ \vdash p = p+p$ holds for all terms which have as a basic term a term from $\mathcal{B}_+$. This condition guarantees that communication (in the case of DyPR) and merge (in the case of DyM) will not occur before all possibilities of applying axioms $PrCM6$, $PrCM7$ and $PrMM2$, $PrMM3$, respectively, have been exhausted. Moreover in the model, Lemma 22 shows that the property $p \leftrightarrow p + p$ is fulfilled by all processes which cannot do probabilistic transitions to different equivalent classes.

Elimination of $\parallel$, $\mathbin{\lfloor\!\lfloor}$, $\mid$, ∂_H and $\,]\!\![\,$ operators from closed ACP_π^+ terms is guaranteed by the following theorem:

Theorem 15 *(Elimination theorem of ACP_π^+)* Let p be a closed ACP_π^+ term. Then there is a closed prBPA term q such that $ACP_\pi^+ \vdash p = q$.   □

$$z = z + z \Rightarrow (x + y) \mid z = x \mid z + y \mid z$$
$$z = z + z \Rightarrow z \mid (x + y) = z \mid x + z \mid y$$

Table 6. Communication merge for Dynamic Processes (DyPR).

3.2   Structured Operational Semantics of ACP_π^+

In ACP_π^+, as in $prBPA$, we need to distinguish static from dynamic processes. Indeed, we obtain the term model of ACP_π^+ as an extension of the term model of $prBPA$, that is, by extension of the signature and the set of deduction rules of the term deduction system and the probability distribution function given in Section 2.1. We consider the signature: $\check{\Sigma}_{ACP_\pi^+} = (A_\delta \cup \check{A}_\delta, +, \cdot, \uplus_\pi, \parallel, \lfloor\!\lfloor, \mid, \partial_H, \mathbb{I})$.

Analogously, we extend the sets of static and dynamic processes as follows:

Definition 16 *A set of static processes* $SP(ACP_\pi^+)$ *in* ACP_π^+ *is the set of all closed terms over the signature of* ACP_π^+, Σ_{prACP}.

A set of dynamic processes $DP(ACP_\pi^+)$ *over the signature* $\check{\Sigma}_{ACP_\pi^+}$ *is defined inductively as follows:*

1. $\check{A}_\delta \subseteq DP(ACP_\pi^+)$;
2. $s, t \in DP(ACP_\pi^+) \Rightarrow s + t, s \mid t, \partial_H(s) \in DP(ACP_\pi^+)$;
3. $s \in DP(ACP_\pi^+), t \in SP(ACP_\pi^+) \Rightarrow s \cdot t, s \lfloor\!\lfloor t \in DP(ACP_\pi^+)$.

The operational semantics is defined by the deduction rules for the new operators in ACP_π^+ given in Table 7, where a, b, c range over A and $H \subseteq A$, and the probability distribution function (Definition 4 and Definition 17).

Definition 17 *The probability distribution function*
$\mu : \mathcal{PR}(prACP) \times \mathcal{PR}(prACP) \to [0, 1]$ *is defined with the equalities given in Definition 4 and the following:*

$$
\begin{aligned}
\mu(p \parallel q, x' \lfloor\!\lfloor q + x'' \lfloor\!\lfloor p + x' \mid x'') &= \mu(p, x')\mu(q, x''), \\
\mu(p \lfloor\!\lfloor q, x' \lfloor\!\lfloor q) &= \mu(p, x'), \\
\mu(p \mid q, x' \mid x'') &= \mu(p, x')\mu(q, x''), \\
\mu(\partial_H(p), \partial_H(x')) &= \mu(p, x'), \\
\mu((p, z) \mathbb{I} (q, w), x' \lfloor\!\lfloor w + x'' \lfloor\!\lfloor z + x' \mid x'') &= \mu(p, x')\mu(q, x'').
\end{aligned}
$$

3.3   Soundness and Completeness

Definition 18 *The probabilistic bisimulation in* ACP_π^+ *is defined in the same way as in* $prBPA$.

$$\dfrac{p \rightsquigarrow x, q \rightsquigarrow y}{p \parallel q \rightsquigarrow x \Lleft q + y \Lleft p + x \mid y} \qquad \dfrac{p \rightsquigarrow x, q \rightsquigarrow y}{(p, z) \parallel\!\!\mid (q, w) \rightsquigarrow x \Lleft w + y \Lleft z + x \mid y}$$

$$\dfrac{p \rightsquigarrow x}{p \Lleft q \rightsquigarrow x \Lleft q} \qquad \dfrac{p \rightsquigarrow x, q \rightsquigarrow y}{p \mid q \rightsquigarrow x \mid y} \qquad \dfrac{p \rightsquigarrow x}{\partial_H(p) \rightsquigarrow \partial_H(x)}$$

$$\dfrac{x \xrightarrow{a} p}{x \Lleft y \xrightarrow{a} p \parallel y} \qquad \dfrac{x \xrightarrow{a} \sqrt{}}{x \Lleft y \xrightarrow{a} y} \qquad \dfrac{x \xrightarrow{a} p, y \xrightarrow{b} q, \gamma(a,b) = c}{x \mid y \xrightarrow{c} p \parallel q}$$

$$\dfrac{x \xrightarrow{a} p, y \xrightarrow{b} \sqrt{}, \gamma(a,b) = c}{x \mid y \xrightarrow{c} p} \qquad \dfrac{x \xrightarrow{a} \sqrt{}, y \xrightarrow{b} q, \gamma(a,b) = c}{x \mid y \xrightarrow{c} q} \qquad \dfrac{x \xrightarrow{a} \sqrt{}, y \xrightarrow{b} \sqrt{}, \gamma(a,b) = c}{x \mid y \xrightarrow{c} \sqrt{}}$$

$$\dfrac{x \xrightarrow{a} p, a \notin H}{\partial_H(x) \xrightarrow{a} \partial_H(p)} \qquad \dfrac{x \xrightarrow{a} \sqrt{}, a \notin H}{\partial_H(x) \xrightarrow{a} \sqrt{}}$$

Table 7. Operational semantics of ACP_π^+.

Theorem 19 $\underline{\leftrightarrow}$ is a congruence relation on ACP_π^+. □

Lemma 20 If $p \in SP(ACP_\pi^+)$ and $p \rightsquigarrow x$ for some closed term x over the signature $\breve{\Sigma}_{ACP_\pi^+}$, then $x \in DP(ACP_\pi^+)$. □

Lemma 21 If $x \in DP(ACP_\pi^+)$ then $x \underline{\leftrightarrow} x + x$. □

Lemma 22 Let p be a closed ACP_π^+ term such that $p \underline{\leftrightarrow} p + p$. Then if $p \rightsquigarrow x'$ and $p \rightsquigarrow x''$ for some $x', x'' \in DP(ACP_\pi^+)$, then $x' \underline{\leftrightarrow} x''$. □

Theorem 23 (Soundness) Let p and q be closed ACP_π^+ terms.
If $ACP_\pi^+ + DyPR + DyM \vdash p = q$ then $p \underline{\leftrightarrow} q$. □

In order to prove completeness we use the method given in [17], [8], [4]. By a trivial check of the conditions in Theorem 4.8 in [8] we can prove the following result:

Theorem 24 (Operational conservative extension) The term deduction system determined by the signature and operational rules of ACP_π^+ is an operational conservative extension of the one for prBPA. □

As we need to get an operational conservative extension up to the probabilistic bisimulation, we need to check if this relation is defined "in terms of predicate and relation symbols". Besides the fourth clause in Definition 7, the probabilistic bisimulation relates terms level by level, that is, transition by transition. Using the previous theorem for operational conservative extension we obtain that for each closed *prBPA* term s, its term-relation-predicate diagrams (in our terminology it is a transition system) in both *prBPA* and ACP_π^+ are the same. Because $\leftrightarrow$ is defined in the same way for transitions in *prBPA* and ACP_π^+ and the term-transition diagrams of s and t ($s, t \in \mathcal{SP}$) are the same in both term deduction systems, we have that $prBPA \vdash s \leftrightarrow t \Leftrightarrow ACP_\pi^+ \vdash s \leftrightarrow t$.

Theorem 25 *(Completeness) Let p and q be closed ACP_π^+ terms. If $p \leftrightarrow q$ then* $ACP_\pi^+ + DyPR + DyM \vdash p = q$. $\qquad\qquad\qquad\qquad\qquad\qquad\square$

3.4 An Equivalent Axiomatization

In this section we give an axiom system that can be considered as equivalent one to ACP_π^+ in the sense that a equation of terms that do not contain $\lVert$, $\mid$ and $\rVert\!\rVert$ operators holds in one theory if and only if it holds in the other theory. The main idea for proposing a new axiom system is to find an appropriate theory which does not have any extra operators. As it has been already mentioned, in order to obtain a complete axiom system of the term model determined by the deduction rules in Table 3 and Table 7 the merge with memory operator has been added to ACP_π^+.

We denote the new process algebra by ACP_π. The signature of ACP_π consists of the operators of *prBPA*, three binary operators: $\parallel$ (merge), $\lVert$ (left merge) and $\mid$ (communication merge) and an unary operator ∂_H (encapsulation) where $H \subseteq A$. The axioms of these operators are given in Table 8 together with the axioms $D1 - D4$ and $PrD4$ in Table 4 and the conditional axioms given in Table 6.

$$x \parallel y = x \lVert y + y \lVert x + x \mid y$$
$$(x \uplus_\pi x') \lVert z + y \lVert w + (x \uplus_\pi x') \mid y = (x \lVert z + y \lVert w + x \mid y) \uplus_\pi (x' \lVert z + y \lVert w + x' \mid y)$$
$$x \lVert z + (y \uplus_\pi y') \lVert w + x \mid (y \uplus_\pi y') = (x \lVert z + y \lVert w + x \mid y) \uplus_\pi (x \lVert z + y' \lVert w + x \mid y')$$

$$a \lVert x = a \cdot x$$
$$a \cdot x \lVert y = a \cdot (x \parallel y)$$
$$(x + y) \lVert z = x \lVert z + y \lVert z$$

$$a \mid b \cdot x = (a \mid b) \cdot x$$
$$a \cdot x \mid b = (a \mid b) \cdot x$$
$$a \cdot x \mid b \cdot y = (a \mid b) \cdot (x \parallel y)$$

Table 8. Additional axioms for ACP_π.

It can be noticed that the distribution laws $PrCM1$, $PrCM6$ and $PrCM7$ are not included in this axiom system. As a result of this, if we consider this theory as an extension of *prBPA* then the Elimination theorem does not hold anymore.

4   PAR Protocol

In this section we consider the PAR protocol (Positive Acknowledgement with Retransmission protocol) as it is described in [15]. We give a specification in ACP_π^+ of the constituent processes of the protocol and of the whole system. In order to do a performance analysis of the system non-determinism has to be resolved. Using only a partial ordering of the set of atomic actions and pre-abstraction we derive the recursive specification of the behaviour of the protocol which can be viewed as a Markov chain.

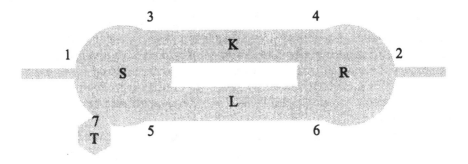

Fig. 3. Components of the protocol

The protocol is modeled as five processes, one sender process S, which is equipped with the timer T, one receiver R and two communication channels K and L, Figure 3. The sender sends a message to the receiver via a communication channel, starts the timer and after that it waits for an acknowledgement. After having received a message the receiver writes the message at the output port and sends an acknowledgement to the sender. A control bit is used in order to avoid multiple writing of a message at the output port. If a message or acknowledgement is sent via the (unreliable) channels K or L three situations can happen: 1) the message is transmitted correctly 2) the message is damaged in transit 3) the message gets lost in the channel. If the sender receives a damaged acknowledgement it sends a duplicate of the sent message. If the sent message or the acknowledgement has been lost in the channel no other action can be performed except the time-out communication action between T and S. When the sender gets the time-out message from the timer it sends a duplicate of the sent message. Unreliability of the channel K (in the similar way it is specified for the channel L) is specified by the probabilistic choice operator: correct transmission of a message with probability π, corruption of a message with probability σ and loss of a message with probability $1 - \pi - \sigma$.

Let D be a finite set of data. The set of atomic actions A contains read, send and communication action and k and l actions which present loss of a message and acknowledgement, respectively. We use the standard read/send communication function given by $r_k(x) \,|\, s_k(x) = c_k(x)$ for communication port k and message x. The specifications of the five processes are given by the recursive equations in Figure 4.

Sender :

$$S \quad = S_0$$
$$S_b \quad = \sum_{d \in D} r_1(d) \cdot S_b^d \qquad\qquad (b = 0, 1)$$
$$S_b^d \quad = s_3(db) \cdot s_7(st) \cdot W S_b^d$$
$$W S_b^d = r_5(ack) \cdot S_{1-b} + (r_5(\bot) + r_7(to)) \cdot S_b^d \quad (b = 0, 1, d \in D)$$

Receiver :

$$R \quad = R_0$$
$$R_b \quad = r_4(\bot) \cdot R_b + \sum_{d \in D} r_4(d\,1-b) \cdot SR_b + \sum_{d \in D} r_4(db) \cdot s_2(d) \cdot SR_{1-b} \quad (b = 0, 1)$$
$$SR_b = s_6(ack) \cdot R_b \qquad\qquad\qquad\qquad\qquad\qquad\qquad (b = 0, 1)$$

Timer :

$$T \ = r_7(st) \cdot T^r$$
$$T^r = r_7(st) \cdot T^r + s_7(to) \cdot T$$

Channels :

$$K = \sum_{d \in D, b \in \{0,1\}} r_3(db) \cdot (s_4(db) \boxplus_\pi s_4(\bot) \boxplus_\sigma k) \cdot K$$
$$L \ = r_6(ack) \cdot (s_5(ack) \boxplus_\rho s_5(\bot) \boxplus_\eta l) \cdot L$$

Fig. 4. Specification of the five components of the protocol.

As it is proposed in [15], in order to verify the protocol we use a unary priority operator Θ in the given specification, as well. In Table 9 and Table 10 we give the axioms of the priority operator and axioms of the auxiliary unless operator $\lhd$. We note that the Elimination theorem of the priority operator holds for closed terms, but it is not the case with the unless operator because distribution laws with probabilistic choice are missing. But in the theory we do not consider this as a problem, because in specification of processes this operator appears only as an auxiliary operator of the priority operator and conditional axiom $DyTH3$ guarantees that this operator does not appear between probabilistic processes.

On the set of atomic actions A the following partial ordering is defined:

1. $a < c_7(st)$, for each $a \in A \setminus \{c_7(st)\}$;
2. $c_7(to) < a$, for each $a \in A \setminus \{c_7(to)\}$.

The action $c_7(to)$ has a lower priority than every other atomic action because a premature time-out can disturb the functioning of the protocol. In order to express that immediately after sending a message the timer is started the action $c_7(st)$ has been given a higher priority than the other actions. (This assumption is very realistic because in such a system a communication between the sender and the timer is usually faster than a communication between other processes in the system.)

$$\Theta(a) \quad = a \qquad\qquad TH1$$
$$\Theta(x \cdot y) \quad = \Theta(x) \cdot \Theta(y) \quad TH2$$
$$\Theta(x \,\pitchfork_{\overline{\pi}}\, y) = \Theta(x) \,\pitchfork_{\overline{\pi}}\, \Theta(y) \;\; PrTH4$$

$$x = x + x, y = y + y \Rightarrow \Theta(x + y) = \Theta(x) \triangleleft y + \Theta(y) \triangleleft x \;\; DyTH3$$

Table 9. Axioms for the priority operator.

$$a \triangleleft b \quad = a \qquad\qquad\quad \text{if } \neg(a < b) \;\; P1$$
$$a \triangleleft b \quad = \delta \qquad\qquad\quad \text{if } a < b \qquad P2$$
$$x \triangleleft (y \cdot z) \;\; = x \triangleleft y \qquad\qquad\qquad\qquad P3$$
$$x \triangleleft (y + z) = (x \triangleleft y) \triangleleft z \qquad\qquad\qquad P4$$
$$x \cdot y \triangleleft z \quad = (x \triangleleft z) \cdot y \qquad\qquad\qquad\quad P5$$
$$(x + y) \triangleleft z = (x \triangleleft z) + (y \triangleleft z) \qquad\qquad P6$$

Table 10. Axioms for the unless operator.

The behaviour of the protocol is obtained by composition of the five processes:

$$PAR = t_I \circ \Theta \circ \partial_H (S \| T \| K \| L \| R),$$

where
$H = \{r_i(x), s_i(x) | i \in \{3, 4, 5, 6, 7\}, x \in (D \times \{0, 1\}) \cup \{ack, \perp, st, to\}\}$
is the set of encapsulated atomic actions and t_I is the pre-abstraction operator
([2]), that renames all internal action from the set
$I = \{c_i(x) | i \in \{3, 4, 5, 6, 7\}, x \in (D \times \{0, 1\}) \cup \{ack, \perp, st, to\}\} \cup \{k, l\}$
into t.

Shortly, we will describe how non-determinism is resolved in the derivation of the recursive specification given below. First of all, non-determinism which occurs as a result of conditional axiom DyM is resolved by using the encapsulation operator. Then, by merge of atomic actions of processes in the parallel composition, two sub-processes which contain non-determinism between processes are obtained. In the first case, we obtain the following sub-process:
$c_7(st) \cdot Q + (c_4(db) \cdot X \,\pitchfork_{\overline{\pi}}\, c_4(\perp) \cdot Y \,\pitchfork_{\overline{\sigma}}\, k \cdot Y)$, for some processes Q, X and Y.
Then, applying the distribution laws and the axioms of Θ operator, by taking into account the partial ordering of the set of atomic actions, we obtain that

$\Theta(c_7(st) \cdot Q + (c_4(db) \cdot X \uplus_\pi c_4(\bot) \cdot Y \uplus_\sigma k \cdot Y)) = c_7(st) \cdot \Theta(Q)$. (This situation corresponds to the state of the system in which in parallel the timer might be started or the message might be delivered to the receiver and as a result of the interleaving model non-determinism occurs. Under the assumption that the timer is started immediately after sending the message from the sender, it follows that this non-deterministic choice actually is deterministic.)

In the second situation we obtain non-deterministic choice between $c_7(to) \cdot R$ process and some other process P which may be in a form $a \cdot Z \uplus_\rho b \cdot U \uplus_\eta c \cdot V$ or $a \cdot Z$ for certain processes R, Z, U, V and atomic actions a, b and c. (There are more variants where non-determinism with $c_7(to) \cdot R$ occurs and we consider all of them in general.) Again, using the axioms of Θ operator and axioms of ACP_π^+ and the partial ordering defined on the set A we obtain that $\Theta(c_7(to) \cdot R + P) = \Theta(P)$ and P does not have non-determinism as a top operator.

We can derive the following recursive specification for PAR:

$$
\begin{aligned}
P_0 &= \sum_{d \in D} r_1(d) \cdot P_1 & P_4 &= t \cdot t \cdot P_6 \\
P_1 &= t \cdot t \cdot (t \cdot P_2 \uplus_\pi t \cdot t \cdot P_1) & P_5 &= t \cdot t \cdot t \cdot P_6 \\
P_2 &= s_2(d) \cdot P_3 & P_6 &= t \cdot P_3 \uplus_\pi t \cdot P_5 \\
P_3 &= t \cdot (t \cdot P_0 \uplus_\rho t \cdot P_4 \uplus_\eta t \cdot P_5)
\end{aligned}
$$

The behaviour of the whole process is depicted in Figure 5. In order to obtain a clearer transition system we omit the labels that present probability 1 and we join a probabilistic and an action transition into one edge. If we abstract from the content of message sent from the environment this transition system can be considered as a labelled Markov chain. Further using Markov chain analysis various results for the behaviour of the protocol can be obtained. We can prove liveness of the protocol by showing that state P_0 in Figure 5 is a recurrent state. Moreover, because t_I operator does not reduce the number of internal actions we can compute the mean number of actions that are executed between reading of two successive data (between two read actions from environment) of the protocol by computing the mean recurrence time of state P_0. For example, for $\pi = 0.95$, $\rho = 0.92$ and $\eta = 0.07$ this mean number of atomic actions is 7.71.

5   Conclusions and Future Work

The objective of this paper is to introduce a probabilistic version of ACP where non-determinism and probability are combined. The presented probabilistic process algebra ACP_π^+ improves the variant of probabilistic process algebra proposed in [1]. In order to get a more effective axiom system we have proposed a new variant of an extension of $prBPA$ with parallel composition. Following the idea of ACP-like process algebras for the interleaving model we have given the axiom system where only parallel dynamic processes are merged. In order to realise this concept we have added an extra quaternary operator, $\parallel$ called merge with memory.

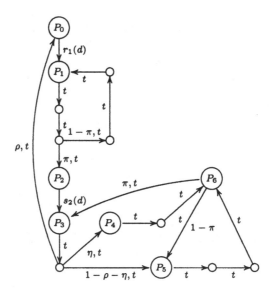

Fig. 5. The behaviour of the whole system.

The operational semantics of ACP_π^+ is based on the alternating model and it has been defined by a term deduction system of which the signature contains an extended set of constants (each atomic action has a dynamic counterpart) and of which the deduction rules include two transition types: probabilistic and action transition. Instead of labelled probabilistic transitions we have defined the probability distribution function which gives a probability with which one probabilistic transition may occur. In the construction of the term models we have used probabilistic bisimulation and we have shown soundness and completeness of the term model with respect to the proposed axiom systems.

Dealing with the PAR protocol with unreliable channels we have investigated the applicability of ACP_π^+. We have given a specification in ACP_π^+ of the constituent processes of the protocol and of the whole system. In order to do a performance analysis non-determinism has to be resolved. Using in addition only the priority operator and the pre-abstraction operator we have obtained a recursive specification of the behaviour of the protocol that can be viewed as a Markov chain. Our results indicate that for more complex protocols where pre-abstraction does not help, in order to verify some properties of a system, non-determinism can be resolved by standard methods used in ACP, for instance abstraction, applied only for sub-processes where non-determinism occurs. In that sense one of the directions in our further research is to investigate possibilities of combining abstraction and probability.

We mention as a possible option for future work the integration of a timed and probabilistic version of ACP.

Acknowledgments. I would like to thank Jos Baeten, Kees Middelburg and Michel Reniers for help during the work on this paper. I also thank Chris Verhoef and Pedro D'Argenio for fruitful discussion.

References

1. S. Andova, *Process algebra with interleaving probabilistic parallel composition,* Eindhoven University of Technology, CSR 99-xx, 1999.
2. J.C.M. Baeten, J. A. Bergstra, *Global renaming operators in concrete process algebra,* Information and Computation 78, pp. 205-245, 1988.
3. J.C.M. Baeten, W. P. Weijland, *Process algebra,* Cambridge University Press, 1990.
4. J.C.M. Baeten, C. Verhoef, *Concrete process algebra,* Handbook of Logic in Computer Science, volume 4: "Semantic Modelling", Oxford University Press, 1995.
5. J.C.M. Baeten, J.A. Bergstra, *Process algebra with partial choice,* Proc. CONCUR '94, Uppsala, B. Jonsson & J. Parrow, eds., LNCS 836, Springer Verlag, pp. 465-480, 1994.
6. J.C.M. Baeten, J.A. Bergstra, S.A. Smolka, *Axiomatizing probabilistic processes: ACP with generative probabilities,* Information and Computation 121(2), pp. 234-255, Sep. 1995.
7. J.A. Bergstra, J.W. Klop, *Process algebra for synchronous communication,* Information and Control 60, pp. 109-137, 1984.
8. P.R. D'Argenio, C. Verhoef, *A general conservative extension theorem in process algebra with inequalities,* Theoretical Computer Science 177, pp. 351-380, 1997.
9. P.R. D'Argenio, H. Hermanns, J.-P. Katoen *On generative parallel composition,* Preliminary Proc. of PROBMIV'98, Indianopolis, USA, C. Baier & M. Huth & M Kwiatkowska & M. Ryan ed., pp. 105-121, 1998.
10. A. Giacalone, C.-C. Jou, S. A. Smolka, *Algebraic reasoning for probabilistic concurrent systems,* Proc. Working Conference on Programming Concepts and Methods, IFIP TC 2, Sea of Galilee, Israel, M. Broy & C.B. Jones ed., pp. 443-458, 1990.
11. R. J. van Glabbeek, S. A. Smolka, B. Steffen, C. M. N. Tofts, *Reactive, generative and stratified models of probabilistic processes,* Proc. of 5th Annual IEEE Symp. on Logic in Computer Science, Philadelphia, PA, pp. 130-141, 1990.
12. H. Hansson, *Time and probability in formal design of distributed systems,* Ph.D. thesis, DoCS 91/27, University of Uppsala, 1991.
13. C.-C. Jou, S. A. Smolka *Equivalences, congruences and complete axiomatizations for probabilistic processes,* Proc. CONCUR '90, LNCS 458, Springer Verlag, Berlin, pp. 367-383, 1990.
14. K.G.Larsen, A.Skou, *Bisimulation through probabilistic testing,* Proc. of 16th ACM Symp. on Principles of Programming Languages, Austin, TX, 1989.
15. F. W. Vaandrager, *Two simple protocols,* In: *Applications of Process algebra,* Cambridge University Press, J.C.M. Baeten ed., pp. 23-44, 1990.
16. M.Y. Vardi, *Automatic verification of probabilistic concurrent finite state programs,* Proc. of 26th Symp. on Foundations of Com. Sc., IEEE Comp. Soc. Press, pp. 327-338, 1985.
17. C. Verhoef, *A general conservative extension theorem in process algebra,* Proc. of PROCOMET'94, IFIP 2 Working Conference, San Miniato, E.-R. Olderog ed., pp. 149-168, 1994.

An Axiomatization of Probabilistic Testing*

Manuel Núñez

Dept. de Sistemas Informáticos y Programación
Universidad Complutense de Madrid, Spain
manuelnu@eucmax.sim.ucm.es

Abstract. In this paper we present a sound and complete axiom system for a probabilistic process algebra with recursion. Soundness and completeness of the axiomatization is given with respect to the testing semantics defined in [19].

1 Introduction

During this decade researchers in process algebras have tried to close the gap between formal models and real systems. In particular, features which were abstracted before have been introduced in these models. This is the case of probabilistic information. Several models have introduced probabilities into process algebras, and in [22] models are classified with respect to the interpretation of probabilities in three groups: *reactive, generative,* and *stratified.* In the reactive model there is a different probability distribution for every action, that is, there is no probabilistic relation between different actions. In the generative model there is one probability distribution for all the actions. The stratified model is similar to the generative model but taking into account the probabilistic branching. We will try to explain the differences among these models by means of a few simple examples. Consider the (reactive) process $P = (a; P_1 +_{\frac{1}{3}} a; P_2) + (b; Q_1 +_{\frac{1}{4}} b; Q_2)$. If the environment offers a then P will execute a and then it will behave as either P_1 or P_2 with probabilities $\frac{1}{3}$ and $\frac{2}{3}$, respectively. Something similar happens if the environment offers the action b. Nevertheless, it is not specified how this process would behave if both actions were offered simultaneously. Consider the (generative) process $P' = (a; P_1 +_{\frac{1}{3}} b; P_2)$. If the environment offers a then P' will execute a with a probability 1 and then it will behave as P_1; if the environment offers b then P' will execute b with a probability 1 and then it will behave as P_2; if the environment offers both a and b then P' will execute a, with a probability $\frac{1}{3}$, or it will execute b, with a probability $\frac{2}{3}$. Finally, the processes $(a +_{\frac{1}{2}} b) +_{\frac{2}{3}} c$ and $a +_{\frac{1}{3}} (b +_{\frac{1}{2}} c)$ are equivalent in the generative model but they are not in the stratified one. In this paper we consider a generative interpretation of probabilities based on the following approach: it allows to specify probabilistic systems more precisely that the reactive interpretation, while the (semantic) models are not so complicated as the ones based on the stratified interpretation.

---

* Research partially supported by the CICYT projects TIC 94-0851-C02-02 and TIC 97-0669-C03-01.

J.-P. Katoen (Ed.): ARTS'99, LNCS 1601, pp. 130–150, 1999.
© Springer-Verlag Berlin Heidelberg 1999

Regarding the testing framework, there have been several proposals for probabilistic extensions (e.g. [3,5,23,19,18,4,10,11]). In this paper we will consider an extension of the language PPA described in [19]. PPA is a probabilistic process algebra featuring two (probabilistic) choice operators: external and internal. Sometimes it has been argued that the external choice operator should not be extended with a probability, and in fact there are proposals featuring a probabilistic internal choice while the external choice operator does not have a probability parameter (e.g. [23]). Instead, we consider useful to have probabilities in both operators for a number of reasons. First, in order to have the same expressive power with our language as with a CCS-like language[1] we need to include probabilities in both operators. For example, we could not simulate the simple (generative) process $a +_p b$ which relate a and b probabilistically, with a nonprobabilistic external choice. Second, by working with two choice operators we automatically get that the testing equivalence is a congruence, and so we can axiomatize it (working with a CCS-like operator we need, as usual, to consider the largest congruence contained in the testing equivalence). Finally, there are behaviors which can be specified more precisely by using a probabilistic external choice operator. We will illustrate this by means of a simple example. Suppose that we want to specify the behavior of a library where two users can request books. If only one user requests a book then the book is given to him, but if both users request the same book the library must give *priority* to one of the users. On the other hand, the system must be somehow *fair*, avoiding the possibility that if the two users request the same book, this book is always given to the same person. A simplified version of the system can be specified as $P = a; P +_{\frac{1}{4}} b; P$, indicating that if both users request the same book, it will be given with a probability $\frac{1}{4}$ to the user a and with a probability $\frac{3}{4}$ to the user b. Note that if we use a probabilistic internal choice then there is no guarantee that if only one user requests the book, it is given to him, while if we use a nonprobabilistic external choice then we cannot specify the notion of *priority*.

An interesting alternative appears in [16] where the probabilistic external choice operator is considered as an operator derived from the probabilistic internal choice and the *priority* operators. Nevertheless it is also necessary to include some kind of *probability* (the *extremal* value 1) in the external choice operator.

Besides, PPA allows the definition of recursive processes. Moreover, in this paper we extend the language described in [19] with a parallel operator. Our parallel operator is parameterized by a set of actions (the synchronization set). Regarding probability parameters, no agreement has been reached about the parallel operator (see [7] for a discussion on the different possibilities). There are proposals with a probability parameter which assigns weights to the *interleaving* actions of both components (e.g. [6,18]); alternatively, there are proposals adding two probability parameters assigning weights to the interleaving actions with respect to the synchronization actions, and assigning weights to the interleaving actions of both components, respectively (e.g. [1]). In any case, we claim that

---

[1] Actually, most of probabilistic models are based on CCS, or in labeled transition systems (which can be easily interpreted as CCS processes).

these parameters only change the probability with which actions are executed, while the *operational* behavior remains the same. Taking this into account, and for the sake of simplicity, in this paper we consider a parallel operator without any probability parameter, but other alternatives can be easily included in our framework (they are discussed in [17]).

The main goal of this paper is to provide a complete and sound axiomatization of testing equivalence for PPA. In [19] a probabilistic extension of the classical testing semantics [8,12] was defined. Besides, an alternative characterization of the testing semantics (based on an extension of acceptance sets) as well as a fully abstract denotational semantics (based on acceptance trees) were given. So in order to conclude the *semantic trilogy* (alternative characterization, denotational semantics, and axiomatic semantics), a suitable axiomatization of the probabilistic testing semantics should be defined. The starting point for the definition of this axiomatization is (as it was for the other semantics) [12]. As it will be shown in this paper, some of the axioms are (more or less complicated) probabilistic versions of the axioms corresponding to the nonprobabilistic case, while we must add new axioms in order to cope with the specific problems introduced by probabilities.

There have been previous proposals for probabilistic axiom systems. For example, using Synchronous PCCS and *generative* probabilities [9,13,21], or with *reactive* probabilities [15]. An axiomatization for a subset of PCCS is presented in [20], and in [1] an axiomatization for ACP finite processes is given. These two proposals also use generative probabilities. Nevertheless, there exists an important difference between all these previous axiomatizations and ours: all of them axiomatize (strong) probabilistic bisimulation, in which there is no *abstraction* of internal movements (i.e. τ actions, or equivalently internal transitions). In fact, observational semantics cannot be directly translated from the nonprobabilistic setting, and a suitable definition of probabilistic *weak* bisimulation for general probabilistic systems was an open problem until [2]. The problem is that there exists some kind of *fairness* in these semantics. Consider $P = recX.\,(a;Nil) \oplus_p X$ (or $P = fix\,X.(a;Nil) +_p (\tau;X)$ using a CCS-like notation). If we *forget* probabilities, P is must equivalent to *divergence* (because of the τ loop), but in a probabilistic setting we would expect that if the environment offers a then P would execute it with probability 1, and so, P should be (probabilistic) testing equivalent to $a; Nil$. This example illustrates why the axiomatization of our testing equivalence cannot be a simple adaptation of the one for nonprobabilistic processes. We will need a rule to express that this kind of recursively defined processes have the same *meaning* as a finite one (in the previous case, $a; Nil$).

The work presented in [6] is the most similar to ours. The main differences between their work and ours are that while our testing semantics is defined following the classical approach (i.e. parallel composition of tested process and test), theirs is defined in an unusual (*ad hoc*) way; besides, they use a reactive interpretation of probabilities (within a probabilistic external choice) which leads to a simplification of the external choice treatment, but complicates the intuitive interpretation of some processes.

As far as we know, the axiomatization presented in this paper is the first one for a semantics abstracting internal movements (in this case a testing semantics), where recursive processes are allowed and probabilites are interpreted using the *generative* model.

The rest of the paper is structured as follows. In Section 2 we recall previous results for our calculus. In Section 3 we present a sound and complete axiomatization for finite processes without parallel composition. In Section 4 we consider recursion, and the previous axiomatization is extended to deal with recursive processes. In Section 5 we give axioms for the parallel operator, showing that this operator can be considered as a derived one. Finally, in Section 6 we present our conclusions and a discussion about the inclusion of hiding in our language.

The full proofs of the results in this paper can be found in [17].

2   Preliminaries

In this section we review our previous results for PPA. The only difference between the language described in this paper and the one presented in [19] is that here we have included a parallel operator. The composition of a process and a test will be defined using the parallel operator of the language. Besides, negative premises in our former operational semantics have been replaced by a syntactic predicate *stable*, and a new function *live*. Anyway, the induced labeled transition systems remains the same as previously.

Definition 1 Given a set of actions Act and a set of identifiers Id, the set of PPA processes is defined by the BNF expression:

$$P ::= Nil \mid \Omega \mid X \mid a; P \mid P \oplus_p P \mid P +_p P \mid P \parallel_A P \mid recX.P$$

where $p \in (0,1)$, $a \in Act$, $A \subseteq Act$, and $X \in Id$.   □

From now on, except if noted, we only consider closed processes, that is processes without free occurrences of variables, and we will omit trailing occurrences of *Nil*. In this process algebra *Nil* is a deadlocked process, Ω is a divergent process, $a; P$ denotes the action a prefixing the process P, $P \oplus_p Q$ denotes an internal choice between P and Q with associated probability p, $P +_p Q$ is an external choice between P and Q with associated probability p, $P \parallel_A Q$ is the parallel composition of P and Q with synchronization alphabet A, and finally $recX.P$ is used to define recursive processes.

Next, we give a syntactic definition for the *stability* of a process. It expresses that a process has not unguarded internal choices, or equivalently that a process will not be able to execute an internal transition. We also define a function *live* computing whether a stable process is operationally equivalent to *Nil*.

Definition 2 We define the predicate $stable(P)$ over PPA processes as:

- $stable(Nil) = stable(a; P) = True$
- $stable(\Omega) = stable(X) = stable(P_1 \oplus_p P_2) = stable(recX.P) = False$
- $stable(P_1 +_p P_2) = stable(P_1 \parallel_A P_2) = stable(P_1) \wedge stable(P_2)$

$$(PRE)\frac{}{a;P\xrightarrow{a}_1 P} \qquad (INT1)\frac{}{P\oplus_p Q \succ\!\!\longrightarrow_p P} \qquad (INT2)\frac{}{P\oplus_p Q \succ\!\!\longrightarrow_{1-p} Q}$$

$$(EXT1)\frac{P\succ\!\!\longrightarrow_q P' \wedge stable(Q)}{P+_p Q \succ\!\!\longrightarrow_q P'+_p Q} \qquad\qquad (EXT2)\frac{Q\succ\!\!\longrightarrow_q Q' \wedge stable(P)}{P+_p Q \succ\!\!\longrightarrow_q P+_p Q'}$$

$$(EXT3)\frac{P\succ\!\!\longrightarrow_{q_1} P' \wedge Q\succ\!\!\longrightarrow_{q_2} Q'}{P+_p Q \succ\!\!\longrightarrow_{q_1\cdot q_2} P'+_p Q'}$$

$$(EXT4)\frac{P\xrightarrow{a}_q P' \wedge stable(Q)}{P+_p Q \xrightarrow{a}_{p\cdot\hat q} P'} \qquad\qquad (EXT5)\frac{Q\xrightarrow{a}_q Q' \wedge stable(P)}{P+_p Q \xrightarrow{a}_{(1-p)\cdot\hat q} Q'}$$

$$(PAR1)\frac{P\succ\!\!\longrightarrow_p P' \wedge stable(Q)}{P\parallel_A Q \succ\!\!\longrightarrow_p P'\parallel_A Q} \qquad\qquad (PAR2)\frac{Q\succ\!\!\longrightarrow_p Q' \wedge stable(P)}{P\parallel_A Q \succ\!\!\longrightarrow_p P\parallel_A Q'}$$

$$(PAR3)\frac{P\succ\!\!\longrightarrow_p P' \wedge Q\succ\!\!\longrightarrow_q Q'}{P\parallel_A Q \succ\!\!\longrightarrow_{p\cdot q} P'\parallel_A Q'} \qquad\qquad (PAR4)\frac{P\xrightarrow{b}_p P' \wedge stable(Q) \wedge b\notin A}{P\parallel_A Q \xrightarrow{b}_{r_1} P'\parallel_A Q}$$

$$(PAR5)\frac{Q\xrightarrow{b}_p Q' \wedge stable(P) \wedge b\notin A}{P\parallel_A Q \xrightarrow{b}_{r_1} P\parallel_A Q'} \qquad\qquad (PAR6)\frac{P\xrightarrow{a}_p P' \wedge Q\xrightarrow{a}_q Q' \wedge a\in A}{P\parallel_A Q \xrightarrow{a}_{r_2} P'\parallel_A Q'}$$

$$(REC)\frac{}{rec\,X.P \succ\!\!\longrightarrow_1 P\{rec\,X.P/X\}} \qquad\qquad (DIV)\frac{}{\Omega \succ\!\!\longrightarrow_1 \Omega}$$

where $\hat q = \frac{q}{p\cdot live(P)+(1-p)\cdot live(Q)}$, $r_1 = \frac{p}{\mu(P,Q,A)}$, and $r_2 = \frac{p\cdot q}{\mu(P,Q,A)}$.

Fig. 1. Operational Semantics of PPA.

We define the function $live(P)$ over PPA processes as:

- $live(Nil) = 0$
- $live(a;P) = 1$
- $live(P_1 +_p P_2) = live(P_1 \parallel_A P_2) = max(live(P_1), live(P_2))$

$\square$

Note that $live(\_)$ is not defined for non stable processes. The set of rules defining the operational semantics is given in Figure 1. There are two types of transitions. The intuitive meaning of an *external* transition $P \xrightarrow{a}_p Q$ is that if the environment offers all the actions in Act, then the probability with which P executes a and then behaves as Q equals p; the meaning of an internal transition $P \succ\!\!\longrightarrow_p Q$ is that the process P evolves to Q with probability p, without interaction with the environment.

In order to avoid the problem of deriving the same transition in different ways, we use multisets of transitions. For example, consider $P = a +_{\frac{1}{2}} a$. If we are not careful, we will have the transition $P \xrightarrow{a}_{\frac{1}{2}} Nil$ only once, while we should have this transition twice (that is why we use multisets). This problem is similar for the $\oplus_p$ and $\parallel_A$ operators. So, in our model, if a transition can be derived in several ways, we consider that each derivation generates a different instance. In particular, when we define the testing semantics we will consider multisets of computations as well. Other approaches to solve this problem are to index transitions (e.g. [9]), to increase the number of rules (e.g. [14]), to define a transition probability function (e.g. [4,20]), or to add the probabilities associated with the same transition (e.g. [23]).

While the rules for prefix, internal choice, divergence and recursion do not need any explanation, we will briefly explain the rest of the rules. $(EXT1 - 3)$ indicate that whenever any of the arguments of an external choice can evolve via an internal transition, these transitions are performed until both arguments become *stable*. $(EXT4 - 5)$ are applied when both processes are stable and (at least) one of them may execute some observable action. The value $\hat{q}$ is obtained by normalizing the probability q of performing this external transition, taking into account whether one or both processes can perform external transitions.

Example 1 Let $P = (a; Nil) +_p Nil$. We have $P \xrightarrow{a}_1 Nil$, while if we would not use this *normalization* we would obtain $P \xrightarrow{a}_p Nil$.   □

Rules $(PAR1 - 3)$ are similar to $(EXT1 - 3)$. If none of the processes can perform internal transitions, then rules $(PAR4 - 6)$ are applied. $(PAR4 - 5)$ deal with *interleaving* actions, while $(PAR6)$ deals with *synchronization* actions. As usual, in these last three rules we use a *normalization factor*, $\mu(P, Q, A)$, in order to obtain that the sum of all the external transitions is 1 (or zero if no transition is possible):

$$\mu(P,Q,A) = \sum_{a \in A} \{ p \cdot q \mid \exists P', Q' : P \xrightarrow{a}_p P' \wedge Q \xrightarrow{a}_q Q' \}$$
$$+ \sum_{b \notin A} \{ p \mid \exists P' : P \xrightarrow{b}_p P' \} + \sum_{b \notin A} \{ q \mid \exists Q' : Q \xrightarrow{b}_q Q' \}$$

As a consequence of this definition of operational semantics, we have that internal and external transitions are not mixed, and then we have the following

Lemma 1 Let P be a process. If there exist p, P' such that $P \succ\!\!\!\longrightarrow_p P'$ then there do not exist q, a, P'' such that $P \xrightarrow{a}_q P''$, or equivalently if there exist p, a, P' such that $P \xrightarrow{a}_p P'$ then there do not exist q, P'' such that $P \succ\!\!\!\longrightarrow_q P''$.   □

We finish this section generalizing the choice operators to deal with an arbitrary (finite) number of arguments. For the generalized external choice we will use a restricted form, in which all the arguments are prefixed by different actions. These operators will be used, in particular, when we define the notion of normal form.

Definition 3 Let $P_1, P_2, \ldots, P_n$ be processes, and $a_1, a_2, \ldots, a_n \in Act$ different actions. We inductively define the *generalized external choice* by

1. $\sum_{i=1}^{1} [1] a_1; P_1 = a_1; P_1$ 2. $\sum_{i=1}^{n} [p_i] a_i; P_i = (a_1; P_1) +_{p_1} (\sum_{i=1}^{n-1} [\frac{p_{i+1}}{1-p_1}] a_{i+1}; P_{i+1})$

where $p_1, p_2, \ldots, p_n > 0$ are such that $\sum p_i = 1$.
We inductively define the *generalized internal choice* by

1. $\bigoplus_{i=1}^{0} [p_i] P_i = \Omega$ 2. $\bigoplus_{i=1}^{1} [1] P_1 = P_1$

3. $\bigoplus_{i=1}^{n} [p_i] P_i = \bigoplus_{i=1}^{n} [\frac{p_i}{p}] P_i \oplus_p \Omega$ [if $p = \sum p_i < 1 \wedge n > 0$]

4. $\bigoplus_{i=1}^{n}[p_i]\,P_i = P_1 \oplus_{p_1} (\bigoplus_{i=1}^{n-1}[\frac{p_{i+1}}{1-p_1}]\,P_{i+1})$ [if $\sum p_i = 1 \wedge n > 1$]

where $p_1, p_2, \ldots, p_n > 0$ are such that $\sum p_i \leq 1$.   □

Let us remark that the sum of the probabilities associated with a generalized internal choice may be less than 1. The difference between 1 and this value indicates the probability of divergence. In this case the third clause is applied first so that the sum of the probabilities associated with the remaining generalized internal choice is equal to 1 (afterwards the second or the fourth clauses will be used). We consider that the empty summation (i.e. $\sum_{i=1}^{0} P_i$) represents the process *Nil*.

2.1   Testing Semantics

As in the nonprobabilistic case tests will be just processes where the alphabet *Act* is extended with a new action ω indicating *successful* termination. The operational semantics of tests is the same as the one for processes (considering ω as an ordinary action). Now we have to define how a process interacts with a test. As usual, this interaction is modeled by the parallel composition of the process and the test. We will denote the composition of a process P and a test T by $P\,|\,T$, and it is defined as $P\,|\,T = P\,\|_{Act}\,T$. Note that ω is not included in the synchronization alphabet. Now we will define a function computing the probability with which a test is passed by a process.

Definition 4 Let P_0 be a process and T_0 be a test. A *computation* is a sequence of transitions $C = P_0\,|\,T_0 \longmapsto_{p_1} P_1\,|\,T_1 \longmapsto_{p_2} \cdots P_{n-1}\,|\,T_{n-1} \longmapsto_{p_n} P_n\,|\,T_n \cdots$, where $\longmapsto_p$ denotes either $\succ\!\!\longrightarrow_p$, or $\overset{a}{\longrightarrow}_p$ for some $a \in Act \cup \{\omega\}$. If C is finite we say that $length(C) = n$.

Let C be a computation such that $length(C) = n$. We say that C is *successful* if $P_{n-1}\,|\,T_{n-1} \overset{\omega}{\longrightarrow}_p P_n\,|\,T_n$, and there is no other occurrence of ω in C, that is, $\not\exists n' < n, p' : P_{n'-1}\,|\,T_{n'-1} \overset{\omega}{\longrightarrow}_{p'} P_{n'}\,|\,T_{n'}$.

We denote by $\tilde{C}_{P|T}$ the *multiset* of *successful computations* of $P\,|\,T$. We define the *probability of a successful computation* S as $Pr(S) = \prod_{i=1}^{length(S)} p_i$. Finally, we define the *probability* with which the process P *passes* the test T as $pass(P, T) = \sum_{S \in \tilde{C}_{P|T}} Pr(S)$.

Given two processes P and Q, we say that they are *testing equivalent*, and we write $P \approx Q$, iff for all test T we have $pass(P, T) = pass(Q, T)$.   □

Note that $pass(P, T) = \lim_{n \to \infty} \sum \{ Pr(S) \,|\, S \in \tilde{C}_{P|T} \wedge length(S) < n \}$. Let us remark that the role played by tests of the form $a +_p (\tau; \omega)$ in other models (e.g. [5,24]) is played in our model by tests of the form $a +_p \omega$, which are not trivially passed within our framework. For example, the process $P = a$ *passes* the test above with a probability $1 - p$.

In the following, we will show that the whole family of tests can be reduced to a simpler class of tests. Although this fact is not important for the axiomatic semantics, it strongly simplifies soundness proofs. First, we have that *infinite* tests (i.e. tests having occurrences of recursion) are not necessary.

Lemma 2 $P \approx Q$ iff for all *finite* test T we have $pass(P,T) = pass(Q,T)$.   □

Now we define a set of *essential* tests, called *probabilistic barbs*, with sufficient discriminatory power to distinguish any pair of non-equivalent processes. These probabilistic barbs are very similar to *probabilistic traces* [24] if we consider the latter as probabilistic tests.

Definition 5 The set of *probabilistic barbs*, denoted by $\mathcal{PB}$, is defined by means of the following BNF expression:

$$T ::= \sum_{i=1}^{s} [p_i] \, (a_i; Nil) +_p \omega \;\; \Big| \;\; \sum_{i=1}^{s} [p_i] \, a_i; T_i \qquad \text{where } T_i = \begin{cases} T & \text{if } i = s \\ Nil & \text{otherwise} \end{cases}$$

where $p \in (0,1)$, $\sum p_i = 1$, and $a_i \in Act$.   □

Theorem 1 $P \approx P'$ iff for all $T \in \mathcal{PB}$ we have $pass(P,T) = pass(P',T)$.   □

In the rest of this paper, mainly in some of the proofs, we will use the denotational semantics for PPA given in [19]. Anyway, previous knowledge of this semantics is not necessary in order to understand the bulk of this paper. In this paper we use the following:

- The denotational semantics of a syntactic process P is denoted by $[\![P]\!]$.
- The semantic order relation and its induced equivalence are denoted by $\sqsubseteq_{\text{PAT}}$ and $=_{\text{PAT}}$ respectively.
- The probability with which a process P reaches a node labeled by the state A of its semantic tree after a sequence s is denoted by $p([\![P]\!], s, A)$. In particular, if $P = P_1 \oplus_p P_2$, then $p([\![P]\!], s, A) = p \cdot p([\![P_1]\!], s, A) + (1-p) \cdot p([\![P_2]\!], s, A)$.
- The denotational semantics of recursive processes is given by their finite approximations.
- *(Full Abstraction)* Let P, Q be PPA processes. Then, $P \approx Q$ iff $[\![P]\!] =_{\text{PAT}} [\![Q]\!]$.

3   Axiomatization for Finite Processes

In this section we will define an axiom system inducing an equivalence relation, denoted by $\equiv$, among the terms of the language PPA$_{fin}$ which is the subset of PPA where neither $\|_A$ nor $recX.P$ have been included. We will also use an order relation $\sqsubseteq$ to define this equivalence relation. This system includes axioms expressing algebraic properties of the operators as well as relations among the operators like distributivity. We will also present some axioms which are sound in the nonprobabilistic framework but not in our case. Soundness of rules (axioms) dealing with $\equiv$ will be shown with respect to the testing equivalence, and we will frequently use Theorem 1, while soundness of the ones corresponding to $\sqsubseteq$ will be shown with respect to the fully abstract denotational semantics equivalence defined in [19]. Although we will mix soundness (and completeness) proofs with respect to either the testing or the denotational semantics, this process is correct.

First, we will prove $[P] \sqsubseteq_{\text{PAT}} [Q]$ iff $\vdash P \sqsubseteq Q$. From this result, given that both $\sqsubseteq_{\text{PAT}}$ and $\sqsubseteq$ are preorders, we will trivially get $[P] =_{\text{PAT}} [Q]$ iff $\vdash P \equiv Q$ an so, by full abstraction, we finally obtain the desired result $P \approx Q$ iff $\vdash P \equiv Q$.

The first axioms of our system are similar to those in [12], and they express that internal choice is idempotent, commutative and associative, while external choice is commutative and *Nil* is its identity element. Commutativity and associativity are intended up to a suitable rebalance of probabilities. Soundness is trivial.

(II) $P \oplus_p P \equiv P$ $\qquad\qquad\qquad$ **(CI)** $P \oplus_p Q \equiv Q \oplus_{1-p} P$

(AI) $P \oplus_p (Q \oplus_q R) \equiv (P \oplus_{p'} Q) \oplus_{q'} R$, where $q' = p + q - p \cdot q$ and $p' = \frac{p}{q'}$

(CE) $P +_p Q \equiv Q +_{1-p} P$ $\qquad$ **(NE)** $P +_p Nil \equiv P$

Now, we present some *axioms* that are not sound in our probabilistic model, although they were in nonprobabilistic testing models. First, in general, the external choice operator is not idempotent as the following example shows:

Example 2 Consider the processes $P = a \oplus_{\frac{1}{2}} b$ and $P' = P +_{\frac{1}{2}} P$, and the test $T = a; \omega$. We have $pass(P, T) = \frac{1}{2}$ while $pass(P', T) = \frac{3}{4}$. $\qquad\qquad\square$

This fact also appears in models dealing with *replication* where the choice between the same process is not equivalent to the original process. On the other hand we have the following:

Proposition 1 Let P be a stable process. Then, for any $p \in (0, 1)$ we have $P \approx (P +_p P)$. $\qquad\qquad\square$

Moreover, associativity of the external choice does not hold, even if we introduce a rebalance of probabilities similar to that used in axiom **(AI)**.

Example 3 Consider $P = a +_{\frac{1}{2}} (b +_{\frac{1}{2}} Nil)$ and $P' = (a +_{\frac{2}{3}} b) +_{\frac{3}{4}} Nil$, and let $T = a; \omega +_{\frac{1}{2}} b; Nil$. We have $pass(P, T) = \frac{1}{2}$, but $pass(P', T) = \frac{2}{3}$. This is so because $P \approx (a +_{\frac{1}{2}} b)$ while $P' \approx (a +_{\frac{2}{3}} b)$, and obviously $(a +_{\frac{1}{2}} b) \not\approx (a +_{\frac{2}{3}} b)$. $\qquad\square$

This lack of associativity could create problems when trying to define normal forms, but fortunately non-associativity only appears in the presence of *Nil*. We can easily solve the problem since, by axiom **(NE)**, we can remove all the occurrences of the process *Nil* in external choices. In short, we have a restricted form of associativity that will be enough in order to transform any finite process into normal form.

Proposition 2 Let P_1, P_2, P_3 be processes such that for all i we have $P_i \longrightarrow$, that is, stable processes which are not operationally equivalent to *Nil*. Then, $P_1 +_p (P_2 +_q P_3) \approx (P_1 +_{p'} P_2) +_{q'} P_3$, where $q' = p + q - p \cdot q$ and $p' = \frac{p}{q'}$. $\quad\square$

Next we will introduce axioms dealing with divergence. Soundness proofs with respect to $\sqsubseteq_{\textbf{PAT}}$ are again trivial.

$$\textbf{(D)}\ \Omega \sqsubseteq P \qquad \textbf{(DI)}\ P \oplus_p \Omega \sqsubseteq P \qquad \textbf{(DE)}\ P +_p \Omega \equiv \Omega$$

Note that, in contrast with the nonprobabilistic case, $P \oplus_p \Omega \not\equiv \Omega$. For example, consider $P = a; Nil$, and $T = a; \omega$. We have $pass(P \oplus_p \Omega, T) = p$, while $pass(\Omega, T) = 0$.

Now, we will consider the distributive laws between the external and the internal choice operators. The soundness of the following axiom is easy to prove:

$$\textbf{(DEI)}\ P_1 +_p (P_2 \oplus_q P_3) \equiv (P_1 +_p P_2) \oplus_q (P_1 +_p P_3)$$

The previous axiom can be generalized to deal with generalized internal choices:

$$\textbf{(DEIG)}\ P +_p \left(\bigoplus_{i=1}^{n}[p_i]\, P_i\right) \equiv \bigoplus_{i=1}^{n}[p_i]\, (P +_p P_i)$$

On the contrary, the converse distributivity does not hold in general. This is illustrated by the following example.

Example 4 Let $P = a \oplus_{\frac{1}{2}} (b +_{\frac{1}{2}} c)$ and $Q = (a \oplus_{\frac{1}{2}} b) +_{\frac{1}{2}} (a \oplus_{\frac{1}{2}} c)$. We have $pass(P, a; \omega) = \frac{1}{2}$ while $pass(Q, a; \omega) = \frac{3}{4}$. $\qquad\square$

As in the nonprobabilistic case, in order to prove the completeness of the logic system we will introduce the adequate notion of normal form. Given that in our normal forms we will have generalized external choices instead of binary ones, we need an axiom for composing two generalized external choices by a binary external choice, called $(\textbf{EBE})$, and one for composing two generalized external choices having the same associated actions and the same probabilities by an internal choice, called $(\textbf{IBE})$.

Let $A = \{a_1, \ldots, a_n\} \subseteq Act$ and $B = \{b_1, \ldots, b_m\} \subseteq Act$. Let us consider the processes $P = \sum_{i=1}^{n}[p_i]\, a_i; P_i$ and $Q = \sum_{j=1}^{m}[q_j]\, b_j; Q_j$. Then, the following axiom is sound:

$$\textbf{(EBE)}\ P +_p Q \equiv R$$

where $R = \sum_{k=1}^{l}[r_k]\, c_k; R_k$, $C = \{c_1, \ldots, c_l\} = A \cup B$, and

$$r_k = \begin{cases} p \cdot p_i & \text{if}\ c_k = a_i \in A - B \\ (1 - p) \cdot q_j & \text{if}\ c_k = b_j \in B - A \\ p \cdot p_i + (1 - p) \cdot q_j & \text{if}\ c_k = a_i = b_j \in A \cap B \end{cases}$$

$$R_k = \begin{cases} P_i & \text{if}\ c_k = a_i \in A - B \\ Q_j & \text{if}\ c_k = b_j \in B - A \\ P_i \oplus_{p'} Q_j & \text{if}\ c_k = a_i = b_j \in A \cap B \ \wedge\ p' = \frac{p \cdot p_i}{p \cdot p_i + (1 - p) \cdot q_j} \end{cases}$$

Let $\{(a_1, p_1), (a_2, p_2), \ldots, (a_n, p_n)\}$ be a non empty state. Then the following axiom is sound:

$$\textbf{(IBE)} \ (\sum_{i=1}^{n}[p_i]\, a_i; P_i) \oplus_p \sum_{i=1}^{n}[p_i]\, a_i; Q_i \equiv \sum_{i=1}^{n}[p_i]\, a_i; (P_i \oplus_p Q_i)$$

Next we present the soundness proof of the axiom **EBE** (the proof of **IBE** is easier). First, we give an auxiliary definition.

Definition 6 Let $T = \sum_{i=1}^{u}[s_i]\,(t_i; Nil) +_s \omega \mid \sum_{i=1}^{u}[s_i]\, t_i; T_i$ be a probabilistic barb. We define its *set of initial actions*, denoted by $\tilde{T}$, as $\tilde{T} = \{t_1, \ldots, t_u\}$. Given a set of actions $C \subseteq Act$, we define the set T_C as $T_C = \{t_i \mid t_i \in C \cap \tilde{T}\}$.
$\square$

Lemma 3 The axiom (**EBE**) is sound.

Proof. In order to clarify the notation, $p(P, a_i)$ stands for p_i and $p(Q, b_j)$ stands for q_j. Note that applying the rules $(EXT4)$ and $(EXT5)$ we have $P \xrightarrow{a}_q P'$ implies $P +_p Q \xrightarrow{a}_{p \cdot q} P'$ and $Q \xrightarrow{a}_q P'$ implies $P +_p Q \xrightarrow{a}_{(1-p) \cdot q} P'$. We will show that for any $T \in \mathcal{PB}$ we have $pass(P +_p Q, T) = pass(R, T)$.

If T is a probabilistic barb of the form $T = \sum_{i=1}^{u}[s_i]\,(t_i; Nil) +_s \omega$, then

$$pass(P +_p Q, T) =$$

$$= \frac{1-s}{(1-s) + \sum\limits_{t_i \in T_A} s \cdot s_i \cdot p \cdot p(P, t_i) + \sum\limits_{t_i \in T_B} s \cdot s_i \cdot (1-p) \cdot p(Q, t_i)}$$

$$= \frac{1-s}{(1-s) + \sum\limits_{t_i \in T_{A-B}} s \cdot s_i \cdot p \cdot p(P, t_i) + \sum\limits_{t_i \in T_{B-A}} s \cdot s_i \cdot (1-p) \cdot p(Q, t_i) + \sum\limits_{t_i \in T_{A \cap B}} s \cdot s_i \cdot (p \cdot p(P, t_i) + (1-p) \cdot p(Q, t_i))}$$

$$= pass(R, T)$$

Let $T = \sum_{i=1}^{u}[s_i]\, t_i; T_i$ be a probabilistic barb such that if $i = u$ then $T_i = T'$ for some probabilistic barb T', while $T_i = Nil$ otherwise, we distinguish four cases:

1. $\exists\, 1 \le i \le n:\ a_i = t_u \in A - B$
2. $\exists\, 1 \le j \le m:\ b_j = t_u \in B - A$
3. $\exists\, 1 \le i \le n,\ 1 \le j \le m: a_i = b_j = t_u \in A \cap B$
4. $t_u \notin A \cup B$.

In the last case we trivially get $pass(P +_p Q, T) = pass(R, T) = 0$. The proof for the first three cases is very similar, so we present, as an example, the proof for the third case:

$$\textbf{(O1)}\ \frac{P\sqsubseteq Q\ \wedge\ Q\sqsubseteq P}{P\equiv Q}\qquad \textbf{(O2)}\ \frac{P\equiv Q}{P\sqsubseteq Q,\ Q\sqsubseteq P}\qquad \textbf{(O3)}\ \frac{P\sqsubseteq Q\ \wedge\ Q\sqsubseteq R}{P\sqsubseteq R}$$

$$\textbf{(C1)}\ \frac{P\sqsubseteq Q}{a;P\sqsubseteq a;Q}\qquad \textbf{(C2)}\ \frac{P\sqsubseteq Q\ \wedge\ P'\sqsubseteq Q'}{P+_pP'\sqsubseteq Q+_pQ'}\qquad \textbf{(C3)}\ \frac{P\sqsubseteq Q\ \wedge\ P'\sqsubseteq Q'}{P\oplus_pP'\sqsubseteq Q\oplus_pQ'}$$

$$\textbf{(RE)}\ \frac{}{P\equiv P}\qquad \textbf{(OI1)}\ \frac{P\sqsubseteq Q}{P\sqsubseteq P\oplus_pQ}\qquad \textbf{(OI2)}\ \frac{P\sqsubseteq Q}{P\oplus_pQ\sqsubseteq Q}$$

Fig. 2. Inference Rules.

$$pass(P +_p Q, T)$$

$$= \frac{s_u\cdot p\cdot p_i\cdot pass(P_i,T')+s_u\cdot(1-p)\cdot q_j\cdot pass(Q_j,T')}{\displaystyle\sum_{t_i\in T_A}s_i\cdot p\cdot p(P,t_i)\ +\ \sum_{t_i\in T_B}s_i\cdot(1-p)\cdot p(Q,t_i)}$$

$$= \frac{s_u\cdot(p\cdot p_i+(1-p)\cdot q_j)\cdot pass(P_i\oplus_{q'}Q_j,T')}{\displaystyle\sum_{t_i\in T_{A-B}}s_i\cdot p\cdot p(P,t_i)\ +\ \sum_{t_i\in T_{B-A}}s_i\cdot(1-p)\cdot p(Q,t_i)\ +\ \sum_{t_i\in T_{A\cap B}}s_i\cdot(p\cdot p(P,t_i)+(1-p)\cdot p(Q,t_i))}$$

$$= pass(R,T),\qquad \text{where } q'=\frac{p\cdot p_i}{p\cdot p_i+(1-p)\cdot q_j}$$

$\square$

In addition to the previous axioms, we need a set of rules indicating that the relation $\equiv$ fulfills some *good* properties. The inference rules of our logic system are given in Figure 2. Rules **(O1-3)** indicate that $\sqsubseteq$ is an order relation. Rules **(C1-3)** say that $\sqsubseteq$ is a precongruence with respect to the basic operators of the language. **(RE)** says that $\equiv$ is reflexive. Finally, **(OI1-2)** indicate that internal choice occupies an intermediate position between the corresponding processes. Soundness of **(O1-3)**, **(C1-3)**, and **(RE)** rules is trivial with respect to $\sqsubseteq_{\textbf{PAT}}$, given that the latter is defined compositionally, while the soundness of **(OI1-2)** can be easily shown with respect to $\sqsubseteq_{\textbf{PAT}}$.

Definition 7 Given two processes P and Q, we write $\vdash P\sqsubseteq Q$ (resp. $\vdash P\equiv Q$) if $P\sqsubseteq Q$ (resp. $P\equiv Q$) can be derived from the axioms given before and the rules given in Figure 2. $\square$

Given that the previous axioms and rules are sound, we automatically get

Theorem 2 (Soundness for PPA$_{fin}$)
For any $P,\ Q\in \text{PPA}_{fin}$ we have $\vdash P\sqsubseteq Q$ implies $[\![P]\!]\sqsubseteq_{\textbf{PAT}}[\![Q]\!]$. As a corollary, we also have $\vdash P\equiv Q$ implies $[\![P]\!]=_{\textbf{PAT}}[\![Q]\!]$, and by using full abstraction of $=_{\textbf{PAT}}$, $\vdash P\equiv Q$ implies $P\approx Q$. $\square$

This result indicates that if we can derive the equivalence between two finite processes from the axiom system, then these two processes are testing equivalent. In the remainder of the section we will prove that our axiomatization is also *complete*, that is, if two finite processes are testing equivalent, then the equivalence of these processes with respect to $\equiv$ can be derived from the given axiomatization.

In order to simplify the completeness proof we will use a notion of *normal form*, and we will prove that every PPA$_{fin}$ process can be transformed into a normal form by applying the axioms and rules of our axiom system. Our normal forms are similar to those in [12], that is, they will be generalized internal choices of generalized external choices. The actions associated with the generalized external choices *prefix* normal forms, so that normal forms will be processes which have a strict alternation between generalized internal choices and generalized external choices. Moreover, we will not allow two generalized external choices associated with the same internal choice to have the same set of actions and the same probability distribution associated with them. Actually, our normal forms are the syntactic expression of the semantic processes described in [19].

Definition 8 *Normal Forms* are those PPA$_{fin}$ processes defined by means of the following BNF expression:

$$N ::= \bigoplus_{i=1}^{n} [p_i] \sum_{j=1}^{r_i} [p_{i,j}] \, a_{i,j} \, ; N$$

where $n \geq 0$, $\sum_{i=1}^{n} p_i \leq 1$, and
- $\forall\, 1 \leq i \leq n : p_i > 0 \wedge r_i \geq 0$, and if $r_i > 0$ then $\sum_{j=1}^{r_i} p_{i,j} = 1 \wedge \forall\, 1 \leq j \leq r_i : p_{i,j} > 0$
- $\forall\, 1 \leq i \leq n : \forall\, 1 \leq k, l \leq r_i, k \neq l : a_{i,k} \neq a_{i,l}$
- $\forall\, 1 \leq u, v \leq n, u \neq v : \{(a_{u,j}, p_{u,j})\}_{j=1}^{r_u} \neq \{(a_{v,j}, p_{v,j})\}_{j=1}^{r_v}$ □

Note that, in contrast with [12], we do not force the continuations after the same action in different states to be equal. We will use the following alternative notation for normal forms:

$$N ::= \bigoplus_{A \in \mathcal{A}} [p_A] \sum_{(a, p_a) \in A} [p_a] \, a; N_{a,A}$$

where $\mathcal{A}$ is a finite subset of $\mathcal{P}(Act \times (0, 1])$ such that for all $A \in \mathcal{A}$, if $A \neq \emptyset$ then $\sum \{\, p_a \mid (a, p_a) \in A \,\} = 1$. The next result states that any PPA$_{fin}$ process can be transformed into a normal form by using the axiom system.

Theorem 3 Given $P \in$ PPA$_{fin}$, there exists a normal form N such that $\vdash P \equiv N$.

Proof. The proof is done by structural induction, and we only present the case for internal choice. The proof for *Nil*, Ω, and prefix is trivial, while the proof for external choice is similar to the one for internal choice.

If $P = P_1 \oplus_p P_2$, then by induction hypothesis P_1 and P_2 can be transformed into normal forms N_1 and N_2 respectively, such that $P_1 \equiv N_1$ and $P_2 \equiv N_2$, where

$$N_1 = \bigoplus_{A \in \mathcal{A}} [p_A] \sum_{(a, p_a) \in A} [p_a] \, a; P_{a,A} \qquad \text{and} \qquad N_2 = \bigoplus_{B \in \mathcal{B}} [q_B] \sum_{(b, q_b) \in B} [q_b] \, b; Q_{b,B}$$

Applying the rules (**C3**) and (**O1-2**) we obtain $P_1 \oplus_p P_2 \equiv N_1 \oplus_p N_2$. Now, applying the axiom (**IBE**), if necessary, and given that any generalized internal choice can be decomposed into binary internal choices and vice versa, we obtain the normal form

$$N = \bigoplus_{C \in \mathcal{C}} [r_C] \sum_{(c,r_c) \in C} [r_c]\, c;\, R_{c,C}$$

where $\mathcal{C} = \mathcal{A} \cup \mathcal{B}$ and for any $C \in \mathcal{C}$ we have three possibilities:

$$
\begin{aligned}
C = A \in \mathcal{A} - \mathcal{B} &\Rightarrow r_C = p \cdot p_A \wedge \forall c \in C: R_{c,C} = P_{c,A} \\
C = B \in \mathcal{B} - \mathcal{A} &\Rightarrow r_C = (1-p) \cdot q_B \wedge \forall c \in C: R_{c,C} = Q_{c,B} \\
C = A = B \in \mathcal{A} \cap \mathcal{B} &\Rightarrow r_C = p \cdot p_A + (1-p) \cdot q_B \wedge \forall c \in C: R_{c,C} = P_{c,A} \oplus_{\frac{p \cdot p_A}{r_C}} Q_{c,B}
\end{aligned}
$$

In the first two cases we obtain that $R_{c,C}$ are already normal forms, while in the last case we can apply the induction hypothesis to the corresponding processes $P_{c,A}$ and $Q_{c,B}$ in order to get a normal form. Therefore, we have got a normal form N such that $N_1 \oplus_p N_2 \equiv N$, and so, applying the rules (O1-3), we obtain $P_1 \oplus_p P_2 \equiv N$. □

Next we present a result stating that if two (semantic) processes are related by $\sqsubseteq_{\mathbf{PAT}}$, then the corresponding syntactic processes are also related by $\sqsubseteq$.

Lemma 4 Let $P, Q \in \mathrm{PPA}_{fin}$. Then, $[\![P]\!] \sqsubseteq_{\mathbf{PAT}} [\![Q]\!]$ implies $P \sqsubseteq Q$.

Proof. By Theorem 3, P and Q can be transformed into normal forms by using the axiom system. So we can restrict ourselves to the study of the equivalent normal forms. Let us take

$$P = \bigoplus_{A \in \mathcal{A}} [p_A] \sum_{(a,p_a) \in A} [p_a]\, a;\, P_{a,A} \quad \text{and} \quad Q = \bigoplus_{B \in \mathcal{B}} [q_B] \sum_{(b,q_b) \in B} [q_b]\, b;\, Q_{b,B}$$

where $\mathcal{A}, \mathcal{B} \subseteq \mathcal{P}(\Sigma \times (0,1])$. Note that $p(P, \epsilon, A) = p_A$ and $p(Q, \epsilon, B) = q_B$. The proof is done by using structural induction over the *complexity* of processes. By complexity we mean the *depth* of processes, that is, the maximum number of times that a generalized internal choice (followed by a generalized external choice) appears in a row. If two processes have the same depth, we consider that a process is more complex than another one if the reachable states of the latter are contained in the ones of the former. We have three possibilities:

- $\mathcal{A}$ and $\mathcal{B}$ are different   • $\mathcal{A} = \mathcal{B}$ and $\exists C: p_C \neq q_C$ • $\mathcal{A} = \mathcal{B}$ and $\forall C \in \mathcal{A}: p_C = q_C$

We present the proof only for the first case. So we suppose that $\mathcal{A} \neq \mathcal{B}$. Given that $[\![P]\!] \sqsubseteq_{\mathbf{PAT}} [\![Q]\!]$, there exists a state B' such that $B' \in \mathcal{B} - \mathcal{A}$. Moreover, the probability in Q of any state belonging to $\mathcal{B}$ must be greater than or equal to the corresponding one in P. Moreover, since $[\![P]\!] \sqsubseteq_{\mathbf{PAT}} [\![Q]\!]$, we have $\mathcal{A} \subseteq \mathcal{B}$. Then we have

$$\sum_{A \in \mathcal{A}} p_A \leq \sum_{A \in \mathcal{A}} q_A < \sum_{A \in \mathcal{A}} q_A + q_{B'} \leq \sum_{B \in \mathcal{B}} q_B \leq 1$$

and so the probability of P diverging in its first step is greater than or equal to $q_{B'}$. Now, using the axiom (**AI**), we can rewrite P and Q as:

$$P \equiv \left(\bigoplus_{A \in \mathcal{A}} \left[\frac{p_A}{1-q_{B'}} \right] \sum_{(a,p_a) \in A} [p_a]\, a; P_{a,A} \right) \oplus_{1-q_{B'}} \Omega$$

$$Q \equiv \left(\bigoplus_{B \in \mathcal{B}-\mathcal{B}'} \left[\frac{q_B}{1-q_{B'}} \right] \sum_{(b,q_b) \in B} [q_b]\, b; Q_{b,B} \right) \oplus_{1-q_{B'}} \left(\sum_{(b',q_{b'}) \in B'} [q_{b'}]\, b'; Q_{b',B'} \right)$$

Applying axiom (**D**), we have

$$\Omega \sqsubseteq \sum_{(b',q_{b'}) \in B} [q_{b'}]\, b'; Q_{b',B'} \tag{1}$$

Given that $[P] \sqsubseteq_{\textbf{PAT}} [Q]$, we obtain

$$[\bigoplus_{A \in \mathcal{A}} [\frac{p_A}{1-q_{B'}}] \sum_{(a,p_a) \in A} [p_a]\, a; P_{a,A}] \sqsubseteq_{\textbf{PAT}} [\bigoplus_{B \in \mathcal{B}-\mathcal{B}'} [\frac{q_B}{1-q_{B'}}] \sum_{(b,q_b) \in B} [q_b]\, b; Q_{b,B}]$$

and applying the induction hypothesis, given that the states of the right hand side process are contained in those of the process Q, we have

$$\bigoplus_{A \in \mathcal{A}} [\frac{p_A}{1-q_{B'}}] \sum_{(a,p_a) \in A} [p_a]\, a; P_{a,A} \sqsubseteq \bigoplus_{B \in \mathcal{B}-\mathcal{B}'} [\frac{q_B}{1-q_{B'}}] \sum_{(b,q_b) \in B} [q_b]\, b; Q_{b,B} \tag{2}$$

Then applying the rule (**C3**) to equations (1) and (2) we conclude $P \sqsubseteq Q$.   □

By using the equivalence between $=_{\textbf{PAT}}$ and $\approx$, and this result we obtain

Theorem 4 (Completeness for PPA$_{fin}$)
For any processes $P, Q \in \text{PPA}_{fin}$ we have $P \approx Q$ implies $\vdash P \equiv Q$.   □

4   Extension of the System to Infinite Processes

In this section we extend the previous results to deal with recursion, adding to PPA$_{fin}$ recursive processes (we call this language PPA$_{rec}$). We will work with the approximations by *finite processes* of recursive processes, which are defined like in [12].

Definition 9 Let P be a PPA$_{rec}$ process. For any $n \in \mathbb{N}$, we define the n-th *finite approximation* of P as $P^0 = \Omega$, and for $n \geq 0$:

- $X^{n+1} = X$, if $X \in Id$
- $(a; P)^{n+1} = a; P^{n+1}$
- $(recX.P)^{n+1} = P^{n+1}\{(recX.P)^n/X\}$

- $Nil^{n+1} = Nil$
- $(P \oplus_p Q)^{n+1} = P^{n+1} \oplus_p Q^{n+1}$
- $(P +_p Q)^{n+1} = P^{n+1} +_p Q^{n+1}$

- $\Omega^{n+1} = \Omega$

□

Note that for PPA$_{fin}$ processes it holds that their finite approximations are equal to themselves. Also note that each finite approximation is a finite process, and therefore we can use the results given in the previous section when reasoning about finite approximations. The previous axiom system is extended with three new rules:

$$\textbf{(R1)} \quad \frac{}{P\{recX.P/X\} \sqsubseteq recX.P} \qquad \textbf{(R2)} \quad \frac{\forall\, n \in \mathbb{N}:\ P^n \sqsubseteq R}{P \sqsubseteq R}$$

$$\textbf{(R3)} \quad \frac{\forall\, n \in \mathbb{N}:\ P \oplus_{\frac{n-1}{n}} \Omega \sqsubseteq R}{P \sqsubseteq R}$$

The first two rules already appeared in [12], and their soundness proofs easily follow from the definition of the denotational semantics of recursive processes.[2] Concretely, soundness of **(R1)** is trivial because $[\![P\{recX.P/X\}]\!] = \bigsqcup_{n=1}^{\infty} [\![P^n]\!]$, while **(R2)** is sound because we are working within a *cpo*, and so $[\![P]\!]$ is the least upper bound of $\{[\![P^i]\!]\}_{i=0}^{\infty}$.

The rule **(R3)** is added to our system because of *technical* reasons. This rule is necessary because the semantics of finite syntactic processes (i.e. without occurrences of the recursion operator) is given by non compact elements in the semantic domain. We will comment more thoroughly this rule when we use it.

Lemma 5 The rule **(R3)** is sound.

Proof. Let us suppose that for all $n \in \mathbb{N}$ we have $[\![P \oplus_{\frac{n-1}{n}} \Omega]\!] \sqsubseteq_{\textbf{PAT}} [\![R]\!]$. That is, for any $n \in \mathbb{N}$, any sequence s, and any state A, $p([\![P \oplus_{\frac{n-1}{n}} \Omega]\!], s, A) \leq p([\![R]\!], s, A)$. From the definition of the internal choice semantic function, we have $p([\![P \oplus_{\frac{n-1}{n}} \Omega]\!], s, A) = \frac{n-1}{n} \cdot p([\![P]\!], s, A) + \frac{1}{n} \cdot p([\![\Omega]\!], s, A) = \frac{n-1}{n} \cdot p([\![P]\!], s, A)$. Taking into account the two previous facts, we have that for any s and A:

$$p([\![P]\!], s, A) = \lim_{n \to \infty} \frac{n-1}{n} \cdot p([\![P]\!], s, A) \leq p([\![R]\!], s, A)$$

which implies $[\![P]\!] \sqsubseteq_{\textbf{PAT}} [\![R]\!]$. $\qquad\qquad\square$

Theorem 5 (Soundness for PPA$_{rec}$)
Let P, Q be PPA$_{rec}$ processes. We have that $\vdash P \equiv Q$ implies $P \approx Q$. $\qquad\square$

Now we will prove completeness of the axiomatization. First we present a result (whose proof is essentially like in [12]), and then we extend Lemma 4 for the case when one of the processes is not finite.

Lemma 6 Let $P \in$ PPA$_{rec}$. For any approximation P^n of P we have $\vdash P^n \sqsubseteq P$. $\qquad\qquad\square$

Lemma 7 Let $P \in$ PPA$_{rec}$, and $Q \in$ PPA$_{fin}$. $[\![P]\!] \sqsubseteq_{\textbf{PAT}} [\![Q]\!]$ implies $P \sqsubseteq Q$.

---

[2] As usually, the (denotational) semantics of a recursive process is given by the limit of its finite approximations, that is, $[\![recX.\, P]\!] = \bigsqcup_{n=0}^{\infty} [\![P^n]\!]$.

Proof. Given that the finite approximations of P are a chain, such that $[P]$ is its least upper bound, we have $[P^0] \sqsubseteq_{\textbf{PAT}} \cdots \sqsubseteq_{\textbf{PAT}} [P^n] \cdots \sqsubseteq_{\textbf{PAT}} [P] \sqsubseteq_{\textbf{PAT}} [Q]$. Given that the processes P^n and Q are finite, we can apply the previous results for finite processes, concluding that for all n we have $P^n \sqsubseteq Q$, and applying (**R2**) we have $P \sqsubseteq Q$. □

Now, let us consider the case where P is finite but Q is not. Given that the usual way to assign semantics to recursive processes is by means of their finite approximations, the most straight way for proving $P \sqsubseteq Q$ would be to guarantee that there exists m such that the m-th finite approximation of the process Q fulfills $[P] \sqsubseteq_{\textbf{PAT}} [Q^m]$. Then, given that P and Q^m are finite, we can apply Lemma 4, deducing $P \sqsubseteq Q^m$. Besides, we have $Q^m \sqsubseteq Q$ (Lemma 6), and so, applying (**O3**), we would obtain $P \sqsubseteq Q$. If finite processes were mapped into compact (also called finite) elements in the semantic domain, then the existence of such an m would be guaranteed, given that if R is a compact element and $R \sqsubseteq_{\textbf{PAT}} \sqcup R^n$ then there exists R^i such that $R \sqsubseteq_{\textbf{PAT}} R^i$, but unfortunately this is not the case, as the following example shows.

Example 5 Consider $P = recX.((a; Nil) \oplus_{\frac{1}{2}} X)$, and $Q = a; Nil$. It is easy to check that the finite approximations of P are given by $P^n = (a; Nil) \oplus_{1-\frac{1}{2^n}} \Omega$.

By definition we have $[P] = \sqcup [P^n]$, and so we trivially get $[P] \sqsubseteq_{\textbf{PAT}} \sqcup [P^n]$. Moreover, $[P]$ *describes* a syntactic finite process, because $[P] =_{\textbf{PAT}} [Q]$, and so, we should be able to conclude $P \equiv Q$. By the previous lemma we have $P \sqsubseteq Q$, but there does not exist m such that $[Q] \sqsubseteq_{\textbf{PAT}} [P^m]$, otherwise we would have

$$1 = p([Q], \epsilon, \{(a, 1)\}) \leq p([P^m], \epsilon, \{(a, 1)\}) = 1 - \frac{1}{2^m}$$

which is not the case. So, we have found a finite (syntactic) process, $a; Nil$, which semantics is the least upper bound of the infinite nontrivial chain $\{[P^n]\}_{n=1}^{\infty}$. □

The previous example shows that in general we must use another way in order to deduce $P \sqsubseteq Q$ from $[P] \sqsubseteq_{\textbf{PAT}} [Q]$. This is the reason why the rule (**R3**) was included in our logic system. This is an important difference with respect to [12] where finite processes are mapped into compact elements. Note that even if we delete probabilities, the previous example is not correct in the classical testing theory, given that Ω is a *zero* of $\oplus$ (Ω is also a zero of the external choice and parallel operators), and so the rule (**R3**) is not sound in that setting. Let us remark that the only compact element of the semantic domain is the one corresponding to divergence, given that for any process P different from Ω we can always construct a succession, for instance $P^n = P \oplus_{\frac{n}{n+1}} \Omega$, such that P is *lower* than the limit (actually $[P] = \sqcup [P^n]$) while for any n we have $[P] \sqsubseteq_{\textbf{PAT}} [P^n]$ does not hold.

Lemma 8 Let $P \in \text{PPA}_{fin}$ and $Q \in \text{PPA}_{rec}$. $[P] \sqsubseteq_{\textbf{PAT}} [Q]$ implies $P \sqsubseteq Q$.

Proof. We have $[P] \sqsubseteq_{\textbf{PAT}} [Q] = \sqcup [Q^n]$. If there exists m such that $[P] \sqsubseteq_{\textbf{PAT}} [Q^m]$, then the proof can be done as previously indicated. So, let us suppose that there does not exist such an m. Given that $\{Q^n\}$ are a chain, for any sequence s and any state A, we have $p(\llbracket P\rrbracket, s, A) \leq p(\llbracket Q\rrbracket, s, A) = \lim_{n\to\infty} p(\llbracket Q^n\rrbracket, s, A)$.

Let us consider those sequences s and those states A such that $p(\llbracket P\rrbracket, s, A) > 0$. We have that for all $k > 0$, $(1 - \frac{1}{k}) \cdot p(\llbracket P\rrbracket, s, A) < \lim_{n\to\infty} p(\llbracket Q^n\rrbracket, s, A)$. Note that $(1 - \frac{1}{k}) \cdot p(\llbracket P\rrbracket, s, A) = p(\llbracket P \oplus_{1-\frac{1}{k}} \varOmega\rrbracket, s, A)$.

Given that P is a finite process, the set of (s, A) pairs verifying $p(\llbracket P\rrbracket, s, A) > 0$ is finite. So, for each $k \in \mathbb{N}$ there exists $n_k \in \mathbb{N}$ such that for any sequence s and any state A, such that $p(\llbracket P\rrbracket, s, A) > 0$, we have $p(\llbracket P \oplus_{1-\frac{1}{k}} \varOmega\rrbracket, s, A) \leq p(\llbracket Q^{n_k}\rrbracket, s, A)$. Obviously, if $p(\llbracket P\rrbracket, s', A') = 0$ then the previous result also holds, and so we have $\llbracket P \oplus_{1-\frac{1}{k}} \varOmega\rrbracket \sqsubseteq_{\textbf{PAT}} \llbracket Q^{n_k}\rrbracket$ and given that $P \oplus_{1-\frac{1}{k}} \varOmega$ and Q^{n_k} are finite processes, we can apply Lemma 4 obtaining $P \oplus_{1-\frac{1}{k}} \varOmega \sqsubseteq Q^{n_k}$, for all $k \in \mathbb{N}$. Again, given that for all $n \in \mathbb{N}$, $Q^n \sqsubseteq Q$, we have for all $k \in \mathbb{N}$, $P \oplus_{1-\frac{1}{k}} \varOmega \sqsubseteq Q$, and so, applying (**R3**), we conclude $P \sqsubseteq Q$.   □

Theorem 6 Let P, Q be PPA$_{rec}$ processes. $\llbracket P\rrbracket \sqsubseteq_{\textbf{PAT}} \llbracket Q\rrbracket$ implies $P \sqsubseteq Q$.

Proof. If either P or Q is finite, then we apply Lemmas 4, 7, and 8. Otherwise, by the definition of (semantic) finite approximations we have that for all $n \in \mathbb{N}$, $\llbracket P^n\rrbracket \sqsubseteq_{\textbf{PAT}} \llbracket P\rrbracket$, and given that $\sqsubseteq_{\textbf{PAT}}$ is a preorder, we have $\llbracket P^n\rrbracket \sqsubseteq_{\textbf{PAT}} \llbracket Q\rrbracket$. Now, by Lemma 8, we have $P^n \sqsubseteq Q$, and applying (**R2**) we conclude $P \sqsubseteq Q$.   □

Again, by the previous result and the equivalence between $=_{\textbf{PAT}}$ and $\approx$ we get

Theorem 7 (Completeness for PPA$_{rec}$)
For any processes $P, Q \in$ PPA$_{rec}$, we have $P \approx Q \implies \vdash P \equiv Q$.   □

5   Extension of the System to the Parallel Operator

In this section we give some axioms for the parallel operator showing that it can be considered as a derived one in the sense that it can be completely eliminated in finite processes (by transforming processes where the parallel operator appears into equivalent processes without occurrences of the parallel operator), and that the occurrences of the parallel operator in recursive processes can be *sunk* in such a way that there will be occurrences of the parallel operator but not in the *head* of the expression (that is, these processes can be transformed into *head normal form*).

These axioms indicate that the parallel operator is commutative and distributes over the internal choice. Moreover, we have an axiom indicating that the parallel operator is strict, and that it can be eliminated if both processes are *Nil*. We also have an *expansion* axiom similar to that in nonprobabilistic process algebras. Finally, we have a rule indicating that this operator is congruent. Let us comment that even though a parallel operator was not included in [19], and so its (denotational) semantic function is not included there, this function is not used in this paper given that soundness proofs of the following axioms are easy with respect to $\approx$ (the corresponding semantic function is given in [17]).

$$\textbf{(CP)} \ P \parallel_A Q \equiv Q \parallel_A P \qquad\qquad \textbf{(DPIG)} \ P \parallel_A \left(\bigoplus_{i=1}^{n}[p_i]\, P_i\right) \equiv \bigoplus_{i=1}^{n}[p_i]\, (P \parallel_A P_i)$$

$$\textbf{(DP)} \ P \parallel_A \Omega \equiv \Omega \qquad\qquad\quad \textbf{(NP)} \ Nil \parallel_A Nil \equiv Nil$$

Let $A = \{a_1, \ldots, a_n\} \subseteq Act$ and $B = \{b_1, \ldots, b_m\} \subseteq Act$. If we consider the processes $P = \sum_{i=1}^{n}[p_i]\, a_i; P_i$ and $Q = \sum_{j=1}^{m}[q_j]\, b_j; Q_j$, then the following axiom is sound

$$\textbf{(EP)} \ P \parallel_X Q \equiv R$$

where $R = \sum_{k=1}^{l}\left[\frac{r_k}{\mu(P,Q,X)}\right] c_k; R_k$, $C = \{c_1, \ldots, c_l\} = (A \cup B) - X \cup (A \cap B \cap X)$, and

$$r_k = \begin{cases} p_i \cdot q_j & \text{if } c_k = a_i = b_j \in X \\ p_i & \text{if } c_k = a_i \in (A - B) - X \\ q_j & \text{if } c_k = b_j \in (B - A) - X \\ p_i + q_j & \text{if } c_k = a_i = b_j \in (A \cap B) - X \end{cases}$$

$$R_k = \begin{cases} P_i \parallel_X Q_j & \text{if } c_k = a_i = b_j \in X \\ P_i \parallel_X Q & \text{if } c_k = a_i \in (A - B) - X \\ P \parallel_X Q_j & \text{if } c_k = b_j \in (B - A) - X \\ (P_i \parallel_X Q) \oplus_{p'} (P \parallel_X Q_j) & \text{if } c_k = a_i = b_j \in (A \cap B) - X \ \wedge \ p' = \frac{p_i}{p_i + q_j} \end{cases}$$

Note that this last axiom can be applied to the process *Nil* (i.e. empty generalized external choices), so that the combination of **(NP)**, **(DP)**, and **(EP)** will allow to remove trailing occurrences of the parallel operator.

Finally, we have that $\equiv$ is a congruence for the parallel operator, that is, we have the following rule:

$$\textbf{(C4)} \ \frac{P \equiv P'}{P \parallel_A Q \equiv P' \parallel_A Q}$$

6 Conclusions

We have presented a sound and complete axiomatization of probabilistic testing with generative probabilities. The rules and axioms have been presented in three steps: first, we studied finite processes without parallel composition, then, we extended the previous axiomatization to deal with recursively defined processes, and finally, we gave sound axioms which indicate that the parallel operator can be considered as a derived one from the rest of operators.

A possible extension of our work would be to include some kind of *hiding* or *restriction* operator. Our results in [17] show that such inclusion is far from easy if we want to have this operator as a derived one. Specifically, consider the following processes

$$P = (a +_p c; b)\backslash c \qquad Q = b \oplus_{p'} \left(\bigoplus_{i=1}^{n} [q_i](a +_{p_i} b) \right)$$

If we make an interpretation of hiding *a la* CCS, that is, considering that P behaves like $a +_p \tau; b$, and we use a suitable definition of testing (e.g. [5]) we have that given p, in general, there do not exist values $0 < p', q_1 \ldots q_n, p_1 \ldots p_n < 1$ such that P and Q are probabilistic testing equivalent. We have an additional result. After a complicated redefinition of the parallel operator (using *prenormalization* factors) we got that P could be equivalent to the process $(a +_1 b) \oplus_p b$, where $+_1$ indicates a priority operator similar to that in [16]. We worked out a definition of the new semantic model but it was so unmanageable that we decided not to include priorities in our framework.

Acknowledgments: I would like to thank my advisor, David de Frutos, for his advice and encouragement. I also would like to thank Scott Smolka for many valuable comments as member of my PhD thesis committee which have improved the quality of this paper.

References

1. J.C.M. Baeten, J.A. Bergstra, and S.A. Smolka. Axiomatizing probabilistic processes: ACP with generative probabilities. *Information and Computation*, 121(2):234–255, 1995.
2. C. Baier and H. Hermanns. Weak bisimulation for fully probabilistic processes. In *Computer Aided Verification'97, LNCS 1254*, pages 119–130. Springer, 1997.
3. I. Christoff. Testing equivalences and fully abstract models for probabilistic processes. In *CONCUR'90, LNCS 458*, pages 126–140. Springer, 1990.
4. R. Cleaveland, I. Lee, P. Lewis, and S.A. Smolka. A theory of testing for soft real-time processes. In *8th International Conference on Software Engineering and Knowledge Engineering*, 1996.
5. R. Cleaveland, S.A. Smolka, and A.E. Zwarico. Testing preorders for probabilistic processes. In *19th ICALP, LNCS 623*, pages 708–719. Springer, 1992.
6. F. Cuartero, D. de Frutos, and V. Valero. A sound and complete proof system for probabilistic processes. In *4th International AMAST Workshop on Real-Time Systems, Concurrent and Distributed Software, LNCS 1231*, pages 340–352. Springer, 1997.
7. P. R. D'Argenio, H. Hermanns, and J.-P. Katoen. On generative parallel composition. In *Workshop on Probabilistic Methods in Verification, PROBMIV'98*, pages 105–121, 1998.
8. R. de Nicola and M.C.B. Hennessy. Testing equivalences for processes. *Theoretical Computer Science*, 34:83–133, 1984.
9. A. Giacalone, C.-C. Jou, and S.A. Smolka. Algebraic reasoning for probabilistic concurrent systems. In *Proceedings of Working Conference on Programming Concepts and Methods, IFIP TC 2*. North Holland, 1990.

10. C. Gregorio, L. Llana, M. Núñez, and P. Palao. Testing semantics for a probabilistic-timed process algebra. In *4th International AMAST Workshop on Real-Time Systems, Concurrent, and Distributed Software, LNCS 1231*, pages 353–367. Springer, 1997.
11. C. Gregorio and M. Núñez. Denotational semantics for probabilistic refusal testing. In *Workshop on Probabilistic Methods in Verification, PROBMIV'98*, pages 123–137, 1998.
12. M. Hennessy. *Algebraic Theory of Processes*. MIT Press, 1988.
13. C.-C. Jou and S.A. Smolka. Equivalences, congruences and complete axiomatizations for probabilistic processes. In *CONCUR'90, LNCS 458*, pages 367–383. Springer, 1990.
14. K. Larsen and A. Skou. Bisimulation through probabilistic testing. *Information and Computation*, 94(1):1–28, 1991.
15. K.G. Larsen and A. Skou. Compositional verification of probabilistic processes. In *CONCUR'92, LNCS 630*, pages 456–471. Springer, 1992.
16. G. Lowe. Probabilistic and prioritized models of timed CSP. *Theoretical Computer Science*, 138:315–352, 1995.
17. M. Núñez. *Semánticas de Pruebas para Álgebras de Procesos Probabilísticos*. PhD thesis, Universidad Complutense de Madrid, 1996.
18. M. Núñez and D. de Frutos. Testing semantics for probabilistic LOTOS. In *Formal Description Techniques VIII*, pages 365–380. Chapman & Hall, 1995.
19. M. Núñez, D. de Frutos, and L. Llana. Acceptance trees for probabilistic processes. In *CONCUR'95, LNCS 962*, pages 249–263. Springer, 1995.
20. E.W. Stark and S.A. Smolka. A complete axiom system for finite-state probabilistic processes, 1996.
21. C. Tofts. A synchronous calculus of relative frequency. In *CONCUR'90, LNCS 458*, pages 467–480. Springer, 1990.
22. R. van Glabbeek, S.A. Smolka, and B. Steffen. Reactive, generative and stratified models of probabilistic processes. *Information and Computation*, 121(1):59–80, 1995.
23. W. Yi and K.G. Larsen. Testing probabilistic and nondeterministic processes. In *Protocol Specification, Testing and Verification XII*, pages 47–61. North Holland, 1992.
24. S. Yuen, R. Cleaveland, Z. Dayar, and S.A. Smolka. Fully abstract characterizations of testing preorders for probabilistic processes. In *CONCUR'94, LNCS 836*, pages 497–512. Springer, 1994.

Verification of Hybrid Systems

Frits Vaandrager

Computing Science Institute
University of Nijmegen
P.O. Box 9010, 6500 GL Nijmegen
The Netherlands
Frits.Vaandrager@cs.kun.nl

Abstract. The next stage of the computer revolution consists in the proliferation of sophisticated and cheap digital controllers into almost every aspect of man-made systems. Informatics is expected to shift its focus of attention from computers performing internal computations, or communicating with human users and with other computers, toward computers interacting in real-time with physical processes. In such settings, the proper functioning of the whole system depends critically on the interaction between the discrete dynamics of the digital controller and the continuous dynamics of the environment in which it is embedded. Models of hybrid systems suggest a framework for modelling, simulation, verification, synthesis and implementation of such systems.

The main activity of the Esprit LTR project VHS — Verification of Hybrid Systems — consists of analysing academic and industrial case studies, taken from the process control industry, in order to define formal models of plants. These models are then used to verify properties concerning their behaviour. The project uses, among others, the models of timed and hybrid automata to express hybrid phenomena. Several tools for analysing systems expressed in this formalism have been built, and are used within the project for automatic verification.

The VHS project started in 1998. The consortium is composed of five CS partners (Verimag, Weizmann, Nijmegen, Brics and Kiel), two chemical engineering and process control partners (Dortmund, LAG), two partners from control theory (CWI and Ghent) and three industrial partners (Sidmar, Nylstar, Krupp).

In this talk, I will report on some initial results obtained by the project, and discuss the challenges ahead of us.

J.-P. Katoen (Ed.): ARTS'99, LNCS 1601, pp. 151–151, 1999.
© Springer-Verlag Berlin Heidelberg 1999

A Parallel Operator for Real-Time Processes with Predicate Transformer Semantics

Karl Lermer

Software Verification Research Centre
The University of Queensland, Qld. 4072 Australia
lermer@csee.uq.edu.au

Abstract. We present a high level specification and refinement framework for concurrent real-time processes with strict message passing based on predicate transformer semantics. Four different parallel operators are defined and we investigate conditions under which they are monotone and associative. Refinement rules for single process components are derived. We also give rules and strategies for the development of a process from an abstract specification to a multi-component specification. This allows the individual refinement of process components under the maintenance of the global process behaviour. A specification and refinement example is included to illustrate the refinement rules.

1 Introduction

Mahony [9] developed a specification and refinement framework for data-flow processes with predicate transformer semantics in the style of Morgan [15,16]. This framework focussed on the application to real-time processes. The central idea was to describe a data-flow, or as it turned out in many cases, a real-time process with two predicates called the assumption and the effect. Any features of the environment relevant to the process are specified in the assumption. The effect is used to describe the desired outcome of the process. In the assumption effect specification statement

$$z[A, E] \, ,$$

z denotes a set of variables called the constructed variables, the assumption A is a predicate over the free variables w which must be disjoint from z, and the effect E is a predicate with free variables $z \cup w$. With disjointness of the process variable sets w and z, a conventional message passing model was evident; the environment supplies the processes input via w and the process supplies output values via z. Predicate transformer semantics for specification statements

$$z[A, E](P) = A \wedge \forall z(E \Rightarrow P) \tag{1}$$

were given in [9] and used to specify and refine real-time processes [10,12,11,5,18,6]. This was in analogy to Morgan's work [16], with the difference that no zero-subscripted variables were used to represent values on the prestate.

J.-P. Katoen (Ed.): ARTS'99, LNCS 1601, pp. 152–171, 1999.

This high level specification technique made it possible to integrate assumptions on the environment into the specification of a process component. For instance, a process that receives binary input values over time and changes its output binary value if 0 comes in, can be specified with the help of the predicate

$$E \equiv (\, z, w : \mathbb{N} \to \{0, 1\} \land \forall n : \mathbb{N} \bullet$$
$$w(n) = 1 \Rightarrow z(n+1) = z(n) \land w(n) = 0 \Rightarrow z(n+1) \neq z(n) \,)$$

and the specification statement $z[true, E]$. If it is known that the environment provides only a selected set of input values w, for instance when w is stable for a certain period $p \in \mathbb{N}$, we can incorporate this as an assumption A,

$$A \equiv (\, w : \mathbb{N} \to \{0, 1\} \land \forall n : \mathbb{N} \bullet$$
$$w(n) \neq w(n+1) \Rightarrow (\forall k : \mathbb{N} \bullet 1 \leq k \leq p \Rightarrow w(n+k) = w(n+1)) \,)$$

in the above specification statement and obtain $z[A, E]$.

Nevertheless, one of the major issues of this approach was how to define a parallel operator which was consistent with the above specification and refinement framework, such that different process specifications can be composed in parallel and independently refined.

In many low level specification and refinement models it is common to restrict the language and the refinement notions to guarantee monotonicity and associativity of the corresponding parallel operator. This prevents assumptions on the environment being included in the process specification [7,13,8,1,17]. Lamport's refinement of TLA formulae is based on logical implication [8] with parallel composition being conjunction of TLA formulae [1]. In TLA, any reasoning in a complex refinement relies on so-called assumption/guarantee specifications. To incorporate properties of the surrounding processes, assumptions are included in an ad hoc manner (see [1] Ths. 2, 3). CSP [7] and CCS [13] are specification languages with refinement notions that are based on failures/divergences and bisimulation. Assumptions upon the environment are commonly incorporated using a dummy process that specifies the desired property.

Motivation for this paper came from ongoing work on real-time processes with trace semantics [10,12,11,4,2,3,18,5,6] and the search for a parallel operator which is consistent with the refinement and specification theory in [9,18,5]. We pursue two main goals: first, we recall and elaborate upon a promising specification and refinement theory [9] for data-flow processes with strict message passing; and second, we complete this theory by providing the notion of a parallel operator which resolves the above issues. We compare four different versions of a parallel operator and single out two appropriate candidates. Due to the generality of the approach, these operators are not necessarily monotone or associative. However, we will describe a natural design methodology for specification statements such that associativity and monotonicity are always maintained within refinements.

The remainder of the paper is organised as follows. Section 2 reviews the central concept of a specification statement for data-flow processes. We provide predicate transformer semantics and characterise refinement of specification statements. The third section states central refinement rules for specification statements. In section 4, four different versions of a parallel operator for specification statements are defined. Monotonicity issues are studied and rules are stated for the partitioning of a process into several components. The correspondence to the classical notion of a specification statement and its extension to real-time is discussed in section 5. Associativity is in the focus of section 6. Due to their generality, the parallel operators are not necessarily associative. We present obligations that guarantee associativity for parallel compositions. Section 7 gives an example specification and refinement where the refinement rules and principles of the previous sections are applied. The paper concludes with final remarks in section 8.

2 Preliminaries

Throughout this paper we assume familiarity with basic notions of the refinement calculus [15,16]. By $Pred_v$ we denote the set of all predicates over the variable set v. $Pred_v$ is a complete lattice with ordering $\preceq$,

$$A \preceq B \text{ iff } \forall v (A \Rightarrow B) .$$

If $A \preceq B$ and $B \preceq A$ we write $A \equiv B$. The set $T(Pred_v, Pred_w)$ of all monotone predicate transformers $S : Pred_v \to Pred_w$ is a complete lattice with the *refinement* ordering [19]

$$S \sqsubseteq T \text{ iff } \forall P \in Pred_v : S(P) \preceq T(P) .$$

In case $S \sqsubseteq T$ and $T \sqsubseteq S$ we write $S \sqsupseteq T$.

The following semantics for specification statements is taken from [9].

Definition 1. *Assume variable sets u, z and w, and predicates $A \in Pred_w$, $E \in Pred_{w;z}$, where $w; z$ abbreviates the union of the disjoint variable sets w and z. The set of all specification statements $z[A, E]$ shall be denoted by*

$$\mathcal{S}(z, Pred_{z;w}) .$$

The semantics of specification statements is given by the function

$$\Theta^{z,w,u} : \mathcal{S}(z, Pred_{z;w}) \to T(Pred_{u;z}, Pred_{u \cup w})$$
$$\Theta^{z,w,u}(z[A, E])(P) = A \wedge \forall z(E \Rightarrow P) .$$

In the following, $\overline{E}^z$ denotes the closure of predicate E with respect to the variables z, i.e., $\overline{E}^z = \exists z\, E$, and $w; z$ always denotes the union of disjoint variable sets. If w and z are not necessarily disjoint, their union will be denoted by $w \cup z$.

In a specification statement as above, the variables in z are called observables or constructed variables of the process. Heuristically, they are constructed via the predicate E, called the effect predicate of the specification statement.

The assumption A, a predicate with free variables in w, is used to incorporate assumptions on the environment into the process specification. The interface to the environment is provided by w.

Another helpful identity is the following equality when the predicate transformer is restricted to a smaller set of predicates with free variables in $v \subseteq u$,

$$\Theta^{z,w,u}(z[A,E])|_{Pred_{v;z}} \sqsubseteq \Theta^{z,w,v}(z[A,E])$$

Furthermore, the following characterisation of refinement between specification statements will be one of our essential tools.

Proposition 1 *Let* $A_i \in Pred_w$, $E_i \in Pred_{w;z}$, $i = 1, 2$. *Then the following conditions are equivalent*

    i) $\Theta^{z,w,u}(z[A_1,E_1]) \sqsubseteq \Theta^{z,w,u}(z[A_2,E_2])$, *for some* u *with* $u \cap z = \emptyset$
    ii) $A_1 \preceq A_2$ *and* $(A_2 \Rightarrow E_2) \preceq (A_1 \Rightarrow E_1)$
    iii) $A_1 \preceq A_2$ *and* $(A_1 \wedge E_2) \preceq E_1$
    iv) $\Theta^{z,w,u}(z[A_1,E_1]) \sqsubseteq \Theta^{z,w,u}(z[A_2,E_2])$, *for all* u *with* $u \cap z = \emptyset$

An important consequence of Proposition 1 is that $\mathcal{S}(z, Pred_{z;w})$ can be identified with a subset of $\mathcal{S}(z, Pred_{z;v})$, as long as $w \subseteq v$ and $v \cap z = \emptyset$. Note that this embedding preserves the refinement ordering given by $\sqsubseteq$.

Definition 2. *For specification statements* $z[A_i, E_i] \in \mathcal{S}(z, Pred_{z;w})$, $i = 1, 2$, *we write* $z[A_1, E_1] \vdash z[A_2, E_2]$ *iff* $\Theta^{z,w,\emptyset}(z[A_1,E_1]) \sqsubseteq \Theta^{z,w,\emptyset}(z[A_2,E_2])$. *When we do not intend to mention the predicate transformer we write* $z[A_i, E_i](P)$ *instead of* $\Theta^{z,w,\emptyset}(z[A_i,E_i])(P)$.

Note that $\vdash$ defines a preorder on $\mathcal{S}(z, Pred_{z;w})$. If $z[A_1, E_1] \vdash z[A_2, E_2]$ and $z[A_2, E_2] \vdash z[A_1, E_1]$, we write the abbreviation $z[A_1, E_1] \cong z[A_2, E_2]$. Thus we distinguish between equivalence classes of specification statements in $\mathcal{S}(z, Pred_{z;w})/\cong$, rather than specification statements themselves. The following commutative diagram states the correspondences between the involved monotone mappings for the case $v \subseteq u$.

$$
\begin{array}{ccc}
\mathcal{S}(z, Pred_{z;w}) & \xrightarrow{\;\Theta^{z,w,u}\;} & \mathcal{T}(Pred_{u;z}, Pred_{u \cup w}) \\[4pt]
& \searrow{\scriptstyle \Theta^{z,w,v}} & \\[2pt]
\nu(z[A,E]) = z[A,E] \bmod \cong \quad \Big\downarrow \nu & & \rho \Big\downarrow \quad \rho(T) = \exists u \setminus (v \cup w) \bullet T|_{Pred_{v;z}} \\[4pt]
\mathcal{S}(z, Pred_{z;w})/\cong & \xrightarrow[\;\overline{\Theta}^{z,w,v}\;]{} & \mathcal{T}(Pred_{v;z}, Pred_{v \cup w})
\end{array}
$$

$$\overline{\Theta}^{z,w,v}(z[A,E] \bmod \cong) = \Theta^{z,w,v}(z[A,E])$$

Note that for specification statements with the above semantics,

$$z[A,E](true) \equiv A \;,\; z[A,E](false) \equiv \neg(A \Rightarrow \overline{E}^z)\,.$$

Definition 3. *A statement $z[A, E]$ is called feasible if $z[A, E](false) \equiv false$. Otherwise, it is called infeasible.*

Hence we can say, $z[A, E]$ is feasible iff $A \preceq \overline{E}^z$. In a refinement it is often of no practical use to start with or refine to an infeasible specification. In order to reach an implementation it is desirable to work with feasible specifications [15,9]. Nevertheless, that infeasible specification statements can be successfully used in refinements was shown in [14,18].

3   Refinement Laws

This section presents basic refinement rules for specification statements with the above defined predicate transformer semantics. The majority of the rules have the form of characterisations, which means that the involved conditions are both necessary and sufficient for the corresponding refinement. Definition 4, Propositions 4, 5 and 6 can be found in altered or weaker versions in [9].

If constructed variables are irrelevant to the outside view of the specification they can be hidden with the following technique.

Definition 4. *Let v, z and w be pairwise disjoint variable sets. For every specification statement $z, v[A, E] \in \mathcal{S}(z; v, Pred_{z;v;w})$, we introduce the syntactic object $z, v[A, E] \setminus \{v\}$ and define its meaning by extending $\Theta^{z,w,u}$ as follows,*

$$\Theta^{z,w,u}(z, v[A, E] \setminus \{v\}) = \Theta^{(z;v),w,u}(z, v[A, E])|_{Pred_{u;z}}$$

We say that v is hidden in $z, v[A, E] \setminus \{v\}$. This is a way of separating internal variables from output variables. It can be shown that any refinement relation remains valid under hiding.

Proposition 2 *Let $z[A_i, E_i] \in \mathcal{S}(v; z, Pred_{v;z;w})$, $i = 1, 2$. Then, the relation $\Theta^{z;v,w,u}(z, v[A_1, E_1]) \sqsubseteq \Theta^{z;v,w,u}(z, v[A_2, E_2])$ implies $\Theta^{z,w,u}(z, v[A_1, E_1] \setminus \{v\}) \sqsubseteq \Theta^{z,w,u}(z, v[A_2, E_2] \setminus \{v\})$.*

A specification statement with hidden variables can be rewritten as a pure specification statement. The following proposition states that hiding of observables is nothing else than hiding in the effect predicate using the existential quantifier.

Proposition 3 *$\Theta^{z,w,u}(z, v[A, E] \setminus \{v\}) \sqsubseteq \Theta^{z,w,u}(z[A, \overline{E}^v])$, for $A \in Pred_w$ and $E \in Pred_{v;z;w}$.*

As a consequence of Proposition 3 we obtain the following proposition for introducing fresh variables to a specification.

Proposition 4 (Introduce Variable) *Let $(z; w) \cap v = \emptyset$, $A \in Pred_w$ and $E \in Pred_{w;z}$. Then, $\Theta^{z,w,u}(z[A, E]) \sqsubseteq \Theta^{z,w,u}(z, v[A, E] \setminus \{v\})$.*

Weakening of pre conditions and strengthening of post conditions are two well-known refinement strategies in the conventional refinement calculus [15]. Their equivalents in the data-flow setting are the following rules for weakening assumptions [9] and strengthening effects.

Proposition 5 (Weaken Assumption) *Let $A_i \in Pred_w$, $i = 1,2$ and $E \in Pred_{w;z}$. Then, $z[A_1, E] \vdash z[A_2, E]$ iff $A_1 \preceq A_2$.*

Proposition 6 (Strengthen Effect) *Let $A \in Pred_w$, $E_i \in Pred_{w;z}$, $i = 1,2$. Then, $z[A, E_1] \vdash z[A, E_2]$ iff $(E_2 \wedge A) \preceq E_1$.*

From the previous result we deduce the following special case. It expresses refinement without respecting any properties of the environment.

Corollary 1. *$z[true, E_1] \vdash z[true, E_2]$ iff $E_2 \preceq E_1$.*

In this special case refinement is logical implication of the underlying formulae.

Rules for splitting a specification statement into a sequence of specification statements are handled in [15] and in [5,18] for real-time processes. We mention the central rule that concerns the sequential composition of specification statements.

Definition 5. *For $(z_1; w_1) \cap z_2 = \emptyset$, the operator*

$$-\mathbin{\overset{\circ}{\circ}}- : \mathcal{S}(z_1, Pred_{z_1;w_1}) \times \mathcal{S}(z_2, Pred_{z_2;w_2}) \to \mathcal{S}(z_1; z_2, Pred_{z_1;z_2;(w_1 \cup w_2)\setminus z_1})$$
$$z_1[A_1, E_1] \mathbin{\overset{\circ}{\circ}} z_2[A_2, E_2] = z_1, z_2[A_1 \wedge \forall z_1(E_1 \Rightarrow A_2), E_1 \wedge E_2]$$

defines the sequential composition of specification statements.

Let the operator $\circ$ denote the common sequential composition of predicate transformers. It is helpful to recognise what sequential composition of specification statements means in terms of the underlying predicate transformer semantics.

Proposition 7 *Let $z_i[A_i, E_i] \in \mathcal{S}(z_i, Pred_{z_i;w_i})$. $i = 1,2$, with $(z_1; w_1) \cap z_2 = \emptyset$. Then, with $u_1 = w_2 \setminus z_1$ and $w = (w_1 \cup w_2) \setminus z_1$, the following identity is valid*
$$\Theta^{z_1;z_2,w,\emptyset}(z_1[A_1, E_1] \mathbin{\overset{\circ}{\circ}} z_2[A_2, E_2]) \sqsubseteq \Theta^{z_1,w_1,u_1}(z_1[A_1, E_1]) \circ \Theta^{z_2,w_2,z_1}(z_2[A_2, E_2]) .$$

We can conclude that $-\mathbin{\overset{\circ}{\circ}}-$ is a monotone operator in both arguments and thus invariant under equivalence $\cong$ of specification statements.

4   The Parallel Operator

Two major issues with respect to any parallel operator within a refinement are: the partitioning of a system into several parallel conjoined components; and the refinement of the individual components separately. With a monotone parallel operator, any individual component can be refined separately and the conjunction of the resulting specifications is a refinement of the entire system. In this section we present four different notions for the parallel composition of several assumption-effect specification statements.

Let us begin with a few heuristic observations. Assume that we have two processes pr_1 and pr_2 with input w and outputs z_1 and z_2, respectively. Further assume that they communicate with each other via the variables z_1 and z_2. When represented as specification statements they may have the form $z_i[A_i, E_i]$, $i = 1, 2$ with predicates $A_1 \in Pred_{w;z_2}$, $A_2 \in Pred_{w;z_1}$ and $E_i \in Pred_{w;z_1;z_2}$. What is the specification statement of their parallel composition? Due to the generality of our approach with arbitrary assumption predicates and the underlying predicate transformer semantics there is no ultimate answer to this question. We favour the predicate

$$\overline{A_1 \wedge A_2}^{z_1 z_2}$$

as the resulting assumption on the environment when pr_1 and pr_2 are joined. In calculating the effect of their parallel composition both individual effect predicates must be considered and, importantly, also A_1 and A_2 could induce assumptions on z_2 and z_1 and thus have to be respected as well. In our approach, we will take either

$$A_1 \wedge A_2 \wedge E_1 \wedge E_2$$

or

$$(A_1 \Rightarrow E_1) \wedge (A_2 \Rightarrow E_2)$$

as the effect predicate of the parallel composition of pr_1 and pr_2 .

Definition 6. *For $i \in \{1, 2, 3, 4\}$ the parallel operators on specification statements*

$$\_||_{i\_} : S(z_1, Pred_{z_1;w_1;z_2}) \times S(z_2, Pred_{z_2;w_2;z_1}) \to S(z_1; z_2, Pred_{z_1;z_2;w_1 \cup w_2})$$

are defined by $z_1[A_1, E_1]||_1 z_2[A_2, E_2] = z_1, z_2[\overline{A_1 \wedge A_2}^{z_1 z_2}, A_1 \wedge A_2 \wedge E_1 \wedge E_2]$
$z_1[A_1, E_1]||_2 z_2[A_2, E_2] = z_1, z_2[\overline{A_1 \wedge A_2}^{z_1 z_2}, (A_1 \Rightarrow E_1) \wedge (A_2 \Rightarrow E_2)]$
$z_1[A_1, E_1]||_3 z_2[A_2, E_2] = z_1, z_2[\overline{A_1 \vee A_2}^{z_1 z_2}, (A_1 \Rightarrow E_1) \wedge (A_2 \Rightarrow E_2)]$
$z_1[A_1, E_1]||_4 z_2[A_2, E_2] = z_1, z_2[\overline{A_1 \vee A_2}^{z_1 z_2}, A_1 \wedge A_2 \wedge E_1 \wedge E_2].$

These operators are defined using two well-known principles: hiding and conjunction. Hiding of observables is used to specify the assumption of the parallel composition. Conjunction is used to define the assumption and effect predicates of the parallel composition. Undoubtedly, conjunction constitutes the abstract principle behind parallel composition without incorporated assumptions on the environment [7,13,1,17]. When assumptions are included in specifications, it becomes necessary to combine two assumptions into one assumption for the entire process. We do this by conjoining the individual assumption predicates and by hiding the observables.

All parallel operators are clearly commutative. A more subtle issue is whether they are monotone, associative and invariant under equivalence $\cong$ of specification statements.

Proposition 8 (Monotonicity) *The parallel operators $\|_2$ and $\|_3$ are monotone in each argument with respect to the ordering $\vdash$ on specification statements.*

Without any restrictions on the involved predicates, parallel composition with $\_\|_1\_$ or $\_\|_4\_$ is not monotone with respect to the refinement ordering on the individual components. Nevertheless, as long as we obey certain design rules for the involved predicates, monotonicity can be ensured.

Proposition 9 (Monotonicity of $\|_1$) *Let $z_1[A_{1j}, E_{1j}] \in S(z_1, Pred_{z_1;w_1;z_2})$ and $z_2[A_{2j}, E_{2j}] \in S(z_2, Pred_{z_2;w_2;z_1})$, $j = 1, 2$. Assume further that $z_i[A_{i1}, E_{i1}] \vdash z_i[A_{i2}, E_{i2}]$, $i = 1, 2$. Then, the following two properties are equivalent.*

   i) $z_1[A_{11}, E_{11}]\|_1 z_2[A_{21}, E_{21}] \vdash z_1[A_{12}, E_{12}]\|_1 z_2[A_{22}, E_{22}]$

  ii) $A_{12} \wedge A_{22} \wedge E_{12} \wedge E_{22} \wedge \overline{A_{11}}^{z_2} \wedge \overline{A_{21}}^{z_1} \preceq A_{11} \wedge A_{21}$

The above stated obligation *ii)* characterises monotonicity of the parallel operator $\_\|_1\_$. Note that $\_\|_4\_$ obeys a similar monotonicity rule to $\_\|_1\_$. From this abstract condition more practical monotonicity rules can be deduced. For example, $\_\|_1\_$ is monotone if the individual components are refined by strengthening effect predicates using Proposition 6.

From the above monotonicity principles it is possible to deduce the invariance of the parallel operators with respect to equivalence of specification statements.

Corollary 2. *For specification statements $z_1[A_{j1}, E_{j1}] \in S(z_1, Pred_{z_1;w_1;z_2})$, $z_2[A_{j2}, E_{j2}] \in S(z_2, Pred_{z_2;w_2;z_1})$, $j = 1, 2$, with $z_i[A_{1i}, E_{1i}] \cong z_i[A_{2i}, E_{2i}]$ we have, $z_1[A_{11}, E_{11}]\|_l z_2[A_{12}, E_{12}] \cong z_1[A_{21}, E_{21}]\|_l z_2[A_{22}, E_{22}]$, $1 \leq l \leq 4$.*

If the assumptions do not refer to any constructed variables, parallel composition with $\_\|_i\_$, $i = 1, 2$, is the same as conjoining the assumptions and conjoining the effects.

Corollary 3. *If z_2 does not occur free in A_1 and z_1 does not occur free in A_2, then $z_1[A_1, E_1]\|_i z_2[A_2, E_2] \cong z_1, z_2[A_1 \wedge A_2, E_1 \wedge E_2]$, $i = 1, 2$.*

In parallel compositions with $\_\|_1\_$ an implicit causal dependence is introduced that constrains the effect predicates. Note the equalities

$$z_1[A_1, E_1]\|_1 z_2[A_2, E_2] \cong z_1[\overline{A_1}^{z_2}, A_2 \wedge E_1]\|_1 z_2[\overline{A_2}^{z_1}, A_1 \wedge E_2] \qquad (2)$$
$$\cong z_1[A_1, A_2 \wedge E_1]\|_1 z_2[A_2, A_1 \wedge E_2] .$$

Causality is an important issue because of the impact of the surrounding processes on each individual component. Within refinements, these dependencies may be extremely helpful and thus play an essential rôle for well-designed specifications (see section 6). The refinement of a process component may only be possible under those side-conditions provided by the surrounding processes. The notion of causality can be defined for more than two predicates:

Definition 7. *The predicates $A_i, E_i \in Pred_{w;\cup_{1 \leq j \leq n} z_j}$, $1 \leq i \leq n$ are called causal (with respect to z_i, $1 \leq i \leq n$) if $\wedge_{j \neq i}(E_j \wedge A_j) \preceq \overline{A_i}^{z_i}$, for all $i \in \{1, ..., n\}$.*

Recall our simple binary-valued real-time process from the introduction. We now consider what happens if we compose two processes $z[true, E]$ in parallel and connect them via z and w. Let F denote the predicate $E[w/z, z/w]$ that results from E by swapping z and w. Then, we obtain the parallel composition

$$z[true, E]\|_i w[true, F] \cong z, w[true, E \wedge F] \, , \, i \in \{1, 2, 3, 4\}$$

Note that $E \wedge F$ defines the set of input/output pairings $\{(a, a), (b, b), (c, d), (d, c)\}$, where $a = 11111...$, $b = 01111...$, $c = 10111...$, and $d = 00111...$.

Let us introduce a nontrivial assumption predicate that is defined by $A = (w \in \{a, b, c, d\})$. In other words, if z is hidden in $E \wedge F$ we get A. Straight from the definition of the parallel operator we then obtain the following identities.

$$z[A, E]\|_i w[true, F] \cong z, w[\overline{A}^w, E \wedge F \wedge A] \cong z, w[true, E \wedge F]$$
$$\cong z[true, E]\|_i w[true, F] \, , \, i = 1, 4$$
$$z[A, E]\|_i w[true, F] \cong z, w[\overline{A}^w, (A \Rightarrow E) \wedge F] \cong z, w[true, (A \Rightarrow E) \wedge F]$$
$$\cong z[true, A \Rightarrow E]\|_i w[true, F] \, , \, i = 2, 3$$

By the definition of the parallel operator, any statement $z_1, z_2[A_1 \wedge A_2, E_1 \wedge E_2]$ with $A_1 \in Pred_{w; z_2}$, $A_2 \in Pred_{w; z_1}$ and $E_1, E_2 \in Pred_{w; z_1; z_2}$, trivially refines to the parallel composition $z_1[A_1, E_1]\|_1 z_2[A_2, E_2]$. The component $z_1[A_1, E_1]$ takes A_1 as an assumption on its environment, but the effect of process $z_2[A_2, E_2]$ is not incorporated. We will investigate the effect of component $z_2[A_2, E_2]$ on component $z_1[A_1, E_1]$ and prove that it is possible to incorporate the effect of the sibling component if the original specification is feasible. In such cases, the refinement remains valid with much stronger assumptions in the individual processes as stated in the following rule for splitting a process into the parallel composition of several components.

Proposition 10 (Splitting with $\|_1$) *Let w, z_1, z_2 be pairwise disjoint, $A_1, E_2 \in Pred_{w, z_2}$, $A_2, E_1 \in Pred_{w, z_1}$ and $F_1, F_2 \in Pred_{w; z_1; z_2}$ and $E = A_1 \wedge A_2 \wedge E_1 \wedge E_2 \wedge F_1 \wedge F_2$. Then the following two conditions are equivalent*
  i) $z_1, z_2[\overline{A_1 \wedge A_2}^{z_1 z_2}, E] \vdash z_1[A_1 \wedge E_2, E_1 \wedge F_1]\|_1 z_2[A_2 \wedge E_1, E_2 \wedge F_2]$
  ii) $\overline{A_1}^{z_2} \wedge \overline{A_2}^{z_1} \preceq \overline{(A_1 \wedge E_2)}^{z_2} \wedge \overline{(A_2 \wedge E_1)}^{z_1}$
  In any case we have the converse refinement

$$z_1[A_1 \wedge E_2, E_1 \wedge F_1]\|_1 z_2[A_2 \wedge E_1, E_2 \wedge F_2] \vdash z_1, z_2[\overline{A_1 \wedge A_2}^{z_1 z_2}, E]$$

Strengthening assumptions with effects of the sibling processes as above is possible when dealing with the entire process, because a parallel composition may rule out certain behaviours of the individual components.

5   Classical Theory and Real-Time Trace Semantics

In this section we explain how the classical specification and refinement theory [15] and its real-time extension [5,18] can be embedded into the context of the previous sections.

Definition 8. *Let w, z, z_0 be disjoint sets of variables, where z_0 denotes the set of all 0-indexed copies of variables in z. Let $A \in Pred_{z;w}$, $E \in Pred_{z;z_0;w}$. The set of all objects of the form $z[A, E]^{cl}$ shall be denoted by $\mathcal{S}^{cl}(z, Pred_{z;z_0;w})$. The semantics of a specification statement $z[A, E]^{cl}$ is given by the mapping [15]*

$$\Xi^{z,w} : \mathcal{S}^{cl}(z, Pred_{z;z_0;w}) \to \mathcal{T}(Pred_{z;w}, Pred_{z;w})$$
$$\Xi^{z,w}(z[A, E]^{cl})(P) = A \wedge \forall z\, (E \Rightarrow P)[z/z_0]$$

The correspondence between a classical specification statement and a specification statement as used in this paper is depicted in the following commutative diagram.

$$
\begin{array}{ccc}
\mathcal{S}^{cl}(z, Pred_{z;z_0;w}) & \xrightarrow{\;\Xi^{z,w}\;} & \mathcal{T}(Pred_{w;z}, Pred_{w;z}) \\
& \varrho^{-1}\Big\uparrow & \\
\mu(z[A, E]^{cl}) = z[A[z_0/z], E] \quad \mu \Big\uparrow & \Big\downarrow\mu^{-1} & \varrho \quad \varrho(T)(P) = T(P)[z_0/z] \\
\mathcal{S}(z, Pred_{z;z_0;w}) & \xrightarrow[\Theta^{z,z_0;w,\emptyset}]{} & \mathcal{T}(Pred_{w;z}, Pred_{w;z_0})
\end{array}
$$

The common sequential composition of specification statements usually defined via the composition of the underlying predicate transformers can be also defined at the syntactic level.

Definition 9. *Let z, z_0, w be disjoint sets of variables, where z_0 denotes the set of all 0-indexed copies of variables in z. The operator*

$$\_\overset{\bar{\circ}}{9}\_ : \mathcal{S}^{cl}(z, Pred_{z;z_0;w}) \times \mathcal{S}^{cl}(z, Pred_{z;z_0;w}) \to \mathcal{S}^{cl}(z, Pred_{z;z_0;w})$$
$$z[A_1, E_1]^{cl}\,\overset{\bar{\circ}}{9}\,z[A_2, E_2]^{cl} = z[A_1 \wedge \forall z(E_1 \Rightarrow A_2)[z/z_0], \overline{E_1[h/z] \wedge E_2[h/z_0]}^{h}]^{cl}$$

defines the sequential composition of specification statements with 0-indexed variables in the classical sense.

Thus, the semantics of sequential composition of specification statements is nothing else than sequential composition of the underlying predicate transformers. Note also that sequential composition in the classical sense can be expressed with the previously introduced sequential operator $\_\overset{\circ}{9}\_$.

Proposition 11 *The sequential composition operators $\_\overset{\circ}{9}\_$, $\_\overset{\bar{\circ}}{9}\_$ and $\_\circ\_$ are related as follows,*

i) $\Xi^{z,w}(z[A_1, E_1]^{cl}\,\overset{\bar{\circ}}{9}\,z[A_2, E_2]^{cl}) \sqsubseteq \Xi^{z,w}(z[A_1, E_1]^{cl}) \circ \Xi^{z,w}(z[A_2, E_2]^{cl}))$

ii) $\mu(z[A_1, E_1]^{cl}\,\overset{\bar{\circ}}{9}\,z[A_2, E_2]^{cl}) \cong (h[A_1[z_0/z], E_1[h/z]]\,\overset{\circ}{9}\,z[A_2[h/z], E_2[h/z_0]])\backslash\{h\}$

So far, we have seen that everything introduced in the previous sections can be expressed in the classical context [15] and vice versa. It remains to define the real-time extension [5,18] of the classical specification statement which makes it possible to apply all previously introduced operators to real-time specifications. We assume the following abbreviations,

$$stable(v, I) \equiv \forall i_1, i_2 \in I \bullet v(i_2) = v(i_1)$$

$$\breve{A}(p) \equiv dom\,\breve{p} = 0 \ldots \tau$$

$$\breve{E}(p, z) \equiv \tau_0 \leq \tau \wedge dom\,\breve{p} = 0 \ldots \tau \wedge \breve{p}_0 = (0 \ldots \tau_0) \triangleleft \breve{p} \wedge stable(\breve{p} \setminus z, \tau_0 \ldots \tau)$$

Definition 10. *Let p, w be disjoint sets of variables with a distinguished time variable τ occurring in p. The variables $p \setminus \{\tau\}$ shall be denoted by $\breve{p}$. We assume that $\breve{p}$ consists of trace variables ranging over time τ. As above p_0 denotes all 0-indexed copies of variables in p. Let $A \in Pred_{p;w}$, $E \in Pred_{p;p_0;w}$. The set of all real-time specification statements of the form $\{p\} * z[A, E]$ with $z \subseteq \breve{p}$, is denoted by $S^r(p, Pred_{p;p_0;w})$ and its semantics is given in terms of the classical semantics [18],*

$$\Pi^{p,w} : S^r(p, Pred_{p;p_0;w}) \rightarrow S^{cl}(p, Pred_{p;p_0;w})$$

$$\Pi^{p,w}(\{p\} * z[A, E]) = p[A \wedge \breve{A}(p), E \wedge \breve{E}(p, z)]^{cl}$$

The sequential and parallel composition operators $\_\overset{\breve{}}{\S}\_$, $\_\|_i\_$ for real-time specification statements are defined by transformation into the classical context.

$$\Pi^{p,w}(\{p\} * z[A, E]\overset{\breve{}}{\S}\{p\} * v[A, E]) = \Pi^{p,w}(\{p\} * z[A, E])\,\overline{\S}\,\Pi^{p,w}(\{p\} * v[A, E])$$

Let p, q be variable sets with $\breve{p} \cap \breve{q} = \emptyset$ and $i \in \{1, 2, 3, 4\}$. Then,

$$\Pi^{p \cup q, w}(\{p\} * z_1[A_1, E_1]\,\|_i\,\{q\} * z_2[A_2, E_2]) =$$
$$\mu^{-1}(\,\mu(\Pi^{p,w}(\{p\} * z_1[A_1, E_1])) \setminus \{\tau\}\,\|_i\,\mu(\Pi^{q,w}(\{q\} * z_2[A_2, E_2])) \setminus \{\tau\}\,)$$

The sequential composition of several real-time specification statements determines the involved traces on consecutive time intervals. This can be seen with the following simple example where the trace $z : \mathbb{N} \rightarrow \mathbb{Z}$ is defined for the values 1 and 0 by two specification statements in sequence and τ ranges over $\mathbb{N}$. By applying Props. 3 and 11 and abbreviating $Tr = \mu \circ \Pi^{\{z, \tau\}, \emptyset}$ we obtain

$$Tr(\{z, \tau\} * z[\tau \leq 1, z(1) = 0 \wedge \tau \leq 2]\overset{\breve{}}{\S}\{z, \tau\} * z[\tau \leq 2, z(2) = 1 \wedge \tau \geq 2])$$
$$\cong Tr(\{z, \tau\} * z[\tau \leq 1, z(1) = 0 \wedge z(2) = 1 \wedge \tau \geq 2])$$

6 Associativity

Associativity holds for the parallel operator of many well-known specification and refinement frameworks [7,13,1,17]. This is guaranteed because no assumptions are incorporated in the specifications of process components. In our high level model the parallel operators $\_\|_1\_$ and $\_\|_2\_$ are not associative due to the generality of the underlying refinement notion. The ability to incorporate arbitrary assumptions in specification statements adds much complexity to the specification model and causes the loss of associativity.

We investigate associativity of $\_\|_1\_$ in detail and introduce what we will call perfect specification statements. The notion of perfect specifications proves to be central for the associativity of $\_\|_1\_$; maintaining and creating perfect specification statements during the refinement guarantees associativity in every parallel composition. We will also see that associativity relies on causality and feasibility assumptions on the involved specifications. Thus, a careful design during the refinement ensures associativity in parallel compositions with $\_\|_1\_$. Associativity criteria for $\_\|_2\_$ are more complicated and will not be discussed here.

As a first step, we investigate associativity on parallel compositions of three specification statements.

Proposition 12 *For* $z_i[A_i, E_i] \in \mathcal{S}(z_i, Pred_{z_i;w;(z_1;z_2;z_3)\setminus z_i})$, $i = 1, 2, 3$, *the parallel compositions* (a) $(z_1[A_1, E_1]\|_1 z_2[A_2, E_2])\|_1 z_3[A_3, E_3]$,
(b) $z_1[A_1, E_1]\|_1 (z_2[A_2, E_2]\|_1 z_3[A_3, E_3])$ *and*
(c) $(z_1[A_1, E_1]\|_1 z_3[A_3, E_3])\|_1 z_2[A_2, E_2]$ *are equal w.r.t.* $\cong$ *iff the following predicates are equivalent*

$$(a') \quad \overline{(\overline{A_1}^{z_2} \wedge \overline{A_2}^{z_1})}^{z_3} \wedge \overline{A_3}^{z_1 z_2}$$
$$(b') \quad \overline{(\overline{A_2}^{z_3} \wedge \overline{A_3}^{z_2})}^{z_1} \wedge \overline{A_1}^{z_2 z_3} \qquad (3)$$
$$(c') \quad \overline{(\overline{A_1}^{z_3} \wedge \overline{A_3}^{z_1})}^{z_2} \wedge \overline{A_2}^{z_1 z_3}$$

From Proposition 12 we know that three specification statements $z_i[A_i, E_i]$, $i = 1, 2, 3$, are associative if the predicates in (3) are equivalent. Thus, associativity is a property that relies only on the involved assumptions. Informally, associativity holds if A_1 and A_2 make no contradictory assumptions on z_3, if A_2 and A_3 make no contradictory assumptions on z_1 and if A_1 and A_3 make no contradictory assumptions on z_2.

The above observations inspire the following definitions. To generalise Proposition 12 for more than three specification statements we use the abbreviation $\mathcal{D}_{(i_1,...,i_n)}[(A_i)_{1 \le i \le n}] :=$

$$\overline{(...((\overline{\overline{A_{i_1}}^{z_{i_2}} \wedge \overline{A_{i_2}}^{z_{i_1}})}^{z_{i_3}} \wedge \overline{A_{i_3}}^{z_{i_1} z_{i_2}})}^{z_{i_4}} \wedge ...)}^{z_{i_n}} \wedge \overline{A_{i_n}}^{z_{i_1} z_{i_2}...z_{i_{n-1}}}$$

Note, that under the assumptions of Prop. 12, the predicates $\mathcal{D}_{(1,2,3)}[(A_i)_{1 \le i \le 3}]$, $\mathcal{D}_{(2,3,1)}[(A_i)_{1 \le i \le 3}]$ and $\mathcal{D}_{(1,3,2)}[(A_i)_{1 \le i \le 3}]$ denote the predicates (a'), (b') and (c') of (3).

Definition 11. *Assume pairwise disjoint variable sets* z_i *and predicates* $A_i \in Pred_{w;\cup_{j \ne i} z_j}$, $E_i \in Pred_{w;\cup_j z_j}$, $1 \le i \le n$.
(a) *The predicates* A_i, $1 \le i \le n$, *are called associative (w.r.t.* z_i, $1 \le i \le n$) *if the predicates*

$$\mathcal{D}_{(i_1,...,i_n)}[(A_i)_{1 \le i \le n}], \quad (i_1, ..., i_n) \text{ permutation of } \{1, ..., n\}$$

are all equivalent. They are called perfect (w.r.t. z_i, $1 \leq i \leq n$) if for every $1 \leq l < n$, $1 \leq i \leq n$ and natural numbers $1 \leq i_1 < i_2 < ... < i_l \leq n$ the following equality holds

$$\overline{\wedge_{1 \leq k \leq l} A_{i_k}}^{z_{i_1}...z_{i_l} z_i} \wedge \overline{A_i}^{z_{i_1}...z_{i_l}} \equiv \overline{(\wedge_{1 \leq k \leq l} A_{i_k}) \wedge A_i}^{z_{i_1}...z_{i_l} z_i} .$$

(b) The specification statements $z_i[A_i, E_i]$, $1 \leq i \leq n$, are called perfect if for every set $M \subseteq \{1, ..., n\}$, the specifications $z_i[A_i, E_i]$, $i \in M$ are associative under the parallel operator $\_\|_1\_$ and their composition equals

$$(\cup_{i \in M} z_i) [\overline{\wedge_{i \in M} A_i}^{\cup_{i \in M} z_i}, \wedge_{i \in M} (A_i \wedge E_i)]$$

In case (b) we will speak of the parallel composition of $z_i[A_i, E_i]$, $1 \leq i \leq n$ and denote it by $\|_1 i \in M : z_i[A_i, E_i]$.

Obviously, if $A_1 \in Pred_{w;z_2}$, $A_2 \in Pred_{w;z_1}$, $E_1, E_2 \in Pred_{w;z_1;z_2}$, the two specifications $z_1[A_1, E_1]$, $z_2[A_2, E_2]$ are perfect.

With the above notations we can generalise Proposition 12 and formulate the correspondence between associative (perfect) specifications and predicates.

Proposition 13 (Associativity for $\|_1$) *The specifications $z_i[A_i, E_i]$, $1 \leq i \leq n$, are associative (perfect) under $\_\|_1\_$ iff the predicates A_i, $1 \leq i \leq n$ are associative (perfect) with respect to z_i, $1 \leq i \leq n$.*

To have maximal control at each design or refinement level it is desirable to work with perfect specifications. Therefore arguments are required that ensure perfect specifications in refinements. Of course, an immediate resolution of this issue is to drop all assumptions. If all assumptions are true, then associativity is no issue any more: the parallel operators are associative without any restrictions on specifications with true assumptions. We can extend this trivial observation for assumption predicates that do not refer to any of the observables:

Proposition 14 *If $A_i \in Pred_w$, $E_i \in Pred_{w;\cup_{1 \leq j \leq n} z_j}$, then the specifications $z_i[A_i, E_i]$, $1 \leq i \leq n$, are perfect.*

We proceed with two simple observations concerning the creation of perfect specifications with the monotonicity laws, Props. 9 and 8.

Proposition 15 *Let $z_i[A_i, E_i]$, $1 \leq i \leq n$, be perfect specifications.*

i) If $z_1[A_1, E_1] \vdash z_1[A_1, E_1']$ then the specifications $z_1[A_1, E_1']$, $z_i[A_i, E_i]$, $2 \leq i \leq n$ are perfect with

$$\|_1 1 \leq i \leq n : z_i[A_i, E_i] \vdash z_1[A_1, E_1'] \|_1 (\|_1 2 \leq i \leq n : z_i[A_i, E_i]) .$$

ii) If $A_1 \equiv A_1^1 \wedge A_2^1$ (neither A_1^1 nor A_2^1 refers to $z_1 = z_1^1; z_2^1$) and $z_1[A_1, E_1] \vdash z_1^1[A_1^1, E_1^1] \|_1 z_2^1[A_2^1, E_2^1]$ then the specifications $z_i^1[A_i^1, E_i^1]$, $i = 1, 2$, $z_i[A_i, E_i]$, $2 \leq i \leq n$ are perfect with

$$\|_1 1 \leq i \leq n : z_i[A_i, E_i] \vdash z_1^1[A_1^1, E_1^1] \|_1 z_2^1[A_2^1, E_2^1] \|_1 (\|_1 2 \leq i \leq n : z_i[A_i, E_i])$$

Obligation i) states that perfect specifications are stable under strengthening postconditions and obligation ii) is a simple rule to increase the number of perfect specification statements by splitting assumptions.

Causality, as defined in Definition 7, and feasibility under certain conditions guarantee perfect specification statements. The following proposition explicitly states these conditions for parallel compositions of three perfect specification statements.

Proposition 16 *Three specifications* $z_i[A_i, E_i]$, $i = 1, 2, 3$, *are perfect if the predicates* A_i, E_i $i = 1, 2$ *are causal with respect to* z_1, z_2 *and if each of the specifications* $z_i[A_i, E_i]$, $i = 1, 2$, $(\, z_1[A_1, E_1] |||_1 z_2[A_2, E_2] \,) |||_1 z_3[A_3, E_3]$ *is feasible.*

With Propositions 9 and 16 we can derive the following monotonicity law that reflects a refinement process beginning with one, then two and finally three specification statements with nontrivial assumptions.

Corollary 4. *Assume feasible specifications* $z_i[A_i, E_i]$, $i = 1, 2$, *with causal predicates* $A_1 \in Pred_{w;z_2}$, $A_2 \in Pred_{w;z_1}$, $E_i \in Pred_{w;z_1;z_2}$, $i = 1, 2$, *and feasible composition* $z_1[A_1, E_1] |||_1 z_2[A_2, E_2]$. *Assume further disjoint variable sets* z_1^1, z_2^1 *with* $z_1 = (z_1^1; z_2^1)$ *and predicates* $A_1^1 \in Pred_{w;z_2;z_2^1}$, $A_2^1 \in Pred_{w;z_2;z_1^1}$, $E_i^1 \in Pred_{w;z_2;z_1}$, $i = 1, 2$. *If* $z_1[A_1, E_1] \vdash z_1^1[A_1^1, E_1^1] |||_1 z_2^1[A_2^1, E_2^1]$ *and* $A_1 \equiv \overline{A_1^1}^{z_2^1} \wedge \overline{A_2^1}^{z_1^1}$, *then the specifications* $z_2[A_2, E_2]$, $z_i^1[A_i^1, E_i^1]$, $i = 1, 2$, *are perfect and* $z_1[A_1, E_1] |||_1 z_2[A_2, E_2] \vdash z_1^1[A_1^1, E_1^1] |||_1 z_2^1[A_2^1, E_2^1] |||_1 z_2[A_2, E_2]$.

We may split a feasible specification statement $z[A, E]$ into two components with causal predicates, $z_1[A_1, E_1]$ and $z_2[A_2, E_2]$, via equality (2) in section 4. If the resulting two components are feasible then we may refine them individually by strengthening postconditions as in Proposition 6. Corollary 4 ensures that the resulting specifications are perfect.

Thanks to the $\vee$-operator in the assumption predicates, parallel composition with $\_||_{3\_}$ and $\_||_{4\_}$ is always associative.

Proposition 17 *The parallel operators* $\_||_{3\_}$ *and* $\_||_{4\_}$ *are associative.*

7   Example

In a simple case study we show how the rules of the previous sections can be used to refine a single specification statement to a multi-component specification. For more complex examples about the sequential refinement of specification statements in the real-time setting we refer to [11,10,12,5].

A process should compute repeatedly the mode value of six binary input values $in_1, ..., in_6$ and output this value after three time units. If more than two inputs are 1 then the output will be 1. The effect

$$E \equiv (\, out : \mathbb{N} \to \{0,1\} \wedge (\forall n : \mathbb{N} \bullet out(n+3) = 1 \iff |\{i \bullet in_i(n) = 1\}| \geq 3)\,)$$

will be achieved under the assumption that the environment never supplies odd numbers of 0 and 1 at any time, as in the following.

$$A \equiv (\,in_1, .., in_6 : \mathbb{N} \to \{0,1\} \wedge (\forall n : \mathbb{N} \bullet 0 = (\sum_{i=1}^{6} in_i(n)) mod2\,))$$

The specification of the entire process can be given as $out[A, E]$. To split this specification further into three components we introduce the following new effect predicates:

$$E_0 \equiv (\,out : \mathbb{N} \to \{0, 1, \perp\} \wedge out(0) = out(1) = 0 \wedge (\forall n : \mathbb{N} \bullet$$
$$(\,out(n+2) = 0 \iff 0 \le h_1(n) + h_2(n) < 3 \wedge out(n+2) = 1$$
$$\iff 3 < h_1(n) + h_2(n)\,)\,)\,)$$
$$E_1 \equiv (\,h_1 : \mathbb{N} \to \mathbb{Z} \wedge h_1(0) = 0 \wedge (\forall n : \mathbb{N} \bullet$$
$$h_1(n+1) = in_1(n) + in_2(n) + in_3(n)\,)\,)$$
$$E_2 \equiv (\,h_2 : \mathbb{N} \to \mathbb{Z} \wedge h_2(0) = 0 \wedge (\forall n : \mathbb{N} \bullet$$
$$h_2(n+1) = in_4(n) + in_5(n) + in_6(n)\,)\,)$$

The variables h_1 and h_2 are initialised by 0 and then set to the sum of in_1, in_2 and in_3, respectively in_4, in_5 and in_6. In E_0, the output set for out is increased by $\perp$ to denote an input failure in the cases $h_1 + h_2 = 3$ and $h_1 + h_2 < 0$. Note that this can never happen under assumption A, nevertheless it increases the usability of the process component if A is removed.

The internal variable set $\{h_1, h_2\}$ shall be abbreviated by IV. Then, the refinement

$$out[A, E] \vdash out, h_1, h_2[A, E_0 \wedge E_1 \wedge E_2] \setminus IV$$

holds because of $A \wedge \overline{E_0 \wedge E_1 \wedge E_2}^{\,h_1\,h_2} \preceq E$, and Propositions 2, 3 and 6. For this refinement step we obviously need the assumption A on the environment.

We proceed with

$$out, h_1, h_2[A, E_0 \wedge E_1 \wedge E_2]$$
$$\{\text{Prop. } 10\} \cong out[A \wedge E_1 \wedge E_2, E_0]|||_1 h_1, h_2[A, E_1 \wedge E_2]$$
$$\{\text{Def. of } |||_1\} \cong out[A \wedge E_1 \wedge E_2, E_0]|||_1 (\,h_1[A, E_1]|||_1 h_2[A, E_2]\,)$$
$$\{\text{Prop. } 15\,\text{ii})\} \cong out[A \wedge E_1 \wedge E_2, E_0]|||_1 h_1[A, E_1]|||_1 h_2[A, E_2]\,.$$

Next, the process $out[A \wedge E_1 \wedge E_2, E_0]$ will be split into 2 components,

$$E_3 \equiv (\,out : \mathbb{N} \to \{0, 1, \perp\} \wedge out(0) = 0 \wedge (\forall n : \mathbb{N} doti$$
$$(\,out(n+1) = 0 \iff 0 \le pr(n) < 3 \wedge out(n+1) = 1$$
$$\iff 3 < pr(n) \le 6\,)\,)\,)$$
$$E_4 \equiv (\,pr : \mathbb{N} \to \mathbb{Z} \wedge pr(0) = 0 \wedge (\forall n : \mathbb{N} \bullet$$
$$(\,(\,h_1(n) < 0 \vee h_2(n) < 0\,) \Rightarrow pr(n+1) < 0 \wedge$$
$$(\,h_1(n) \ge 0 \wedge h_2(n) \ge 0\,) \Rightarrow pr(n+1) = h_1(n) + h_2(n)\,)\,)\,)$$

With these new predicates we obtain $A \wedge E_1 \wedge E_2 \wedge \overline{E_3 \wedge E_4}^{pr} \preceq E_0$. Hence,

$$out[A \wedge E_1 \wedge E_2, E_0]$$
$$\{ \text{Props. 2, 3, 6} \} \vdash out, pr[A \wedge E_1 \wedge E_2, E_3 \wedge E_4] \setminus \{pr\}$$
$$\{\text{Def. of } \|_1 \} \cong (out[A \wedge E_1 \wedge E_2, E_3] \|_1 pr[A, E_4]) \setminus \{pr\}$$
$$\{\text{Props. 5, 9}\} \vdash (out[A, E_3] \|_1 pr[A, E_4]) \setminus \{pr\} .$$

The whole refinement chain can now be stated as

$$out[A, E]$$
$$\vdash out, h_1, h_2[A, E_0 \wedge E_1 \wedge E_2] \setminus IV$$
$$\cong (out[A \wedge E_1 \wedge E_2, E_0] \|_1 h_1[A, E_1] \|_1 h_2[A, E_2]) \setminus IV$$
$$\{\text{Prop. 9}\} \vdash ((out[A, E_3] \|_1 pr[A, E_4]) \setminus \{pr\} \|_1 (h_1[A, E_1] \|_1 h_2[A, E_2])) \setminus IV$$
$$\{\text{Prop. 14}\} \vdash (out[A, E_3] \|_1 pr[A, E_4] \|_1 h_1[A, E_1] \|_1 h_2[A, E_2]) \setminus (IV \cup \{pr\}) .$$

8   Conclusions

We have extended the specification and refinement calculus [9,5,18] by providing more refinement rules and a parallel operator notion for specification statements. Due to the generality of the underlying specification and refinement notion, parallel composition is not necessarily associative or monotone. However, we described a design methodology for specification statements that guarantees monotonicity and associativity in parallel compositions and their refinements. We introduced the notion of perfect specifications and pointed out how this guarantees associativity during refinements with nontrivial assumption predicates.

Many well-known specification and refinement models [7,13,8,1,17] restrict their language and refinement notions to guarantee monotonicity and associativity. There is a common recipe for this: process specifications make no assumptions on the environment. In analogy to standard low level parallel operators, $\_\|_1\_$ is monotone and associative when no assumptions occur in the specification statements (see Props. 9, 14). Nevertheless, the power to incorporate assumptions in process components in the very abstract level of a refinement process justifies the loss of monotonicity or associativity of the parallel operator: if a design methodology for specifications can guarantee monotonicity and associativity there is no need to ensure both desired principles in the general case.

Note that there is no unique definition of the parallel operator and there are several candidates with properties of varying desirability. It seems that there is no ultimate answer to the issue of a parallel operator in the predicate transformer setting. In this paper four different operator notions have been investigated. We are in favour of the operators $\_\|_1\_$ and $\_\|_2\_$ where the former probably has better features than the latter. The operator $\_\|_2\_$ behaves very similarly to $\_\|_1\_$. In general, it lacks associativity and obeys similar refinement laws. It is monotone and weaker than $\_\|_1\_$, i.e., $z_1[A_1, E_1] \|_2 z_2[A_2, E_2] \vdash z_1[A_1, E_1] \|_1 z_2[A_2, E_2]$.

Nevertheless, the splitting into process components and the formulation of associativity criteria turn out to be more complicated than for $_-\|_{1-}$ in Proposition 10 and 13.

Thanks to the $\vee$-operator, $_-\|_{3-}$ is associative and monotone. But $_-\|_{3-}$ and $_-\|_{4-}$ fail to abort the entire process if one of the sibling processes aborts, i.e.,

$$z_1[false, E_1]\|_3 z_2[A_2, E_2](P) \equiv \overline{A_2}^{z_1} \wedge \forall z_1, z_2((A_2 \Rightarrow E_2) \Rightarrow P) \text{ and}$$
$$z_1[false, E_1]\|_4 z_2[A_2, E_2](P) \equiv \overline{A_2}^{z_1} .$$

The individual features of the different parallel operators are listed in the following table.

Operator	monotone w.r.t. $\vdash$	associative	abort $\|$ abort $\cong$ abort	splitting into components	invariant w.r.t. $\cong$
$\|_1$	no/Prop 9	no/Prop 13	yes	easy/Prop 10	yes/Prop 2
$\|_2$	yes/Prop 8	no/complex	yes	complex	yes/Prop 2
$\|_3$	yes/Prop 8	yes/Prop 17	no	complex	yes/Prop 2
$\|_4$	no	yes/Prop 17	no	complex	yes/Prop 2

Acknowledgements: Many thanks to Mark Bofinger, Colin Fidge and Axel Wabenhorst for valuable comments on drafts of this paper. I am also indebted to Graeme Smith who inspired the investigations of the parallel operators $_-\|_{2-}$, $_-\|_{3-}$ and $_-\|_{4-}$. This research was done partly under Australian Research Council grant A49600176.

References

1. M. Abadi and L. Lamport. Conjoining specifications. *ACM Transactions on Programming Languages and Systems*, 17(3):507–534, 1995.
2. C. J. Fidge. Refinement rules for real-time multi-tasking programs. In Michael Johnson, editor, *Algebraic Methodology and Software Technology (AMAST'97)*, volume 1349 of *Lecture Notes in Computer Science*, pages 199–215. Springer-Verlag, December 1997.
3. C. J. Fidge, I. J. Hayes, A. P. Martin, and A. K. Wabenhorst. A set-theoretic model for real-time specification and reasoning. In J. Jeuring, editor, *Mathematics of Program Construction (MPC'98)*, volume 1422 of *Lecture Notes in Computer Science*, pages 188–206. Springer-Verlag, 1998.
4. C. J. Fidge, M. Utting, P. Kearney, and I. J. Hayes. Integrating real-time scheduling theory and program refinement. In M.-C. Gaudel and J. Woodcock, editors, *FME'96: Industrial Benefit and Advances in Formal Methods*, volume 1051 of *Lecture Notes in Computer Science*, pages 327–346. Springer-Verlag, 1996.
5. I. J. Hayes and M. Utting. A sequential real-time refinement calculus. Technical Report 97-33, Software Verification Research Centre, University of Queensland, August 1997. http://svrc.it.uq.edu.au/Publications/Technical_reports_1997.html.
6. I. J. Hayes and M. Utting. Deadlines are termination. In D. Gries and W.-P. de Roever, editors, *IFIP International Conference on Programming Concepts and Methods (PROCOMET '98)*, pages 186–204. Chapman and Hall, 1998.
7. C.A.R. Hoare. *Communicating sequential processes*. Prentice-Hall International, UK, LTD, 1985.

8. L. Lamport. The temporal logic of actions. *ACM Transactions on Programming Languages and Systems*, 16(3):872–923, 1994.
9. B. Mahony. Using the refinement calculus for dataflow processes. Technical Report 94-32, Software Verification Research Centre, University of Queensland, October 1994. http://svrc.it.uq.edu.au/Publications/Technical_reports_1994.html.
10. B. Mahony and I. J. Hayes. A case study in timed refinement: A central heater. In J. M. Morris and R. C. Shaw, editors, *Fourth Refinement Workshop*, pages 138–149. Springer-Verlag, 1991.
11. B. Mahony, C. Millerchip, and I. J. Hayes. A boiler control system: Overview of a case-study in timed refinement. In D. Del Bel Belluz and H. C. Ratz, editors, *Software Safety: Everybody's Business—Proc. 1993 International Workshop on Design and Review of Software Controlled Safety-Related Systems*, pages 189–208, 1994.
12. B. P. Mahony and I. J. Hayes. A case-study in timed refinement: A mine pump. *IEEE Transactions on Software Engineering*, 18(9):817–826, September 1992.
13. R. Milner. *Communication and Concurrency*. Prentice-Hall, 1989.
14. C. Morgan. Data refinement by miracles. In C. Morgan and T. Vickers, editors, *On the Refinement Calculus*, pages 59–64. Springer-Verlag, 1994.
15. C. Morgan. *Programming from Specifications*. Prentice-Hall, second edition, 1994.
16. C.C. Morgan and T. Vickers. *On the Refinement Calculus*. Springer-Verlag, 1994.
17. D. Scholefield. Real-time refinement in Manna and Pnueli's temporal logic. *Formal Aspects of Computing*, 8(4):408–427, 1996.
18. M. Utting and C. J. Fidge. Refinement of infeasible real-time programs. In L. Groves and S. Reeves, editors, *Formal Methods Pacific '97*, pages 243–262. Springer-Verlag, 1997.
19. J. von Wright. The lattice of data refinement. *Acta Informatica*, 31(10):105–135, 1994.

Appendix: This appendix contains the proofs of the main propositions.

Proof of Proposition 1: $i)$ $\Rightarrow$ $ii)$: The first part, $A_1 \preceq A_2$, is a consequence of $\Theta^{z,w,u}(z[A_1, E_1])(true) \preceq \Theta^{z,w,u}(z[A_2, E_2])(true)$. For the remaining assertion note the following equivalences for $P \in Pred_{u;z}$:

$$\Theta^{z,w,u}(z[A_1, E_1])(P) \preceq \Theta^{z,w,u}(z[A_2, E_2])(P)$$
$$A_1 \wedge \forall z(\neg E_1 \vee P) \preceq A_2 \wedge \forall z(\neg E_2 \vee P) \tag{4}$$

We proceed by contradiction and assume $\neg\forall z, w \; (A_2 \Rightarrow E_2) \Rightarrow (A_1 \Rightarrow E_1)$. Hence, by setting $Q = (A_1 \wedge \neg E_1 \wedge E_2)$ we can find bindings a, b for z, w with

$$Q(a, b) \equiv true .$$

By setting $P_0 = (z \neq a)$ we obtain a predicate in $Pred_z$, but the identities

$$(A_1 \wedge \forall z(\neg E_1 \vee P_0)) \, (b) \equiv true , \; (A_2 \wedge \forall z(\neg E_2 \vee P_0)) \, (b) \equiv false$$

are in contradiction to (4). For implication $ii)$ $\Rightarrow$ $iv)$ assume $A_1 \preceq A_2$ and $(\neg E_1 \wedge A_1) \preceq (\neg E_2 \wedge A_2)$. Then, for u with $u \cap z = \emptyset$ and $P \in Pred_{u;z}$,

$$\begin{aligned}
\Theta^{z,w,u}(z[A_1, E_1])(P) &\equiv A_1 \wedge \forall z(E_1 \Rightarrow P) \equiv A_1 \wedge \forall z(A_1 \wedge (P \vee \neg E_1)) \\
&\equiv A_1 \wedge \forall z((A_1 \wedge P) \vee (A_1 \wedge \neg E_1)) \\
&\preceq A_2 \wedge \forall z((A_2 \wedge P) \vee (A_2 \wedge \neg E_2)) \\
&\equiv \Theta^{z,w,u}(z[A_2, E_2])(P)
\end{aligned}$$

The equivalence $ii) \Longleftrightarrow iii)$ is a trivial tautology and $iv) \Rightarrow i)$ is obvious. $\quad\square$

Proof of Proposition 3: Hiding v means restricting the predicate transformer $\Theta^{z;v,w,u}(z, v[A, E])$ to $Pred_{u;z}$. For $P \in Pred_{u;z}$,

$$\Theta^{z;v,w,u}(z, v[A, E])|_{Pred_{u;z}}(P) \equiv A \wedge \forall z, v(\neg E \vee P) \equiv A \wedge \forall z((\forall v \neg E) \vee P)$$
$$\equiv A \wedge \forall z(\overline{E}^v \Rightarrow P)$$
$$\equiv z[A, \overline{E}^v](P) \qquad\qquad \square$$

Proof of Proposition 5: According to Proposition 1, $z[A_1, E] \vdash z[A_2, E]$ is equivalent to $A_1 \preceq A_2$ and $A_2 \Rightarrow E \preceq A_1 \Rightarrow E$ which implies the assertion. $\quad\square$

Proof of Proposition 9: According to Proposition 1, $z_i[A_{i1}, E_{i1}] \vdash z_i[A_{i2}, E_{i2}]$ is equivalent to the two conditions

$$A_{i1} \preceq A_{i2} \qquad\qquad (5)$$
$$A_{i2} \Rightarrow E_{i2} \preceq A_{i1} \Rightarrow E_{i1} \qquad\qquad (6)$$

for $i = 1, 2$. By definition, we get for the above parallel compositions,

$$z_1[A_{11}, E_{11}]|||_1 z_2[A_{21}, E_{21}] \cong z_1, z_2[\overline{A_{11}}^{z_2} \wedge \overline{A_{21}}^{z_1}, A_{11} \wedge A_{21} \wedge E_{11} \wedge E_{21}]$$
$$z_1[A_{12}, E_{12}]|||_1 z_2[A_{22}, E_{22}] \cong z_1, z_2[\overline{A_{12}}^{z_2} \wedge \overline{A_{22}}^{z_1}, A_{12} \wedge A_{22} \wedge E_{12} \wedge E_{22}]$$

Once more with Proposition 1 we see that the refinement

$$z_1[A_{11}, E_{11}]|||_1 z_2[A_{21}, E_{21}] \vdash z_1[A_{12}, E_{12}]|||_1 z_2[A_{22}, E_{22}] \qquad\qquad (7)$$

is equivalent to the two conditions

$$\overline{(A_{11} \wedge A_{21})}^{z_1 z_2} \preceq \overline{A_{12} \wedge A_{22}}^{z_1 z_2} \qquad\qquad (8)$$
$$\overline{A_{12} \wedge A_{22}}^{z_1 z_2} \Rightarrow (A_{12} \wedge A_{22} \wedge E_{12} \wedge E_{22}) \qquad\qquad (9)$$
$$\preceq \overline{A_{11} \wedge A_{21}}^{z_1 z_2} \Rightarrow (A_{11} \wedge A_{21} \wedge E_{11} \wedge E_{21})$$

The first property (8) is satisfied because of (5). The second condition (9), under our assumptions, is obviously equivalent to (7). By using the condition (8) and the conditions (5) and (6), it can be checked that the condition (9) is equivalent to property $ii)$. $\quad\square$

Proof of Proposition 10: According to definition,

$$z_1[A_1 \wedge E_2, E_1 \wedge F_1]|||_1 z_2[A_2 \wedge E_1, E_2 \wedge F_2]$$
$$= z_1, z_2[\overline{A_1 \wedge E_2 \wedge A_2 \wedge E_1}^{z_1 z_2}, A_1 \wedge A_2 \wedge E_1 \wedge E_2 \wedge F_1 \wedge F_2] .$$

From Propositon 1 $iii)$ we know that $z_1[A_1 \wedge E_2, E_1 \wedge F_1]|||_1 z_2[A_2 \wedge E_1, E_2 \wedge F_2] \vdash z_1, z_2[\overline{A_1 \wedge A_2}^{z_1 z_2}, A_1 \wedge A_2 \wedge E_1 \wedge E_2 \wedge F_1 \wedge F_2]$ is equivalent to the two conditions

$$\overline{A_1 \wedge E_2 \wedge A_2 \wedge E_1}^{z_1 z_2} \preceq \overline{A_1 \wedge A_2}^{z_1 z_2}$$

and

$$(\overline{A_1 \wedge E_2 \wedge A_2 \wedge E_1}^{z_1 z_2} \wedge A_1 \wedge A_2 \wedge E_1 \wedge E_2 \wedge F_1 \wedge F_2)$$
$$\preceq (A_1 \wedge A_2 \wedge E_1 \wedge E_2 \wedge F_1 \wedge F_2)$$

which are obviously true. So it remains to prove $i) \iff ii)$.

The refinement $z_1, z_2[\overline{A_1 \wedge A_2}^{z_1 z_2}, A_1 \wedge A_2 \wedge E_1 \wedge E_2 \wedge F_1 \wedge F_2] \vdash z_1[A_1 \wedge E_2, E_1 \wedge F_1]|||_1 z_2[A_2 \wedge E_1, E_2 \wedge F_2]$ is equivalent to the properties

$$\overline{A_1 \wedge A_2}^{z_1 z_2} \preceq \overline{A_1 \wedge E_2 \wedge A_2 \wedge E_1}^{z_1 z_2}$$
$$(\overline{A_1 \wedge A_2}^{z_1 z_2} \wedge A_1 \wedge E_2 \wedge A_2 \wedge E_1 \wedge F_1 \wedge F_2) \preceq (A_1 \wedge A_2 \wedge E_1 \wedge E_2 \wedge F_1 \wedge F_2)$$

which are clearly equivalent to assertion ii. □

Proof of Proposition 12: The corresponding specifications to the parallel compositions are, respectively,

(a) $z_1, z_2, z_3[\overline{(\overline{A_1}^{z_2} \wedge \overline{A_2}^{z_1})}^{z_3} \wedge \overline{A_3}^{z_1 z_2}, A_1 \wedge A_2 \wedge A_3 \wedge E_1 \wedge E_2 \wedge E_3]$

(b) $z_1, z_2, z_3[\overline{(\overline{A_2}^{z_3} \wedge \overline{A_3}^{z_2})}^{z_1} \wedge \overline{A_1}^{z_2 z_3}, A_1 \wedge A_2 \wedge A_3 \wedge E_1 \wedge E_2 \wedge E_3]$

(c) $z_1, z_2, z_3[\overline{(\overline{A_1}^{z_3} \wedge \overline{A_3}^{z_1})}^{z_2} \wedge \overline{A_2}^{z_1 z_3}, A_1 \wedge A_2 \wedge A_3 \wedge E_1 \wedge E_2 \wedge E_3]$

Applying Proposition 1 we get $(a) \equiv (b)$ iff the following equivalence holds,

$$\overline{(\overline{A_1}^{z_2} \wedge \overline{A_2}^{z_1})}^{z_3} \wedge \overline{A_3}^{z_1 z_2} \equiv \overline{(\overline{A_2}^{z_3} \wedge \overline{A_3}^{z_2})}^{z_1} \wedge \overline{A_1}^{z_2 z_3}$$

Hence, necessary and sufficient conditions for the equivalence $(a) \equiv (b) \equiv (c)$ are the equivalences in (3). □

Proof of Proposition 16: We have $(z_1[A_1, E_1]|||_1 z_2[A_2, E_2])|||_1 z_3[A_3, E_3] \cong$

$$\cong z_1 z_2[\overline{A_1}^{z_2} \wedge \overline{A_2}^{z_1}, A_1 \wedge A_2 \wedge E_1 \wedge E_2]|||_1 z_3[A_3, E_3]$$
$$\cong z_1 z_2 z_3[\overline{(\overline{A_1}^{z_2} \wedge \overline{A_2}^{z_1})}^{z_3} \wedge \overline{A_3}^{z_1 z_2}, \wedge_{1 \le i \le 3}(A_i \wedge E_i)]$$

and thus, our assumptions can be stated as:

$$A_1 \wedge E_1 \preceq A_2 , \quad A_2 \wedge E_2 \preceq A_1 ,$$
$$A_i \preceq \overline{A_i \wedge E_i}^{z_i} , \quad i = 1, 2 ,$$
$$\overline{(A_1 \wedge A_2)}^{z_1 z_2 z_3} \wedge \overline{A_3}^{z_1 z_2} \preceq \overline{\wedge_{1 \le i \le 3}(A_i \wedge E_i)}^{z_1 z_2 z_3} .$$

Using this we find

$$\overline{(A_1 \wedge A_3)}^{z_1 z_2 z_3} \wedge \overline{A_2}^{z_1 z_3} \preceq \overline{(\overline{A_1 \wedge E_1}^{z_1} \wedge A_3)}^{z_1 z_2 z_3} \wedge \overline{A_2}^{z_1 z_3}$$
$$\preceq \overline{(\overline{A_1 \wedge A_2}^{z_1} \wedge A_3)}^{z_1 z_2 z_3} \wedge \overline{A_2}^{z_1 z_3}$$
$$\preceq \overline{(A_1 \wedge A_2)}^{z_1 z_2 z_3} \wedge \overline{A_3}^{z_1 z_2}$$
$$\preceq \overline{A_1 \wedge A_2 \wedge A_3}^{z_1 z_2 z_3} .$$

The remaining case can be treated similarly. □

Comparing the Efficiency of Asynchronous Systems*

Lars Jenner** and Walter Vogler

Institut für Informatik, Universität Augsburg, D-86135 Augsburg, Germany
{jenner, vogler}@informatik.uni-augsburg.de

Abstract. A timed process algebra is developed for evaluating the temporal worst-case efficiency of asynchronous concurrent systems. For the sake of simplicity, we use a classical CCS-like algebra where actions may occur arbitrarily within a continuous time interval, yielding arbitrary relative speeds of the components. Via the timed testing approach, asynchronous systems are then related w.r.t. their worst-case efficiency, yielding an efficiency preorder. We show that this preorder can just as well be based on much simpler discrete time and that it can be characterized with some kind of refusal traces. Finally, precongruence results are provided for all operators of the algebra, where prefix, choice and recursion require special attention.

1 Motivation and Introduction

Classical process algebras like CCS model asynchronous systems, where the components have arbitrary relative speeds. To consider the temporal behaviour, several timed process algebras have been proposed, where usually systems are regarded as *synchronous*, i.e. have components with fixed speeds. The easiest of these is SCCS [Mil89]: terms are essentially the same as for CCS; the natural choice to fix the speeds of components is to assume that each action takes one unit of time; so SCCS-semantics differs from CCS-semantics essentially by excluding runs where one component performs many actions while another performs just one. Our aim is to evaluate the temporal worst-case efficiency of *asynchronous* concurrent systems modeled with a process algebra, and – as in the case of SCCS – we want to keep things simple by using just classical CCS-like process terms. Furthermore, we will use a variant of (must-) testing [DNH84], where the testing preorder can be interpreted as comparing efficiency.

A usual treatment of asynchronous systems with a timed process algebra is to allow arbitrary idling before each action [Mil89, MT91]; this achieves arbitrary relative speeds, but is not suitable for defining worst-case runs since each action already can take arbitrarily long. Here, we assume each action to be performed within a given time – and to keep things simple as in SCCS, we take 1 as a common upper time bound for all actions. This enforces some progress, but

---

* A preliminary version of this paper appeared in the proceedings of PAPM'98 [Pri98]
** This work was supported by the DFG–project 'Halbordnungstesten'

J.-P. Katoen (Ed.): ARTS'99, LNCS 1601, pp. 172–191, 1999.

different from SCCS, actions may also be performed faster than necessary; hence, components have arbitrary relative speeds and we take into account all runs of an asynchronous system; see e.g. [Lyn96] for an approach with upper time bounds.

We compare processes via the testing approach developed by [DNH84] and extended to timed testing in a Petri net framework in [Vog95, JV95]. A timed test is an environment together with a time bound. A process is embedded into the environment essentially via parallel composition and satisfies a timed test, if success is reached before the time bound in *every* run of the composed system, i.e. even in the worst case. If some process P satisfies each timed test satisfied by a process Q, then P may be successful in more environments than specified by Q, but it may also be successful in the same environments within a shorter time; therefore, we call it a *faster implementation* of Q, and the testing preorder is naturally an efficiency preorder. In order to help intuition, we anticipate the following example: let $P_a \equiv \mu X.a.X$ be a process which is ready to engage in activity a repeatedly, let $P_b \equiv \mu X.b.X$ be analogous with b and let $P_+ \equiv \mu X.(a.X + b.X)$ be ready to engage repeatedly either in a or b one at a time; then we expect the parallel composition without synchronization $P_* \equiv P_a \parallel_\emptyset P_b$ to be faster than P_+, since simultaneous requests for both a and b from an environment can be served simultaneously by P_* but not by P_+.

To define timed testing formally, we have to define runs of asynchronous systems. In Section 2, we develop a suitable semantics with upper time bound on actions where time is continuous; we try to formalize our intuitive ideas as directly as possible without anticipating any specific treatment that might be necessary to obtain a precongruence in the end. As regards the definition of testing, the classical embedding in the test environment leads to a testing preorder which – surprisingly – is not a precongruence for prefixing; instead of refining the preorder to the coarsest such precongruence (cf. [Jen96]), we get this precongruence directly by using a slightly different, but also intuitive embedding.

Using continuous time is certainly not as simple as intended; e.g. initially a process can make uncountably many time steps. Our first main result in Section 3 reconciles realism and simplicity: we define an analogous efficiency preorder based on discrete time behaviour and show its coincidence with the first one. In Section 4, as usual in a testing approach, we characterize the efficiency preorder – here with some kind of refusal traces. The important point with this second main result is that test environments are asynchronous systems, hence 'temporally weak', but nevertheless reveal the temporal behaviour of tested processes quite in detail; correspondingly, the construction of revealing tests is a little involved.

We also provide precongruence results for parallel composition, hiding, relabeling and prefixing. Finally, in Section 5 we refine the efficiency preorder to a precongruence also for choice: as usual, we additionally have to take into account the (initial) stability of processes. Quite surprisingly, although we consider a preorder, the additional condition on stability is not only an implication but an equivalence. The refined efficiency preorder is then shown to be the coarsest precongruence for all operators of our process algebra that respects inclusion of discrete behaviour. We also provide a precongruence result for recursion. Here, we avoid the introduction of least elements (Ω-terms) and application of cpo-techniques (cf. [Hen88]) and thereby gain some degree of self-containment, but our technique exploits the restriction to guarded recursion.

We have translated the results for Petri nets from [JV95] to a process algebra setting for two reasons: on the one hand, it is shown that the underlying ideas are not model-dependent; on the other hand, the developments here are quite different – see e.g. the progress preorder in Section 3 – and process algebras are much more powerful than finite safe Petri nets by providing TURING-power.

For an interesting application of our approach see [JV95], where different implementations of a bounded buffer are distinguished w.r.t. their efficiency; we intend to carry over this example into our process algebra setting, expecting the same results. Due to lack of space, most proofs are omitted in this paper. (A full version is available as technical report.)

2 Continuously Timed Processes and Tests

We will use a CCS-like process algebra with TCSP-like $\|_A$ parallel composition, where A is a set of actions and components have to synchronize on all actions from A. Processes will perform (atomic) actions instantaneously within time 1; time passes continuously (in this section) in between their occurrences. For example, process $a.P$ will idle and then perform action a at some time point in the real interval $[0;1]$, evolving to P. To model this, we introduce continuously timed actions $\langle a, r \rangle$, which carry a 'timer' r whose initial value can be chosen from the interval $[0;1]$ of real numbers. When time passes globally by a certain amount, the timer of a locally activated action will be decreased accordingly. Timer value 0 denotes that the idle time of the respective action has elapsed, hence it must either occur or be deactivated before time may pass further *(urgency)* – unless it has to wait for synchronization with another component *(patience)*. E.g., process $a.P$ corresponds to $\langle a, 1 \rangle.P$ and can idle, process $\langle a, 0 \rangle.Q$ can neither idle nor wait, but component $\langle a, 0 \rangle.Q$ in $(\langle a, 0 \rangle.Q)\|_{\{a\}}(\langle a, 1 \rangle.P)$ has to wait for synchronization on a while component $\langle a, 1 \rangle.P$ still may idle.

We also use two distinguished actions: τ represents internal activity and ω is reserved for observers (test processes) only, which use this action in order to signal success of a test.

Definition 2.1   Let $\mathbb{A}$ be an infinite set of actions and let $\omega, \tau \notin \mathbb{A}$ be the *success* and *internal* action resp. We define $\mathbb{A}_\omega = \mathbb{A} \cup \{\omega\}$ and $\mathbb{A}_{\omega\tau} = \mathbb{A}_\omega \cup \{\tau\}$. Elements of $\mathbb{A}_{\omega\tau}$ are denoted by $a, b, c, \ldots$ (including τ and ω). Let $\mathbb{T}$ be the set of real numbers in $[0;1]$. Elements from $\mathbb{T}$ are denoted by $\rho, r, \ldots$. Let $Act = \mathbb{A}_{\omega\tau} \times \mathbb{T} = \{\alpha, \beta, \ldots\}$ be the set of *continuously timed actions*, where e.g. $\alpha = \langle a, r \rangle \in Act$. We use a as a shorthand for $\langle a, 1 \rangle$ and $\underline{a}$ as a shorthand for $\langle a, 0 \rangle$, which we call an *urgent* action.

A *(continuously timed) c-process term* P is generated by the following grammar:

$$P ::= \mathbf{0} \mid X \mid \langle a, r \rangle.P \mid P + P \mid P\|_A P \mid P[\Phi] \mid \mu X.P$$

where $\mathbf{0}$ *(Nil)* is a constant, $X \in \mathcal{X} = \{X, Y, Z, \ldots\}$ is a *(process) variable*, $\langle a, r \rangle \in Act$ and $A \subseteq \mathbb{A}_\omega$ possibly infinite; $\Phi : \mathbb{A}_{\omega\tau} \to \mathbb{A}_{\omega\tau}$ is a *general relabeling function* satisfying $\{a \in \mathbb{A} \mid \exists b \neq a : \Phi(b) = a\}$ is finite, $\Phi^{-1}(\omega) \subseteq \{\omega\}$ and $\Phi(\tau) = \tau$. Additionally, we only allow *guarded* recursion. $\mathbb{P}_c$ is the set of c-process terms $P, Q, \ldots$. We distinguish several cases: P is an *initial* process term, if the choice of r is restricted to $r = 1$; $\tilde{\mathbb{P}}_1$ is the set of initial process terms. P is a *(continuously timed) c-process*, if P is closed, i.e. all variables X in P are bound by the corresponding μX-operator; the set of c-processes is denoted by $\mathbb{P}_c$. $\mathbb{P}_1 = \mathbb{P}_c \cap \tilde{\mathbb{P}}_1$ is the set of *initial processes*. ∎

0 is the Nil-process, which cannot perform any action, but may let pass time without limit. $X \in \mathcal{X}$ is a process variable used for recursion. $\alpha.P$ is action-prefixing known from CCS: $\langle a, r \rangle$ stands for the action a which has to be performed within time r. To evaluate worst-case behaviour, such an upper time bound has to be assumed; if detailed information is missing, it is natural that in the processes under consideration all actions have the same time bound, which one can take as unit of time. Thus, we will be able to translate ordinary CCS-like process terms into our setting by replacing each a by $\langle a, 1 \rangle$.

$P_1 + P_2$ models nondeterministic choice between P_1 and P_2 and $P_1 \|_A P_2$ is the parallel composition of two processes P_1 and P_2 that run in parallel and have to synchronize on all actions from A; this is inspired from TCSP. The general relabeling operation $P[\Phi]$ subsumes the classically distinguished operations relabeling and hiding: if Φ satisfies $\Phi^{-1}(\tau) = \{\tau\}$, then Φ is a *(classical) relabeling function*; if Φ maps some (possibly infinite) $A \subseteq \mathbb{A}$ to $\{\tau\}$ and is the identity otherwise, then $P[\Phi]$ *hides* A in P and is also written P/A. The finiteness of the set $\{a \in \mathbb{A} \mid \exists b \neq a : \Phi(b) = a\}$ will ensure that the number of different actions ever performable by a c-process is finite. $\mu X.P$ models recursion; some $X \in \mathcal{X}$ is *guarded* in a c-process term $P \in \tilde{\mathbb{P}}_c$, if each occurrence of X is in a subterm $\alpha.Q$ of P, where the guard $\alpha \in Act$ may *also be an internal* timed action $\langle \tau, r \rangle$. In this paper, we only consider c-process terms $\mu X.P$ where X is guarded in P. We say that $P \in \tilde{\mathbb{P}}_c$ is *guarded* if all $X \in \mathcal{X}$ are guarded in P. Whenever we perform syntactical substitution $P\{Q/X\}$, we assume that no free variable of Q is bound in P (BARENDREGT convention). If S is a function $S : \mathcal{X} \mapsto \tilde{\mathbb{P}}_c$, then S denotes a *simultaneous substitution* of all variables, and we write $[P]_S$ for $P\{S(X)/X, S(Y)/Y, \ldots\}$, i.e. application of S to P.

The precedence of the operators in decreasing order is as follows: relabeling, prefix, recursion, parallel composition, choice. We intend choice and parallel composition to be commutative and choice to be associative, and we anticipate this by a syntactical congruence:

Definition 2.2 *Syntactical congruence* $\equiv \subseteq \tilde{\mathbb{P}}_c \times \tilde{\mathbb{P}}_c$ is the least congruence of c-process terms satisfying for all $P_1, P_2, P_3 \in \tilde{\mathbb{P}}_c$ and $A \subseteq \mathbb{A}$:

$$P_1 + P_2 \equiv P_2 + P_1 \qquad (P_1 + P_2) + P_3 \equiv P_1 + (P_2 + P_3) \qquad P_1 \|_A P_2 \equiv P_2 \|_A P_1$$

We regard syntactically congruent c-process terms as equal. Therefore, $\sum_{i \in I} P_i$ is used as a shorthand for the sum of all $P_i \in \tilde{\mathbb{P}}_c$, where i is in a finite indexing set I. We define $\sum_{i \in \emptyset} P_i \equiv \mathbf{0}$, and if $|I| = 1$, then $\sum_{j \in \{i\}} P_j \equiv P_i$. ∎

Now the purely functional behaviour of process terms (i.e. which actions they can perform) is given by the following operational semantics, where syntactical congruence enables us to use only one SOS-rule for choice and two SOS-rules for parallel composition:

Definition 2.3   Relation $\rightarrow \subseteq (\tilde{\mathbb{P}}_c \times \mathbb{A}_{\omega\tau} \times \tilde{\mathbb{P}}_c)$ is defined inductively:

$$\frac{}{\langle a,r \rangle.P \overset{a}{\rightarrow} P} \qquad \frac{a \notin A,\ P_1 \overset{a}{\rightarrow} P_1'}{P_1\|_A P_2 \overset{a}{\rightarrow} P_1'\|_A P_2} \qquad \frac{a \in A,\ P_1 \overset{a}{\rightarrow} P_1',\ P_2 \overset{a}{\rightarrow} P_2'}{P_1\|_A P_2 \overset{a}{\rightarrow} P_1'\|_A P_2'}$$

$$\frac{P_1 \overset{a}{\rightarrow} P_1'}{P_1 + P_2 \overset{a}{\rightarrow} P_1'} \qquad \frac{P \overset{a}{\rightarrow} P'}{P[\Phi] \overset{\Phi(a)}{\rightarrow} P'[\Phi]} \qquad \frac{P \overset{a}{\rightarrow} P'}{\mu X.P \overset{a}{\rightarrow} P'\{\mu X.P/X\}}$$

For c-process terms P, P' and $a \in \mathbb{A}_{\omega\tau}$, we write $P \overset{a}{\rightarrow} P'$ if $(P, a, P') \in \rightarrow$ and $P \overset{a}{\rightarrow}$ if there exists a P'' such that $(P, a, P'') \in \rightarrow$. Finally, we let $\mathcal{A}(P) = \{a \in \mathbb{A}_{\omega\tau} \mid P \overset{a}{\rightarrow}\}$ be the set of *activated actions* of P.   ∎

Except for prefix and recursion, these rules are standard. The first one allows an activated action to occur disregarding the value of its timer; since passage of time will never deactivate actions or activate new ones, we capture all behaviour that is possible in the standard CCS-like setting without time. Note that the recursion rule implicitly makes use of guarded recursion [BD91]; this simplifies proofs of operational properties by connecting induction on inferences with induction on the structure of a c-process.

The set of activated actions of a c-process term P describes its immediate functional behaviour; it will be preserved along passage of time. It is empty for process variables $X \in \mathcal{X}$, reflecting that unbound occurrence of a variable means incomplete specification. We have defined $\mathcal{A}(P)$ via operational semantics, but it can equivalently be determined inductively from the syntactical structure of P alone. Observe that $\mathcal{A}(P)$ records only actions, not the possibly various timer values associated with the same action in a process. Furthermore, due to the image-finiteness of general relabeling functions, $\mathcal{A}(P)$ is always finite, which will be used for the characterization of our testing preorder.

Proposition 2.4   Let $P \in \tilde{\mathbb{P}}_c$ be a process term. Then $\mathcal{A}(P)$ is finite.   ∎

As a first step to define timed behaviour, we now give operational rules for the passage of 'wait-time': all components of a system participate in a global time step, and this passage of time is recorded for locally activated actions by decreasing their annotated timer by the prefix rule. Note that time passes disregarding elapsed timers; this might be necessary for a component when waiting for a synchronization partner, and this explains the notion 'wait-time'.

Definition 2.5   Relation $\leadsto_c \subseteq (\tilde{\mathbb{P}}_c \times \mathbb{T} \times \tilde{\mathbb{P}}_c)$ is defined inductively:

$$\frac{}{0 \overset{\rho}{\leadsto}_c 0} \qquad \frac{r' = \max(r - \rho, 0)}{\langle a,r \rangle.P \overset{\rho}{\leadsto}_c \langle a,r' \rangle.P} \qquad \frac{P_1 \overset{\rho}{\leadsto}_c P_1',\ P_2 \overset{\rho}{\leadsto}_c P_2'}{P_1 + P_2 \overset{\rho}{\leadsto}_c P_1' + P_2'}$$

$$\frac{P \overset{\rho}{\leadsto}_c P'}{P[\Phi] \overset{\rho}{\leadsto}_c P'[\Phi]} \qquad \frac{P_1 \overset{\rho}{\leadsto}_c P_1',\ P_2 \overset{\rho}{\leadsto}_c P_2'}{P_1\|_A P_2 \overset{\rho}{\leadsto}_c P_1'\|_A P_2'} \qquad \frac{P \overset{\rho}{\leadsto}_c P'}{\mu X.P \overset{\rho}{\leadsto}_c P'\{\mu X.P/X\}}$$

For c-process terms $P, P' \in \tilde{\mathbb{P}}_c$ and $\rho \in \mathbb{T}$, we write $P \overset{\rho}{\leadsto}_c P'$ if $(P, \rho, P') \in \leadsto_c$. We write $P \overset{\rho}{\leadsto}_c$, if there exists a $P'' \in \tilde{\mathbb{P}}_c$ such that $(P, \rho, P'') \in \leadsto_c$.   ∎

Note that a process variable $X \in X$ has no time semantics, again reflecting the fact that unbound occurrence of a variable means incomplete specification.

The operational semantics of wait-time allows c-processes to wait forever, but our intention was that an urgent action has to occur or be disabled, unless it has to wait for a synchronization partner. We will enforce this using an auxiliary function that calculates for a given action a its residual time $\mathcal{R}(a, P)$ in a c-process term P, i.e. the time until it becomes urgent.

Definition 2.6   The *residual time* of an action $a \in \mathbb{A}_{\omega\tau}$ in a c-process term $P \in \tilde{\mathbb{P}}_c$ is given by the following inductively defined function $\mathcal{R} : \mathbb{A}_{\omega\tau} \times \tilde{\mathbb{P}}_c \to \mathbb{T}$:

Nil: $\mathcal{R}(a, \mathbf{0}) = 1$ for all $a \in \mathbb{A}_{\omega\tau}$
Var: $\mathcal{R}(a, X) = 1$ for all $a \in \mathbb{A}_{\omega\tau}$
Pref: $\mathcal{R}(a, \alpha.P)$ is r if $\alpha = \langle a, r \rangle$ and 1 otherwise
Sum: $\mathcal{R}(a, P_1 + P_2) = \min(\mathcal{R}(a, P_1), \mathcal{R}(a, P_2))$
Par: $\mathcal{R}(a, P_1 \|_A P_2)$ is $\max(\mathcal{R}(a, P_1), \mathcal{R}(a, P_2))$ if $a \in A$ and
        $\min(\mathcal{R}(a, P_1), \mathcal{R}(a, P_2))$ if $a \notin A$
Rel: $\mathcal{R}(a, P[\Phi]) = \min\{\mathcal{R}(b, P) \,|\, b \in \Phi^{-1}(a)\}$
Rec: $\mathcal{R}(a, \mu X.P) = \mathcal{R}(a, P)$

Finally, we let $\mathcal{R}(P) = \min\{\mathcal{R}(a, P) \,|\, a \in \mathcal{A}(P)\}$, where $\min \emptyset := 1$.   ∎

We have chosen $\mathcal{R}(a, X) = \mathcal{R}(a, \mathbf{0}) = 1$ mainly for technical reasons (cf. 2.7 below). The Par-case will realize the desired behaviour of waiting in a parallel composition: if P_1 and P_2 have to synchronize on a, then the residual time of a in $P_1 \|_A P_2$ is determined by the 'slower' component with larger residual time; if P_1 and P_2 do not have to synchronize on a, the 'faster' component determines the maximal possible delay of a in $P_1 \|_A P_2$.

Observe that in the Rel-case $\Phi^{-1}(a)$ may be empty or infinite; for the latter case, we will see below that for any c-process term P there are only finitely many actions b with $\mathcal{R}(b, P) \neq 1$ (2.7 together with 2.4), such that the set $\{\mathcal{R}(b, P) \,|\, b \in \Phi^{-1}(a)\}$ is finite and $\mathcal{R}(a, P[\Phi])$ exists. Similarly, $\mathcal{R}(P)$ exists for each c-process term P, and, hence, the residual time is well-defined and we have $\mathcal{R}(a, P) \in \mathbb{T}$ and $\mathcal{R}(P) \in \mathbb{T}$ in all cases.

Proposition 2.7   If $\mathcal{R}(a, P) \neq 1$, then $a \in \mathcal{A}(P)$ for $P \in \tilde{\mathbb{P}}_c$ and $a \in \mathbb{A}_{\omega\tau}$.   ∎

Using the residual time of a c-process term, we are now able to restrict wait-time to the timed behaviour we had in mind originally and which we call 'idle-time'. Alternatively, idle-time could have been defined via SOS-rules intertwined with the rules for wait-time.

Definition 2.8   We write $P \overset{\rho}{\to}_c P'$ (and $P \overset{\rho}{\to}_c$) if $P \overset{\rho}{\leadsto}_c P'$ and $\rho \leq \mathcal{R}(P)$.   ∎

Consider the example from the beginning of this section: it is $\mathcal{R}(\langle a, 1 \rangle.P) = \mathcal{R}(a, \langle a, 1 \rangle.P) = 1$, so $\langle a, 1 \rangle.P \overset{1}{\leadsto}_c \langle a, 0 \rangle.P$ and $\langle a, 1 \rangle.P \overset{1}{\to}_c \langle a, 0 \rangle.P$. Similarly, we have $\mathcal{R}(\langle a, 0 \rangle.Q) = \mathcal{R}(a, \langle a, 0 \rangle.Q) = 0$, hence only $\langle a, 0 \rangle.Q \overset{1}{\leadsto}_c \langle a, 0 \rangle.Q$ but not $\langle a,0\rangle.Q \xrightarrow{1}_c \langle a,0\rangle.Q$; however, we have $\mathcal{R}(\langle a,0\rangle.Q \|_{\{a\}} \langle a,1\rangle.P) = 1$ and, thus, $\langle a,0\rangle.Q \|_{\{a\}} \langle a,1\rangle.P \xrightarrow{1}_c \langle a,0\rangle.Q \|_{\{a\}} \langle a,0\rangle.P$.

Proposition 2.9 gathers some properties of our timing discipline; by *termination*, *urgency* and *persistence*, c-processes without activated actions may idle for an arbitrary amount of time, but if there are activated actions, they may idle at most for time 1 by *progress*, *urgency* and *persistence*:

Proposition 2.9   Let $P, P', P'' \in \tilde{\mathbb{P}}_c$ and $\rho, \rho', \rho + \rho' \in \mathbb{T}$.

1. *(urgency)* $P \xrightarrow{\rho}_c$ iff P guarded and $\rho \leq \mathcal{R}(P)$, and P' guarded if $P \xrightarrow{\rho}_c P'$.
2. *(persistence)*   If $P \xrightarrow{\rho}_c P'$, then $\mathcal{A}(P) = \mathcal{A}(P')$.
3. *(termination)*   If $\mathcal{A}(P) = \emptyset$ and $P \xrightarrow{\rho}_c P'$, then $\mathcal{R}(P) = \mathcal{R}(P') = 1$.
4. *(progress)*   If $\mathcal{A}(P) \neq \emptyset$ and $P \xrightarrow{\rho}_c P'$, then $\mathcal{R}(P) - \mathcal{R}(P') = \rho$.
5. *(continuity)* $P \xrightarrow{\rho+\rho'}_c P''$ if and only if $P \xrightarrow{\rho}_c P' \xrightarrow{\rho'}_c P''$ for some P'.
6. *(determinism)* If $P \xrightarrow{\rho}_c P'$ and $P \xrightarrow{\rho}_c P''$, then $P' \equiv P''$.   ∎

Purely functional and timed behaviour of processes are combined in the continuous language of processes. As usual, we abstract from internal behaviour; note that internal actions gain some 'visibility' in timed behaviour, since their presence possibly allows to pass more time in between the occurrence of visible actions. For later proofs (cf. 3.7) we also need a language that records τ's.

Definition 2.10   Let $P, P' \in \tilde{\mathbb{P}}_c$ be c-process terms. We write $P \xrightarrow{\varepsilon}_c P'$ if either $\varepsilon \in \mathbb{A}_{\omega\tau}$ and $P \xrightarrow{\varepsilon} P'$, or $\varepsilon \in \mathbb{T}$ and $P \xrightarrow{\varepsilon}_c P'$. We extend this to sequences w and write $P \xrightarrow{w}_c P'$ if $P \equiv P'$ and $w = \lambda$ (empty sequence) or there exist $Q \in \mathbb{P}_c$ and $\varepsilon \in (\mathbb{A}_{\omega\tau} \cup \mathbb{T})$ such that $P \xrightarrow{\varepsilon}_c Q \xrightarrow{w'}_c P'$ and $w = \varepsilon w'$. For a $w \in (\mathbb{A}_{\omega\tau} \cup \mathbb{T})^*$ let w/τ be the sequence w with all τ's removed, let $act(w)$ be the sequence of elements from $\mathbb{A}_{\omega\tau}$ in w, and let $\zeta(w)$ be the sum of time steps in w; note that $\zeta(w/\tau) = \zeta(w)$. We write $P \xRightarrow{v}_c P'$, if $P \xrightarrow{w}_c P'$ and $v = w/\tau$.

For a c-process $P \in \mathbb{P}_c$ we define $\mathsf{CL}_\tau(P) = \{w \mid P \xrightarrow{w}_c\}$ to be the *continuous τ-language*, containing the *continuous τ-traces* of P, and $\mathsf{CL}(P) = \{w \mid P \xRightarrow{w}_c\}$ to be the *continuous language*, containing the *continuous traces* of P.   ∎

We state in passing that the set of c-processes is closed under occurrence of actions or passage of time, i.e. $P \in \mathbb{P}_c$ and $P \xrightarrow{w}_c P'$ implies $P' \in \mathbb{P}_c$ again.

Based on the continuous language of c-processes, we are now ready to define timed testing and to relate c-processes w.r.t. their efficiency:

Definition 2.11   An *initial* process $P \in \mathbb{P}_1$ is *testable* if ω does not occur in P. Any initial process $O \in \mathbb{P}_1$ may serve as a *test process (observer)*. A *c-timed test* is a pair (O, R), where O is a test process and $R \in \mathbb{R}_0^+$ is the *real time bound*. A testable process P *c-satisfies* a c-timed test (P must_c (O, R)), if each $v \in \mathsf{CL}(\tau.P\|_\mathbb{A}O)$ with $\zeta(v) > R$ contains some ω. For testable processes P and Q, we call P a *continuously faster implementation* of Q, written $P \sqsupseteq_c Q$, if P c-satisfies all c-timed tests that Q c-satisfies. $\sqsupseteq_c$ is the *efficiency preorder*.   ∎

In contrast to e.g. [DNH84], execution and not only activation of an ω is necessary for satisfaction of a c-timed test. Note that $\tau.P\|_\mathbf{A}O$ is a shorthand for $(\langle\tau,1\rangle.P)\|_\mathbf{A}O$. Usually, one considers the behaviour of $P\|_\mathbf{A}O$ when defining a test. This is also done in [Jen96], where it is shown that surprisingly the resulting efficiency preorder is not a precongruence for prefix and therefore has to be refined afterwards. In order to avoid this complication, we have chosen $\tau.P\|_\mathbf{A}O$ instead, gaining the same result directly. From an intuitive point of view, the additional τ-prefix represents some internal setup activity before the actual test begins.

As an example consider observer $O \equiv a.\omega.\mathbf{0}\|_{\{\omega\}}b.\omega.\mathbf{0}$ and P_* and P_+ from Section 1: we have $11a1b1 \in \mathsf{CL}(\tau.P_+\|_\mathbf{A}O)$, hence P_+ not $must_c\ (O,3)$; but $\tau.P_*\|_\mathbf{A}O \overset{11a}{\to}_c (\mu X.a.X\|_\mathbf{0}\underline{b}.\mu X.b.X)\|_\mathbf{A}(\omega.\mathbf{0}\|_{\{\omega\}}\underline{b}.\omega.\mathbf{0})$ which in the worst case performs $b1$ before an ω; thus $P_+\ must_c\ (O,3)$. (Recall that $\underline{b}$ is $\langle b,0\rangle$.)

Runs with duration less than R may not contain all actions that occur up to time R; hence we only consider runs with a duration greater than the time bound R for test satisfaction. This definition of c-satisfaction would be of questionable usefulness, if c-processes were able to stop time, i.e. to reach a state from where no time step is possible any more; we will see later on (cf. 3.4.4) that this doubt is unsubstantiated.

At this point, it is by no means clear how to check $P \sqsupseteq_c Q$ for given testable P and Q. Obviously, the definition cannot be applied directly, since there are uncountably many time bounds and, hence, c-timed tests to apply. Even if we could decide $P \sqsupseteq_c Q$ from $\mathsf{CL}(P)$ and $\mathsf{CL}(Q)$ only (which is not the case), $\mathsf{CL}(P)$ and $\mathsf{CL}(Q)$ are still uncountable and hard to handle.

3   Discretization

Intuitively, satisfaction of a c-timed test essentially depends on the 'slowest' sequences in $\mathsf{CL}(\tau.P\|_\mathbf{A}O)$; in this section, we will show that these are generated by discrete behaviour only, i.e. those traces with only time steps of duration 1. This will yield a simple theory.

Definition 3.1   Let $P, P' \in \tilde{\mathbb{P}}_c$ be c-process terms. We write $P \overset{\varepsilon}{\to}_d P'$ if either $\varepsilon \in \mathbb{A}_{\omega\tau}$ and $P \overset{\varepsilon}{\to} P'$, or $\varepsilon = 1$ and $P \overset{\varepsilon}{\to}_c P'$; in the latter case we say that P performs a *unit time step*. For sequences $w \in (\mathbb{A}_{\omega\tau} \cup \{1\})^*$, we define $P \overset{w}{\to}_d$ and $P \overset{w/\tau}{\Rightarrow}_d$ analogously to 2.10. For a c-process $P \in \mathbb{P}_c$ we define $\mathsf{DL}_\tau(P) = \{w \mid P \overset{w}{\to}_d\}$ to be the *discrete τ-language*, containing the *discrete τ-traces* of P, and $\mathsf{DL}(P) = \{w/\tau \mid w \in \mathsf{DL}_\tau(P)\}$ to be the *discrete language*, containing the *discrete traces* of P. Observe that $\mathsf{DL}(P) \subseteq \mathsf{CL}(P)$ and $\mathsf{DL}_\tau(P) \subseteq \mathsf{CL}_\tau(P)$.   ∎

We are mainly interested in initial processes (which can be seen as the processes of an ordinary untimed process algebra). Therefore, we will first characterize syntactically those c-processes in $\mathbb{P}_c$ that are reachable from an initial process by only discrete behaviour. These terms represent a discretely timed process algebra and their structure is important e.g. in the proof of 3.3.

Definition 3.2   An *urgent process term* U is generated by the grammar:

$$U ::= \mathbf{0} \mid \underline{a}.I \mid U + U \mid U \|_A U \mid U[\Phi] \qquad \text{(recall that } \underline{a} \text{ is } \langle a, 0 \rangle)$$

where $I \in \tilde{\mathbb{P}}_1$ is an *initial* process term, $a \in \mathsf{A}_{\omega\tau}$, $A \subseteq \mathsf{A}_\omega$ and Φ a general relabeling function. The set of urgent process terms is denoted by $\tilde{\mathbb{P}}_0$, and $\mathbb{P}_0 = \tilde{\mathbb{P}}_0 \cap \mathbb{P}_c$ is the set of *urgent processes*. A *(discretely timed) process term* P is generated by the following grammar:

$$P ::= I \mid U \mid P \|_A P \mid P[\Phi]$$

where I, A, Φ are as above and $U \in \tilde{\mathbb{P}}_0$ is an *urgent* process term. $\tilde{\mathbb{P}}$ is the set of process terms and $\mathbb{P} = \tilde{\mathbb{P}} \cap \mathbb{P}_c$ is the set of (discretely timed) processes.   ■

Intuitively, an urgent process term is reached whenever a process term performs a unit time step. Hence, an urgent process term usually must not let time pass further; but this is allowed for process terms without activated actions: consider $\mathbf{0} \in \mathbb{P}_0 \cup \mathbb{P}_1$ for this case, which can be seen as both, initial and urgent. Process variables $X \in \mathcal{X}$ are always initial, since they may not let pass time at all, hence cannot be reached by a time step.

Proposition 3.3   Let $P \in \tilde{\mathbb{P}}$ be a process term and $a \in \mathsf{A}_{\omega\tau}$.

1. $\mathcal{R}(a, P) \in \{0, 1\}$, thus $\mathcal{R}(P) \in \{0, 1\}$; if $P \in \tilde{\mathbb{P}}_1$, then $\mathcal{R}(a, P) = \mathcal{R}(P) = 1$.
2. If $P \xrightarrow{a}_d P'$, then $P' \in \tilde{\mathbb{P}}$ and $\forall_{b \in \mathsf{A}_{\omega\tau}} \mathcal{R}(b, P) \leq \mathcal{R}(b, P')$.
3. If $P \xrightarrow{1}_d P'$, then $P' \in \tilde{\mathbb{P}}_0$.
4. There are $P_1 \in \tilde{\mathbb{P}}_1$ and $w \in \{\tau\}^*$ with $P_1 \xrightarrow{1w}_d P$, where $w = \lambda$ if $P \in \tilde{\mathbb{P}}_0$.
5. There are $P' \in \tilde{\mathbb{P}}$ and $w \in \{a\}^*$, such that $P \xrightarrow{w}_d P'$ and $\mathcal{R}(a, P') = 1$.   ■

Proposition 3.3 states technical properties of (discrete) process terms and discrete behaviour; they are crucial in the proofs of many further developments and are gathered for processes in a more readable manner in 3.4 below.

First, in 3.3.1, we ascertain that the residual time of (actions in) process terms is always either 0 or 1, reflecting that process terms can perform either no time step or a unit time step. Properties 2. and 3. ensure that discrete behaviour of a process term yields a process term again, validating the match between the operational Definition 3.1 of discrete behaviour and the syntactical Definition 3.2 of discrete process terms. Additionally, occurrence of actions can only increase the residual time of (actions in) a process term. Properties 4. and 5. are of rather technical nature, but their statements are of intuitive interest, too: any process term is reachable from an initial process term by a $\xrightarrow{1}_d$ step only, and repetition of a single action will eventually yield a process term, in which this action is not urgent any more. This will be important when characterizing the testing preorder in the next section.

Corollary 3.4

1. The set $\mathbb{P}$ contains exactly processes that are reachable from some initial process $P \in \mathbb{P}_1$ by only discrete behaviour.
2. The set $\mathbb{P}_0$ contains exactly those processes that are reachable from some initial process $P \in \mathbb{P}_1$ by performing only a 1-time-step.

3. Each $P \in \mathbb{P}$ has a discretely reachable successor $P' \in \mathbb{P}$ with $\mathcal{R}(P') = 1$.
4. If $P \xrightarrow{w}_d P'$ for some $P, P' \in \mathbb{P}$ and $w \in \mathsf{DL}(P)$, then for each $R \in \mathbb{R}_0^+$ there is a $w' \in \mathsf{DL}(P')$ (hence $ww' \in \mathsf{DL}(P)$), such that $\zeta(ww') > R$. ∎

From 3.4.1 follows that the set of processes is closed under discrete behaviour, i.e. $P \in \mathbb{P}$ and $P \xrightarrow{w}_d P'$ for some $w \in \mathsf{DL}_\tau(P)$ implies $P' \in \mathbb{P}$ again. Furthermore, 3.4.4 states that at least discrete behaviour never yields a time stop. Theorem 3.9 will indicate that this is sufficient also for our definition of c-timed tests to make sense.

So far, we only know that discrete behaviour of an initial process is part of its continuous behaviour. We now aim to show that discrete behaviour already contains enough information for checking $P \sqsupseteq_c Q$ for testable P and Q. For this purpose, we will map each continuous trace of an initial (c-)process to a discrete trace of the same process. Related traces will exhibit the same behaviour, but at different points in time. We first relate the intermediate c-processes reached when performing such traces.

Definition 3.5 The *progress preorder* is the least $\vdash_\delta \subseteq (\tilde{\mathbb{P}}_c \times \mathbb{T} \times \tilde{\mathbb{P}}_c)$ satisfying:

Nil:	$\mathbf{0} \vdash_\delta \mathbf{0}$ for all $\delta \in \mathbb{T}$
Var:	$X \vdash_\delta X$ for all $\delta \in \mathbb{T}$
Pref:	$\langle a, r_1 \rangle.P \vdash_\delta \langle a, r_2 \rangle.P$ if $r_2 - r_1 \leq \delta$
Sum:	$P_1 + P_2 \vdash_\delta Q_1 + Q_2$ if $\forall_{i=1,2}\ P_i \vdash_\delta Q_i$
Par:	$P_1 \|_A P_2 \vdash_\delta Q_1 \|_A Q_2$ if $\forall_{i=1,2}\ P_i \vdash_\delta Q_i$
Rel:	$P[\Phi] \vdash_\delta Q[\Phi]$ if $P \vdash_\delta Q$
Rec:	a) $\mu X.P \vdash_\delta \mu X.P$ for all $\delta \in \mathbb{T}$
	b) $P'\{\mu X.P/X\} \vdash_\delta \mu X.P$ if $P' \vdash_\delta P$
	c) $\mu X.P \vdash_\delta P'\{\mu X.P/X\}$ if $P \vdash_\delta P'$ ∎

Intuitively, $P \vdash_\delta Q$ means that P and Q are essentially identical up to the values of timers, and if P is ahead of Q, then for at most time δ. However, Q may be ahead of P for an arbitrary amount of time, which is realized locally in the Pref-case, where we allow $r_2 < r_1$. In cases Rec b) and c), $\mu X.P$ and $P'\{\mu X.P/X\}$ are regarded as structurally identical in two specific situations; this is necessary to make 3.6.4.a) below true: if $P \equiv \mu X.R \vdash_\delta \mu X.R \equiv Q$ and Q makes a time step, then only for Q recursion is unfolded by the recursion rule.

Proposition 3.6 For c-process terms $P, P', Q, Q' \in \tilde{\mathbb{P}}_c$ and $\delta, \delta' \in \mathbb{T}$ let $P \vdash_\delta Q$. Furthermore, let $a \in \mathbb{A}_{\omega\tau}$ and $\rho, \rho_1, \rho_2 \in \mathbb{T}$.

1. $P \vdash_0 P$ for all $P \in \tilde{\mathbb{P}}_c$.
2. $\mathcal{R}(Q) - \mathcal{R}(P) \leq \delta$ and $P \vdash_{\delta'} Q$ if $\delta' \geq \delta$.
3. If $P \xrightarrow{a} P'$, then there exists Q' with $Q \xrightarrow{a} Q'$ and $P' \vdash_\delta Q'$, and vice versa.
4. a) If $Q \xrightarrow{\rho}_c Q'$ and $0 \leq \delta - \rho$, then $P \vdash_{\delta - \rho} Q'$.
   b) If $P \xrightarrow{\rho_1}_c P'$, $Q \xrightarrow{\rho_2}_c Q'$ and $0 \leq \delta + \rho_1 - \rho_2 \leq 1$, then $P' \vdash_{\delta + \rho_1 - \rho_2} Q'$. ∎

Proposition 3.6 provides the elements for emulating each continuous trace of an initial process by a discrete trace that exhibits the same behaviour but consumes more time:

Lemma 3.7   Let $P \in \mathbb{P}_1$ be an initial process; then for each $w \in \mathsf{CL}(P)$ there is a $v \in \mathsf{DL}(P)$, such that $act(v) = act(w)$ and $\zeta(v) \geq \zeta(w)$.

Proof:

We will construct for each $w \in \mathsf{CL}_\tau(P)$ a $v \in \mathsf{DL}_\tau(P)$, such that $act(v) = act(w)$ and $\zeta(v) \geq \zeta(w)$; furthermore, we will show that for P_w and P_v reached after w and v we have $P_v \vdash_{\zeta(v)-\zeta(w)} P_w$; by 3.4.1, this will imply $P_v \in \mathbb{P}$. Then $w/\tau \in \mathsf{CL}(P)$, $v/\tau \in \mathsf{DL}(P)$, $act(v/\tau) = act(w/\tau)$ and $\zeta(v/\tau) = \zeta(v) \geq \zeta(w) = \zeta(w/\tau)$. The proof is by induction on $|w|$, where for $w = \lambda$ we can choose $v = \lambda$; then $P \vdash_0 P$ by 3.6.1, hence $P_v \vdash_{0-0} P_w$. Now assume that for $w \in \mathsf{CL}_\tau(P)$ we have constructed $v \in \mathsf{DL}_\tau(P)$ as desired and consider $w' = w\varepsilon \in \mathsf{CL}_\tau(P)$. We denote the processes reached after w' and v' by $P_{w'}$ and $P_{v'}$.

If $\varepsilon = a \in \mathbb{A}_\omega$, then $v' = va$ with $act(v') = act(w')$ and $\zeta(v') = \zeta(v) \geq \zeta(w) = \zeta(w')$. We have $P_w \xrightarrow{a} P_{w'}$ and by 3.6.3, there is a $P_{v'}$ such that $P_v \xrightarrow{a} P_{v'}$ and $P_{v'} \vdash_{\zeta(v)-\zeta(w)} P_{w'}$, i.e. $P_{v'} \vdash_{\zeta(v')-\zeta(w')} P_{w'}$.

Now let $\varepsilon = \rho \in \mathbb{T}$. If $\rho \leq \zeta(v) - \zeta(w)$ we choose $v' = v$; obviously, $act(v') = act(w')$ and $\zeta(v') = \zeta(v) \geq \rho + \zeta(w) = \zeta(w')$. Furthermore, $\zeta(v') - \zeta(w') = \zeta(v) - \zeta(w) - \rho \geq 0$, hence $P_v \vdash_{\zeta(v)-\zeta(w)} P_w$ and 3.6.4.a) yield $P_{v'} \equiv P_v \vdash_{\zeta(v')-\zeta(w')} P_{w'}$. If on the other hand $\rho > \zeta(v) - \zeta(w)$, we choose $v' = v1$. With 3.6.2 from $P_v \vdash_{\zeta(v)-\zeta(w)} P_w$ we conclude $\mathcal{R}(P_v) + \zeta(v) - \zeta(w) \geq \mathcal{R}(P_w)$ and $\mathcal{R}(P_w) \geq \rho > \zeta(v) - \zeta(w)$ by 2.8, i.e. $\mathcal{R}(P_v) > 0$ and $\mathcal{R}(P_v) = 1$ by 3.3.1. Now by 2.9.1, the time step 1 is allowed after v and $v' = v1 \in \mathsf{DL}_\tau(P)$ with $act(v') = act(w')$. Furthermore, $\zeta(v') = \zeta(v) + 1 \geq \zeta(w) + \rho = \zeta(w')$, and finally, $\rho \leq 1$ and $0 \leq \zeta(v) - \zeta(w)$ give $0 \leq \zeta(v) - \zeta(w) + 1 - \rho$, and $\zeta(v) - \zeta(w) < \rho$ gives $\zeta(v) - \zeta(w) + 1 - \rho \leq 1$; so with 3.6.4.b) we conclude $P_{v'} \vdash_{\zeta(v)-\zeta(w)+1-\rho} P_{w'}$, i.e. $P_{v'} \vdash_{\zeta(v')-\zeta(w')} P_{w'}$. ∎

As an example we consider again process P_* from Section 1 and show how from one of its continuous traces (upper line) the corresponding discrete trace (lower line) is constructed; additionally, we use $\perp_\delta$ (middle line) to denote the progress relation of the intermediate states:

$$P_* \xrightarrow{0.5a}_c \mu X.a.X \|_\emptyset \langle b, 0.5 \rangle . \mu X.b.X \xrightarrow{0.5b}_c \langle a, 0.5 \rangle . \mu X.a.X \|_\emptyset \mu X.b.X \xrightarrow{0.5a}_c$$
$$\perp_0 \qquad\qquad \perp_{0.5} \qquad\qquad\qquad\qquad \perp_0$$
$$P_* \xrightarrow{1a}_d \mu X.a.X \|_\emptyset \underline{b} . \mu X.b.X \xrightarrow{b}_d \mu X.a.X \|_\emptyset \mu X.b.X \xrightarrow{1a}_d$$

Initially, P_* is related with itself via $\vdash_0$ as stated in 3.6.1. Then continuous $0.5a$ is matched by discrete $1a$, yielding states related by $\vdash_{0.5}$ according to 3.5(mainly Pref-case), validating 3.6.4.b) and 3.6.3. A further $0.5b$ is matched by simple b, yielding states related by $\vdash_0$ according to 3.5, where now mainly case Rec c) and the Pref-case with $r_2 - r_1 = 0.5 - 1 = -0.5 \leq 0$ apply; this also validates 3.6.4.a) and 3.6.3. We finally get $act(0.5a0.5b0.5a) = act(1ab1a) = aba$ and $\zeta(0.5a0.5b0.5a) = 1.5 \leq 2 = \zeta(1ab1a)$.

The same discretization result is shown in a Petri net setting for actions without upper time bound in [Jen98] and for actions with varying (integer) lower and upper time bounds in [Bih98]; for nets of the latter type, [Pop91] already shows how to transform continuous runs to *shorter* discrete runs.

With our emulation result we can restrict attention to discretely timed testing based on discrete behaviour and discrete time bounds:

Definition 3.8   For a testable process $P \in \mathbb{P}_1$, an observer $O \in \mathbb{P}_1$ and $D \in \mathbb{N}_0$ define $P \; must_d \; (O, D)$, if each $w \in DL(\tau.P\|_A O)$ with $\zeta(w) > D$ contains some ω. The relation $\sqsupseteq_d$ is defined accordingly.   ∎

We now give our first main result: although $\sqsupseteq_d$ is based on fewer tests and much more restricted behaviour than $\sqsupseteq_c$, it turns out that both relations define the same efficiency preorder. By this, we have also reached simplicity: we can now work with a CCS-like untimed algebra, extended syntactically by urgent terms (see Definition 3.2) and semantically by 1-time-steps.

Theorem 3.9   The relations $\sqsupseteq_c$ and $\sqsupseteq_d$ coincide.
Proof: Let $P, Q \in \mathbb{P}_1$ be testable, O an observer and $R \in \mathbb{R}_0^+$. We first show $P \; must_c \; (O, R)$ iff $P \; must_d \; (O, \lfloor R \rfloor)$: assume $P \; \not must_c \; (O, R)$; then there is a $w \in CL(\tau.P\|_A O)$ without ω and $\zeta(w) > R$; now by 3.7, there is a $v \in DL(\tau.P\|_A O)$ without ω and $\zeta(v) \geq \zeta(w) > \lfloor R \rfloor$, hence $P \; \not must_d \; (O, \lfloor R \rfloor)$. Now assume $P \; \not must_d \; (O, \lfloor R \rfloor)$; then there is a $w \in DL(\tau.P\|_A O)$ without ω and $\zeta(w) > \lfloor R \rfloor$, hence $\zeta(w) \geq \lfloor R \rfloor + 1 > R$; since $DL(\tau.P\|_A O) \subseteq CL(\tau.P\|_A O)$, the same w causes $P \; \not must_c \; (O, R)$. With this result we conclude $Q \; must_c \; (O, R) \Rightarrow P \; must_c \; (O, R)$ iff $Q \; must_d \; (O, \lfloor R \rfloor) \Rightarrow P \; must_d \; (O, \lfloor R \rfloor)$, hence $P \sqsupseteq_c Q$ iff $P \sqsupseteq_d Q$.   ∎

Checking $P \sqsupseteq_c Q$ now reduces to checking $P \sqsupseteq_d Q$. But as for testing in general, it is impossible to apply the definition of $\sqsupseteq_d$ directly, since there are still infinitely many tests to apply. And as indicated in Section 2, we cannot decide $P \sqsupseteq_d Q$ from $DL(P)$ and $DL(Q)$ only, since $DL(\tau.P\|_A O)$ generally cannot be determined from $DL(P)$ and $DL(O)$ alone: e.g. synchronization allows urgent actions in one component to wait for a partner in the other one, which is not the case in stand-alone behaviour of a single component, recorded in $DL(P)$, $DL(O)$ resp. Consider $P \equiv a.b.0\|_{\{b\}}(b.0 + c.0)$ and $Q \equiv a.0\|_\emptyset(b.0 + c.0)$; we first argue that $DL(P) \subseteq DL(Q)$: P differs from Q in that b can only be performed synchronously in both components of P and its left component can delay b after a; but in any case, non-synchronized c has to occur before time 2, hence conflicting b can only occur before time 2 in both P and Q, thus P cannot delay b longer than Q. Now consider P_* as in Section 1: we have $1a1b \in DL(P\|_A P_*) \setminus DL(Q\|_A P_*)$ since $c \in \mathbb{A}$ cannot be synchronized with P_* and, hence, cannot deactivate b any more which can now occur in P later than in Q.

In the next section we will refine the discrete language to a kind of refusal traces; their inclusion will both be a precongruence for parallel composition and characterize $\sqsupseteq_d$ denotationally; for the latter result, we also need that the number of different actions ever performable by a process is finite:

Definition 3.10   For a c-process $P \in \mathbb{P}_c$ and $x \in \{c, d\}$ let $\ell_x(P) = \{a \in \mathbb{A}_{\omega\tau} \mid \exists w \in CL_\tau(P), P' \in \mathbb{P}_c : P \xrightarrow{w}_x P' \xrightarrow{a}_x\}$. Then $\ell_c(P) \; (\ell_d(P))$ is the *continuous (discrete) semantic sort* of P.   ∎

Proposition 3.11   Continuous and discrete semantic sort of a c-process P coincide and will both be denoted $\ell(P)$. Furthermore, $\ell(P)$ is finite.   ∎

4 Characterization

As a consequence of the last section, from now on we let $\sqsupseteq$ denote the (coinciding) preorders $\sqsupseteq_c$ and $\sqsupseteq_d$. Furthermore, we will merely deal with discrete processes and their discrete behaviour.

We first modify the SOS-rules for wait-time as follows: we only allow unit time steps and record at each time step a so-called *refusal set* Σ of actions which are *not* waiting; i.e. these actions are *not* urgent, they do not have to be performed and can be refused at this moment. Note that additionally and in contrast to passage of wait-time we now prohibit passage of time if there are urgent τ's. This time semantics is also a relaxation of (discrete) idle time: all actions in $\Sigma \cup \{\tau\}$ are treated correctly w.r.t. passage of idle time.

Definition 4.1 $\rightarrow_r \subseteq (\tilde{\mathbb{P}} \times 2^{\mathbb{A}_\omega} \times \tilde{\mathbb{P}})$ is defined inductively, where $\Sigma, \Sigma_i \subseteq \mathbb{A}_\omega$:

$$\frac{}{0 \xrightarrow{\Sigma}_r 0} \qquad\qquad \frac{}{a.P \xrightarrow{\Sigma}_r a.P} \qquad\qquad \frac{a \notin \Sigma \cup \{\tau\}}{\underline{a}.P \xrightarrow{\Sigma}_r \underline{a}.P}$$

$$\frac{\forall_{i=1,2}\ P_i \xrightarrow{\Sigma_i}_r P_i',\ \Sigma \subseteq (A \cap \bigcup_{i=1,2} \Sigma_i) \cup ((\bigcap_{i=1,2} \Sigma_i) \setminus A)}{P_1 \|_A P_2 \xrightarrow{\Sigma}_r P_1' \|_A P_2'}$$

$$\frac{\forall_{i=1,2}\ P_i \xrightarrow{\Sigma}_r P_i'}{P_1 + P_2 \xrightarrow{\Sigma}_r P_1' + P_2'} \qquad \frac{P \xrightarrow{\Phi^{-1}(\Sigma \cup \{\tau\}) \setminus \{\tau\}}_r P'}{P[\Phi] \xrightarrow{\Sigma}_r P'[\Phi]} \qquad \frac{P \xrightarrow{\Sigma}_r P'}{\mu X.P \xrightarrow{\Sigma}_r P'\{\mu X.P/X\}}$$

For $P, P' \in \tilde{\mathbb{P}}$, we write $P \xrightarrow{\Sigma}_r P'$ if $(P, \Sigma, P') \in \rightarrow_r$ and call this a *time step*. We write $P \xrightarrow{\Sigma}_r$, if there exists a $P'' \in \tilde{\mathbb{P}}$ such that $(P, \Sigma, P'') \in \rightarrow_r$.   ■

By 4.2.1 below, the set of possible refusal sets at a time step is downward closed w.r.t. set inclusion, and by 4.2.2, not activated actions can always be refused; finally, 4.2.3 provides the link between time steps and unit-time-waiting, unit-time-idling resp:

Proposition 4.2   Let $P, Q \in \tilde{\mathbb{P}}$ be process terms and let $\Sigma, \Sigma' \subseteq \mathbb{A}_\omega$.

1. If $P \xrightarrow{\Sigma}_r Q$ and $\Sigma' \subseteq \Sigma$, then $P \xrightarrow{\Sigma'}_r Q$.
2. If $P \xrightarrow{\Sigma}_r Q$ and $\Sigma' \cap \mathcal{A}(P) = \emptyset$, then $P \xrightarrow{\Sigma \cup \Sigma'}_r Q$.
3. $P \xrightarrow{\Sigma}_r Q$ iff $P \xrightarrow{1}_c Q$ and $\forall_{a \in \Sigma \cup \{\tau\}}\ \mathcal{R}(a, P) = 1$, i.e. $P \xrightarrow{\mathbb{A}_\omega}_r Q$ iff $P \xrightarrow{1}_d Q$.   ■

Combining time steps and occurrence of actions, we now define refusal traces of processes, which refine the discrete language due to 4.2.3 (part 2).

Definition 4.3   Let $P, P' \in \mathbb{P}$ be processes. We write $P \xrightarrow{\varepsilon}_r P'$, if either $\varepsilon = a \in \mathbb{A}_{\omega\tau}$ and $P \xrightarrow{a} P'$, or $\varepsilon = \Sigma \subseteq \mathbb{A}_\omega$ and $P \xrightarrow{\Sigma}_r P'$. For sequences w, we define $P \xrightarrow{w}_r P'$ and $P \overset{w}{\Rightarrow}_r P'$ analogously to 2.10. Then $\mathsf{RT}_\tau(P) = \{w \mid P \xrightarrow{w}_r\}$ is the set of τ-*refusal traces* of P, and the set $\mathsf{RT}(P) = \{w \mid P \overset{w}{\Rightarrow}_r\}$ are the *refusal traces* of P. Functions $act(w)$ and $\zeta(w)$ are extended to elements from $\mathsf{RT}_\tau(P)$ and $\mathsf{RT}(P)$, i.e. $\zeta(w)$ is the number of time steps (sets) in w.   ■

As for discrete traces, we note that $\mathbb{P}$ is closed under performance of refusal traces, i.e. $P \in \mathbb{P}$ and $P \xrightarrow{w}_r P'$ for some $w \in \mathsf{RT}_\tau(P)$ implies $P' \in \mathbb{P}$ again.

Theorem 4.4 $\mathsf{RT}(P) \subseteq \mathsf{RT}(Q)$ implies $\mathsf{DL}(P) \subseteq \mathsf{DL}(Q)$ for $P, Q \in \mathbb{P}$.   ∎

In order to see that RT-inclusion is strictly finer than DL-inclusion, consider for example the processes P and Q from the end of Section 3 again: we have $\mathsf{DL}(P) \subseteq \mathsf{DL}(Q)$ but there is e.g. $\mathbb{A}_\omega\{b\} \in \mathsf{RT}(P) \setminus \mathsf{RT}(Q)$.

The information on temporal and nondeterministic behaviour of a process provided by refusal traces is quite similar to the one e.g. contained in the 'barbs' of TPL (see [HR95]; more precisely, the resulting preorders are quite similar). Remarkably, we will be able to observe this information with asynchronous – i.e. weak – test processes. A notable difference between the settings is that only in our setting an action can be both activated and refusable at the same time: consider $a.P$ with $a \in \mathcal{A}(P)$ and $a.P \xrightarrow{\{a\}}_r \underline{a}.P$ as an example.

From now on we denote refusal-trace-inclusion and -equivalence also by $\leq_r$, $=_r$ resp. and lift these relations to process terms as usual via closed substitutions:

Definition 4.5   Let $P, Q \in \tilde{\mathbb{P}}$. We write $P \leq_r Q$ if for all closed substitutions $\mathcal{S} : X \mapsto \mathbb{P}$ where $[P]_\mathcal{S}, [Q]_\mathcal{S} \in \mathbb{P}$ we have $\mathsf{RT}([P]_\mathcal{S}) \subseteq \mathsf{RT}([Q]_\mathcal{S})$. We write $P =_r Q$ if $P \leq_r Q$ and $Q \leq_r P$.   ∎

The following developments are concerned with (pre)congruence properties of refusal-trace-equivalence (-inclusion). We note that all these also hold for RT_τ-semantics; this will be important when deriving the precongruence property of RT-inclusion w.r.t. recursion. We first show that refusal-trace-inclusion (in contrast to DL-inclusion) is a precongruence for parallel composition:

Theorem 4.6   Let $u, v \in (\mathbb{A}_{\omega\tau} \cup 2^{\mathbb{A}_\omega})^*$ and $A \subseteq \mathbb{A}$; then $u \|_A v$ is the set of all $w \in (\mathbb{A}_{\omega\tau} \cup 2^{\mathbb{A}_\omega})^*$ such that $u = u_1 \ldots u_n$, $v = v_1 \ldots v_n$, $w = w_1 \ldots w_n$ for some n and for all $k = 1, \ldots, n$ one of the following cases applies:

1. $u_k = v_k = w_k = a \in A$
2. $u_k = w_k = a \in \mathbb{A}_\omega \setminus A$ and $v_k = \lambda$
3. $v_k = w_k = a \in \mathbb{A}_\omega \setminus A$ and $u_k = \lambda$
4. $u_k = \Sigma_u \subseteq \mathbb{A}_\omega$, $v_k = \Sigma_v \subseteq \mathbb{A}_\omega$,
   $w_k = \Sigma \subseteq \mathbb{A}_\omega$ and $\Sigma \subseteq (A \cap (\Sigma_u \cup \Sigma_v)) \cup ((\Sigma_u \cap \Sigma_v) \setminus A)$

For sets $R_1, R_2 \subseteq (\mathbb{A}_{\omega\tau} \cup 2^{\mathbb{A}_\omega})^*$ we define $R_1 \|_A R_2 = \bigcup \{u \|_A v \mid u \in R_1, v \in R_2\}$. Then for processes $P_1, P_2 \in \mathbb{P}$, we have $\mathsf{RT}(P_1 \|_A P_2) = \mathsf{RT}(P_1) \|_A \mathsf{RT}(P_2)$. In particular, RT-inclusion is a precongruence for parallel composition.   ∎

We now show that refusal-trace-inclusion is also a precongruence for prefix, relabeling and hiding; these results are needed for the characterization.

Theorem 4.7   Let $R \subseteq (\mathbb{A}_{\omega\tau} \cup 2^{\mathbb{A}_\omega})^*$, $a \in \mathbb{A}_\omega$ and let

1. $a.R$ be the set of prefixes of
   $\{\Sigma_1 \ldots \Sigma_n a \mid n \in \mathbb{N}_0, \Sigma_1 \subseteq \mathbb{A}_\omega, \Sigma_2, \ldots, \Sigma_n \subseteq \mathbb{A}_\omega \setminus \{a\}\} \circ R$,
2. $\underline{a}.R$ be the set of prefixes of $\{\Sigma_1 \ldots \Sigma_n a \mid n \in \mathbb{N}_0, \Sigma_1, \ldots, \Sigma_n \subseteq \mathbb{A}_\omega \setminus \{a\}\} \circ R$,
3. $\tau.R = \{\Sigma, \lambda \mid \Sigma \subseteq \mathbb{A}_\omega\} \circ R$,
4. $\underline{\tau}.R = R$.

Then $\mathsf{RT}(a.P) = a.\mathsf{RT}(P)$ and $\mathsf{RT}(\underline{a}.P) = \underline{a}.\mathsf{RT}(P)$ for $P \in \mathbb{P}_1$ and $a \in \mathbb{A}_{\omega\tau}$. Moreover, RT-inclusion is a precongruence for prefixing of (initial) processes. ∎

Theorem 4.8 Let Φ be a general relabeling function, $a \in \mathbb{A}_{\omega\tau}$, $\Sigma \subseteq \mathbb{A}_\omega$ and define $a[\Phi]^{-1} = \Phi^{-1}(a)$ and $\Sigma[\Phi]-1 = \{\Phi^{-1}(\Sigma \cup \{\tau\}) \setminus \{\tau\}\}$; we extend $[\Phi]^{-1}$ to sequences $w \in (\mathbb{A}_\omega \cup 2^{\mathbb{A}_\omega})^*$ via concatenation $\circ$, where we additionally let $\lambda[\Phi]^{-1} = \Phi^{-1}(\tau) \setminus \{\tau\}$.

Then for a process $P \in \mathbb{P}$ we have $\mathsf{RT}(P[\Phi]) = \{w \in (\mathbb{A}_\omega \cup 2^{\mathbb{A}_\omega})^* \mid w[\Phi]^{-1} \cap \mathsf{RT}(P) \neq \emptyset\}$. Moreover, RT-inclusion is a precongruence for general relabeling $P[\Phi]$ of processes, hence also for relabeling and hiding. ∎

A further property needed for the characterization of $\sqsupseteq$ is that $\mathbf{0}$ is a zero element for both choice and parallel composition without synchronization:

Proposition 4.9 Let $P \in \tilde{\mathbb{P}}$. Then $P \|_\emptyset \mathbf{0} =_r P$ and $P + \mathbf{0} =_r P$. ∎

Finally, we state that refusal traces can always be extended by a time step (after performing all urgent internal activity) and that time steps can be omitted:

Proposition 4.10 Let $P \in \mathbb{P}$, let $w, w' \in (\mathbb{A}_\omega \cup 2^{\mathbb{A}_\omega})^*$ and let $\Sigma \subseteq \mathbb{A}_\omega$.
1. $w \in \mathsf{RT}(P)$ if and only if $w\emptyset \in \mathsf{RT}(P)$.
2. $w\Sigma w' \in \mathsf{RT}(P)$ implies $ww' \in \mathsf{RT}(P)$. ∎

We now have gathered all elements for characterizing the efficiency preorder, which is our second main result:

Theorem 4.11 Let $P_1, P_2 \in \mathbb{P}_1$ be testable. Then $P_1 \sqsupseteq P_2$ iff $P_1 \leq_r P_2$.
Proof: (sketch)
'if': Let (O, D) be a timed test. Then $\mathsf{RT}(P_1) \subseteq \mathsf{RT}(P_2)$ implies $\mathsf{DL}(\tau.P_1\|_\mathbb{A}O) \subseteq \mathsf{DL}(\tau.P_2\|_\mathbb{A}O)$ by 4.7, 4.6 and 4.4. Thus, if P_1 fails the test due to some $w_1 \in \mathsf{DL}(\tau.P_1\|_\mathbb{A}O)$, then so does P_2.

'only if': We assume $P_1 \sqsupseteq P_2$ and take some $w_1 \in \mathsf{RT}(P_1)$. Then all actions in w_1 are in $\ell(P_1) \cup \ell(P_2)$ by 4.3, 4.2.3 and 3.11. Furthermore, by 4.2.1 and 4.2.2 and $\mathcal{A}(P) \subseteq \ell(P)$, we may assume that for all refusal sets Σ in w_1 we have $\Sigma \subseteq \ell(P_1) \cup \ell(P_2)$, which is finite due to 3.11. Now let $w = \lambda$ if $w_1 = \lambda$ and $w = w_1\emptyset$ otherwise; then also $w \in \mathsf{RT}(P_1)$ by 4.10.1. Furthermore, $\Sigma w \in \mathsf{RT}(\tau.P_1)$ for each $\Sigma \subseteq \ell(P_1) \cup \ell(P_2)$ by 4.7.3; we will only consider the case $\Sigma = \emptyset$.

We will construct a timed test $(O_{\Sigma w}, \zeta(w))$ that is failed by a testable process $P \in \mathbb{P}_1$ if and only if $\Sigma w \in \mathsf{RT}(\tau.P)$. Hence, P_1 fails $(O_{\Sigma w}, \zeta(w))$, thus by assumption P_2 fails $(O_{\Sigma w}, \zeta(w))$, too, and we conclude $\Sigma w \in \mathsf{RT}(\tau.P_2)$. But then $\Sigma w_1 \in \mathsf{RT}(\tau.P_2)$ by 4.10.1 and $w_1 \in \mathsf{RT}(P_2)$ or $\Sigma w_1 \in \mathsf{RT}(P_2)$ by 4.7.3, i.e. $w_1 \in \mathsf{RT}(P_2)$ by Proposition 4.10.2, and we are done.

Here, we give the inductive construction of $O_{\Sigma w}$ and then only describe informally the function and the interplay of its parts. To make induction work, we define $O_{\Sigma w}$ for sequences Σw that end with $\emptyset$ but may start with an arbitrary $\Sigma \subseteq \ell(P_1) \cup \ell(P_2)$. Furthermore, all actions of Σw are in $\ell(P_1) \cup \ell(P_2)$ and all refusal sets are subsets of $\ell(P_1) \cup \ell(P_2)$. $O_{\Sigma w}$ will consist of several components that communicate via synchronized actions which must not occur in the sort of P_1 or P_2. Hence, let $H = \{b_0, c_0, b_1, c_1, \dots\} \subseteq \mathbf{A}$ be an infinite set such that $H \cap (\ell(P_1) \cup \ell(P_2)) = \emptyset$; H exists since $\ell(P_1)$ and $\ell(P_2)$ are finite and $\mathbf{A}$ is infinite.

We first let $T_{\Sigma w} \equiv Q_{\Sigma w} \parallel_H S_{\Sigma w} \parallel_H R_{\Sigma w}$ with $R_{\Sigma w} \equiv (X_{\Sigma w} \parallel_\emptyset c_{\zeta(w)}.\mathbf{0})$ and the components $Q_{\Sigma w}$, $S_{\Sigma w}$ and $X_{\Sigma w}$ are defined inductively as follows, where in the base case $\Sigma w = \emptyset$ we let $Q_\emptyset \equiv \omega.\mathbf{0}$, $S_\emptyset \equiv \mathbf{0}$ and $X_\emptyset \equiv \mathbf{0}$. Now let the general case be $\Sigma w = \Sigma a_1 \dots a_n \Sigma' w'$, where $\Sigma' w'$ ends with $\emptyset$. We define:

$$Q_{\Sigma w} \equiv (b_{\zeta(w)}.Q_{\Sigma' w'}) \parallel_\emptyset (c_{\zeta(w)}.\mathbf{0} + \omega.\mathbf{0})$$
$$S_{\Sigma w} \equiv b_{\zeta(w)}.a_1 \dots a_n.c_{\zeta(w)}.S_{\Sigma' w'}$$
$$X_{\Sigma w} \equiv (b_{\zeta(w)}.X_{\Sigma' w'}) \parallel_\emptyset (c_{\zeta(w)-1}.\mathbf{0} + \textstyle\sum_{x \in \Sigma'} x.\mathbf{0})$$

Finally, we let $O_{\Sigma w} \equiv T_{\Sigma w}/H$.

The part $\Sigma a_1 \dots a_n$ of $\Sigma w = \Sigma a_1 \dots a_n \Sigma' w'$ is called the $\zeta(w)$-th round of Σw, started by occurrence of Σ, whereas occurrence of Σ' marks the begin of the $(\zeta(w) - 1)$-th round.

$Q_{\Sigma w}$ is the 'clock'-part of the test, which for each round i of Σw enables an ω that is urgent after the time step starting round i and can only be deactivated by performing the auxiliary action c_i (*completion* of round i) before the next time step. The 'action-sequence'-part $S_{\Sigma w}$ will ensure that c_i can only occur after performance of the action sequence $a_1 \dots a_n$, which itself must be preceded by the auxiliary action b_i (*begin* of round i). Furthermore, occurrence of b_i triggers the activation of the ω for the next round by enabling $Q_{\Sigma' w'}$. This must not happen too early, i.e. b_i and hence c_i will be performed after the time step starting round i and before the next one. At the beginning of the present round, the 'refusal-set'-part $X_{\Sigma w}$ enables all actions x from the refusal set Σ' of the following round in conflict with the auxiliary action c_{i-1} which has to occur only at completion of the following round. After the time-step of the present round, all x from Σ' have become urgent, but may not occur – i.e. must be refusable by the tested process at the time-step starting the following round. Finally, $X_{\Sigma w}$ is augmented to $R_{\Sigma w}$ for proof-technical reasons, $T_{\Sigma w}$ puts all three parts via synchronization together, and $O_{\Sigma w}$ hides the auxiliary actions away. Otherwise, they would have to synchronize with the tested process, which is of course impossible by the definition of H.   ∎

5   Full Abstraction

Refusal-trace-inclusion not only characterizes the efficiency preorder, but also makes just the necessary refinements to discrete behaviour of (initial) processes in order to gain a precongruence for parallel composition and prefix:

Corollary 5.1   RT-semantics is fully abstract w.r.t. DL and parallel composition and prefixing of initial processes, i.e. gives the coarsest congruence for initial processes and these operators that respects DL-equivalence. For process terms, $\leq_r$ is a precongruence for these operators, and also for hiding and relabeling.   ∎

As usual, RT-inclusion alone is not a precongruence for choice: e.g. we have $\mathbf{0} \leq_r \tau.\mathbf{0}$ and $\tau.\mathbf{0} \leq_r \mathbf{0}$, but for $a \neq \tau$, we have neither $\mathbf{0} + a.\mathbf{0} \leq_r \tau.\mathbf{0} + a.\mathbf{0}$

(since $\emptyset\emptyset a \in RT(0 + a.0) \setminus RT(\tau.0 + a.0)$), nor $\tau.0 + a.0 \leq_r 0 + a.0$ (since $\{a\}\{a\} \in RT(\tau.0+a.0)\setminus RT(0+a.0)$). Thus, we also have to consider the (initial) stability of processes, where the example indicates that although we consider a preorder this additional condition is not an implication but an equivalence:

Definition 5.2   A process $P \in \mathbb{P}$ is *stable* if $\tau \notin \mathcal{A}(P)$. For process terms $P, Q \in \tilde{\mathbb{P}}$ we write $P \leq Q$ if for all $\mathcal{S} : \mathcal{X} \mapsto \mathbb{P}$ where $[P]_\mathcal{S}, [Q]_\mathcal{S} \in \mathbb{P}$ we have: $RT([P]_\mathcal{S}) \subseteq RT([Q]_\mathcal{S})$ (hence $P \leq_r Q$) and additionally $[P]_\mathcal{S}$ stable iff $[Q]_\mathcal{S}$ stable. We write $P = Q$ if $P \leq Q$ and $Q \leq P$.

For $n \in \mathbb{N}$ we write $P \leq_\tau^n Q$ if for all $\mathcal{S} : \mathcal{X} \mapsto \mathbb{P}$ where $[P]_\mathcal{S}, [Q]_\mathcal{S} \in \mathbb{P}$ we have: $v \in RT_\tau([P]_\mathcal{S})$ and $|v| < n$ implies $v \in RT_\tau([Q]_\mathcal{S})$. We write $P =_\tau^n Q$ if $P \leq_\tau^n Q$ and $Q \leq_\tau^n P$. We write $P \leq_\tau Q$ ($P =_\tau Q$) if $\forall_{n \in \mathbb{N}} P \leq_\tau^n Q$ ($P =_\tau^n Q$).   ∎

The class of RT_τ-inclusions ($\leq_\tau^n$) will support an approximation technique when treating recursion later on. The following two results yield that we have defined $\leq$ adequately in order to gain the coarsest precongruence w.r.t. choice that respects RT-inclusion, hence the efficiency preorder:

Theorem 5.3   Let $\mathcal{P} \subseteq \mathbb{P}_1$ or $\mathcal{P} \subseteq \mathbb{P}_0$ and $\mathcal{P} = \{P_i \mid i \in I\}$ for some finite I, hence $\sum_{i \in I} P_i \in \mathbb{P}$. For each $n \in \mathbb{N}_0$ let $RT^n(\mathcal{P}) = \{\Sigma_1 \dots \Sigma_n w \in \bigcup_{i \in I} RT(P_i) \mid \Sigma_1 \dots \Sigma_n \in \bigcap_{i \in I} RT(P_i), \Sigma_i \subseteq \mathbb{A}_\omega, w$ does not start with a set$\}$. Finally, let $P \equiv \sum_{i \in I} P_i$ and let $I = S \dot{\cup} \overline{S}$, such that P_i is stable iff $i \in S$.

1. If $S = I$, then $RT(P) = \bigcup_{n \in \mathbb{N}_0} RT^n(\mathcal{P})$.
2. If $S \neq I$ and $P \in \mathbb{P}_0$, then $RT(P) = \bigcup_{i \in \overline{S}} RT(P_i) \cup RT^0(\mathcal{P})$.
3. If $S \neq I$ and $P \in \mathbb{P}_1$, then $RT(P) = \bigcup_{i \in \overline{S}} RT(P_i) \cup RT^0(\mathcal{P}) \cup RT^1(\mathcal{P})$.   ∎

Theorem 5.4   Both $\leq_\tau$ and $\leq$ are precongruences for parallel composition, prefixing, hiding and relabeling and choice of process terms, and $\leq_\tau$ is strictly finer than $\leq$. For initial processes, $\leq$ is fully abstract w.r.t. choice and $\leq_r$.   ∎

One might argue that the constructions in 5.3 require more information than provided by $\leq$ in order to gain the refusal traces of a sum from the refusal traces of its components: additionally to the stability of the components we have to know whether they are initial or urgent in order to choose correctly from cases 2 and 3. We only indicate here that this information is indeed provided by RT-semantics: if there is no stable component, then cases 2 and 3 coincide, hence assume P_i to be a stable component; if $\mathcal{A}(P_i) = \emptyset$ then it can be omitted from the sum, hence assume $\mathcal{A}(P_i) \neq \emptyset$; then $P_i \in \mathbb{P}_0 \cup \mathbb{P}_1$ implies that $\mathbb{A}_\omega \in RT(P_i)$ if and only if $P_i \in \mathbb{P}_1$.

We finally aim to show that $\leq$ is also a precongruence for (guarded) recursion. Following [Hen88], we consider (initial) process terms as functions in the domain of (τ-)refusal-traces and will exploit their monotonicity w.r.t. $\leq$ and $\leq_\tau$, which essentially results from 5.4.

Definition 5.5   For closed substitutions $\mathcal{S}, \mathcal{S}' : \mathcal{X} \mapsto \mathbb{P}$ we write $\mathcal{S} \leq \mathcal{S}'$ if $\mathcal{S}(X) \leq \mathcal{S}'(X)$ for all $X \in \mathcal{X}$, and $\mathcal{S} \leq_\tau \mathcal{S}'$ if $\mathcal{S}(X) \leq_\tau \mathcal{S}'(X)$ for all $X \in \mathcal{X}$. An initial process term $P \in \tilde{\mathbb{P}}_1$ is *monotonic*, if $[P]_\mathcal{S} \leq [P]_{\mathcal{S}'}$ whenever $\mathcal{S} \leq \mathcal{S}'$ for any closed *initial* substitutions $\mathcal{S}, \mathcal{S}' : \mathcal{X} \mapsto \mathbb{P}_1$. τ-monotonicity is defined analogously with $\leq_\tau$ instead of $\leq$.

For each $n \in \mathbb{N}$, $X \in \mathcal{X}$ and $P \in \tilde{\mathbb{P}}_1$ let P_X^n denote the initial process term defined inductively by $P_X^1 \equiv P$ and $P_X^{n+1} \equiv \tilde{P}\{P_X^n/X\} \equiv P_X^n\{P/X\}$.   ∎

Now $\mathsf{RT}_\tau(\mu X.P)$ is a fixpoint of the RT_τ-function defined by the initial process term P, and τ-monotonicity of this function carries over to its iterated applications, where the guardedness of X allows us even to ignore up to a certain degree the relation of the arguments for X:

Lemma 5.6   Let $P \in \tilde{\mathbb{P}}_1$ be a τ-monotonic initial process term and let $X \in \mathcal{X}$ be guarded in P. Furthermore, let $\mathcal{S}_1, \mathcal{S}_2 : \mathcal{X} \mapsto \mathbb{P}_1$ be closed initial substitutions with $\mathcal{S}_1(Y) \leq_\tau \mathcal{S}_2(Y)$ for all $Y \not\equiv X$. Then for all $n \in \mathbb{N}$:

1. $\mu X.P =_\tau P_X^n\{\mu X.P/X\}$.
2. $[P_X^n]_{\mathcal{S}_1} \leq_\tau^n [P_X^n]_{\mathcal{S}_2}$.   ∎

We now can derive the precongruence property for τ-monotonic and monotonic initial process terms, where we use the fact that for all refusal traces $w \in \mathsf{RT}(\mu X.P)$ there is an underlying τ-refusal trace $v \in \mathsf{RT}_\tau(\mu X.P)$, such that $w = v/\tau$ and $|v| < n$ for some $n \in \mathbb{N}$:

Proposition 5.7   Let $P, Q \in \tilde{\mathbb{P}}_1$ be initial process terms that are both τ-monotonic and monotonic, and let $X \in \mathcal{X}$ be guarded in both P and Q.

1. $P \leq_\tau Q$ implies $\mu X.P \leq_\tau \mu X.Q$.
2. $P \leq Q$ implies $\mu X.P \leq \mu X.Q$.   ∎

Showing the τ-monotonicity and monotonicity of all initial process terms by induction on the term structure using 5.6 and 5.4, we end up with the result:

Theorem 5.8   Both $\leq_\tau$ and $\leq$ are precongruences for recursion.   ∎

We are currently working on an axiomatization of the $\leq$-preorder which turns out to be somewhat involved due to handling with both initial and urgent actions; whereas basic axioms like $a.P \leq a.\tau.P$ (but in general $a.\tau.P \not\leq a.P$) can be justified by our theorems quite straightforward, parallel composition with synchronization seems to require some more technical effort: we not only seek a semantically founded expansion law but a truly syntactic axiom which apparently requires the introduction of some auxilliary operator. Using our theorems we can already derive that $\tau.a\|_{\{a\}}\tau.a$ is *strictly* faster than $\tau.\tau.a$; this is in accordance with our intuition, where we expect the simultaneous execution of two independent actions to be faster than their sequentialisation.

6   Related Work

In the literature, several approaches to efficiency preorders have been proposed, from which only representative samples can be considered here.

For untimed CCS-like terms, efficiency preorders based on testing have been investigated in [CZ91] and [NC96a], and bisimulation-based ones in [AKH92] and [AKN95]; in all these approaches, efficiency is measured by counting internal actions, where runs of a parallel composition are seen to be the interleaved runs of the components; consequently, in all cases, $\tau.a\|_{\{a\}}\tau.a$ is as efficient as $\tau.\tau.a$, in contrast to the above result in our setting.

TPL is a CCS-based discretely timed process algebra developed in [HR95], where systems are also related via a must-testing approach. In [NC96b], the resulting preorder is interpreted as to relate systems w.r.t. their temporal and functional 'predictability' rather than efficiency. Systems in TPL can be considered as synchronous, since maximal progress is forced in test application. This gives the test environment more direct control over the temporal behaviour than in our setting. As a consequence, no time bounds are needed for tests; rather, these can be build in the test itself. TPL can also be seen as a discrete part of the continuously timed process algebra TimedCSP (cf. [Sch95]), where e.g. the discrete unit delay σ is replaced by *WAIT 1* constructs.

In the discretely timed algebra ℓTCCS of [MT91], components may have arbitrary relative speeds, but there is no progress assumption at all and the efficiency preorder is based on a sort of bisimulation; an interpretation in terms of worst-case behaviour is not obvious. [CGR97] gives a different bisimulation based approach, where component speeds are fixed with respect to local clocks (modulo patience for communication in [Cor98]). Here, the operational semantics realizes local passage of time, hence this idea is hard to compare to our or any other approach.

The idea of associating time intervals to actions in distributed systems can be found e.g. in [MF76] and – in a process algebraic setting – e.g. in [Zic94]; the latter is (what is sometimes called) a 'soft-real-time' approach, where time can exceed the upper time bound of an action, which disables this action; this is in contrast to our approach where actions are persistent.

[Bur92] discusses how (the more realistic) continuously timed behaviour can be approximated with discretely timed behaviour; the aim is to ensure that each implementation in the discrete view is indeed an implementation in the continuous view (but not necessarily vice versa). There is no result showing that discrete time gives *complete* information as in our setting.

References

[AKH92] S. Arun-Kumar and M. Hennessy. An Efficiency Preorder for Processes. *Acta Informatica*, 29:737–760, 1992.

[AKN95] S. Arun-Kumar and V. Natarajan. Conformance: a Precongruence close to Bisimilarity. In J. Desel, editor, *Structures in Concurrency Theory*, Worksh. in Computing, 55–68. Springer, 1995.

[BD91] E. Badouel and P. Darondeau. On Guarded Recursion. *TCS*, 81:403–408, 1991.

[Bih98] E. Bihler. Effizienzvergleich bei verteilten Systemen (German). Master's thesis, Institut für Informatik, Universität Augsburg, 1998.

[Bur92] Jerry R. Burch. *Trace Algebra for Automatic Verification of Real-Time Concurrent Systems*. PhD thesis, School of CS, Carnegie Mellon Univ., 1992.

[CGR97] F. Corradini, R. Gorrieri, and M. Roccetti. Performance preorder and competitive equivalence. *Acta Informatica*, 34 no. 11:805–835, 1997.

[Cor98]   F. Corradini. On the Coarsest Congruence within Global-Clock-Bounded equivalence. *TCS*, 19:225–237, 1998.

[CZ91]   R. Cleaveland and A. Zwarico. A theory of testing for real-time. In *Proc. 6th Symp. on Logic in Computer Science*, pages 110–119. IEEE Computer Society Press, 1991.

[DNH84]   R. De Nicola and M.C.B. Hennessy. Testing equivalence for processes. *TCS*, 34:83–133, 1984.

[Hen88]   M. Hennessy. *An algebraic theory of processes*. the M.I.T. Press, 1988.

[HR95]   M. Hennessy and T. Regan. A process algebra for timed systems. *Information and Computation*, 117:221–239, 1995.

[Jen96]   L. Jenner. Modular construction of fast asynchronous systems. Technical Report 1996-2, Inst. f. Informatik, Univ. Augsburg, 1996.

[Jen98]   L. Jenner. Further studies on timed testing of concurrent systems. Technical Report 1998-4, Inst. f. Informatik, Univ. Augsburg, 1998.

[JV95]   L. Jenner and W. Vogler. Fast asynchronous systems in dense time. Technical Report Nr. 344, Inst. f. Mathematik, Univ. Augsburg, 1995. Extended abstract appeared in Proc. ICALP 96.

[Lyn96]   N. Lynch. *Distributed Algorithms*. Morgan Kaufmann Publishers, San Francisco, 1996.

[MF76]   P. Merlin and D. Farber. Recoverability of communication protocols – implications of a theoretical study. *IEEE Trans. Comm.*, 24:1036–1043, 1976.

[Mil89]   R. Milner. *Communication and Concurrency*. Prentice Hall, 1989.

[MT91]   F. Moller and C. Tofts. Relating processes with respect to speed. In J. Baeten and J. Groote, editors, *CONCUR '91*, Lect. Notes Comp. Sci. 527, 424–438. Springer, 1991.

[NC96a]   V. Natarajan and R. Cleaveland. An algebraic theory of process efficiency. In *Proc. LICS'96*. 11th Annual IEEE Symposium, 1996.

[NC96b]   V. Natarajan and R. Cleaveland. Predictability of real-time systems: A process-algebraic approach. In *Proc. RTSS'96*. 17th IEEE Real-Time Systems Symposium, 1996.

[Pop91]   L. Popova. On time Petri nets. *J. Inform. Process. Cybern. EIK*, 27:227–244, 1991.

[Pri98]   In Corrado Priami, editor, *Proceedings PAPM'98, sixth international workshop on Process Algebras and Performance Modelling, Nice, France*, pages 137–151. Universita degli studi di Verona, Facolta di Scienze, Istituto Policattedra, September 1998.

[Sch95]   S. Schneider. An operational semantics for timed CSP. *Information and Computation*, 116(2), pp.193-213, 1995.

[Vog95]   W. Vogler. Timed testing of concurrent systems. *Information and Computation*, 121:149–171, 1995.

[Zic94]   J. Zic. Time constrained buffer specifications in CSP+T and timed CSP. *ACM TOPLAS*, 16-6:1661–1674, 1994.

A Formal Model of Real-Time Program Compilation

Karl Lermer and Colin Fidge

Software Verification Research Centre,
The University of Queensland,
Queensland 4072, Australia
{lermer,cjf}@it.uq.edu.au

Abstract. Program compilation can be formally defined as a sequence of equivalence-preserving transformations, or refinements, from high-level language programs to assembler code. Recent models also incorporate timing properties, but the resulting formalisms are prohibitively complex. Here we take advantage of a new, simple model of real-time refinement to present a straightforward formalism for compilation that incorporates real-time constraints.

1   Introduction

Compiler correctness is a significant concern for developers of safety-critical systems. In an attempt to improve confidence in compiler quality, numerous attempts have been made to represent code generation as a formal transformation, or *refinement*, process [14,21,1,2]. This has proven to be surprisingly challenging, and the results disappointingly complex. Since many safety-critical systems have strict timing constraints, some models also add the concept of time to the formalism, thus increasing this complexity even further [7,10,20].

A significant disadvantage of these formalisms is that they differ markedly from the widely-known refinement calculus defined by Morgan [18]. Recently, however, Hayes and Utting proposed a real-time formalism for sequential, imperative programs that presents a modest increment on the established calculus [12]. Furthermore, we have already shown that, with care, the standard refinement calculus can be used to model compiler code generation [15,4]. The goal of this paper, therefore, is to combine these two outcomes to produce a simple refinement formalism for representing compilation of programs with hard real-time constraints.

2   Languages

In this section we describe the modelling, source and target languages used for defining our real-time compilation formalism. To support a refinement calculus, both the source and target languages must be well-defined subsets of the overall modelling language.

J.-P. Katoen (Ed.): ARTS'99, LNCS 1601, pp. 192–210, 1999.

2.1 Real-Time Refinement Calculus

Here we review a simplified variant of the real-time refinement calculus [12], which will form the modelling language for our real-time compilation formalism.

As usual, the calculus operates on a wide-spectrum language, allowing abstract specifications and concrete statements to coexist. The concrete language is Dijkstra's guarded command language with statements for assignment (:=), sequential composition (;), alternation (**if** $\cdots$ **fi**), iteration (**do** $\cdots$ **od**), and variable (**var**) and logical constant (**con**) declarations. Unrefined code segments are defined via *specification statements*

$$\tilde{v}: [P\,,\,Q]$$

consisting of a *frame* $\tilde{v}$, which lists those variables that the statement may change, a *precondition* P, which defines the assumed pre-state, and a *postcondition* Q, which defines the required post-state. If the precondition is 'true' it may be omitted. A specification with empty frame and postcondition 'true' is written as an *assumption* $\{P\}$. A specification with empty frame and precondition 'true' is written as a *coercion* $[Q]$. The refinement relation $\sqsubseteq$ then defines valid transformations from specification to concrete statements as those that preserve the desired properties, while possibly adding more or decreasing nondeterminism [18].

From its user's perspective, the real-time calculus [12] extends the familiar, untimed refinement calculus [18] in two significant ways.

1. There is a distinguished specification variable τ denoting the current time. It is of type $\mathbb{T}$, which represents the time domain.
2. Other variables are divided into three classes.
   (a) *Local* variables $\tilde{v}$ cannot be observed outside the block in which they are declared. A local variable must appear in the frame of a specification statement if that statement is to change it, and it may appear in zero-subscripted form in a postcondition to represent its initial value [18].
   (b) *Input* variables $\tilde{u}$ are controlled by some process outside the current program segment. An input variable may not appear in the frame of a specification statement, nor in zero-subscripted form. Each appearance of an input variable in a pre or postcondition must be indexed by a time-valued expression to yield the value of the input at that time.
   (c) *Output* variables $\tilde{w}$ are controlled by the current program segment. An output variable may not appear in the frame of a specification statement, nor in zero-subscripted form, and must be indexed in pre and postconditions to describe its value at that time.

Formally, input and output variables actually denote functions from the time domain. They trace the entire history of interactions with the current program segment. Each consecutive statement in a program fragment accesses, or constrains, a distinct segment of these *timed traces* [24].

2.2   Real-Time Programming Language

Here we define the source language for our compilation formalism. It consists of a small, imperative programming language with special real-time statements. Figure 1 shows the correspondence between programming language statements and their underlying modelling language definitions [12]. Here S is a high-level language statement, E an arbitrary expression, B a boolean expression, and D a time-valued expression. Importantly, B, E and D may refer to local variables only. Predicate P may refer to any variable, including the current time τ.

$$
\begin{aligned}
v := E \ &\hat{=}\ \tau, v : [\tau_0 \leqslant \tau \wedge v = E_0 \wedge stable(\tilde{w}, \tau_0, \tau)] \\
S_1 \; ; \; S_2 \ &\hat{=}\ S_1 \; ; \; S_2
\end{aligned}
$$

$$
\begin{array}{ll}
\textbf{if } B \textbf{ then} & \hat{=}\ \textbf{if } B \to \textbf{idle} \; ; \; S_1 \; ; \textbf{idle} \\
\quad S_1 & \quad [\!] \ \neg B \to \textbf{idle} \; ; \; S_2 \; ; \textbf{idle} \\
\textbf{else} & \quad \textbf{fi} \\
\quad S_2 & \\
\textbf{end if} &
\end{array}
$$

$$
\begin{array}{ll}
\textbf{while } B \textbf{ loop} & \hat{=}\ \textbf{do} \\
\quad S & \qquad B \to \textbf{idle} \; ; \; S \; ; \textbf{idle} \\
\textbf{end loop} & \quad \textbf{od}; \\
& \quad \textbf{idle}
\end{array}
$$

$$
\begin{aligned}
\textbf{read}(u, v) \ &\hat{=}\ \tau, v : [stable(\tilde{w}, \tau_0, \tau) \wedge (\exists\, t : \mathbb{T} \bullet \tau_0 \leqslant t \leqslant \tau \wedge v = u(t))] \\
\textbf{write}(w, E) \ &\hat{=}\ \tau : [\tau_0 \leqslant \tau \wedge w(\tau) = E \wedge stable(\tilde{w} \setminus \{w\}, \tau_0, \tau)] \\
\textbf{delay until } D \ &\hat{=}\ \tau : [D \leqslant \tau \wedge stable(\tilde{w}, \tau_0, \tau)] \\
\textbf{gettime}(v) \ &\hat{=}\ \tau, v : [\tau_0 \leqslant v \leqslant \tau \wedge stable(\tilde{w}, \tau_0, \tau)] \\
\textbf{deadline } D \ &\hat{=}\ : [\tau \leqslant D] \\
\textbf{assume } P \ &\hat{=}\ : [P\,, \textbf{true}]
\end{aligned}
$$

Fig. 1. Definition of high-level programming language statements.

The assignment statement ':=' definition tells us that the assignment may change local variable v, and will finish with v equal to the value of expression E evaluated at the time the statement began. Here E_0 is expression E with all local variables it contains subscripted by 0. The definition also says that the current time τ may change, but that its final value must be no less than the starting time τ_0. The *stable* predicate applies to the list $\tilde{w}$ of all *output* variables visible at this point in the program. It is defined as follows.

$$
stable(\tilde{x}, a, b) \ \hat{=}\ \forall\, t : \mathbb{T} \bullet a < t \leqslant b \Rightarrow \tilde{x}(t) = \tilde{x}(a)
$$

In other words, given a list of timed-trace variables $\tilde{x}$, and two times a and b, then *stable* states that these variables remain unchanged throughout this interval. (Even though the assignment statement does not act on the output variables $\tilde{w}$, the semantics of the timed refinement calculus require us to explicitly state the behaviour of each timed-trace variable in all time intervals [24].) We allow assignment to be generalised to multiple assignment in the usual way [18].

Sequential composition ';' does not consume time, so its definition is the standard one.

In the **if** statement definition, statement S_1 is selected if B is true, and S_2 is selected if B is false, as one would expect. An unusual feature, however, are the **idle** statements. This auxiliary statement is defined as one that may change the time, but leaves high-level language variables unaffected.

$$\textbf{idle} \ \hat{=} \ \tau\colon [\tau_0 \leqslant \tau \wedge stable(\tilde{w}, \tau_0, \tau)]$$

It is used whenever we want to state that time may pass due to low-level actions that are not visible to the high-level program [12]. The **idle** preceding statement S_1, for instance, models the time required to evaluate expression B and branch to this statement. The **idle** following statement S_1 models the time required to branch past the second alternative once the first has been executed. Similarly for the **idle** statements before and after statement S_2.

The definition of the iterative **while** statement follows in the same vein. The **idle** before statement S represents the time required to evaluate expression B and reach statement S, and the **idle** after S represents the time required to branch back to the top of the loop. The **idle** statement following the **do** loop accounts for the time required to evaluate B for the last time, when it is false, and exit the loop.

The **read** statement takes a value from input variable u and places it in local variable v. Its definition states that it leaves all output variables $\tilde{w}$ unchanged, and that the final value of v will equal the value of u at time t, where t occurs between the starting τ_0 and finishing τ times of the statement. We do not know exactly when the input will be sampled during the execution of the statement.

The **write** statement takes the value of an expression E involving local variables and sends it to output variable w. Apart from possibly consuming time, it has the effect of leaving the final value of the output variable, i.e., $w(\tau)$, equal to the value of expression E. The definition also states that all other output variables are unchanged. While the **write** statement is executing, the value of output variable w is unspecified.

The **delay until** statement stops progress of the program until at least time D. Its definition merely says that the finishing time τ may be no less than D, and that all output variables $\tilde{w}$ are unchanged.

The **gettime** statement reads the current time into a local variable v. Its definition states that the final value of v will be somewhere between the starting and finishing times of the statement itself, and that the output variables are unchanged.

So far, none of the definitions has placed any bound on how long each statement may take to execute. To allow for this, a striking feature of the real-time refinement calculus is a special **deadline** statement added to the programming language to allow such bounds to be expressed [12]. A deadline statement with argument D requires the program to reach the point in the code where the statement appears by time D. The definition requires that the current time τ must be no greater than D. However, since τ may not be changed by the deadline statement itself (the frame is empty), it is formally a constraint on the *preceding* statement to achieve this effect [12]. A deadline statement is not executable, but represents a compile-time requirement to prove that the program has this desired timing property. Such proofs are possible for sequential programs using static analysis techniques [9]. This method of introducing timing requirements to a program is an important advance because it is machine-independent and allows the functional and timing constraints on programs to be kept distinct [11].

The programmer may also use the **assume** statement to document conditions that are expected to be true at a certain point in the program, including time-dependent properties [12].

The frames of both the **deadline** and **assume** statements are empty, reflecting the fact that they do not change any high-level language variables. They could be written as a coercion and an assumption, respectively. Nevertheless, we shall see below that our intermediate language model adds new variables to the frame of each statement. In doing so it is convenient to treat the **deadline** and **assume** statements in the same way as other statements, so in Figure 1 we leave their empty frames explicit.

$$\text{declare var } v : T \text{ begin } S \text{ end } \;\widehat{=}\; |[\text{var } v : T \bullet \text{idle} ; S ; \text{idle}]|$$

$$\text{declare con } c : T \text{ begin } S \text{ end } \;\widehat{=}\; |[\text{con } c : T \bullet S]|$$

$$\text{declare input } u : T \text{ begin } S \text{ end } \;\widehat{=}\; \text{Add variable } u \text{ of type } \mathbb{T} \to T$$
$$\text{to input variable list } \tilde{u} \text{ in } \alpha S$$

$$\text{declare output } w : T \text{ begin } S \text{ end } \;\widehat{=}\; \text{Add variable } w \text{ of type } \mathbb{T} \to T$$
$$\text{to output variable list } \tilde{w} \text{ in } \alpha S$$

Fig. 2. High-level programming language declarations.

As shown in Figure 2, it is also important to consider the effect of timing concerns on declarations. When declaring a local high-level language variable v, of type T, its definition must account for the time required to allocate space for this variable when the block is entered, and deallocate this space when the block is left [12]. This is done by adding two **idle** statements. The declaration of a compile-time constant c, however, does not consume *run* time, so does not need special treatment.

We have already noted that each input variable u and output variable w is modelled as a function over the time domain. Therefore, when such a variable is declared with type T, it is semantically interpreted to be a function of type $\mathbb{T} \rightarrow T$ [12]. Once declared, such variables may be used in statement S. This is noted here by adding them to the *alphabet* αS of state variables known to S [6].

2.3   Real-Time Intermediate Language

Here we define a target language for the compilation process. It is an *intermediate representation* language, close to, but more abstract than, the final machine code [5]. This approach supports machine-independent definitions [8,22]. In particular, instruction addresses are handled symbolically, and a simple stack-machine model is used [17], rather than anticipating a particular register set.

$$ldi_\omega \; i \;\; \widehat{=} \;\; pc, st := \omega, st \;^\frown \langle i \rangle$$

$$ldt_\omega \; d \;\; \widehat{=} \;\; pc, st := \omega, st \;^\frown \langle R_{\mathrm{T}}(d) \rangle$$

$$sti_\omega \; v \;\; \widehat{=} \;\; \{\#st \geqslant 1\} \,; pc, st, v := \omega, fr(st), lt(st)$$

$$add_\omega \;\; \widehat{=} \;\; \{\#st \geqslant 2\} \,; pc, st := \omega, fr2(st) \;^\frown \langle lt(st) + lt2(st) \rangle$$

$$sub_\omega \;\; \widehat{=} \;\; \{\#st \geqslant 2\} \,; pc, st := \omega, fr2(st) \;^\frown \langle lt2(st) - lt(st) \rangle$$

$$leq_\omega \;\; \widehat{=} \;\; \{\#st \geqslant 2\} \,; pc, st := \omega, fr2(st) \;^\frown \langle max\{lt2(st) - lt(st) + 1, 0\} \rangle$$

$$jmp \; \ell \;\; \widehat{=} \;\; pc := \ell$$

$$fjp_\omega \; \ell \;\; \widehat{=} \;\; \{\#st \geqslant 1\} \,; \mathbf{if} \; lt(st) = 0 \rightarrow pc, st := \ell, fr(st)$$
$$[\!] \; lt(st) \neq 0 \rightarrow pc, st := \omega, fr(st)$$
$$\mathbf{fi}$$

$$evi_\omega \; E \;\; \widehat{=} \;\; pc, st := \omega, st \;^\frown \langle E \rangle$$

$$evb_\omega \; B \;\; \widehat{=} \;\; pc, st := \omega, st \;^\frown \langle R_{\mathrm{B}}(B) \rangle$$

$$evt_\omega \; D \;\; \widehat{=} \;\; pc, st := \omega, st \;^\frown \langle R_{\mathrm{T}}(D) \rangle$$

$$all_\omega \; s \;\; \widehat{=} \;\; my := my \cup \{s\}$$

$$dal_\omega \; s \;\; \widehat{=} \;\; my := my \setminus \{s\}$$

$$tim_\omega \;\; \widehat{=} \;\; pc, st: [pc = \omega \wedge stable(\tilde{w}, \tau_0, \tau) \wedge$$
$$(\exists \, t : \mathbb{T} \bullet \tau_0 \leqslant t \leqslant \tau \wedge st = st_0 \;^\frown \langle R_{\mathrm{T}}(t) \rangle)]$$

$$sdi_\omega \; w \;\; \widehat{=} \;\; pc, st: [\#st \geqslant 1 \,, pc = \omega \wedge stable(\tilde{w} \setminus \{w\}, \tau_0, \tau) \wedge$$
$$st = fr(st_0) \wedge w(\tau) = lt(st_0)]$$

Fig. 3. Intermediate language instruction definitions.

The target intermediate language is a distinguished subset of the modelling notation. Firstly, we consider individual instructions [21,13]. Each instruction is represented by updates to machine-level constructs as shown by the selection of instructions in Figure 3. Importantly, the assignment statements in Figure 3 are "timed" assignments of the form defined in Figure 1 so that time may pass while an instruction executes. Here, i is an integer-valued constant or variable name, d is a time-valued constant or variable name, v is a local high-level language variable of type integer, w is a high-level language integer output variable, ℓ and ω are instruction-memory locations, E is an integer-valued high-level language expression, B is a boolean-valued high-level language expression, D is a time-valued high-level language expression, and s is a string corresponding to the name of a high-level language variable.

The low-level constructs introduced are as follows.

- A program counter pc is used for control flow of the low-level program. It is of type $\mathbb{A}$, denoting the set of memory addresses.
- A data stack st is used to hold temporary values. It is a sequence of integers, i.e., type 'seq $\mathbb{Z}$'. Let $\langle i_1, i_2, \ldots \rangle$ represent a sequence, operator '$\frown$' concatenate two sequences, operator fr return the front of a sequence, i.e., all but the last element, operator $fr2$ return all but the last two elements, operator lt return the last element of a sequence, and operator $lt2$ return the second last element. When non-integer values are stored on the stack they must be translated into an appropriate integer representation. For each type T, we assume an appropriate *representation relation* R_T, of type $T \to \mathbb{Z}$, which achieves the necessary translation [20], and preserves any essential algebraic properties of the original type.
- A 'memory' variable my is used to keep track of those high-level language variables which will ultimately be stored in main memory. Here it is merely a set containing the names of variables currently in scope, where names are represented by character strings from set $\mathbb{S}$. At this level of abstraction we continue to use high-level language variables as our 'storage medium'. (This has the advantage that their type declarations are available to us during the refinement [19].) Ultimately, however, these variables will be 'refined away' and their role taken by elements in a memory array. In this paper, variable my is a first step towards this.

The load-integer instruction ldi loads integer value i onto the stack st. Executing the instruction also changes the program counter pc. Since instructions at the intermediate level have yet to be assigned to specific addresses in memory, the symbolic address ω of the *following* instruction is provided as a subscripted parameter to each instruction's definition. The load-time instruction ldt does the same thing for a time value d; it uses the representation relation R_T to translate time d to an appropriate integer representation so that it can be stored on the stack.

The store-integer instruction sti takes the last value from the stack and stores it in high-level language variable v. The definition is protected by an assertion that the stack contains at least one element—otherwise the instruction's behaviour would be undefined.

The add and subtract instructions, add and sub, respectively add and subtract the last two elements on the stack, destroying these operands, and leaving the result on the stack. Both require the stack to initially contain at least two elements.

The less-or-equal instruction *leq* compares the last two stack elements, returning 'true' only if the last element is less than or equal to the second last one. We follow the tradition of encoding 'false' by 0 and allowing any other number to represent 'true' [25, §7.3.3]. Expression $lt2(st) - lt(st) + 1$ will be positive only if inequality $lt2(st) \geqslant lt(st)$ is true, otherwise the *max* operator ensures that the result is 0.

The jump instruction *jmp* unconditionally changes the program counter to address ℓ. The jump-if-false instruction *fjp* does so only if the last value on the stack is 'false', otherwise it just advances to the next location ω.

All of these instructions can be translated easily into equivalent machine code. However, the intermediate language's evaluate-integer-expression instruction *evi* denotes evaluation of a *high-level language* expression E, with the result left on the stack. It is a very useful modelling aid, but needs to be decomposed into more primitive instructions before machine code generation is possible. The *evb* and *evt* instructions do the same thing for boolean and time-valued expressions, respectively.

The allocate and deallocate instructions, *all* and *dal*, manipulate the memory variable *my* in order to keep track of which variable names are currently in scope. Here s is the name of a variable which is respectively added to and removed from the *my* set. (In subsequent refinements, these instructions would be replaced with operations on a more complicated *my* data structure representing the run-time heap.)

The final two instructions cannot be represented by assignments because their definitions must refer to the current time. They are therefore both expressed as specification statements so that they can access the special time variable τ. The read-time instruction *tim* reads the current (hardware clock) time and places it on the stack. Its predicate says that it updates the program counter pc and leaves all output variables $\tilde{w}$ unchanged. It also adds a time value t to the stack, where t is some time between the starting τ_0 and finishing τ times of the instruction. Relation R_T is used to convert the time to an integer representation.

The send-integer instruction *sdi* sends the value on the top of the stack to output variable w, representing a hardware output port. Its precondition requires the stack to contain at least one element. Its postcondition updates the program counter, leaves all output variables other than w unchanged, pops the stack, and ensures that w equals the value from the top of the stack by the time the instruction finishes.

The intermediate language model is completed by providing a way of constructing target programs from the individual instructions introduced above. This requires both a way of labelling instructions with their (symbolic) locations, and of linking lists of instructions together, despite the presence of jump instructions which may mean that instructions are not executed in their textual order.

Firstly, we allow any statement S in our modelling language to be *labelled* by an instruction memory location ℓ.

$$\ell : S \;\hat{=}\; \{pc = \ell\} \,;\, S$$

Thus a label states that we assume the program counter equals ℓ when statement S begins.

A symmetric operator allows us to express the intention that statement S must leave the program counter equal to ℓ when it terminates.

$$S \downarrow \ell \;\hat{=}\; S \,;\, [pc = \ell]$$

This is a coercion, forcing S to terminate with an appropriate program counter value. (The definition assumes that pc is in the alphabet of statement S.)

Lastly, we define the meaning of vertically-displayed lists of labelled instructions, allowing for the fact that jumps may mean that the instructions are not necessarily executed in their order of appearance, but are actually controlled by the program counter.

$$\begin{array}{cc} \ell_1 : S_1 \\ \ell_2 : S_2 \end{array} \;\hat{=}\; \begin{array}{l} \mathbf{do}\ pc = \ell_1 \to S_1 \\ \ \| \ pc = \ell_2 \to S_2 \\ \mathbf{od} \end{array}$$

This generalises to an arbitrary number of statements in the obvious way. In effect, the **do** statement acts as an interpreter for the list of labelled instructions, as controlled by the special variable pc. Execution of this imaginary loop does not itself consume time. All execution time overheads are accounted for in the individual instructions in Figure 3. Although each statement S_i on the right is no longer explicitly labelled, it can still be treated as a labelled statement $\ell_i : S_i$ when refined in the context of the enclosing loop construct, thanks to the preceding guard $pc = \ell_i$.

3   Compilation Laws

Here we show a selection of refinement laws for compilation of real-time programs.

The first law is intended for use with a complete high-level language program S. It declares and initialises the new low-level variables. The program is assumed to be placed at location a and is required to leave the program counter pointing to location z. Whenever a law requires a 'fresh' address, we assume it is a constant from set $\mathbf{A}$ that has not been used previously. Let statement S' be statement S extended so that the new low-level variables are part of its alphabet, i.e., $\{pc, st, my\} \subseteq \alpha S'$, and list '$pc, st, my$' is added to the frame of each statement within S. (Strictly speaking, this step is an example of data refinement [6].)

Law 1 (Introduce low-level constructs) *Let a and z be fresh addresses, and pc, st and my be fresh variable names.*

$$S \sqsubseteq \textbf{var } pc : \mathbb{A} := a; \\ st : seq\,\mathbb{Z} := \langle\rangle; \\ my : \mathbb{P}\mathbb{S} := \varnothing \bullet \\ a : S' \downarrow z$$

The following laws show how typical high-level language statements, bracketed by starting a and final z symbolic addresses, can be compiled to instruction lists, controlled by the program counter. Thanks to the way the real-time refinement calculus achieves a clean separation of timing and functional concerns [12], the laws are a straightforward representation of typical compilation strategies. Here E is an integer-valued high-level language expression, v is a high-level language variable of type integer, B is a boolean-valued high-level language expression, and each S is a high-level language statement.

Law 2 (Compile integer assignment) *Let b be a fresh address.*

$$a : (v := E) \downarrow z \sqsubseteq a : evi_b\,E \\ b : sti_z\,v$$

Law 3 (Compile sequence) *Let b be a fresh address.*

$$a : (S_1\ ;\ S_2) \downarrow z \sqsubseteq a : S_1 \downarrow b \\ b : S_2 \downarrow z$$

Law 4 (Compile choice) *Let b to e be fresh addresses.*

$$a : (\textbf{if } B \textbf{ then} \qquad \sqsubseteq \quad a : evb_b\,B \\ \quad S_1 \qquad\qquad\qquad b : fjp_c\,e \\ \textbf{else} \qquad\qquad\qquad c : S_1 \downarrow d \\ \quad S_2 \qquad\qquad\qquad d : jmp\,z \\ \textbf{end if}) \downarrow z \qquad e : S_2 \downarrow z$$

Law 5 (Compile iteration) *Let b to d be fresh addresses.*

$$a : (\textbf{while } B \textbf{ loop} \quad \sqsubseteq \quad a : evb_b\,B \\ \quad S \qquad\qquad\qquad b : fjp_c\,z \\ \textbf{end loop}) \downarrow z \qquad c : S \downarrow d \\ d : jmp\,a$$

In the following law, string 'v' is used to represent the *name* of high-level language variable v, not its value. Here v is a high-level language variable, and T is its type.

Law 6 (Compile variable block) *Let b and c be fresh addresses.*

$$
\begin{array}{ll}
a : (\texttt{declare} & \sqsubseteq \;\; \mathbf{var}\; v : T\; \bullet \\
\quad\quad \mathbf{var}\; v : T & (a : \mathrm{all}_b\; 'v' \\
\quad\quad \texttt{begin} & \; b : S \downarrow c \\
\quad\quad\quad S & \; c : \mathrm{dal}_z\; 'v') \\
\quad\quad \texttt{end)} \downarrow z &
\end{array}
$$

On the right, the modelling language's **var** operator declares a 'logical' version of variable v, equivalent to the programming language's **var** declaration. For the purposes of this paper we use this modelling-language declaration to represent memory storage for the high-level language variable, but subsequent refinements will replace all occurrences of v with a particular data memory element.

The law for compiling an integer output statement is similarly straightforward. Here w is a high-level language output variable of type integer.

Law 7 (Compile integer write) *Let b be a fresh address.*

$$
a : (\texttt{write}(w, E)) \downarrow z \;\sqsubseteq\;
\begin{array}{l}
a : \mathrm{evi}_b\; E \\
b : \mathrm{sdi}_z\; w
\end{array}
$$

We can also easily define a law for compiling a delay statement into a busy wait. Here D is a time-valued high-level language expression.

Law 8 (Compile delay until) *Let b to d be fresh addresses.*

$$
a : (\texttt{delay until}\; D) \downarrow z \;\sqsubseteq\;
\begin{array}{l}
a : \mathrm{tim}_b \\
b : \mathrm{evt}_c\; D \\
c : \mathrm{leq}_d \\
d : \mathrm{fjp}_z\; a
\end{array}
$$

This is a rather inefficient compilation strategy since it re-evaluates the static expression D at every iteration, and thus unnecessarily increases the potential overrun of the delay, but is sufficient for the purposes of exposition. (A subtle consequence of our use of the *integer* less-or-equal instruction to compare times, is that we are assuming the representation relation R_T preserves the ordering of time constants.)

For brevity, the above laws rely on the *evi*, *evb* and *evt* instructions to evaluate high-level language expressions. The following laws mimic code generation strategies for expression evaluation [25, §7.3.2] and thus allow these instructions to be eliminated. Let E_1 and E_2 be integer-valued expressions, i and j be integer constants or the names of integer-valued variables, D_1 and D_2 be time-valued expressions, and d be a time constant or the name of a time-valued variable.

Law 9 (Evaluate integer addition) *Let b and c be fresh addresses.*

$$
a : \mathrm{evi}_z\; (E_1 + E_2) \;\sqsubseteq\;
\begin{array}{l}
a : \mathrm{evi}_b\; E_1 \\
b : \mathrm{evi}_c\; E_2 \\
c : \mathrm{add}_z
\end{array}
$$

Law 10 (Evaluate time difference) *Let b and c be fresh addresses.*

$$a : evt_z (D_1 - D_2) \quad \sqsubseteq \quad \begin{array}{l} a : evt_b\ D_1 \\ b : evt_c\ D_2 \\ c : sub_z \end{array}$$

Law 11 (Evaluate integer less or equal) *Let b and c be fresh addresses.*

$$a : evb_z (E_1 \leqslant E_2) \quad \sqsubseteq \quad \begin{array}{l} a : evi_b\ E_2 \\ b : evi_c\ E_1 \\ c : leq_z \end{array}$$

Law 12 (Evaluate integer)

$$a : evi_z\ i \quad \sqsubseteq \quad a : ldi_z\ i$$

Law 13 (Evaluate time)

$$a : evt_z\ d \quad \sqsubseteq \quad a : ldt_z\ d$$

When the above refinement laws are repeatedly applied to a program segment, they result in a nested set of labelled instruction lists. To eliminate this nesting, and achieve a program structure closer to the final machine code, the following law allows 'inner' statements to be moved to the 'outer' list.

Law 14 (Flatten nested instruction lists)

$$\{pc \neq c\}\,;\, (a : (S_1\,;\,[pc \neq c]) \quad \sqsubseteq \quad (a : (S_1\,;\,[pc \neq c]) \\ \phantom{\{pc \neq c\}\,;\,}\ b : (b : S_2 b : S_2 \\ \phantom{\{pc \neq c\}\,;\,xxx}\ c : S_3)) c : S_3)$$

On the left is a list of two statements, where the second statement is itself a list. (This second statement is labelled by b, as is its first component—application of the preceding laws will always generate nested labels of this form.) The goal is to refine this to the single list shown on the right. Care must be taken, however, that the control flow of the program remains unaffected. To enforce this, two restrictions are introduced on the left to ensure that when the statement labelled c is moved to the outer list, it cannot be executed in situations where it could not have been previously. Firstly, an assumption states that the program counter must not initially equal the inner address c. Secondly, a coercion is used to ensure that the outer statement labelled a does not leave the program counter equal to c. As long as these two conditions hold, we are free to move the inner statement labelled c as shown. (Moreover, the rules defined above always generate lists that obey these two constraints, so Law 14 can be applied at any time, without the need to test these conditions.) This rule generalises readily to the case where there are multiple 'inner' and 'outer' statements.

4 Example

As a concrete example, consider the high-level language program in Figure 4. It is a 'transmitter' intended to send a sequence of numbers from 1 to 10 via output port x. However it also has a strict timing requirement to satisfy the demands of a receiver program at the other end. The nth number must be placed in the output buffer by at least time n, and must remain there for at least 0.8 seconds. In Figure 4 this timing requirement is expressed by three special real-time statements. Firstly, an assumption states that the program is expected to be started by no later than time 0. If the program is started too late, it would be impossible to transmit the first value in time. Secondly, a **deadline** statement documents the requirement that writing the nth number must be completed by time n. This is a constraint on the **write** statement preceding this point in the program. Thirdly, the requirement that the output buffer remains undisturbed for at least 0.8 seconds is achieved by the **delay until** statement which prevents the program from proceeding, and possibly overwriting x, until 0.2 seconds before the $(n+1)^{\text{st}}$ character is due to appear. (The expression is '$n-0.2$', not '$n+0.8$', because n has been incremented.)

Compilation of this program proceeds by mechanical application of the laws defined above, and other established program refinement principles [18]. As a first step the low-level variables are introduced and the outermost sequential composition operator is compiled. (We treat the **output** declaration implicitly here.)

$$\text{Program from Figure 4} \sqsubseteq \text{'by Laws 1 and 3'}$$

> **var** $pc : \mathbb{A} := a;$
> $\quad st : \text{seq}\,\mathbb{Z} := \langle\rangle;$
> $\quad my : \mathbb{P}\,\mathbb{S} := \varnothing \bullet$
> $(a : (\text{assume}\,\tau \leqslant 0) \downarrow b$
> $\quad b : (\text{declare var}\ n \ \cdots \text{end}) \downarrow z)$

Next the block that declares integer variable n is compiled into instructions representing allocation and deallocation of memory space for the variable.

$$\text{Statement } b \sqsubseteq \text{'by Law 6'}$$

> **var** $n : \mathbb{Z} \bullet$
> $(b : \text{all}_c\ \text{'}n\text{'}$
> $\quad c : (n := 1\ ;\ \text{while}\ \cdots\ \text{end loop}) \downarrow d$
> $\quad d : \text{dal}_z\ \text{'}n\text{'})$

Another application of the sequential composition law partitions the body of the block into the initial assignment statement and the **while** loop.

$$\text{Statement } c \sqsubseteq \text{'by Law 3'}$$

> $c : (n := 1) \downarrow e$
> $\quad e : (\text{while}\ \cdots\ \text{end loop}) \downarrow d$

```
declare
  output x : integer
begin
  assume τ ≤ 0;              -- Assumed starting time
  declare
    var n : integer
  begin
    n := 1;
    while n ≤ 10 loop
      write(x, n);
      deadline(n);           -- Complete writing nth value by time n
      n := n + 1;
      delay until(n − 0.2)   -- Don't overwrite nth value until time n + 0.8
    end loop
  end
end
```

Fig. 4. High-level language transmitter.

Compilation of the assignment statement that initialises n to 1 is completed using two laws.

$$\text{Statement } c \sqsubseteq \text{ 'by Laws 2 and 12'}$$
$$c : ldi_f\ 1$$
$$f : sti_e\ n$$

Compilation of the while loop also proceeds by straightforward application of the appropriate law.

$$\text{Statement } e \sqsubseteq \text{ 'by Law 5'}$$
$$e : evb_g\ (n \leq 10)$$
$$g : fjp_h\ d$$
$$h : (\text{write} \cdots \text{delay until}(n − 0.2)) \downarrow i$$
$$i : jmp\ e$$

Evaluation of the boolean expression guarding the loop is also straightforward.

$$\text{Statement } e \sqsubseteq \text{ 'by Laws 11 and 12'}$$
$$e : ldi_j\ 10$$
$$j : ldi_k\ n$$
$$k : leq_g$$

The four high-level language statements in the loop body can be formed into an 'instruction' list. (Clearly, the ability to mix high-level and low-level concepts is crucial in a compilation-as-refinement formalism.)

Statement $h \sqsubseteq$ 'by Law 3'

$$h : \texttt{write}(x, n) \downarrow \ell$$
$$\ell : \texttt{deadline}(n) \downarrow m$$
$$m : (n := n + 1) \downarrow p$$
$$p : \texttt{delay until}(n - 0.2) \downarrow i$$

Compilation of the assignment statement that increments n again exercises the laws for assignment statements and expression evaluation. For readability, we also flatten the resulting nested lists.

Statement $m \sqsubseteq$ 'by Laws 2, 9, 12, and 14'

$$m : ldi_q \, n$$
$$q : ldi_r \, 1$$
$$r : add_s$$
$$s : sti_p \, n$$

The statement that writes the value of variable n to output port x is compiled in two steps.

Statement $h \sqsubseteq$ 'by Laws 7 and 12'

$$h : ldi_t \, n$$
$$t : sdi_\ell \, x$$

The delay statement is compiled into a tight loop that waits for the time on the hardware clock to equal or exceed the delay expression.

Statement $p \sqsubseteq$ 'by Law 8'

$$p : tim_u$$
$$u : evt_v \, (n - 0.2)$$
$$v : leq_w$$
$$w : fjp_i \, p$$

Finally, the time-valued delay expression itself must be evaluated.

Statement $u \sqsubseteq$ 'by Laws 10 and 13'

$$u : ldt_o \, n$$
$$o : ldt_y \, 0.2$$
$$y : sub_v$$

At this point we have compiled all executable high-level language statements to a nested series of intermediate language instructions. Our formalised 'compilation' is completed by expanding the scope of the nested declaration for variable n, and applying Law 14 to flatten the program structure. The resulting intermediate language program is shown in Figure 5.

```
var pc : A := a;
    st : seq Z := ⟨⟩;
    my : PS := ∅;
    n : Z •
(a : (assume τ ⩽ 0) ↓ b    — Assumed starting time
 b : all_c 'n'              — Enter variable block
 c : ldi_f 1               — Initialise n
 f : sti_e n
 e : ldi_j 10              — Evaluate loop condition
 j : ldi_k n
 k : leq_g
 g : fjp_h d
 h : ldi_t n               — Write n to output port x
 t : sdi_ℓ x
 ℓ : deadline(n) ↓ m       — Reach here by time n
 m : ldi_q n               — Increment n
 q : ldi_r 1
 r : add_s
 s : sti_p n
 p : tim_u                 — Delay until time n − 0.2
 u : ldt_o n
 o : ldt_y 0.2
 y : sub_v
 v : leq_w
 w : fjp_i p
 i : jmp e                 — Return to top of loop
 d : dal_z 'n')            — Exit variable block
```

Fig. 5. Compiled intermediate language code for transmitter.

5   Translation to Machine Code

The intermediate language program in Figure 5 is not directly executable, but the steps required to translate such a program to executable machine code, or even to directly interpret it [17], are well established in compiler technology. For instance, recent representations of particular machine instruction sets, like MIPS R3000, SPARC, Alpha or Intel Pentium Instructions within a unified model [23,22] show how intermediate representations such as ours can be instantiated for specific architectures.

1. Symbolic instruction locations must be instantiated with actual addresses. (In doing so, no addresses need be reserved for the non-executable **assume** and **deadline** instructions, since no machine code will be produced for them.)

2. Above we allowed high-level language variables to appear in load and store instructions. Ultimately, these must be replaced with the data memory addresses corresponding to these variables, and instructions with appropriate addressing modes introduced to access them. Formally, this will involve data refinement [6] of the *my* variable to a memory array structure whose elements can take on the role of the corresponding high-level language variables, followed by elimination of the now redundant high-level language variables themselves. Also the actions of the allocate and deallocate instructions, *all* and *dal*, must be extended to perform appropriate manipulation of the new memory data structure.

3. The stack of integers used to hold temporary variables must be replaced by the particular set of registers available on the target machine. This may involve introducing code for spilling register contents to main memory [3] if the number of registers available is less than the maximum depth of the stack. Furthermore, the range of data values must be restricted to the particular word size of the target machine, and appropriate checks undertaken to ensure that arithmetic operations will not cause overflow.

Since we started with a high-level language program with timing constraints, it is important to observe that these still appear in Figure 5 as non-executable `assume` and `deadline` instructions at locations a and ℓ, respectively. Neither of these will generate machine code, so they will not occupy memory space. Symbolic locations a and b are synonyms, as are ℓ and m. Nevertheless, these statements represent undischarged proof obligations. We cannot remove them until flow-analysis and cycle-counting has been performed on the final machine code to guarantee that the stated timing requirements will always be met [9,16].

6   Conclusion

We have combined an existing compilation formalism [15,4] with a new real-time refinement calculus [12,9] to create a formal compilation model for real-time programs. The approach avoided machine-specific detail by exploiting the real-time refinement calculus' ability to express machine-independent timing constraints. Instead, a significant degree of abstraction was maintained by targeting an intermediate, stack-machine representation, with embedded timing statements. The outcome was significantly simpler than previous real-time compilation formalisms, and closer to already-familiar refinement methods.

Acknowledgements

The method of modelling local variables in the timed calculus like untimed ones was suggested by Brendan Mahony, and brought to our attention by Ian Hayes. We wish to thank Ian Hayes for correcting errors in this work, and Antonio Cerone for reviewing a draft of this paper. The ARTS'99 referees suggested a number of improvements to the presentation. This research was funded by ARC Large Grant A49600176, *Verified Compilation Rules for Real-Time Programs via Program Refinement*.

References

1. J. A. Bergstra, T. B. Dinesh, J. Field, and J. Heering. A complete transformational toolkit for compilers. Technical Report CS-R9601, Computer Science, Centrum voor Wiskunde en Informatica, January 1996.
2. E. Börger and I. Durdanović. Correctness of compiling occam to transputer code. *The Computer Journal*, 39(1):52–92, 1996.
3. G. J. Chaitin. Register allocation and spilling via graph coloring. *ACM SIGPLAN Notices*, 17(6), June 1982.
4. C. J. Fidge. Modelling program compilation in the refinement calculus. In D. J. Duke and A. S. Evans, editors, *2nd BCS-FACS Northern Formal Methods Workshop*, Electronic Workshops in Computing. Springer-Verlag, 1997. http://ewic.springer.co.uk/workshops/NFM97/.
5. C. N. Fischer and R. J. LeBlanc, Jr. *Crafting a Compiler*. Benjamin/Cummings, 1988.
6. P. H. B. Gardiner and C. C. Morgan. Data refinement of predicate transformers. *Theoretical Computer Science*, 87:143–162, 1991.
7. M. Gordon. A formal method for hard real-time programming. In J. M. Morris and R. C. Shaw, editors, *4th Refinement Workshop*, pages 378–410. Springer-Verlag, 1991.
8. K. J. Gough. Multi-target compiler development: Evolution of the Gardens Point compiler project. In H. Mössenböck, editor, *Modular Programming Languages*, volume 1204 of *Lecture Notes in Computer Science*. Springer-Verlag, 1997.
9. S. Grundon, I. J. Hayes, and C. J. Fidge. Timing constraint analysis. In C. McDonald, editor, *Computer Science '98: Proc. 21st Australasian Computer Science Conference*, pages 575–586. Springer-Verlag, 1998.
10. R. W. S. Hale. Program compilation. In J. Bowen, editor, *Towards Verified Systems*, volume 2 of *Real-Time Safety Critical Systems*, chapter 7, pages 131–146. Elsevier, 1994.
11. I. J. Hayes. Separating timing and calculation in real-time refinement. In J. Grundy, M. Schwenke, and T. Vickers, editors, *International Refinement Workshop & Formal Methods Pacific '98*, Discrete Mathematics and Theoretical Computer Science, pages 1–16. Springer-Verlag, 1998.
12. I. J. Hayes and M. Utting. A sequential real-time refinement calculus. Technical Report 97-33, Software Verification Research Centre, University of Queensland, August 1997. http://svrc.it.uq.edu.au/Bibliography/svrc-tr.html?97-33.
13. He Jifeng. *Provably Correct Systems*. McGraw-Hill, 1995.
14. C. A. R. Hoare. Refinement algebra proves correctness of compiling specifications. In C. Morgan and J. Woodcock, editors, *3rd Refinement Workshop*, pages 33–48. Springer-Verlag, 1990.
15. K. Lermer and C. J. Fidge. Compilation as refinement. In L. Groves and S. Reeves, editors, *Formal Methods Pacific '97*, pages 142–164. Springer, 1997.
16. K. Lermer and C. J. Fidge. A methodology for compilation of high-integrity real-time programs. In C. Lengauer, M. Griebel, and S. Gorlatch, editors, *Euro-Par'97: Parallel Processing*, volume 1300 of *Lecture Notes in Computer Science*, pages 1274–81. Springer-Verlag, 1997. Longer version available as Software Verification Research Centre Technical Report 96-18.
17. K. C. Louden. *Compiler Construction: Principles and Practice*. PWS Publishing Company, 1997.
18. C. Morgan. *Programming from Specifications*. Prentice-Hall, second edition, 1994.

19. G. Morrisett, D. Walker, K. Crary, and N. Glew. From System F to Typed Assembly Language. In *Proc. 1998 Symposium on Principles of Programming Languages*, San Diego, 1998.
20. M. Müller-Olm. *Modular Compiler Verification: A Refinement-Algebraic Approach Advocating Stepwise Abstraction*, volume 1283 of *Lecture Notes in Computer Science*. Springer-Verlag, 1997.
21. T. S. Norvell. Machine code programs are predicates too. In D. Till, editor, *Sixth Refinement Workshop*, pages 188–204. Springer-Verlag, 1994.
22. N. Ramsey and M. F. Fernández. Specifying representations of machine instructions. *ACM Transactions on Programming Languages and Systems*, 19(3):492–524, May 1997.
23. S. Sendall. Semantics of machine instructions. Honours thesis, Department of Computer Science and Electrical Engineering, The University of Queensland, October 1997.
24. M. Utting and C. J. Fidge. A real-time refinement calculus that changes only time. In He Jifeng, John Cooke, and Peter Wallis, editors, *BCS-FACS Seventh Refinement Workshop*, Electronic Workshops in Computing. Springer-Verlag, 1996. http://ewic.springer.co.uk/workshops/7RW/.
25. D. Watson. *High-Level Languages and Their Compilers*. Addison-Wesley, 1989.

Specifying Performance Measures for PEPA

Graham Clark, Stephen Gilmore, and Jane Hillston

Laboratory for Foundations of Computer Science,
The University of Edinburgh, Kings Buildings, Edinburgh EH9 3JZ.
Telephone: +44 131 650 1000. Fax: +44 131 667 7209.
{gcla, stg, jeh}@dcs.ed.ac.uk

Abstract. Stochastic process algebras such as PEPA provide ample support for the component-based construction of models. Tools compute the numerical solution of these models; however, the stochastic process algebra methodology lacks support for the specification and calculation of complex performance measures. This paper addresses that problem by presenting a performance specification language which supports high level reasoning about PEPA models, allowing the description of equilibrium (steady-state) measures. The meaning of the specification language can be made formal by examining its foundations in a stochastic modal logic. A case-study is presented to illustrate the approach.

1   Introduction

Performance Evaluation Process Algebra (PEPA) [1] is an expressive formal language for modelling distributed computer and telecommunications systems. PEPA models are constructed by the composition of components which perform individual activities or cooperate on shared ones. To each activity is attached a stochastic estimate of the rate at which it may be performed. Using such a model, a system designer can determine whether a candidate design meets both the behavioural and the temporal requirements demanded of it.

Stochastic process algebras such as PEPA provide ample support for the component-based construction of models. Robust tools such as the PEPA Workbench [2] facilitate the numerical solution of these models when calculating the effective performance of the system under study. However, two important parts of the modelling process are at present insufficiently well supported:

i). the specification and checking of performance properties which are to be satisfied by a model; and
ii). the formulation and calculation of the complex performance measures which are to be derived from the model's numerical solution.

Without additional support for these parts of the modelling process there is a danger that the difficulty of checking correctness and calculating the performance measurements will discourage system designers from undertaking a quantitative analysis. If this were the case, the benefits which are to be gained from a thorough initial investigation of system correctness and responsiveness would be lost.

J.-P. Katoen (Ed.): ARTS'99, LNCS 1601, pp. 211–227, 1999.
© Springer-Verlag Berlin Heidelberg 1999

This paper presents the preliminary results of our attempts to remedy these omissions through the creation of a companion language for PEPA which supports high-level reasoning about PEPA models and provides a suitably-tailored syntax for the description of performance measures over them. This language has foundations in a stochastic logic, the aim being to give a precise definition to specifications in terms of a well-understood theory.

Simple models of a computer system can be constructed without explicit notational support. However, as computer systems become more complex so do their models and the use of a high-level language to aid in their expression becomes necessary. Stochastic process algebras offer attractive features which were not available in previous performance modelling paradigms. The most important of these are *compositionality*, the ability to model a system as the interaction of subsystems, *formality*, giving a precise meaning to all terms in the language, and *abstraction*, the ability to build up complex models from detailed components, disregarding the details when it is appropriate to do so. Queueing networks offer compositionality but not formality; stochastic extensions of Petri nets offer formality but not compositionality; neither offer abstraction mechanisms.

Markovian process algebras are enhanced with information about the duration of activities and, via a race policy, their relative probabilities. Several such languages have appeared in the literature; these include PEPA [1], TIPP [3] and EMPA [4]. Essentially these all propose the same approach to performance modelling: a corresponding continuous time Markov chain (CTMC) is generated via a structured operational semantics; linear algebra can then be used to solve the model in terms of equilibrium behaviour. This behaviour is represented as a probability distribution over all the possible states of the model.

This distribution is seldom the ultimate goal of performance analysis; instead the modeller is interested in performance *measures* which must be derived from this distribution via a *reward structure* defined over the CTMC [5]. A recent case study by first-time users of PEPA [6] reported that a significant proportion of the effort was spent in deriving the performance measures once steady state analysis was complete.

Earlier work by Clark proposed the use of a modal logic to define the reward structure over a PEPA model [7, 8]. While demonstrating feasibility, this work suffered from two major drawbacks. Firstly, the logic used did not include any representation of the timing aspects of PEPA and consequently does not have a clear relationship to the equivalence relations which have been established for the language, such as *Markovian bisimulation* (which is also called *strong equivalence*). Secondly, although the logic formalised an aspect of the PEPA modelling methodology which had previously been carried out in an *ad hoc* manner, it did so in a way which is inaccessible to system designers, the intended users of PEPA. In the current work we aim to address these problems by developing both a stochastic logic which takes full account of the random variables used to represent the duration of activities in PEPA and a model specification language designed to allow the modeller to express, in a high-level way, properties against which the model should be checked.

1.1   Structure of This Paper

In the next section we give a succinct summary of the PEPA language and
motivate the need for a formal notation for specifying the performance of a
PEPA model. Since we provide only a brief summary of PEPA here, the reader
should consult [1] for full details. In Section 3 we introduce a formal notation for
describing performance measures. This will allow the modeller to make queries
about the equilibrium behaviour of a PEPA model. A logical foundation for
the specification notation is illustrated in Section 4 where we reveal that the
language has a particular relationship to probabilistic modal logic. In Section 5
we illustrate our ideas with a simple, yet realistic, example. Finally, conclusions
and future directions for the work are presented at the end of the paper.

2   PEPA

PEPA (Performance Evaluation Process Algebra) extends classical process algebra with the capacity to assign rates to activities, which are described in an
abstract model of a system. It is a concise formal language with a small number
of grammar rules which define the well-formed terms in the language. An activity of action type α performed at rate r preceding P is denoted by $(\alpha, r).P$.
Using the symbol $\top$ instead of a rate denotes *passive* participation in a shared
activity. Choices are separated by $+$. Cooperation between P and Q over a set L
of action types is $P \bowtie_L Q$ or $P \parallel Q$ if L is empty. Hiding the activities in L and
thus denying their availability for cooperation gives the term P/L. The notation
for definitional equality is $\stackrel{def}{=}$. The syntax may be formally introduced by means
of the following grammar:

$$S ::= (\alpha, r).S \mid S + S \mid C_S$$
$$P ::= P \bowtie_L P \mid P/L \mid C$$

where S denotes a *sequential component* and P denotes a *model component*
which executes in parallel. C stands for a constant which denotes either a sequential or a model component, as introduced in a definition. C_S stands for
constants which denote sequential components. The effect of this syntactic separation between these types of constants is to constrain legal PEPA components
to be cooperations between sequential processes. PEPA is a high-level notation
for Markov modelling because it is possible to generate directly from a PEPA
model a continuous time Markov chain (CTMC) which faithfully encodes the
temporal aspects of the PEPA model.

One reason to fix on a formal notation for a task such as performance modelling is to avoid misunderstanding and misinterpretation of a model. Of course,
even when a notation is carefully defined, as PEPA is, there may still be errors
of misrepresentation of parts of the system within the model but all of the users
of the model can at least agree on the correct interpretation of a given model
through recourse to the formal definition of the language. However, when we
come to undertake a careful consideration of properties of a model we see that

we now have a need for a formal notation for *analysis* of performance models expressed in PEPA. Without this, we would not be able to state performance measures precisely.

It is our intention that each of these specifications should be expressed with reference to a PEPA model. This model is converted to an equivalent encoding as a CTMC for analysis. Different types of analysis of the Markov process may be performed, but for this work, we will require steady-state analysis. This is done through the compilation of the infinitesimal generator matrix of the Markov process and the solution of this by Gaussian elimination or another technique from linear algebra. This leads to a steady state *probability vector*, expressing for each state the long-run probability that the model will be found in that state. For many performance measures, a *reward vector* can be specified, associating particular rewards with particular states. The performance measure can be calculated by the simple scalar product of the probability and reward vectors. For example, if we are considering a lift system, utilisation can be calculated from a steady state analysis, by considering those states in which the lift is utilised to have a reward of 1, and otherwise 0. Timing measures, such as average waiting time, cannot be found directly in this way but can be calculated via an application of Little's Law. However some performance measures cannot be calculated from the steady state information. For example, the percentage of lift requests satisfied in under two minutes requires a *transient analysis*, since we are not interested in long-run probabilities in this case. A preliminary notation for the expression of transient performance measures for PEPA models was given in [9], but is not explored further here.

In earlier work we have considered the problem of specifying reward structures corresponding to PEPA models using a modal logic [7, 8]. However that logic ignored the stochastic elements of the model, namely the random variables used to specify activity durations. In this work we extend work on process logics into this exciting new area, and show links between an established probabilistic logic, and the specification language.

3 A High-Level Notation for Steady State Properties

Our objective is to design a high-level notation for expressing steady state properties of a PEPA model. This should provide a straightforward means for the modeller to make quantitative queries about the behaviour of the model, without having to descend into the details of the state space or a reward structure.

Clearly our language must be capable of expressing properties based on those performance measures which can be computed directly by steady state analysis. Typically we wish to know the probability that some condition holds. To express this we use a combination of standard mathematical notation, notation of equivalence relations from PEPA, and a new notation expressing the potential to perform an action of a given type. The use of equivalence relations in this way can focus our queries directly on states, rather than actions. This is unusual within the process algebra literature where notions of state are generally abstracted, and where only potential actions are used to distinguish models. However in Markov processes there is no notion of actions, only states, and all views of the behaviour of a process are phrased in terms of the states it can visit. Stochastic process algebras sit between these two worlds and consequently it is important that our notation has the capabilities to express properties that seem natural within both.

A state based property may mean that we wish to specify the probability that component P is in state P_1—in our notation this is expressed simply as: $\Pr(P = P_1)$. Such a specification is interpreted relative to a model in which P occurs and it succinctly describes the summation of the probabilities of the states of the system where sub-component P is in state P_1. To be pedantic, we should write $\Pr(P \equiv P_1)$ if we intend to require P to be literally P_1 and not just isomorphic to P_1. Similarly, we would write $\Pr(P \cong P_1)$ if we wished to denote the probability that P is in a state which is Markovian bisimilar to P_1. These probabilities may then be used in further calculation such as $r \times \Pr(P = P_1)$ and those results used in comparisons as in $r \times \Pr(P = P_1) > M$. More complex descriptions of states may be expressed via logical operations as in $\Pr(P = P_1 \wedge Q = Q_1)$ or $\Pr(P = P_1 \vee P = P_2)$. For clarity, we may negate relational operators with $\Pr(P \not\equiv Q)$ instead of $\Pr(\neg(P \equiv Q))$.

PEPA allows the modeller to replicate components so that there may be, say, several copies of P in the system description. Thus, we introduce a notion of *situation* (or *location*) of a copy of a component within a PEPA model. It could be the case that the component of interest occurs as a sub-component of another which has only one instance. If so, we use dot notation to identify the sub-component. If not, we number the copies by following a pre-order traversal of the abstract syntax tree of the term.

In order to describe properties in terms of the performance of activities we introduce a term for the probability that a type of activity is enabled. We use the notation $\Pr(\alpha\uparrow)$ for this, whenever the action type of the activity is α. Thus the interpretation of an activity name as a predicate is that the predicate is satisfied whenever the model is in a state S and there is both a state S' and a rate r such that $S \xrightarrow{(\alpha,r)} S'$. A convenient extension to this notation is $\Pr(\alpha\uparrow P)$, meaning that activity α could be performed by component P of the model. However, we shall regard these two forms of *activity probability* as simply convenient abbreviations for a much more complex predicate where the components are constrained (or a given component is constrained) to those states where they may perform an activity of action type α. The cases where the meanings of these two expressions would differ arise whenever the model is not *PEPA live* or not *fully live* [10]. A fully live PEPA model is one such that, for each reachable state, and each syntactic occurrence of an activity within a sequential component, there exists another state which is reachable where this occurrence of the activity can be performed. For the remainder of this paper we restrict consideration to fully live models.

We now have performance measure *expressions* ε, probability *terms* τ, *predicates* ϕ and *situations* σ. These are expressed in the syntax presented in Fig. 1.

$$
\begin{aligned}
\varepsilon ::= {} & \varepsilon + \varepsilon \mid \varepsilon - \varepsilon \mid \varepsilon \times \varepsilon \mid \varepsilon/\varepsilon && \text{(arithmetic expressions)} \\
& \mid \ \varepsilon \geq \varepsilon \mid \varepsilon > \varepsilon \mid \varepsilon \leq \varepsilon \mid \varepsilon < \varepsilon && \text{(comparison expressions)} \\
& \mid \ \mathbb{R} \mid \tau && \text{(constants and terms)} \\
\tau ::= {} & \Pr(\phi) && \text{(probability terms)} \\
\phi ::= {} & \phi \vee \phi \mid \phi \wedge \phi \mid \neg\phi && \text{(logical operators)} \\
& \mid \ \sigma \equiv \sigma \mid \sigma = \sigma \mid \sigma \cong \sigma && \text{(local state conditions)} \\
& \mid \ \alpha{\uparrow} \mid \alpha{\uparrow}\sigma && \text{(activity predicates)} \\
\sigma ::= {} & \sigma \underset{L}{\bowtie} \sigma \mid \sigma/L \mid \sigma.C \mid C\#\mathbb{N} \mid C && \text{(situations)}
\end{aligned}
$$

Fig. 1. Syntax of notation for steady state properties

The characteristics of this notation are that it allows the modeller to inspect internal local states of model components and to consider the steady state probability of attaining significant states of interest. Under the interpretation of activity probabilities as abbreviations for more complex predicates over states we may consider this notation to be entirely based on model states.

4   A Logical Foundation for the Specification Language

In this section, we illustrate how the specification language, introduced in Section 3 may be seen to have a formal underpinning, in terms of a probabilistic modal logic. In particular, the expression, and testing for satisfaction of equilibrium properties, can be seen to be closely related to the specification, and model checking of a formula expressed in *probabilistic modal logic* (PML [11]). We give a modified interpretation of such formulae suitable for reasoning about PEPA's continuous time models.

The study of temporal and modal logics in conjunction with models of concurrency is well established. These logics express properties of systems which have a number of states, and in which there is a relation of succession. A modal logic is used to express a finite behaviour. In a temporal logic operators are introduced to allow reasoning over infinite behaviour.

Over the last decade, work on probabilistic verification has accelerated in line with stochastic extensions to models, as used in the performance community. Various modifications to logics allow properties to be expressed which reflect the additional model information. Recent work by Huth and Kwiatkowska [12] gives the temporal logic the *modal mu-calculus* [13] a non-standard semantics, where the meaning of a formula is a function from states to $[0, 1]$. This is intended to express the 'confidence' that a formula is true, for a given state, although the semantics cannot be interpreted directly as probabilities. Their approach results in their model checking procedure giving lower bounds for the probabilities of properties (these may serve the user as a 'guarantee'). Further they note that the work may be modified to deal with *generative* (essentially, autonomous) models such as those described in PEPA. If it was possible to generate true probabilities in this way, it would seem a useful first step in generating performance measures. A differing approach is taken by Hansson and Jonsson [14], whereby probabilistic operators are added to the temporal logic CTL. For example, the formula $[\phi]_{>p}$ is satisfied for a given state if a measure over the set of paths from the state satisfying ϕ is greater than p. Since the formula will either be satisfied by a state, or not, this leads to a classical predicative semantics. A variant of Hansson and Jonsson's model checking procedure is used in the Probabilistic VERUS tool [15]. This is a variant of VERUS, a BDD-based model checker for real-time systems [16]. A VERUS program is a collection of sequential randomised processes; the authors adapt the language to replace non-determinism with discrete probability distributions. With a probabilistic logic similar to that mentioned above, they are able to specify probabilistic properties, and to check whether these properties are satisfied or not. However, as Huth and Kwiatkowska point out, a user's specification of the threshold probability may be inappropriate for the task at hand, where the information required is such a threshold itself. These varying styles of probabilistic verification suggest avenues of exploration for a PEPA reward logic.

An alternative approach to performance evaluation for stochastic process algebras is described by Bernardo [17]. Instead of using a separate logical notation, the author extends the syntax of the stochastic process algebra *EMPA* such that activities include a notion of reward. In order to generate performance measures, a reward structure for the underlying stochastic process is generated; the reward assigned to each state is the sum of the rewards associated with the activities the model enables in that state. By assigning different values (and different interpretations) to the reward field in appropriate activities, one is able to calculate rewards several kinds of performance measure, such as utilisation and throughput. The advantages of the method are that it is relatively simple to use and apply, and is reasonably expressive. In addition, Bernardo has constructed an equivalence relation which respects the additional reward information. An extension of strong Markovian equivalence, for each pair of states in an equivalence class, the total reward accrued by moving into another equivalence class is the same for each state. This will allow the theory of *EMPA* to be extended smoothly to incorporate rewards. However, we can argue that a specification language based on a logical approach too has its advantages. Firstly, it has the potential to be more expressive than an algebra-based technique. By exploiting the operators a modal logic supplies, it is possible to be more discriminating about which states should contribute to the reward measure. In particular, it is possible to select a state based on model behaviour not immediately local to the state. Some examples of such performance measures were presented in [7]. Philosophically, we may also take the point of view that structure for measuring the performance of a model should be separated from the model itself. A disadvantage of a purely logic-based approach is that it may be seen by a user to be esoteric, and requiring of more effort in order to understand and apply. This motivates one of the aims of our current work, to provide a high-level specification language which abstracts from an underlying logic, and provides the user with a framework which is simpler to apply.

We proceed by describing the principle behind using a logic to generate a performance measure. Following that, we highlight why PML may be a suitable logic for our purposes.

4.1   Using Logic to Specify Performance Measures

Previous work by Clark [7] proposed an approach to generating measures using traditional Hennessy-Milner logic (HML [18]). The idea was to capture the set of 'interesting' states of the model by partitioning the state space with a formula of the logic—those states that enjoy the property are then assigned a reward, such as a number, or a value based on 'local state' information, such as the rate at which the state may perform a particular activity. All uninteresting states are given a reward of 0. In this way, a reward vector is formally specified, and equilibrium measures such as utilisation and throughput may be calculated. However, the method was not ideal for several reasons. Firstly, it was ad hoc—the logic provided an initial partition only, meaning that a calculational technique was required in addition, in order to assign reward values. Secondly, the logic was qualitative only, in that it disregarded the *rate* at which a PEPA process could perform an activity, and only captured the fact that an activity was possible. We believe these issues can be addressed by using a more appropriate logic, namely Larsen and Skou's PML.

4.2   Probabilistic Modal Logic

The syntax of PML formulas is given by

$$F ::= \mathbf{tt} \mid \nabla_\alpha \mid \neg F \mid F_1 \wedge F_2 \mid \langle\alpha\rangle_\mu F$$

The models described in [11] are *probabilistic*, in that for any state P and any action α, there is a (discrete) probability distribution over the α-successors of P. Informally, the semantics of a formula ∇_α is the set of states unable to perform an α activity; and the semantics of $\langle\alpha\rangle_\mu F$ is the set of states such that each can make an α-transition with probability *at least* μ to a set of successors each of which satisfies F. We choose to modify slightly the interpretation of these formulae with respect to PEPA models. First we give a simple definition

Definition 1. $P\overset{(\alpha,\nu)}{\longrightarrow}S$ *if and only if for all* $P' \in S$, $P \overset{\alpha}{\longrightarrow} P'$, *and* $\sum\{r \mid P\overset{(\alpha,r)}{\longrightarrow}P', P' \in S\} = \nu$.

Now let P be a model of a PEPA process. Then

$$P \models \mathbf{tt}$$
$$P \models \neg F \text{ if } P \not\models F$$
$$P \models F_1 \wedge F_2 \text{ if } P \models F_1 \text{ and } P \models F_2$$
$$P \models \nabla_\alpha \text{ if } P \xrightarrow{\alpha}\!\!\!\!\!\!/$$

$$P \models \langle \alpha \rangle_\mu F \text{ if } P \xrightarrow{(\alpha,\nu)} S \text{ for some } \nu \geq \mu, \text{ and for all } P' \in S, P' \models F$$

Therefore, the subscript μ present in formulae of the form $\langle \alpha \rangle_\mu F$ is now interpreted as a rate rather than a probability; if a state P is capable of doing activity α *quickly enough* arriving at a set of states S each of which satisfies F, then P satisfies $\langle \alpha \rangle_\mu F$.

4.3   Relation of PML to the Specification Language

If we use PML as a vehicle for the semantics of the specification language, it will address one of the criticisms of the original PEPA reward language work—that the logic was badly suited to the models. Now it is possible to distinguish model states that differ only in the rate at which they may perform activities. But how does this logic relate to the specification language? This can be made clearer by first showing the precise nature of the relation of PML to PEPA. In [11], Larsen and Skou show that PML exactly characterises *probabilistic bisimulation*, in the sense that two probabilistic processes are bisimilar if and only if they satisfy exactly the same set of PML formulae. With our modification to the semantics of PML, an analogous result holds for PEPA processes:

Theorem 1 (Modal characterisation of strong equivalence). *Let P be a model of a PEPA process. Then*

$$P \cong Q \text{ if and only if for all } F, P \models F \text{ iff } Q \models F$$

That is to say that two PEPA processes are *strongly equivalent* (in particular, their underlying Markov chains are *lumpably equivalent* [1]) if and only if they both satisfy, in our modified setting, the same set of PML formulae.

Instantly, this gives us an understanding of the notation for specifying equilibrium properties. For example, probability terms may take the form $\Pr(P \cong P_1)$. Model checking a logical characterisation of state P_1 via PML would provably capture all and only those states P which are strongly equivalent to P_1, and thus with the steady state vector would immediately lead to a computed value for the term $\Pr(P \cong P_1)$. Another example is provided by the term $\Pr(\alpha\!\uparrow)$. We can instantly characterise, up to strong equivalence, those states which should be included in the computation of this measure—they are those which satisfy the PML formula $\neg \nabla_\alpha$.

As discussed in Section 3, the performance specification language makes use of the idea of model states, as well as model behaviour *in* a state. This can be smoothly reconciled with the use of a probabilistic logic, and the computation of the reward vector can thus be seen as a two-stage procedure. The method is simple, and standard in the theory of process logics—it is to extend the syntax of PML with a set of *variables* V, and for a given model P with state space S, to extend the semantics with a *valuation* function $\mathcal{V} : V \to 2^S$.

$$F ::= \mathtt{tt} \mid \nabla_\alpha \mid \neg F \mid F_1 \wedge F_2 \mid \langle \alpha \rangle_\mu F \mid X$$

$$P \models X \text{ iff } P \in \mathcal{V}(X)$$

The intuition is that a variable $X \in V$ represents a property which is true in a particular subset of the state space. This allows formulae such as $\neg(\langle \mathtt{transmit}_{120} \rangle FailState)$, where $FailState$ is understood to represent an undesirable portion of the state space—"it is not the case that it is possible to efficiently transmit a network packet and finish in a failure state". Given a model, and an expression given in the specification language, the two stage generation of the reward vector can be understood as:

i). calculating the valuation function according to any 'local state' requirements, by e.g. strong equivalence aggregation [1]; then
ii). computing the satisfaction of the PML formula corresponding to the specification, using a model-checking style technique.

The use of PML suggests ways in which the specification language could be extended, if these features would be useful to users. It will certainly be possible to reason about more complex behaviour than the ability to perform a single activity, and it will be possible to reason directly about the rate at which activities are performed. For example, a user may wish to verify that the percentage of time that a component in his model is transmitting network packets efficiently is higher than 40%. Our notation could be extended to allow $\Pr((\mathtt{transmit}, 120) \uparrow) \geq 0.4$. The states to be included in the computation of the measure would be those captured by the formula $\langle \mathtt{transmit} \rangle_{120} \mathtt{tt}$.

Due to the predicative semantics of PML, we note that it is straightforward to specify utilisation and reliability measures using this approach. The relation of PML to throughput measures is not so direct. This is because in previous approaches, the reward structure for a throughput measure associates rates of activity with particular states. In this paper, we choose not to formally develop the link to throughput measures further. However, the specification language will provide the necessary level of abstraction to generate throughput measures, and could do so using PML as the underlying logic. For example, with our suggested extension above, we may determine whether the throughput of our network is greater than some threshold with the expression

$$r \times \Pr((\mathtt{transmit}, r) \uparrow) > M$$

Although the logic of Huth and Kwiatkowska [12] does not support a direct interpretation of formulae as probabilities, we envisage making use of the underlying ideas to extend our approach in order to cover a wider range of equilibrium measures.

Our choice of PML was motivated by its simplicity, and its link to PEPA's strong equivalence. Other research in the area of probabilistic verification has links to our approach. Recent work by de Alfaro [19] addresses the problem of specifying "long-run" average properties of probabilistic systems. The author points out that logics such as those presented by Hansson and Jonsson [14] are able to specify bounds on probabilistic properties, but crucially these are probabilities over behaviours from a specified state. De Alfaro's approach is inspired by process algebraic tests; *experiments* are defined to represent interesting model behaviour patterns. These experiments associate a real-valued outcome with a pattern of behaviour, and are considered to occur infinitely often. The author shows how these experiments can thus be used to specify long-run behaviour. His looks to be a fruitful approach to the problem of probabilistic verification, and we too plan to focus on a concept of stochastic test. Currently work in progress, we are studying the specification of *transient* measures by considering a PEPA model in cooperation with a stochastic test [9]. However our tests do not specify long-run behaviour as do de Alfaro's experiments; rather we seek to examine the point at which a PEPA model first passes a test.

The next section demonstrates how a modeller may use the specification language, by presenting a case study of a *location tracking* system.

5   Case Study: A Location Tracking System

As an example here we consider the problem of modelling a system where the location of people and equipment within a building is monitored by a central tracking system. Such a system is being considered for the James Clerk Maxwell Building at The University of Edinburgh. The building is notoriously confusing to navigate and the tracking system would be helpful in finding those visitors who get lost in the maze of corridors. The system would also help secretaries find professors who may be in any number of teaching and meeting rooms or colleagues' offices and would be an invaluable aid in the hunt for the (non-networked) laptop computers which can be borrowed for the secure preparation of examination papers.

Location tracking systems such as these are implemented by the use of *active badges*, credit-card sized devices which transmit unique infra-red signals which are detected by networked sensors. Systems such as these are already in use in several European universities and in research laboratories in the USA.

The University of Edinburgh issues "smart" enrolment cards at the start of each academic year. These are used both for electronic cash and as swipe-cards for door entry. It is planned that these would be superseded by cards which may also be used for location tracking. The battery life of such a device has typically been found to be around a year [20] so it is necessary to tune the performance of the system by adjusting the rate at which registration is performed in order to conserve battery power while simultaneously ensuring that the system gives accurate location information.

A Markovian stochastic process algebra such as PEPA is well suited to modelling this system because exponential registration intervals are used to prevent the repeated collisions between transmitting badges which would result in lost messages [21]. This is the same use of randomness as found in the Aloha packet-switching network: without it, a collision would inevitably be followed by another collision.

To keep the example small we will consider the simple case of tracking the progress of a single person around a single floor of a building. The floor has three corridors which are numbered 14, 15 and 16, and we assume that there is only a single sensor in each corridor. The corridors are arranged in a U-shape so that it is possible to go from the 14 corridor to the 15 corridor and then to the 16 corridor (and the other way, of course) but it is not possible to go from the 14 to the 16 corridor directly.

The behaviour of a person P who is wearing an active badge can be described in terms of their movement from one corridor to a neighbouring one and the registration of their badge with the nearest sensor.

$$P_{14} \stackrel{def}{=} (reg_{14}, r).P_{14} + (move_{15}, m).P_{15}$$
$$P_{15} \stackrel{def}{=} (reg_{15}, r).P_{15} + (move_{14}, m).P_{14} + (move_{16}, m).P_{16}$$
$$P_{16} \stackrel{def}{=} (reg_{16}, r).P_{16} + (move_{15}, m).P_{15}$$

Sensors accept registration information and report this back to the central database.

$$S_{14} \stackrel{def}{=} (reg_{14}, \top).(rep_{14}, s).S_{14}$$
$$S_{15} \stackrel{def}{=} (reg_{15}, \top).(rep_{15}, s).S_{15}$$
$$S_{16} \stackrel{def}{=} (reg_{16}, \top).(rep_{16}, s).S_{16}$$

For a system with only one person to be tracked the database need only store the most recently reported position.

$$DB_{14} \stackrel{def}{=} (rep_{14}, \top).DB_{14} + (rep_{15}, \top).DB_{15} + (rep_{16}, \top).DB_{16}$$
$$DB_{15} \stackrel{def}{=} (rep_{14}, \top).DB_{14} + (rep_{15}, \top).DB_{15} + (rep_{16}, \top).DB_{16}$$
$$DB_{16} \stackrel{def}{=} (rep_{14}, \top).DB_{14} + (rep_{15}, \top).DB_{15} + (rep_{16}, \top).DB_{16}$$

In the complete system the badge-wearer will move asynchronously but will register with the sensors. The sensors are independent but they all report back to the database. We can initialise the system in any state we wish, perhaps with the badge-wearer in the 14 corridor and the database also recording this.

$$P \stackrel{def}{=} P_{14} \qquad DB \stackrel{def}{=} DB_{14} \qquad System \stackrel{def}{=} P \bowtie_{\{reg_i\}} (S_{14} \parallel S_{15} \parallel S_{16}) \bowtie_{\{rep_i\}} DB$$

5.1   Analysing the Performance of the Location Tracking System

In tuning the system to provide the best balance between accuracy and increased battery life we would investigate the probability of the database incorrectly recording the position of the badge-wearer and increase or decrease the registration rate in order to attain an acceptable threshold. Moreover, failure to register a move is not the only source of inaccurate data within the system. It is possible that reports to the database occur in the wrong order, giving a false impression of the location of the badge wearer. In either case the error can be characterised by the wearer being able to register in a location and the database not recording their presence there. If it has been decided that an acceptable level of accuracy is to have a 1% error rate then, in our high level notation, we would investigate the adequacy of our implementation as follows:

$$\Pr(reg_{14}\uparrow \wedge DB \not\equiv DB_{14})$$
$$+ \Pr(reg_{15}\uparrow \wedge DB \not\equiv DB_{15})$$
$$+ \Pr(reg_{16}\uparrow \wedge DB \not\equiv DB_{16}) \geq 0.01$$

We have investigated the alteration of the probability of error as the rates of badge registration and sensor reporting (variables r and s) are changed while the rate of movement of the badge-wearer (variable m) remains constant. The results are presented in Fig. 2. With the values chosen, the probability of error in the system varies between 0.02 and 0.18. These values were computed by first using the PEPA Workbench to investigate the state space of the location tracking system and then using the PEPA State Finder to select the states of interest. We then used the Maple computer algebra package both to find the steady-state probability distribution of the system and to plot the results.

As a consistency check on our work we also used the PEPA State Finder to compute the probability that the database correctly recorded the location of the badge-wearer and checked that the probabilities of database correctness and incorrectness summed to 1, which they did. The PEPA State Finder at present only implements a subset of the specification language which is described here but it is our intention to extend this to a complete implementation of the language.

The location tracking system with only a single person is a very simple system with only 72 states but we have also considered the effect of adding another person, with a correspondingly more complex database model. The state space of the system increases quickly, of course, and the extended system has 2187 states. More complex performance measures are applicable to the more complex model.

6   Further Work and Discussion

We are confident that the notion of probabilistic logic can be used to give a formal semantics to the specification language as described in Section 3. However,

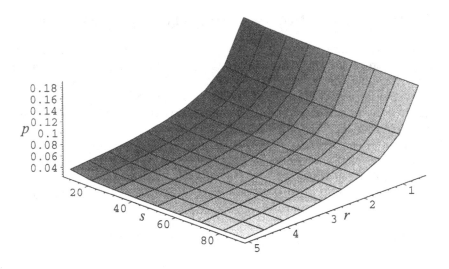

Fig. 2. Investigation of the probability p of error against rates r and s (with $m = 0.1$)

the utility of PML in interpreting transient specifications, as initially proposed in [9] has not been investigated, and remains as future work. Furthermore, we are currently developing the theory behind calculating transient measures. The satisfaction of a transient property is determined by the construction of an appropriate *stochastic test*, consisting of an ancillary PEPA process; the analysis of the original model is done in concert with the stochastic test. Therefore, the longer term aim is to provide the PEPA user and modeller with a rigorous and formally defined specification language for the computation of both equilibrium and transient performance measures.

Initial work on this notation for specifying performance measures was carried out in a *feature interaction* framework. We view a *feature* as being a significant aspect or property of the system which could be used to compare this one to another. Most importantly, features are qualities which can *interact* and which can be *measured*. Therefore the feature interaction framework represents the idea that a system may be built by composing a number of well-engineered features, and is a useful paradigm for both system designers—who are concerned with a compositional or structured approach to the construction of a system—and to system users—who wish to learn and understand complex systems in terms of substantive concepts. The widespread acceptance of the importance of features makes them a very desirable concept to build into a specification language since one of the uses of a specification language can be to provide a common working language between designers and users. Our original setting meant that by using the specification language, a user could formally describe within the model a particular feature enjoyed by the system.

7   Conclusions

Despite impressive improvements in the computational power which is now available to end-users of computer systems, computer equipment remains expensive to purchase and maintain. Consequently, making cost-effective use of limited resources remains one of the motivating concerns of computer system managers. Analysis of computer systems through construction and solution of descriptive models is a hugely profitable activity: brief analysis of a model can provide as much insight as hours of simulation and measurement [22].

We have presented a notation for the description of performance specifications which relate to stochastic process algebra models expressed in the PEPA modelling notation. Our notation for performance specification focuses on models in equilibrium, and concentrates on internally measurable quantities of the system. We are currently developing the framework for specifying transient measures, which will focus on externally observable patterns in the system's transient behaviour. Further, in this paper, we have highlighted how a meaning may be given to equilibrium specifications by using the probabilistic modal logic PML. The location tracking case study illustrates the way in which a modeller would use the PEPA specification language to reason about the performance of a model.

Acknowledgements

Graham Clark and Jane Hillston are supported by the EPSRC 'COMPA' grant. Stephen Gilmore is supported by the 'Distributed Commit Protocols' grant from the EPSRC and by Esprit Working group FIREworks.

References

[1] J. Hillston. *A Compositional Approach to Performance Modelling*. Cambridge University Press, 1996.

[2] S. Gilmore and J. Hillston. The PEPA Workbench: A Tool to Support a Process Algebra-based Approach to Performance Modelling. In G. Haring and G. Kotsis, editors, *Proceedings of 7th Conf. on Mod. Techniques and Tools for Computer Perf. Eval.*, volume 794 of *LNCS*, pages 353–368, 1994.

[3] N. Götz, U. Herzog, and M. Rettelbach. Multiprocessor and Distributed System Design: The Integration of Functional Specification and Performance Analysis using Stochastic Process Algebras. In *Performance'93*, 1993.

[4] M. Bernardo, L. Donatiello, and R. Gorrieri. Integrating Performance and Functional Analysis of Concurrent Systems with EMPA. Technical Report UBLCS-95-14, University of Bologna, 1995.

[5] R. A. Howard. *Dynamic Probabilistic Systems*, volume II: Semi-Markov and Decision Processes, chapter 13, pages 851–915. John Wiley & Sons, New York, 1971.

[6] H. Bowman. Analysis of a Multimedia Stream using Stochastic Process Algebra. In Priami [23], pages 51–69.

[7] G. Clark. Formalising the Specification of Rewards with PEPA. In *Proceedings of the Fourth Process Algebras and Performance Modelling Workshop*, pages 139–160, July 1996.

[8] G. Clark and J. Hillston. Towards Automatic Derivation of Performance Measures from PEPA Models. *Proceedings of UKPEW*, September 1996.

[9] S. Gilmore and J. Hillston. Feature Interaction in PEPA. In Priami [23], pages 17–26.

[10] S. Gilmore, J. Hillston, and L. Recalde. Elementary structural analysis for PEPA. Technical Report ECS-LFCS-97-377, Laboratory for Foundations of Computer Science, Department of Computer Science, The University of Edinburgh, 1997.

[11] K. G. Larsen and A. Skou. Bisimulation through probabilistic testing. *Information and Computation*, 94(1):1–28, September 1991.

[12] M. Huth and M. Kwiatkowska. Quantitative analysis and model checking. In *Proceedings, Twelth Annual IEEE Symposium on Logic in Computer Science*, pages 111–122, Warsaw, Poland, 29 June–2 July 1997. IEEE Computer Society Press.

[13] D. Kozen. Results on the propositional mu-calculus. *Theoretical Computer Science*, 27:333–354, 1983.

[14] H. Hansson and B. Jonsson. A logic for reasoning about time and reliability. *Formal Aspects of Computing*, 6(5):512–535, 1994.

[15] V. Hartonas-Garmhausen. *Probabilistic Symbolic Model Checking with Engineering Models and Applications*. PhD thesis, Carnegie Mellon University, 1998.

[16] S. Campos, E. Clarke, and M. Minea. The Verus tool: A quantitative approach to the formal verification of real-time systems. *Lecture Notes in Computer Science*, 1254, 1997.

[17] M. Bernardo. An Algebra-Based Method to Associate Rewards with EMPA Terms. In *to appear in 24th Int. Colloquium on Automata, Languages and Programming*, July 1997.

[18] M. Hennessy and R. Milner. Algebraic laws for nondeterminism and concurrency. *Journal of the ACM*, 32(1):137–161, January 1985.

[19] L. de Alfaro. How to specify and verify the long-run average behavior of probabilistic systems. In *LICS: IEEE Symposium on Logic in Computer Science*, 1998.

[20] A. Harter and A. Hopper. A distributed location system for the active office. *IEEE Network Magazine*, 8(1):62–70, 1994.

[21] Y-B. Lin and P. Lin. Performance modeling of location tracking systems. *Mobile Computing and Communications Review*, 2(3):24–27, 1998.

[22] I. Mitrani. *Probabilistic Modelling*. Cambridge University Press, 1998.

[23] C. Priami, editor. *Proceedings of the Sixth International Workshop on Process Algebras and Performance Modelling*, Nice, France, September 1998.

A Proof of Modal Characterisation of Strong Equivalence

Case 1 Assume $P \cong Q$. We proceed by induction on the size of F, as in [11].

    Case $F \equiv \langle a \rangle_\mu G$: Let $P \models F$. Then by definition, there exists a set S such that $P \overset{(a,\nu)}{\longrightarrow} S$, where $\nu \geq \mu$, and for all $P' \in S$, $P' \models G$.

Since $P \cong Q$, there exists some strong equivalence $\mathcal{R}$, such that for all $a \in \mathcal{A}$, for all $S \in \mathcal{C}/\mathcal{R}, q[P, S, a] = q[Q, S, a]$. For each $P' \in S$, let $\mathcal{R}_{P'}$ be the equivalence class in $\mathcal{C}/\mathcal{R}$ which contains P'. Furthermore, let $S'' = \bigcup_{P' \in S} \mathcal{R}_{P'}$. Now, for each $P'' \in S''$, $P'' \mathcal{R} P'$, and thus $P'' \cong P'$, for some $P' \in S$, and so by the hypothesis, for all $P'' \in S''$, $P'' \models G$.

Since $S \subseteq S''$, $P \overset{(a,\nu)}{\longrightarrow} S''$, where $\nu' \geq \nu$. Since $P \mathcal{R} Q$, for all $T \in \mathcal{C}/\mathcal{R}$, $q[P, T, a] = q[Q, T, a]$. However, note that for all $s, s' \in S$, $\mathcal{R}_s = \mathcal{R}'_s$ or $\mathcal{R}_s \cap \mathcal{R}_{s'} = \emptyset$. Therefore, by construction of S'', $q[P, S'', a] = q[Q, S'', a]$. Therefore, $Q \overset{(a,\nu')}{\longrightarrow} S''$, where $\nu' \geq \nu \geq \mu$; and for all $Q' \in S''$, $Q' \models G$. Therefore, $Q \models \langle a \rangle_\mu F$. By symmetry of $\cong$, this case is complete.

    Case $F \equiv \nabla_a$: Let $P \models F$. Therefore $P \overset{a}{\nrightarrow}$. Since $P \cong Q$ it is the case that for some strong equivalence $\mathcal{R}$, for all $a \in \mathcal{A}$, for all $S \in \mathcal{C}/\mathcal{R}, q[P, S, a] = q[Q, S, a]$. However, for all $S' \subseteq 2^{\mathcal{C}}$, $q[P, S', a] = 0$. Since for all $S \in \mathcal{C}/\mathcal{R}$, $S \subseteq 2^{\mathcal{C}}$, it is the case that $q[Q, S, a] = q[P, S, a] = 0$ for any $S \in \mathcal{C}/\mathcal{R}$, for any $\mathcal{R}$ which is a strong equivalence. Therefore there does not exist a C such that $q[Q, C, a] > 0$ and therefore, $Q \overset{a}{\nrightarrow}$. By symmetry of $\cong$, this case is complete. All other cases are straightforward.

Case 2 Assume that for all F, $P \models F$ if and only if $Q \models F$. Let $\mathcal{R} = \{(P, Q) \mid$ for all F, $P \models F$ if and only if $Q \models F\}$. The result will hold if $\mathcal{R}$ can be shown to be a strong equivalence. By simple inspection, $\mathcal{R}$ is clearly an equivalence relation. Thus, it must be shown that for all $a \in \mathcal{A}$, for all $S \in \mathcal{C}/\mathcal{R}$, $q[P, S, a] = q[Q, S, a]$.

Let $S \in \mathcal{C}/\mathcal{R}$. Assume that for some $a \in \mathcal{A}$, $P \overset{(a,\mu)}{\longrightarrow} S$ for some μ. Now consider the a-derivatives of Q, labelled $Q'_1, \ldots, Q'_m, Q'_{m+1}, \ldots, Q'_n$, where $n \geq 0$, $0 \leq m \leq n$. These derivatives are labelled such that $Q'_1, \ldots, Q'_m \in S$ and $Q'_{m+1}, \ldots, Q'_n \notin S$. For each Q'_i, let the rate at which Q makes an a-transition to Q'_i be denoted by μ_i. Since S is an equivalence class under $\mathcal{R}$, it is the case that for each $Q'_j, m + 1 \leq j \leq n$, there exists a formula F'_j such that $Q'_j \models F'_j$, and for each $Q'_i, 0 \leq i \leq m$, $Q'_i \nvDash F'_j$. From a lemma by Larsen and Skou [11], it is possible to construct a dual formula to each F'_j, named here $\overline{F}'_j$ such that for $Q'_j, m + 1 \leq j \leq n$, $Q'_j \models F'_j$ if and only if $Q'_j \nvDash \overline{F}'_j$. Now it is the case that $Q \models \langle a \rangle_{\mu'} (\overline{F}'_{m+1} \wedge \ldots \wedge \overline{F}'_n)$, where $\mu' = \sum_{i=1}^m \mu_i$. However, by the initial assumption, it is also the case that $P \models \langle a \rangle_{\mu'} (\overline{F}'_{m+1} \wedge \ldots \wedge \overline{F}'_n)$, and therefore, $\mu' \geq \mu$. This then gives that $q[Q, S, a] = \mu' \geq \mu$. However, $\mathcal{R}$ is symmetrical, and so by such an argument, it is the case that $\mu \geq \mu'$, and thus that $\mu = \mu'$. Hence $q[P, S, a] = q[Q, S, a]$, as required. $\qquad\square$

Semi-numerical Solution of Stochastic Process Algebra Models*

Henrik C. Bohnenkamp and Boudewijn R. Haverkort

Laboratory for Performance Evaluation and Distributed Systems
Department of Computer Science
RWTH Aachen
{henrik|haverkort}@informatik.rwth-aachen.de

Abstract. A solution method for solving Markov chains for a class of stochastic process algebra terms is presented. The solution technique is based on a reformulation of the underlying continuous-time Markov chain (CTMC) in terms of semi-Markov processes. For the reformulation only local information about the processes running in parallel is needed, and it is therefore never necessary to generate the complete global state space of the CTMC. The method works for a fixed number of sequential processes running in parallel and which all synchronize on the same *global* set of actions. The behaviour of the processes is expressed by the embedded Markov chain of a semi-Markov process and by distribution functions (exponomials) which describe the times between synchronizations. The solution method is exact, hence, the state space explosion problem for this class of processes has been solved. A distributed implementation of the solution technique is straightforward.

1 Introduction

Formal verification and the evaluation of performance models have been proven to be important stages in the design of distributed and communication systems. Stochastic process algebras (SPA) are an attempt to integrate the qualitative (functional) and quantitative (temporal or stochastic) specifications within one formal modeling framework. The advantages of this approach are obvious: the formal verification and performance evaluation are carried out on the same basis, so that temporal as well as functional results relate to the same model.

SPA are action-based modeling formalisms, where the SPA terms describe *global* states of the specified system. The most common semantic domain of the functional specification are transition systems. The *stochastic behaviour* is usually a continuous-time Markov chain (CTMC). Unfortunately, SPA are, as any formalism referring to the global state space, subject to the *state space explosion problem*. That means, the state space of the model often increases exponentially with increasing degree of parallelism of the specified system. Thus,

---

* An earlier version of this paper has been presented on the PAPM '98 workshop [1] in Nice, France.

J.-P. Katoen (Ed.): ARTS'99, LNCS 1601, pp. 228–243, 1999.

verification as well as performance evaluation is often impossible due to the vast memory requirements even for medium scale problems. In this paper we develop an approach to tackle the state space explosion problem in the *temporal* domain.

There have already been made several attempts to reduce the memory requirements for the solution of the CTMC of performance models. According to [12], these can be classified as *product-form* solution techniques and *aggregation* techniques. In the field of product-form solutions, the solution of an SPA models is carried out componentwise. The results are combined afterwards. Aggregation techniques generally aim at state-space reduction of the underlying CTMC by means of state aggregation. For a detailed overview of the techniques developed so far we refer to [12].

In this paper we will present another approach to tackle the state space explosion. We will exploit the compositional structure of SPA specifications in the solution of the underlying stochastic process. We reformulate the stochastic process expressed by the underlying CTMC by means of semi-Markov processes. Times between synchronizations of processes can be characterized by phase-type distributions[1], which can be expressed by *exponomials*. The synchronization behaviour is expressed by the *embedded Markov chains* of the semi-Markov processes. Since synchronizations are generally more seldom then local actions, the embedded Markov chain is most often much smaller than the original CTMC of the considered SPA specification.

Our approach, which is strictly oriented at the compositional structure of the SPA specification, has the following characteristics:

- Generation of the global state space is avoided.
- The approach is only applicable to a restricted class of SPA terms.
- We obtain *exact* throughputs and *local* steady-state probabilities.
- Interesting but of minor importance for this paper is the fact that a distributed implementation of the approach is straightforward.

The paper is structured as follows: In Section 2 we introduce the fundamentals necessary to understand the rest of the paper. In Section 3 we present our approach. In Section 4 we discuss the pro and cons of the approach and give an overview of our further work.

2   Preliminaries

We start in Section 2.1 by defining the stochastic process algebra *SPA* which serves us as the basic formalism to describe the kind of processes apt to be solved by our approach. In Section 2.2 we briefly explain the usefulness of throughputs for the computation of steady-state probabilities of CTMCs. In Section 2.3 we discuss the relations between local and global state probabilities. In Section 2.4 we will introduce basic facts of semi-Markov processes. Section 2.5 gives a short description of the kind of distributions (exponomials) we will be concerned with in the rest of this paper.

---

[1] The *time to absorption* of an absorbing Markov chains has a distribution, which commonly is referred to as *phase-type distribution*.

2.1   Stochastic Processes Algebra $\mathcal{SPA}$

The stochastic process algebra $\mathcal{SPA}$ is an extension of TCSP [3] by anonymous timed actions which are intended to model a stochastic passing of time between visible actions. Functional and temporal behaviour is treated separately, as in [7]. The operational semantics is rather similar to that of IM-TIPP [18].

First, we will define a general syntax of $\mathcal{SPA}$. For the resulting language we define a structural operational semantics. Finally, we restrict the language of $\mathcal{SPA}$ such that the resulting terms are apt to be solved by our method.

Syntax of $\mathcal{SPA}$. Let $Com = \{a, b, c, \ldots\}$ be a set of actions with $\tau \notin Com$ and $Act := Com \cup \{\tau\}$.

Definition 1. *The language $\mathcal{L}_{SPA}$ is defined by the following grammar:*

$$P \quad \longrightarrow \quad Stop \mid a.P \mid (\lambda).P \mid P + P \mid P\|_S P \mid P \setminus L \mid X \mid recX : P \quad (1)$$

with $a \in Act$, $L, S \subseteq Com$, $\lambda \in \mathbb{R}$ with $\lambda > 0$, and X a process variable. $\mathcal{L}_{SPA}$ is additionally restricted by the following rules:

1. *Recursion over static operators $(\|_S, \cdot \setminus L)$ is not allowed*
2. *The recursion operator $recX$ binds the process variables X and, as usual, we only consider terms without any free occurrence of a process variable.*
3. *Each occurrence of a process variable X is preceded by an action $a \in Act$ or $\lambda \in \mathbb{R}$.*

If necessary, we use parentheses to mark the scope of recX-operators or the bounds of choices.

The prefixes $a. \cdot$ have to be seen as *immediate* actions which do not consume time. The prefixes $(\lambda). \cdot$ with λ being a positive real number denote anonymous timed actions with a duration which is distributed according to a negative exponential distribution with rate λ. These actions are subsequently called *Markovian*. Synchronization is possible only between immediate actions. Hence the synchronization mechanism used here is *timeless synchronization* as described in [11].

Structural Operational Semantics for $\mathcal{SPA}$. The definition of a operational semantics requires first the definition of appropriate *transistion systems*:

Definition 2 ($\mathcal{SPA}$ transition system).
A SPA transition system is a tuple

$$(S, s_0, \longrightarrow, \cdots\cdots\blacktriangleright),$$

where $S \subseteq \mathcal{L}_{SPA}$, $s_0 \in S$ is the starting state and $\longrightarrow, \cdots\cdots\blacktriangleright$ are labelled transition relations:

$$\longrightarrow \subseteq S \times \mathbb{R}^+ \times Lab \times S$$
$$\cdots\cdots\blacktriangleright \subseteq S \times Act \times S,$$

and $Lab = \{+_l, +_r, \|_l, \|_r\}^*$.

$$\langle . \rangle \frac{}{(\lambda).P \xrightarrow{\lambda, \varepsilon} P}$$

$$\langle +_l \rangle \frac{P \xrightarrow{\lambda, w} P'}{P + Q \xrightarrow{\lambda, +_l.w} P'} \qquad \langle +_r \rangle \frac{Q \xrightarrow{\lambda, w} Q'}{P + Q \xrightarrow{\lambda, +_r.w} Q'}$$

$$\langle \|_l \rangle \frac{P \xrightarrow{\lambda, w} P'}{P\|_S Q \xrightarrow{\lambda, \|_l.w} P'\|_S Q} \qquad \langle \|_r \rangle \frac{Q \xrightarrow{\lambda, w} Q'}{P\|_S Q \xrightarrow{\lambda, \|_r.w} P\|_S Q'}$$

$$\langle rec \rangle \frac{P\{recX : P/X\} \xrightarrow{\lambda, w} P'}{recX \ : \ P \xrightarrow{\lambda, w} P'}$$

Fig. 1. Operational semantics for $\mathcal{SPA}$: Markovian actions

The semantics of a term $P \in \mathcal{L}_{\mathcal{SPA}}$ is given by the smallest transition system obeying the semantic rules given in Figure 1 and Figure 2. We denote this transition system subsequently by $[\![P]\!]$.

We will now define some more terms which we will use in the subsequent sections.

Definition 3. *Let $P \in \mathcal{L}_{\mathcal{SPA}}$ and $[\![P]\!] = (\mathcal{S}, P, \longrightarrow, \dashrightarrow\,)$. Then*

$$Reach(P) := \mathcal{S}$$

is called the reachability set *of P.*

The inclusion $P' \in Reach(P)$ is sometimes informally stated as "the state P' belongs to process P".

Definition 4. *The set of synchronizing states of $P \in \mathcal{L}_{\mathcal{SPA}}$ is given by:*

$$S_{syn}(P) \quad = \quad \{P' \mid P' \in Reach(P) \wedge \exists P'' : P' \dashrightarrow^{a} P'' \ for \ a \in Com\} \quad (2)$$

The set $S_{syn}(P)$ for $P \in \mathcal{L}_{\mathcal{SPA}}$ contains all those states of $Reach(P)$ where an immediate action is enabled. These states are also known as *vanishing states*, since they are usually eliminated from the reachability graph when the underlying CTMC is generated.

Definition 5. *With $\equiv$ we denote syntactic equivalence.*

Syntactic Restrictions. The solution method we want to explain in Section 3 is only applicable to a restricted class of $\mathcal{SPA}$-terms. Here we want to define this class.

$$\langle .^I \rangle \frac{}{a.P \overset{a}{\cdots\!\!\rightarrow} P} \quad (a \in Act)$$

$$\langle +_l^I \rangle \frac{P \overset{a}{\cdots\!\!\rightarrow} P'}{P + Q \overset{a}{\cdots\!\!\rightarrow} P'} \qquad\qquad \langle +_r^I \rangle \frac{Q \overset{a}{\cdots\!\!\rightarrow} Q'}{P + Q \overset{a}{\cdots\!\!\rightarrow} Q'}$$

$$\langle \|_l^I \rangle \frac{P \overset{a}{\cdots\!\!\rightarrow} P'}{P\|_sQ \overset{a}{\cdots\!\!\rightarrow} P'\|_sQ} \quad (a \notin S) \qquad \langle \|_r^I \rangle \frac{Q \overset{a}{\cdots\!\!\rightarrow} Q'}{P\|_sQ \overset{a}{\cdots\!\!\rightarrow} P\|_sQ'} \quad (a \notin S)$$

$$\langle \|^I \rangle \frac{P \overset{a}{\cdots\!\!\rightarrow} P' \quad Q \overset{a}{\cdots\!\!\rightarrow} Q'}{P\|_sQ \overset{a}{\cdots\!\!\rightarrow} (P'\|_sQ')} \quad (a \in S)$$

$$\langle rec^I \rangle \frac{P\{recX : P/X\} \overset{a}{\cdots\!\!\rightarrow} P'}{recX : P \overset{a}{\cdots\!\!\rightarrow} P'}$$

$$\langle \backslash_{no}^I \rangle \frac{P \overset{b}{\cdots\!\!\rightarrow} P'}{P \backslash a \overset{b}{\cdots\!\!\rightarrow} P' \backslash a} \quad (a \neq b) \qquad\qquad \langle \backslash_{yes}^I \rangle \frac{P \overset{a}{\cdots\!\!\rightarrow} P'}{P \backslash a \overset{\tau}{\cdots\!\!\rightarrow} P' \backslash a}$$

Fig. 2. Operational semantics for SPA: Immediate actions

Definition 6. *The language $\mathcal{L}_{RSPA} \subseteq \mathcal{L}_{SPA}$ is defined by the following grammar:*

$$Q \longrightarrow \underbrace{P\|_sP\|_s \dots \|_sP}_{n \text{ times}} \tag{3}$$

$$P \longrightarrow Stop \mid a.P \mid (\lambda).P \mid T + T \mid P \backslash L \mid X \mid recX : P \tag{4}$$

$$T \longrightarrow Stop \mid (\lambda).P \mid T + T \mid T \backslash L \mid X \mid recX : T \tag{5}$$

where $n = 2, 3, \dots$, and $L, S \subseteq Com$.

- The rule Q describes the global structure of the processes we want to consider. We always deal with n processes which are synchronized over the same synchronization set S.
- The second rule, P, confirms that we do not allow a choice between local (timed) and synchronizing (immediate) actions. Stated in an intuitive way, this means that we do not allow local *timeouts*. A process willing to synchronize has to wait until all other participants are ready to synchronize. We need this restriction, because the time between the executions of untimed actions must be phase-type distributed. This requirement would be violated if a choice between timed and untimed actions is allowed.
- The rule T describes processes which are only able to perform timed actions as next step.

Additionally, we demand that the resulting CTMC underlying the SPA terms have to be ergodic. This requires at least that the SPA process is deadlock free.

As a consequence we can see that the synchronizational behaviour of synchronizing processes must be deterministic: once they have synchronized it has to be known on which action type they will synchronize next. Since choices between immediate actions lead to nondeterministic behaviour we have to forbid this possibility.

Other Stochastic Process Algebras. Though we consider only timeless synchronization in this paper, it is possible to use other SPA like MTIPP [8] or PEPA [10] as well. In these SPA, synchronizations are considered as actions with an associated exponentially distributed delay. The rate of the delay depends on the rates of the synchronizing actions which take part in the synchronization. Though these timed synchronizations seem to be inconsistent with our notion of untimed synchronization, they actually are not. The timed synchronisations are inherently composed of two timeless synchronisations and a delay which is shared by all parties which take part in the synchronization. We do not consider this further here, but we claim that the "classical" timed synchronizations can be expressed by means of SPA with timeless synchronization, like $\mathcal{SPA}$. This capability has been extensively used in [6], to which we refer the reader for more details. Since $\mathcal{SPA}$ is hence a SPA which is as powerfull as others, we decide to consider only timeless synchronization in the future.

2.2   Throughputs and State Probabilities

The throughput (or *probability flow*) τ_s of a CTMC state s is defined as

$$\tau_s = \pi_s \cdot q_s,$$

where π_s is the steady-state probability of being in state s and q_s the rate sum of the outgoing transitions of s. Given a generator matrix Q of an irreducible CTMC the knowledge of the throughput of one state does not give much information to aid the solution of Q. On the other hand, if we have a CTMC where the rate of a transition is not known, but its throughput is, we can use the throughput to derive the steady-state solution of the CTMC. CTMCs with unknown rates will appear naturally in the next sections.

2.3   Local vs. Global State Probabilities

Consider a process $\mathcal{P} = P_1\|_S \ldots \|_S P_n \in \mathcal{L_{RSPA}}$. We call the probabilities to be in state Q for all $Q \in Reach(\mathcal{P})$ *global state probabilities*. *Local state probabilities* are defined for the components P_i, $i = 1, \ldots, n$ of $\mathcal{P}$ and denote the probabilities for component P_i to be in state R for all $R \in Reach(P_i)$. The local probabilities depend not only on P_i itself but also on the environment of P_i, i.e. the other components of $\mathcal{P}$. The local state probabilities of a component P_i are strongly dependent on its CTMC and from the influence the other components have on P_i.

Many performance measures relate to individual components and can be expressed by means of local state probabilities of the components itself (e.g. the mean number of customers of an individual station in a queuing network). For cases in which such measures are needed it is desirable to compute the local state probabilities directly.

The influence of the environment on a component P_i can be expressed by the mean counts of synchronizations in unit time which P_i performs. These mean counts can be seen as throughputs of the synchronizing states of P_i, hence, for each synchronizing state of P_i such a throughput can be defined. Knowing them, the system of global balance equations of the CTMC underlying P_i can be modified in a way that its solution yields the local state probabilities of P_i. In Section 3 we will present a method to compute these throughputs.

2.4   Semi-Markov Processes

The concept of semi-Markov processes is a generalization of the common Markov process. The main difference is that the state sojourn times of a semi-Markov process are no longer described by negative exponential distributions but by arbitrary ones. Only at times where state changes occur the Markov property is obeyed. The next state to enter is determined according to the current state and transition probabilities which are described by the so-called *embedded Markov chain* (EMC). The EMC is an ordinary DTMC, which has the same states and transitions as the semi-Markov process but which gives only the transition probabilities from state to state. In the following, we denote the steady-state solution of the EMC, which is needed to solve the semi-Markov process, as $(\pi_1, \ldots, \pi_n)$.

For the each state i of a semi Markov process, a distribution function F_i for the sojourn time in the state has to be defined. With τ_i, $i = 1, \ldots, n$, being the mean values of these F_i-distributed random variables, the steady-state solution vector $(\phi_1, \ldots, \phi_n)$ of the semi-Markov process is given by the following quotient:

$$\phi_i \quad = \quad \frac{\pi_i \cdot \tau_i}{\sum_{j=1}^{n} \pi_j \cdot \tau_j}, \qquad\qquad i = 1, \ldots, n.$$

(6)

For an overview of semi-Markov processes see [5]. A more complete description is given in [13], [4] and [14].

2.5   Exponomials

This section is devoted to a special class of functions, which can be used to express phase-type distributions: *exponential polynomials* or *exponomials* for short. Exponomials will be used in Section 3 to express the state sojourn time distributions for the semi-Markov process we want to define. Exponomials have the following form:

$$f(t) = \sum_{i=1}^{n} a_i t^{k_i} e^{\gamma_i t}, \qquad\qquad k_i \in \mathbb{N}, \gamma_i, a_i \in \mathbb{R} \text{ for } i = 1, \ldots, n.$$

Note that not all exponomials describe distribution functions, for example $f(t) = e^t$.

The fact that exponomials are closed under multiplication will become very important in the following sections. Remember, that the distribution of the maximum of a set of random variables, $\mathbf{X} = \max\{X_1, \ldots, X_n\}$ is easily to express by the distributions F_i, $i = 1 \ldots, n$ of the individual random variables, as follows:

$$F_{\max_i\{X_i\}}(t) \quad = \quad \prod_{i=1}^{n} F_i(t). \tag{7}$$

Hence, $\mathbf{X}$ has an exponomial distribution function.

In [19] more information on exponomials can be found. There are algorithms known to derive exponomial distribution functions for the *time to absorption* of absorbing Markov chains. See e.g. [15] and [17].

3 The Solution Method

In this section we describe our solution method. The main goal of our approach is to reduce the computations on the global state space of the CTMC. We do this by reformulating the mathematical problem in terms of semi-Markov processes. The time instants at which a state change in the SMP occurs represent the times of synchronization. The sojourn times of the SMP represent the times between two synchronizations.

Throughout this section we will assume a process

$$\mathcal{P} = P_1\|_S \ldots \|_S P_n \in \mathcal{L}_{\mathcal{RSPA}}.$$

The solution algorithm comprises 3 major steps:

1. Definition of (local) embedded Markov chains for the semi-Markov process underlying the considered system.
2. Definition of the sojourn time distributions in terms of exponomials for the (local) EMC states.
3. Computation of mean sojourn times of the defined SMPs, their steady-state state probabilities, the computation of the throughputs and local steady-state probabilities and, finally, computation of the desired performance measures.

To simplify the understanding of our approach we accompany the technical parts with a running example, which we introduce now.

Example (a): Introduction. Consider two processes P and Q which have three possibilities to synchronize:

$$P \equiv recX : a.(rp_1).b.(rp_2).X$$
$$Q \equiv recY : a.((rq_1).b.(rq_3).Y + (rq_2).b.(rq_4).Y)$$
$$\mathcal{P} \equiv P\|_{\{a,b\}}Q.$$

The process P is very simple: after performing an immediate action a, it lets pass some time (negative exponentially distributed with rate rp_1). Then, after immediate action b it waits a time interval (with rate rp_2) and behaves then again like P.

Process Q is only slightly different: after performing an immediate action a it has the choice between two timed actions: rq_1 and rq_2. The choice takes a time which is exponentially distributed with rate $rq_1 + rq_2$. In either cases an immediate action b is executed. After that it takes some time (with rate rq_3 or rq_4) until the process behaves again like Q.

Finally, $\mathcal{P}$ is the parallel composition of P and Q, where P and Q synchronize themselves via the actions a and b.

3.1   Step 1: Finding the EMC

The states of the EMC (and the semi-Markov process as well) are strongly connected to the times where synchronizations take place in the original model.

Let $m_i = |\mathcal{S}_{syn}(P_i)|$ the cardinality of the set of synchronizing states. For each P_i we define an intermediate DTMC MC_{P_i} for which the state spaces are the sets $\mathcal{M}_i := \{1, \ldots, m_i\}$. The (bijective) function $\sigma_i : \mathcal{M}_i \to \mathcal{S}_{syn}(P_i)$ defines which state of MC_{P_i} belongs to the respective synchronizing state of P_i.

The transition probabilities for MC_{P_i} shall be defined as follows: if we are in state $j \in \mathcal{S}_{syn}(P_i)$ (that means in the state $\sigma_i(j) \in Reach(P_i)$) we can derive from P_i the probability p_{jk} that the next EMC state [that means the next synchronizing state] that is visited will be k [$\sigma_i(k)$]. MC_{P_i} is completely described by the transition probability matrix

$$\mathbf{P}_i \quad = \quad (p_{jk})_{j,k \in \{1,\ldots,m_i\}}. \qquad (8)$$

Now that we have defined the MC_{P_i} we can proceed with the definition of the desired EMC. Its state space is simply the cross-product of all the MC_{P_i}. We denote the transition probability matrix of the overall EMC as $\mathbf{P}_{||}$. In terms of Kronecker operators the transition probability matrix $\mathbf{P}_{||}$ is given by $\mathbf{P}_{||} = \otimes_{i=1}^{n} \mathbf{P}_i$.

We can describe the states of the EMC as tuples

$$(i_1, i_2, \ldots, i_n) \in \mathcal{M}_1 \times \ldots \times \mathcal{M}_n =: \mathcal{M}_{||}.$$

When the stochastic process described by $\mathbf{P}_{||}$ enters $(i_1, i_2, \ldots, i_n)$ this reflects the fact that between the processes $P_1, \ldots, P_n$ a synchronization has taken place, where P_1 was in synchronizing state $\sigma_1(i_1)$, P_2 in synchronizing state $\sigma_2(i_2)$ and so on.

The state graph of $\mathbf{P}_{||}$ is not necessarily connected, i.e. it may consist of disjoint parts, where no state in one part can reach a state in a different one. In this case we have to decide which part is the interesting one. Generally, this is determined by a starting distribution of the DTMC, which describes the probabilities to be in a certain state at the beginning of the observation. In our case we have to choose the part which contains at least one state $(i_1, i_2, \ldots, i_n) \in \mathcal{M}_{\parallel}$ with

$$\sigma_1(i_1) \|_S \ldots \|_S \sigma_n(i_n) \in Reach(\mathcal{P}).$$

Demanding that at least one state has to have this property is sufficient, since every state reachable from $(i_1, i_2, \ldots, i_n)$ has this property, either.

Below we will calculate the steady state probabilities of the EMC. Since the EMC has been built from the *independent* DTMCs MC_{P_i} it is also possible to obtain the steady-state solutions for the MC_{P_i} individually. The solution vector for the complete EMC can be obtained thereafter by simple elementwise multiplication of the n solution vectors. This is not shown in the example below.

Example (b): Finding the EMC. We want to express the temporal behaviour of $\mathcal{P}$ by means of a semi-Markov process. The first thing to do is to define the state space and transition structure of this SMP. That means to define the EMC of the SMP.

First we define the discrete time Markov chains MC_P and MC_Q, which describe the synchronization behaviour of P and Q by means of probabilities. MC_Q has a very simple structure as shown in Figure 3(b). MC_P is even simpler, as Figure 3(a) proves.

The overall EMC is depicted in Figure 4. It consists of two disjoint parts. Only the left part is needed, since it contains the starting state $(1,1)$. Hence we have to solve the DTMC with the states $(1,1)$, $(2,2)$, and $(2,3)$. The solution is $\underline{\pi}^{EMC} = (\pi_1^{EMC}, \pi_2^{EMC}, \pi_3^{EMC})$ with

$$\pi_{(1,1)}^{EMC} = \frac{1}{2},$$

$$\pi_{(2,2)}^{EMC} = \frac{rq_1}{2(rq_1 + rq_2)},$$

$$\pi_{(2,3)}^{EMC} = \frac{rq_2}{2(rq_1 + rq_2)}.$$

3.2   Step 2: How To Determine Distributions for the Sojourn Times

Now that we know the EMC we also know the structure of the SMP. All we have to define now are the sojourn time distributions of the SMP states. To do this we begin once again with the EMC MC_{P_i}. First we define distribution functions for each state of the MC_{P_i}: the distributions of the *time to next synchronization*, identified by the random variables T. To distinguish them we write T_j^i for the random variable which describes the time to next synchronization starting in state $\sigma(j)$ of process P_i. The distributions of the T_j^i can be expressed by phase-type Markov chains derived from the process P_i. An explicit semi-symbolic expression in exponomial form can be derived of the distribution of the time to absorption (as mentioned in Section 2.5).

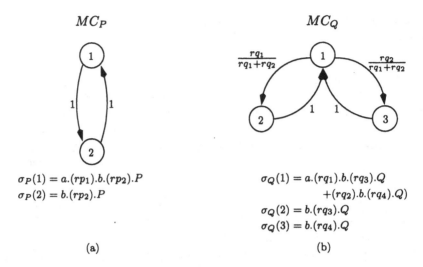

$\sigma_P(1) = a.(rp_1).b.(rp_2).P$

$\sigma_P(2) = b.(rp_2).P$

$\sigma_Q(1) = a.(rq_1).b.(rq_3).Q$

$+ (rq_2).b.(rq_4).Q)$

$\sigma_Q(2) = b.(rq_3).Q$

$\sigma_Q(3) = b.(rq_4).Q$

(a)   (b)

Fig. 3. MC_P and MC_Q for the example

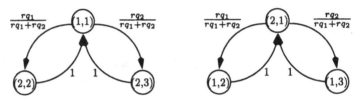

Fig. 4. The (overall) EMC of the example

We denote the distribution function of T_j^i as F_j^i. Now that we have defined them we can proceed with the distribution functions of the complete SMP. For a state $(j_1, j_2, \ldots, j_n)$ of the complete Markov chain we define the distribution function

$$F_{(j_1, j_2, \ldots, j_n)}(t) := \prod_{k=1}^{n} F_{j_k}^{k}(t) \qquad (9)$$

The distribution $F_{(j_1, j_2, \ldots, j_n)}(t)$ describes the *maximum of the individual times to next synchronizations*, i.e., it is the distribution of the random variable

$$T_{(j_1, j_2, \ldots, j_n)} := \max \left\{ T_{j_1}^1, T_{j_2}^2, \ldots, T_{j_n}^n \right\}.$$

This random variable describes the temporal behaviour of the overall system between two synchronization events.[2]

---

[2] It should be noted that the distributions F_j^i and $F_{(j_1, j_2, \ldots, j_n)}$ do not take into account which synchronizing states take part in the *next* synchronization. That means that we have defined *unconditional* distributions. There is also another variant of semi-

Example (c): Sojourn Time Distributions. To define the distributions of SMP states we begin by considering the intermediate EMCs MC_P and MC_Q. First we define the sojourn time distributions for both of them. According to the last section we denote the *times to next synchronization* as T_i^X, where X is either P or Q and i one of the respective state numbers.

We start with MC_P. Since P is very simple this is easy: the time to leave state 1 and to enter 2 is described by the same distribution as for the time that a state change from

$$a.(rp_1).b.(rp_2).X$$

to

$$b.(rp_2).X$$

takes. This is a negative exponential distribution with mean $\frac{1}{rp_1}$. Hence the distribution function is

$$F_1^P(t) = 1 - e^{-rp_1 t}.$$

It is nearly the same for state 2, hence

$$F_2^P(t) = 1 - e^{-rp_2 t}.$$

For MC_Q the considerations are very similar. If MC_Q is in state 1 the fact is mirrored that process Q is in state $\sigma_Q(1)$ (cf. Fig. 3). The process has the choice to execute either (rq_1) or (rq_2). In both cases a synchronizing state is reached, hence the distribution we are looking for is again negative exponential with rate $rq_1 + rq_2$:

$$F_1^Q(t) = 1 - e^{-(rq_1 + rq_2)t}.$$

For states 2 and 3 a similar reasoning holds: the T is in both cases negative exponentially distributed with parameter rq_3 and rq_4, respectively. Hence

$$F_2^Q(t) = 1 - e^{rq_3 t}$$
$$F_3^Q(t) = 1 - e^{rq_4 t}.$$

With the sojourn time distributions for MC_P and MC_Q we are ready to define the respective distributions for the overall SMP. The times where state changes occur in the SMP are synchronization instants. The time to the next state change is then determined by the slowest participant. For state $(1,1)$ this is $T_{(1,1)} = \max\{T_1^P, T_1^Q\}$, which is distributed, as we know from Section 2.5, with

$$F_{(1,1)}(t) = F_1^P(t)F_1^Q(t) = 1 - e^{-rp_1 t} - e^{-(rq_1+rq_2)t} + e^{-(rp_1+rq_1+rq_2)t}.$$

For $F_{(2,2)}(t)$ and $F_{(2,3)}(t)$ the results look similar:

$$F_{(2,2)}(t) = F_2^P(t)F_2^Q(t) = 1 - e^{-rp_2 t} - e^{-rq_3 t} + e^{-(rp_2+rq_3)t}$$
$$F_{(2,3)}(t) = F_2^P(t)F_3^Q(t) = 1 - e^{-rp_2 t} - e^{-rq_4 t} + e^{-(rp_2+rq_4)t}$$

Markov processes, where distributions for individual pairs of synchronizing states (i.e. *conditional* distributions) have to be given, but we do not dwell on this topic here.

3.3   Steps 3-5: Solving the Semi-Markov Process

The solution of the semi-Markov process is now straightforward. From the distributions $F_{(j_1,j_2,...,j_n)}$ obtained in Section 3.2 we must now compute the mean values, i.e.,

$$\tau_{(j_1,j_2,...,j_n)} = \int_0^\infty t f_{(j_1,j_2,...,j_n)}(t)dt, \tag{10}$$

where $f_{(j_1,j_2,...,j_n)}(t) = F'_{(j_1,j_2,...,j_n)}(t)$.

With these mean sojourn times of the respective states, and the probabilities $\pi_{(j_1,j_2,...,j_n)}$, obtained in Section 3.1 we only have to employ (6) to obtain the steady state probability distribution of the semi-Markov process. The steady-state probability, that the semi-Markov process is in state $(j_1, j_2, \ldots, j_n)$ equals

$$\phi_{(j_1,j_2,...,j_n)} = \frac{\pi_{(j_1,j_2,...,j_n)} \cdot \tau_{(j_1,j_2,...,j_n)}}{\sum_{(k_1,k_2,...,k_n)\in\mathcal{M}_1\times\mathcal{M}_2\times\cdots\times\mathcal{M}_n} \pi_{(k_1,k_2,...,k_n)} \cdot \tau_{(k_1,k_2,...,k_n)}}$$

With the steady-state probabilities we are now ready to compute throughputs of the overall system. The throughput $\theta_{(j_1,j_2,...,j_n)}$ of the state $(j_1, j_2, \ldots, j_n)$ is given as

$$\theta_{(j_1,j_2,...,j_n)} = \frac{\phi_{(j_1,j_2,...,j_n)}}{\tau_{(j_1,j_2,...,j_n)}}. \tag{11}$$

$\theta_{(j_1,j_2,...,j_n)}$ gives us the mean number of synchronizations in which the synchronizing states $\sigma_i(j_i)$ $(i = 1,\ldots,n)$ are involved. With these throughputs we are now able to compute *local* steady-state probabilities of the processes P_i.

Example (d): Solving the SMP. To solve the SMP we have to compute the mean values of the distribution functions $F_{(1,1)}$, $F_{(2,2)}$, and $F_{(2,3)}$. This is accomplished by differentiation of the distribution functions and applying the usual well-known formula for mean values of continuous distributions. We define

$$f_{(1,1)}(t) = \frac{d}{dt}F_{(1,1)}(t) = rp_1 e^{-rp_1 t} + (rq_1 + rq_2)e^{-(rq_1+rq_2)t}$$
$$- (rp_1 + rq_1 + rq_2)e^{-(rp_1+rq_1+rq_2)t},$$

$$f_{(2,2)}(t) = \frac{d}{dt}F_{(2,2)}(t) = rp_2 e^{-rp_2 t} + rq_3 e^{-rq_3 t} - (rp_2 + rq_3)e^{-(rp_2+rq_3)t},$$

$$f_{(2,3)}(t) = \frac{d}{dt}F_{(2,3)}(t) = rp_2 e^{-rp_2 t} + rq_4 e^{-rq_4 t} - (rp_2 + rq_4)e^{-(rp_2+rq_4)t}.$$

Symbolic integration yields as mean values

$$\tau_{(1,1)} = \frac{1}{rp_1} + \frac{1}{rq_1 + rq_2} - \frac{1}{rp_1 + rq_1 + rq_2},$$

$$\tau_{(2,2)} = \frac{1}{rp_2} + \frac{1}{rq_3} - \frac{1}{rp_2 + rq_3},$$

$$\tau_{(2,3)} = \frac{1}{rp_2} + \frac{1}{rq_4} - \frac{1}{rp_2 + rq_4}.$$

Now we are ready to compute the steady-state probabilities according to (6). To simplify the formulas we set

$$\tau := \sum_{i \in \{(1,1),(2,2),(2,3)\}} \pi_i \tau_i.$$

Then

$$\phi_{(1,1)} = \frac{\pi_{(1,1)} \tau_{(1,1)}}{\tau},$$

$$\phi_{(2,2)} = \frac{\pi_{(2,2)} \tau_{(2,2)}}{\tau},$$

$$\phi_{(2,3)} = \frac{\pi_{(2,3)} \tau_{(2,3)}}{\tau}.$$

From this we can compute the throughputs of our semi-Markov process:

$$\theta_{(1,1)} = \frac{\phi_{(1,1)}}{\tau_{(1,1)}} = \frac{\pi_{(1,1)}}{\tau},$$

$$\theta_{(2,2)} = \frac{\phi_{(2,2)}}{\tau_{(2,2)}} = \frac{\pi_{(2,2)}}{\tau,}$$

$$\theta_{(2,3)} = \frac{\phi_{(2,3)}}{\tau_{(2,3)}} = \frac{\pi_{(2,3)}}{\tau}.$$

Now that the throughputs are known the state probabilities of P and Q can be computed.

4 Discussion and Further Work

In the following we discuss some of the features of our solution technique.

- The solution method yields exact results. That means, the throughputs obtained are the same as the ones obtained by solving the system of linear equations of the original Markov process.
- There is never the need to construct the overall, global state space of the stochastic process. That means, the state space explosion problem for this class of processes does not occur.
- The technique is easy to parallelize. This is due to the fact that many computation steps have to be performed on independent Markov chains and their solution vectors. To develop a distributed, parallel computation algorithm is hence straightforward.
- The computations of the semi-numerical representations of the sojourn time distributions are not always numerically stable. The stability depends on the eigenvalues of the absorbing Markov chains under consideration. Though this is not really a disadvantage of *our* approach it might limit its practical applicability.

Henrik C. Bohnenkamp and Boudewijn R. Haverkort

- The main limitation of our approach is that the class of the processes which are apt to be solved by our method is rather small. Since the assumption that all processes have to synchronize over the same set of actions is very restrictive, it seems that only processes $P\|_S Q$ can profit from our approach.

The work presented here has to be seen as a first step in the development of compositional solution technique for SPA models. To overcome the structural restrictions we incur in this paper, we have decided to abandon the field of semi-Markov processes in favour of iterative computation schemes which allow the asymptotical exact derivation of steady-state probabilities. Our new developments are based on the iterative approximation of waiting time distributions of processes participating in a synchronization. This new ideas allow for the solution of processes which synchronize over *different* synchronization sets, which enriches the class of solvable processes enormously ([2]).

Nevertheless, we will adopt some ideas presented in this paper for our further work:

- We are still convinced that the distinction between timed anonymous and immediate visible actions in conjunction with timeless synchronization is a reasonable assumption. As is illustrated in [7] and [6], this type of synchronization is easily extendible to other, timed synchronization types.
- The use of phase-type distributions between the occurrence of synchronizations (the "no-timeouts-restriction") is a restriction that should be relaxed in the future. For the time being, anyway, it is a reasonable and easy to check restriction.
- We will continue to use explicit distributions to describe the behaviour of processes between synchronizations.
- Although the idea to derive local steady-state measures from SPA models is a restriction, since we want avoid the state space explosion problem, we are forced to continue to restrict ourselves here.

References

[1] Henrik Bohnenkamp and Boudewijn Haverkort. Semi-numerical solution of stochastic process algebra models. In Priami [16], pages 71–84.
[2] Henrik Bohnenkamp and Boudewijn Haverkort. Stochastic event structures for the decomposition of stochastic process algebra models. Submitted for presentation at the PAPM '99 workshop, Feb 1999.
[3] Stephen D. Brookes, C. A. R. Hoare, and A. W. Roscoe. A theory of communicating sequential processes. *Journal of the ACM*, 31(3):560–599, July 1984.
[4] Erhan Çinlar. *Introduction to Stochastic Processes*. Prentice Hall, Inc., Englewood Cliffs, New Jersey, 1975.
[5] Ricardo Fricks, Miklós Telek, Antonio Puliafito, and Kishor Trivedi. Markov renewal theory applied to performability evaluation. Technical Report TR-96/11, The Center for Advanced Computing and Communication, North Carolina State University, Raleigh, NC, USA, 1996. http://www.ece.ncsu.edu/cacc/tech_reports/abs/abs9611.html.

[6] H. Hermanns and J.-P. Katoen. Automated compositional Markov chain generation for a plain-old telephone system. *Science of Computer Programming*, Oct 1998. accepted for publication.

[7] Holger Hermanns. *Interactive Markov chains*. PhD thesis, Universität Erlangen-Nürnberg, Germany, 1998.

[8] Holger Hermanns and Michael Rettelbach. Syntax, Semantics, Equivalences, and Axioms for MTIPP. In Herzog and Rettelbach [9].

[9] Ulrich Herzog and Michael Rettelbach, editors. *Proceedings of the 2nd workshop on process algebras and performance modelling*. FAU Erlangen-Nürnberg, 1994.

[10] Jane Hillston. *A Compositional Approach to Performance Modelling*. PhD thesis, University of Edinburgh, 1994.

[11] Jane Hillston. The nature of synchronization. In Herzog and Rettelbach [9], pages 51–70.

[12] Jane Hillston. Exploiting structure in solution: Decomposing composed models. In Priami [16], pages 1–15.

[13] Ronald A. Howard. *Dynamic Probabilistic Systems.*, volume 2: Semimarkov and Decision Processes. John Wiley & Sons, Inc., New York, London, Syndney, Toronto, 1971.

[14] Vidyadhar G. Kulkarni. *Modeling and Analysis of Stochastic Systems*. Chapman & Hall, London, Glasgow, Weinheim, 1995.

[15] Raymond Marie, Andrew L. Reibman, and Kishor S. Trivedi. Transient analysis of acyclic Markov chains. *Performance Evaluation*, 7:175–194, 1987.

[16] Corrado Priami, editor. *Proceedings of the sixth workshop on process algebras and performance modelling*. Universita Degli Studi di Verona, 1998.

[17] A. V. Ramesh and K. Trivedi. Semi-numerical transient analysis of Markov models. In *Proceedings of the 33rd ACM Southeast Conference*, pages 13–23, 1995.

[18] Michael Rettelbach. *Stochastische Prozessalgebren mit zeitlosen Aktivitäten und probabilistischen Verzweigungen*. PhD thesis, Friedrich-Alexander-Universität Erlangen-Nürnberg, April 1996.

[19] Robin A. Sahner, Kishor S. Trivedi, and Antonio Puliafito. *Performance and Reliability Analysis of Computer Systems. An Example-Based Approach Using the SHARPE Software Package*. Kluwer Academic Publishers, Boston, London, Dordrecht, 1996.

Bisimulation Algorithms for Stochastic Process Algebras and Their BDD-Based Implementation[*]

Holger Hermanns[1] and Markus Siegle[2]

[1] Systems Validation Centre, FMG/CTIT, University of Twente,
P.O. Box 217, 7500 AE Enschede, The Netherlands
hermanns@cs.utwente.nl
[2] Informatik 7, IMMD, University of Erlangen-Nürnberg,
Martensstraße 3, 91058 Erlangen, Germany
siegle@informatik.uni-erlangen.de

Abstract. Stochastic process algebras have been introduced in order to enable compositional performance analysis. The size of the state space is a limiting factor, especially if the system consists of many cooperating components. To fight state space explosion, various proposals for compositional aggregation have been made. They rely on minimisation with respect to a congruence relation. This paper addresses the computational complexity of minimisation algorithms and explains how efficient, BDD-based data structures can be employed for this purpose.

1 Introduction

Compositional application of stochastic process algebras (SPA) is particularly successful if the system structure can be exploited during Markov chain generation. For this purpose, congruence relations have been developed which justify minimisation of components without touching behavioural properties. Examples of such relations are strong equivalence [22], (strong and weak) Markovian bisimilarity [16] and extended Markovian bisimilarity [2]. Minimised components can be plugged into the original model in order to circumvent the state space explosion problem. This strategy, known as *compositional aggregation* has been applied successfully to handle, for instance, a telephony system model [18]. Without compositional aggregation, the state space turned out to consist of more than 10 million states, while only 720 states were actually required using compositional aggregation.

Applicability of compositional aggregation relies on the existence of *algorithms* to compute minimised components. In this paper, we discuss efficient algorithms for strong equivalence, and (strong and weak) Markovian bisimulation. The algorithms are variants of well-known partition refinement algorithms [29,11,24]. They compute partitions of equivalent states of a given state space by iterative refinement of partitions, until a fixed point is reached.

---

[*] A preliminary version of this paper has been presented at the PAPM'98 workshop [20].

J.-P. Katoen (Ed.): ARTS'99, LNCS 1601, pp. 244–264, 1999.
© Springer-Verlag Berlin Heidelberg 1999

For the practical realisation of the algorithms we introduce BDD-based data structures. During the recent years, BDDs [6] have been shown to enable an efficient, *symbolic* encoding of state spaces. In particular, the parallel composition operator can be defined on BDDs in a way which avoids the usually observed exponential blow-up due to interleaving of causally independent transitions [10]. In this paper, we highlight how parallel composition and compositional aggregation can both be performed symbolically in a stochastic setting.

This paper is organised as follows: Sec. 2 contains the definition of the languages and of the bisimulation relations which we consider. Sec. 3 presents the basic bisimulation algorithm for non-stochastic process algebras. Sec. 4 and Sec. 5 do the same for the purely Markovian case and for the case where both Markovian and immediate transitions are allowed. In Sec. 6, we focus on BDDs and introduce a novel stochastic extension, DNBDDs. Furthermore, we show how algorithms for parallel composition and bisimulation can benefit from the use of these data structures. The paper concludes with Sec. 7.

2   Basic Definitions

This section introduces the scenario that will be considered in the sequel. We define a language and its operational semantics. In addition, we recall the notions of strong and weak Markovian bisimilarity. We refer to [16] for more details and motivating examples.

Definition 1. *Let Act be the set of valid action names and Pro the set of process names. We distinguish the action* i *as an internal, invisible activity. Let* $a \in Act$, P, $P_i \in \mathcal{L}$, $A \subseteq Act \setminus \{i\}$, *and* $X \in Pro$. *The set* $\mathcal{L}$ *of expressions consists of the following language elements:*

stop	inaction		
$a \,;\, P$	action prefix	$(a, \lambda) \,;\, P$	Markovian prefix
$P_1 \,[]\, P_2$	choice	$P_1 \,|[A]|\, P_2$	parallel composition
hide a in P	hiding	X	process instantiation

A set of process definitions (of the form $X := P$*) constitutes a process environment.*

The following operational semantic rules define a labelled transition system (LTS) containing action transitions, $\dashrightarrow^{a}\!\!\rightarrow$, and Markovian transitions, $\xrightarrow{a,\lambda}$. The semantic rule for synchronisation of Markovian transitions is parametric in a function ϕ determining the rate of synchronisation, in response to the fact that different synchronisation policies (minimum, maximum, product, ...) are possible. Note, however, that the apparent rate construction of PEPA [22] requires a function $\phi(P, Q, \lambda, \mu)$ instead.

$$\frac{}{a; P \xrightarrow{a} P} \qquad \frac{P \xrightarrow{a} P'}{P [] Q \xrightarrow{a} P'} \qquad \frac{Q \xrightarrow{a} Q'}{P [] Q \xrightarrow{a} Q'} \qquad \frac{P \xrightarrow{a,\lambda} P'}{P [] Q \xrightarrow{a,\lambda} P'} \qquad \frac{Q \xrightarrow{a,\lambda} Q'}{P [] Q \xrightarrow{a,\lambda} Q'} \qquad \frac{}{(a,\lambda); P \xrightarrow{a,\lambda} P}$$

$$\frac{P \xrightarrow{a} P'}{P |[A]| Q \xrightarrow{a} P' |[A]| Q} \; a \notin A \qquad \frac{Q \xrightarrow{a} Q'}{P |[A]| Q \xrightarrow{a} P |[A]| Q'} \; a \notin A \qquad \frac{P \xrightarrow{a} P' \quad Q \xrightarrow{a} Q'}{P |[A]| Q \xrightarrow{a} P' |[A]| Q'} \; a \in A$$

$$\frac{P \xrightarrow{a,\lambda} P'}{P |[A]| Q \xrightarrow{a,\lambda} P' |[A]| Q} \; a \notin A \qquad \frac{Q \xrightarrow{a,\lambda} Q'}{P |[A]| Q \xrightarrow{a,\lambda} P |[A]| Q'} \; a \notin A \qquad \frac{P \xrightarrow{a,\lambda} P' \quad Q \xrightarrow{a,\mu} Q'}{P |[A]| Q \xrightarrow{a,\phi(\lambda,\mu)} P' |[A]| Q'} \; a \in A$$

$$\frac{P \xrightarrow{a} P'}{\text{hide } a \text{ in } P \xrightarrow{i} \text{hide } a \text{ in } P'} \qquad \frac{P \xrightarrow{b} P'}{\text{hide } a \text{ in } P \xrightarrow{b} \text{hide } a \text{ in } P'} \; a \neq b \qquad \frac{P \xrightarrow{a} P'}{X \xrightarrow{a} P'} \; X := P$$

$$\frac{P \xrightarrow{a,\lambda} P'}{\text{hide } a \text{ in } P \xrightarrow{i,\lambda} \text{hide } a \text{ in } P'} \qquad \frac{P \xrightarrow{a,\lambda} P'}{\text{hide } b \text{ in } P \xrightarrow{a,\lambda} \text{hide } a \text{ in } P'} \; a \neq b \qquad \frac{P \xrightarrow{a,\lambda} P'}{X \xrightarrow{a,\lambda} P'} \; X := P$$

Strong and weak Markovian bisimilarity are defined in a variant of Larsen & Skou style [27], using the function $\gamma : \mathcal{L} \times Act \times 2^{\mathcal{L}} \mapsto \mathbb{R}$, often called the *cumulative rate*, defined as follows (we use $\{\!|$ and $|\!\}$ to denote multiset brackets):

$$\gamma(P, a, C) := \sum_{\lambda \in E(P,a,C)} \lambda, \text{ where } E(P, a, C) := \{\!| \, \lambda \mid P \xrightarrow{a,\lambda} P' \wedge P' \in C \, |\!\}.$$

Definition 2. *An equivalence relation* $\mathcal{B}$ *is a strong Markovian bisimulation, if* $(P, Q) \in \mathcal{B}$ *implies that*
(i) $P \dashrightarrow^{a} P'$ *implies* $Q \dashrightarrow^{a} Q'$, *for some* Q' *with* $(P', Q') \in \mathcal{B}$,
(ii) for all equivalence classes C *of* $\mathcal{B}$ *and all actions* a *it holds that*
$$\gamma(P, a, C) = \gamma(Q, a, C).$$
Two expressions P *and* Q *are strong Markovian bisimilar (written* $P \sim Q$*) if they are contained in a strong Markovian bisimulation.*

Weak bisimilarity is obtained from strong bisimilarity by basically replacing $\dashrightarrow^{a}$ with $\Longrightarrow^{a}$. Here, $\Longrightarrow^{a}$ denotes an observable a transition that is preceded and followed by an arbitrary number (including zero) of invisible activities, i.e. $\Longrightarrow^{a} := \xrightarrow{i^*} \xrightarrow{a} \xrightarrow{i^*}$. If a is internal ($a = i$), $\Longrightarrow^{a}$ abbreviates $\xrightarrow{i^*}$. As discussed in [16], the extension from strong to weak Markovian bisimilarity has to take into account the interplay of Markovian and immediate transitions. Priority of *internal* immediate transitions gives rise to the following definition [15].

Definition 3. *An equivalence relation* $\mathcal{B}$ *is a weak Markovian bisimulation, if* $(P, Q) \in \mathcal{B}$ *implies that*
(i) $P \Longrightarrow^{a} P'$ *implies* $Q \Longrightarrow^{a} Q'$, *for some* Q' *with* $(P', Q') \in \mathcal{B}$,
(ii) if $P \Longrightarrow^{i} P' \not\xrightarrow{i}$ *then there exists* Q' *such that* $Q \Longrightarrow^{i} Q' \not\xrightarrow{i}$, *and for all equivalence classes* C *of* $\mathcal{B}$ *and all actions* a
$$\gamma(P', a, C) = \gamma(Q', a, C).$$
Two expressions P *and* Q *are weak Markovian bisimilar (written* $P \approx Q$*) if they are contained in a weak Markovian bisimulation.*

In this definition, $P \not\xrightarrow{\quad i \quad}$ denotes that P does not possess an outgoing internal immediate transition. We call such a state a *tangible* state, as opposed to *vanishing* states which may internally and immediately evolve to another behaviour (denoted $P \dashrightarrow^{i}$).

It can be shown that strong Markovian bisimilarity is a congruence with respect to the language operators, provided that ϕ is distributive over summation of real values. The same result holds for weak Markovian bisimilarity except for congruence with respect to choice, see [15].

In the sequel, we consider two distinct sub-languages of $\mathcal{L}$. The first, $\mathcal{L}_1$, arises by disallowing Markovian prefix. This sub-language gives rise to an ordinary, non-stochastic process algebra, a subset of Basic LOTOS [3] where only action transitions appear in the underlying LTS. On this language, strong and weak Markovian bisimilarity coincide with Milner's non-stochastic strong and weak bisimilarity [28]. The complementary subset, $\mathcal{L}_2$, is obtained by disallowing the other prefix, action prefix. The resulting language coincides with MTIPP à la [17] (if ϕ is instantiated with multiplication), and both strong and weak Markovian bisimilarity coincide with Markovian bisimilarity on MTIPP. Note that Markovian bisimilarity agrees with Hillston's strong equivalence [22]. The semantics of $\mathcal{L}_2$ only contains Markovian transitions, and we will refer to such a transition system as a stochastic LTS (SLTS). The complete language, where both prefixes coexist involves both types of transitions, and we shall call such a transition system an extended SLTS (ESLTS).

3   Bisimulation Minimisation in Non-stochastic Process Algebras

In this section, we introduce the general idea of iterative partition refinement, working with the language $\mathcal{L}_1$. We aim to set the ground for an understanding of the following sections. To illustrate the key ideas, we use as an example a queueing system, consisting of an arrival process and a finite queue. First, we model an arrival process as an infinite sequence of incoming arrivals ($arrive$), each followed by an enqueue action (enq).

$$Arrival := arrive;\ enq;\ Arrival$$

The behaviour of the queue is described by a family of processes, one for each value of the current queue population.

$$Queue_0 := enq;\ Queue_1$$
$$Queue_i := enq;\ Queue_{i+1}\ []\ deq;\ Queue_{i-1} \qquad 1 \leq i < max$$
$$Queue_{max} := deq;\ Queue_{max-1}$$

These separate processes are combined by parallel composition in order to describe the whole queueing system. Hiding is used to internalise actions as soon as they are irrelevant for further synchronisation.

$$System := \textbf{hide}\ enq\ \textbf{in}\ \Big(Arrival\ ||[enq]||\ Queue_0 \Big)$$

Fig. 1 (top) shows the LTS associated with the $System$ specified above for the case that the maximum queue population is $max = 3$. The LTS has 8 states, the initial state being emphasised by a double circle. Fig 1 (bottom) shows an equivalent representation, minimised with respect to weak bisimilarity. The original state space is reduced by replacing every class of weakly bisimilar states by a single state.

Most algorithms for computing bisimilarity require a *finite* state space. Traditionally, they follow an iterative refinement scheme [29,11,24]. This means that starting

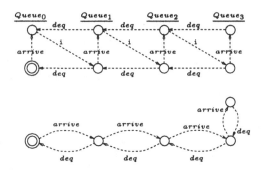

Fig. 1. LTS of the queueing system example, before and after applying weak bisimilarity

from an initial partition of the state space which consists of a single class (containing all states), classes are refined until the obtained partition corresponds to a bisimulation equivalence. The result thus obtained is the largest existing bisimulation, in a sense the "best" such bisimulation, since it has a minimal number of equivalence classes.

For the refinement of a partition, the notion of a "splitter" is very important. A splitter is a pair (a, C_{spl}), consisting of an action a and a class C_{spl}. During refinement, a class C is split with respect to a splitter, which means that subclasses C^+ and C^- are computed, such that subclass C^+ contains all those states from C which can perform an a-transition leading to class C_{spl}, and C^- contains all remaining states.

In the following, an algorithm for strong bisimulation is presented. The algorithm uses a dynamic set of splitters, denoted $Splitters$. Note that here we only present a basic version of the algorithm which can be optimised in many ways [11,29]. By a deliberate treatment of splitters, it is possible to obtain a time complexity $\mathcal{O}(m \log n)$, where n is the number of states and m is the number of transitions.

1. **Initialisation**
   $Partition := \{S\}$
   /* the initial partition consists of only one class which contains *all* states */
   $Splitters := Act \times Partition$
   /* all pairs of actions and classes have to be considered as splitters */
2. **Main loop**
   while $(Splitters \neq \emptyset)$
       choose splitter $(a, C_{spl}) \in Splitters$
       forall $C \in Partition$ $split(C, a, C_{spl}, Partition, Splitters)$
       /* all classes (including C_{spl} itself) are split */
       $Splitters := Splitters - (a, C_{spl})$
       /* the processed splitter is removed from the splitter set */

It remains to specify the procedure $split$. Its task is to split a class C, using (a, C_{spl}) as a splitter. If splitting actually takes place, the input class C is split into subclasses C^+ and C^-.

procedure $split(C, a, C_{spl}, Partition, Splitters)$
    $C^+ := \{P \mid P \in C \wedge \exists Q : (P \dashrightarrow^{a} Q \wedge Q \in C_{spl})\}$

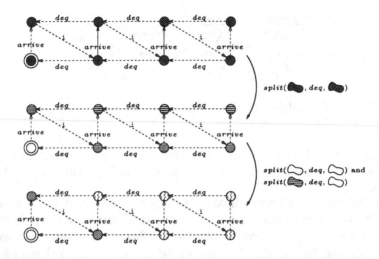

Fig. 2. Initialisation, first and second refinement step of the algorithm

```
/* the subclass C⁺ is computed */
if (C⁺ ≠ C ∧ C⁺ ≠ ∅)
    /* only continue if class C actually needs to be split */
    C⁻ := C − C⁺
    /* C⁻ is the complement of C⁺ with respect to C */
    Partition := Partition ∪ {C⁺, C⁻} − {C}
    Splitters := Splitters ∪ (Act × {C⁺, C⁻}) − Act × {C}
    /* the partition and the splitter set are updated */
```

We illustrate the algorithm by means of the above queueing example. In fact, we shall compute *weak* instead of strong bisimilarity. The only change that is necessarry for this purpose concerns the transition relation $\xrightarrow{a}$ used in procedure *split*, which is replaced by the weak relation $\overset{\ell}{\Longrightarrow}$. However, this requires the computation of $\overset{\ell}{\Longrightarrow}$ during the initialisation phase. As a matter of fact, the computation of $\overset{\ell}{\Longrightarrow}$ dominates the complexity of partition refinement, basically because the reflexive and transitive closure $\xrightarrow{i^*}$ of internal moves has to be computed in order to build the weak transition relation. The usual way of computing a transitive closure has cubic complexity. (Some slight improvements are known for this task, see for instance [9]. In any case, this is the computationally expensive part.)

The LTS is depicted in Fig. 2 (top) where we have used a particular shading of states in order to visualize the algorithm. In the beginning all states are assumed to be equivalent, and hence, all states are shaded with the same pattern. We use ● to refer to the set of states shaded like ●. So, *Partition* := {●}, and *Splitters* is initialised accordingly.

After computing the weak transition relation ⇢, we start partition refinement by choosing a splitter, say (*deq*, ●) and computing *split*(●, *deq*, ●). The initial state has no possibility to perform a $\overset{deq}{\Longrightarrow}$ transition in contrast to all other states. Therefore ●⁺ = ◒ and ●⁻ = ○. As a consequence, *Partition* becomes {○, ◒} and

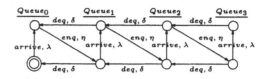

Fig. 3. Semantic model of the Markovian queueing system, isomorphic to a CTMC

new splitters are added to *Splitters* while the currently processed one, $(deq, \clubsuit)$, is removed. This completes the first iteration and leads to the situation depicted in Fig. 2 (middle).

By choosing a different splitter, say $(deq, \oslash)$, we start the next iteration. Since *Partition* now contains two elements, we compute $split(\oslash, deq, \oslash)$ and $split(\Leftrightarrow, deq, \oslash)$. $\oslash$ cannot be split any further, while splitting of $\Leftrightarrow$ returns $\Leftrightarrow^+ = \Leftrightarrow$ and $\Leftrightarrow^- = \oslash$. Updating *Partition* to $\{\oslash, \Leftrightarrow, \oslash\}$ and adding new splitters leads to the situation depicted in Fig. 2 (bottom). Subsequent iterations of the algorithm will divide $\oslash$ further, leading to five partitions in total. The algorithm terminates once the set *Splitters* is empty.

4   The Markovian Case

In this section, we consider the MTIPP-style language $\mathcal{L}_2$ where *all* actions are associated with a delay which is an exponentially distributed random variable. In addition, MTIPP instantiates ϕ with the product of rates, for reasons discussed (for instance) in [16]. The semantic model of a process from the language $\mathcal{L}_2$ is an SLTS, only containing transitions of the form $\xrightarrow{a,\lambda}$.

We return to our example of a queueing system. The arrival process is now modelled as follows, employing the Markovian action prefix:
$$Arrival := (arrive, \lambda); (enq, 1); Arrival$$
Action *arrive* occurs with rate λ, whereas for action *enq* we specified the (passive) rate 1, the neutral element of multiplication. The queue process determines the actual rate of *enq*, occuring as a result of synchronisation via *enq*.

$$Queue_0 := (enq, \eta); Queue_1$$
$$Queue_i := (enq, \eta); Queue_{i+1} \; [] \; (deq, \delta); Queue_{i-1} \qquad 1 \le i < max$$
$$Queue_{max} := (deq, \delta); Queue_{max-1}$$

Fig. 3 depicts the SLTS obtained from the parallel composition of processes *Arrival* and $Queue_0$ synchronised over action *enq*.

From a given SLTS one can immediately construct a continuous time Markov chain (CTMC [25]). The arcs of the CTMC are given by the union of all the transitions joining the LTS nodes (regardless of their labels), and the transition rate is the sum of the individual rates. This is justified by the properties of the exponential distribution, in particular the fact that the minimum of two exponentially distributed random variables with rates λ_1, λ_2 is again exponentially distributed with rate $\lambda_1 + \lambda_2$. Transitions leading back to the same node (loops) can be neglected, since they would have no effect on the balance equations of the CTMC. The CTMC carries only the (cumulated) rate labels.

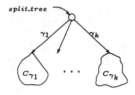

Fig. 4. *split_tree* used by procedure *split'*

Performance measures can then be derived by calculating the steady-state or transient state probabilities of the CTMC.

As already mentioned, both strong and weak Markovian bisimilarity coincide with Markovian bisimilarity à la MTIPP on this language. The technical reason is that the first clauses of Definition 2 and Definition 3 are irrelevant, while the respective second clauses both boil down to $\gamma(P, a, C) = \gamma(Q, a, C)$ for all actions a and classes C. This equivalence notion has a direct correspondence to the notion of *lumpability* on CTMCs [25,22]. As a consequence, the algorithm which we develop can be used to efficiently compute *lumpable partitions* of an SPA description (as well as a CTMC in isolation). The basic bisimulation algorithm is the same as in Sec. 3, only the procedure *split* needs to be modified. Procedure *split'* now uses a data structure *split_tree* which is shown in Fig. 4. It essentially sorts states according to their γ-values. During refinement, when a class C is split by means of a splitter (a, C_{spl}), possibly more than two subclasses $C_{\gamma_1}, C_{\gamma_2}, \ldots, C_{\gamma_k}$ will be generated. Input class C is split such that the cumulative rate $\gamma(P, a, C_{spl}) = \gamma_j$ is the same for all the states P belonging to the same subclass C_{γ_j}, a leaf of the *split_tree*.

procedure *split'*$(C, a, C_{spl}, Partition, Splitters)$
    forall $P \in C$
        $\gamma := \gamma(P, a, C_{spl})$
        /* the cumulative rate from state P to C_{spl} is computed */
        $insert(split\_tree, P, \gamma)$
        /* state P is inserted into the *split_tree* */
    /* now, *split_tree* contains k leaves $C_{\gamma_1}, \ldots, C_{\gamma_k}$ */
    if $(k > 1)$
        /* only continue if C has been split into $k > 1$ subclasses */
        $Partition := Partition \cup \{C_{\gamma_1}, C_{\gamma_2}, \ldots, C_{\gamma_k}\} - \{C\}$
        $Splitters := Splitters \cup (Act \times \{C_{\gamma_1}, C_{\gamma_2}, \ldots, C_{\gamma_k}\}) - Act \times \{C\}$
        /* the partition and the splitter set are updated */

In the **forall** loop of procedure *split'*, the cumulative rate γ is computed for every state P in class C, and state P is inserted into the *split_tree* such that states with the same cumulative rate belong to the same leaf (procedure *insert*). The *split_tree* has k leaves, i.e. k different values of γ have appeared. If splitting has taken place (i.e. if $k > 1$), the partition must be refined and the set of splitters has to be updated.

Theorem 1. *The above algorithm computes Markovian bisimilarity on a given SLTS. It can be implemented such that the time complexity is of order $\mathcal{O}(m \log n)$ and the space complexity is of order $\mathcal{O}(m + n)$, where n is the number of states and m is the number of transitions.*

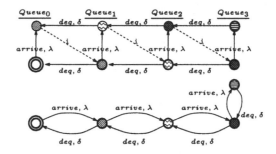

Fig. 5. ESLTS of the queueing system example, before and after applying weak Markovian bisimilarity

The detailed proof is given in [15]. As in [23], the crucial point to obtain the time complexity of non-stochastic strong bisimilarity is that all but one of the largest subclasses C_{γ_i} are actually inserted into the set *Splitters* of potential splitters. (No assumptions about the time complexity of arithmetic operations are required).

5   Markovian and Immediate Actions

In this section, we consider the complete language $\mathcal{L}$ where both immediate and Markovian actions coexist. Again, we return to our queueing system example. In the arrival process, action *arrive* has an exponential delay, whereas action *enq* is immediate.

$$Arrival := (arrive, \lambda); enq; Arrival$$

The specification of the Queue is again modified with respect to Sec. 3, i.e. action *enq* is immediate and action *deq* has exponential delay.

$$Queue_0 := enq; Queue_1$$
$$Queue_i := enq; Queue_{i+1} \,[]\, (deq, \delta); Queue_{i-1} \qquad 1 \le i < max$$
$$Queue_{max} := (deq, \delta); Queue_{max-1}$$

The overall system is again given by the composition of *Arrival* and $Queue_0$, where *enq* is hidden after synchronisation. The semantic model of such a specification from the language $\mathcal{L}$ is an ESLTS with two types of transitions: Markovian transitions $\longrightarrow$, and action transitions $\dashrightarrow$. Fig. 5 (top) depicts the ESLTS for the example queueing system. In the context of our complete language $\mathcal{L}$, the notion of weak Markovian bisimilarity is central for associating a CTMC to a given specification. The reason is that immediate transitions do not have a counterpart on the level of the CTMC. Weak Markovian bisimilarity justifies to eliminate *internal* immediate transitions such that a SLTS, and hence an (action labelled) CTMC results from the quotient transition system (the transition system obtained by representing each equivalence class by a single state). The details of this strategy are described in [18,15]. In order to illustrate how the relation can be used to achieve this, the equivalence classes of weak Markovian bisimilarity are indicated in Fig. 5 (bottom). Note, however, that this effect relies on abstraction of immediate actions before applying weak Markovian bisimilarity. Furthermore, a unique CTMC exists only if nondeterminism is absent after applying weak Markovian bisimilarity. The absence of nondetermininsm is easy to check on the quotient transition system.

Accordingly, an algorithm to compute weak Markovian bisimilarity is central for deriving the quotient transition system, and hence the CTMC. (In principle, the CTMC could also be derived from a specification by purely syntactic transformations, using the complete axiomatisation from [19].) Our algorithm is based on the one given in the previous section, but proceeds in a different way. The technical reason is that, similar to the computation of branching bisimilarity [12], refining a partition by means of a splitter might cause that the refinement with respect to already processed splitters has to be repeated for this partition.[1] This is a crucial difference with respect to the algorithms we have described before, for which termination is only guaranteed because refinement with respect to an already processed splitter is never repeated for that splitter. For branching bisimilarity, the problem is tackled in [13], by introducing a distinct treatment of vanishing states. Bouali has adopted this machinery to compute also weak bisimilarity [4]. Indeed our algorithm is based on this adaption.

We use $P \searrow^{i} P'$ to indicate that P may internally and immediately evolve to a tangible state P', i.e. where no further internal immediate transition is possible. Formally, $P \searrow^{i} P'$ iff $P \dashrightarrow^{i} P'$ for some P' with $P' \not\xrightarrow{i}$. If there is at least one tangible state P' that can be reached from P via a (possibly empty) sequence of internal immediate transitions we use the predicate $P \searrow^{i}$. Note that $P \searrow^{i}$ whenever P is tangible. The converse situation, where a (vanishing) state P has no possibility to internally and immediately evolve to a tangible state, is denoted $P \nsearrow^{i}$. We refer to such states as *divergent* states, as opposed to *convergent* states (satisfying $P \searrow^{i}$). For the presentation of the algorithm, we first restrict to transition systems that do not contain divergent states. This is done to simplify the exposition, the general case is discussed afterwards. Restricted to divergence-free ESLTS, the basic algorithm is as follows.

1. **Initialisation** as before in Sec. 3. In addition, weak transitions $\dashrightarrow$ are computed from $\dashrightarrow$.
2. **Main loop**

    while $(Splitters \neq \emptyset)$
        choose splitter (a, C_{spl})
        forall $C \in Partition$ $split(C, a, C_{spl}, Partition, Splitters)$
        /* all classes are split with respect to weak transitions */
        forall $C \in Partition$ $split''(C, a, C_{spl}, Partition, Splitters)$
        /* all classes are split with respect to Markovian transitions */
        $Splitters := Splitters - (a, C_{spl})$
        /* the processed splitter is removed from the splitter set */

The main loop contains two different procedures, *split* and *split''* requiring further explanation. The first, $split(C, a, C_{spl}, Partition, Splitters)$, refines with respect to clause *(i)* of Definition 3. This is achieved using the procedure *split* of Section 3, but applied on weak transitions, as in the example of Sec. 3. The second procedure, $split''(C, a, C_{spl}, Partition, Splitters)$, is more complicated. It refines with respect to the second clause of Definition 3. The details are given below.

---

[1] In terms of [13], stability is not inherited under refinement.

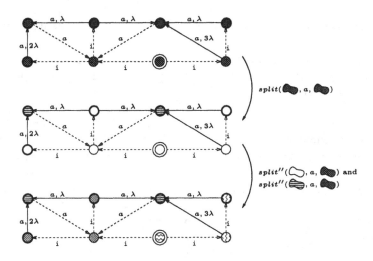

Fig. 6. Initialisation and first refinement step of the algorithm

procedure $split''(C, a, C_{spl}, Partition, Splitters)$

   forall $P \in C \land P \not\xrightarrow{i} $
      /* P is a tangible state */
      $\gamma := \gamma(P, a, C_{spl})$
      /* the cumulative rate to C_{spl} is computed */
      $insert(split\_tree, P, \gamma)$
      /* state P is inserted into the $split\_tree$ */
   /* now, $split\_tree$ contains k leaves $C_{\gamma_1}, \ldots, C_{\gamma_k}$ */

   forall $P \in C \land P \dashrightarrow^{i} $
      /* P is a vanishing state */
      if $(\exists \gamma_j : P \overset{i}{\searrow} Q \Rightarrow Q \in C_{\gamma_j})$
         /* P can internally and immediately reach tangible states of class C_{γ_j} only */
         $insert(split\_tree, P, \gamma_j)$
   $Partition := Partition \cup \{C_{\gamma_1}, C_{\gamma_2}, \ldots, C_{\gamma_k}\} - \{C\}$
   $Splitters := Splitters \cup (Act \times \{C_{\gamma_1}, C_{\gamma_2}, \ldots, C_{\gamma_k}\}) - Act \times \{C\}$
   /* the partition and the splitter set are updated */
   if $(C \neq \bigcup_1^k C_{\gamma_j})$
      /* some vanishing states have not been covered yet */
      $Partition := Partition \cup \{C - \bigcup_1^k C_{\gamma_j}\}$
      $Splitters := Splitters \cup (Act \times \{C - \bigcup_1^k C_{\gamma_j}\})$
      /* all remaining vanishing states form a new class, since they can internally
         and immediately evolve to tangible states belonging to different classes */

The reader is invited to check the result depicted in Fig. 5 by means of this algorithm. In order to facilitate the inspection, tangible states are highlighted by bold circles in the figure. In order to illustrate the algorithm on a nontrivial example, where all the distinctions between different types of vanishing states matter, we consider a different example, depicted in Fig. 6 (top).

The initialisation proceeds as usual, after computing the weak transition relation ⇢⇢, we start the algorithm by choosing a splitter, say $(a, \bullet)$ and computing $split(\bullet, a, \bullet)$. Two states may perform a $\cdots\!\stackrel{a}{\cdots}\!\rightarrow$ transition in contrast to all other states. Therefore $\bullet^{+} = \Longleftrightarrow$ and $\bullet^{-} = \circlearrowright$. *Partition* and *Splitters* are updated accordingly, leading to the situation depicted in Fig. 6 (middle).

The subsequent invocation of $split''(\circlearrowright, a, \bullet)$ is most interesting (as opposed to $split''(\Longleftrightarrow, a, \bullet)$). First, the three tangible markings (indicated by bold circles) in class $\circlearrowright$ are inserted into *split_tree*, according to their cumulative rates of moving into (former) class $\bullet$. This leads to a tree with two leaves, $C_{2\lambda}$ and C_λ, containing two, respectively one state. Now the three remaining vanishing states are treated: The righmost vanishing states can internally and immediately evolve only to tangible states of class C_λ (note that according to Definition 3 the transition $\xrightarrow{a, 3\lambda}$ is irrelevant since it originates in a vanishing state). For the same reason, the left vanishing state is inserted into class $C_{2\lambda}$. Only the initial state is not covered yet, since it has an internal, nondeterministic choice of behaving as a member of either of the classes. Hence, this state forms a new class, $\Longleftrightarrow$. In total, $split''(\circlearrowright, a, \bullet)$ has split $\circlearrowright$ into $\Longleftrightarrow$, $\Longleftrightarrow$ (representing $C_{2\lambda}$ and C_λ), and $\Longleftrightarrow$, leading to the situation depicted in Fig. 6 (bottom)(the *Partition* and *Splitters* are updated accordingly). This situation incidentally coincides with the classes of weak Markovian bisimilarity, because subsequent refinement steps do not reveal any distinction in one of these four classes. The algorithm terminates once the set *Splitters* is emptied.

To overcome the restriction to divergence-free ESLTS, a few modifications in the initialisation and the main loop of the algorithm are necessary. Algorithmically, the second clause of Definition 3 needs not to be checked at all for divergent states, while the first clause is still relevant. Furthermore, the second clause of Definition 3 implies that no convergent state is weakly Markovian bisimilar to a divergent state. These facts justify to (1) separate convergent and divergent states during inititalisation, and to (2) exclude the refinement of classes of divergent states by means of procedure $split''$ in the main loop of the algorithm. Recall that $split''$ implements refinement with respect to the second clause of Definition 3. So, for the general case, the algorithm becomes as follows, where $split$ and $split''$ are as before:

1. **Initialisation**
   Weak transitions ⇢⇢ are computed from ⇢⇢.
   $Con := \{\{P \in S \mid P \stackrel{i}{\searrow}\}\}$
   $Div := \{\{P \in S \mid P \stackrel{i}{\nearrow}\}\}$
   /* the initial partition consists of two disjoint classes */
   $Splitters := Act \times (Con \cup Div)$
   /* all pairs of actions and classes have to be considered as splitters */
2. **Main loop**
   while($Splitters \neq \emptyset$)
       choose splitter (a, C_{spl})
       forall $C \in Con$ $split(C, a, C_{spl}, Con, Splitters)$
       /* all classes of convergent states are split with respect to weak transitions */
       forall $C \in Div$ $split(C, a, C_{spl}, Div, Splitters)$
       /* all classes of divergent states are split with respect to weak transitions */

forall $C \in Con$ $split''(C, a, C_{spl}, Con, Splitters)$
/* only the classes of convergent states are split with respect to Markovian transitions */
$Splitters := Splitters - (a, C_{spl})$
/* the processed splitter is removed from the splitter set */

An implementation of this algorithm, based on [23,13,4,1] has a cubic time complexity.

Theorem 2. *The above algorithm computes weak Markovian bisimilarity on a given ESLTS. It can be implemented such that it requires $\mathcal{O}(n^3)$ time and $\mathcal{O}(n^2)$ space, where n is the number of states.*

The proof is given in [15], for the divergence-free as well as the general case. It is worth pointing out that non-stochastic weak bisimulation essentially has the same complexity, due to the fact that a transitive closure operation is needed to compute weak transitions in either case.

6 Symbolic Representation with BDDs

In this section, we discuss details of a BDD-based implementation of the above algorithms. BDDs are specific representations of Boolean functions and have recently gained remarkable attention as efficient encodings of very large state spaces. In a process algebraic context, this efficiency is mainly due to the fact that the parallel composition operator can be implemented on BDDs in such a way that the size of the data structure only grows linearly in the number of parallel components, especially for loosely coupled components. This compares favourably to the exponential growth caused by the usual operational semantics, due to the interleaving of causally independent transitions. We explain how LTSs can be encoded as BDDs and illustrate a way to include the rate information of (E)SLTS into this data structure and the bisimulation algorithms. To complete the picture, we also discuss parallel composition on BDDs.

6.1 Binary Decision Diagrams and the Encoding of LTSs

A Binary Decision Diagram (BDD) [6] is a symbolic representation of a Boolean function $f : \{0,1\}^n \rightarrow \{0,1\}$. Its graphical interpretation is a rooted directed acyclic graph, essentially a collapsed binary decision tree in which isomorphic subtrees are merged and "don't care" nodes are skipped (a node is called "don't care" if the truth value of the corresponding variable is irrelevant for the truth value of the overall function). It is known that BDDs provide a canonical representation for Boolean functions, assuming a fixed ordering of the Boolean variables. Algorithms for BDD construction from a Boolean expression and for performing Boolean operations (and, or, not, ...) on BDD arguments all follow a recursive scheme.

A LTS can be represented symbolically by a BDD. The idea is to encode states and actions by Boolean vectors (for the moment, we look at the non-stochastic case where it is not necessary to consider information about transition rates). One transition of the LTS then corresponds to a conjunction of $n_a + 2n_s$ literals (a literal is either a Boolean

$$
\begin{array}{ll}
 & a_1, a_2, s_1, t_1, s_2, t_2 \\
0 \xrightarrow{enq} 1 \rightarrow & (0, 1, 0, 0, 0, 1) \\
1 \xrightarrow{enq} 2 \rightarrow & (0, 1, 0, 1, 1, 0) \\
2 \xrightarrow{enq} 3 \rightarrow & (0, 1, 1, 1, 0, 1) \\
1 \xrightarrow{deq} 0 \rightarrow & (1, 0, 0, 0, 1, 0) \\
2 \xrightarrow{deq} 1 \rightarrow & (1, 0, 1, 0, 0, 1) \\
3 \xrightarrow{deq} 2 \rightarrow & (1, 0, 1, 1, 1, 0)
\end{array}
$$

Fig. 7. LTS, transition encoding and corresponding BDD for $Queue_0$

variable or the negation of a Boolean variable) $\bigwedge_{i=1}^{n_a} a_i \bigwedge_{j=1}^{n_s} s_j \bigwedge_{j=1}^{n_s} t_j$, where literals $a_1 \ldots a_{n_a}$ encode the action, $s_1 \ldots s_{n_s}$ identify the source state and $t_1 \ldots t_{n_s}$ the target state of the transition (we assume that the number of distinct actions to be encoded is between 2^{n_a-1} and $2^{n_a} + 1$, so that n_a bits are suitable to encode them, and similarly for the number of states). The overall LTS corresponds to the disjunction of the terms for the individual transitions. The size of a BDD is highly dependent on the chosen variable ordering. In the context of transition systems, experience has shown that the following variable ordering yields small BDD sizes [10]:
$$ a_1 < \ldots < a_{n_a} < s_1 < t_1 < s_2 < t_2 < \ldots < s_{n_s} < t_{n_s} $$
i.e. the variables encoding the action come first, followed by the variables for source and target state interleaved. In particular, this ordering is advantageous in view of the parallel composition operator discussed below.

To illustrate the encoding, Fig. 7 shows the LTS corresponding to the $Queue_0$ process from Sec. 3 (assuming, again, that $max = 3$), the way transitions are encoded and the resulting BDD (in the graphical representation of a BDD, one-edges are drawn solid, zero-edges dashed, and for reasons of simplicity, the terminal false-node and its adjacent edges are omitted). Since there are only two different actions (enq and deq), one bit would be enough to encode the action. However, in view of action $arrive$ which will be needed for process $Arrival$, we use two bits to encode the action, i.e. $n_a = 2$. The LTS has four states, therefore two bits are needed to represent the state, i.e. $n_s = 2$. In the BDD, one can observe the interleaving of the Boolean variables for the source and target state.

The parallel composition operator can be realised directly on the BDD representation of the two operand processes. Consider the parallel composition of two processes, $P = P_1 \,|[A]|\, P_2$, and assume that the BDDs which correspond to processes P_1 and P_2 have already been generated and are denoted $\mathcal{P}_1$ and $\mathcal{P}_2$. The set A can also be coded as a BDD, namely $\mathcal{A}$. The BDD $\mathcal{P}$ which corresponds to the resulting process P can then be written as a Boolean expression:
$$
\begin{aligned}
\mathcal{P} = \ & (\mathcal{P}_1 \wedge \mathcal{A}) \wedge (\mathcal{P}_2 \wedge \mathcal{A}) \\
& \vee (\mathcal{P}_1 \wedge \overline{\mathcal{A}} \wedge Stab_{P_2}) \\
& \vee (\mathcal{P}_2 \wedge \overline{\mathcal{A}} \wedge Stab_{P_1})
\end{aligned}
$$

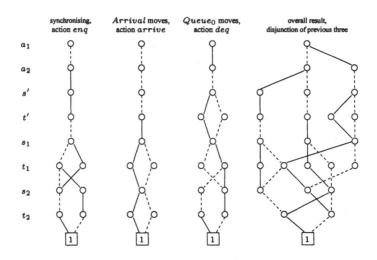

Fig. 8. Intermediate and final BDD results for parallel composition of *Arrival* and $Queue_0$

The term on the first line is for the synchronising actions in which both P_1 and P_2 participate. The term on the second (third) line is for those actions which P_1 (P_2) performs independently of P_2 (P_1) — these actions are all from the complement of A. The meaning of $Stab_{P_2}$ ($Stab_{P_1}$) is a BDD which expresses stability of the non-moving partner of the parallel composition, i.e. the fact that the source state of process P_2 (P_1) equals its target state.

We illustrate parallel composition by means of our queueing example. Fig. 8 shows the intermediate and final BDDs when performing BDD-based parallel composition of processes *Arrival* and $Queue_0$. In the second (third) BDD one can observe the parts which express stability of process $Queue_0$ (*Arrival*). Even in this small example we observe the general tendency that the size of the resulting BDD (25 nodes, including the terminal false-node not shown) is in the order of the sum of the sizes of the two partner BDDs (15 nodes for $Queue_0$ and 8 nodes for *Arrival*, cf. Fig. 7 and Fig. 9). Thus, using BDD-based parallel composition, the typically observed exponential growth of memory requirements can be avoided.

The BDD resulting from the parallel composition, $\mathcal{P}$, describes all transitions which are possible in the product space of the two partner processes. Given a pair of initial states for P_1 and P_2, only part of the product space may be reachable due to synchronisation constraints. Reachability analysis can be performed on the BDD representation, restricting $\mathcal{P}$ to those transitions which originate in reachable states.

6.2 Symbolic Bisimulation

The basic bisimulation algorithm of Sec. 3 and its various optimisations can be realised efficiently using BDD-based data structures. For convenience, the transition system is represented not by a single BDD, but by a set of BDDs $T_a(s,t)$, one for each action a

(here, s and t denote vectors of Boolean variables of length n_s). The current partition is stored as a set of BDDs $\{C_1(s), C_2(s), \ldots\}$, one for each class. When class C is split into subclasses C^+ and C^- during execution of procedure *split*, those subclasses are also represented by BDDs. The dynamic set of splitters, *Splitters*, is realised as a pointer structure. The computation of the subclass C^+ in procedure *split* is formulated as a Boolean expression on BDD arguments

$$C^+(s) := C(s) \wedge \exists\, t: \ (T_a(s, t) \wedge C_{spl}(t))$$

where the existential quantification is also performed on BDDs.

6.3   BDDs with Rate Information

Clearly, pure BDDs are not capable of representing the numerical information about the transition rates of a *stochastic* LTS. In the literature, several modifications and augmentations of the BDD data structure have been proposed for representing functions of the type $f : \{0, 1\}^n \to \mathbb{R}$. Most prominent among these are multi-terminal BDDs [8], edge-valued BDDs [26] and Binary Moment Diagrams (BMD) [7]. In all of these approaches, the basic BDD structure is modified and the efficiency of the data structure, due to the sharing of isomorphic subtrees, may be diminished. Based on this observation, we developed a different approach which we call decision-node BDD (DNBDD) [30]. The distinguishing feature of DNBDDs is that the basic BDD structure remains completely untouched when moving from an LTS encoding to an SLTS encoding. The additional rate information is attached to specific edges of this BDD in an orthogonal fashion.

In a BDD representing a LTS, a *path* p from the root to the terminal true-node corresponds to 2^k transitions of the transition system, where k is the number of "don't care" variables on that path (for an example of a "don't care" see Fig. 10 below). Since these transitions are labelled by 2^k distinct rates, we need to assign a rate list of length 2^k to that path. Let $rates(p)$ denote a list of real values $(\lambda_0, \ldots, \lambda_{2^k-1})$, where k is the number of "don't cares" on path p. The correspondence between transitions and individual rates of such a list is implicitly given by the valuation of the encoding of the transitions on "don't care" nodes, which ranges from 0 to $2^k - 1$.

For the practical realisation of this concept, and in order to make our representation canonical, we must answer the question of where to store the rate lists. This leads to the following consideration: Instead of characterising a path by all its nodes, we observe that a path is fully characterised by its *decision nodes*.

Definition 4. *A decision node is a non-terminal BDD node whose successor nodes are both different from the terminal false-node. A decision node BDD (DNBDD) is a BDD enhanced by a function*

$$rates : Paths \to (\mathbb{R})^+$$

where Paths is the set of paths from the root node to the terminal true-node (and $(\mathbb{R})^+$ is the set of finite lists of real values), such that for any such path p,

$$rates(p) \in (\mathbb{R})^{2^k}$$

if k is the number of "don't cares" on path p. The list $rates(p) = (\lambda_0, \ldots, \lambda_{2^k-1})$ is attached to the outgoing edge of the last decision node on path p, i.e. the decision node nearest to the terminal true-node.

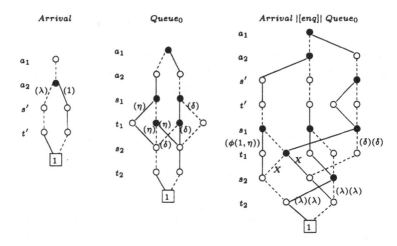

Fig. 9. DNBDDs for the queueing example (shorthand notation: $X = (\phi(1, \eta))(\delta)(\delta)$)

To illustrate the DNBDD concept, we return to our queueing example. Fig. 9 shows the DNBDDs associated with processes $Arrival$, $Queue_0$ and $Arrival \|[enq]\| Queue_0$ (in the figure, decision nodes are drawn black). On the left, rates λ and 1 are attached to the outgoing edges of the (single) decision node of the BDD. In the middle, six individual rates are attached to the appropriate edges. On the right hand side, up to three rate lists, each consisting of a single rate, are attached to BDD edges. For instance, the rate lists $(\delta)(\delta)$ specify the rates of the two transitions encoded as bitstrings 10110010 and 10000010 whose paths share the last decision node.

In the case where several rate lists are attached to the same BDD edge (because several paths share their last decision node) it is important to preserve the one-to-one mapping between paths and rate lists. This could simply be accomplished by the lexicographical ordering of paths. For algorithmic reasons, however, we use a so-called rate tree, an unbalanced binary tree which makes it possible to access rate lists during recursive descent through the BDD [30]. In our current implementation of DNBDDs, the rate tree is implemented as illustrated in Fig. 10. This figure (left) shows the encoding of the transitions of some SLTS, each of the transition being associated with a rate. The first two transitions share the same path, a path which has a "don't care" in the Boolean variable s. Therefore, the corresponding rate list (λ_0, λ_1) has length two. The other four paths do not have any "don't care" variables, they each correspond to exactly one transition of the SLTS and the corresponding rate lists have length one. The latter four paths all share their last decision node. Therefore each of the outgoing edges of that decision node carries two rate lists (of length one). The rate tree is built as a separate data structure from the BDD. However, its internal nodes and the rate lists are associated with the decision nodes of the BDD as indicated in Fig. 10 (right). The rate tree is manipulated by an appropriate extension of the procedures which manipulate the BDD. This implementation of the rate tree has the drawback that it requires the explicit

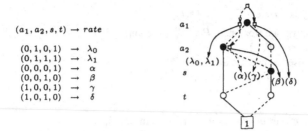

$$
\begin{array}{ccc}
(a_1,a_2,s,t) & \to & rate \\
\\
(0,1,0,1) & \to & \lambda_0 \\
(0,1,1,1) & \to & \lambda_1 \\
(0,0,0,1) & \to & \alpha \\
(0,0,1,0) & \to & \beta \\
(1,0,0,1) & \to & \gamma \\
(1,0,1,0) & \to & \delta
\end{array}
$$

Fig. 10. Encoded transitions with rates, and corresponding DNBDD with rate tree

storage of one rate for each encoded transition which may cause considerable overhead. We are currently investigating this issue.[2]

Parallel composition of two SLTSs based on their symbolic representation follows the same basic algorithm as sketched in Sec. 6.1. Similar to the fact that the operational rules in Sec. 2 are parametric in the synchronisation policy, the concept of DNBDDs is not bound to a particular choice of function ϕ, any arithmetic expression of the two individual rates can be employed.

6.4 Symbolic Markovian Bisimulation

We now discuss aspects of a DNBDD-based algorithm which computes Markovian bisimulation on SLTSs. The basic bisimulation algorithm is the same as in Sec. 4, only the procedure $split'$ needs to be adapted. When using DNBDDs, the cumulative rate of action a from state P to class C_{spl} is computed in the following way: We compute $T_{P \xrightarrow{a} C_{spl}}(s,t)$, the DNBDD which represents all a-transitions from state P to states from class C_{spl}. It can be obtained by restricting $T_a(s,t)$ to the single source state P and to target states from class C_{spl} (again, the transition relation is represented by individual DNBDDs $T_a(s,t)$, one for every action a, and class C is represented by a BDD $C(t)$):

$$
T_{P \xrightarrow{a} C_{spl}}(s,t) := T_a(s,t) \wedge (s \stackrel{\cdot}{=} P) \wedge C_{spl}(t)
$$

We use the notation $s \stackrel{\cdot}{=} P$ to denote that state P is encoded as Boolean vector s. The cumulative rate $\gamma(P, a, C_{spl})$ is then computed by applying the function $sum\_of\_all\_rates$ to $T_{P \xrightarrow{a} C_{spl}}(s,t)$. This function simply sums up all the entries of all rate lists of a DNBDD. For example, application of the function $sum\_of\_all\_rates$ to the DNBDD in Fig. 10 yields $\lambda_0 + \lambda_1 + \alpha + \beta + \gamma + \delta$. Furthermore, in the $split\_tree$ used by procedure $split'$ (Fig. 4) the subclasses $C_{\gamma_1}, \ldots, C_{\gamma_k}$ are now also represented by BDDs.

procedure $split'(C, a, C_{spl}, Partition, Splitters)$
    forall $P \in C$
        $T_{P \xrightarrow{a} C_{spl}}(s,t) := T_a(s,t) \wedge (s \stackrel{\cdot}{=} P) \wedge C_{spl}(t)$

---

[2] In order to avoid such redundancies, an efficient data structure to represent rate trees might itself be based on BDDs.

$\gamma := sum\_of\_all\_rates(T_{P \xrightarrow{a} C_{spl}}(s,t))$

/* the cumulative rate from state P to C_{spl} is computed */

$insert(split\_tree, P, \gamma)$

/* state P is inserted into the $split\_tree$ */

/* now, $split\_tree$ contains k leaves $C_{\gamma_1}, \ldots, C_{\gamma_k}$ */

if $(k > 1)$

$\ldots$

/* the remaining part of procedure $split'$ is as in Sec. 4, */

/* but $Partition$ and $Splitters$ are represented as BDDs */

6.5   BDDs with and without Rate Information

The semantics of the complete language $\mathcal{L}$ comprises both types of transitions, action transitions $\dashrightarrow{}^{a}\dashrightarrow$ and Markovian transitions $\xrightarrow{a,\lambda}$, in one transition system, an ESLTS. Using the knowledge developed in the previous sections, an ESLTS can be encoded by means of two separate data structures, using BDDs to encode action transitions and DNBDDs to encode Markovian transitions. Also, during parallel composition, the component BDDs are treated separately from the component DNBDDs. Therefore the treatment of ESLTS does not pose specific problems. Furthermore, the computation of weak Markovian bisimilarity (Sec. 5) can be lifted to this combination of BDD and DNBDD. The computation of the weak transition relation $\bullet\!\!\bullet\!\!\rightarrow$ from $\dashrightarrow$ during the initialisation step can easily be performed on the BDD for the action transitions. Only the first part of function $split''$ requires the DNBDD information, in order to sort tangible markings in a $split\_tree$ (the tangibility predicate is encoded as a BDD as well), in analogy to the implementation of function $split'$ given in Sec. 6.4. The subsequent steps work completely on BDDs.

7   Conclusion

In this paper, we have discussed efficient algorithms to compute bisimulation style equivalences for Stochastic Process Algebras. In addition, we have presented details of a BDD-based implementation of these algorithms, introducing DNBDDs to represent the additional rate information which is relevant for the analysis of the underlying Markov chain.

The complexity results established in this paper allow the following simple conclusion: the computational complexity of computing bisimulation equivalences *does not* increase when moving from a non-stochastic to a stochastic setting. For Markovian bisimilarity this fact is also mentioned (in similar settings) in [23] and in [2].

The usefulness of BDDs to encode transition systems has been stressed by many authors. However, we would like to point out that the myth, saying that BDDs always provide a more compact encoding than the ordinary representation (as a list or a sparse matrix data structure), does not hold in general. A naïve encoding of transition systems as BDDs does not save space. Heuristics for encodings are needed, exploiting the structure of the specification. The implementation of parallel composition on BDDs is indeed such a heuristics, and a very successful one, since an exponential blow-up can be turned into a linear growth.

Apart from encoding transition systems as (DN)BDDs and parallel composition on (DN)BDDs, we have described how bisimulation algorithms can be implemented on these data structures. As a consequence, all the ingredients are at hand for carrying out compositional aggregation of SPA specifications in a completely BDD-based framework. In this way, the state space explosion problem can be alleviated. We are currently implementing all these ingredients in a prototypical tool written in C, based on our own DNBDD package [5]. However, in order to obtain performance results, the (minimised) BDD representation still has to be converted back to the ordinary representation, since we do not yet have a Markov chain analyser which works directly on DNBDDs. Numerical analysis based on DNBDDs is one of our topics for future work. For this purpose, it seems beneficial to investigate the actual relation between DNBDDs and MTBDDs, since MTBDD-based numerical analysis methods have already been developed [14,21].

Acknowledgments   The authors acknowledge insightful comments of the reviewers that helped to improve the quality of paper. The second author is supported by the DAAD-Project AZ 313-ARC-XII-98/38 on stochastic modelling and verification.

References

1. C. Baier and H. Hermanns. Weak Bisimulation for Fully Probabilistic Processes. In *Proc. CAV '97*, Springer LNCS 1254:119–130, 1997.
2. M. Bernardo and R. Gorrieri. A Tutorial on EMPA: A Theory of Concurrent Processes with Nondeterminism, Priorities, Probabilities and Time. *Theoretical Computer Science* 202:1-54, 1998.
3. T. Bolognesi and E. Brinksma. Introduction to the ISO Specification Language LOTOS. *Computer Networks and ISDN Systems* 14:25-59, 1987.
4. A. Bouali. Weak and branching bisimulation in FCTOOL. Rapports de Recherche 1575, INRIA Sophia Antipolis, Valbonne Cedex, France, 1992.
5. H. Bruchner. Symbolische Manipulation von stochastischen Transitionssystemen. Internal study, Universität Erlangen–Nürnberg, IMMD VII, 1998. in German.
6. R.E. Bryant. Graph-based Algorithms for Boolean Function Manipulation. *IEEE Transaction on Computers*, C-35(8):677–691, August 1986.
7. R.E. Bryant and Y. Chen. Verification of Arithmetic Functions with Binary Moment Diagrams. In *Proc. 32nd Design Automation Conference*, 535-541, ACM/IEEE, 1995.
8. E.M. Clarke, M. Fujita, P. McGeer, K. McMillan, J. Yang, and X. Zhao. Multi-terminal Binary Decision Diagrams: An efficient data structure for matrix representation. In *Proc. International Workshop on Logic Synthesis*, Tahoe City, May 1993.
9. D. Coppersmith and S. Winograd. Matrix Multiplication via Arithmetic Progressions. In *Proc. 19th ACM Symposium on Theory of Computing*, 1987.
10. R. Enders, T. Filkorn, and D. Taubner. Generating BDDs for symbolic model checking in CCS. *Distributed Computing*, 6:155–164, 1993.
11. J.C. Fernandez. An Implementation of an Efficient Algorithm for Bisimulation Equivalence. *Science of Computer Programming*, 13:219–236, 1989.
12. R. J. van Glabbeek and W. Weijland:. Branching Time and Abstraction in Bisimulation Semantics. *Journal of the ACM*, 43(3):555–600, 1996.
13. J.F.Groote and F.W.Vaandrager. An efficient algorithm for branching bisimulation and stuttering equivalence. In *Proc. ICALP '90*, Springer LNCS 443:626-638, 1990.

14. G.D. Hachtel, E. Macii, A. Pardo, and F. Somenzi. Markovian Analysis of Large Finite State Machines. *IEEE Transactions on CAD*, 15(12):1479–1493, 1996.

15. H. Hermanns. *Interactive Markov Chains*. PhD thesis, Universität Erlangen-Nürnberg, 1998.

16. H. Hermanns, U. Herzog, and V. Mertsiotakis. Stochastic Process Algebras - Between LOTOS and Markov Chains. *Computer Networks and ISDN Systems*, 30(9-10):901–924, 1998.

17. H. Hermanns and M. Rettelbach. Syntax, Semantics, Equivalences, and Axioms for MTIPP. In *Proc. 2nd PAPM Workshop*. University of Erlangen-Nürnberg, IMMD 27(4):71-87, 1994.

18. H. Hermanns and J.P. Katoen. Automated Compositional Markov Chain Generation for a Plain Old Telephony System. to appear in *Science of Computer Programming*, 1998.

19. H. Hermanns and M. Lohrey. Priority and maximal progress are completely axiomatisable. In *Proc. CONCUR'98*, Springer LNCS 1466:237-252, 1998.

20. H. Hermanns and M. Siegle. Computing Bisimulations for Stochastic Process Algebras using Symbolic Techniques. In *Proc. 6th Int. PAPM Workshop*, 103-118, Nice, 1998.

21. H. Hermanns, J. Meyer-Kayser and M. Siegle. Multi Terminal Binary Decision Diagrams to Represent and Analyse Continuous Time Markov Chains. submitted for publication, 1999.

22. J. Hillston. *A Compositional Approach to Performance Modelling*. Cambridge University Press, 1996.

23. T. Huynh and L. Tian. On some Equivalence Relations for Probabilistic Processes. *Fundamenta Informaticae*, 17:211–234, 1992.

24. P. Kanellakis and S. Smolka. CCS Expressions, Finite State Processes, and Three Problems of Equivalence. *Information and Computation*, 86:43–68, 1990.

25. J.G. Kemeny and J.L. Snell. *Finite Markov Chains*. Springer, 1976.

26. Y.-T. Lai and S. Sastry. Edge-Valued Binary Decision Diagrams for Multi-Level Hierarchical Verification. In *29th Design Automation Conference*,608-613, ACM/IEEE, 1992.

27. K. Larsen and A. Skou. Bisimulation through Probabilistic Testing. *Information and Computation*, 94(1):1-28, 1991.

28. R. Milner. *Communication and Concurrency*. Prentice Hall, London, 1989.

29. R. Paige and R. Tarjan. Three Partition Refinement Algorithms. *SIAM Journal of Computing*, 16(6):973–989, 1987.

30. M. Siegle. Technique and tool for symbolic representation and manipulation of stochastic transition systems. TR IMMD 7 2/98, Universität Erlangen-Nürnberg, March 1998.

Probabilistic Linear-Time Model Checking:
An Overview of the Automata-Theoretic Approach

Moshe Y. Vardi*

Rice University, Department of Computer Science, Houston, TX 77005-1892, USA

Abstract. We describe the automata-theoretic approach to the algorithmic verification of probabilistic finite-state systems with respect to linear-time properties.
The basic idea underlying this approach is that for any linear temporal formula
we can construct an automaton that accepts precisely the computations that satisfy the formula. This enables the reduction of probabilistic model checking to
ergodic analysis of Markov chains.

1 Introduction

Temporal logics, which are modal logics geared towards the description of the temporal
ordering of events, have been adopted as a powerful tool for specifying and verifying
concurrent systems [Pnu81]. One of the most significant developments in this area is the
discovery of algorithmic methods for verifying temporal logic properties of *finite-state*
systems [CE81, QS81, LP85, CES86]. This derives its significance both from the fact
that many synchronization and communication protocols can be modeled as finite-state
programs, as well as from the great ease of use of fully algorithmic methods. Finite-
state programs can be modeled by transition systems where each state has a bounded
description, and hence can be characterized by a fixed number of Boolean atomic propositions. This means that a finite-state program can be viewed as a finite *propositional*
Kripke structure and that its properties can be specified using *propositional* temporal
logic. Thus, to verify the correctness of the program with respect to a desired behavior,
one only has to check that the program, modeled as a finite Kripke structure, satisfies (is
a model of) the propositional temporal logic formula that specifies that behavior. Hence
the name *model checking* for the verification methods derived from this viewpoint. Sur-
veys can be found in [CG87, CGL93, Wol89].

For linear temporal logics, a close and fruitful connection with the theory of automata over infinite words has been developed [VW86, VW94, Var96]. The basic idea
is to associate with each linear temporal logic formula a finite automaton over infinite
words that accepts exactly all the computations that satisfy the formula. This enables
the reduction of various decision problems, such as satisfiability and model-checking,
to known automata-theoretic problems, yielding clean and asymptotically optimal algorithms. Furthermore, these reductions are very helpful for implementing temporal-logic
based verification methods, and are the key to techniques such as *on-the-fly* verification
[CVWY92] that help coping with the "state-explosion" problem.

* Supported in part by NSF grants CCR-9628400 and CCR-9700061, and by a grant from the
Intel Corporation. URL: http://www.cs.rice.edu/~vardi.

J.-P. Katoen (Ed.): ARTS'99, LNCS 1601, pp. 265–276, 1999.
© Springer-Verlag Berlin Heidelberg 1999

In view of the attractiveness of the model-checking approach, one would like to extend its applicability as much as possible. In particular, we would like to extend the model-checking approach to deal with *probabilistic* systems, since the introduction of probabilistic randomization into protocols has been shown to be extremely useful (see, for example, [LR81]). For probabilistic systems the situation becomes more complex. In such systems there is a probability measure defined on the set of computations. The notion of correctness now becomes probabilistic: we study here the notion that the program is correct if the probability that a computation satisfies the specification is one. (For investigations of quantitative notions of correctness, see, for example, [HJ94].) Even in this setting, the automata-theoretic approach is very useful, as was shown in [Var85, VW86, CY90, CY95]. In this paper we provide an overview of the automata-theoretic approach to probabilistic model checking of linear temporal properties. We show how it provides essentially optimal algorithms in most cases, and highlight one case where it does not.

2 Automata Theory

A *nondeterministic automaton* words is a tuple $A = (\Sigma, S, S_0, \rho, \alpha)$, where

- Σ is a finite alphabet,
- S is a finite set of states,
- $S_0 \subseteq S$ is a set of initial states,
- $\rho : S \times \Sigma \to 2^S$ is a (nondeterministic) transition function, and
- α is an *acceptance condition* (will be defined precisely later).

A state $s \in S$ is *deterministic* if $|\rho(s,a)| = 1$ for all $a \in \Sigma$. The automaton A is said to be *semi-deterministic* if all states are deterministic. If in addition $|S_0| = 1$, then A is said to be *deterministic*.

A *run* of A over a infinite word $w = a_1 a_2 \ldots$, is a sequence $s_0, s_1, \ldots$, where $s_0 \in S_0$ and $s_i \in \rho(s_{i-1}, a_i)$, for all $i \geq 1$. Acceptance is defined in terms of *limits*. The limit of a run $r = s_0, s_1, \ldots$ is the set $\lim(r) = \{s \mid s = s_i \text{ infinitely often}\}$. A *Büchi* acceptance condition is a set $F \subseteq S$ of *accepting states*. A set $T \subseteq S$ is *accepting* if $T \cap F \neq \emptyset$. Note that when $F = S$, all sets are accepting; we call such an accepting condition a *trivial* acceptance condition. A *Rabin* condition is a subset G of $2^S \times 2^S$, i.e., it is a collection of pairs of sets of states, written $[(L_1, U_1), \ldots, (L_k, U_k)]$. A set T is accepting if for some i we have that $T \cap L_i \neq \emptyset$ and $T \cap U_i = \emptyset$. A *Streett* condition is also a subset G of $2^S \times 2^S$, written $[(L_1, U_1), \ldots, (L_k, U_k)]$. A set T is accepting if for for all i we have that if $T \cap L_i \neq \emptyset$, then $T \cap U_i \neq \emptyset$ (thus, Streett acceptance is dual to Rabin acceptance). Note that Büchi acceptance is a special case of both Rabin acceptance (the pair $\langle F, \emptyset \rangle$), and Streett acceptance (the pair $\langle S, F \rangle$). A Büchi (resp., Rabin, Streett) automaton is an automaton on infinite words with Büchi (resp., Rabin, Streett) acceptance condition. Büchi, Rabin, and Streett conditions can all be viewed as *fairness* conditions, which are limit conditions on runs [Fra86]. A run r is accepting if $\lim(r)$ is accepting. An infinite word w is *accepted* by A if there is an accepting run of A over w. The set of infinite words accepted by A, called the *language of A*, is denoted $L(A)$.

It is known that Rabin and Streett automata are not more expressive than Büchi automata. More precisely, if A is a Rabin or Streett automaton, then there is a Büchi automaton A^b such that $L(A) = L(A^b)$ [Tho90]. When A is a Rabin automaton, the translation to a Büchi automaton is quadratic, but when A is a Streett automaton, the translation is exponential [SV89].

An automaton A is *nonempty* if $L(A) \neq \emptyset$. One of the most fundamental algorithmic issues in automata theory is testing whether a given automaton is nonempty. The *nonemptiness problem* for automata is to decide, given an automaton A, whether A is nonempty.

Proposition 1. [CES86] *The nonemptiness problem for Büchi automata is decidable in linear time.*

Proof: Let $A = (\Sigma, S, S_0, \rho, F)$ be the given automaton. Consider the directed graph $G_A = (S, E_A)$, where $E_A = \{\langle s, t \rangle \mid t \in \rho(s, a), a \in \Sigma\}$. It can be shown that A is nonempty iff G_A has a nontrivial maximal strongly connected component that is reachable from S_0 and intersects F nontrivially. As a depth-first-search algorithm can construct a decomposition of the graph into strongly connected components in linear time [CLR90], the claim follows. ∎

Since there is a quadratic translation of Rabin automata to Büchi automata, Proposition 1 yields a quadratic algorithm for nonemptiness of Rabin automata. For Streett automata, a direct algorithm is needed.

Proposition 2. [Eme85] *The nonemptiness problem for Streett automata is decidable in polynomial time.*

Proof: Let $A = (\Sigma, S, S_0, \rho, G)$ be the given automaton. Again we start by decomposing G_A into maximal strongly connected components reachable from S_0. We then iterate the following operation

For a component Q and a pair $\langle L, U \rangle \in G$, if $Q \cap L \neq \emptyset$ and $Q \cap U = \emptyset$, then delete the states in L from G_A and recompute the decomposition into maximal strongly connected components.

Since each iteration deletes states from G_A, the above operations can be applied only $|S|$ times. $L(A)$ is nonempty iff the final decomposition contains a nontrivial component. ∎

As we shall see, closure under Boolean operations plays in important role in the application to verification. We first consider closure under intersection.

Proposition 3. [Cho74] *Let A_1, A_2 be Büchi automata. Then there is a Büchi automaton A such that $L(A) = L(A_1) \cap L(A_2)$.*

Proof: We show the construction explicitly for the case that A_1 has a trivial acceptance condition. Let $A_1 = (\Sigma, S_1, S_1^0, \rho_1, S_1)$ and $A_2 = (\Sigma, S_2, S_2^0, \rho_2, F_2)$. Let $A = (\Sigma, S, S^0, \rho, F)$, where $S = S_1 \times S_2$, $S^0 = S_1^0 \times S_2^0$, $F = S_1 \times F_2$, and $(s', t') \in \rho((s, t), a)$ if $s' \in \rho_1(s, a)$ and $t' \in \rho_2(t, a)$. ∎

We denote the intersection automaton by $A_1 \cap A_2$.

Büchi automata are also closed under complementation.

Proposition 4. [Büc62, Kla91, KV97b] *Let A be a Büchi automaton over an alphabet Σ. Then there is a Büchi automaton A^c such that $L(A^c) = \Sigma^\omega - L(A)$.*

If A has n states, then A^c has $n^{O(n)}$ states, which is known to be tight [Mic88].

Unlike automata on finite words, Büchi automata are not closed under determinization, i.e., nondeterministic Büchi automata are more expressive than deterministic Büchi automata [Tho90]. In contrast, Rabin and Streett automata are closed under determinization. In fact, they are also closed under co-determinization.

Proposition 5. [McN66, Saf89] *Let A be a Büchi automaton. There are deterministic Rabin (resp., Streett) automata A_d and A^{cd} such that $L(A^d) = L(A)$ and $L(A^{cd}) = \Sigma^\omega - L(A)$*

If A has n states, then A_d and A^{cd} have $n^{O(n)}$ states and $O(n)$ pairs.

3   Verification

We focus here on *finite-state systems*, i.e., systems in which the variables range over finite domains. The significance of this class follows from the fact that a significant number of the communication and synchronization protocols studied in the literature are in essence finite-state systems [Liu89, Rud87].

A finite-state system over a set $Prop$ of atomic propositions is a structure of the form $M = (W, w_0, R, V)$, where W is a finite set of states, $w_0 \in W$ is the initial state, $R \subseteq W^2$ is a total transition relation, and $V : W \to 2^{Prop}$ assigns truth values to propositions in a set $Prop$ for each state in W. The intuition is that W describes all the states that the program could be in (where a state includes the content of the memory, registers, buffers, location counter, etc.), R describes all the possible transitions between states (allowing for nondeterminism), and V relates the states to the propositions (e.g., it tells us in what states the proposition request is true). The assumption that R is total (i.e., that every state has a child) is for technical convenience. We can view a terminated execution as repeating forever its last state.

Let **u** be an infinite sequence $u_0, u_1, \ldots$ of states in W such that $u_0 = w_0$, and $u_i R u_{i+1}$ for all $i \geq 0$. Then the sequence $V(u_0), V(u_1) \ldots$ is a *computation* of M. If we take Σ to be 2^{Prop}, then a computation of M is a word in Σ^ω. We denote the set of computations of M by $L(M)$. A *specification* for M is a language $\sigma \subseteq \Sigma^\omega$. M *satisfies* σ if every computation of M is in σ.

A finite-state system $M = (W, w_0, R, V)$ can be viewed as a Büchi automaton $A_M = (\Sigma, W, \{w_0\}, \rho, W)$, where $\Sigma = 2^{Prop}$ and $s' \in \rho(s, a)$ iff $(s, s') \in R$ and $a = V(s)$. As this automaton has a set of accepting states equal to the whole set of states, every infinite run of the automaton is accepting; that is, $L(A_M) = L(M)$. If σ is expressed in terms of a *specification automaton* A_σ, then M satisfies σ iff $L(M) \subseteq L(A_\sigma)$. This is called the *language-containment* approach to verification [Kur94]. Note that $L(M) \subseteq L(A_\sigma)$ iff $L(M) \cap (\Sigma^\omega - L(A_\sigma)) = \emptyset$ iff $L(M) \cap L(A_\sigma^c)) = \emptyset$ iff $L(A_M \cap A_\sigma^c) = \emptyset$, where A_σ^c is an automaton that complement A_σ and $A_M \cap A_\sigma^c$ is the intersection of A_M and A_σ^c. Thus, verification is ultimately reducible to the emptiness problem. Using Propositions 1 and 4, we get:

Theorem 6. *Checking whether a Büchi automaton A_σ with n states is satisfied by a finite-state program M can be done in time $O(\|M\| \cdot n^{O(n)})$.*

We note that a time upper bound that is polynomial in the size of the program and exponential in the size of the specification is considered here to be reasonable, since the specification is usually rather short [LP85]. It is unlikely that the exponential bound can be improved, as the problem is PSPACE-complete [Wol83].

4 Temporal Logic and Automata

Formulas of *linear time propositional temporal logic* (LPTL) are built from a set *Prop* of atomic propositions and are closed under the application of Boolean connectives, the unary temporal connective X (next), and the binary temporal connective U (until) [Pnu77, GPSS80]. LPTL is interpreted over *computations*. A computation is a function $\pi : \omega \to 2^{Prop}$, which assigns truth values to the elements of *Prop* at each time instant (natural number). For a computation π and a point $i \in \omega$, we have that:

- $\pi, i \models p$ for $p \in Prop$ iff $p \in \pi(i)$.
- $\pi, i \models \xi \wedge \psi$ iff $\pi, i \models \xi$ and $\pi, i \models \psi$.
- $\pi, i \models \neg\varphi$ iff not $\pi, i \models \varphi$
- $\pi, i \models X\varphi$ iff $\pi, i + 1 \models \varphi$.
- $\pi, i \models \xi U\psi$ iff for some $j \geq i$, $\pi, j \models \psi$ and for all k, $i \leq k < j$ $\pi, k \models \xi$.

We say that π *satisfies* a formula φ, denoted $\pi \models \varphi$, iff $\pi, 0 \models \varphi$. We say that a finite-state system $M = (W, w_0, R, V)$ satisfies φ if $\pi \models \varphi$ for every computation π of M.

As we observed computations can also be viewed as infinite words over the alphabet 2^{Prop}. The following theorem establishes the correspondence between LPTL and Büchi automata.

Proposition 7. [VW94] *Given an LPTL formula φ, one can build a Büchi automaton $A_\varphi = (\Sigma, S, S_0, \rho, F)$, where $\Sigma = 2^{Prop}$ and $|S| \leq 2^{O(|\varphi|)}$, such that $L(A_\varphi)$ is exactly the set of computations satisfying the formula φ.*

It follows that $M \models \varphi$ iff $L(M) \subseteq L(A_\varphi)$ iff $L(M) \cap (\Sigma^\omega - L(A_\varphi)) = \emptyset$ iff $L(M) \cap L(A_\varphi^c)) = \emptyset$ iff $L(A_M \cap A_\varphi^c) = \emptyset$. Note that rather than construct first A_φ and then A_φ^c, involving a doubly exponential blow-up, we can construct directly $A_{\neg\varphi}$, as, clearly, $L(A_{\neg\varphi}) = L(A_\varphi^c)$. By Proposition 7, the number of states of $A_{\neg\varphi}$ is $2^{O(|\varphi|)}$. Consequently, the automaton $A_M \cap A_{\neg\varphi}$ has $|W| \cdot 2^{O(|\varphi|)}$ states. Using Proposition 1, we get:

Theorem 8. *Checking whether a formula φ is satisfied by a finite-state program M can be done in time $O(\|M\| \cdot 2^{O(|\varphi|)})$,*

It is unlikely that the exponential bound can be improved, as the problem is PSPACE-complete [SC85]. Note that regardless of whether the specification is expressed using a Büchi automaton or an LPTL formula, the complexity is linear in the size of the system and exponential in the size of the specifiation.

5 Probabilistic Systems

We model probabilistic systems by (finite-state) *Markov chains*. The basic intuition is that transition between states is governed by some probability distribution. A Markov chain $M = (W, P, P_0)$ consists of a finite *state space* W; a *transition probability function* $P : W^2 \rightarrow [0, 1]$, such that $Sum_{v \in W} P(u, v) = 1$ for all $u \in W$; and an *initial probability distribution* $P_0 : W \rightarrow [0, 1]$, such that $Sum_{u \in W} P_0(u) = 1$.

As in the standard theory of Markov processes (see [KS60, KSK76]), we define a probability space called the *sequence space* $\Psi_M = (\Omega, \Delta, \mu)$, where $\Omega = W^\omega$ is the set of all infinite sequences of states, Δ is a Borel field generated by the *basic cylindric sets*

$$\Delta(w_0, w_1, \ldots, w_n) = \{\mathbf{w} \in \Omega \mid \mathbf{w} = w_0, w_1, \ldots, w_n, \ldots\},$$

and μ is a probability distribution defined by

$$\mu(\Delta(w_0, w_1, \ldots, w_n)) =$$

$$P_0(w_0) \cdot P(w_0, w_1) \cdot P(w_1, w_n) \cdot \ldots P(w_{n-1}, w_n).$$

Consider a language $\sigma \subseteq W^\omega$, viewed as specification, that is measurable wrt the sequence space Ψ_M. We say that M *almost surely satisfies* σ if $\mu(\sigma) = 1$, that is, if "almost" all computations of M are in σ.

Suppose that σ is expressed in terms of a deterministic automaton $A = (W, S, s_0, \rho, G)$. It can be shown that in this case σ is measurable [Var85]. We define the product chain $M \times A = (W \times S, P', P'_0)$, where $P'_0(\langle w, s_0 \rangle) = P_0(w)$ and $P'_0(\langle w, s \rangle) = 0$ if $s \neq s_0$, and $P'(\langle u, s \rangle, \langle v, t \rangle) = P(u, v)$ if $t = \rho(s, u)$ and $P'(\langle u, s \rangle, \langle v, t \rangle) = 0$ if $t \neq \rho(s, u)$. If G is the acceptance condition $[(L_1, U_1), \ldots, (L_k, U_k)]$ (Rabin or Streett), then take $W \times G$ to be $[(W \times L_1, W \times U_1), \ldots, (W \times L_k, W \times U_k)]$. Let $sat(W \times G)$ be the set of sequences that satisfy the acceptance condition $W \times G$, i.e., whose limit is accepting.

Lemma 9. $\mu_M(L(A)) > 0$ *iff* $\mu_{M \times A}(sat(W \times G) > 0$

Lemma 9 enables us to focus on the behavior of the Markov chain in the limit. Let $M = (W, P, P_0)$ be a Markov chain and let $\alpha \subseteq 2^W \times 2^W$ be a Streett acceptance condition. Consider the graph $G_M = (W, W_0, E_M)$, where $W_0 = \{w \mid P_0(w) > 0\}$ and $E_M = \{\langle u, v \rangle \mid P(u, v) > 0\}$. An *ergodic set* in G_M is a terminal maximal strongly connected component that is reachable from W_0. Such a set is closed with respect to all positive transitions of M.

Lemma 10. $\mu_M(sat(\alpha)) > 0$ *iff some ergodic set of* G_M *is accepting wrt* α.

Note that in this analysis the exact transition probabilities are irrelevant. All that counts is whether a transition probability is 0 or not.

Ergodic analysis can be also viewed from an automata-theoretic perspective. Define the Streett automaton $A_M = (\{a\}, W, W_0, \rho_P, \alpha \cup \beta)$, where $\{a\}$ is a singleton alphabet, $\rho_P(u, a) = \{v \mid P(u, v) > 0\}$, and $\beta = \{(\{u\}, \{v\}) \mid P(u, v) > 0\}$.

Lemma 11. $\mu_M(sat(\alpha)) > 0$ *iff* $L(A_M) \neq \emptyset$.

The intuition behind the lemma is that probabilistic behavior is essentially a "fair" behavior.

We can now consider the algorithmic aspect of verifying probabilistic systems. Suppose that we are given a Markov chain M and a nondeterministic automaton A_σ. We want to check whether M almost surely satisfies σ. We construct the co-deterministic Streett automaton A_σ^{cd}, per Proposition 5. We know that M almost surely satisfies A_σ iff $\mu_M(L(A_\sigma^{cd})) = 0$. Thus, we can form the product chain $M \times A_\sigma^{cd}$ and then apply Lemma 11.

Theorem 12. *Checking whether a Büchi automaton A_σ with n states is almost surely satisfied by a Markov chain M can be done in time polynomial in $\|M\|$ and exponential in $\|A_\sigma\|$.*

It is unlikely that the exponential bound can be improved, as the problem is PSPACE-complete [Var85].

Suppose now that we have an assignment $V : W \to 2^{Prop}$ and the specification is given by an LPTL formula over $Prop$. Let $L(\varphi)$ consists of all sequences $\mathbf{w} \in \Omega$ such that $V(\mathbf{w})$ satisfies φ. It can be shown that $L(\varphi)$ is measurable [Var85]. We want to verify that M almost surely satisfies φ, i.e., M almost surely satisfies $L(\varphi)$. We can apply Proposition 7 and construct A_φ and then proceed with the algorithm of Theorem 12. The resulting algorithm is polynomial in the size of M, but is doubly exponential in the size of φ. Courcoubetis and Yannakakis [CY95] showed how almost-sure satisfaction of LPTL formulas over Markov chains can be checked in time that is exponential in the size of the specification. The algorithm does not use the translation of LPTL formulas to Büchi automata. We will return to this point in the concluding discussion.

6 Reactive Probabilistic Programs

So far we viewed systems as Markov chains. This model assumes that all the transitions of a system are probabilistic. This is adequate for *closed* systems, whose transitions are internally driven. In *reactive* systems, which interact with their external environments [HP85], some transitions are inherently nondeterministic.

A (finite-state) *reactive Markov chain* $M = (W, N, P, P_0)$ is a Markov chain (W, P, P_0) with a set $N \subseteq W$ of *nondeterministic states* (the states in $W - N$ are the *probabilistic states*). The idea is that $W - N$ is the set of states where a probabilistic transition has to be made and N is the set of states where a nondeterministic transition has to be made. If $u \in N$, then we interpret $P(u, v)$ to mean that there is a possible transition from u to v if and only if $P(u, v) > 0$.

This model, originally named *concurrent Markov chain*, was proposed in [Var85], based on earlier ideas in [HSP83]. It turns out, however, that is simply another guise of *Markov decision processes* [Der70].

To define the sequence space of a reactive Markov chain it is convenient to imagine a *scheduler*, which makes all the nondeterministic choices. A scheduler for a reactive Markov chain $M = (W, N, P, P_0)$ is a function $\tau : W^*N \to W$, i.e., a function that assigns a state to each sequence of states that end with a nondeterministic state, such that $\tau(w_0, \ldots, w_n) = w$ only if $P(w_n, w) > 0$.

Let $M = (W, N, P, P_0)$ be a reactive Markov chain. A scheduler τ for M gives rise to an infinite Markov chain $M^\tau = (W^+, P^\tau, P_0^\tau)$, where

- $P_0^\tau(w) = P_0(w)$ for all $w \in W$ and $P^\tau(x) = 0$ for all $x \in W^+ - W$,
- $P^\tau : W^+ \times W^+ \to [0, 1]$ is defined as follows (where x and y are arbitrary members of W^+):
  - $P^\tau(xu, xuv) = P(u, v)$ if $u \in W - N$,
  - $P^\tau(xu, xuv) = 1$, if $u \in N$ and $\tau(xu) = v$, and
  - $P^\tau(x, y) = 0$, otherwise.

Intuitively, M^τ describes the behavior of the system under the scheduler τ.

Consider a specification $\sigma \subseteq W^\omega$. We need to "lift" σ to the level of M^τ. To that end, we define a mapping $V : W^+ \to W$ by $V(u_1 u_2 \ldots u_n) = u_n$. Now take $L(\sigma) \subseteq (W^+)^\omega$ as the set of sequences $\mathbf{u} \in (W^+)^\omega$ such that $V(\mathbf{u}) \in \sigma$. We now say that M almost surely satisfy σ if $\mu_{M^\tau}(L(\sigma)) = 1$ for all schedulers τ. The intution is that σ almost surely holds regardless of the environment decisions. Dually, we can ask whether the exists a scheduler τ such that $\mu_{M^\tau}(L(W^\omega - \sigma)) > 0$.

Suppose that σ is given in terms of a deterministic Streett automaton A with acceptance condition G. Then, as in Lemma 9, almost sure satisfaction of A can be reduced to checking a limit property.

Lemma 13. *There exists a scheduler τ such that $\mu_{M^\tau}(L(A)) > 0$ iff there exists a scheduler τ such that $\mu_{(M \times A)^\tau}(sat(W \times G) > 0$*

As we did with Markov chains, we use ergodic analysis to check limit properties. Let $M = (W, N, P, P_0)$ be a reactive Markov chain and let $\alpha \subseteq 2^W \times 2^W$ be a Streett acceptance condition. Consider the graph $G_M = (W, W_0, E_M)$, where $W_0 = \{w \mid P_0(w) > 0\}$ and $E_M = \{\langle u, v \rangle \mid P(u, v) > 0\}$. An *ergodic set* in G_M is a strongly connected component of G_M that is reachable from W_0 and is closed under the positive probabilistic transitions of M, i.e., under $E_M \cap ((W - N) \times W)$.

Lemma 14. *There exists a scheduler τ such that $\mu_{M^\tau}(sat(\alpha)) > 0$ iff some ergodic set of G_M is accepting wrt α.*

Again, the ergodic analysis can be also viewed from an automata-theoretic perspective. Define the Streett automaton $A_M = (\{a\}, W, W_0, \rho_P, \alpha \cup \beta)$, where $\{a\}$ is a singleton alphabet, $\rho_P(u, a) = \{v \mid P(u, v) > 0\}$, and $\beta = \{(\{u\}, \{v\}) \mid u \in W - N$ and $P(u, v) > 0\}$.

Lemma 15. *There exists a scheduler τ such that $\mu_{M^\tau}(sat(\alpha)) > 0$ iff $L(A_M) \neq \emptyset$.*

To check that a reactive Markov chain almost surely satisfies a Büchi automaton A_σ or an LPTP formula φ we proceed as we did with Markov chains. We first construct a deterministic Streett automaton for the complementary specification. The cost is exponential for Büchi automata and doubly exponential for LPTL formuas. We then take the product with the chain and perform ergodic analysis. The resulting complexity is polynomial in the size of the chain, exponential in the size of A_σ and doubly exponential in the size of φ. A 2EXPTIME lower bound in [CY95] shows that the latter bound is asymptotically optimal.

We note that the automata-theoretic framework lends itself easily to the incorporation of fairness. The intuition underlying fairness is that we want to restruct attention to only "well-behaved" schedulers [BK97]. For example, we may want to assume that if a transition is enabled infinitely often then it is taken infinitely often. Streett conditions enable us to express rather general fairness properties [Fra86]. We say that a scheduler τ is *fair* wrt a fairness condition G if $\mu_{M^\tau}(sat(G)) = 1$. We can now modify the definition of almost-sure satisfaction by quantifying universally only over fair schedulers. It turns out that the algorithmic modification required to handle fairness is rather straightforward; all we have to do is to add the Streett condition describing the fairness condition to the Streett condition used in Lemmas 14 and 15.

7 Concluding Remarks

Over the last 15 years, the automata-theoretic approach to verification has proven itself to be a rather powerful paradigm. Essentially, almost all decision problems related to specification and verification of finite-state systems can be expressed and solved using automata-theoretic tools. See [VW86, EJ91, VW94, BVW94, CY95, KV97a] for numerous examples. The result in Section 5 is a rare exception. As we saw there, using the automata-theoretic approach we obtained an algorithm for checking almost-sure satisfaction of LPTL formulas over Markov chains whose complexity is doubly exponential in the size of the input formula. A non-automata-theoretic algorithm, whose complexity is exponentially lower (i.e., a single exponential) is described in [CY95]. Can the improved algorithm be given an automata-theoretic account? We believe that the answer is positive and suspect that such account can be given in terms of "weak alternating automata" [Var95, KV97b].

References

[BK97]   C. Baier and M.Z. Kwiatowska. Automatic verification of liveness properties of randomized systems. In *ACM Symp. on Principles of Distributed Systems (PODC)*, 1997.

[Büc62]   J.R. Büchi. On a decision method in restricted second order arithmetic. In *Proc. Internat. Congr. Logic, Method and Philos. Sci. 1960*, pages 1–12, Stanford, 1962. Stanford University Press.

[BVW94]   O. Bernholtz, M.Y. Vardi, and P. Wolper. An automata-theoretic approach to branching-time model checking. In D. L. Dill, editor, *Computer Aided Verification, Proc. 6th Int. Conference*, volume 818 of *Lecture Notes in Computer Science*, pages 142–155, Stanford, June 1994. Springer-Verlag, Berlin.

[CE81]   E.M. Clarke and E.A. Emerson. Design and synthesis of synchronization skeletons using branching time temporal logic. In *Proc. Workshop on Logic of Programs*, volume 131 of *Lecture Notes in Computer Science*, pages 52–71. Springer-Verlag, 1981.

[CES86]   E.M. Clarke, E.A. Emerson, and A.P. Sistla. Automatic verification of finite-state concurrent systems using temporal logic specifications. *ACM Transactions on Programming Languages and Systems*, 8(2):244–263, January 1986.

[CG87]   E.M. Clarke and O. Grumberg. Avoiding the state explosion problem in temporal logic model-checking algorithms. In *Proc. 6th ACM Symposium on Principles of Distributed Computing*, pages 294–303, Vancouver, British Columbia, August 1987.

[CGL93]   E.M. Clarke, O. Grumberg, and D. Long. Verification tools for finite-state concurrent systems. In J.W. de Bakker, W.-P. de Roever, and G. Rozenberg, editors, *Decade of Concurrency – Reflections and Perspectives (Proceedings of REX School)*, volume 803 of *Lecture Notes in Computer Science*, pages 124–175. Springer-Verlag, 1993.

[Cho74]   Y. Choueka. Theories of automata on ω-tapes: A simplified approach. *Journal of Computer and System Sciences*, 8:117–141, 1974.

[CLR90]   T.H. Cormen, C.E. Leiserson, and R.L. Rivest. *Introduction to Algorithms*. MIT Press, 1990.

[CVWY92]   C. Courcoubetis, M.Y. Vardi, P. Wolper, and M. Yannakakis. Memory efficient algorithms for the verification of temporal properties. *Formal Methods in System Design*, 1:275–288, 1992.

[CY90]   C. Courcoubetis and M. Yannakakis. Markov decision processes and regular events. In *Proc. 17th Int. Coll. on Automata Languages and Programming*, volume 443, pages 336–349, Coventry, July 1990. Lecture Notes in Computer Science, Springer-Verlag.

[CY95]   C. Courcoubetis and M. Yannakakis. The complexity of probabilistic verification. *J. ACM*, 42:857–907, 1995.

[Der70]   C. Derman. *Finite-State Markovian Decision Processes*. Academic Press, New York, 1970.

[EJ91]   E.A. Emerson and C. Jutla. Tree automata, Mu-calculus and determinacy. In *Proc. 32nd IEEE Symposium on Foundations of Computer Science*, pages 368–377, San Juan, October 1991.

[Eme85]   E.A. Emerson. Automata, tableaux, and temporal logics. In *Proc. Workshop on Logic of Programs*, volume 193 of *Lecture Notes in Computer Science*, pages 79–87. Springer-Verlag, 1985.

[Fra86]   N. Francez. *Fairness*. Texts and Monographs in Computer Science. Springer-Verlag, 1986.

[GPSS80]   D. Gabbay, A. Pnueli, S. Shelah, and J. Stavi. On the temporal analysis of fairness. In *Proc. 7th ACM Symposium on Principles of Programming Languages*, pages 163–173, January 1980.

[HJ94]   H. Hansson and B. Jonsson. A logic for reasoning about time and probability. *Formal Aspects of Computing*, 6:512–535, 1994.

[HP85]   D. Harel and A. Pnueli. On the development of reactive systems. In K. Apt, editor, *Logics and Models of Concurrent Systems*, volume F-13 of *NATO Advanced Summer Institutes*, pages 477–498. Springer-Verlag, 1985.

[HSP83]   S. Hart, M. Sharir, and A. Pnueli. Termination of probabilistic concurrent programs. *ACM Trans. on Programming Languages*, 5:356–380, 1983.

[Kla91]   N. Klarlund. Progress measures for complementation of ω-automata with applications to temporal logic. In *Proc. 32nd IEEE Symposium on Foundations of Computer Science*, pages 358–367, San Juan, October 1991.

[KS60]   J.G. Kemeny and J.L. Snell. *Finite Markov Chains*. Van Nostrad, Princeton, 1960.

[KSK76]   J.G. Kemeny, J.L. Snell, and A.W. Knapp. *Denumerable Markov Chains*. Springer-Verlag, New York, 1976.

[Kur94]   R.P. Kurshan. *Computer Aided Verification of Coordinating Processes*. Princeton Univ. Press, 1994.

[KV97a]   O. Kupferman and M.Y. Vardi. Synthesis with incomplete informatio. In *2nd International Conference on Temporal Logic*, pages 91–106, Manchester, July 1997. Kluwer Academic Publishers.

[KV97b]   O. Kupferman and M.Y. Vardi. Weak alternating automata are not that weak. In *Proc. 5th Israeli Symposium on Theory of Computing and Systems*, pages 147–158. IEEE Computer Society Press, 1997.

[Liu89]   M.T. Liu. Protocol engineering. *Advances in Computing*, 29:79–195, 1989.

[LP85]   O. Lichtenstein and A. Pnueli. Checking that finite state concurrent programs satisfy their linear specification. In *Proc. 12th ACM Symposium on Principles of Programming Languages*, pages 97–107, New Orleans, January 1985.

[LR81]   D. Lehman and M. O. Rabin. On the advantage of free choice: A fully symmetric and fully distributed solution to the dining philosophers problem. In *Proc. 8th ACM Symposium on Principles of Programming Languages*, pages 133–138, 1981.

[McN66]   R. McNaughton. Testing and generating infinite sequences by a finite automaton. *Information and Control*, 9:521–530, 1966.

[Mic88]   M. Michel. Complementation is more difficult with automata on infinite words. CNET, Paris, 1988.

[Pnu77]   A. Pnueli. The temporal logic of programs. In *Proc. 18th IEEE Symposium on Foundation of Computer Science*, pages 46–57, 1977.

[Pnu81]   A. Pnueli. The temporal semantics of concurrent programs. *Theoretical Computer Science*, 13:45–60, 1981.

[QS81]   J.P. Queille and J. Sifakis. Specification and verification of concurrent systems in Cesar. In *Proc. 5th International Symp. on Programming*, volume 137, pages 337–351. Springer-Verlag, Lecture Notes in Computer Science, 1981.

[Rud87]   H. Rudin. Network protocols and tools to help produce them. *Annual Review of Computer Science*, 2:291–316, 1987.

[Saf89]   S. Safra. *Complexity of automata on infinite objects*. PhD thesis, Weizmann Institute of Science, Rehovot, Israel, 1989.

[SC85]   A.P. Sistla and E.M. Clarke. The complexity of propositional linear temporal logic. *Journal ACM*, 32:733–749, 1985.

[SV89]   S. Safra and M.Y. Vardi. On ω-automata and temporal logic. In *Proc. 21st ACM Symposium on Theory of Computing*, pages 127–137, Seattle, May 1989.

[Tho90]   W. Thomas. Automata on infinite objects. *Handbook of Theoretical Computer Science*, pages 165–191, 1990.

[Var85]   M.Y. Vardi. Automatic verification of probabilistic concurrent finite-state programs. In *Proc. 26th IEEE Symp. on Foundations of Computer Science*, pages 327–338, Portland, October 1985.

[Var95]   M.Y. Vardi. Alternating automata and program verification. In *Computer Science Today –Recent Trends and Developments*, volume 1000 of *Lecture Notes in Computer Science*, pages 471–485. Springer-Verlag, Berlin, 1995.

[Var96]   M.Y. Vardi. An automata-theoretic approach to linear temporal logic. In F. Moller and G. Birtwistle, editors, *Logics for Concurrency: Structure versus Automata*, volume 1043 of *Lecture Notes in Computer Science*, pages 238–266. Springer-Verlag, Berlin, 1996.

[VW86]   M.Y. Vardi and P. Wolper. An automata-theoretic approach to automatic program verification. In *Proc. First Symposium on Logic in Computer Science*, pages 322–331, Cambridge, June 1986.

[VW94]   M.Y. Vardi and P. Wolper. Reasoning about infinite computations. *Information and Computation*, 115(1):1–37, November 1994.

[Wol83]   P. Wolper. Temporal logic can be more expressive. *Information and Control*, 56(1–2):72–99, 1983.

[Wol89]   P. Wolper. On the relation of programs and computations to models of temporal logic. In B. Banieqbal, H. Barringer, and A. Pnueli, editors, *Proc. Temporal Logic in Specification*, volume 398, pages 75–123. Lecture Notes in Computer Science, Springer-Verlag, 1989.

Formal Verification of a Power Controller Using the Real-Time Model Checker UPPAAL

Klaus Havelund[1], Kim Guldstrand Larsen[2], and Arne Skou[2]

[1] NASA Ames Research Center, Recom Technologies, CA, USA
havelund@ptolemy.arc.nasa.gov
[2] BRICS, Aalborg University, Denmark
{kgl,ask}@cs.auc.dk

Abstract. A real-time system for power-down control in audio/video components is modeled and verified using the real-time model checker UPPAAL. The system is supposed to reside in an audio/video component and control (read from and write to) links to neighbor audio/video components such as TV, VCR and remote–control. In particular, the system is responsible for the powering up and down of the component in between the arrival of data, and in order to do so in a safe way without loss of data, it is essential that no link interrupts are lost. Hence, a component system is a multitasking system with hard real-time requirements, and we present techniques for modeling time consumption in such a multitasked, prioritized system. The work has been carried out in a collaboration between Aalborg University and the audio/video company B&O. By modeling the system, 3 design errors were identified and corrected, and the following verification confirmed the validity of the design but also revealed the necessity for an upper limit of the interrupt frequency. The resulting design has been implemented and it is going to be incorporated as part of a new product line.

1 Introduction

Since the basic results by Alur, Courcoubetis and Dill [3,4] on decidability of model checking for real–time systems with dense time, a number of tools for automatic verification of hybrid and real–time systems have emerged [7,14,10]. These tools have by now reached a state, where they are mature enough for application on industrial development of real-time systems as we hope to demonstrate in this paper.

One such tool is the real–time verification tool UPPAAL[1] [7] developed jointly by BRICS[2] at Aalborg University and Department of Computing Systems at Uppsala University. The tool provides support for automatic verification of safety and bounded liveness properties of real–time systems and contains a number of additional features including graphical interfaces for designing and simulating system models. The tool has been applied successfully to a number of case–studies [13,18,5,6,16,9] which can roughly be divided in two classes: real–time controllers and real–time communication protocols.

---

[1] See URL: http://www.docs.uu.se/docs/rtmv/uppaal for information about UPPAAL.
[2] BRICS – Basic Research in Computer Science – is a basic research centre funded by the Danish government at Aarhus and Aalborg University.

J.-P. Katoen (Ed.): ARTS'99, LNCS 1601, pp. 277–298, 1999.
© Springer-Verlag Berlin Heidelberg 1999

Industrial developers of embedded systems have been following the above work with great interest, because the real–time aspects of concurrent systems can be extremely difficult to analyze during the design and implementation phase. One such company is Bang & Olufsen (B&O) – having development and production of fully integrated home audio/video systems as a main activity.

The work presented in this paper documents a collaboration between AAU (Aalborg University) – under the BRICS project – and B&O on the development of one of the company's new designs: a system for audio/video power control. The system is supposed to reside in an audio/video component and control (read from and write to) links to neighbor audio/video components such as TV, VCR and remote–control. In particular, the system is responsible for the powering up and down of the component in between the arrival of data, and in order to do so, it is essential that no link interrupts are lost. The work is a continuation of an earlier successful collaboration [13] between the same two organizations, where an existing audio/video protocol for detecting collisions on a link between audio/video components was analyzed and found to contain a timing error causing occasional data loss. The interesting point was, that the error was a decade old, like the protocol, and that it was known to exist – but normal testing had never been sufficient in tracking down the reason for the error.

The collaboration between B&O and AAU spanned 3 weeks (4 including report writing), and was very intense the first week, where a representative from B&O visited AAU, and a first sketch of the model was produced. During the next two weeks, the model was refined, and 15 properties formulated by B&O in natural language were formalized and then verified using the UPPAAL model checker. During a meeting, revisions to the model and properties were suggested, and a final effort was spent on model revision, re-verification and report writing. The present paper is an intensive elaboration of the preliminary report [12][3].

The paper is structured as follows. Section 2 contains an informal description of the B&O protocol, and in section 3 we present the UPPAAL modeling language and tool. In section 4 we present our techniques for modeling timed transitions and interrupts in the UPPAAL language. Section 5 presents the formal modeling of this protocol in the UPPAAL language, while section 6 presents the verification results. Finally section 7 provides an evaluation of the project and points out future work.

2   Informal Description of the Power Down Protocol

In this section, we provide an informal description of the designed protocol for power down control in an audio/video component. As advocated in [15], we divide the description into environment, syntax, and protocol rules.

2.1   Protocol Environment

A typical B&O configuration consists of a number of components, which are interconnected by different kinds of links carrying audio/video data and (or) control information. Each component is equipped with two processors controlling audio/video devices

---

[3] A full version of the paper is available at
   http://ic-www.arc.nasa.gov/ic/projects/amphion/people/havelund.

and links, and among other tasks, the processors must minimize the energy consumption when the component goes stand by. Each processor may be in one of two modes: (1) active, where it is operational and can handle its devices and links, (2) stand by, where it is unable to do anything except wake up and enter active mode. One of the processors acts as a master in the sense that it may order the other processor (the slave) to enter stand by mode (and thereby reduce energy consumption). Due to physical laws[4] a processor cannot leave stand by mode via one atomic action, and the purpose of the protocol is to ensure that stand by operation is handled in a consistent way, i.e. when one of the processors enters or leaves stand by mode, this is also recognized by the other processor. Furthermore, whenever a processor senses valid data on an external link, it must leave stand by operation. Also, the real-time duration for switching between the modes may not exceed a given upper limit in order not to lose messages.

Figure 1 illustrates the processor interconnection and our model of the software architecture for one of the processors. Each processor communicates with devices and other components via external links[5], and the two processors are interconnected via an internal link. The software architecture will be almost identical for the two processors, and in this report we concentrate on the IOP3212 processor – the slave processor. The main software module is the IOP process which communicates with the AP processor, the external link drivers, and the interrupt handlers according to the protocol rules described below. The protocol forms the crucial part of the software design, because it must assure that no data and interrupts are lost (in order to leave stand by operation at due time).

2.2 Protocol Syntax

The power down protocol entity (the IOP process) communicates with its environment (AP processor, link drivers and interrupt handlers) via the protocol commands in the set: {ap_down, ap_active, ap_down_ack, ap_down_nack, data, no_data, interrupt, no_interrupt}. The *ap_down* command is sent from the AP processor and commands the IOP processor to enter stand by operation. The *data* command is sent from a link driver and indicates that meaningful input has been detected on the link, whereas the *no_data* command indicates that there is no input from the link. Likewise, the *interrupt (no_interrupt)* command is sent from from the link interrupt handler and indicates that an interrupt (or no interrupt) has been received at the link interrupt interface. The commands *ap_active, ap_down_ack, ap_down_nack* informs the AP3002 processor about state changes of the protocol, that is, *ap_active* is sent when the IOP3212 processor becomes active, *ap_down_ack* is sent when it accepts to enter stand by mode, and *ap_down_nack* is sent when stand by cannot be entered.

2.3 Protocol Rules

In order to give an intuitive explanation of the protocol, we describe below in an informal way the major protocol rules, which must be obeyed by the IOP protocol entity. We

---

[4] It takes e.g. approx. 1 ms to make the processor operational when it has been in stand by operation.
[5] The figure illustrates a configuration with one external link, the LSL link.

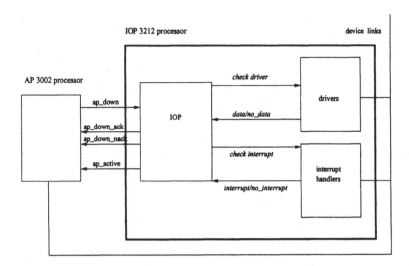

Fig. 1. Software architecture of the power down protocol. The protocol entity process (IOP) receives protocol commands (left arrows) from the drivers and interrupt handlers by issuing check commands (right arrows).

leave out the details on communication with interrupt handlers and drivers, which will be described in the formalization section. In order to structure the description, we define the following major phases (see Figure 2 below) for the entity: the *active phase*, where the IOP is in normal (active) operation, the *check driver phase*, where the IOP process is waiting for a driver status (no data/data) in order to decide whether or not to leave the active phase, the *stand_by phase*, where the IOP processor is out of operation, and the *check interrupts phase*, where the IOP processor is waiting for an interrupt handler status (no interrupt/interrupt) in order to decide whether or not to enter the stand by phase. We use ?/! to indicate protocol input/output in the usual way.

Active rule In the active phase, the IOP protocol entity must enter the check driver phase, whenever a *ap_down* command is received from the AP processor.

Check driver rule In the check driver phase, the IOP protocol entity commands the drivers to check whether or not meaningful data are received from the links. The outcome of the check defines the succeeding phase according to Figure 2.

Stand_by rule Whenever an interrupt is received in the stand by phase, the IOP protocol entity must enter the check driver phase.

Check interrupts rule In the check interrupts phase, the protocol entity commands the interrupt handlers to check for pending interrupts. If no interrupts are pending, the stand by phase can safely be entered. Otherwise, the check driver phase is entered.

The above rules have to be implemented in such a way, that (1) Whenever an interrupt is received and meaningful data is present on the given link, the active phase must be entered, and (2) Whenever a down signal is received from the AP processor and no interrupts and valid data are present, the stand by phase must be entered. The

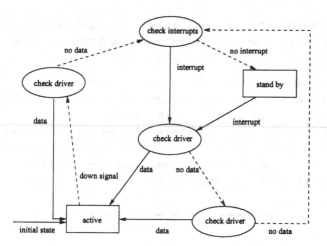

Fig. 2. Major protocol phases. The dotted lines indicate transitions leading towards power down. The full lines are leading towards power up. The two neighboring 'check driver' phases are necessary in order to be able to ignore noise from the communication lines.

delay caused by software of these transitions may not exceed $1500\mu s$ since otherwise data may be lost.

The informal rules form the basis for the model design, and in the analysis section, we present a complete list of protocol requirements in terms of properties of the formal protocol model.

3   The UPPAAL Model and Tool

UPPAAL is a tool box for symbolic simulation and automatic verification of real–timed systems modeled as networks of timed automata [4] extended with global shared integer variables. More precisely, a model consists of a collection of non–deterministic processes with finite control structure and real–valued clocks communicating through channels and shared integer variables. The tool box is developed in collaboration between BRICS at Aalborg University and Department of Computing Systems at Uppsala University, and has been applied to several case–studies [13,18,5,6,16,9].

The current version of UPPAAL is implemented in C++, XFORMS and MOTIF and includes the following main features:

- A graphical interface based on Autograph [8] allowing graphical descriptions of systems.
- A compiler transforming graphical descriptions into a textual programming format.
- A simulator, which provides a graphical visualization and recording of the possible dynamic behaviors of a system description. This allows for inexpensive fault detection in the early modeling stages.
- A model checker for automatic verification of safety and bounded–liveness properties by on–the–fly reachability analysis.

– Generation of (shortest) diagnostic traces in case verification of a particular real–time system fails. The diagnostic traces may be graphically visualized using the simulator.

A system description (or model) in UPPAAL consists of a collection of automata modeling the finite control structures of the system. In addition the model uses a finite set of (global) real–valued clocks and integer variables.

Consider the model of Figure 3. The model consists of two components A and B with control nodes {A0, A1, A2, A3} and {B0, B1, B2, B3} respectively. In addition to these discrete control structures, the model uses two clocks x and y, one integer variable n and a channel a for communication.

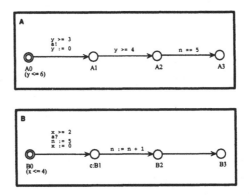

Fig. 3. An example UPPAAL model

The edges of the automata are decorated with three types of labels: a *guard*, expressing a condition on the values of clocks and integer variables that must be satisfied in order for the edge to be taken; a synchronization *action* which is performed when the edge is taken forcing as in CCS [19] synchronization with another component on a complementary action[6], and finally a number of *clock resets* and *assignments* to integer variables. All three types of labels are optional: absence of a guard is interpreted as the condition *true*, and absence of a synchronization action indicates an internal (non–synchronizing) edge similar to τ–transitions in CCS. Reconsider Figure 3. Here the edge between A0 and A1 can only be taken, when the value of the clock y is greater than or equal to 3. When the edge is taken the action a! is performed thus insisting on synchronization with B on the complementary action a?; that is for A to take the edge in question, B must simultaneously be able to take the edge from B0 to B1. Finally, when taking the edge, the clock y is reset to 0.

In addition, control nodes may be decorated with so–called *invariants*, which express constraints on the clock values in order for control to remain in a particular node. Thus, in Figure 3, control can only remain in A0 as long as the value of y is no more than 6.

[6] Given a channel name a, a! and a? denote complementary actions corresponding to *sending* respectively *receiving* on the channel a.

Formally, states of a UPPAAL model are of the form $(\bar{l}, v)$, where $\bar{l}$ is a *control vector* indicating the current control node for each component of the network and v is an *assignment* given the current value for each clock and integer variable. The *initial state* of a UPPAAL model consists of the initial node of all components[7] and an assignment giving the value 0 for all clocks and integer variables. A UPPAAL model determines the following two types of *transitions* between states:

Delay transitions As long as none of the invariants of the control nodes in the current state are violated, time may progress without affecting the control node vector and with all clock values incremented with the elapsed duration of time. In Figure 3, from the initial state $\langle(A0, B0), x = 0, y = 0, n = 0\rangle$ time may elapse 3.5 time units leading to the state $\langle(A0, B0), x = 3.5, y = 3.5, n = 0\rangle$. However, time cannot elapse 5 time units as this would violate the invariant of B0.

Action transitions If two complementary labeled edges of two different components are enabled in a state then they can synchronize. Thus in state $\langle(A0, B0), x = 3.5, y = 3.5, n = 0\rangle$ the two components can synchronize on a leading to the new state $\langle(A1, B1), x = 0, y = 0, n = 5\rangle$ (note that x, y, and n have been appropriately updated). If a component has an internal edge enabled, the edge can be taken without any synchronization. Thus in state $\langle(A1, B1), x = 0, y = 0, n = 5\rangle$, the B–component can perform without synchronizing with A, leading to the state $\langle(A1, B2), x = 0, y = 0, n = 6\rangle$.

Finally, in order to enable modeling of atomicity of transition–sequences of a particular component (i.e. without time–delay and interleaving of other components) nodes may be marked as *committed* (indicated by a c–prefix). If in a state one of the components is in a control node labeled as being committed, no delay is allowed to occur and any action transition (synchronizing or not) *must* involve the particular component (the component is so–to–speak committed to continue). In the state $((A1, B1), x = 0, y = 0, n = 5)$ B1 is committed; thus without any delay the next transition must involve the B–component. Hence the two first transitions of B are guaranteed to be performed atomically. Besides ensuring atomicity, the notion of *committed* nodes also helps in significantly reducing the space–consumption during verification. Channels can in addition be defined as *urgent*: when two components can synchronize on an urgent channel no further delay is allowed before communication takes place.

In this section and indeed in the modeling of the audio/video protocol presented in the following sections, the values of all clocks are assumed to increase with identical speed (perfect clocks). However, UPPAAL also supports analysis of timed automata with varying and drifting time–speed of clocks. This feature was crucial in the modeling and analysis of the Philips Audio–Control protocol [5] using UPPAAL.

UPPAAL is able to check for reachability properties, in particular whether a certain combination of control-nodes and constraints on clock and data variables is reachable from an initial configuration. The properties that can be analyzed are of two forms: "A[ ]p" and "E<>p", where p is a formula over clock variables, data variables, and control-node positions. Intuitively for "A[ ]p" to be satisfied, all reachable states must satisfy p. Dually, for "E<>p" to be satisfied, some reachable state must satisfy p.

---

[7] indicated graphically by a double circled node.

4   Timed Transitions and Interrupts

In this section, we shall introduce techniques for dealing with a couple of concepts that appear in the protocol, and which are not supported directly by the UPPAAL notation. These concepts are on the one hand *time slicing* in combination with *time consuming transitions*, and on the other hand prioritized *interrupts*. We refer to time slicing as the activity of delegating and scheduling execution rights to processes that all run on the same single processor. Transitions normally don't take time in UPPAAL, but this occurs in the protocol. Interrupts is a well known concept.

First, we give a small example illustrating what we need. Then we suggest the techniques that we shall apply in the modeling of the protocol.

4.1   The Problem

Assume a system with two processes A and B running on a single processor. Assume further, that these processes can be interrupted by an interrupt handler. The situation is illustrated in Figure 4, which is *not* expressed in the UPPAAL language, but rather in some informal extension of the language.

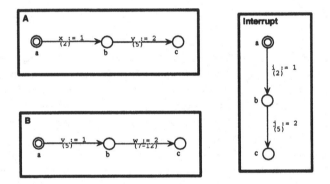

Fig. 4. What we want to express

Each edge modifies a variable (A modifies x and y, B modifies v and w, and the interrupt handler modifies i and j). These assignments only serve to identify the edges and have no real importance for the example. Each edge is furthermore labeled with a time slot within parenthesis (2, 5, 7-12), indicating the amount of time units the edge takes. The slot 7-12 means anywhere between 7 and 12 time units.

Suppose the interrupt handler does not interrupt. Then the semantics should be the following: A and B execute in an interleaved manner modeling the time slicing of the processor – each transition taking the amount of time it is labeled with. No unnecessary time is spent in intermediate nodes (except waiting for the other process to execute). At the end, as soon as both A and B are in the node c, at least 19 $(2 + 5 + 5 + 7)$ and at most 24 $(2 + 5 + 5 + 12)$ time units will have passed.

An interrupt can occur at any moment and executes "to the end" when occurring. That is, it goes from node a to c without neither A nor B being allowed to execute in the meantime. If we assume that the interrupt handler can also interrupt, then it will change the above numbers to 26 $(19 + 2 + 5)$ and 31 $(24 + 2 + 5)$.

Or goal is now to formulate this in the UPPAAL language. Consider an approach where nodes are annotated with time constraints on local clocks, expressing the time consumed by the *previous* edge. This solution does not work since the two automata may consume time "together", and does not reflect the desired behavior, since they are supposed to run on a single processor. Let us first model time consuming transitions, ignoring the interrupts for a moment.

4.2 Modeling Timed Transitions

In a single processor setting it is natural to hand over time control to a single "operating system" process. Figure 5 illustrates such a process, called Timer, using a local clock k.

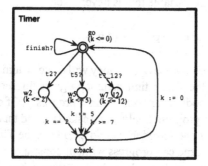

Fig. 5. The Timer

It has a start node, named go, in which time is constrained to not progress at all. This means that in order for time to progress, one of the edges t2?, t5? or t7_12? must be taken. These edges then lead to nodes where time can progress the corresponding number of time units, where after control returns immediately (back is a committed node just used to collect the edges) to the go node.

Now let us turn to the processes A and B, which are shown in Figure 6. These now communicate with the Timer, asking for time slots. Every time unit T that in the informal model, Figure 4, was in brackets (T) is now expressed as tT!. When for example A takes the edge from node a to node b, the Timer goes into the node w2, and stays there for 2 time units while A stays in node b. Hence, the time consumed by an edge is really consumed in the node it leads to. We have, however, guaranteed that B for example, cannot go to the node b and consume time "in parallel" since that would require a communication with Timer, and this is not ready for that before it returns to the node go.

When A reaches the node c, it has not yet consumed 7 time units $(2 + 5)$, it has only consumed 2. The 5 will be consumed while in node c. In order to reach a state where we for sure know that all the time has been consumed, we add an extra d node, which is reached by communicating finish! to the Timer. This forces the Timer to "finish"

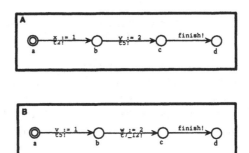

Fig. 6. A and B communicating with the Timer

the last time consumption. Now we can express and verify the following true property, where gc is a global clock variable that is never reset:

```
A[] (A.d and B.d) imply ((19 <= gc) and (gc <= 24))
```

That is, if both A and B reach node d, then they will do so within 19−24 time units. Note that due to the design of the Timer, time cannot progress further when that happens (the Timer will be in the go node where time cannot progress). Of course one can design a Timer that allows time to progress freely when asked to, and that is in fact what happens in the protocol. Basically one introduces an idle node in the Timer, that can be entered upon request, and where time can progress without constraints.

It is possible to model such single processor time scheduling in model checkers lacking real-time features, such as for example SPIN [15]. However, when trying to formulate and verify properties where time ticks are summed up, such explicit modeling easily leads to state space explosion.

4.3 Modeling Interrupts

Now we incorporate the interrupt handler. The basic idea is to give a priority to each process, and then maintain a variable, which at any moment contains the priority currently active. Processes with a priority lower than the current cannot execute. When an interrupt occurs, the current priority is set to a value higher than those of the processes interrupted.

Processes A and B can for example have priority 0 while the interrupt handler gets priority 1. When the interrupt occurs, the current priority is then set to 1, preventing priority 0 processes from running. We introduce the variable cur for this purpose, see Figure 7. The Timer stays unchanged.

Note how the variable cur occurs in guards of A and B, and how it is assigned to by the interrupt handler. In this model, we can verify the following property to be true:

```
A[] (A.d and B.d and Interrupt.d) imply
   (26 <= gc and gc <= 31)
```

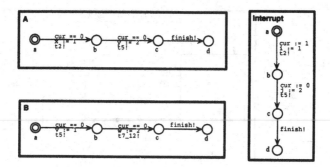

Fig. 7. Dealing with interrupts

5 Formalization in UPPAAL

In this section, we shall formalize the system in UPPAAL. We start with an overview of the components and their interaction via channels and shared variables. Then we describe the IOP in detail.

5.1 Component Overview

The system consists of 7 automata, as illustrated in Figure 8. The Timer controls the time slicing between the components using the technique described in section 4.2. In addition, there is an environment which generates interrupts corresponding to data arriving on the links; hence this environment is referred to as the Interrupt Generator.

The components communicate via channel synchronization and via shared variables. The figure illustrates the channel connections by fully drawn arcs, each going from one component (the one that does a send "!") to another (the one that does a receive "?"). Also, all shared variables are plotted into the figure, in italics, with dotted lines indicating their role as message carriers, from the process that typically writes to the variable to the process that typically reads the variable. This notation is informal, but it should give an overview of the shared variables and the role they play in communication. Channels and variables are described below.

5.2 The Channels

The AP signals the IOP to go down by issuing an ap_down! (which the IOP then consumes by performing a dual ap_down?). The channels ap_down_ack and ap_down_nack correspond to the IOP's response to such an ap_down signal from the AP. They represent the acknowledgment (ack) respectively the negative acknowledgment (nack) that the closing down has succeeded respectively not succeeded. The ap_active channel is used by the IOP to request the AP to become active.

The channels reset, wait, wait_int, i_reset, i_wait are all used to operate the timer. Basically, the reset and i_reset channels are used to activate the timer, to start delivering time slots, while the wait, wait_int and i_wait channels are used to dis-activate the timer, to stop delivering time slots. Different channels for resetting (reset and i_reset) respectively waiting (wait, wait_int and i_wait)

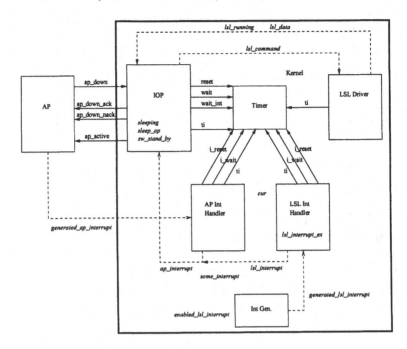

Fig. 8. The components

are needed due to different interpretations of these commands in different contexts. Whenever activated, the timer then delivers time slots to the IOP, the LSL (Low Speed Link) driver, and the interrupt handlers when these issue signals on the t_i channels.

5.3 The Shared Variables

The interrupt generator generates interrupts corresponding to data arriving on the links. Such an interrupt is generated by setting the variable generated_lsl_interrupt to 1 (*true*). The LSL interrupt handler then reacts on this by interrupting the IOP or the driver, whichever is running. A result of such an interrupt is that the variable lsl_interrupt is set to 1. The IOP reads the value of this variable, and hence is triggered to deal with new data if it equals 1. In order for the interrupt generator to generate interrupts at all, the variable enabled_lsl_interrupt must be 1. Concerning the AP, there is a generated_ap_interrupt and an ap_interrupt, but there is no enabled_ap_interrupt. The AP itself plays the role as AP interrupt generator, and hence sets the generated_ap_interrupt to 1, while the AP interrupt handler reacts to this by setting the ap_interrupt to 1. The variable some_interrupt is 1 whenever either ap_interrupt or lsl_interrupt is 1.

    The variable cur is used to secure that an interrupt handler gets higher priority than the process it interrupts. Note that in this sense, the IOP and the driver have the lowest priority (0), while the LSL interrupt handler has one higher (1), and the AP interrupt handler has the highest (2). Hence, whenever the value of cur is 0, the IOP and the LSL driver are allowed to execute. When the LSL interrupt handler starts executing, it sets the value to 1, whereby the IOP and driver are no longer allowed to execute. The AP interrupt handler can further interrupt all the previous processes, assigning 2 to cur, whereby all other processes with lower priority are denied to execute.

We said that the AP interrupt handler can interrupt the LSL interrupt handler. This is a truth with modifications. In fact, it is not allowed to interrupt during the initialization phase of the LSL interrupt handler. This is modeled by introducing a semaphore lsl_interrupt_ex. It is used to exclude the AP interrupt handler from interrupting the LSL interrupt handler during the latter's first activities.

The IOP sends messages to the LSL driver by assigning values to the variable lsl_command with the following meanings: 1 = *Initialize the driver*, 2 = *Close down the driver*, and 3 = *Activate the driver*. After initialization of the driver, the IOP can read the results of the driver's activity (whether it is still running and whether there are data or not) in the variables lsl_running and lsl_data. Since the model is a reduction from a bigger model also involving the AP driver, we had early in the design a need for maintaining a variable some_running, being true if either ap_running or lsl_running was true, and likewise we needed a variable some_data, being true if either lsl_data or other similar variables were true. These two variables have survived after we have reduced the model.

The three variables sw_stand_by, sleeping and sleep_op are central to the closing down procedure, and the interaction between the IOP and the interrupt handlers. Figure 9 illustrates the relevant pieces of code in the IOP (when approaching stand by mode), respectively the Interrupt handlers. To start with the IOP, the variable sleep_op is a kind of *"emergency break"* which can be "pulled" by the interrupt handler. The IOP assigns *true* to this variable, and it has to be *true* before going to sleep. The interrupt handler can change the value of *sleep_op* "in last micro second". Next, the IOP assigns *true* to the variable sw_stand_by when approaching the stand_by node. Hence this variable is *true* in a certain critical time zone just before closing down[8]. When the IOP finally goes down (enters the stand_by mode), the variable sleeping becomes *true*.

The value of sw_stand_by is used by the interrupt handlers when activated to see whether the IOP is in its critical closing down zone. If so, they assign the value *false* to the variable sleep_op, and this will then prevent the IOP from going to sleep. The interrupt handlers also "wake up" (sleeping := 0) the IOP in case it is sleeping (sleeping == 1). The sleeping variable is used by the interrupt handler to direct the amount of time used to restart the IOP. If sleeping == 1 it takes 900 micro seconds, otherwise it is instantaneous. We shall see the IOP algorithm formulated in UPPAAL below.

5.4   The IOP

The IOP, Figure 10, is obtained by refining (in an informal sense) the abstract model presented in Figure 2. The model is refined using *state refinement* as well as *action refinement*. By state refinement we mean that certain states (the ovals) are expanded out to sub–transition systems with new states connected with new (labeled) arcs. We have

---

[8] In the C-implementation, the variable sw_stand_by is a register informing the processor hardware about the approaching close down.

```
IOP:                              Interrupt Handler:
  sleep_op := 1;                    If sleeping == 1 Then
  sw_stand_by := 1;                   ''spend 900 ms''
  If sleep_op == 1 Then               sleeping := 0
    sleeping := 1;                  End;
    ''stand by''                    If sw_stand_by == 1 Then
  End;                                sleep_op := 0;
  ''after interrupt'':                sw_stand_by := 0
  sw_stand_by := 0                  End;
  ''go up''
```

Fig. 9. The variables sw_stand_by, sleeping and sleep_op

enclosed these new sub–systems in boxes on Figure 10 such that they can be easier related to Figure 2. Note, however, that this is not formal UPPAAL notation. By action refinement we mean that also arcs are expanded out to such sub–transition systems. Concerning state refinement, we have expanded each *"check driver"* state into a couple of states: driver_call – representing the point where a driver has been called – and driver_return – representing the point where the driver returns. The state *"check interrupts"* has been expanded out to a small transition system consisting of the four states: insert_noop, set_stand_by, check_interrupts and check_noop.

The IOP starts being active, in the node active. In this node it does not need time slots, hence the timer is supposed to be inactive. Note that although the IOP is in the node active, and hence intuitively is active, from a technical point of view, we don't see it as requiring time slots, since it does not take any transitions.

Now it can receive an ap_down signal from the AP, ordering it to close down. It then proceeds (up, left – referring to the approximate position on the figure) by resetting the timer – reset!, indicating that now it wants processor time slots necessary to close down. It then initializes the variables lsl_running (to 1) and lsl_data (to 0) preparing the activation of the LSL driver, initially assuming that there are no data. Note the *"priority 0"* guard – cur == 0 – and the time slot demand – t6! – requiring 6 micro seconds to initialize these variables. The time constant, and all other time constants in the model, have been estimated by the protocol developers at B&O. When the driver later returns, it will have set the variable lsl_running to 0, and now the IOP can check the value of lsl_data. The driver is, however, first activated with the assignment of 2 (close down) to the variable lsl_command in the edge leading to the node driver_call1.

In this node the IOP waits for the driver to finish its job. If at that point, in node driver_return1, lsl_data equals 1 there is data, and the IOP must activate the driver – lsl_command is assigned the value 3 – and it must respond to the AP with a negative acknowledgment – ap_down_nack!. If on the other hand lsl_data equals 0, then there are no data on the link, and the IOP can proceed successfully to close down, next checking whether there are any interrupts. First, however, it acknowledges via an ap_down_ack! signal to the AP, and then goes to the node insert_noop (up, right) to check interrupts. A possible trace from here leads to the node stand_by, where the IOP is sleeping, and can only be wakened by an interrupt. The waiting for an interrupt is done by issuing a wait_int! signal to the timer just before entering the stand_by node. When an interrupt occurs thereafter, the timer will ensure that the IOP is re-activated immediately.

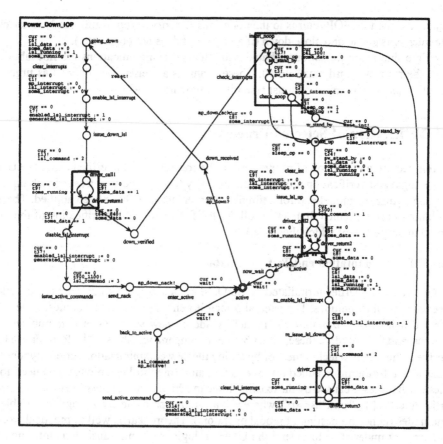

Fig. 10. The IOP

If on the other hand, before reaching the stand_by node, an interrupt has already occurred, then the IOP will avoid going into that node and instead go directly to the wake_up node. Hence, in this node we assume that an interrupt has occurred, and now the LSL driver has to be re-started, since apparently there must be data. This means re-initializing the variables lsl_running and lsl_data, and then assigning the value 1 (initialize) to lsl_command. In the node driver_call2, the IOP then waits for the LSL driver to return. If there is data – lsl_data equals 1 – the AP is asked to become active – ap_active! – and the IOP goes into the node active. Note that when entering this node, a wait! signal is issued to the timer to dis-activate it. If on the other hand there are no data – lsl_data equals 0 – then what has been encountered is noise, and the node noise is entered. In this node the IOP wants to close down, but before doing this, the driver is asked to close down – lsl_command is assigned the value 2. The IOP then waits in the node driver_return3 for the drivers response.

Now, if there is data – lsl_data equals 1 the AP is activated – ap_active! – and the node active is entered. If on the other hand there are no data – lsl_data equals 0 – then the IOP returns to the node `insert_noop` (up, right), ready to check the interrupts again, and close down (if an interrupt does not occur, etc.).

Note that some transitions labeled with channel communications are not labeled with the priority guard `cur == 0`. These channels are elsewhere defined as urgent, meaning that communication must take place immediately whenever enabled.

6 Verification of Selected Properties

In this section a collection of properties will be formulated and verified using the UP-PAAL logic and verification tool. In order to verify these properties, a set of techniques for annotating the model and for defining observer automata have been applied. These techniques are presented first. Then follows the formulation and verification of the individual properties of which there are 15.

6.1 Model Annotation and Test Automata

Amongst the properties formulated by B&O, in particular three kinds were typical and needed special techniques. The general principle behind the three techniques, to be described below, is to *annotate* the model by adding new variables or communication actions, and then observe these, either by mentioning the variables in the formulae to be verified (the first two techniques) or by letting the new communication actions synchronize with a furthermore added observer automaton (the third technique). The need for these techniques is caused by the existing logic in which it only is possible to state properties like: "A[]p" and "E<>p", where p is an atomic predicate over program variables and nodes (hence no nesting of modal operators). Theoretical as well as practical work is currently undertaken to extend the UPPAAL logic, defining translations into model annotations and observers as outlined below.

The FLAG Technique The first technique, called the FLAG technique for later reference, is illustrated in Figure 11. Suppose we have an automaton A containing two states (amongst others): a and b, and suppose we want to verify, that *"there is a path from a to b"*.

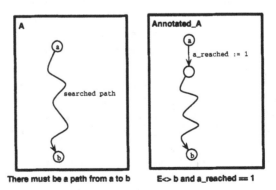

Fig. 11. Automaton A and its annotation

Note, that the current logic does not allow nested modal operators, hence it is for example not possible to state this as: "E<> (a and E<>b)" saying that there exists a path such that eventually node a is reached and from there node b can be reached. The technique consists of annotating automaton A, obtaining automaton Annotated_A, by adding a boolean *flag* variable a_reached, which initially has the value 0, and which is assigned the value 1 when passing through a. The property can now be formally stated as follows: "E<>(b and a_reached == 1)". That is, eventually node b is reached, after having passed through node a.

The DEBT technique The second technique, called the DEBT technique, is illustrated in Figure 12. Suppose we have an automaton B containing three states (amongst others): a, b and x, and suppose we want to verify, that *"every path from a to b must pass through x"*.

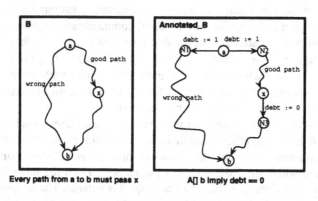

Fig. 12. Automaton B and its annotation

In an imagined extended logic this could be formulated as follows:
"A[] (a imply ((not b) Until x))" saying that if at any time a is reached, then "not b" will hold until x has been reached[9]. The technique consists of annotating automaton B, obtaining automaton Annotated_B, by adding a boolean variable debt, which initially has the value 0, and which is assigned the value 1 when passing through a. Furthermore, when passing through x it is reset to 0 – the debt has been "cashed". The property can now be formally stated as follows: "A[] b imply debt == 0". That is, if at any point node b is reached, then debt must not be 1, since that would indicate that node a had been reached before, but not x in between.

The OBSERVER Technique The last technique, called the OBSERVER technique, is illustrated in Figure 13. Suppose we have an automaton C containing two nodes (amongst others): a and b, and suppose we want to verify, that *"from node a, node b must be reached within T time units"*.

In an extended logic this could be formulated as follows: "A[] (a imply A<T> b)" saying that if at any time a is reached, then eventually – within T time units – node

---

[9] Note that the Until operator here must be *weak* in the sense that node x need not be reached at all, and hence node b need not be reached neither, which is what we want.

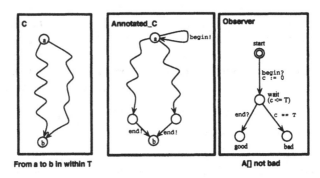

Fig. 13. Automaton C, its annotation and observer

b will be reached. The technique consists of annotating automaton C, obtaining automaton Annotated_C, by adding two kinds of communication actions, each of which communicates with an added observer that measures time. Let's first look at Annotated_C. When in node a, a begin! signal can be issued, telling the observer to start measure time. When reaching node b, no matter along which path, an end! signal is issued, telling the observer to stop measure time. The channel end is declared as *urgent*, hence it will be taken as soon as node b is reached.

The Observer automaton rests in the start node until it receives a begin? signal (node a reached), where after it initializes its local clock c and enters the node wait where time can progress. Time can, however, only progress T time units due to the node invariant, where after the node bad is entered. If on the other hand an end? signal is received before that, then the node good is entered. The property can now be formally stated as a property of the observer: "A[] not bad". That is, the Observer will never reach node bad: an end? signal will always be received (b reached) before T time units.

6.2 Property Verification

In this section we shall present the results of analyzing in UPPAAL various desired properties. The properties as directly formulated by B&O are listed below, with explanatory comments in brackets. The listing is just supposed to give the reader a general feeling of the kinds of properties formulated.

1. sleeping must not change from 0 to 1 while sleep_op has the value 0. *(The IOP must not go to sleep if there has been an interrupt – see Figure 9 for an explanation of these variables.)*

2. There must be a path from active to stand_by and vice versa. *(It must be possible for the IOP to switch between its two final states.)*

3. Every path from active to noise must pass through stand_by *(The IOP must have been asleep before reaching the noise state where it on its way up due to an interrupt discovers that the interrupt is "false", and hence caused by noise only.)*

4. The variable sleeping must not change from 0 to 1 while lsl_interrupt is 1 or ap_interrupt is 1 *(The IOP must not go to sleep as long as there is an untreated interrupt.)*

5. The shortest way from driver_return1 to driver_call2 does not take more than 1500 µs *(If the IOP on its way down verifies that the link is empty by calling the driver, and then immediately thereafter data arrive (an interrupt occurs) no more than 1500 µs must pass before the driver is called again.)*

6. The shortest way from driver_return1 to active does not take more than 1500 µs *(If the IOP on its way down discovers data on the link by calling the driver, then no more than 1500 µs must pass before the IOP is active again.)*

7. The shortest way from driver_return3 to driver_call2 does not take more than 1500 µs *(Like 5, but in a different place in the protocol's execution.)*

8. The shortest way from driver_return3 to active does not take more than 1500 µs *(Like 6, but in a different place in the protocol's execution.)*

9. If the last value of the variable lsl_command has been 1 or 3 (driver starting commands), then the value of sleeping must not change from 0 to 1 *(If the last command issued to the driver was a "start command", then the IOP must not go to sleep.)*

10. If the last value of lsl_command has been 3 (activate driver), then the next value must not be 1 (initialize driver), and vice versa *(In between two driver starting commands must come a driver closing command.)*

11. No more than 1500 µs must pass from an interrupt occurs until all drivers are active

12. It must be possible for both interrupt handlers to want to assign 0 to sleep_op at the same time, while in addition this variable's value is already 0 *(Intuition missing – "technical" property.)*

13. If both interrupt handlers want to assign 0 to sleep_op at the same time, then the IOP will be in one of the nodes: set_stand_by, check_interrupts, check_noop, w_stand_by, stand_by, or wake_up *(If both an LSL and an AP interrupt occur, and both interrupt handlers believe that the IOP is approaching stand by mode, then this is the case.)*

14. It must be possible to come from the node noise to the node stand_by *(In case IOP has discovered noise on the link, it will reach stand by mode and go to sleep, unless data arrive.)*

15. I should not be possible to come from the node stand_by to the node active without synchronizing on the channel ap_active *(The IOP cannot get from stand by mode to active mode without activating the AP.)*

Figure 14 shows the verification results, indicating the outcome (satisfied or not) and the verification technique used. Those properties not verified using any of the three techniques outlined in section 6.1 have been verified using other and simpler techniques: *"trivial"* means the property was seen correct without verification. *"formula"* means that the property could be directly stated in the UPPAAL temporal logic. Finally, *"formula + aux. variable"* means that by adding an additional variable being updated in appropriate places, the property could be directly stated in the UPPAAL temporal logic. The properties were verified using UPPAAL version 2.17 from March 1998, on a Sun Ultra Sparc 60 with 512 MB main memory.

Properties 3 and 12 turned out not to be satisfied, and after having examined the error traces B&O recognized that these properties were wrongly formulated and hence the "error" traces showed valid behaviors.

Properties 5–8, on the other hand, are interesting in the sense that their verifications failed and caused B&O to reconsider their design. In particular property 5 gave an error trace, where a single LSL interrupt and 18 AP interrupts, all consuming time, are generated before the next driver call. As a result, B&O decided to only allow one AP interrupt to occur in their implementation.

No.	Satisfied?	Technique	Comment	Memory (MB)	Time (min:sec)
1	YES	trivial			
2	YES	FLAG		5.3	0:5
3	NO	DEBT	should not be satisfied	4.1	0:2
4	YES	formula		8.2	0:9
5	NO	OBSERVER	18 AP interrupts causes error	36.0	1:42
6	NO	OBSERVER	24 AP interrupts causes error	22.0	0:56
7	?	OBSERVER	state explosion		
8	NO	OBSERVER	79 AP interrupts causes error	157.0	33:39
9	YES	formula + aux. variable		8.3	0:9
10	YES	formula + aux. variable		8.7	0:25
11	YES	OBSERVER		16.0	0:41
12	NO	formula	should not be satisfied	7.9	0:8
13	YES	formula		8.2	0:9
14	YES	FLAG		8.0	0:8
15	YES	trivial			

Fig. 14. Verification results

7   Conclusion

During a period of 3 weeks, a model of B&O's Power Down protocol was developed and verified using the UPPAAL language and model checker. The first week consisted of an intense collaboration between AAU and B&O, where the B&O representative visited AAU. During this week, a first sketch of the model was written down in UPPAAL's language. The model was based on an initial design sketch made by the company representative. The work carried out during the following two weeks was mainly carried out by AAU. Hence, during the second week, a technique was introduced for dealing with timed transitions and interrupts. During this same week, the model was reduced by omitting certain components in order to obtain a model being verifiable within reasonable time and memory space. In other words, at the end of the second week, a model was produced that was ready for verification. At the beginning of the third (and last) week, various properties to be verified were formulated by B&O in natural language. These were then translated into the UPPAAL temporal logic, together with various modifications to the model, and all verifications were then carried out.

After the collaboration, the company made a C-code implementation, and after a testing phase (which did not reveal any design errors), the implementation is by now ready to be put into operation in the new company product.

During the development of models, we found that the notion of timed automata and their graphical representation served extremely well as a communication medium between the industrial protocol designer and the tool expert doing the simulation and verification. In addition, the graphical simulation features of UPPAAL lead to fast detection of (obvious) errors in the early models.

The protocol was verified correct wrt. the 15 properties formulated by B&O, and although no bugs were identified, various critical time constants were identified, which should be obeyed in order to keep the protocol correct. Various unexpected, but correct, behaviors were furthermore demonstrated, challenging the understanding of the protocol. Overall, the experience appeared to increase B&O's confidence in their design. The fact that 3 errors were caught during the modeling phase suggests that just specifying a system can be very informative. In fact, B&O claimed they had got a better understanding of their system this way.

The collaboration has been beneficial for both partners: B&O now considers tools like UPPAAL as viable means to improve the design process for time-critical software. Also, in order to model the system, we have developed techniques for modeling timed transitions and prioritized interrupts. A timed transition is a transition which consumes time, like code in a program which takes time to execute. It is a special circumstance, that several processes run on a single processor. To the best of our knowledge, such techniques have not been presented elsewhere.

What concerns the UPPAAL tool set, we anticipate investigating techniques for version control, (keeping track of several related models), and we consider tool support for defining abstractions. Both themes appear non-trivial in fact. Concerning the UPPAAL language, a technical contribution of the work is a way of modeling timed transitions and interrupts in a setting where several processes share one processor. In the forthcoming new version of UPPAAL, the introduction of *parameterized* timed automatons will support a more structural way to define time consuming transitions than we have presented in this paper. In [11], the problem of supporting task scheduling is treated. It is likely that this work will be included in later versions of UPPAAL.

In this work, we have sketched a number of patterns which may be used to define properties of real-time systems. In [1,2] the limits of UPPAAL's model checking language are characterized. In future versions of UPPAAL, its timed logic will be modified according to these results - thereby supporting the definition of the patterns in a more direct way.

Acknowledgments The B&O representative was Johnny Kudahl, who we thank for being extremely collaborative and productive, as well during the model building as in formulating the properties to be verified. Also thanks to the reviewers.

References

1. L. Aceto, A. Bergueno, and K. G. Larsen. Model Checking via Reachability Testing for Timed Automata. In B. Steffen, editor, *Proceedings of TACAS'98*, volume 1384 of *Lecture Notes in Computer Science*, pages 263–280, 1998.

2. L. Aceto, P. Bouyer, A. Burgueno, and K. G. Larsen. The Limit of Testing for Timed Automata. In *Proceedings of FST TCS'98*, Lecture Notes in Computer Science, 1998.

3. R. Alur, C. Courcoubetis, and D. Dill. Model-checking for Real-Time Systems. In *Proc. of Logic in Computer Science*, pages 414–425. IEEE Computer Society Press, 1990.

4. R. Alur and D. Dill. Automata for Modelling Real-Time Systems. In *Proc. of ICALP'90*, volume 443 of *Lecture Notes in Computer Science*, 1990.

5. J. Bengtsson, D. Griffioen, K. Kristoffersen, K. G. Larsen, F. Larsson, P. Pettersson, and W. Yi. Verification of an Audio Protocol with Bus Collision Using UPPAAL. In *Proc. of CAV'96*, volume 1102 of *Lecture Notes in Computer Science*. Springer–Verlag, 1996.

6. J. Bengtsson, K. G. Larsen, F. Larsson, P. Pettersson, and W. Yi. UPPAAL — A Tool Suite for Symbolic and Compositional Verification of Real-Time Systems. In *Proc. of the 1st Workshop on Tools and Algorithms for the Construction and Analysis of Systems*, volume 1019 of *Lecture Notes in Computer Science*. Springer–Verlag, May 1995.

7. J. Bengtsson, K. G. Larsen, F. Larsson, P. Pettersson, and W. Yi. UPPAAL in 1995. In *Proc. of the 2nd Workshop on Tools and Algorithms for the Construction and Analysis of*

Systems, number 1055 in Lecture Notes in Computer Science, pages 431–434. Springer–Verlag, March 1996.

8. A. Bouali, A. Ressouche, and V. Roy R. de Simone. The FC2Toolset. *Lecture Notes in Computer Science*, 1102, 1996.

9. P.R. D'Argenio, J.-P. Katoen, T. Ruys, and J. Tretmans. Modelling and Verifying a Bounded Retransmission Protocol. *In Proc. of COST 247, International Workshop on Applied Formal Methods in System Design*, 1996.

10. C. Daws, A. Olivero, S. Tripakis, and S. Yovine. The tool KRONOS. In *Hybrid Systems III, Verification and Control*, volume 1066 of *Lecture Notes in Computer Science*, pages 208–219. Springer-Verlag, 1996.

11. C. Ericsson, A. Wall, and W. Yi. Timed Automata as Task Models for Event-Driven Systems. In *Proceedings of Nordic Workshop on Programming Theory*, 1998. To appear in a special issue of Nordic Journal of Computing.

12. K. Havelund, K. G. Larsen, and A. Skou. Documentation of the Modeling and Verification of Bang & Olufsens's IOP Power Down Module in UPPAAL. Internal AUC document delivered to B&O. Early version of this report., September 1997.

13. K. Havelund, A. Skou, K. G. Larsen, and K. Lund. Formal Modeling and Analysis of an Audio/Video Protocol: An Industrial Case Study Using UPPAAL. In *Proc. of the 18th IEEE Real-Time Systems Symposium*, pages 2–13, Dec 1997. San Francisco, California, USA.

14. P.-H. Ho and H. Wong-Toi. Automated Analysis of an Audio Control Protocol. In *Proc. of CAV'95*, volume 939 of *Lecture Notes in Computer Science*. Springer–Verlag, 1995.

15. G. Holzmann. *The Design and Validation of Computer Protocols*. Prentice Hall, 1991.

16. H.E. Jensen, K.G. Larsen, and A. Skou. Modelling and Analysis of a Collision Avoidance Protocol Using SPIN and UPPAAL. In *The Second Workshop on the SPIN Verification System*, volume 32 of *DIMACS, Series in Discrete Mathematics and Theoretical Computer Science*. American Mathematical Society, 1996.

17. K. G. Larsen, P. Pettersson, and W. Yi. Diagnostic Model Checking for Real-Time Systems. In *Proceedings of the 4th DIMACS Workshop on Verification and Control of Hybrid Systems*, 1995.

18. M. Lindahl, P. Pettersson, and W. Yi. Formal Design and Analysis of a Gear-Box Controller. In Bernhard Steffen, editor, *Proc. of the 4th International Workshop on Tools and Algorithms for the Construction and Analysis of Systems – LNCS 1384*, pages 281–297. Gulbelkian Foundation, March 1998. Lisbon, Portugal.

19. R. Milner. *Communication and Concurrency*. Prentice Hall, Englewood Cliffs, 1989.

20. S. Tripakis. Timed Diagnostics for Reachability Properties. In *Proceedings of TACAS'99*, Lecture Notes in Computer Science, 1999.

Verifying Progress in Timed Systems

Stavros Tripakis *

VERIMAG

Abstract. In this paper we study the issue of progress for distributed timed systems modeled as the parallel composition of timed automata. We clarify the requirements of discrete progress (absence of *deadlocks*) and time progress (absence of deadlocks and *timelocks*) and give static sufficient conditions for a model of TA to be deadlock- and timelock-free. We also present dynamic techniques for deadlock and timelock detection. The techniques are based on *forward symbolic reachability* and are on-the-fly, that is, they can return an answer as soon as possible, without necessarily having to construct and store the whole state space.

1 Introduction

Distributed timed systems are systems consisting of a number of communicating components, the behavior of which depends on timing constraints. Distributed timed systems have become increasingly interesting because on the one hand they are used in critical applications and on the other hand they are complex enough so that it is not obvious to prove their correctness. Formal verification techniques are used for this purpose: the system and its desired properties are described formally using mathematical models; then, it is checked whether the system's model satisfies the properties.

What is implicit (thus, informal) in the verification process is modeling. There are few ways to ensure that the system's model captures correctly the behaviors of the system and that the property's model corresponds to the expected property. An obvious way is by trial-and-error: the models are built in stages, and are modified during the verification process, until they are believed to be realistic enough. A more systematic way to ensure sanity of the system's model is to check that it satisfies the property of *progress*, that is, the ability to execute forever. Progress is usually a minimal requirement: if it does not hold, then the model is probably wrong, since the real system is not supposed to stop [1].

In this paper we study the issue of progress for timed systems modeled as *timed automata* (TA) [ACD93, HNSY94]. The requirement of progress is particularly relevant in this model, especially in cases where the system is composed by

---

* This work has been done at Verimag. Currently, the author is at UC Berkeley as a post-doctoral scholar. Current address: 275M Cory Hall, UC Berkeley, 94720 US. Tel. +1 510 642 5649, Fax. +1 510 642 6330. E-mail: stavros@eecs.berkeley.edu.

[1] This is a convenient simplifying hypothesis, which does not result in loss of generality: if the system may terminate execution in some legal *end state*, we can assume that it can continue performing infinitely often "dummy" actions which do not modify its state.

J.-P. Katoen (Ed.): ARTS'99, LNCS 1601, pp. 299–314, 1999.
© Springer-Verlag Berlin Heidelberg 1999

more than one components (this is most usually the case for realistic systems). The parallel composition operator typically used in TA involves *conjunctive synchronization* semantics, which can lead to unexpected behaviors of non-progress. Therefore, a need for methods to detect this problems during modeling has been expressed by users of TA verification tools (see, for instance, [BFK+98]).

After recalling TA (section 2) we clarify the notion of progress in timed systems (section 3). Unlike untimed systems which have only one type of evolution by discrete state changes, TA evolve in two possible ways, namely, either by taking a discrete transition or by letting time pass. Accordingly, there are two progress requirements related to TA, namely, discrete and time progress.

The discrete progress requirement states that it should be possible to take discrete transitions infinitely often. It corresponds to the (unique) progress requirement in untimed systems, that is, *deadlock-freedom*. In the timed context, deadlocks are states from which no discrete transition is possible, even after letting time pass.

The time progress requirement states that it should be possible for time to *diverge*, that is, elapse without upper bound. This requirement is justified by our intuition about the physical world we are trying to model, summarized in the following hypothesis:

Any physical process, no matter how fast, cannot be infinitely fast.

The above hypothesis implies that only a finite (possibly unbounded) number of events can occur in a certain (positive) amount of time. Executions which violate this property are called *zeno*. In a deadlock-free model, time progress corresponds to the absence of *timelocks*, that is, states from which all possible infinite executions are zeno.

In section 3 we give conditions ensuring that a TA model is deadlock- and timelock-free. These conditions are sufficient but not necessary, since they are *static*, that is, they take into account the discrete structure of the TA but not the reachable state space in the presence of timing constraints. On the other hand, they can be quite useful in practice, since they are not expensive to check.

In section 4 we present dynamic techniques for detecting deadlocks and timelocks. These techniques are both sound and complete, that is, they only detect true deadlocks or timelocks, whereas they fail only when the model is deadlock- or timelock-free. The techniques are also *on-the-fly*: they are based on a *forward symbolic reachability* which covers all reachable state space. In the case of deadlocks, they are detected locally on each visited node in the symbolic reachability graph. In the case of timelocks, they are detected using a nested reachability starting from each visited node. In both cases an answer can be returned as soon as possible, and diagnostics can also be provided.

Related work. Although progress is not explicitly discussed in the original work of Alur et al. [ACD93], their *region graph* construction can be used for deadlock and timelock detection: viewing the region graph as an untimed graph, deadlocks can be detected as usual, by finding sink nodes in this graph; timelocks can be detected by encoding non-zenoness as a *generalized Büchi acceptance condition* and solving an untimed emptiness problem. Although theoretically possible, both these approaches are too expensive in practice, mainly due to the very large size of the region graph.

Timelock-freedom is handled in [HNSY94] using a symbolic technique based on a backward fix-point computation [2]. Informally, a TA is timelock-free iff it satisfies the TCTL formula init $\Rightarrow \forall\Box\,\exists\Diamond_{\geq 1}$ true. Although this approach is feasible, it has some important drawbacks, namely:

- It is not on-the-fly, since the fix-point computation must terminate before an answer can be returned.
- It does not provide diagnostics, except in a very primitive form, namely, the characteristic set of a formula. Usually what is needed as diagnostics is sample executions.
- It considers the whole potential state space, whereas what is interesting is only the reachable part of the state space.

More recently, the work of Sifakis et al. [SY96, BS97, BST98] treats the problem from a different perspective. Instead of checking that the model satisfies progress, this work aims at developing a theory of composition of timed systems which guarantees progress as much as possible.

2   Background

2.1   Dense State Spaces

Clocks and valuations. Let R be the set of non-negative reals and $\mathcal{X} = \{x_1, ..., x_n\}$ be a set of variables in R, called *clocks*. An $\mathcal{X}$-*valuation* is a function $\mathbf{v} : \mathcal{X} \mapsto$ R. We write $\mathbf{0}$ the valuation that assigns zero to all clocks. For some $X \subseteq \mathcal{X}$, $\mathbf{v}[X := 0]$ is the valuation $\mathbf{v}'$, such that $\forall x \in X \, . \, \mathbf{v}'(x) = 0$ and $\forall x \notin X \, . \, \mathbf{v}'(x) = \mathbf{v}(x)$. For every $\delta \in$ R, $\mathbf{v} + \delta$ (resp. $\mathbf{v} - \delta$) is a valuation such that for all $x \in \mathcal{X}$, $(\mathbf{v} + \delta)(x) = \mathbf{v}(x) + \delta$ (resp. $(\mathbf{v} - \delta)(x) = \mathbf{v}(x) - \delta$). Given $c \in$ N, two valuations $\mathbf{v}$ and $\mathbf{v}'$ are called c-*equivalent* if:

- for any clock x, either $\mathbf{v}(x) = \mathbf{v}'(x)$, or $\mathbf{v}(x) > c$ and $\mathbf{v}'(x) > c$;
- for any pair of clocks x, y, either $\mathbf{v}(x) - \mathbf{v}(y) = \mathbf{v}'(x) - \mathbf{v}'(y)$, or $\mathbf{v}(x) - \mathbf{v}(y) > c$ and $\mathbf{v}'(x) - \mathbf{v}'(y) > c$.

Polyhedra. An *atomic constraint* on $\mathcal{X}$ is an expression of the form $x \sim c$ or $x - y \sim c$, where $x, y \in \mathcal{X}$, $\sim \in \{<, \leq, \geq, >\}$ and $c \in$ N. An $\mathcal{X}$-valuation $\mathbf{v}$ *satisfies* the constraint $x \sim c$ if $\mathbf{v}(x) \sim c$; $\mathbf{v}$ satisfies $x - y \sim c$ if $\mathbf{v}(x) - \mathbf{v}(y) \sim c$.

An $\mathcal{X}$-*hyperplane* is a set of valuations satisfying an atomic clock constraint. The class $\mathcal{H}_{\mathcal{X}}$ of $\mathcal{X}$-*polyhedra* is defined as the smallest subset of $2^{R^{\mathcal{X}}}$ which contains all $\mathcal{X}$-hyperplanes and is closed under set union, intersection and complementation.

---

[2]   Deadlocks are not considered, since they are meaningless in the TA model of [HNSY94] (see remark 1).

We often use the following notation for polyhedra: we write $x < 5$ for the hyperplane defined by the constraint $x < 5$, $x < 5 \land y = 2$ for the polyhedron defined as the intersection of $x < 5$ and $y = 2$, and so on. We also write true for $R^{\mathcal{X}}$ (equivalently, $\bigwedge_{x \in \mathcal{X}} x \geq 0$), false for $\emptyset$ (equivalently, $\bigwedge_{x \in \mathcal{X}} x < 0$) and zero for $\{\mathbf{0}\}$ (equivalently, $\bigwedge_{x \in \mathcal{X}} x = 0$).

A polyhedron ζ is called *convex* if for all $\mathbf{v}_1, \mathbf{v}_2 \in \zeta$, for any $0 < \delta < 1$, $\delta \mathbf{v}_1 + (1 - \delta) \mathbf{v}_2 \in \zeta$. A polyhedron is convex iff it can be defined as the intersection of a finite number of hyperplanes. On the other hand, if ζ is non-convex then it can be written as $\zeta_1 \cup \cdots \cup \zeta_k$, where $\zeta_1, ..., \zeta_k$ are all convex. We denote the set $\{\zeta_1, ..., \zeta_k\}$ by convex(ζ).

Operations on polyhedra. By definition, intersection, union and complementation are well-defined operations on polyhedra. Polyhedra difference is defined via complementation as: $\zeta_1 \setminus \zeta_2 = \zeta_1 \cap \overline{\zeta_2}$. The test for inclusion $\zeta_1 \subseteq \zeta_2$ is equivalent to $\zeta_1 \setminus \zeta_2 = \emptyset$. We now define some more operations which will be used in the sequel. Examples of operations are shown in figure 1.

c-closure. This operation is necessary for guaranteeing termination of the reachability algorithms given in section 4.

Given a convex $\mathcal{X}$-polyhedron ζ and a natural constant c, the *c-closure* of ζ, denoted close(ζ, c), is the greatest convex $\mathcal{X}$-polyhedron $\zeta' \supseteq \zeta$, such that for all $\mathbf{v}' \in \zeta'$ there exists $\mathbf{v} \in \zeta$ such that $\mathbf{v}$ and $\mathbf{v}'$ are c-equivalent. Intuitively, ζ' is obtained by ζ by "ignoring" all bounds which involve constants greater than c. ζ is said to be *c-closed* if close(ζ, c) = ζ.

Lemma 1. *1. If ζ is c-closed then it is c'-closed, for any $c' > c$.*

2. If ζ_1 and ζ_2 are c-closed then $\zeta_1 \cap \zeta_2$ is also c-closed.

3. For any ζ, there exists a constant c such that ζ is c-closed.

From now on, $c_{max}(\zeta)$ will denote the smallest constant c such that ζ is c-closed.

Lemma 2. *For any constant c, there is a finite number of c-closed $\mathcal{X}$-polyhedra.*

Clock resets. We define the operations $\zeta[Y := 0]$ and $[Y := 0]\zeta$ of *forward* and *backward clock reset*, respectively, as follows:

$$\zeta[Y := 0] \stackrel{\text{def}}{=} \{\mathbf{v}[Y := 0] \mid \mathbf{v} \in \zeta\}$$

$$[Y := 0]\zeta \stackrel{\text{def}}{=} \{\mathbf{v} \mid \mathbf{v}[Y := 0] \in \zeta\}$$

Intuitively, $\zeta[Y := 0]$ contains all valuations which can be obtained from some valuation in ζ by resetting clocks in Y. It contains all valuations which, after resetting clocks in Y, yield a valuation in ζ.

Time elapse. We define the operations of *backward* and *forward time elapse* of an $\mathcal{X}$-polyhedron ζ to be the $\mathcal{X}$-polyhedra $\swarrow\zeta$ and $\nearrow\zeta$, respectively, such that:

$$\mathbf{v}' \in \swarrow\zeta \text{ iff } \exists\delta \in \mathsf{R} . \mathbf{v}' + \delta \in \zeta$$
$$\mathbf{v}' \in \nearrow\zeta \text{ iff } \exists\delta \in \mathsf{R} . \mathbf{v}' - \delta \in \zeta$$

The following result is easy to derive from the definitions.

Lemma 3. *If ζ is convex and $Y \subseteq \mathcal{X}$ then $\zeta[Y := 0]$, $[Y := 0]\zeta$, $\swarrow\zeta$ and $\nearrow\zeta$ are also convex.*

Effective representation. $\mathcal{X}$-polyhedra can be effectively represented using the *difference bound matrix* (DBM) data structure, first proposed by [Dil89]. Convex $\mathcal{X}$-polyhedra can be represented by a single DBM, which can be reduced to a *minimal* (or *canonical*) *form* using an $O(|\mathcal{X}|^3)$ algorithm. A non-convex polyhedron ζ is the union of k convex polyhedra $\zeta = \zeta_1 \cup \cdots \cup \zeta_k$. Therefore, ζ can be represented (in a non-canonical way) by a list of k DBMs, one for each polyhedron $\zeta_1, ..., \zeta_k$. Semantic operations on polyhedra can be implemented as syntactic DBM transformations [Yov93, Oli94, Daw98, Tri98].

It is more interesting to work with convex polyhedra, since they admit a memory-efficient representation (quadratic in the number of clocks) and time-efficient operations (cubic in the number of clocks). Non-convex polyhedra are more expensive (exponential worst-case time and space complexity). However, sometimes non-convex polyhedra are indispensable, for example, when the algorithms involve complementations or unions. In this paper we manage to use convex polyhedra as much as possible. In particular, the reachability analyses of section 4 are performed on convex polyhedra. Non-convex polyhedra are used temporarily, for instance, to check inclusion of a convex polyhedron in a union of convex polyhedra (section 4.2).

2.2   Timed Automata

In the sequel, *Labels* denotes a finite set of labels.

A *timed automaton* (TA) [ACD93, HNSY94] is a tuple $A = (\mathcal{X}, Q, q_0, E, \mathsf{invar})$, where:

- $\mathcal{X}$ is a finite set of clocks.
- Q is a finite set of *discrete states*.
- q_0 is the *initial discrete state*.
- E is a finite set of *edges* of the form $e = (q, \zeta, a, X, q')$. $q, q' \in Q$ are the *source* and *target* discrete states. $a \in Labels$ is a label. ζ is a conjunction of atomic constraints on $\mathcal{X}$ defining a convex $\mathcal{X}$-polyhedron, called the *guard* of e. $X \subseteq \mathcal{X}$ is a set of clocks to be reset upon crossing the edge.
- invar is a function associating with each discrete state q a convex $\mathcal{X}$-polyhedron called the *invariant* of q.

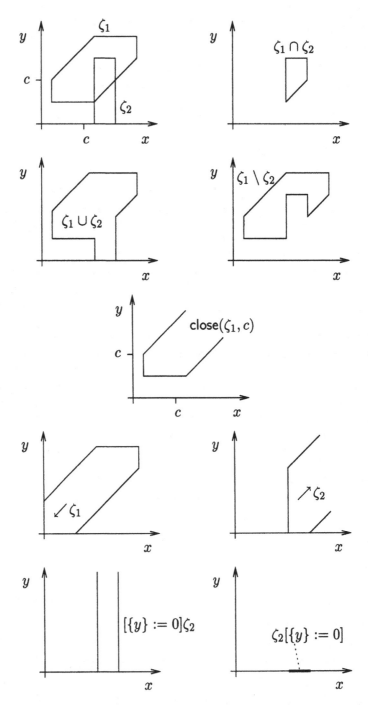

Fig. 1. Polyhedra on $\{x, y\}$ and their operations.

Given an edge $e = (q, \zeta, a, X, q')$, we write source(e), target(e), guard(e), label(e) and reset(e) for q, q', ζ, a and X, respectively. Given a discrete state q, we write in(q) (resp. out(q)) for the set of edges of the form $(\_, \_, \_, \_, q)$ (resp. $(q, \_, \_, \_, \_)$). We assume that for each $e \in$ out(q), guard(e) $\subseteq$ invar(q). Finally, $c_{max}(A)$ is defined as the maximum of $c_{max}(\zeta)$, where ζ is a guard or an invariant of A.

States. A *state* of A is a pair $(q, \mathbf{v})$, where $q \in Q$ is a location, and $\mathbf{v} \in$ invar(q) is a valuation satisfying the invariant of q. The *initial state* of A is $(q_0, \mathbf{0})$. Two states $(q, \mathbf{v_1})$ and $(q, \mathbf{v_2})$ are c-equivalent if $\mathbf{v_1}$ and $\mathbf{v_2}$ are c-equivalent.

Transitions. Consider a state $s = (q, \mathbf{v})$. We write $s + \delta$ instead of $(q, \mathbf{v} + \delta)$. A *timed transition* from s has the form $s \xrightarrow{\delta} s + \delta$, where $\delta \in \mathsf{R}$ and $\mathbf{v} + \delta \in$ invar(q). $s + \delta$ is called the δ-*successor* of s. Given an edge $e = (q, \zeta, a, X, q')$ such that $\mathbf{v} \in \zeta$, a *discrete transition* with respect to e has the form $s \xrightarrow{e} s'$, where $s' = (q', \mathbf{v}[\text{reset}(e) := 0])$. s' is called the e-*successor* of s.

We write $s \xrightarrow{e \ \delta} s'$ if, either $\delta = 0$ and $s \xrightarrow{e} s'$ is a discrete transition, or $\delta > 0$, and $s \xrightarrow{e} s''$ is a discrete transition and $s'' \xrightarrow{\delta} s'$ is a timed transition.

Runs. A *run* of A starting from state s is a finite or infinite sequence $\rho = s_1 \xrightarrow{\delta_1} s_1 + \delta_1 \xrightarrow{e_1} s_2 \xrightarrow{\delta_2} s_2 + \delta_2 \xrightarrow{e_2} \cdots$, such that $s_1 = s$ and for all $i = 1, 2, ..., s_i + \delta_i$ is the δ-successor of s_i and s_{i+1} is the e_i-successor of $s_i + \delta_i$. The i-th point of ρ, denoted $\rho(i)$, is defined to be s_i, for $i = 1, 2, ...$ The *waiting delay of ρ at point i*, denoted delay(ρ, i), is defined to be δ_i. All states $\rho(i)$ where the run spends no time, that is, where delay(ρ, i) $= 0$, are called *transient* states. The *elapsed time until point i*, denoted time(ρ, i), is defined to be the sum $\Sigma_{j < i}$delay(ρ, j). The *total elapsed time during ρ*, denoted time(ρ), is defined to be the limit of the sequence time(ρ, i), if the sequence converges and ∞ otherwise.

A state s is *reachable* if there exists a finite run $s_0 \xrightarrow{\delta_0 \ e_0} \cdots \xrightarrow{\delta_l \ e_l} s_l \xrightarrow{\delta} s$, for $l \geq 0$, where s_0 is the initial state of A. Let $Reach(A)$ be the set of all reachable states of A.

Remark 1. Our TA model differs from the one of [ACD93] in two points: first, we use invariants; second, we permit transient states. Invariants are useful for specifying the *urgency* of actions, especially in the context of many TA executing in parallel. Transient states are also useful when modeling sequences of actions that take a negligible amount of time.

Our model is also different from the one of [HNSY94]: in our semantics of runs there is an implicit requirement that discrete transitions are taken infinitely often, whereas [HNSY94] permit executions where the TA stays forever in the same discrete state. Our definition is more general, since it permits to distinguish between the following cases:

(1) an event a occurs eventually but we do not know when; and

(2) an event a may never occur.

We model case (1) by having an edge labeled a going out of a discrete state with invariant true. We model case (2) by adding a "dummy" self-loop edge to the state. Using the definition of [HNSY94], case (1) cannot be modeled since a true invariant implies that there exists an infinite run staying forever in the corresponding state.

Parallel composition of TA. A system is usually divided in parts, therefore, it is indispensable to be able to describe systems *compositionally*, that is, as a set of components which execute in parallel and communicate in a certain way. We adopt the usual model of parallelism for TA, based on the synchronous passage of time for all components and *interleaving* of discrete actions. Communication is modeled via action synchronization.

More precisely, consider two TA $A_i = (\mathcal{X}_i, Q_i, q_i, E_i, \mathsf{invar}_i)$, $i = 1, 2$, such that $\mathcal{X}_1 \cap \mathcal{X}_2 = \emptyset$. Let $Labels_i$ be the set of labels *local* to A_i, that is, $Labels_i = \{\mathsf{label}(e) \mid e \in E_i\}$, for $i = 1, 2$.

Given two edges $e_i = (q_i, a_i, \zeta_i, X_i, q_i') \in E_i$, $i = 1, 2$, we define the following *composite* edges:

- If $a_1 = a_2 \in Labels_1 \cap Labels_2$, then the synchronization of e_1 and e_2 yields the edge

$$e_1 \| e_2 \overset{\text{def}}{=} ((q_1, q_2), a_1, \zeta_1 \cap \zeta_2, X_1 \cup X_2, (q_1', q_2'))$$

  where ζ_1, ζ_2 are viewed as polyhedra on $\mathcal{X}_1 \cup \mathcal{X}_2$ so that the intersection $\zeta_1 \cap \zeta_2$ is well defined.
- If $a_i \notin Labels_1 \cap Labels_2$ for both $i = 1, 2$, then the interleaving of e_1 and e_2 yields the edges

$$e_1 \| \bot \overset{\text{def}}{=} ((q_1, q_2), a_1, \zeta_1, X_1, (q_1', q_2))$$
$$\bot \| e_2 \overset{\text{def}}{=} ((q_1, q_2), a_2, \zeta_2, X_2, (q_1, q_2'))$$

The *parallel composition* of A_1 and A_2, denoted $A_1 \| A_2$, is defined to be the TA $(\mathcal{X}_1 \cup \mathcal{X}_2, Q_1 \times Q_2, (q_1, q_2), E, \mathsf{invar})$, where, for $q \in Q_1$ and $q' \in Q_2$, $\mathsf{invar}(q, q') = \mathsf{invar}_1(q) \cap \mathsf{invar}_2(q')$, and the set of edges E contains all composite edges of the form $e_1 \| e_2$, $e_1 \| \bot$, $\bot \| e_2$, for $e_1 \in E_1, e_2 \in E_2$. That is, the two automata synchronize on their common labels and interleave on their local labels.

3   The Requirement of Progress in Timed Systems

In this section we define formally the requirements of discrete and time progress, under the notions of deadlock- and timelock-freedom, respectively. We also give sufficient but not necessary conditions to ensure deadlock- and timelock-freedom in a model of one or more TA. These conditions are *static*, that is, they take into account the discrete structure of the TA but not the reachable state space in the presence of timing constraints. This is why the conditions are not necessary: an untimed behavior of the TA which does not satisfy the conditions might not be valid when the timing constraints are considered.

3.1   Discrete Progress

Discrete progress is captured by the notion of deadlocks.

Deadlocks. A state s of a TA A is a *deadlock* if there is no delay $\delta \in R$ and edge $e \in E$ such that $s \xrightarrow{\delta} \xrightarrow{e} s'$. A is *deadlock-free* if none of its reachable states is a deadlock.

We can characterize deadlock-freedom of A by a *local* condition on its reachable states. Let q be a discrete state of A and define:

$$\mathsf{free}(q) \stackrel{\text{def}}{=} \bigcup_{e \in \mathsf{out}(q)} \swarrow \left(\mathsf{guard}(e) \cap ([\mathsf{reset}(e) := 0]\mathsf{invar}(\mathsf{target}(e))) \right)$$

Intuitively, $\mathsf{free}(q)$ contains all valuations $\mathbf{v}$ such that the state $(q, \mathbf{v})$ is not a deadlock. The following lemma follows from the definitions.

Lemma 4. *A is deadlock-free iff for each* $(q, \mathbf{v}) \in Reach(A)$, $\mathbf{v} \in \mathsf{free}(q)$.

A static sufficient condition for deadlock-freedom. Based on the above characterization, a static sufficient condition for deadlock-freedom is given in the following lemma.

Lemma 5. *A is deadlock-free if for each discrete state* q *and for all* $e \in \mathsf{in}(q)$, *the following condition holds:*

$$((\mathsf{guard}(e))[\mathsf{reset}(e) := 0]) \cap \mathsf{invar}(q) \subseteq \mathsf{free}(q)$$

We should note that the above condition is not *compositional*, that is, two TA might satisfy the condition while their parallel composition does not. However, it is still useful, since it can be checked on the syntactic parallel product of a set of TA, which is usually much smaller than a semantic graph which also contains clock information, such as the graph defined in the next section.

3.2   Time Progress

Zeno runs. Consider an infinite run ρ such that $\mathsf{time}(\rho) \neq \infty$, that is, there exists $t \in R$ such that for all i, $\mathsf{time}(\rho, i) < t$. Such a run is called *zeno*, and corresponds to a pathological situation, since it violates the first of the above time-progress requirements. As an example, consider the TA A_1 shown in figure 2. Its run $\rho = (q_0, x = 1) \xrightarrow{\frac{1}{2}} \xrightarrow{a} (q_0, x = 1.5) \xrightarrow{\frac{1}{4}} \xrightarrow{a} (q_0, x = 1.75) \cdots$, where $\mathsf{time}(\rho) = 2$, is zeno. In fact, any run of A_1 taking only a-transitions is zeno.

Timelocks. Timelocks are states violating the time-progress requirement. Formally, a state s of a TA A is a *timelock* if all infinite runs starting from s are zeno. A is *timelock-free* if none of its reachable states is a timelock.

Notice that a deadlock is not necessarily a timelock, neither the reverse. For example, the TA A_1 of figure 2 is deadlock-free, but all its states $(q_0, 1 < x \leq 2)$

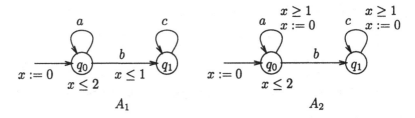

Fig. 2. A TA with timelocks (left) and a strongly non-zeno TA (right).

are timelocks since they are bound to stay to q_0 taking forever a-transitions. On the other hand, if the a-edge was missing, these states would be deadlocks but not timelocks, since they would have no infinite runs starting from them at all.

The following lemma characterizing timelock-freedom of a TA A is inspired from [HNSY94].

Lemma 6. *A is timelock-free iff for each $s \in Reach(A)$, there exists a run ρ starting from s, and some point i in ρ, such that $\mathsf{time}(\rho, i) \geq 1$.*

Strongly non-zeno TA. Consider a TA A. A *structural loop* of A is a sequence of distinct edges $e_1 \cdots e_m$ such that $\mathsf{target}(e_i) = \mathsf{source}(e_{i+1})$, for all $i = 1, ..., m$ (the addition $i + 1$ is modulo m). A is called *strongly non-zeno* if for every structural loop there exists a clock x and some $0 \leq i, j \leq m$ such that:

1. x is reset in step i, that is, $x \in \mathsf{reset}(e_i)$; and
2. x is bounded from below in step j, that is, $(x < 1) \cap \mathsf{guard}(e_j) = \mathsf{false}$.

Intuitively, this means that at least one unit of time elapses in every loop of A. For example, the TA A_2 of figure 2 is strongly non-zeno (this would not be the case if any of the guards $x \geq 1$ was missing).

Strong non-zenoness is interesting since it dispenses us with the burden of ensuring time progress. Another nice characteristic of strong non-zenoness is that it is preserved by parallel composition, so that it can be efficiently checked on large systems.

Lemma 7. *1. If A is strongly non-zeno then every infinite run of A is non-zeno.*
2. If A, A' are strongly non-zeno, so is $A \| A'$.

The above lemma provides a static sufficient condition for timelock-freedom. By part 1 of the lemma, a strongly non-zeno TA is also timelock-free. By part 2 of the lemma, the test for strong non-zenoness can be done in a compositional way. By definition, the test for strong non-zenoness is static.

Remark 2. When modeling a system, it is often the case that some of its components are untimed, that is, they can be modeled using simple finite-state machines without clocks. These components can be considered strongly non-zeno by convention, so that their parallel composition with the rest of the system does not affect the strong non-zenoness of the global system.

The meaning of different variants of zenoness. We finish this section by summarizing the meaning of notions related to time progress introduced above.

- Deadlocks and timelocks correspond to modeling errors, since any TA assumed to capture the behavior of a real system correctly should act infinitely often and not block time.
- TA which are not strongly non-zeno model systems where an unbounded number of events can occur in a finite amount of time. For example, the TA A_1 on figure 2 can perform an unbounded number of a-transitions in 2 time units. Such systems are useful sometimes, for instance, when modeling a sender which can emit messages arbitrarily fast.
- Strongly non-zeno TA model systems where only a bounded number of events can occur in a finite amount of time. For example, the TA A_2 on figure 2 can perform at most two a-transitions in 2 time units. Most systems in practice are strongly non-zeno.

4 On-the-Fly Deadlock and Timelock Detection

In this sections we present algorithms for deadlock and timelock detection. The algorithms are *on-the-fly*, that is, they return an answer as soon as possible, without necessarily building the whole state space. Both algorithms are based on a *symbolic reachability* [DT98], where the state space represented as a graph the nodes of which are sets of states (symbolic states) and the edges of which correspond to symbolic successor operations. For simplicity, the algorithms are presented taking as input a single TA A. It is straightforward to extend them to take as input the parallel composition $A_1 \| \cdots \| A_k$ of a number of TA and generate on-the-fly the symbolic state space of the composite automaton.

The algorithm for deadlock detection uses a simple depth-first search (DFS) to generate the symbolic graph and check at the same time that for each visited symbolic state S, no state in S is a deadlock.

The algorithm for timelock detection is more sophisticated. It is based on lemma 6 and uses a nested reachability: at the outer level, a DFS is performed to generate the symbolic graph; for each visited symbolic state S, an inner-level reachability is performed, to compute the states of S from which time can elapse at least by one time unit. If some states in S do not satisfy this property, then these states are timelocks.

4.1 Symbolic Reachability

Consider a TA A with discrete states Q and clocks $\mathcal{X}$. A *symbolic state* of A is a set of states $S = \{(q, \mathbf{v}) \mid \mathbf{v} \in \zeta\}$, where $q \in Q$ and ζ is an $\mathcal{X}$-polyhedron. For simplicity, we denote S as (q, ζ). If ζ is convex, then S is called a *zone*. If ζ is non-convex, we write $\mathsf{convex}(S)$ instead of $\{(q, \zeta') \mid \zeta' \in \mathsf{convex}(\zeta)\}$.

Given a zone $S = (q, \zeta)$, two edges $e_1 = (q, \zeta_1, X_1, q_1)$ and $e_2 = (q_2, \zeta_2, X_2, q)$ of A, and a natural constant $c \geq c_{max}(A)$, we define the following successor and predecessor operations:

$$\text{post}(S, e_1) \stackrel{\text{def}}{=} \left(q_1, \text{close}(\nearrow((\zeta \cap \zeta_1)[X_1 := 0]), c) \right)$$
$$\text{pre}(S, e_2) \stackrel{\text{def}}{=} \left(q_2, ([X_2 := 0](\swarrow \zeta)) \cap \zeta_2 \right)$$

Intuitively, post() contains all states (and their c-equivalents) that can be reached from some state in (q, ζ), by taking an e-transition, then letting some time pass; pre() contains all states that can reach some state in (q, ζ) by taking an e-transition, then letting some time pass. Since all operations preserve convexity of polyhedra, the result of post() and pre() is a zone.

Based on the above operations, we present the algorithm for symbolic reachability shown in figure 3. The algorithm takes as input an initial zone S_0 and a set of *target* zones $\mathcal{Z}$. It returns as output a zone $S \subseteq S_0$, such that all states in S can reach some state in some zone in $\mathcal{Z}$. If $S = \emptyset$, then no state in S_0 can reach a state in some zone in $\mathcal{Z}$. *Visit* is the set of currently visited nodes, initially empty.

The algorithm works by exploring on-the-fly *symbolic paths*, that is, sequences of the form $\pi = S_0 \stackrel{e_0}{\to} \cdots \stackrel{e_{l-1}}{\to} S_l$, where for $i = 0, ..., l-1$, $S_{i+1} = \text{post}(S_i, e_i)$. When the last zone in the path, S_l, intersects the target zones, then the whole path is *pre-stabilized* in a backward way, to compute all states of S_0 which can lead to the target zone along this path. This operation yields $S \subseteq S_0$ such that

$$\forall s \in S . \exists \rho = s \stackrel{\delta_0}{\to} \stackrel{e_0}{\to} s_1 \stackrel{\delta_1}{\to} \stackrel{e_1}{\to} \cdots \stackrel{\delta_{l-1}}{\to} \stackrel{e_{l-1}}{\to} s_l, \text{ where } s_i \in S_i, \text{ for } i = 1, ..., l.$$

It is important to notice that *not all* states of S_0 which can reach $\mathcal{Z}$ are included in S, that is, it might be the case that some states in $S_0 \setminus S$ can still reach $\mathcal{Z}$ by another path. On the other hand, if a target zone is hit, then S is guaranteed to be non-empty, by the properties of the post() operator [Tri98]. Termination of the algorithm is ensured by lemma 2.

```
Reach (S₀, Z) {
    let S₀ = (q₀, ζ₀) ;
    if (∃(q,ζ) ∈ Z . q = q₀ ∧ ζ ∩ ζ₀ ≠ ∅) then return (q, ζ ∩ ζ₀) ; (1)
    Visit := Visit ∪ {S₀} ;
    for each (e ∈ out(q₀)) do
        (q₁, ζ₁) := post(S₀, e) ;                                    (2)
        if (ζ₁ = ∅) then continue ;
        else if (∃(q₁, ζ₁') ∈ Visit . ζ₁ ⊆ ζ₁') then continue ;      (3)
        else
            S₁ := Reach((q₁, ζ₁), Z) ;
            if (S₁ ≠ ∅) then return S₀ ∩ pre(S₁, e) ;                (4)
        end if
    end for each
    return ∅ ;                                                       (5)
}
```

Fig. 3. Symbolic reachability.

4.2   Deadlock Detection

The procedure Reach can be directly used for deadlock detection. Given a TA $A = (\mathcal{X}, Q, q_0, E, \text{invar})$, it suffices to define the set of target states as follows:

$$\mathcal{Z}^\dagger = \bigcup_{q \in Q} \text{convex}(q, \text{invar}(q) \setminus \text{free}(q))$$

Then, by lemma 4, A is deadlock-free iff $\text{Reach}((q_0, \text{zero}), \mathcal{Z}^\dagger)$ returns $\emptyset$.

In fact, the test of line (1) in the algorithm of figure 3 can be optimized as follows. Since, by definition, each visited zone (q, ζ) is such that $\zeta \subseteq \text{invar}(q)$, testing $\zeta \cap (\text{invar}(q) \setminus \text{free}(q)) = \emptyset$ is equivalent to testing $\zeta \setminus \text{free}(q) = \emptyset$.

Finally, it is worth noticing that in case a deadlock is found, the algorithm can be extended in a straightforward way to provide diagnostics showing how the deadlock can be reached.

4.3   Timelock Detection

Complete Symbolic Reachability. As mentioned above, the reachability procedure $\text{Reach}(S_0, \mathcal{Z})$ of figure 3 is not complete, in the sense that it does not return the greatest subset of S_0 which can reach $\mathcal{Z}$, but only some non-empty subset. On the other hand, the algorithm is sound in the sense that if it returns an empty subset, then no states in S_0 can reach $\mathcal{Z}$.

To find timelocks, we develop a complete reachability procedure, called CompleteReach, based on the partial reachability procedure Reach. CompleteReach is shown in figure 4. It takes as input an initial zone S_0 and a set of target zones $\mathcal{Z}$ and returns the greatest subset $S \subseteq S_0$ such that no state in S can reach $\mathcal{Z}$. S is not necessarily convex, thus, it is represented as a set of zones $\mathcal{Z}_0$.

```
CompleteReach(S₀, Z) {
    Z₀ := {S₀} ;
    while (∃S = (q,ζ) ∈ Z₀) do
        S' := Reach(S, Z) ;
        Z₀ := (Z₀ \ {S}) ∪ convex(S \ S') ;
    end while
    return Z₀ ;
}
```

Fig. 4. Complete symbolic reachability.

Starting from $S = S_0$, the algorithm first computes using Reach a subset S' of S reaching the target zones. Since it might be that the symbolic state $S \setminus S'$ is not empty, and some states in it can still reach the target zones, the algorithm substitutes S by $S \setminus S'$ and repeats the procedure. $S \setminus S'$ is not always a zone, that is, if $S = (q, \zeta)$ and $S' = (q, \zeta')$, then $\zeta \setminus \zeta'$ is not always convex. Since Reach performs reachability only on zones, $\zeta \setminus \zeta'$ has to be "split" into a number of convex polyhedra using the convex() operator. Then, Reach is called for each of the resulting zones.

Nested Reachability for Timelock Detection. To detect timelocks on a TA A, we use a nested combination of the partial reachability procedure of figure 3 and the complete reachability procedure of figure 4. At the outer level, Reach is applied to generate the reachable zones of A one by one. For each zone S, an inner-level complete reachability is performed on an extended TA A^+. A^+ uses an auxiliary clock z to find which of the states in S cannot let time elapse for one time unit.

More precisely, consider a TA $A = (\mathcal{X}, Q, q_0, E, \text{invar})$ and let A^+ be the TA $(\mathcal{X} \cup \{z\}, Q, q_0, E, \text{invar})$, where $z \notin \mathcal{X}$. Also let $\mathcal{Z}_{\geq 1}$ be the set of zones $\{(q, z \geq 1) \mid q \in Q\}$.

```
TimelockReach(S) {
    let S = (q, ζ) ;
    Z := CompleteReach_{A+}((q, ζ ∩ z = 0), Z_{≥1})) ;
    if (Z ≠ ∅) then return ''YES'' ;
    Visit := Visit ∪ {S} ;
    for each (e ∈ out(q)) do
        (q₁, ζ₁) := post(S, e) ;
        if (ζ₁ = ∅) then continue ;
        else if (∃(q₁, ζ₁') ∈ Visit . ζ₁ ⊆ ζ₁') then continue ;
        else if (TimelockReach((q₁, ζ₁)) = ''YES'') then return ''YES'' ;
        end if
    end for each
    return ''NO'' ;
}
```

Fig. 5. Nested reachability for timelock detection.

The algorithm for timelock-detection is shown in figure 5. The outer-most reachability procedure, TimelockReach, is identical to procedure Reach of figure 3, except that instead of checking the intersection of the currently visited zone S with a set of target zones, it checks whether there are states in S from which not even one time unit can elapse. For this, CompleteReach is called on A^+ with initial zone $(q, \zeta \cap z = 0)$ and target zones $\mathcal{Z}_{\geq 1}$. CompleteReach returns a set of zones $\mathcal{Z}$ which cannot reach any zone in $\mathcal{Z}_{\geq 1}$. If $\mathcal{Z}$ is non-empty, then S contains timelocks. Notice that the outer-most reachability is performed on A, while the inner-most reachability is performed on A^+.

By lemma 6, A is timelock-free iff TimelockReach((q_0, zero)) returns ''NO''.

5   Conclusions

We have presented static and dynamic techniques for ensuring progress in a system modeled as the parallel composition of a set of timed automata. Our focus has been given on practicality. In the case of deadlocks, the static technique is interesting when the syntactic parallel product of the system is small, that is, the number of reachable discrete states is much smaller than the number of possible discrete states in the product. Otherwise, the dynamic technique is preferable.

In the case of timelocks, the static technique (test for strong non-zenoness) is very efficient since it can be applied compositionally. Although not complete, this technique is useful in practice since most realistic systems are strongly non-zeno.

The techniques are currently being implemented in the real-time verification tool KRONOS. This tool already uses the forward symbolic reachability analysis to check safety properties such as invariance and bounded response. Experiments have proven that the size of the symbolic reachability graph is quite small in practice (see, for instance, [DT98]). Since both dynamic detection techniques are based on this graph, they are expected to be efficient in practice.

References

[ACD93]   R. Alur, C. Courcoubetis, and D.L. Dill. Model checking in dense real time. *Information and Computation*, 104(1):2–34, 1993.

[BFK+98] H. Bowman, G. Faconti, J-P. Katoen, D. Latella, and M. Massink. Automatic verification of a lip synchronisation algorithm using uppaal. In *3rd International Workshop on Formal Methods for Industrial Critical Systems*, 1998.

[BS97]   S. Bornot and J. Sifakis. Relating time progress and deadlines in hybrid systems. In *International Workshop, HART'97*, pages 286–300, Grenoble, France, March 1997. Lecture Notes in Computer Science 1201, Spinger-Verlag.

[BST98]   S. Bornot, J. Sifakis, and S. Tripakis. Modeling urgency in timed systems. In *Compositionality*, LNCS 1536, 1998. To appear.

[Daw98]   C. Daws. *Méthodes d'analyse de systèmes temporisés: de la théorie à la pratique*. PhD thesis, Institut National Polytechnique de Grenoble, 1998. In french.

[Dil89]   D.L. Dill. Timing assumptions and verification of finite-state concurrent systems. In J. Sifakis, editor, *Automatic Verification Methods for Finite State Systems*, Lecture Notes in Computer Science 407, pages 197–212. Springer–Verlag, 1989.

[DT98]   C. Daws and S. Tripakis. Model checking of real-time reachability properties using abstractions. In *Tools and Algorithms for the Construction and Analysis of Systems '98, Lisbon, Portugal*, volume 1384 of *LNCS*. Springer-Verlag, 1998.

[HNSY94] T.A. Henzinger, X. Nicollin, J. Sifakis, and S. Yovine. Symbolic model checking for real-time systems. *Information and Computation*, 111(2):193–244, 1994.

[Oli94]   A. Olivero. *Modélisation et analyse de systèmes temporisés et hybrides*. PhD thesis, Institut National Polytechnique de Grenoble, 1994. In french.

[SY96]   J. Sifakis and S. Yovine. Compositional specification of timed systems. In *13th Annual Symposium on Theoretical Aspects of Computer Science, STACS'96*, pages 347–359, Grenoble, France, February 1996. Lecture Notes in Computer Science 1046, Spinger-Verlag.

[Tri98]   S. Tripakis. *The formal analysis of timed systems in practice*. PhD thesis, Université Joseph Fourrier de Grenoble, 1998. To be published.

[Yov93]   S. Yovine. *Méthodes et outils pour la vérification symbolique de systèmes temporisés*. PhD thesis, Institut National Polytechnique de Grenoble, 1993. In french.

Proof Assistance for Real-Time Systems Using an Interactive Theorem Prover

Paul Z. Kolano

Computer Science Department, University of California
Santa Barbara, CA 93106 U.S.A.
kolano@cs.ucsb.edu

Abstract. This paper discusses the adaptation of the PVS theorem prover for performing analysis of real-time systems written in the ASTRAL formal specification language. A number of issues were encountered during the encoding of ASTRAL that are relevant to the encoding of many real-time specification languages. These issues are presented as well as how they were handled in the ASTRAL encoding. A translator has been written that translates any ASTRAL specification into its corresponding PVS encoding. After performing the proofs of several systems using the encoding, PVS strategies have been developed to automate the proofs of certain types of properties. In addition, the encoding has been used as the basis for a transition sequence generator tool.

1 Introduction

A real-time system is a system that must perform its actions within specified time bounds. With the advent of cheap processing power and increasingly sophisticated consumer demands, real-time systems have become commonplace in everything from refrigerators to automobiles. Besides such numerous everyday uses, real-time systems are also being employed in more complex and potentially deadly applications such as weapons systems and nuclear reactor controls where deviation from critical timing requirements can result in disastrous loss of lives and/or property. It is thus desirable to extensively test and verify the designs of these systems to gain assurance that such disasters will not occur. A number of formal methods for real-time systems have been proposed [14] that provide a framework under which developers can eliminate ambiguity, reason rigorously about system design, and prove that critical requirements are met using well-defined mathematical techniques. Real-time systems are characterized by concurrency, asynchrony, nondeterminism, and dependence upon the external operating environment. Thus, the formal proofs of even simple real-time systems can be nontrivial. To make the verification of real-world real-time systems practical, mechanical proof assistance is necessary.

One such form of assistance is an interactive theorem prover. Interactive theorem provers provide mechanical support for deductive reasoning. Each theorem prover is associated with a specification language in which a system and associated theorems are expressed. A theorem prover uses a collection of axioms and inference rules about its specification language to reduce a high-level proof into simpler subproofs that can eventually be discharged by basic built-in decision procedures that support

J.-P. Katoen (Ed.): ARTS'99, LNCS 1601, pp. 315-333, 1999.
© Springer-Verlag Berlin Heidelberg 1999

arithmetic and boolean reasoning. Theorem provers provide a number of forms of assistance, including preserving the soundness of proofs, finishing off proof details automatically, keeping track of proof status, and recording proofs for reuse.

This paper discusses the adaptation of the PVS theorem prover [8] for performing analysis of real-time systems written in the ASTRAL [5] formal specification language. A number of issues were encountered during the encoding of ASTRAL that are relevant to the encoding of many real-time specification languages. These issues are presented as well as how they were handled in the ASTRAL encoding. A translator has been written that translates any ASTRAL specification into its corresponding PVS encoding. After performing the proofs of several systems using the encoding, PVS strategies have been developed to automate the proofs of certain types of properties. In addition, the encoding has been used as the basis for a transition sequence generator tool.

The remainder of this paper is organized as follows. In sections 2 and 3, brief overviews of ASTRAL and PVS are given. In section 4, the issues encountered during the encoding of ASTRAL are discussed. Section 5 describes the ASTRAL to PVS translator. Strategies for automating ASTRAL proofs and the use of PVS to develop a transition sequence generator are presented in section 6. Section 7 discusses related work. Finally, section 8 provides some conclusions and directions for future research.

2 ASTRAL

In ASTRAL [5], a real-time system is described as a collection of state machine specifications, each of them representing a process type of which there may be multiple statically generated instances. There is also a *global specification*, which contains declarations for types and constants that are shared among more than one process type, as well as assumptions about the global environment and critical requirements for the whole system.

An ASTRAL *process specification* consists of a sequence of *levels*. Each level is an abstract data type view of the system being specified. The first („top level") view is a very abstract model of what constitutes the process (types, constants, variables), what the process does (state transitions), and the critical requirements the process must meet (invariants and schedules). Lower levels are increasingly more detailed with the lowest level corresponding closely to high level code. Figure 1 shows one of the process types of an elevator control system. The Elevator_Button_Panel process represents the button panel located within an elevator car.

The process being specified is thought of as being in various *states*, with one state differentiated from another by the values of its *state variables*, which can be changed only by means of *state transitions*. Transitions are described in terms of entry and exit assertions, where *entry assertions* describe the constraints that state variables must satisfy in order for the transition to fire, and *exit assertions* describe the constraints that are fulfilled by state variables after the transition has fired. Variables are changed atomically at the end of a transition's execution with variables not referenced in the exit assertion remaining unchanged. An explicit non-null duration is associated with each transition. A transition is executed as soon as it is enabled (i.e. when its entry assertion is satisfied), assuming no other transition for that process instance is executing. In the Elevator_Button_Panel process, the clear_floor_request transition is enabled when the elevator is currently stopped with its door opening at a floor that has been requested.

PROCESS Elevator_Button_Panel
  IMPORT
    floor, request_dur, clear_dur,
    elevator, elevator.position,
    elevator.door_open,
    elevator.door_moving
  EXPORT
    floor_requested, request_floor
  VARIABLE
    floor_requested(floor): boolean
  INITIAL
    FORALL f: floor
      (~floor_requested(f))
  TRANSITION request_floor(f: floor)
    ENTRY   [TIME: request_dur]
      ~floor_requested(f)
    EXIT
      floor_requested(f)
        Becomes TRUE

TRANSITION clear_floor_request
  ENTRY   [TIME: clear_dur]
    floor_requested(elevator.position)
  &   ~elevator.door_open
  &   elevator.door_moving
  EXIT
    floor_requested(elevator.position)
      Becomes FALSE
INVARIANT
  FORALL f: floor
  (Change(floor_requested(f), now)
  &   ~floor_requested(f)
 →   EXISTS t: time
    ($Change_2$(floor_requested(f)) < t
    &   t ≤ now
    &   past(elevator.position, t) = f
    &   ~past(elevator.door_open, t)
    &   past(elevator.door_moving, t)))

Fig. 1. The Elevator_Button_Panel process

Every process can export both state variables and transitions; as a consequence, the former are readable by other processes and the external environment while the latter are executable from the external environment. Interprocess communication is accomplished by broadcasting the values of exported variables and the start and end times of exported transitions. In the Elevator_Button_Panel process, the floor_requested variable and the request_floor transition are exported. The position, door_open, and door_moving variables of the elevator process are imported.

In addition to specifying system state (through process variables and constants) and system evolution (through transitions), an ASTRAL specification also defines system critical requirements and assumptions about the behavior of the environment that interacts with the system. The behavior of the environment is expressed by means of *environment clauses*, which describe assumptions about the pattern of invocation of external transitions. Critical requirements are expressed by means of *invariants* and *schedules*. Invariants represent requirements that must hold in every state reachable from the initial state, no matter what the behavior of the external environment is, while schedules represent additional properties that must be satisfied provided that the external environment behaves as assumed.

The requirement and assumption clauses are expressed using a combination of first-order logic and ASTRAL-specific constructs. The main constructs are the timed operators used to express timing requirements. The *start* operator, Start(trans1, t1), takes a transition trans1 and a time t1 and returns true iff the last start of trans1 was at t1. Similarly, the *end* and *call* operators, End(trans1, t1) and Call(trans1, t1), return true iff the last end or the last call of trans1 was at t1. The *change* operator,

Change(A, t), takes an expression A and a time t and returns true iff the last time A changed value was at t. The *past* operator, past(A, t), takes an expression A and a time t and returns the value of A at t. In addition to these operators, a special global variable *now* is used to denote the current time, where the time domain is the nonnegative real numbers.

Using these operators, a variety of complex properties can be expressed. For example, the invariant of the Elevator_Button_Panel process states that between a change to floor_requested(f) and a change back to ~floor_requested(f) for any floor f, the elevator has been at f and its door has started opening. An introduction and complete overview of the ASTRAL language can be found in [5]. For the complete description and specification of the elevator system, see [16].

Rather than implementing a theorem prover for ASTRAL from scratch, it was decided to take advantage of an existing general-purpose theorem prover adapted for use with ASTRAL. PVS was considered ideal for ASTRAL given its powerful typing system, higher-order facilities, heavily automated decision procedures, and ease of use. Other theorem provers were also considered, including HOL [12] and ACL2 [15]. HOL does not have the usability of PVS and its decision procedures are not as powerful [11]. ACL2 is also not as usable as PVS and has limited or no support for arbitrary quantification and real numbers [20].

3 PVS

The Prototype Verification System (PVS) [8] is a powerful interactive theorem prover based on typed higher-order logic. A PVS specification consists of a modular collection of *theories*, where a theory is defined by a set of type, constant, axiom, and theorem declarations. PVS has a very expressive typing language, which includes functions, arrays, sets, tuples, enumerated types, and predicate subtypes. Types may be *interpreted* or *uninterpreted*. Interpreted types are defined based on existing types, while uninterpreted types must be defined axiomatically. Predicate subtypes allow the expression of complex types that must satisfy a given constraint. For example, the even numbers can be defined „even_int: TYPE = {i: int | EXISTS (j: int): 2 * j = i}".

For any assignment or substitution that involves a predicate subtype, PVS generates *type correctness conditions* (TCCs), which are obligations that must be proved in order for the rest of the proof to be valid. For example, for the declaration „e_plus_2(e: even_int): even_int = e + 2", PVS generates the following TCC:

```
% Subtype TCC generated (line 7) for e + 2
    e_plus_2_TCC1: OBLIGATION
        (FORALL (e: even_int): (EXISTS (j: int): 2 * j = e + 2));
```

That is, it must be shown that adding two to an even number is still an even number. Otherwise, the definition of e_plus_2 violates its stated type.

Like types, constants can either be interpreted or uninterpreted. The value of an interpreted constant is stated explicitly, whereas the value of an uninterpreted constant is defined axiomatically. Besides types and constants, a theory declaration contains axioms, which are basic „truths" of the theory and theorems, which are hypotheses that are thought to be true, but that need to be proven with the prover.

When the PVS prover is invoked on a theorem, the theorem is displayed in the form of a *sequent*. A sequent consists of a set of *antecedents* and a set of *consequents*, where if A_1, ..., A_n are antecedents and C_1, ..., C_m are consequents in the current sequent, then the current goal is $(A_1 \& ... \& A_n) \to (C_1 \mid ... \mid C_m)$. It is the user's job to direct PVS with prover commands such as instantiating quantifiers and introducing lemmas to show that either (1) there exists an i such that A_i is false, (2) there exists an i such that C_i is true, or (3) there exists a pair (i, j) such that $A_i = C_j$. PVS maintains a proof tree, which consists of all of the subgoals generated during a proof. Initially, when the prover is invoked on a theorem, the proof tree contains only the sequent form of that theorem. As the proof proceeds, subgoals may be generated and proved. To prove that a particular goal in the proof tree is true, all its subgoals must be proved true. PVS allows the user to define *strategies*, which are collections of prover commands that can be used to automate frequently occurring proof patterns.

4 Encoding Issues

While encoding ASTRAL within PVS, a number of issues arose that needed to be handled. Several of these issues are not exclusive to ASTRAL and occur in many different real-time specification languages. The following sections discuss some of these issues and how they were handled in the ASTRAL encoding.

4.1 Formulas as Types

In many real-time specification languages, a single formula may have multiple values depending on the temporal context in which it is evaluated. Depending on the language, the temporal context may be an explicit clock variable, or implicitly derivable from the formula. To encode such languages into a theorem prover, it is necessary to define formulas as types that can be evaluated in different contexts.

Two different approaches have been used to encode formulas as types in PVS. In the TRIO to PVS encoding [1], an uninterpreted „TRIO_formula" type is introduced to handle this issue. In TRIO, the current time is always implicit, but the values of formulas in the past and future can be obtained relative to the current time using the *dist* operator, dist(A, t), which takes a formula A and a relative time t and gives the value of A at t time units from the current time. In the TRIO encoding, the dist operator is defined as a function of type [[TRIO_formula, time] $\to$ TRIO_formula]. Axioms are defined to transform elements of type TRIO_formula to other elements of type TRIO_formula. Eventually, there must be a valuation from TRIO_formulas to real-world values (i.e. booleans, integers, etc.) so that the decision procedures of PVS can be invoked. Hence a valuation function is defined that takes a TRIO_formula and produces the corresponding boolean value assuming an initial context of the current time instant.

The Duration Calculus (DC) is another real-time language that has been encoded into PVS [18]. DC is an implicit-time interval temporal logic in which the current interval is not explicitly known. Rather than using uninterpreted types to define formulas, however, the DC encoding takes advantage of the higher-order capabilities of PVS and defines formulas as functions of type [Interval $\to$ bool]. DC operators are defined as Curried functions, which when given their original operands, return a function from an Interval to the original range of the operator. For example, the disjunction operator „$\lor$" is defined as „$\lor$(A, B)(i): bool = A(i) OR B(i)", where A and B are of the type [Interval $\to$ bool] and i is of type Interval. Using this technique, the resulting functions can be combined normally, while still delaying the evaluation of the whole expression until a temporal context is given. Eventually, when a specific interval is given, an actual boolean value is obtained.

For ASTRAL, the DC approach was chosen for several reasons. Since TRIO is an implicit-time temporal logic, one of the main motivations of the TRIO encoding was to keep the actual current time hidden. In ASTRAL, the current time can be explicitly referenced using the variable now, thus it was unnecessary to keep the time hidden. Another disadvantage of the TRIO encoding is that all of the axioms of first-order logic needed to be explicitly encoded into PVS to manipulate the TRIO_formula type. Using the DC encoding style, however, the built-in PVS framework could be utilized, which includes all first-order logic axioms.

All ASTRAL operators have been defined as Curried functions from their operand domains to the type [time → range]. For example, the ASTRAL operator Start(trans1, t1) takes a transition trans1 and a time t1 and returns true iff the last start of trans1 was at t1. Its PVS counterpart, Start1(trans1, at1) takes a transition trans1 and an operand at1 of type [time → time] and returns a function of type [time → bool] such that when an evaluation time t1 is given will return true iff the last start of trans1 at time t1 was at time at1(t1). In the Start1 definition, shown below, as well as the definitions of all ASTRAL operators that take a time operand, the time operand is itself of type [time → time] and is only evaluated after an evaluation context is provided.

```
Start1(trans1: transition, at1: [time → time])(t1: {t1: time | at1(t1) ≤ t1}): bool =
    Fired(trans1, at1(t1)) AND
    (FORALL (t2):
        at1(t1) < t2 AND t2 ≤ t1 IMPLIES
            NOT Fired(trans1, t2))
```

With the operators defined in this manner, it is possible to combine ASTRAL operators in standard ways and yet still produce an expression that will only be evaluated once its temporal context is given. The explicit operator definitions also allow all expressions translated from ASTRAL to PVS to be easily expanded and reduced via the built-in mechanisms of PVS. The resulting encoding is very close to the ASTRAL base logic with only slight syntactic differences and allows a specifier who is familiar with the ASTRAL language to easily read the PVS expressions of ASTRAL formulas.

4.2 Partial Functions

Some specification languages such as Z [19] allow the definition of partial functions (i.e. functions that are only well defined at certain points) within specifications. Unlike some other theorem provers, PVS does not support the use of partial functions directly. To encode languages that allow the definition of partial functions or whose operators themselves may be partial functions into PVS, alternative approaches must be used. In lieu of partial functions, PVS has a very powerful predicate subtyping system that allows functions to be declared with domains of only those elements satisfying a given predicate, such as only those elements for which a function is well defined. The user then proves TCC obligations that the operand of each function satisfies the given predicate. For a specific class of functions, such as boolean functions, an alternative to predicate subtyping is to define a new domain that contains an additional undefined element and then modify the operators for that class of functions to use the new domain. For example, for boolean partial functions, a three-valued domain of {true, false, undefined} can be defined in PVS with boolean operators modified to work with the new domain.

The partial functions in ASTRAL are the operators that take a time as an argument. In ASTRAL, only times in the past may be referenced, thus any formula that references a time beyond the value of now is undefined. In encoding these operators into PVS, the choice was made to use the subtyping mechanism of PVS for similar reasons as the choice to use the DC encoding style. Namely, it was preferable to rely on the existing PVS framework as much as possible. There were also a number of disadvantages to explicitly adding an undefined value and then modifying the appropriate operators. For instance, many additional axioms needed to be added to derive and manipulate expressions containing the undefined element. The main drawback, however, is that the ASTRAL *past* operator, past(A, t), which takes an expression A and a time t and returns the value of A at t, is a polymorphic function. That is, the past operator can have multiple types depending on the type of A. Since past takes a time, it is undefined when t is greater than now. Since A can be of any type, essentially every type in the specification and hence every operator in the language would need to be redefined using an undefined element. This was highly undesirable and would have unnecessarily complicated both the encoding and the resulting proofs.

Instead, by using the PVS subtyping mechanism, the user must prove TCCs showing that the time operand of any timed operator used in a specification is less than or equal to the temporal context given to the operator. Most of these obligations will be trivial given that the time operands are usually based on now directly or on a quantified time variable that was appropriately limited.

The definition of the Start1 operator in the previous section demonstrates the use of the subtyping mechanism. The time operand of the Start1 function, at1, is of type [time → time] and is only evaluated after an evaluation context is provided. Since it is not known whether at1(t1) will be a valid operand or not (i.e. will cause the expression to be undefined), t1 is limited by the PVS typing system to be greater than or equal to at1(t1). It is then the user's job to show via a TCC obligation that any evaluation times of a Start1 expression occurring in a specification are permissible. The other timed operators of ASTRAL are defined in a similar manner.

4.3 Noninterleaved Concurrency

Concurrency in real-time systems can be represented by either an interleaved or a noninterleaved model. In an interleaved model, concurrent events occur sequentially between changes to time, while in a noninterleaved model, concurrent events occur simultaneously without an implied ordering. Timed state-machine languages that use an interleaved model of concurrency use an explicit „tick" transition to change time. The combination of the implied ordering of interleaved concurrency and the use of a tick transition allows the semantics of interleaved timed state-machine languages to be simplified significantly over their noninterleaved counterparts because a system execution can be represented as a sequence of transitions rather than an interval of time in which one or more events occur or do not occur at each time. The proof obligations for such languages are also correspondingly simplified since they can be inductive on the nth transition to fire rather than a full induction on a possibly dense time domain.

In ASTRAL, the proof obligations are carried out modularly by proving the properties of each process individually and then proving global properties based on the collection of process properties. Although the sequence of transitions that fire in a particular process can be represented by an interleaved model since transition execution is nonoverlapping, this sequence is not enough to discharge the proof obligations of the process. Transition entry assertions and process properties can reference calls from the external environment, changes to the values of imported variables, and call/start/end times of imported transitions. These events can occur at any time with respect to the sequence of transitions in a particular process. Thus, the semantic representation of ASTRAL needs to handle multiple concurrent events as well as gaps in time in which no events occur, which requires a noninterleaved model of concurrency.

The semantics of ASTRAL are based on the predicates *Called* and *Fired*. Called(trans1, t1) is true iff transition trans1 was called from the external environment at time t1. Fired(trans1, t1) is true iff trans1 fired at t1. Since a different transition may be executing on each process instance, each process instance has a separate Fired and Called predicate. In ASTRAL, a given process instance „knows" its own execution history completely, but only knows the portion of the execution history of other process instances that pertains to the exported transitions of those instances. In the semantics, for a given process instance, the Fired and Called predicates of the process can be used to derive information about the state variables of the process and vice-versa. The predicates of other process instances, however, can only be used to derive a limited amount of information about those processes. Namely, if an imported transition ended, then it is known there was a corresponding start and similarly, if an imported transition started, then it was called.

Two of the ten axioms of the ASTRAL axiomatization are shown below. The axiomatization of ASTRAL into PVS is a much revised and expanded version of the ASTRAL axiomatization of [7] and includes corrections for both soundness and completeness. The full version of the semantics presented in this paper defines the current formal semantics of the ASTRAL language. The trans_fire axiom states that if some transition is enabled and the process is idle (i.e. no transition in the middle of execution), then some transition fires. The trans_mutex axiom states that whenever a transition fires, no other transition can fire until its duration has elapsed (i.e. until the transition ends). This axiom combined with trans_fire is sufficient to show that a single unique transition fires on a particular process instance when some transition is enabled and the process is idle. Note that since the semantics cannot be represented by a sequence of transitions as in an interleaved model, it is necessary to assure that a process is actually idle in order for a transition to fire.

```
trans_fire: AXIOM                          trans_mutex: AXIOM
  (FORALL (t1):                              (FORALL (trans1, t1):
    (EXISTS (trans1):                          Fired(trans1, t1) IMPLIES
      Enabled(trans1, t1)) AND                 (FORALL (trans2):
    (FORALL (trans2, t2):                        trans2 ≠ trans1 IMPLIES
      t1 - Duration(trans2) < t2 AND               NOT Fired(trans2, t1)) AND
      t2 < t1 IMPLIES                        (FORALL (trans2, t2):
        NOT Fired(trans2, t2)) IMPLIES         t1 < t2 AND
    (EXISTS (trans1):                          t2 < t1 + Duration(trans1) IMPLIES
      Fired(trans1, t1)))                        NOT Fired(trans2, t2)))
```

Since ASTRAL is based on noninterleaved concurrency, the intra-level proof obligations [7] (i.e. the proof obligations necessary to show that the invariant and schedule of a level hold) are inductive on ASTRAL's time domain. Since the time domain of ASTRAL is the nonnegative real numbers, however, and simple induction on that domain is not valid, the induction must be performed on nonempty intervals of the nonnegative reals. That is, the induction hypothesis is assumed up to some arbitrary time T0 and the user must show that it holds for a constant length of time Δ > 0 afterwards. The induction case of the invariant proof obligation is shown below.

```
invariant_induct: THEOREM
    (FORALL (T1): T1 ≤ T0 IMPLIES Invariant(T1)) IMPLIES
    (FORALL (T1): T0 < T1 AND T1 < T0 + Δ IMPLIES Invariant(T1))
```

For the induction to be reasonable, Δ must be bounded because the bigger Δ becomes, the more difficult it is to prove that the property holds at the times close to the upper bound T0 + Δ. This is because at those times, more and more time has elapsed since the last known state of the system (i.e. when the inductive hypothesis held). In translating the proof obligations into PVS, it was not possible to say that Δ is „as small as possible". Instead, an explicit upper bound needed to be chosen to restrict Δ. The upper bound chosen for the ASTRAL encoding was a value less than the smallest transition duration. That is, the conjunct „(FORALL (trans1: transition): Δ < Duration(trans1))" was added to the proof obligation above.

This bound is satisfactory for a number of reasons. The main justification is that with Δ bounded by the smallest duration, only a single transition can fire or complete execution within the proof interval. This is advantageous because if only a single transition can end, then the state variables can only change once within the interval. Additionally, if a transition did end within the interval, then the inductive hypothesis held when the transition began firing. These qualities are useful for automating the proofs of certain types of properties as will be shown in section 6.1.

5 PVS Library and Translator

The axiomatization and operator definitions discussed in section 4 have been incorporated into an ASTRAL-PVS library. The library contains the specification-independent core of the ASTRAL language. In the axiomatization and operators, some of the theories are parameterized by type and function constants. For example, to define the trans_fire axiom, the type „transition" and the function „Duration" need to be supplied to the axiomatization. In order to use the axiomatization, the appropriate types and functions must be defined based on the specification to be verified. An ASTRAL to PVS translator has been developed to automatically construct all the appropriate definitions.

The major obstacle in translating ASTRAL specifications is translating identifiers with types involving lists and structures. In ASTRAL, it is possible to define arbitrary combinations of structures and lists as types, thus references to variables of these types can become quite complex. For example, consider the following type declarations: „list1: list of integer" and „struct1: structure of (l_one(integer): list1)". If s1 is a variable of type struct1, valid uses of s1 would include s1 by itself, s1[l_one(5)], and s1[l_one(5)][9]. The translation of expressions such as these must result in a Curried time function, so that it can be used with the definitions of the Curried boolean and arithmetic operators. The expression in each bracket can be time-dependent, so it is necessary to define the translation such that an evaluation context (i.e. time) given to the expression as a whole is propagated to all expressions in brackets.

In the translation of this example, s1 is a function of type [time → struct1] and struct1 is a record [# l_one: [integer → list1] #]. The expression „s1[l_one(5)][9]", becomes „(λ(T1: time): nth(((λ(T1: time): l_one((s1)(T1)) ((const(5))(T1))))(T1), (const(9))(T1)))". The lambdas are added to propagate the temporal context given to the formula as a whole. Although the lambda expression generated for s1 looks very difficult to decipher, translated expressions will never actually be used in this „raw" form. In the proof obligations, a translated expression is always evaluated in some context before being used. Once this evaluation occurs, all the lambdas drop out and the expression is simplified to a combination of variables and predicates. For example, the expression above evaluated at time t becomes „nth(l_one((s1)(t))(5), 9)". First, the value of the variable s1 is evaluated at time t. Then, the record member l_one is obtained from the resulting record. This member is parameterized, so it is given a parameter of 5. Finally, element 9 of the resulting list is obtained.

For the full details of the axiomatization of the ASTRAL abstract machine, the operator definitions, and the ASTRAL to PVS translator, see [16].

6 Proof Assistance and Automation

After a specification is translated, the user must prove the inductive proof obligations discussed in section 4.3. In general, the proof obligations are undecidable so they require a fair amount of interaction with the prover. For timed properties, this interaction usually consists of setting up the sequences of transitions that are possible within the prover, proving that each sequence is indeed possible, and then showing that the time of the sequence is less than the required time. Portions of these proofs can be automated with appropriate PVS strategies [16], but the user must still direct PVS during much of the reasoning. There are some property types, however, that can oftentimes be proven fully automatically by PVS. After performing the proofs of several systems using the encoding, PVS strategies have been developed to assist the user in proving these types of properties.

6.1 Untimed Formulas

The *try-untimed* strategy was written to attempt the proofs of properties that do not involve time and only deal with combinations of state variables of a single process instance. For example, in the Elevator process type, one such property in the invariant section is „elevator_moving → ~door_moving". That is, whenever the elevator car is moving, the elevator door should not be in the process of opening or closing. This property was proved completely unassisted by the try-untimed strategy.

The basis of the try-untimed strategy is that in the interval T0 to T0 + Δ of the proof obligations, the state variables either stay the same or one or more of them change. If the variables stay the same, then by the inductive hypothesis, the property holds at all times in the interval. If a variable changes during the interval, then by the semantics of ASTRAL, a transition ended at the time of the change. Furthermore, since transitions are nonoverlapping and, as discussed, Δ has been limited to a constant less than the duration of any transition, only a single transition end can occur within the interval. Figure 2 depicts this situation. Let T1 be the time of such an end. Since no transition ended in the interval [T0, T1), the state variables must have stayed the same during that time period, thus the property holds by the inductive hypothesis. Similarly, since no transition ended in the interval (T1, T0 + Δ], the variables are unchanged in that region, thus the property holds in that region if it holds at T1. The bulk of the strategy is thus devoted to proving that the property holds at T1.

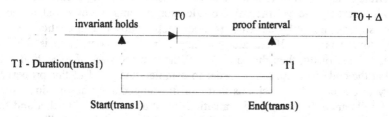

Fig. 2. Proof interval

To prove this, it must be shown that all transition exit assertions preserve the property, thus the proof is split into a case for each transition and the transition's entry and exit clauses are asserted. Once again, since Δ was limited to less than the duration of any transition, the start of the transition occurred before T0, thus the property held at the start of the transition. From this point, a modified version of the PVS *grind* command, which is a heavy-duty decision procedure that performs rewriting, skolemization, and automatic quantifier instantiation, is invoked to finish the proof. Grind in unmodified form rewrites all definitions in a specification. The modified version does not rewrite the timed ASTRAL operators, since it is unlikely that the decision procedures could use the information efficiently, thus expanding the operators would only increase the running time of the strategy.

A side benefit of the try-untimed strategy is that even when it fails, it is still advantageous for the user to run it because usually only very difficult cases will be left for the user to prove. When the strategy fails, it is due to one of three reasons. The first reason is that the user invoked the strategy on a timed property or one that involves imported variables. In this case, it is likely that most of the cases will fail, since try-untimed was not intended to deal with these types of properties. The second reason is that one or more transitions do not preserve the property. In this case, the user knows the exact transitions that failed since PVS will require further interaction to complete those cases. The user can correct the specification before continuing with other proofs. The last reason, which will be the most likely, is that it failed because there was not enough information in the entry assertion of a transition to prove the property. Usually, this occurs when the value of a variable in the formula to be proved is not explicitly stated in the entry assertion of the transition, but instead is implied by the sequences preceding that particular transition. For example, consider the elevator property „elevator_moving → ~door_open". That is, the door must be closed while the elevator car is moving. After running the try-untimed strategy, all the transition cases are proved except for the „door_stop" case. The door_stop transition, shown below, stops the door in either the open or closed position after a suitable length of time from when the door started moving.

```
TRANSITION door_stop
    ENTRY   [TIME: door_stop_dur]
            door_moving
        &   now - t_move_door ≥ Change(door_moving)
    EXIT
            ~door_moving
        &   door_open = ~door_open'
```

The strategy fails for this case because it is possible for door_open to be set to true in the exit assertion and yet the value of elevator_moving is not stated in the entry assertion so can possibly be true if door_stop follows a transition in which elevator_moving is true. If elevator_moving is true and door_open is false when door_stop begins firing, then the formula will hold at the start of execution yet will not hold at the end of execution. In order to complete the proof of this property, it is necessary to consider the transitions that can fire immediately before door_stop. If the proof still cannot be completed, transitions must be considered further and further back in time. Eventually, the formula will be provable or a violation will occur.

6.2 Transition Sequence Generator

Since sequencing is so important to proving some properties, it is useful to provide the user with a tool to view the transition sequences that can occur in a given process type. Such a tool can be used to estimate time delays between states, help the user visualize the operation of the system, and in some cases can be used to prove simple system properties. Unlike graphical state-machine languages in which the successor information is part of the specification, in textual languages such as ASTRAL, sequencing cannot be determined without more in-depth analysis. In addition, determining whether one transition is the successor of another in ASTRAL is undecidable since transition entry/exit assertions may be arbitrary first-order logic expressions. Many successors, however, can be eliminated based only on the simpler portions of the entry/exit assertions, such as boolean and enumerated variables. Based on this fact, a transition sequence generator tool has been developed.

The sequence generator first eliminates as many transition successors as possible. This is done by attempting the proof of an obligation trans1_not_trans2 for each pair of transitions (trans1, trans2) as shown below. Note that this obligation only states that some transition must end between trans1 and trans2 and does not exclude trans1 or trans2 from firing. The obligation is sufficient, however, to prove that a transition besides trans1 and trans2 must fire in between any firing of trans1 and trans2. If only trans1 and trans2 fire in between t1 and t2, then since t2 - t1 is finite and the durations of trans1 and trans2 are constant and non-null, eventually a contradiction can be achieved by applying the theorem below repeatedly on an ever shortening interval.

trans1_not_trans2: THEOREM
    (FORALL (t1, t2):
        t1 + Duration(trans1) ≤ t2 AND
        Fired(trans1, t1) AND
        Fired(trans2, t2) IMPLIES
        (EXISTS (trans3, t3):
            t1 + Duration(trans1) <
                t3 + Duration(trans3) AND
            t3 + Duration(trans3) ≤ t2 AND
            Fired(trans3, t3))))

initial_not_trans1: THEOREM
    (FORALL (t1):
        Fired(trans1, t1) IMPLIES
        (EXISTS (trans2, t2):
            t2 + Duration(trans2) ≤ t1 AND
            Fired(trans2, t2)))

An obligation initial_not_trans1, as shown above, is also attempted to prove that each transition is not the first to fire after the initial state. The PVS strategies *try-seq-gen* and *try-seq-gen-0* were written to automatically discharge these obligations. The try-seq-gen strategy uses abstract machine axioms to introduce the entry and exit assertions of trans1, the entry assertion of trans2, and the fact that if nothing ended between the end of trans1 and the start of trans2, then all variable values remained constant during this time. Once all of this information is present, the strategy invokes the modified grind command as discussed for the try-untimed strategy. The try-seq-gen-0 strategy is similar but uses the initial clause of the process in place of the information about trans1.

Table 1 shows the results of using these strategies to compute the successors for each process type of a set of testbed systems developed in [16], which includes the elevator control system. For each process type, the table shows the maximum number of successors, the number of successors that are provably possible, and the number that were computed automatically using the try-seq-gen strategies.

There are two main factors that contribute to the difference between the number of successors that are provably possible and the number computed by the try-seq-gen strategies in the testbed systems. The first factor is that entry assertions do not usually constrain all of the state variables of a process. For example, the entry assertion of the door_stop transition, shown in section 6.1, constrains the value of door_moving, but does not constrain the value of elevator_moving.

When proving that the arrive transition, shown below, cannot follow door_stop, PVS does not have information about the value of elevator_moving at the start of door_stop, which is only derivable from the transitions preceding door_stop. Thus, PVS must assume an arbitrary symbolic value for elevator_moving. It is possible that elevator_moving is true, thus PVS cannot eliminate the possibility that arrive immediately follows door_stop. It is provable that this is not the case, however, because it is not possible to find a sequence of transitions starting from the initial state in which arrive can immediately follow door_stop. The only possible predecessors to door_stop are open_door and close_door. Open_door sets elevator_moving to false in its exit assertion, thus if open_door immediately precedes door_stop, arrive cannot follow door_stop. Similarly, it is possible to show that close_door must be preceded

by door_stop, which is preceded by open_door.   Thus, arrive cannot follow
door_stop.

```
TRANSITION arrive
    ENTRY   [TIME: arrive_dur]
            elevator_moving
        &   FORALL t: time
                (   t ≤ now
                &   (   End(move_down, t)
                    |   End(move_up, t))
                →       now - t_move ≥ t)
        &   FORALL t, t1: time
                (   t ≤ now
                &   End(arrive, t)
                &   (   End(move_up, t1)
                    |   End(move_down, t1))
                →       t < t1)
    EXIT
            IF   going_up'
            THEN  position = position' + 1
            ELSE  position = position' - 1
            FI
```

In order to improve the accuracy of the sequence generator for these processes, it
would be necessary to examine sequences back to a transition that causes a
contradiction. This is a non-terminating procedure, however, whenever the second
transition of a successor obligation actually is a successor of the first, thus it is
necessary to specify termination conditions such as a specific number of transitions
into the past or similar criteria. In general, this procedure is not worth the additional
time it would require unless the number of successors that could be eliminated using a
small number of backward steps is significantly higher than the number of actual
successors. As an alternative, the user can fully constrain all of the state variables in
the entry assertions.

The second factor that contributes to the difference between the number of
provable successors and the number computed by the try-seq-gen strategies is the use
of timed operators to define the sequencing between different operations.   For
example, the end operator is used in the arrive transition to prevent arrive from
following itself. In the proof of the successor obligation arrive_not_arrive, arrive
fires at t1 and t2 and no other transition fires in between. By the last conjunct of
arrive's entry assertion, there must be an end to move_up or move_down between the
last time arrive ended (t1 + arrive_dur) and the next time it fires (t2), which
contradicts the fact that no transition fires in between t1 and t2. This proof cannot be
carried out without the use of the end operator. The definition of the end operator
within PVS, however, is quite complex with several quantifiers, thus there is little
hope that PVS could automatically prove such an obligation. For this reason, the
modified grind used in the try-seq-gen strategies does not expand any of the timed
operators, which prevents work from being wasted.

Table 1. Transition successors of testbed systems

System	Process Type	maximum successors	actual successors	computed successors
Bakery Algorithm	Proc	42	8	25
Cruise Control	Accelerometer	2	2	2
	Speed_Control	132	76	94
	Speedometer	2	2	2
	Tire_Sensor	2	2	2
Elevator	Elevator	42	13	24
	Elevator_Button_Panel	6	4	4
	Floor_Button_Panel	20	14	14
Olympic Boxing	Judge	2	2	2
	Tabulate	12	4	6
	Timer	6	3	3
Phone	Central_Control	420	235	312
	Phone	110	50	69
Production Cell	P_Crane	156	13	36
	P_Deposit	6	3	3
	P_Deposit_Sensor	6	3	3
	P_Feed	20	14	14
	P_Feed_Sensor	6	3	3
	P_Press	42	7	7
	P_Robot	420	21	129
	P_Table	72	9	21
Railroad Crossing	Gate	20	7	7
	Sensor	6	3	3
Stoplight	Controller	420	84	198
	Sensor	6	3	3
Total		1978	585	986

When a transition is parameterized, such as the request_floor transition of the Elevator_Button_Panel process shown in section 2, each set of parameters represents one possible choice that a process can make. Usually, the start of a transition with one set of parameters does not preclude the start of the same transition with a different set of parameters immediately afterward. Thus, the sequences generated for parameterized transitions do not usually give any helpful information to the user since essentially any transition can follow any other.

Since the standard sequence generator proof obligations do not ordinarily produce a useful result for parameterized transitions, a parameterized extension has been added to the sequence generator. In this extension, if two transitions have the same parameter list (i.e. the same number of parameters and parameter types), the successor proof obligations are attempted assuming that the parameters are the same. That is, the sequences are generated with a fixed set of parameters among consecutive transitions. This is useful for finding the sequence of transitions in a single „thread". For example, by keeping the parameters fixed in the Central_Control process of the phone system of [5], the sequences of transitions that make up the evolution of a call for a particular phone can be computed. The numbers in Table 1 were computed using the parameterized extension. The numbers for the Elevator_Button_Panel,

Central_Control, and Controller processes are the only processes affected by this extension.

After the successors have been computed, the sequence generator constructs transition sequences based on input from the user, which includes the first and last transitions, the direction to generate sequences from the first transition, the maximum number of transitions per sequence, and the maximum number of sequences. There is also an option to disallow sequences in which the same transition appears more than once (besides as the first or last transition). The user must provide the maximum number of transitions per sequence and if the search is backward, must provide the first transition. The sequence generation process is completely automatic and is available as a component of the ASTRAL Software Development Environment (SDE) [17]. The ASTRAL SDE constructs the sequence generator obligations, invokes PVS, runs the proof scripts, retrieves the results, and then generates the sequences according to the user query. Since running the proof scripts can be time-consuming, the results are saved between changes to the specification, so that sequences from previous proof attempts can be quickly displayed.

For each sequence generated, an approximate running time of the sequence is constructed by analyzing the entry assertion of each transition. Entry assertions depend on the values of local and imported variables, the call/start/end times of local and imported transitions, and the current time in the system. Transitions that only depend on local variables and/or the start/end times of local transitions will always fire immediately after another transition. Transitions that reference the current time, however, may be delayed some amount of time before firing. For example, the door_stop transition, shown in section 6.1, fires at least t_move_door after the door starts moving. Similarly, transitions may wait indefinitely for a change to an imported variable, a call/start/end to an imported transition, or a call to a local transition from the external environment. The three types of delays are denoted *delay_T* for a time delay, *delay_O* for a delay because of the other processes in the system, and *delay_E* for a delay due to the external environment.

The sequence generator is complete (i.e. if a sequence is possible it will appear as a result) without the parameterized extension since the successor obligations are performed using the PVS encoding, which will only eliminate a successor if it is derivable that it cannot occur. The sequence generator is not complete with the parameterized extension because it does not display any sequences in which two parameterized transitions with the same parameter lists are given different parameters. In this case, utility was chosen over completeness.

The accuracy of the sequence generator can be improved by manually performing the proofs of those successor obligations that actually can be proved but could not be automatically proved by the try-seq-gen strategies. The time used to run the proof scripts or to refine the performance of the sequence generator is not wasted because any successor eliminated can be used as a lemma in the main proof obligations.

As a simple example of a sequence generator query, consider the door_stop case that failed in the try-untimed proof of „elevator_moving → ~door_open" in section 6.1. The user may wish to view the predecessors to door_stop to see if the proof can be completed quickly or if a violation is possible involving the door_stop transition. Figure 3 shows the sequence generator dialog box and the second of the three sequences generated from the query.

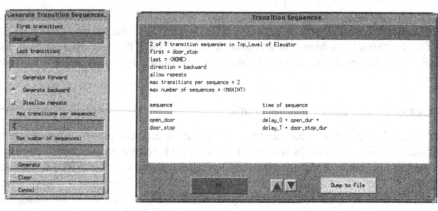

Fig 3. Sequence generator dialog box and query result

Three sequences are returned to the user, which show three possible predecessors to door_stop: close_door, open_door, and arrive. If close_door fires before door_stop, the door is closed when door_stop completes firing, thus the property trivially holds. The open_door transition sets elevator_moving to false, thus the property also trivially holds if open_door fires before door_stop. The arrive transition, shown earlier, requires the elevator car to be moving to fire. By the inductive hypothesis, the door is closed when it fires, thus if arrive precedes door_stop, the invariant can be violated because the elevator car is moving and door_stop sets door_open to true. Therefore, the user knows that to complete the proof, it must be shown that arrive cannot fire immediately before door_stop. The arrive case is another example of a successor that the sequence generator could not eliminate automatically and yet is not actually possible after further analysis. Thus, the user must consider the predecessors of arrive and continue the proof process in a similar manner until the property is proved. Additional uses of the transition sequence generator can be found in [16].

7 Related Work

The temporal logics TRIO [1] and DC [18] have been encoded into PVS as discussed in section 4.1. TRIO is a lower-level formalism than ASTRAL and DC is not as expressive. Several real-time state machine languages have also been encoded into theorem provers. The Timed Automata Model has been encoded into PVS [2] and Timed Transition Systems into HOL [13]. These languages are based on interleaved concurrency, however, which makes their semantics simpler than those of ASTRAL. Additionally, Timed Transition Systems are not defined in terms of arbitrary first-order logic expressions and do not have the complex subtyping mechanisms that are available in ASTRAL.

An encoding of ASTRAL into PVS was reported in [3] and [4], but this encoding is based on a definition of ASTRAL that has been developed independently at Delft University based on earlier ASTRAL work in [9] and [10]. The ASTRAL definition in [9] and [10] did not include the notion of an external environment, thus did not include the call operator, environmental assumptions, or schedules. The Delft definition has diverged from the work reported in [5] and [7] and has essentially become a different language. It includes only a small subset of the full set of

ASTRAL operators and typing options, does not include all of the sections of an ASTRAL specification, and defines only a small fraction of the axiomatization of the ASTRAL abstract machine. In addition, it is based on a discrete time domain and proofs are performed with a global view of the system rather than using a modular approach.

8 Conclusions and Future Work

This paper has discussed the adaptation of the PVS theorem prover for performing analysis of real-time systems written in the ASTRAL formal specification language. A number of issues were encountered during the encoding of ASTRAL that are relevant to the encoding of many real-time specification languages. These issues were presented as well as how they were handled in the ASTRAL encoding. A translator has been written that translates any ASTRAL specification into its corresponding PVS encoding. After performing the proofs of several systems using the encoding, PVS strategies have been developed to automate the proofs of certain types of properties. In addition, the encoding has been used as the basis for a transition sequence generator tool.

A number of issues still need to be addressed in future work. The implementation clause of ASTRAL, which is used to map relationships between upper and lower level specifications, needs to be incorporated into the translator, as well as the inter-level proof obligations used to show that an implementation is consistent with the level above. Currently, the refinement mechanism described in [6] is in a transitional phase, so its translation was postponed until the new refinement mechanism is in place.

A number of enhancements to the sequence generator can be added. For instance, it is useful to provide a more powerful interface. For example, a query interface could be added to answer queries such as whether a given transition can ever occur between two other specified transitions. It is also possible to construct a symbolic expression for the values of the state variables at the end of each sequence by examining the entry and exit assertions of each transition.

In general, more proofs need to be performed for different ASTRAL systems using their PVS translations. In studying the proofs performed for many systems, more proof patterns may be discovered that can be incorporated into suitable PVS strategies. The patterns may also lead to the definition of useful lemmas that can be proven in advance and added to the ASTRAL-PVS library for future use. It is also worthwhile to investigate whether the structure of the ASTRAL specification determines which lemmas and strategies are most applicable to a given formula type.

References

1. Alborghetti, A., A. Gargantini, and A. Morzenti. Providing automated support to deductive analysis of time critical systems. *Proc. 6th European Software Engineering Conf.*, 1997.
2. Archer, M. and C. Heitmeyer. Mechanical verification of timed automata: a case study. *Proc. Real-Time Technology and Applications Symp.*, pp. 192-203, 1996.

3. Bun, L. Checking properties of ASTRAL specifications with PVS. *Proc. 2nd Annual Conf. of the Advanced School for Computing and Imaging*, pp. 102-107, 1996.
4. Bun, L. Embedding Astral in PVS. *Proc. 3rd Annual Conf. of the Advanced School for Computing and Imaging*, pp. 130-136, 1997.
5. Coen-Porisini, A., C. Ghezzi, and R.A. Kemmerer. Specification of realtime systems using ASTRAL. *IEEE Transactions on Software Engineering*, 23(9): 572-598, 1997.
6. Coen-Porisini, A., R.A. Kemmerer, and D. Mandrioli. A formal framework for ASTRAL inter-level proof obligations. *Proc. 5th European Software Engineering Conf.*, pp. 90-108, 1995.
7. Coen-Porisini, A., R.A. Kemmerer, and D. Mandrioli. A formal framework for ASTRAL intralevel proof obligations. *IEEE Transactions on Software Engineering*, 20(8): 548-561, 1994.
8. Crow, J., S. Owre, J. Rushby, N. Shankar, and M. Srivas. A tutorial introduction to PVS. *Workshop on Industrial-Strength Formal Specification Techniques*, 1995.
9. Ghezzi, C. and R.A. Kemmerer. ASTRAL: an assertion language for specifying realtime systems. *Proc. 3rd European Software Engineering Conf.*, pp. 122-140, 1991.
10. Ghezzi, C. and R.A. Kemmerer. Executing formal specifications: the ASTRAL to TRIO translation approach. *Proc. Symp. on Testing, Analysis, and Verification*, 1991.
11. Gordon, M. Notes on PVS from a HOL perspective. Available at <http://www.cl.cam.ac.uk/users/mjcg/PVS.html>, 1995.
12. Gordon, M.J.C. and T.F. Melham (eds.). Introduction to HOL: a theorem proving environment for higher order logic. Cambridge University Press, 1993.
13. Hale, R., R. Cardell-Oliver, and J. Herbert. An embedding of timed transition systems in HOL. *Formal Methods in System Design*, 3(1-2): 151-174, 1993.
14. Heitmeyer, C. and D. Mandrioli (eds.). Formal methods for real-time computing. John Wiley, 1996.
15. Kaufmann, M. and J. Strother Moore. ACL2: an industrial strength version of Nqthm. *Proc. 11th Annual Conf. on Computer Assurance*, pp. 23-34, 1996.
16. Kolano, P.Z. Tools and techniques for the design and systematic analysis of real-time systems. Ph.D. Thesis, University of California, Santa Barbara, 1999.
17. Kolano, P.Z., Z. Dang, and R.A. Kemmerer. The design and analysis of real-time systems using the ASTRAL software development environment. *Annals of Software Engineering*, 7, 1999.
18. Skakkebaek, J.U. and N. Shankar. Towards a duration calculus proof assistant in PVS. *3rd Int. Symp. on Formal Techniques in Real-Time and Fault-Tolerant Systems*, pp. 660-679, 1994.
19. Spivey, J.M. Specifying a real-time kernel. *IEEE Software*, 7(5): 21-28, 1990.
20. Young, W.D. Comparing verification systems: interactive consistency in ACL2. *Proc. 11th Annual Conf. on Computer Assurance*, pp. 35-45, 1996.

Modelling Timeouts without Timelocks

Howard Bowman*

Computing Laboratory, University of Kent at Canterbury,
Canterbury, Kent, CT2 7NF, United Kingdom
H.Bowman@ukc.ac.uk

Abstract. We address the issue of modelling a simple timeout in timed automata. We argue that expression of the timeout in the UPPAAL timed automata model is unsatisfactory. Specifically, the solutions we explore either allow timelocks or are prohibitively complex. In response we consider timed automata with deadlines which have the property that timelocks cannot be created when composing automata in parallel. We explore a number of different options for reformulating the timeout in this framework and then we relate them.

1   Introduction

A timeout is perhaps the most basic and widely arising specification structure in real-time systems. For example, they arise frequently when modelling communication protocols and work on enhancing "first generation" specification techniques with real-time has frequently been directly motivated by the desire to model timeouts in communication protocols [9].

From within the canon of timed specification notations, timed automata [1] are certainly one of the most important. One reason for this is that powerful real-time model checking techniques have been developed for timed automata, as exemplified by the tools, UPPAAL [2], Kronos [7] and HyTech [8].

However satisfactorily modelling timeout structures proves surprisingly difficult in timed automata. Broadly, problems arise because it is difficult to define timeout behaviour in a manner that avoids the possibility of *timelocks*. By way of clarification:

> *we say that a system is timelocked if it has reached a state from which no path can be found to a time passing transition.*

Timelocks are highly degenerate situations because they yield a *global* blockage of the systems evolution. For example, if a completely independent component is composed in parallel with a system that is timelocked, then the entire composition will inherit the timelock. This is quite different from a classic (local)

---

* Howard Bowman is currently on leave at VERIMAG, Centre Equation, 2 rue Vignate, 38610 GIERES, France and CNR-Istituto CNUCE, Via S. Maria 36, 56126 - Pisa - Italy with the support of the European Commission's TMR programme.

deadlock, which cannot affect the evolution of an independent process. These characteristics of timelocks will be illustrated in section 2.

This paper addresses the issue of how to model timeouts without generating timelocks. We illustrate how the difficulty arises in current timed automata models and then we consider a new timed automata model - Timed Automata with Deadlines (TADs) [3] - which guarantee timelock free parallel composition of automata components.

We begin (in section 2) by presenting background material - we introduce timed automata, discuss the nature of timelocks and outline the timeout behaviour that we require. These requirements have been identified during practical study of the specification and verification of a lip-synchronisation algorithm [6]. Then (in section 3) we discuss possible ways to model the timeout in timed automata. As a typical timed automata model we choose the UPPAAL [2] notation. This is one of the most important timed automata approaches. We argue that none of the legal UPPAAL approaches are completely satisfactory. In particular, avoiding the possibility of timelocks is difficult and leads to prohibitively complex solutions.

In response, (in section 4) we consider how the same timeout behaviour can be modelled in Timed Automata with Deadlines [3]. However, it turns out that the standard TADs approach, as presented in [3], resolves the timelock problem, but introduces a new difficulty which is related to the generation of escape transitions. Consequently, we consider a number of different TAD formulations in section 5 which resolve these difficulties in contrasting ways. Finally, in section 6 we relate these solutions and present a concluding discussion.

2   Background

2.1   Timed Automata

We briefly review some basic timed automata notation.

- A is the set of *completed* (or *basic*) actions.
- $\overline{A} = \{\, a?, a! \mid a \in A \,\}$ is the set of *uncompleted* actions. These give a simple CCS style [10] point-to-point communication which has also been adopted in UPPAAL.
- $A^+ = \overline{A} \cup A$ is the set of *all* actions.
- We use a complementation notation over elements of A^+,

$$\overline{a} = a \quad \text{if } a \in A \tag{1}$$

$$\overline{b?} = b! \tag{2}$$

$$\overline{b!} = b? \tag{3}$$

In addition, we let v, v' etc, range over vectors of processes, which are written, $< l_1, ..., l_n >$, $|v|$ denotes the length of the vector, we use a substitution notation as follows: $< l_1, ..., l_j, ..., l_n > [l/l_j] =< l_1, ..., l_{j-1}, l, l_{j+1}, ..., l_n >$ and we write $v[l'_1/l_1][l'_2/l_2]...[l'_m/l_m]$ as $v[l'_1/l_1, l'_2/l_2, ..., l'_m/l_m]$. We assume the a finite set: C

of clocks which range over $\mathbb{R}^+$ and CC is a set of clock constraints[1]. An arbitrary element of $\mathcal{A}$, the set of all timed automata, has the form:

$$(L, l_0, T, P)$$

where,

- L is a finite set of locations (these appear as small circles in our timed automata diagrams, e.g. see figure 1);
- l_0 is a designated *start location*;
- $T \subseteq L \times CC \times A^+ \times \mathbb{P}(\mathcal{C}) \times L$ is a transition relation (where $\mathbb{P}(S)$ denotes the powerset of S). A typical element of T would be, (l_1, g, a, r, l_2), where $l_1, l_2 \in L$ are automata locations; $g \in CC$ is a guard; $a \in A^+$ labels the transition; and $r \in \mathbb{P}(\mathcal{C})$ is a reset set. $(l_1, g, a, r, l_2) \in T$ is typically written, $l_1 \xrightarrow{g,a,r} l_2$, stating that the automata can evolve from location l_1 to l_2 if the (clock) guard g holds and in the process action a will be performed and all the clocks in r will be set to zero. When we depict timed automata, we write the action label first, then the guard and then the reset set, see e.g. figure 4. Guards that are **true** or resets that are empty are often left blank.
- $P : L \rightarrow CC$ is a function which associates a progress condition (often called an invariant) with every location. Intuitively, an automata can only stay in a state while its progress condition is satisfied. Progress conditions are shown adjacent to states in our depictions, see e.g. figure 2.

Timed automata are interpreted over time/action transition systems which are triples, $(S, s_0, \rightarrow)$, where,

- S is set of states;
- s_0 is a start state;
- $\rightarrow \subseteq S \times \textbf{Lab} \times S$ is a transition relation, where $\textbf{Lab} = A^+ \cup \mathbb{R}^+$. Thus, transitions can be of one of two types: *action transitions*, e.g. (s_1, a, s_2), where $a \in A^+$ and *time passing transitions*, e.g. (s_1, x, s_2), where $x \in \mathbb{R}^+$ and denotes the passage of x time units. Transitions are written:

$$s_1 \xrightarrow{a} s_2 \quad \text{respectively} \quad s_1 \xrightarrow{x} s_2$$

A *clock valuation* is a mapping from clock variables $\mathcal{C}$ to $\mathbb{R}^+$. For a clock valuation u and a delay d, $u \oplus d$ is the clock valuation such that $(u \oplus d)(x) = u(x) + d$ for all $x \in \mathcal{C}$. For a reset set r, we use $r(u)$ to denote the clock valuation u' such that $u'(x) = 0$ whenever $x \in r$ and $u'(x) = u(x)$ otherwise. u_0 is the clock valuation that assigns all clocks to the value zero.

The semantics of a timed automaton $A = (L, l_0, T, P)$ is a time/action transition system, $(S, s_0, \rightarrow)$, where S is the set of all pairs $< l, u >$ such that $l \in L$

---

[1] The form that such constraints can take is typically limited, however since we are not considering verification this is not an issue for us.

and u is a clock valuation, $s_0 = <l_0, u_0>$ and $\to$ is given by the following inference rules:-

$$\frac{l \xrightarrow{g,a,r} l' \quad g(u)}{<l,u> \xrightarrow{a} <l',r(u)>} \qquad \frac{\forall d' \le d \,.\, P(l)(u \oplus d')}{<l,u> \xrightarrow{d} <l',u \oplus d>}$$

We assume our system is described as a network of timed automata. These are modelled by a process vector[2] denoted, $|| <A_1, ..., A_n>$. If $\forall i (1 \le i \le n) \,.\, A_i = (L_i, l_{i,0}, T_i, P_i)$ then the product automaton, which characterises the behaviour of $|| <A_1, ..., A_n>$ is given by,

$$(L^p, l_0^p, T^p, P^p)$$

where $L^p = \{ ||v \,|\, v \in L_1 \times ... \times L_n \}$, $l_0^p = || <l_{1,0}, ..., l_{n,0}>$, T^p is as defined by the following two inference rules and $P^p(|| <l_1, ..., l_n>) = P_1(l_1) \wedge ... \wedge P_n(l_n)$.

$$\frac{l_i \xrightarrow{g_i,a?,r_i} l_i' \quad l_j \xrightarrow{g_j,a!,r_j} l_j'}{||v \xrightarrow{g_i \wedge g_j, a, r_i \cup r_j} ||v[l_i'/l_i, l_j'/l_j]} \qquad \frac{l_i \xrightarrow{g,a,r} l_i' \quad a \in A}{||v \xrightarrow{g,a,r} ||v[l_i'/l_i]}$$

where $1 \le i, j \le |v|$, $i \ne j$.

2.2 Timelocks

We can formulate the notion of a timelock in terms of a testing process. Consider, if we take our system which we denote System and compose it completely independently in parallel with the timed automaton, Tester, shown in figure 1, where the zzz action is independent of all actions in the system. Then for any $x \in \mathbb{R}^+$ if the composition ||<Tester(x),System> cannot perform zzz then the system contains a timelock at time x.

This last illustration indicates why timelocks represent such degenerate situations - even though the Tester is in all respects independent of the system, e.g. it could be that Tester is executed on the Moon and System is executed on Earth without any co-operation, the fact that the system cannot pass time prevents the tester from passing time as well. Thus, *time really does stop* and it stops everywhere because of a degenerate piece of *local* behaviour.

This is a much more serious fault than a classical (local) deadlock. For example, the automaton Stop, also shown in figure 1, generates a local deadlock, however, it cannot prevent an independent process from evolving. In the sequel we will use the term *local deadlock* to denote such a non-timeblocking deadlock.

We consider two varieties of timelock which we illustrate by example, see figure 2,

---

[2] Although our notation is slightly different, our networks are a straightforward simplification of those used in UPPAAL. The simplifications arise because we do not consider the full functionality of UPPAAL. For example, we do not consider committed locations or data variables.

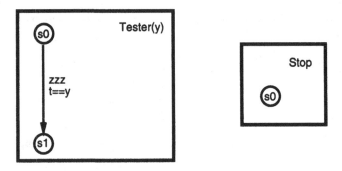

Fig. 1. A tester and a (locally) deadlocked timed automata

1. The first is System1; this is a zeno process which performs an infinite number of aaa actions at time zero. This system is timelocked at time zero and if we compose it independetly in parallel with any other system, the composite system will not be able to pass time. We call such timelocks *zeno timelocks*.
2. The second is the network ||<System2,System3>; this composition contains a timelock at time 2, which arises because System2 must have performed (and thus, synchronised on) action aaa by the time t reaches 2 while System3 does not start offering aaa until t has past 2. Technically the timelock is due to the fact that at time 2 System2 only offers the action transition aaa and importantly, it does not offer a time passing transition. Since the synchronisation cannot be fulfilled the system cannot evolve to a point at which it can pass time. We call such timelocks *composition timelocks*.

The interesting difference between these two varieties of timelock is that the first one locks time, but in the classical sense of untimed systems, is not deadlocked, since actions can always be performed. However, the second reaches a state in which neither time passing or action transitions are possible. Such composition timelocks are the variety we will address in this paper.

2.3 A Bounded Timeout

We describe a rather standard timeout behaviour, which we call a *Bounded Timeout*. The general scenario is that a Timeout process is monitoring a Component and the timeout should expire and enter an error state if the Component does not offer a particular action, which we call good, within a certain period of time.

The precise functionality that we want the timeout to exhibit is[3]:

1. *Basic behaviour.* Assuming Timeout is started at time t, it should generate a timeout action at a time $t + D$ if and only if the action good has not already occured. Thus, if action timeout occurs, it must occur exactly at time $t + D$

---

[3] Our presentation here is similar to that in [6]

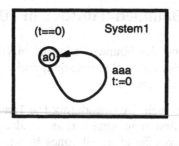

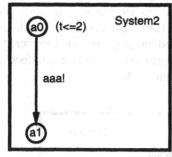
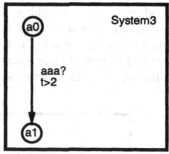

Fig. 2. Timelock Illustrations

and if action **good** occurs, then it must occur at some time from t up to, but not including, $t + D$. Using the terminology of [11] this yields a *strong* timeout. A *weak* timeout would, in contrast, allow a non-deterministic choice between the **good** action and the **timeout** at time $t + D$.

2. *Urgency of* **good** *action.* We also require that if the **good** action is enabled before time $t + D$ then it is taken *urgently*, i.e. as soon as **good** is enabled it happens. This urgency requirement is akin to the "as soon as possible" principle which has been applied in timed process algebra [12].

3. *Timelock Free.* Finally we want our composed system to be free of timelocks, for obvious reasons.

4. *Simple.* We also require that the solution is not "prohibitively" complex.

Notice that in the first two of these requirements, urgency arises in two ways. Firstly, we require that **timeout** is urgent at time $t + D$ and secondly, we require that **good** is urgent as soon as it is enabled. Without the former requirement the timeout might fail to fire even though it has expired and without the latter, even though the **good** action might be able to happen it might nonetheless not occur and thus, for example, the **timeout** may expire even though **good** was possible.

We also emphasize that although our work here was inspired by that in [6], it is somewhat different. In particular, [6] presents a bounded timeout in a discrete time setting, thus, the final time at which the **good** action can be performed and the time of expiry of the **Timeout** are at different discrete time points.

3   Modelling the Bounded Timeout in UPPAAL

In this section we describe the bounded timeout in UPPAAL. However, our discussion is not solely relevant to this notation, and could be extrapolated to timed automata notations in general.

Basic Formulation. We begin by considering the Timeout shown in figure 3. This process realises the first requirement that we identified for modelling the bounded timeout - good is offered at all times in which t<D. Then timeout is performed when t==D, in which case the system passes into state a2 which plays the role of an error state. Importantly, the guard (t<=D) forces the required urgency on the timeout action. Thus, if good has not happened earlier, timeout *must* happen when t==D. Furthermore, it is easy to see that this is indeed a strong timeout - its behaviour is deterministic when t==D.

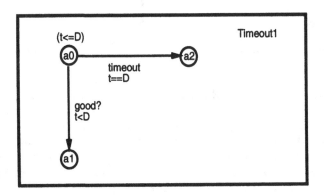

Fig. 3. An UPPAAL Automaton for Timeout1

However on its own, this automaton is not sufficient since nothing forces the good action to be taken if it can be. This was our second requirement. For example, consider Component1 shown in figure 4 which will perform an internal action tau[4] at some time r<=C and then offer the good action. The internal action can be viewed as modelling some internal computation by Component1. The completion of which is signalled by offering good!. Now if we put Timeout1 and Component1 in parallel then even if good could occur while t<D, it might not be taken. Thus, a possible trace of the system:

    ||<Timeout1,Component1>

is, $(\text{tau}, x_1)(\text{timeout}, x_2)$ where, $x_1 < C$, $x_1 < D$ and $x_2 = D$.

---

[4] In fact, internal transitions are left unlabelled in UPPAAL, however, we abuse notation in order that we can refer to the transition.

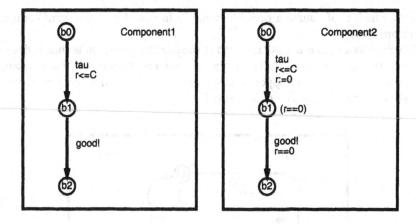

Fig. 4. UPPAAL Automata for Component1 and Component2

Thus, we need some way to make **good** urgent. The standard approach is to enforce urgency in the component. For example, we could use **Component2** shown in figure 4. This automaton will perform the internal action as before and then it *must* immediately perform the **good** action.

Now the problem with the composition:

```
||<Timeout1,Component2>
```

is the relative values of D and C. In particular, if C is larger than D then this system can time-block in the following way:-

1. the timeout could fire when t==D;
2. then if **tau** happens when r==C say, **good!** will become urgent, however it cannot be performed since **Timeout1** is no longer offering it, causing a timelock. **Component2** will not let time pass until **good** is performed, but **good** cannot be performed because of a mis-matched synchronisation.

We would argue that this is a big problem. In particular, it is not generally possible to ensure that C is less than D since our component behaviour would typically be embedded in the complex functioning of a complete system. In fact, writing C as we have done, abstracts from a likely multitude of complexity and deriving such a value from a system would typically require analysis of many components of the complete system, some of which might be time non-deterministic at the level of abstraction being considered.

Furthermore, in some situations we might actually be interested in analysing what happens if the good action arrives after the timeout has fired. Consider, for example, that our timeout behaviour is being used to wait for an acknowledgement in a sender process. The component performing **good** after **timeout** has fired corresponds to the acknowledgement arriving after the timeout has expired, which is of course a possible scenario in practical analysis of communication protocols.

The problem with our ||<Timeout1,Component2> solution is that it does not enable us to analysis this situation, rather the system timelocks when Component2 forces the good action to happen. Unfortunately, as mere mortals, we are unable to analyse systems after the end of time!

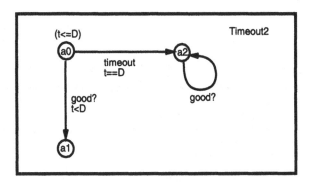

Fig. 5. An UPPAAL Automaton for Timeout2

One way to avoid this timelock is to add "escape" transitions in the timeout. For example, consider the timeout behaviour encapsulated by Timeout2. Now the composition,

||<Timeout2,Component2>

cannot block time. However, this is not a satisfactory solution since rather than Timeout2 just evolving to a single deadlock state, a2, after performing timeout, it could evolve to a complex behaviour; of course in practice it is almost certain to do this. However then, escape transitions would have to be scattered throughout the complex behaviour. This would generate significant specification clutter, which would be compounded if the system contained more than one timeout.

The consequences become particularly severe if the timeout is enclosed in some repetitive behaviour, e.g. see figure 6. This is because, since no assumptions can be made about the time at which the component will want to perform the good action, escape transitions on good will have to be added at a0, a2, b0, b1 (and actually a1 as well). Thus, firstly, the behaviour prior to reaching the timeout has been altered, i.e. escape transitions must be added at b0 and secondly, it is unclear how many escape transitions need to be added to each node in the loop, since state a2 may be reached many times before the first good escape transition is performed.

Urgent Channels. UPPAAL also contains the concept of an urgent channel. The specifier is allowed to denote a particular channel as urgent, which means

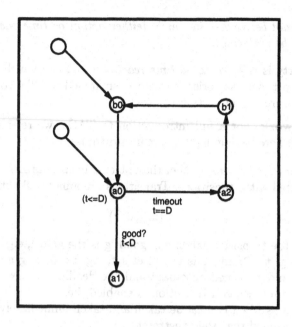

Fig. 6. Timeout2 in a repetitive context

that as soon as synchronisation on that channel can take place, it does. However, UPPAAL restricts the use of such urgent channels. In particular, an urgent transition can only have the guard **true**.

Intuitively, urgent channels seem to be what we require in order to avoid enforcing urgency in the component process. In particular, they enforce urgency in a "global" manner, rather than requiring it to be enforced in the component process. However, it turns out that the restriction on guarding of urgent channels that UPPAAL imposes prevents derivation of a suitable solution, see [5] which investigates possible solutions with urgent channels which were inspired by the solutions presented in [6].

In summary then, although we do not have a formal proof that a completely satisfactory UPPAAL description of the timeout cannot be found, we postulate that if it is possible, the complexity inherent in the solution would be prohibitive.

4   Timed Automata with Deadlines

A more radical approach to realising a satisfactory bounded timeout is to consider the Timed Automata with Deadlines (TAD) framework developed by Bornot et al [3, 4]. The reason for selecting this model is that it is argued that it has very nice properties with regard to time progress and timelocks. In particular, the following property holds, *a state cannot be reached in which neither action or time passing transitions can be performed.*

This property is referred to as *time reactivity* and since such situations (as opposed to zeno timelocks) arise through mismatched parallel compositions, it ensures freedom from composition timelocks.

Basic Framework. For a full introduction to TADs, we refer the interested reader to [3, 4]; here we highlight the main principles:

– *Deadlines on Transitions.* Rather than placing invariants on states, deadlines are associated with transitions. Transitions are annotated with 4-tuples:

$$(a, g, d, r)$$

where a is the transition label, e.g. good; g is the guard, e.g. t<=D; d is the deadline, e.g. t==D; and r is the reset set, e.g. t:=0. a, g and r are familiar from standard timed automata and the deadline is new. Conceptually, the guard states when a transition is enabled, i.e. *may* be taken; while the deadline states when it *must* be taken and taken immediately.
It is also assumed that the constraint,

$$d \implies g$$

holds, which ensures that if a transition is forced to happen it is also able to. Clearly, if this constraint did not hold then we could obtain timelocks because a transition is forced to happen, but it is not enabled.
Since we have deadlines on transitions there is no need for invariants on states. Thus, they are not included in the framework.
– *(Timewise) Priorities.* By restricting guards and deadlines in choice contexts, prioritised choice can be expressed. For example, if we have two transitions:

$$b1 = (a1, g1, d1, r1) \quad and \quad b2 = (a2, g2, d2, r2)$$

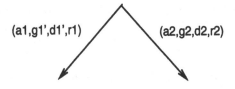

(a1,g1',d1',r1)   (a2,g2,d2,r2)

Fig. 7. A Prioritised Choice

then when placing them in a choice context we can give b2 priority over b1 by restricting the guards and deadlines of b1, see figure 7. [3] considers a variety of priority operators, which ensure that if the higher priority action will *eventually* be enabled within a particular period of time then it takes precedence over competing actions. These different priority mechanisms are obtained by including timed temporal operators in the restricted guards and deadlines. The extreme example of which is to enforce the following restricted guard and deadline:

$$\text{g1}' = \text{g1} \wedge \Box\neg\text{g2} \quad \text{and} \quad \text{d1}' = \text{d1} \wedge \text{g1}'$$

which ensures that **b1** is only enabled if **g1** holds and there is *no point in the future* at which **g2** will hold.

- *Parallel Composition with Escape Transitions.* The TADs framework employs a different parallel composition operator to that arising in standard timed automata. The key idea is that of an *escape transition*. These are the local transitions of automata components that are combined when generating a synchronisation transition. Thus, not only are synchronisations included, but component transitions of the synchronisation are as well. The timewise priority mechanism is then used to give the synchronisation transition highest priority. Intuitively, the escape transitions can only happen if the synchronisation transition will *never* be enabled. We will illustrate this aspect of TADs shortly.
- *Synchronisation Strategies.* [3] also consider a number of different synchronisation strategies, but these are not relevant to our discussion. In terms of [3] we only consider *AND* synchronisation.

In fact, in addition to ensuring time reactivity, the TADs framework limits the occurrence of local deadlocks. Specifically, the escape transitions allow the components of a parallel composition to escape a potential local deadlock by evolving locally. Associated with such avoidance of local deadlocks is the enforcement of *maximal progress*[5], which exactly requires that if a synchronisation is possible, it is always taken in preference to a corresponding escape transition.

Basic Definitions. We now briefly review the definition of timed automata with deadlines. Also, in order to preserve some continuity through the paper we continue to use the UPPAAL synchronisation notation even though it is different to that used in [3].

An arbitrary element of $\mathcal{A}$, the set of TADs, has the form:

$$(L, l_0, T)$$

where, L is a finite set of locations; l_0 is the *start location*; and

- $T \subseteq L \times CC \times CC \times A^+ \times \mathbb{P}(\mathcal{C}) \times L$ is a transition relation. A typical element of which is, $(l_1, \text{g}, \text{d}, \text{a}, \text{r}, l_2)$, where $l_1, l_2 \in L$ are automata locations; $\text{g} \in CC$

---

[5] Note, the term is used in a related but somewhat different way in the timed process algebra setting [12].

is a guard; $d \in \mathcal{CC}$ is a deadline; $a \in A^+$ labels the transition; and $r \in \mathbb{P}(\mathcal{C})$ is a reset set. $(l_1, g, d, a, r, l_2) \in T$ is typically written,

$$l_1 \xrightarrow{g,d,a,r} l_2$$

In addition, we will use the function:

$$\theta_B(l) = \{ (b,g) \mid \exists l' . l \xrightarrow{g,d,b,r} l' \wedge b \in B \}$$

Standard TADs. We will introduce a number of different TADs approaches in this paper. These are distinguished by their rules of parallel composition. Here we consider the basic approach, as introduced in [3, 4], which we call *standard TADs*. A TADs expansion theorem for deriving the product behaviour from a parallel composition is given in [3]. Here we give an equivalent inference rule definition for our state vector notation:-

$$(R1) \quad \frac{l_i \xrightarrow{g_i,d_i,a?,r_i} l'_i \quad l_j \xrightarrow{g_j,d_j,a!,r_j} l'_j}{\begin{array}{l} ||v \xrightarrow{g',d',a,r_i \cup r_j} ||v[l'_i/l_i, l'_j/l_j] \\ ||v \xrightarrow{g'_i,d'_i,a?,r_i} ||v[l'_i/l_i] \\ ||v \xrightarrow{g'_j,d'_j,a!,r_j} ||v[l'_j/l_j] \end{array}}$$

where $1 \le i,j \le |v| \wedge i \ne j$ and,

$$\begin{aligned}
g' &= g_i \wedge g_j \\
d' &= g' \wedge (d_i \vee d_j) \\
g'_i &= g_i \wedge \Box \neg (g_i \wedge g_j) \\
d'_i &= g'_i \wedge d_i \\
g'_j &= g_j \wedge \Box \neg (g_i \wedge g_j) \\
d'_j &= g'_j \wedge d_j
\end{aligned}$$

$$(R2) \quad \frac{l_i \xrightarrow{g,d,a,r} l'_i \quad a \in \overline{A} \Rightarrow \bigcup_{k \in (\{1..|v|\} - \{i\})} \theta_{\{\overline{a}\}}(l_k) = \emptyset}{||v \xrightarrow{g,d,a,r} ||v[l'_i/l_i]}$$

where $1 \le i \le |v|$. (R1) generates synchronisation and escape transitions with the constrained guards and deadlines ensuring that synchronisation has priority in the required manner. (R2) is the interleaving rule, which is straightforward apart from the second condition which ensures that transitions on incomplete actions are only generated by this rule if synchronisation, and hence rule (R1), is not possible.

As an illustration of these inference rules consider ||<A1,A2> where A1 and A2 are shown in figure 8. The unreduced composition arising from directly applying the inference rules is shown in figure 9(a) ($\Box$ is denoted [] and $\neg$ is denoted $\sim$) and figure 9(b) depicts the resulting composed TAD when guards and deadlines have been reduced by expanding out temporal operators and applying propositional logic. In addition, transitions with unfulfillable guards, e.g. false, have been removed.

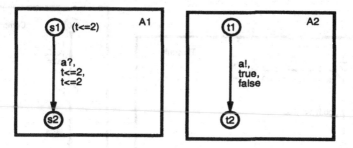

Fig. 8. TADs A1 and A2

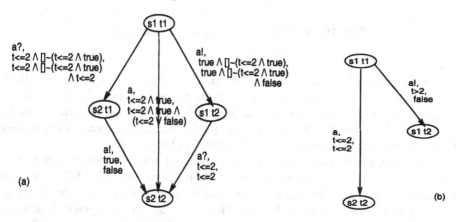

Fig. 9. Unreduced and reduced composition of A1 and A2

We can observe the following:-

1. In figure 9(a) the transition coming from s1 t1 labelled a is the synchronisation transition.

2. In figure 9(a) the two transitions coming from s1 t1 labelled a? and a! respectively, are the escape transitions. The first arises from automaton A1 and the second from automaton A2. The guards of these escape transitions ensure that they can only fire if the synchronisation will never in the future be possible. Thus, synchronisation transitions have priority over escape transitions.

3. Figure 9(b) shows that since the synchronisation transition inherits the guards of a? from A1, no escape transition on a? is possible. If s1 t1 is entered with t>2 then the escape transition on a! can be taken, enabling A2 to escape its local deadlock.

Bounded Timeout in Standard TADs. Now we reformulate our bounded timeout in standard TADs. The component that we consider is Component3 and the timeout is Timeout4 both shown in figure 10.

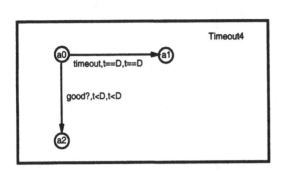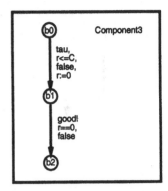

Fig. 10. A TAD for `Timeout4` and `Component3`

So, `Component3` behaves similarly to `Component2` except the `good!` transition is not urgent, i.e. the `good` transition is never forced to happen[6]. In the terminology of [3], such transitions are called *lazy*. In contrast, all the transitions in `Timeout4` are *eager* [3], since their guard and deadline are the same. This implies that as soon as the transition can happen it will happen.

Now by applying the above inference rules and removing impossible transitions, the composite automaton shown in figure 11 results. The full version of this paper [5] presents the intermediate steps required to derive this composition.

If we first focus on state a0 b1 then we can see that this composite behaviour gives priority to the synchronisation between `good?` and `good!` which is indicated by the transition labelled `good`. Thus, while t<D this is the only transition that can fire (notice r==0 automatically when entering state a0 b1) and furthermore it is eager.

Also, if state a0 b1 is entered with t==D then `timeout` is urgent. Furthermore, from this state the action `good!` can happen (but lazily) either at time D or later. This is the escape transition, which allows `Component3` to move out of state b1. Remember the timelock that we obtained previously arose because the component could not exit the state where it wished to perform `good!`[7].

This solution seems to fulfil our requirements - it is a strong timeout, urgency is enforced as required on both `timeout` and `good` and the solution is timelock free. However, there are some peculiarities with the resulting composite behaviour. Consider for example, the transition from a0 b0 labelled `good?`. This represents the timeout performing its `good` escape transition. However, con-

---

[6] We prefer to enforce the urgency of `good` in the timeout because in some of our case studies, e.g. [6], there are situations in which enforcing the urgency of `good` on the system side can cause problems, since nothing ensures that the timeout is ready to synchronise on the `good` exactly when it is offered. In order to avoid this possibility we require the system to passively offer its action and thus, wait until the timeout is ready to receive it.

[7] Actually, the situation is not as severe here since `good!` is lazy.

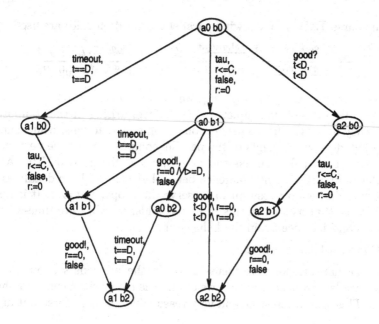

Fig. 11. ||<Timeout4,Component3> in standard TADs

ceptually it is being performed too early - before the synchronisation on **good** is even offered. In fact, if **a0 b0** is entered with **t==0**, which will almost certainly be the case, then **good?** will almost always be selected since it is an eager transition. In response to this observation we consider alternative TADs formulations in the next section.

5   Alternative TAD Formulations

We consider two alternative TAD formulations[8]. [5] actually considers a third formulation, but this turns out to be unsatisfactory. Both satisfy the requirements that we identified in the introduction for our bounded timeout. Thus, in particular, they are both time reactive. However, the solutions vary in the extent to which they limit local deadlocks.

5.1   Sparse Timed Automata with Deadlines

This is a minimal TADs approach, in which we do not generate *any* escape transitions. Furthermore, since escape transitions are not generated, we do not have to enforce any priority between the synchronisation and escape transitions.

---

[8] We still call these timed automata with deadlines, because the basic principles, as concieved by Bornot et al [3, 4], still apply, i.e. placing deadlines on transitions and using prioritised choice.

With sparse TADs the following parallel composition rules are used:

$$\frac{l_i \xrightarrow{a?,g_i,d_i,r_i} l'_i \quad l_j \xrightarrow{a!,g_j,d_j,r_j} l'_j}{||v \xrightarrow{a,g',d',r_i \cup r_j} ||v[l'_i/l_i, l'_j/l_j]} \qquad \frac{l_i \xrightarrow{a,g,d,r} l'_i \quad a \in A}{||v \xrightarrow{a,g,d,r} ||v[l'_i/l_i]}$$

where $1 \leq i, j \leq |v|$, $i \neq j$, $g' = g_i \wedge g_j$ and $d' = g' \wedge (d_i \vee d_j)$.

These rules prevent uncompleted actions from arising in the composite behaviour; they only arise in the generation of completed actions, while completed actions offered by components of the parallel composition can be performed independently. This definition has the same spirit as the normal UPPAAL rules of parallel composition. The difference being that here we have deadlines which we constrain during composition to preserve the property $d \Rightarrow g$. It is straightforward to see that as long as this property holds, we will have time-reactivity.

Let us consider once again the behaviour,

| |<Timeout4,Component3>

which is the network we were focussing on in the previous section. Now with our new parallel composition rules, we obtain the composite behaviour shown in figure 12. This is an interesting and very reasonable solution. Firstly, it meets all

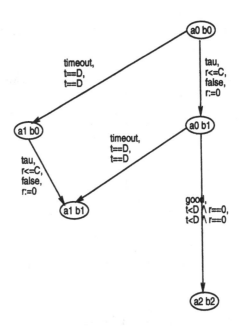

Fig. 12. | |<Timeout4,Component3> in Sparse TADs

the requirements identified at the start of this paper for our bounded timeout. Thus, in particular, it is time-reactive. However, it makes no effort to limit local deadlocks, so communication mis-matches yield local deadlocks rather than timelocks.

5.2   TADs with Minimal Priority Escape Transitions

The idea here is to ensure maximal progress as standard TADs do, but rather than just giving escape transitions lower priority than their corresponding synchronisation, we also give them lower priority than other completed transitions. Thus, a component can only perform an escape transition if the component will never be able to perform a completed transition.

The parallel composition rules are:

$$(R1) \quad \frac{l_i \xrightarrow{a?,g_i,d_i,r_i} l_i' \quad l_j \xrightarrow{a!,g_j,d_j,r_j} l_j'}{||v \xrightarrow{a,g',d',r_i \cup r_j} ||v[l_i'/l_i, l_j'/l_j]}$$

where, $1 \leq i, j \leq |v|$, $i \neq j$, $g' = g_i \wedge g_j$, $d' = g' \wedge (d_i \vee d_j)$. and,

$$(R2) \quad \frac{l_i \xrightarrow{a,g,d,r} l_i' \quad a \in A}{||v \xrightarrow{a,g,d,r} ||v[l_i'/l_i]} \qquad (R3) \quad \frac{l_i \xrightarrow{a,g,d,r} l_i' \quad a \in \overline{A}}{||v \xrightarrow{a,g'',d'',r} ||v[l_i'/l_i]}$$

where, $1 \leq i \leq |v|$ and,

$$g'' = g \wedge \bigwedge_{(b, g') \in \theta_A(l_i)} \Box \neg g' \wedge$$

$$\bigwedge_{(b, g_1) \in \theta_{\overline{A}}(l_i)} \bigwedge_{j \in (\{1..|v|\} - \{i\})} \bigwedge_{(\overline{b}, g_2) \in \theta_{\{\overline{b}\}}(l_j)} \Box \neg(g_1 \wedge g_2)$$

$$d'' = d \wedge g''$$

R1 is the normal synchronisation rule; R2 defines interleaving of completed transitions; and R3 defines interleaving of incomplete, i.e. escape, transitions. In this final rule, g'' holds when,

1. g holds;
2. it is not the case that an already completed transition from l_i could eventually become enabled; and
3. it is not the case that an incomplete transition (including a itself) offered at state l_i could eventually be completed.

Applying these rules to the composition:

    ||<Timeout4,Component3>

and removing impossible transitions, see [5] for a full presentation, yields the composition shown in figure 13. This solution removes the excessively early escape transition from a0 b0, but preserves all other transitions.

6   Discussion and Conclusions

We failed to find a fully satisfactory UPPAAL specification of a bounded timeout. In response, we presented three different TADs solutions - standard TADs, sparse TADs, and TADs with minimal priority escape transitions. The latter two of

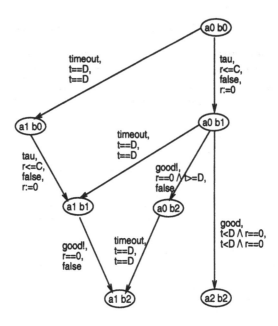

Fig. 13. ||<Timeout4,Component3> in TADs with minimum priority escape transitions

which are new to this paper[9]. All three meet all the requirements we identified at the start of the paper for our timeout. However, our preference is for the 2nd and 3rd solutions. The 2nd is interesting because it gives a timelock free solution but does not seek to minimise local deadlocks, while the 3rd adds escape transitions to limit such local deadlocks.

It is interesting to consider a specific timeout example. In the same way as earlier in the paper, we consider the implications if we view the **good** action as the passing of an acknowledgment from the medium to a waiting sender process. The situation that the component wishes to perform **good** after the timeout has fired corresponds to the medium delivering the acknowledgment too late. The two solutions handle this situation differently.

With the sparse TADs solution, a local deadlock is generated. Conceptually, this indicates that the medium is prevented from delivering the acknowledgement. This is in fact the normal manner in which mis-matched communications are handled in untimed systems - local deadlocks result. In contrast, with TADs with minimal priority escape transitions the late delivery of the acknowledgement yields a local transition in the medium, which could be viewed as the acknowledgement packet being consumed/dropped. This avoids the local dead-

---

[9] In particular, the *stiff* parallel composition of [13] which seem related to our sparse TADS are in fact rather different since they do not ensure that deadlines imply guards when generating the product. Thus, they do not ensure time reactivity.

lock and allows the system to proceed. Choosing between these two should be made according to the application domain under consideration.

Acknowledgements. The author has benefited greatly from discussions with Sebastian Bornot, Joseph Sifakis and Stavros Tripakis and would also like to recognise the contribution of Giorgio Faconti, Joost-Pieter Katoen, Diego Latella and Meike Massink who were involved in preliminary discussions from which this paper has grown. In addition, the reviewers made a number of valuable recommendations.

References

[1] R. Alur and D. Dill. A theory of timed automata. *Theoretical Computer Science*, pages 183–235, 1994.

[2] Johan Bengtsson, Kim G. Larsen, Fredrik Larsson, and Paul Pettersson amd Wang Yi. Uppaal - a tool suite for automatic verification of real-time system. In *Proceedings of the 4th DIMACS Workshop on Verification and Control of Hybrid Systems*, 1995.

[3] S. Bornot and J. Sifakis. On the composition of hybrid systems. In *Hybrid Systems: Computation and Control*, LNCS 1386, pages 49–63, 1998.

[4] S. Bornot, J. Sifakis, and S. Tripakis. Modeling urgency in timed systems. In *Compositionality, COMPOS'97*, LNCS (to appear), 1997.

[5] H. Bowman. Discussion document - modelling timeout behaviour in timed automata. Technical report, Available from author, 1998.

[6] H. Bowman, G. Faconti, J-P. Katoen, D. Latella, and M. Massink. Automatic verification of a lip synchronisation algorithm using UPPAAL. In *Proceedings of the 3rd International Workshop on Formal Methods for Industrial Critical Systems*, 1998. To Appear in Special Issue of Formal Aspects of Computing.

[7] C.Daws, A.Olivero, S.Tripakis, and S.Yovine. The tool KRONOS. In *Hybrid Systems III, Verification and Control*, LNCS 1066. Springer-Verlag, 1996.

[8] Th. A. Henzinger and Pei-Hsin. HyTech: The Cornell HYbrid TECHnology tool. In *Proceedings of TACAS, Workshop on Tools and Algorithms for the Construction and Analysis of Systems*, 1995.

[9] L. Leonard and G. Leduc. An introduction to ET-LOTOS for the description of time-sens itive systems. *Computer Networks and ISDN Systems*, 29:271–292, 1996.

[10] R. Milner. *Communication and Concurrency*. Prentice-Hall, 1989.

[11] X. Nicollin and J. Sifakis. An overview and synthesis on timed process algebra. In *Real-time Theory in Practice*, LNCS 600, pages 549–572. Springer-Verlag, June 1991.

[12] T. Regan. Multimedia in temporal LOTOS: A lip synchronisation algorithm. In *PSTV XIII, 13th Protocol Specification, Testing and Verification*. North-Holland, 1993.

[13] J. Sifakis and S. Yiovine. Compositional specification of timed systems, (extended abstract). In *STACS'96, Proceedings of the 13th Annual Symposium on Theoretical Aspects of Computer Science*, LNCS 1046, pages 347–359. Springer-Verlag, 1996.

Author Index

Lecture Notes in Computer Science

For information about Vols. 1–1520
please contact your bookseller or Springer-Verlag

Vol. 1557: P. Zinterhof, M. Vajteršic, A. Uhl (Eds.), Parallel Computation. Proceedings, 1999. XV, 604 pages. 1999.

Vol. 1558: H. J.v.d. Herik, H. Iida (Eds.), Computers and Games. Proceedings, 1998. XVIII, 337 pages. 1999.

Vol. 1559: P. Flener (Ed.), Logic-Based Program Synthesis and Transformation. Proceedings, 1998. X, 331 pages. 1999.

Vol. 1560: K. Imai, Y. Zheng (Eds.), Public Key Cryptography. Proceedings, 1999. IX, 327 pages. 1999.

Vol. 1561: I. Damgård (Ed.), Lectures on Data Security. VII, 250 pages. 1999.

Vol. 1562: C.L. Nehaniv (Ed.), Computation for Metaphors, Analogy, and Agents. X, 389 pages. 1999. (Subseries LNAI).

Vol. 1563: Ch. Meinel, S. Tison (Eds.), STACS 99. Proceedings, 1999. XIV, 582 pages. 1999.

Vol. 1565: P. P. Chen, J. Akoka, H. Kangassalo, B. Thalheim (Eds.), Conceptual Modeling. XXIV, 303 pages. 1999.

Vol. 1567: P. Antsaklis, W. Kohn, M. Lemmon, A. Nerode, S. Sastry (Eds.), Hybrid Systems V. X, 445 pages. 1999.

Vol. 1568: G. Bertrand, M. Couprie, L. Perroton (Eds.), Discrete Geometry for Computer Imagery. Proceedings, 1999. XI, 459 pages. 1999.

Vol. 1569: F.W. Vaandrager, J.H. van Schuppen (Eds.), Hybrid Systems: Computation and Control. Proceedings, 1999. X, 271 pages. 1999.

Vol. 1570: F. Puppe (Ed.), XPS-99: Knowledge-Based Systems. VIII, 227 pages. 1999. (Subseries LNAI).

Vol. 1571: P. Noriega, C. Sierra (Eds.), Agent Mediated Electronic Commerce. Proceedings, 1998. IX, 207 pages. 1999. (Subseries LNAI).

Vol. 1572: P. Fischer, H.U. Simon (Eds.), Computational Learning Theory. Proceedings, 1999. X, 301 pages. 1999. (Subseries LNAI).

Vol. 1574: N. Zhong, L. Zhou (Eds.), Methodologies for Knowledge Discovery and Data Mining. Proceedings, 1999. XV, 533 pages. 1999. (Subseries LNAI).

Vol. 1575: S. Jähnichen (Ed.), Compiler Construction. Proceedings, 1999. X, 301 pages. 1999.

Vol. 1576: S.D. Swierstra (Ed.), Programming Languages and Systems. Proceedings, 1999. X, 307 pages. 1999.

Vol. 1577: J.-P. Finance (Ed.), Fundamental Approaches to Software Engineering. Proceedings, 1999. X, 245 pages. 1999.

Vol. 1578: W. Thomas (Ed.), Foundations of Software Science and Computation Structures. Proceedings, 1999. X, 323 pages. 1999.

Vol. 1579: W.R. Cleaveland (Ed.), Tools and Algorithms for the Construction and Analysis of Systems. Proceedings, 1999. XI, 445 pages. 1999.

Vol. 1580: A. Včkovski, K.E. Brassel, H.-J. Schek (Eds.), Interoperating Geographic Information Systems. Proceedings, 1999. XI, 329 pages. 1999.

Vol. 1581: J.-Y. Girard (Ed.), Typed Lambda Calculi and Applications. Proceedings, 1999. VIII, 397 pages. 1999.

Vol. 1582: A. Lecomte, F. Lamarche, G. Perrier (Eds.), Logical Aspects of Computational Linguistics. Proceedings, 1997. XI, 251 pages. 1999. (Subseries LNAI).

Vol. 1584: G. Gottlob, E. Grandjean, K. Seyr (Eds.), Computer Science Logic. Proceedings, 1998. X, 431 pages. 1999.

Vol. 1586: J. Rolim et al. (Eds.), Parallel and Distributed Processing. Proceedings, 1999. XVII, 1443 pages. 1999.

Vol. 1587: J. Pieprzyk, R. Safavi-Naini, J. Seberry (Eds.), Information Security and Privacy. Proceedings, 1999. XI, 327 pages. 1999.

Vol. 1590: P. Atzeni, A. Mendelzon, G. Mecca (Eds.), The World Wide Web and Databases. Proceedings, 1998. VIII, 213 pages. 1999.

Vol. 1592: J. Stern (Ed.), Advances in Cryptology – EUROCRYPT '99. Proceedings, 1999. XII, 475 pages. 1999.

Vol. 1593: P. Sloot, M. Bubak, A. Hoekstra, B. Hertzberger (Eds.), High-Performance Computing and Networking. Proceedings, 1999. XXIII, 1318 pages. 1999.

Vol. 1594: P. Ciancarini, A.L. Wolf (Eds.), Coordination Languages and Models. Proceedings, 1999. IX, 420 pages. 1999.

Vol. 1596: R. Poli, H.-M. Voigt, S. Cagnoni, D. Corne, G.D. Smith, T.C. Fogarty (Eds.), Evolutionary Image Analysis, Signal Processing and Telecommunications. Proceedings, 1999. X, 225 pages. 1999.

Vol. 1597: H. Zuidweg, M. Campolargo, J. Delgado, A. Mullery (Eds.), Intelligence in Services and Networks. Proceedings, 1999. XII, 552 pages. 1999.

Vol. 1598: R. Poli, P. Nordin, W.B. Langdon, T.C. Fogarty (Eds.), Genetic Programming. Proceedings, 1999. X, 283 pages. 1999.

Vol. 1599: T. Ishida (Ed.), Multiagent Platforms. Proceedings, 1998. VIII, 187 pages. 1999. (Subseries LNAI).

Vol. 1601: J.-P. Katoen (Ed.), Formal Methods for Real-Time and Probabilistic Systems. Proceedings, 1999. X, 355 pages. 1999.

Vol. 1602: A. Sivasubramaniam, M. Lauria (Eds.), Network-Based Parallel Computing. Proceedings, 1999. VIII, 225 pages. 1999.

Vol. 1605: J. Billington, M. Diaz, G. Rozenberg (Eds.), Application of Petri Nets to Communication Networks. IX, 303 pages. 1999.

Vol. 1609: Z. W. Raś, A. Skowron (Eds.), Foundations of Intelligent Systems. Proceedings, 1999. XII, 676 pages. 1999. (Subseries LNAI).

Vol. 1610: G. Cornuéjols, R.E. Burkard, G.J. Woeginger (Eds.), Integer Programming and Combinatorial Optimization. Proceedings, 1999. IX, 453 pages. 1999.

Vol. 1615: C. Polychronopoulos, K. Joe, A. Fukuda, S. Tomita (Eds.), High Performance Computing. Proceedings, 1999. XIV, 408 pages. 1999.

Vol. 1621: D. Fensel, R. Studer (Eds.), Knowledge Acquisition Modeling and Management. Proceedings, 1999. XI, 404 pages. 1999. (Subseries LNAI).

Vol. 1625: B. Reusch (Ed.), Computational Intelligence. Proceedings, 1999. XIV, 710 pages. 1999.